Shakespeare and the Countess

Shakespeare and the Countess

The Battle that Gave Birth to the Globe

CHRIS LAOUTARIS

PEGASUS BOOKS
NEW YORK LONDON

Dedicated to my parents, John and Thalia,
and to the memory of my brother,
George (1975–2006)

∂∞∂

SHAKESPERE AND THE COUNTESS

Pegasus Books LLC
80 Broad Street, 5th Floor
New York, NY 10004

First Pegasus Books hardcover edition June 2015

ISBN: 978-1-60598-792-7

10 9 8 7 8 6 5 4 3 2 1

Printed in the United States of America
Distributed by W. W. Norton & Company, Inc.

Contents

Contents

Illustrations

11. Monument of Sir Anthony Cooke and Anne Fitzwilliam Cooke, workshop of Cornelius Cure, after 11 June 1576. Church of St Edward the Confessor, Romford, Essex. Photo: Patricia Phillippy

12. Detail from the monument of Sir Anthony Cooke and Anne Fitzwilliam Cooke, with relief engraving of the Cooke sisters, workshop of Cornelius Cure, after 11 June 1576. Church of St Edward the Confessor, Romford, Essex. Photo: Patricia Phillippy

13. Elizabeth Russell's letter to William More, 9 August c.1580–81. Surrey History Centre, Woking, Historical Correspondence, 6729/6/98. By kind permission of the More-Molyneux family

14. Richard Field's lease agreement. Surrey History Centre, Woking, Loseley Manuscripts, LM 333/12, 22 September 1592. By kind permission of the More-Molyneux family

15. Monument of John, Lord Russell, Cure workshop, after 23 July 1584. Westminster Abbey, London. © Dean and Chapter of Westminster

16. Portrait of Robert Devereux, 2nd Earl of Essex, Marcus Gheeraerts the Younger, c.1596. Woburn Abbey, Bedfordshire. The Bridgeman Art Library

17. The remains of Donnington Castle, near Newbury, Berkshire. © Henry Taunt/English Heritage/Arcaid/Corbis

18. Portrait of the Lord Admiral, Charles Howard, 1st Earl of Nottingham, unknown artist, oil on canvas, 1602. © National Portrait Gallery, London

19. Portrait of William Shakespeare, attributed to John Taylor, oil on canvas, 1600s. © National Portrait Gallery, London

20. Detail from an engraving by Cornelius de Visscher, showing a theatre labelled 'The Globe', 1616. British Library, London, UK/© British Library Board. All Rights Reserved/The Bridgeman Art Library

Acknowledgements

Whenever I encountered a seeming dead-end while following a research trail and came close to giving up, I always found myself asking, 'What would Elizabeth Russell do?' 'Elizabeth Russell,' I inevitably, reassuringly, concluded, 'would not give up.' And so I would press on. While her example gave me the impetus to persist where the historical record seemed at first to be too fragmented to allow me to open a window into her world, I know that this book would not have come into being at all had it not been for the generosity and help of so many others.

This project was made possible thanks to the support of the institutions which funded and hosted my research. A post-doctoral fellowship from the British Academy, held at University College London, enabled me to conduct a detailed exploration of Elizabeth Russell's life and the political and religious contexts which gave shape to her activism. A Birmingham Fellowship at The Shakespeare Institute, awarded by the University of Birmingham, allowed me to delve into the complex history of Shakespeare's Blackfriars Theatre and the men who joined Elizabeth Russell's campaign to prevent it from opening in 1596. This award gave me the opportunity to sift through the archives which underpin the discoveries made in this book, including the precise locations of Elizabeth Russell's home and what is almost certainly Richard Field's printing press; Field's professional association with the Church of St Anne's in the Blackfriars and with his landlords (which helped me solve the mystery of the printer's betrayal of Shakespeare); the identities, business dealings and affiliations of some of Elizabeth Russell's backers; and new potential allusions to Elizabeth Russell in Shakespeare's plays. I also owe thanks to the Arts and Humanities Research Council for funding the graduate and doctoral study which set me on the path that led to this book.

I am eternally grateful to all my former colleagues and mentors at University College London for their encouragement and friendship over the years. Special thanks go to René Weis, Helen Hackett, John Sutherland, Alexander Samson, Paul Davis, Henry Woudhuysen, John Mullan, Susan Irvine, Bas Aarts, Juliette Atkinson, Jane Darcy, Kathryn Allan, Anita Garfoot, Chris Stamatakis, Kathryn Metzenthin, Stephen Cadywold and Carol Bowen. My new colleagues at The Shakespeare Institute and the University of Birmingham have been immensely welcoming and have nurtured my research with an unfailing commitment. I owe huge debts in particular to Michael Dobson and John Jowett, whose valuable feedback gave direction to the work conducted since my move to The Shakespeare Institute; to Ewan Fernie, Martin Wiggins, Rebecca White, Juliet Creese, Abigail Rokison and Erin Sullivan; as well as to Tom Lockwood, Helen Laville, Michael Toolan and Zarina Chughtai of the University of Birmingham. I am also very grateful to Claire Preston for her support.

Susan Ronald and Alison Weir have been a special source of inspiration. I have benefited, in ways that words fail me to acknowledge, from their interest in my research, their astute comments on the proposal for this book at the early stages and, most of all, for their belief in me (thank you, thank you!). Lady Elizabeth, Duchess of Buccleuch, has been as generous in her encouragement as she has in her sponsorship of the Tony Lothian Prize. I am so obliged to her and to Kate Williams, Matthew Parris and Benjamin Buchan for shortlisting me for this prize. Warm thanks are also due to Andrew Lownie, Anna Swan, Nicholas Clee, Jane Mays, Philippa Bernard, Anne de Courcy, again to Susan Ronald, and everyone else who has been involved with the Biographers' Club for the wonderful work they have done, and are continuing to do, to promote the craft of biography. My agent, Julian Alexander, has been a joy to work with and I am deeply indebted to him for his sage advice and for his instrumental involvement in this project every step of the way. Thanks are also due to Ben Clark and everyone at Lucas Alexander Whitley for their much appreciated assistance.

I have learned so much from Helen Fry, James Hamilton, Douglas Ronald, Celia Lee, Josephine Ross, Kirsten Ellis and Neil McKenna; they have drawn my fullest admiration, and (naturally inadequate) attempts at emulation, since I began writing this biography. I also feel privileged to be walking in the footsteps of the pioneers of academic study into the Cooke sisters and Elizabeth Russell, including Mary Ellen Lamb, Patricia Phillippy and Jaime Goodrich, whose groundbreaking work and direct guidance have been so helpful to me in more ways than I have room to mention here. Jaime's elegant translations of some of the Latin letters referred to in this book and the poems of Daniel Rogers and Walter Haddon have opened up hidden worlds. Kate Moncrief, Kate McPherson, Caroline Bicks and Elizabeth Hodgson have shared with me their passion for uncovering women's occluded stories, which has been a catalyst for my own research; and the amazing work conducted by Annaliese Connolly and Lisa Hopkins on the Earl of Essex and their willingness to involve me in it has led me to investigate the lives of the rebellious Earl and his sister Lady Penelope Rich in more fruitful detail than I otherwise would have done.

This book has been enriched by those who have generously offered their professional opinions or provided me with their own unpublished research, including Sir Brian Vickers, Karen Hearn, Robin Simon, John Craig, Richard Rex, Arnold Hunt, Margaret Hannay, Jane Lawson, Kevin Colls, Patricia Burstall, Grethe Hauge, Catherine Weiss and Mark Weiss. I am also grateful to the Marquis of Salisbury and everyone at Hatfield House; to Tony Trowles, Christine Reynolds and Claire Mancini of Westminster Abbey Library; Cordelia Morrison of the Globe Theatre/Sam Wanamaker Playhouse; and all the staff at the British Library, National Archives, Shakespeare Institute Library, Shakespeare Birthplace Trust, Lambeth Palace Library, Surrey History Centre, Lincolnshire Archives, College of Arms, Huntington Library, British Museum, the National Portrait Gallery, Warburg Institute, Inner Temple Library, London Metropolitan Archives, Diocese of London, Cambridge University Library and Bodleian and Worcester College Libraries, Oxford, among other institutions which have been central to my research.

Many wonderful friends have been co-travellers on this journey, offering their engaging perspectives and encouragement along the way. I am especially grateful to Shona McNeill, whose love of biography and literature and almost preternatural historical knowledge have been major influences in my career; Yasmin Arshad, whose understanding of early modern culture and art has always been an inspiration (here's to more adventures together in the Renaissance!); and to Yewande Okuleye, Eleni Pilla, Nichole Wong, Claude Fretz, Charlotte Evans, Rob Ellard, Emma Whipday, Sasha Garwood and Josephine Billingham. Their fresh insights and enthusiasm for their own personal or professional projects have been guiding lights for my own undertakings.

If anything has made me realize just how true it is that a book is a collaborative effort it is the amazing team at Penguin. I am overwhelmed by the passionate dedication they have shown to this project and by their willingness to go above and beyond the call of duty to bring my research to press. I am so grateful to Juliet Annan for believing in this book, for her energy, sharp insight and unshakable commitment. Working with her has been a pleasure, a privilege and an honour (thanks for taking a chance on the Dowager Countess!). I similarly owe copious thanks to Sophie Missing for her immensely important assessment of the earlier draft of this book, as well as for her tremendous efficiency in helping to secure images and permissions; to Dave Cradduck for his excellent work on the index; as well as to Ellie Smith, Julia Murday, Bela Cunha and Jeff Edwards for their tireless labours on my behalf. I am utterly in awe of the copy-editing talents of Sarah Day, whose industriousness, meticulous attention to detail and perfectionism have improved this project immeasurably. Thanks to everyone at Penguin not directly mentioned here who has been involved in the editing, production and design of this book. My apologies to anyone I have forgotten to acknowledge.

Shakespeare and the Countess is dedicated to my parents, John and Thalia Laoutaris, and to the memory of my brother, George Laoutaris. They are the foundation of everything I do and, although George did not live to see this book's publication, he has always been, and will continue to be, a silent but shaping influence on all the projects I undertake (especially the really challenging ones!). Like Elizabeth Russell, he had a fighting spirit and never gave up.

Author's Note

It is, I like to think, in accordance with what would have been Elizabeth Russell's wishes (and what would thwart her enemies') that I often refer to her as 'Dowager' or 'Dowager Countess' in this book. Elizabeth insisted that she had every right to use this honorific title, which ordinarily belonged to the widow of an Earl. Elizabeth's second husband, John, Lord Russell, died just before formally acceding to the great Earldom of Bedford; however, Elizabeth maintained that her daughters had already been ratified as heirs to John's father, Francis Russell, 2nd Earl of Bedford. This, she argued, placed her in command of the Bedford inheritance and honours, which would eventually pass to her daughters (and their husbands) when they came of age. Unsurprisingly, this was hotly disputed in court by rival claimants to the Earl of Bedford's estates. Whether or not Elizabeth was successful in her suit would depend on the court's willingness to acknowledge the right of women to inherit over that of men.

History has since sided with Elizabeth's opponents. Today, her strenuous – sometimes even scandalous – efforts to secure the privileges which she fully believed were her due are almost entirely unknown. Yet her claims were not without legal validity. When she decided to wage her battle against the backers of Shakespeare's Blackfriars Theatre, she did so as a Dowager and her demands were met by the Queen's Privy Council. By restoring to public consciousness her preferred Dowager status I hope to counter the view of many of her contemporaries that her adoption of this self-defining title was merely an act of presumption and arrogance. The 'Countess' of this book's title, therefore, has a double significance, alluding both to Elizabeth Russell's personal struggle to be recognized as a Dowager Countess and to Shakespeare's own Countess of

Roussillon (for reasons that will become obvious) in his play *All's Well That Ends Well*.

Throughout this book I often refer to Elizabeth Russell by her first name alone but, to avoid confusion, have endeavoured not to do so for her royal namesake, Queen Elizabeth I. I have also regularly identified elevated individuals, such as Barons and Baronesses, Earls and Countesses, by the title Lord or Lady, which was commonly done during the period. Hence, for example, Henry Carey, 1st Baron Hunsdon, is often called Lord Hunsdon.

Until 1752, the new calendar year in England began on 25 March – Lady Day or the Feast of the Annunciation – although New Year's gifts were still exchanged on 1 January. Throughout, I have converted all dates so that they are in accordance with our own present-day convention of beginning the calendar year on 1 January. For example, a date of 18 February 1589 (when the year began on 25 March) would be presented in this book as 18 February 1590 (with the beginning of the year adjusted to 1 January). When calculating today's approximate equivalent to English Renaissance monetary values, I have primarily used the National Archives 'currency converter' – www.nationalarchives.gov.uk/currency – with additional estimated adjustments made to bring the figure into line with what might be expected today. This is, of course, just a rough guide, since purchasing power was itself governed by contemporary relative values, which are incredibly difficult to represent meaningfully through currency conversion alone.

Throughout, I have modernized spelling and punctuation for all Renaissance and early modern manuscripts and printed works, as well as, where I felt this was appropriate, modern transcriptions of manuscripts and early printed books. I have also modernized the titles of most early works, and presented, as far as possible, a consistent style in such referencing, except where I felt that the title of a work is better known in its original form. I have translated all Elizabeth Russell's poems in Greek and Latin myself. I have sometimes deliberately taken a few liberties with my translations in order to communicate something of the emotional texture of Elizabeth's

expression as well as bring out selected meanings which I have interpreted as inherent in the ambiguous diction of the Greek and Latin
originals; meanings which I believe their author intended. The most
accurate and scholarly transcriptions and translations of all Elizabeth Russell's currently known poems can be found in Patricia
Phillippy's masterly edition, *Elizabeth Cooke Hoby Russell: The Writings of an English Sappho*, with excellent translations by Jaime
Goodrich.

When presenting measurements for the dimensions of buildings
in the Blackfriars I have reproduced the format preserved in the
indentures, leases and sale agreements in which they are described,
rendering these in feet. Other, longer, distances have been recorded
in miles. My calculations of the relative positions of Elizabeth Russell's home and Thomas Vautrollier's/Richard Field's printing press
(as well as my identification of the site in today's Blackfriars,
London, where I believe Elizabeth's home to have once stood) have
been derived from my cross-referencing of the Dowager's descriptions of her property with the tenancy and sale agreements of her
neighbours, and my own inspection of the current Blackfriars. It
goes without saying that any mistakes made in this book are entirely
my own.

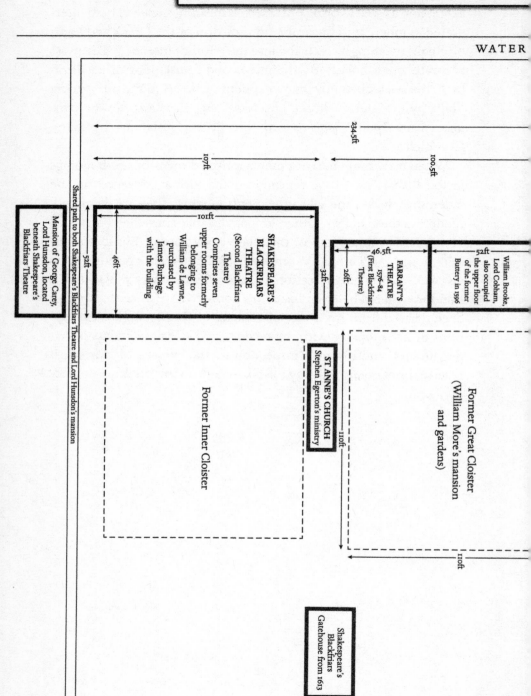

WATER

234.5ft

107ft

100.5ft

Shared path to both Shakespeare's Blackfriars Theatre and Lord Hunsdon's mansion

Mansion of George Carey,
Lord Hunsdon, located
beneath Shakespeare's
Blackfriars Theatre

101ft

52ft

46ft

32ft

**SHAKESSPEARE'S
BLACKFRIARS
THEATRE**
(Second Blackfriars
Theatre)
Comprises seven
upper rooms formerly
belonging to
William de Lawne,
purchased by
James Burbage
with the building

46.5ft

26ft

**FARRANT'S
THEATRE**
1576–84
(First Blackfriars
Theatre)

52ft

William Brooke,
Lord Cobham,
also occupied
the upper floor
of the former
Buttery in 1596

ST ANNE'S CHURCH
Stephen Egerton's ministry

Former Inner Cloister

Former Great Cloister
(William More's mansion
and gardens)

110ft

110ft

Shakespeare's
Blackfriars
Gatehouse from 1613

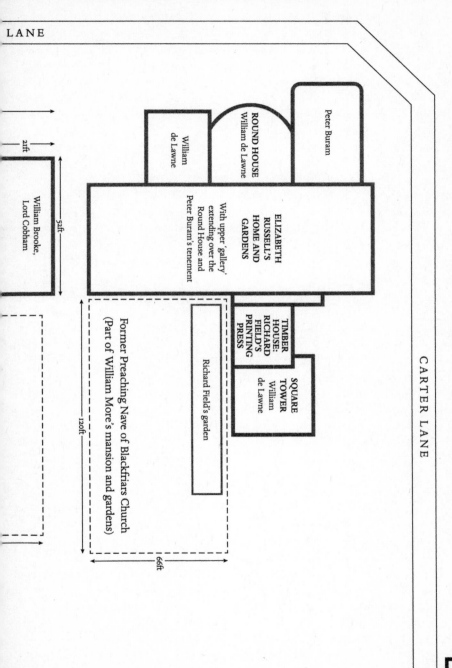

LANE

21ft

52ft

William
de Lawne

ROUND HOUSE
William de Lawne

Peter Buram

William Brooke,
Lord Cobham

ELIZABETH
RUSSELL'S
HOME AND
GARDENS

With upper 'gallery'
extending over the
Round House and
Peter Buram's tenement

TIMBER
HOUSE:
RICHARD
FIELD'S
PRINTING
PRESS

SQUARE
TOWER
William
de Lawne

120ft

Former Preaching Nave of Blackfriars Church
(Part of William More's mansion and gardens)

Richard Field's garden

66ft

CARTER LANE

The
Bell Inn

Principal Persons in Elizabeth Russell's Family Tree

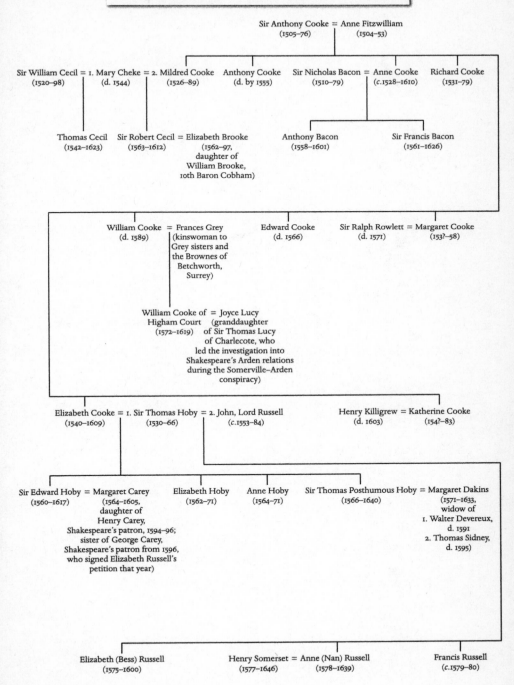

Sir Anthony Cooke = Anne Fitzwilliam
(1505–76)   (1504–53)

Sir William Cecil = 1. Mary Cheke = 2. Mildred Cooke   Anthony Cooke   Sir Nicholas Bacon = Anne Cooke   Richard Cooke
(1520–98)   (d. 1544)   (1526–89)   (d. by 1555)   (1510–79)   (c.1528–1610)   (1531–79)

Thomas Cecil   Sir Robert Cecil = Elizabeth Brooke   Anthony Bacon   Sir Francis Bacon
(1542–1623)   (1563–1612)   (1562–97,   (1558–1601)   (1561–1626)
                                      daughter of
                                      William Brooke,
                                      10th Baron Cobham)

William Cooke = Frances Grey   Edward Cooke   Sir Ralph Rowlett = Margaret Cooke
(d. 1589)   (kinswoman to   (d. 1566)   (d. 1571)   (153?–58)
                Grey sisters and
                the Brownes of
                Betchworth,
                Surrey)

William Cooke of = Joyce Lucy
Higham Court   (granddaughter
(1572–1619)   of Sir Thomas Lucy
                  of Charlecote, who
                  led the investigation into
                  Shakespeare's Arden relations
                  during the Somerville–Arden
                  conspiracy)

Elizabeth Cooke = 1. Sir Thomas Hoby = 2. John, Lord Russell   Henry Killigrew = Katherine Cooke
(1540–1609)   (1530–66)   (c.1553–84)   (d. 1603)   (154?–83)

Sir Edward Hoby = Margaret Carey   Elizabeth Hoby   Anne Hoby   Sir Thomas Posthumous Hoby = Margaret Dakins
(1560–1617)   (1564–1605,   (1562–71)   (1564–71)   (1566–1640)   (1571–1633,
                   daughter of   widow of
                   Henry Carey,   1. Walter Devereux,
                   Shakespeare's patron, 1594–96;   d. 1591
                   sister of George Carey,   2. Thomas Sidney,
                   Shakespeare's patron from 1596,   d. 1595)
                   who signed Elizabeth Russell's
                   petition that year)

Elizabeth (Bess) Russell   Henry Somerset = Anne (Nan) Russell   Francis Russell
(1575–1600)   (1577–1646)   (1578–1639)   (c.1579–80)

I most humbly beseech your Lordship, suffer me not to take any wrong or dishonour by being contemptuously trodden on and over-braved by my malicious inferiors and adversaries ... I am a noblewoman, so near yourself in nature as me thinketh your Lordship should do yourself but right, in showing earnestly your displeasure toward any that to my dishonour contemptuously wrong me by riot or unlawfully distrain upon any land of mine ... A Lady of my place is no way subject to any Justice of [the] Peace ... My Lord, my honour [is] dearer to me than my life.

– Elizabeth Russell, Dowager, to Robert Cecil,
Secretary of State and Lord Treasurer of England, 1608

Prologue

A Blackfriars Mystery

In November 1596 William Shakespeare was engulfed by a catastrophe. The force which stormed into his life and shook it to the core was a woman named Elizabeth Russell. That winter she began a campaign which would nearly destroy the dramatist's career and leave him facing financial ruin. She would lead an uprising against his theatrical troupe and business partners, managing to turn even his closest friends and allies against him. In the process she would spark one of the most baffling mysteries of Shakespeare's life, for Lady Russell's personal army would include the two men who stood to gain the most from his continuing success: his patron, George Carey, Lord Hunsdon, and his boyhood comrade and publisher, Richard Field.

This is the true story of the woman whose battle with Shakespeare and his associates in the Blackfriars of London gave birth to the world's most iconic theatre: the Globe.

Jutting sharply out of the corner of Ireland Yard and St Andrew's Hill in the Blackfriars is the Cockpit Pub. Stand facing it and you are looking at the site of the now vanished Blackfriars Gatehouse, a building purchased by Shakespeare in 1613. Walk a few paces to the west, down the narrow strip of Ireland Yard, and you come to Playhouse Yard. It was here that the playhouse which has since come to be known as Shakespeare's Blackfriars Theatre was constructed in 1596. Loiter in this quiet square, under the shadow of its sombre office blocks, among parked bicycles and office workers taking lunch or cigarette breaks. You will find it requires some effort of the imagination to picture it as the scene of a conflict which would dramatically change the course of Shakespeare's career.

Continue west through Playhouse Yard then turn right into Blackfriars Lane and keep going, for around a minute and a half, until you come to the point at which Ludgate Broadway extends northwards away from you and the ancient Carter Lane beckons to your right. You are standing as close as you ever will to the home of Elizabeth Russell. It was from here that the woman who styled herself with the honorific title Dowager Countess of Bedford coordinated her operation against the backers of the theatre that was built by Shakespeare's business partner, James Burbage. This was to be the new state-of-the-art venue for England's premier theatrical troupe, the Chamberlain's Men. Burbage had staked a fortune on this risky venture after failing to secure an extension to the lease of the company's current premises, the Theatre in Shoreditch, lying just under two miles from the Blackfriars. It was here that Shakespeare cut his teeth as a dramatist and, with the licence on the land upon which the playhouse was built due to expire in April 1597, everything was riding on Burbage's latest scheme. Unlike the more old-fashioned Shoreditch amphitheatre, which was open to the elements and could therefore be used only in the warmer months, the Blackfriars was an indoor playhouse which could open its doors all year round. Full of the latest in special-effects technology and boasting a more luxurious interior, it catered to a deeper-pocketed clientele. The Chamberlain's Men were within reach of greater status and wealth than they had yet known. As the company's leading playwright and sharer, able to claim a percentage of the profits in exchange for paying towards the theatrical team's running costs, Shakespeare now stood at his crossroads moment. Unfortunately for him, the Blackfriars Theatre was built on the doorstep of Elizabeth Russell. Galvanizing the community into action, she led a backlash against the theatrical team behind it, leaving the dramatist and his friends without a home venue and on the verge of bankruptcy.

Sparking one of the most critical turning points in Shakespeare's career, Elizabeth Russell's machinations, it would not be untrue to say, have shaped today's London skyline and with it the playwright's lasting legacy. The Globe Theatre, to which thousands of bardolaters flock from far and wide every year to witness the dramatization of Shakespeare's words, would not now grace the Bankside had it not been for the Dowager's clash with the entrepreneurs who built its predecessor. With the doors to the Blackfriars Theatre shut in his face, Shakespeare was forced into the Globe venture, thus securing his indelible association with this most recognizable of landmarks.

Among the National Archives in Kew there is a bundle of curious documents which were once the cause of a national scandal. Classed among the papers identified with the reference number SP 12/260 are two petitions. The first, beginning on folio 176, is headed by the name 'Elizabeth Russell, Dowager'. Two folios on, another document, apparently in answer to the first, bears the name 'Willm Shakespeare'. Placed together, these petitions seem to speak to each other, or rather to shout, for they echo with raised voices in a heated dialogue between history's most famous playwright and this almost entirely unknown woman.

Both petitions are addressed to Queen Elizabeth I's Privy Council, the most powerful governing body in the land, comprising a committee of learned men whose role was to advise their sovereign on matters of domestic and foreign policy. That submitted under the auspices of Elizabeth Russell reveals a female-led crusade; her endeavour to block the opening of a newly built theatre which Shakespeare was about to occupy in the fashionable London district of the Blackfriars in 1596. The document in which Shakespeare's name appears imbues these events with a combative air, for it is a riposte, a counter-plea by the playwright and some of his fellow actors and sharers in the Chamberlain's Men, including Thomas Pope, John Heminges, Augustine Phillips, Will Kemp, William Sly, Nicholas Tooley and James Burbage's son Richard. Through this document Shakespeare appears to be fighting back against the woman who drew to her side 'certain persons (some of them of honour), inhabitants of the precinct and liberty of the Blackfriars', in a mission to 'shut up' their theatre. This action, as the playwright and his co-petitioners maintained, was prosecuted to their 'manifest great injury . . . who have no other means whereby to maintain their wives and families'. When these petitions came to the attention of the leading palaeographers and archivists in the country in the nineteenth century they caused a storm which would turn the Department of Manuscripts of the British Museum, in the words of one contemporary commentator, into 'a literary Old Bailey'. The accused: the renowned editor and scholar John Payne Collier. The crime: forgery.

On 30 January 1860 an intimidating group of scholars was summoned to the State Paper Office in London by Sir John Romilly, the Master of the Rolls. Their purpose was to undertake a thorough examination of the Shakespeare petition. In 1831 Collier first published the contents of the document which, as he boasted proudly, 'contains the name of our great dramatist', claiming that it had 'never seen the light from the moment it was presented, until it was very recently discovered'. The men who led the investigation into its authenticity were Sir Francis Palgrave, Deputy Keeper of Public Records; Sir Frederick Madden, Keeper of Manuscripts in the British Museum; J. S. Brewer, Reader at the Rolls; T. Duffus Hardy, Assistant Keeper of Records; and N. E. S. A. Hamilton of the British Museum's Department of Manuscripts. Having completed their inspection of the disputed manuscript, they added a note to the bundle in which the petition would remain to this very day: 'We, the undersigned, at the desire of the Master of the Rolls, have carefully examined the document hereunto annexed . . . and we are of opinion, that the document in question, is spurious.'

The scandal that followed kept journalists busy for the next eight months, 'lifting up their voices against Mr. Collier'. Accusations and defences were issued in the *Athenaeum* and *Edinburgh Review* in which the authenticity of the petition was debated, while Hamilton composed a spirited attack on Collier for misdemeanours 'so vile and gross that a man of honour would scarcely whisper them to his own heart'. The story did not end there. Several months after

Collier's exposure, in December of 1860, the archivist Robert Lemon did something strange. Unseen by anyone, he retrieved the document and attached a defiant note to the bundle. Remaining undiscovered until 4 April 1868, it read:

> I, Robert Lemon . . . Assistant Keeper of Records of the First Class, late secretary of the Commission for Printing and Publishing State Papers, and for above Forty years an Officer in Her Majesty's State Paper Office, have carefully examined the Petition of the Players hereunto annexed, and I am of opinion that the document in question is <u>not</u> spurious.

Lemon was not so outspoken in public. His caution may have been due to the fact that he had been roundly condemned in *The Times* on Saturday 14 May 1859 for his sloppy scholarliness and 'unsatisfactory' handling of the project to create a *Calendar of State Papers*. Despite, or rather because of, the damage already done to his reputation, Lemon offered a somewhat lukewarm defence of Collier in a printed letter to the editor of the *Athenaeum* on 14 February 1860, claiming that the Shakespeare petition 'was well known to my father and myself, before Mr. Payne Collier began his researches'. At least he was 'pretty confident' about this. Hardly iron-clad testimony. This was news to the academic community, who knew full well that his father, the archivist Robert Lemon senior, had been close friends with the suspected forger. The younger Robert Lemon's critics therefore surmised that he had merely been 'badgered' into an unconvincing plea on Collier's behalf. 'It must at first strike every one as extraordinary,' wrote one of Collier's chief detractors, C. M. Ingleby, in 1861, 'that the editor of "The Athenaeum," while he was examining Mr. Lemon, should have omitted to ask that palaeographist whether he believed the Players' Petition to be a genuine document.'

The scandal of the Collier forgery put other documents he claimed to have discovered under the spotlight. One of these 'suspected' manuscripts was Elizabeth Russell's petition. Among the

'Jury of Scholars' which presided over Collier's humiliating public trial, there could scarcely be found among them anyone who believed that such a document existed. The reason for this, given with curt dismissiveness by Ingleby, was that 'no petitions to the Privy Council of that period were signed by such an overwhelming array of names', much less ones headed by a woman. Collier stood condemned by his peers. The investigations concluded that, in an attempt to ensure his lasting fame as a great editor and intrepid bringer-into-the-light of Shakespeare's secrets, he had deftly inserted fictionalized documents among the authentic manuscripts to which he had ready access, later insisting that he had unearthed these explosive relics of theatrical history to the view of a grateful scholarly community. The Shakespeare petition was an elaborate hoax.

Elizabeth Russell's petition is now widely regarded by Shakespeare scholars as an accurate copy of a now lost authentic address to the Privy Council. Coming across this document, Collier must have been struck by the uncommon nature of the noblewoman's project. It is probable that his imagination had been fired by an earnest desire to hear Shakespeare's side of the story. His fake counter-petition seemed to give the world what it wanted, the other half of the argument between Elizabeth Russell and the players that raged in the Blackfriars in 1596 and which could be only partially glimpsed through the genuine petition. He had done history a disservice. Touched with the infamy of the Collier forgeries, Lady Russell's petition and her own story dropped out of public consciousness. It is time to restore them, for the truth is far more extraordinary than even Collier's fantasy could devise.

I hope that this book will help repair some of the damage done by Collier, providing incontrovertible proof that Elizabeth Russell's petition is authentic and thereby solving one of the persistent enigmas of Shakespeare's career. Even a cursory look at the petition calls to attention the names over which there hangs an unsettling air of betrayal. 'G. Hunsdon', Shakespeare's patron from 1596 and the man to whom the Burbage family were bound professionally, is given prominence as the second signatory. Two rows down we come to 'Ric: Ffeild', who first brought Shakespeare to print as the author of *Venus and Adonis* in 1593. The playwright's most popular published work during his lifetime, it notched up at least ten separate editions, and was succeeded a year later by *The Rape of Lucrece*, which rolled off the presses in an impressive additional six editions. What could have possessed these men, who by all accounts were damaging their own interests in their support of Elizabeth Russell, to turn against Shakespeare? How did she convince them to join her in evicting him from the playhouse which was his chief hope in one of the most perilous periods of his career? Her petition has never before been explored in detail, but it holds the key to solving this compelling mystery. Alongside new discoveries about Shakespeare's publisher which explain his actions in 1596, this book will unveil the hidden lives of the petitioners who supported Lady Russell. Their stories, their relation to each other and to the woman who broke so spectacularly with contemporary rules of female conduct in her attempt to put Shakespeare's company permanently out of business, will tell us much we did not know about the political, economic and social pressures which governed the dramatist's life and work.

Who was Elizabeth Russell at the precise moment when she took up her pen in the Blackfriars to sign the document which nearly put a stop to Shakespeare's progress as a playwright? Her ability to prevail in her challenge to a successful theatrical consortium led by a group of worldly and talented men, its patron a blood relation of the Queen, did not rest merely on her local powerbase in the Blackfriars. It was determined in large measure by her indomitable will, her unusual education and by the arsenal of skills, contacts and experience she acquired through the many battles in which she had engaged throughout her controversial life. Her personal journey is no less spectacular than her collision with Shakespeare's enterprising theatrical team. She was the first female in the country to become her Queen's soldier, acquiring the Keepership of her own castle – an office with martial responsibilities which had traditionally been the preserve of men alone. A committed religious radical and activist, she operated at the heart of a network of extremists whose secret operations stretched across Europe. She involved herself in the murky world of Elizabethan espionage, becoming a spy and detective for the English intelligence services and wading with alacrity into some of the most infamous conspiracies ever to have rocked the royal throne. Renowned throughout Europe for her uncommon learning, she was a poet, linguist and celebrated designer of the country's most innovative monuments to the great and the good of Elizabethan society. Taking up the gauntlet for those less fortunate than herself, she was a protector of orphans and an early champion of women's rights. Time and again her conflicts led her into scandalous legal suits, acts of rioting, violent affray, kidnapping, breaking and entering, illegal imprisonment and armed combat. To her, warfare had become second nature.

Such a formidable woman, who had a decisive impact on the trajectory of his own vocation, could not fail to have made an impression on Shakespeare. It is my contention that, as well as incorporating allusions to the outrageous exploits of Elizabeth Russell and her kinsmen in a number of plays, the dramatist used her as the model for the Dowager Countess of Roussillon in *All's Well That Ends Well*, the character George Bernard Shaw described affectionately as 'the most beautiful old woman's part ever written'. Recovering the traces of Elizabeth's voice in this play would be some recompense for the damage done to her posthumous reputation. Today, outside of academic circles, the Dowager Countess Elizabeth Russell is popularly remembered as the 'wicked' woman who murdered a son and conspired to conceal the evidence, a crime for which her restless ghost is said still to pay its penance in the halls of Bisham Abbey, Lady Russell's former home in Berkshire. There is no basis to these fictions, yet they have eclipsed Elizabeth's real achievements. The chapters which follow will set the record straight.

In 1596 a woman walked through the streets of the Blackfriars, hurriedly navigating the cluster of private residences and shopping arcades that were part of what was once the monastery of the Dominican order of the Black Friars from which the district took its name. She stopped occasionally at a door, on which she or one of her servants would knock with brisk urgency. Once it was opened, the resident within would be presented with a large sheet of paper, a petition addressed to the honourable Lords of the Privy Council, and their attention would be drawn to the space below it awaiting their signature.

As each door opened, the occupant of the house or shop would have found themselves face to face with Elizabeth Russell. The first thing they would have noticed was her accustomed widow's weeds. She would have been wearing a long black gown fronted with a contrasting white bodice, a black cloak trimmed with white lace flailing out behind her. The most arresting feature would have been her gargantuan widow's hood, stiffened with starch and wire until it resembled the head of a cobra about to strike its victim. Wisps of vibrant auburn-red hair would have peeked from the sides of her tight white headdress. Above a stifling starched ruff the occupant would have noted her small, pursed lips. Beneath the broad brim of her lace-fringed hood, grey-blue eyes, alert and piercing, would have returned their stare.

To reanimate the cast in Elizabeth Russell's battle with the creators and sponsors of the Blackfriars Theatre, I have mapped the homes and businesses of her most influential followers. For centuries, the precise location of the Dowager's home has remained unknown, as has that of the printing press of Shakespeare's publisher, Richard Field. Uncovering Elizabeth Russell's story has allowed me to rediscover these sites, and in doing so reveal the intricate relations and obligations that determined the conditions under which the playwright's supporters and their enemies locked swords in the Blackfriars. With these pieces of the puzzle restored, the streets through which this noblewoman passed as she whipped up support for her campaign spring back to life, resounding again with the footsteps of one of its most notorious residents. Elizabeth's progress can now be followed for the first time in over four centuries, providing us with a greater understanding of the circumstances that fashioned the literary and theatrical heritage which has become global in more than one sense; for the woman who took up arms against the Blackfriars Theatre, with devastating consequences for the 'sweet swan of Avon', set in motion the chain of events that would be the making of Shakespeare as we know him today: the Shakespeare of the Globe.

PART ONE
An Education

I.

A Radical Beginning

In more practised hands, the blow, striking home, would have severed her arm. Narrowly missing its aim, the heavy spiked blade instead sliced through the reins at which Anne Fitzwilliam Cooke clawed for stability as she stumbled from her horse in the Hoddesdon mud. Rising to face her assailant, she took in the proportions of the weapon she had dodged by a hair's breadth. It was a bill, a long battle-pole terminating in a distinctive curved chopping-blade topped with a spear-like barb and engineered to cause maximum carnage. Had the bill's deadly heft fallen inches the other way, Elizabeth Russell would never have been born.

The riot took place on 16 August 1534, six years before Anne Cooke gave birth to Elizabeth. That was the summer in which Anne's father, Sir William Fitzwilliam of Gains Park in Essex, died. A wealthy London merchant, Fitzwilliam had risen to prominence after receiving great favours at the hands of Cardinal Thomas Wolsey, Lord Chancellor and one-time principal advisor to Henry VIII. As well as being appointed to an enviable position as Wolsey's Treasurer, he had become an alderman in 1504 and Sheriff of London two years later. Before his death, on 9 August, he had appointed as one of his executors Anthony Cooke. The latter's father, John Cooke, had added to his substantial landholdings in Essex and Warwickshire when he married Alice Saunders, whose family had accumulated their wealth from the wool trade.

Born in 1505, Anthony was a perfect match for Anne, who was just one year his junior. His attractiveness was no doubt increased by the fact that in 1521 he had inherited a vast estate from his great-uncle Sir Edward Belknap, more than doubling the inheritance that had been left by his father in 1516. The couple were married some time before 1523, the year in which Anthony, at just seventeen years of age, had enrolled in the Inner Temple, the country's premier training ground for a career in the legal profession. The newly-weds moved into the Cooke estate of Gidea Hall in Essex, just ten miles from Gains Park, little knowing that their new home would soon become famous throughout Europe because of the attainments of their remarkable daughters.

Anne Cooke was charged with the heavy task of preparing for her father's funeral, which was to take place in his home parish of Milton, Northamptonshire, on 20 August. She went on ahead to make the necessary arrangements, accompanied by her sister-in-law Anne Sapcote Fitzwilliam; Anthony Cooke's uncle Sir Richard Cooke; four other gentlewomen; and six servants. The journey had been fairly uneventful until they came within one mile of Hoddesdon, in Hertfordshire, where they were forced to slow their pace after finding themselves riding behind Robert Mitchell, a butcher by trade, and his servant. One of Anne Sapcote Fitzwilliam's servants, annoyed by the clouds of dust the pair were kicking up in the faces of those riding immediately behind, politely requested that they draw aside 'that the gentlewomen and their company might the more quietly and surely pass'. This was a mistake.

The butcher shot him a proud look and answered curtly that 'the way was as common and free for him as for them and would not forbear his way for no man's pleasure'. Next to try his luck was Sir Richard Cooke, confident that his superior breeding better equipped him to prevail with the stranger. In grandiloquent tones he offered to 'drink with him at the next town and give him a quart of wine there' if he would allow them to pass out of mere courtesy for the gentlewomen. Then he paused, waiting for an apologetic stream of effusive gratitude from his auditor. None was forthcoming. Instead he was treated to such a torrent of choice profanities that the party thought 'the man had not been well in his wits'.

'Well knave, by God's body,' cursed the butcher, 'I will make thee and all thy company drink when ye come to Hoddesdon, that peradventure ye shall repent it.' With that, he proceeded on his former course with his servant, taking up the entire width of the road. Anne Cooke and her retinue had to endure the rest of the journey to Hoddesdon with the surly butcher swearing, muttering threats and flicking dust at them.

When they reached the town the butcher suddenly turned to face them and they saw, to their utter amazement, that he had 'got a great cudgel in his hand'. Thrusting the weapon in their faces, he summoned his neighbours to his side with an outcry of 'Clubs, clubs! For God's blood, staves, staves! Down with these whoreson courtiers!' A heartbeat later a horde of townsfolk, about two hundred in all, rushed out into the street 'with great force and arms' and 'struck the horses, the servants, and the women, and pulled them off their horsebacks and riotously did beat them and sore wounded divers of them'.

Concerned for her servants, Anne Cooke's sister-in-law charged into the marauding crowd on horseback. 'For the passion of Christ,' she screamed above the din, 'keep the peace for God's sake, and save my men and slay them not!' She then alighted from her horse with the intention of breaking up the rampaging mob, but did not get very far before she felt something hard connect with her face. The world span as Robert Mitchell swung his cudgel before her. For the next assault he dispensed with the weapon and 'like a mad man . . . beat her to the ground' using his fist; a fist well used to carving up flesh. Before she could recover her senses the other rioters, brandishing 'bills, staves, clubs, swords, bucklers, bows and arrows', had encircled her, raining down 'above 20 strokes' and leaving her 'scant able to stand'. It was in this human maelstrom that Anne Cooke came to distinguish herself with her bravery. Despite finding herself 'in the uttermost despair of her life that any creature might be', she rushed to rescue her kinswoman, only to be stopped in her tracks by one of the 'riotous persons', who broke from the rest and rushed towards her wielding the bill that nearly ended her life.

Unluckily for the besieged courtiers, Mitchell was also the town's constable. In the chaos that followed, three of the servants were manhandled from the scene and, 'like thieves and murderers', unceremoniously carted off to gaol, which the locals referred to ominously as 'the Cage'. The visitors knew the game was up, for now at least, and had little choice but to beat a hasty and humiliating retreat. Seeing this, some of the rioters gleefully began to throw mud and dust at their faces and clothes. Others thought it more expedient to send them packing with a cold douche of stale ale and beer. Drenched to the skin, their courtly finery stained and mud-spattered, the exhausted funeral party retreated, egos bruised, revenge in their hearts. And revenge they would have, before too long.

The confidence of the inhabitants of Hoddesdon was, as it transpired, due to the fact that they had the backing of Lord Henry Bourchier, Earl of Essex, the Chief Captain of the King's Forces and a principal landowner in the area. Undaunted, the Cookes and Fitzwilliams brought their case to Thomas Cromwell, who was then just two years into his role as Henry VIII's chief advisor, following the death of Cardinal Wolsey. On 23 September he was informed about the 'rude handling' of Anne Cooke and the other gentlewomen in her party, and reminded that he 'honoured ladies and gentlewomen too much to see these take shame by a villain'. He would see to it that their assailants were punished in the highest court in the land: the Star Chamber. Established to hear the cases of the nobility and gentry, this court was located in the Palace of Westminster and presided over by the King's Privy Councillors. Here, at the heart of the machinery of power, the victims could be certain that their case would be heard among friends. Not even the warlike Bourchier could prevail.

There was more to the Hoddesdon riot than a spiteful butcher's personal prejudices against the fripperies of the court. The battle lines had been drawn as a consequence of the tensions between the Pope and the English King as the latter sought to justify his divorce from Catherine of Aragon and his marriage to Anne Boleyn, which took place in January 1533. Thomas Cromwell had facilitated the union, which outraged the Catholic superpowers of Europe. Just months after the riot Henry would break with the Church of Rome and declare himself Supreme Head of the Church of England. These seismic events were sending ripples through every part of the country, and it is easy to see how the inhabitants of outlying parishes, resistant to change and having lost a beloved Catholic Queen, might have seen the King's courtiers as representatives of the municipal and bureaucratic structures which they felt were meddling in local affairs.

When the Cookes and Fitzwilliams turned to Cromwell, one of the chief architects of the English Reformation, they began to forge a network of allegiances which would fundamentally underpin their political activism for years to come. It was into a world torn apart by the adherents of these conflicting religious ideologies that Elizabeth Cooke, later Lady Russell, was born in 1540. By this year the Dissolution of the Monasteries had swept away some 850 abbeys, priories and friaries. Elizabeth would grow up surrounded by the ghostly ruins of these once bustling edifices, at least two of which would be converted into properties she would inherit and which would become the backdrops to her own battles: Bisham Abbey in Berkshire; and a section of the former Dominican stronghold of the Black Friars in London. The latter was part of a complex in which Shakespeare's Blackfriars Theatre would be built. The chanting of the friars may have been silenced, the wealth of their religious houses plundered by the King and nobility, but the Reformation was not a single event. It was a work-in-progress which continued to unleash violent energies throughout Elizabeth's tumultuous career, in the process giving shape to her identity and sense of vocation, with sometimes shocking results.

As a girl, Elizabeth must have listened with awe to dramatic retellings of the Hoddesdon riot. The involvement of her mother and aunt in such an extraordinary episode, alongside four other gentlewomen of their kinship, would have left an indelible mark on the family's personal mythology. Her sisters Mildred and Anne were, respectively, eight and seven years old when the incident occurred; old enough to remember the scandal and the legal quarrel it sparked.

The valorous conduct of the Cooke and Fitzwilliam women, eventually ratified and rewarded through recourse to the law, would establish a pattern in Elizabeth's own life. A woman's war against angry rioters, prominent local men and even institutions would become a recurring theme in her own story, as would a reliance on the powerhouses that were the Privy Council and the Court of Star Chamber.

The Hoddesdon riot provides a glimpse of the uncommon women who surrounded Elizabeth during her formative years. Among them was Anthony Cooke's stepmother, Margaret Pennington Cooke, who married John Cooke in 1512 when Anthony was only seven years old. Once lady-in-waiting to Catherine of Aragon, she became 'Gentlewoman extra ordinary' under Princess Mary. She remained a committed Catholic her entire life, resisting the pressure to take up the cause of reform in the reigns of Henry VIII and his son Edward VI. A canny businesswoman, she managed extensive property holdings in Essex and, highly unusually, became executor to the will of a powerful male neighbour, a role almost exclusively undertaken by men up until this point.

Margaret Cooke was fervently litigious and had embroiled herself in controversy after controversy in her battle to secure her rights to land she held in Risebridge, within Havering. She had been leasing these from New College, Oxford, from around 1524. When the Lord Chancellor of Oxford, Sir Thomas Audeley, decided to grant the land to one Mr Legat of Hornchurch, Margaret immediately challenged the decision, securing the aid of Thomas Cromwell and Princess Mary herself. Her relationship with the princess was clearly an affectionate one, for she had sent her many gifts of sweet delicacies, puddings and fruit, and Mary was swift to pay back these kindnesses, writing personally on behalf of 'my mother's old servant' to complain that parties involved in the case, particularly the Lord Chancellor, had failed to behave 'gently'. Because Margaret was a very elderly woman in 1537, when the lease to the Risebridge lands expired, her opponents thought her easy pickings. They came up with a cunning compromise which they believed would ultimately work in their favour. They granted a joint lease for the space of ten years, or limited to the term of Margaret's natural life, feeling confident that she was not long for this world and they would soon be in full possession of the disputed lands. Margaret refused to comply. She stunned everyone by managing to outlive the period of the lease.

The formidable Margaret Cooke took over the raising of Anthony and later became godmother to two of his children. She would have been a potent presence during Elizabeth's girlhood, dying in 1552 when the latter was twelve years old. With such a radical beginning, among a family of feisty, fearless and pioneering females, it is hardly surprising that Elizabeth would one day grow to become the kind of woman who would lead her own armed foot soldiers into combat with rioters; convert part of her home into a prison wherein her enemies would be consigned at her pleasure; and take up arms against the entrepreneurs behind the Elizabethan theatre.

The Cambridge scholar Walter Haddon, who would fall in love with the young Elizabeth, summed up her character best when he compared her to a warrior-woman who 'marched in battle-gear'.

The Female University

'Three things there are before whom . . . I cannot do amiss: 1. My Prince. 2. My Conscience. 3. My Children.' So declared Elizabeth Russell's father, Anthony Cooke, according to one of his earliest biographers, David Lloyd, who eulogized him at length in his *Statesmen and Favourites of England* of 1665. Not necessarily in that order, one might say, for Cooke became best known, both during his own age and through the succeeding centuries, for his devotion to his children's education. By the time Elizabeth emerged from the home which has since come to be known among academics and historians as the 'female university', she would be widely recognized as one of the most learned women in Europe.

Cooke's paternal endeavours accelerated his promotion as tutor to Henry VIII's heir, Edward VI, a post which would see him joining the Cambridge scholar John Cheke as recipient of a £100 annuity granted for the purpose. For generations to come Cooke would be memorialized for the care with which he instructed his precious charge. His fellow religious radical Peter Martyr would later write to him in praise of his 'singular piety and learning, and also for the worthy office which you faithfully and with great renown executed in the Christian public wealth, in instructing Edward, that most holy King'. John Strype, Cheke's first biographer, credited Cooke with his pupil's steadfast commitment to reform, insisting that 'particularly his memory is to be preserved, for having been one of those that first imbued the mind of that excellent prince, King Edward VI, with right principles of religion, and an instrument of his extraordinary attainments in learning'.

Cooke's appointment to this most prestigious of posts had been made under the auspices of Edward Seymour, Earl of Hertford, brother to Queen Jane Seymour and hence Edward VI's uncle. A staunch reformer, he was proclaimed Lord Protector of England and Governor of the King's Person on 31 January 1547, just three days after Henry VIII's death. Ruling in the nine-year-old monarch's stead until he reached the end of his minority, he ensured the creation of a deftly revised coronation oath which removed the Crown's obligation to protect the privileges of the clergy. Masterminded in collusion with the Archbishop of Canterbury, Thomas Cranmer, this vested in the King sole power to define the basis for 'law and liberty' within his dominions, opening the way for the Reformation to go further than it ever had under Henry VIII.

Seymour was showered with further honours on 17 February, when he was created Duke of Somerset, and it is no doubt due to his influence that Cooke was included among the leading courtiers made 'Knights of the Bath' during the coronation celebrations, a title believed to have once been conferred through an ancient ceremonial bathing ritual. Anthony was proudly following in the footsteps of his great-grandfather Sir Thomas Cooke, who had held this accolade before him. It was an elevation that formed part of a career trajectory which involved him in the pomp of martial display as much as it did in the grimier aspects of military endeavour and local law enforcement. In 1539 he was made one of Henry VIII's 'spears', his ceremonial bodyguards, and was part of the formal pageantry which welcomed the Admiral of France during his ambassadorial mission in 1546. When horses and footmen were needed for a military campaign in Flanders in 1543 he was called upon to supply ten footmen. A similar number was requested to augment the vanguard in France the following year, coinciding with his appointment as Sheriff of Essex and Hertfordshire. Like his male forebears he had often served as a Havering Justice of the Peace and member of the Essex Commission of the Peace.

As one of Edward VI's knights, symbolically conscripted into the Protestant army being fashioned by the ambitious Duke of Somerset, Cooke was in a prime position to guide the education of the new King in a manner that would serve his patron's interests. His appointment as royal tutor, it has since been said, came about after the Protector had witnessed Cooke offering some chiding precepts to his son. 'Some men govern Families with more skill than others do Kingdoms,' announced the enraptured Duke, before sealing the deal on the spot. Despite this pleasant anecdote, recorded by Lloyd, Cooke's sons – Anthony, Richard, Edward and William – did not in fact distinguish themselves in the public arena to any notable degree, most of them dying relatively early: Anthony by 1555, Edward in 1566, Richard in 1579 and William in 1589. Yet Lloyd makes the intriguing observation that 'Sir Anthony took more pleasure to breed up statesmen than to be one.' While Edward had some minor involvement in diplomatic missions to France, it was left to his sisters to gain the universal approbation and notoriety which had eluded the Cooke boys.

There were five girls in all. The eldest, Mildred Cooke, was born on 25 August 1526, and is the only one of the sisters for whom there is a secure birthdate. Anne arrived around two years later. She was probably followed by Margaret in the mid- to late 1530s. Next came Elizabeth, born around 1540. Finally, there was Katherine, whose birth may have occurred some time between 1542 and 1547. At least four of Cooke's daughters would become famous across Europe for their skills as linguists, translators, poets and religious activists. Elizabeth, the most politically engaged of all the siblings, would later describe herself as a 'courtier and parliament woman', and the sisters' collective endeavours would come to justify their being ranked among the 'statesmen' whom Anthony Cooke had bred.

This is all the more remarkable given that there is no evidence that Anthony Cooke attended university. It is likely that during his early adulthood he began an ambitious, one might say audacious, programme of self-schooling, which he later applied with equal vigour to the education of his children. Elizabeth and her sisters would join Edward VI in Anthony's school. It would be a pedagogical powerhouse.

★

In 1550 Walter Haddon had been invited to stay with his friend Sir Anthony Cooke in the Essex liberty of Havering-atte-Bower, part of what is now the north-east London suburb of Romford. As he crossed over the house's drawbridge he took in the magnificent proportions of Gidea Hall. Something of the aspirations of Sir Thomas Cooke, Anthony Cooke's great-grandfather and the man responsible for entrenching the family in this country seat in the second half of the fifteenth century, could still be discerned in its design. The plans drawn up for its renovation in 1465, which would remain largely unrealized, included the crenellating and fortification of the building. Over successive generations of Cooke men, Gidea Hall would slowly take shape within the confines of the moat first conceived by its early founder, acquiring six domed turrets which protruded majestically above a forest of chimney stacks. Anthony Cooke inherited what his ancestor had hoped would eventually become a grand castle. Under his governance, however, it became a stronghold of learning, and would be lauded across the centuries as an academy for some of the most accomplished women in English history.

When Haddon entered Gidea Hall he witnessed at first hand the training regime that was giving the Cooke sisters the tools to enter the public arena, and he was dumbfounded. These young women were handling ancient and modern languages alike with such aplomb that there could scarce have been a man to rival them. It is possible that Haddon became involved in their schooling, for he later recalled them during one of his lectures at Cambridge University, no doubt hoping to shame some of his less assiduous male students out of their indolence. 'What kind of house did I see there?' he intoned from his lectern, before artfully correcting himself, for this was no ordinary household. 'On the contrary!, [it was] rather a little university. Verily, while employed there, I seemed to be living within a Tusculan villa, except for the fact that in this Tusculum the studies of women were actually thriving.'

It was in a villa in Tusculum, an ancient Roman city in Latium, Italy, that the great rhetorician Cicero was believed to have composed his *Tusculanae Disputationes*, or *Tusculan Disputations*, which propounded his take on Stoic philosophy. Haddon had good reason to invoke the spirit of Cicero, for these female pupils were becoming fearsome rhetoricians thanks to the most cutting-edge educational programmes of the day. To this endeavour, Anthony Cooke and his fellow instructor, John Cheke, Regius Professor in Greek at St John's College, Cambridge, were applying the latest innovations in humanist practice.

Humanism was a pedagogical movement that centred on the revival of classical learning, placing grammar, rhetoric, poetry, history and moral philosophy at the heart of a new curriculum in the liberal arts. These principles spread from the Continent into England, in large measure through the assiduous efforts of Desiderius Erasmus and Sir Thomas More, Renaissance Europe's most celebrated humanist intellectuals. New colleges were founded to put these ideals into practice, among the most important being St John's, Cambridge, which would steep a generation of young men in the study of Greek and Latin; future statesmen such as William Cecil, who enrolled there in 1535, and Thomas Hoby, who arrived in 1545, both of whom were tutored by John Cheke. Hoby would go on to translate one of the most influential books of the Renaissance, Baldassare Castiglione's *Il Libro del Cortegiano*, rendered in English as *The Book of the Courtier*. This placed the humanist ethos at the very heart of the courtier's civic responsibilities and, more radically, it did not exclude women. Rather, it made such attainments a precondition for women's involvement in the public life of the court, arguing that 'many virtues of the mind . . . be as necessary for a woman, as for a man'. Not merely a man's silent consort, a woman should have such qualities in 'common with the Courtier, as wisdom, nobleness of courage', and be able to 'entertain all kind of men with talk worthy the hearing'.

Elizabeth thus received an education in the humanist mode, which was still relatively new to the English sensibility and which exemplified her father's belief 'that souls were equal, and that women are as capable of learning as men'. Behind the walls of

Gidea Hall, where discipline and love were doled out in equal measure, there were lessons in Greek and Latin, along with a smattering of Hebrew, as well as in other European languages, including French and Italian, imparting skills which would have been tested through rigorous exercises in translation. Cooke was himself a translator of some note, who knew how to use this learned art for political as well as pedagogical ends. In 1541 he had presented to Henry VIII the gift of his English rendering of a sermon by one of the early Church Fathers, St Cyprian, using the occasion to praise the King, in his dedicatory epistle, for being 'a valiant prince . . . warlike in strength and furniture for battle' whose reformation of religion had liberated a population 'oppressed with inestimable thraldom'. Cooke made sure his daughters studied St Cyprian alongside other early theologians, including St Chrysostom, St Basil the Great and St Gregory Nazianzen, whose works they would most often have read in Greek. The Greek New Testament and the great tomes produced by contemporary theologians would also have been on the reading list, the girls' appreciation of these texts sharpened by a regimen of prayers, attendance at sermons and spiritual self-examination. The studious routine was broken by other attainments, such as learning about the medicinal qualities of herbs and flowers, dancing and mastering musical instruments, particularly the lute, at which Anne was especially accomplished. When the girls and their mother wanted a moment to themselves they could sit together and chat while producing exquisite pieces of needlework and embroidery, or plying some other housewifely duty.

Religious studies and lessons in household economy were heartily approved by most commentators on women's education, such as the Spanish pedagogue Juan Luis Vives. These subjects assured the cultivation of the more traditional feminine virtues of humility and obedience. Women's access to pagan authors, on the other hand, whose morally questionable subjects included love, romance or war, had to be rigorously controlled, for, as Vives asserted in his pedagogical treatise *The Education of a Christian Woman*, they were not entirely 'prudent and chaste'. Composed for the edification of his pupil, the Princess Mary, Vives' tract was translated by Richard Hyde in 1530 and advocated the study of languages and sacred texts for the improvement of a woman's 'manners', circumscribing the reach of her learning within the strictest limits. While a man should pursue his studies both to 'profit himself and the commonwealth', wrote Vives, it behoved a woman to 'learn for herself alone and her young children, or her sisters in our Lord' and not seek to acquire public influence, for 'it neither becometh a woman to rule a school, nor to live among men, or speak abroad . . . [or] to be a teacher, nor to have authority of the man'.

The zealously Catholic Mary was reluctant to embrace the kind of forward-thinking humanism she associated with more reformist tendencies. The Cooke girls were raised to hold fewer scruples. They were devouring works by the rhetoricians and pagan poets, among them Cicero, Virgil, Livy, Ovid, Homer, Terence and Horace. The last of these became a particular favourite of Elizabeth Cooke – and neither was she reticent about turning her hand to studies of logic and dialectic, texts more familiar to male students as pre-scribed reading for their university courses. A copy of Aristotle's immensely challenging work the *Organon* survives in Hatfield House, Hertfordshire, with Elizabeth's pre-married name inscribed in Greek on the inside. Racier material was to be found among the great tragedians Seneca, Aeschylus, Euripides and Sophocles, with whom the Cooke girls would later demonstrate their familiarity.

This was schooling of the highest order which, despite the humanist revolution, was still largely reserved for men alone. Many of the sisters' male contemporaries would have been scandalized by the books that crowded their bookshelves. Even the indomit-able Anne Fitzwilliam Cooke, who braved two hundred armed Hoddesdon rioters, had some doubts about the regime her daugh-ters were following. The girls would often look up from their studies to find their mother gently chiding them for their bookishness and generally worrying about the effect it would have when the time came for them to cast their beloved books aside in order to take up the reins of their own households, with all the tiresome domestic commitments this entailed. Surely such 'vain study', she would tell them, could not but be 'sown in barren, unfruitful ground'. What practical use could it have for a wife and mother?

Married or not, the girls – particularly Elizabeth – had other ideas. How could they not, being fostered by the same curriculum that was training Edward VI for public life? In this they were in very good company, for other pupils taught by the network of scholars associated with Sir Anthony Cooke and John Cheke were Edward's half-sister, the Princess Elizabeth (the future Queen Elizabeth I), and their cousin Lady Jane Grey, who, as granddaughter of Henry VIII's sister Mary Tudor, would become the controversial claimant to the throne after Edward's death. Instrumental in the fashioning of this pedagogical culture was Queen Catherine Parr, who became Henry VIII's wife in 1543. Sympathetic to the reformist cause, she was patroness to the most renowned humanist scholars in Europe, and under her stewardship Cheke was appointed tutor to Prince Edward in 1544 and became involved in the instruction of Lady Jane Grey two years later. Princess Elizabeth was trained in Greek by Cheke's one-time pupil at Cambridge, William Grindal. When the latter died in 1548, the princess insisted that her schooling be commandeered henceforth by another of the ever-ubiquitous Cheke's former students: the Yorkshire scholar Roger Ascham, a fellow of St John's. 'There are many honourable ladies now who surpass Sir Thomas More's daughters in all kinds of learning,' he wrote, 'but among all of them the brightest star is my illustrious Lady Elizabeth . . . Her study of true religion and learning is most energetic . . . [and] her perseverance is equal to that of a man.'

Sir Thomas More, who had been Lord Chancellor to Henry VIII, was celebrated throughout Europe as the pioneer in female education. Aware that 'erudition in women is a new thing', More wrote to one of his children's tutors, William Gonell, with this sage advice: 'if a woman (and this I desire and hope with you as their teacher for all my daughters) to eminent virtue of mind should add even moderate skill in learning, I think she will gain more real good than if she obtain the riches of Croesus and the beauty of Helen'. To be

grouped among More's learned daughters was a significant accolade, and one that would be accorded the Cooke sisters. As early as
1550 John Coke had firmly entrenched such a comparison in the
public imagination with his *Debate between the Heralds of England and
France*, citing Anne Cooke, beside the More girls, among the 'gentlewomen . . . well studied in the holy scripture, but also in the Greek
and Latin tongues' as evidence that England was far superior to
France.

The association persisted through the centuries and in 1748, when
Thomas Birch composed his *Who's Who* of notable women, 'a catalogue of Ladies Famous for their writings, or skill in the learned
languages', he placed 'Lady Russell' and her sisters in close proximity to More's daughters and Lady Jane Grey. Ascham also had the
Cooke sisters in mind when reflecting on the young Edwardian
radicals who outdid even the More enclave in pedagogical acumen.
In a letter of 14 December 1550 he praised 'two English ladies in particular', the eldest of the Cooke daughters, Mildred, and Lady Jane
Grey. He reminisced about the occasion when he chanced to visit
the fifteen-year-old Lady Jane in Leicester the previous summer. 'I
was immediately admitted into her chamber,' he explained excit-
edly, 'and found the noble damsel – Oh, ye gods! – reading Plato's
Phaedo in Greek, and so thoroughly understanding it that she caused
me the greatest astonishment.' The letter went on:

> The other lady is Mildred [Cooke] Cecil, who understands and talks
> Greek as well as English; so that I am doubtful whether she is the
> more to be envied for her surpassing knowledge, or for having the
> noble Anthony Cook[e] for her father and teacher, the associate of
> John Cheke in instructing our young king, or again for having mar-
> ried William Cecil, a young man it is true, but possessed of such
> prudence beyond his years, such learning, and such moderation . . .

By the end of 1552, when Walter Haddon had publicly lauded
Gidea Hall as a 'little university' of women, the Cooke girls had
become valuable commodities on the marriage market. Sir Anthony

Cooke had insisted that his goal had been to ensure that his daughters 'might have complete Men, and that their husbands might be happy in complete Women: never promising, yet always paying a great dowry'. None came more complete than William Cecil, to whom Mildred was wed on 21 December 1545 at the age of nineteen. Born in 1520, Cecil would eventually become Lord Treasurer Burghley, principal Secretary to Elizabeth I, and the most powerful man in England. He and the Cecils' son, Robert, would become Elizabeth Russell's most potent contacts in the royal court and on the Privy Council, instrumental in her campaign against Shakespeare's Blackfriars Theatre. Mildred was Cecil's second wife, for he had married Mary Cheke in 1541. Though she died within two years, the match had established Cecil's closeness to the figurehead of the new learning, for Mary was his old tutor's sister. Mildred's schooling within the same rigorous disciplines made her an attractive prospect, and would do so for her female siblings, all of whom would marry well.

By 1553 Anne had become the second wife of Nicholas Bacon. At forty-two years of age, he was nearly two decades older, and had six children by his former wife, the late Jane Fernley. His achievements by this date, however, more than made up for his advanced years. His father, Robert Bacon, had left farming to become a sheepreeve, or chief shepherd, for the Abbot of Bury in Suffolk, so Nicholas was from humble stock but had gained a scholarship to attend Corpus Christi College, Cambridge. After graduating, he studied law at Gray's Inn, thereafter swiftly acquiring a succession of prestigious posts, becoming Solicitor of the Court of Augmentations, Attorney of the Court of Wards and, in 1552, Treasurer of Gray's Inn. By this time he was also creating ties with William Cecil, now one of King Edward's principal secretaries, a friendship which may have been instrumental in his marriage to Anne. Like others of his generation, including Philip Hoby, half-brother of Thomas, he had acquired properties made available by the Dissolution of the Monasteries and was reaping the rewards. Greater glories awaited him in the reign of Elizabeth I.

Between 1550 and 1552, when Walter Haddon paid regular visits to Gidea Hall, it could not have escaped his attention that the young girls he saw there were flowering into confident and attractive women, imbued with the most desired gifts of grace and learning. A woman of such qualities was ideal for an ambitious man on the lookout for a suitable wife. There were great advantages to marriage within the reforming circle which had a direct line to the Protector and the King. Anthony Cooke was clearly well liked and in Edward VI's good graces for on 19 June 1552 he was listed as a privileged member of the 'Privy Chamber' and put forward as someone worthy of a royal gift 'in consideration of his service and his charge as shall please His Majesty to appoint'. With two of the Cooke girls now snapped up, Haddon began to assess the qualities of the remaining sisters. His roving eye alighted upon the precocious Elizabeth.

He knew he would have to act quickly if he was to win this inestimable prize. Now aged twelve or thirteen, Elizabeth had reached the age of consent. The average marrying age for girls at this time was their mid-twenties, but it was not unheard of for daughters of elite families to be contracted in dynastic marriages as young as twelve. Haddon's haste may also have been due to the fact that there was another suitor on the horizon. Cecil had become friends with Philip Hoby, who may have been attempting to steer Elizabeth into a match with his brother, Thomas. The same age as Anthony Cooke, Philip was Imperial Ambassador under Henry VIII and a Gentleman Usher of the King's Privy Chamber. Sophisticated, cultured and well travelled, he could boast among his friends the artist Titian and was a committed Protestant to boot. He had been in regular contact with Cecil in 1552 and had been sending gifts to Mildred. In one letter, sent on 21 August, he writes wittily: 'As to the wine, I sent it to my Lady and not to you . . . I pray God it may be as good as I wish it, and then my Lady and I shall agree enough.' The nature of the subject on which he sought Mildred's agreement specifically is not clear. Was he merely referring to the quality of the wine, or to a more serious matter: perhaps the marriage of her sister to his brother?

On 11 November 1552 Haddon made his secret passions known to Elizabeth's brother-in-law, William Cecil. The role of the ardent, courtly lover was one he embraced with characteristic gusto. 'But yet since I am myself in the greatest desire, I think that something ought to be said,' he confessed with passionate hyperbole, 'towards urging your benevolence in this business, to which no other thing ever is equal in the whole course of my future life.' The matter was brought to Elizabeth's father, who flatly refused to give his consent to the match. Haddon was not put off. He decided to appeal to Elizabeth through her sister Anne. The two met in Cambridge to plot their next move, and resolved to collude in the composition of a robust Latin epistle in hopes that flattering the classicist in Elizabeth would win her round. Haddon played secretary to Anne, who dictated the letter to him, for the arguments laid down in favour of the union would be – or so they wanted Elizabeth to believe – entirely her own.

'I saw your Haddon, whom you will love, if you are wise,' she began, assuring her sister that her suitor 'lacks nothing except fortune, nor indeed can this be absent for long in such a great assembly of remaining ornaments'. She would be marrying a man who had just been promoted to the Regius Chair of Magdalen College, Oxford. Why shouldn't she want to be 'raised toward perfection' through such a union? 'Look at me,' she protested, alluding to her recent good luck in being contracted to Nicholas Bacon, 'who although I now have a flowing and fruitful fortune, yet in the beginning, I pursued hope, not circumstance.' Bacon had just been promoted to Treasurer of Gray's Inn and, since a similar success story 'has been repeated in Cheke', who has now 'proceeded to fame of this kind from those same fountains of learning and genius, why should that not follow in your Haddon?' Yes, poor he may be now, but that would not last for ever, and in any case, outward wealth was not everything. 'Haddon is more desirable with these slender resources than six hundred [men] are of this courtly din,' she insisted, adding with satirical verve, 'of whom as if of beasts, it is permitted to see only the outermost spoils of bodies, but you would swear that the mind of a pig, as it were, has been given them for wit.'

Anne then raised the one sticking point: 'Father's will opposes you – certainly a difficult and slippery position.' Against these objections, she interposed her own towering will. 'I would not urge you so eagerly if the matter was not greatly approved by me,' she wrote, in that bold statement encapsulating the independent-mindedness for which Cooke's daughters would one day become famous. Elizabeth resisted the sisterly pressure, decisively rebuffing her admirer's advances. Haddon was furious and in revenge wrote a self-indulgent epistle in Latin in which he extravagantly compared her to that most famed paragon of unfaithfulness, Cressida, who abandoned her lover Troilus for the lascivious embraces of Diomedes:

I, wretched, pursue you with tears, since your Diomedes has dragged you away, and established you in his bosom. Nay, truly I do not pursue, but I bid you farewell, my Cressida . . . O! flower of maidens, O! once my life, now my grief, farewell, farewell . . . God himself indeed cannot grant me anything which I care for now . . . Farewell, one who must never afterwards be named or greeted by me, as much as can be foreseen for any reason; and yet who must always be worshipped and admired and thought of and desired. Would that even as you live pleasantly with your Diomedes, so I will die quickly with Troilus . . . Farewell, farewell, farewell. Yours full of sorrow, yours most profoundly.

This rival suitor, presented in the mythic guise of Diomedes, must have been a reference to Thomas Hoby. Born in 1530, he was ten years older than Elizabeth and as well travelled as his brother, having spent time in Strasbourg with such noted reformers as Martin Bucer, a lecturer in divinity at Cambridge, whose *Gratulation to the Church of England* he translated in 1549. While on the Continent he also absorbed lectures in Greek by Peter Martyr, a close associate of Anthony Cooke. On 6 October 1552 Cooke and Martyr were included among the thirty-two men appointed to 'resolve upon the reformation of the common laws', a commission established to assess and revise ecclesiastical regulations. Significantly, Cooke was described in the commission as a 'divine', appearing on the list alongside John Cheke and the Polish cleric Joannes Alasco. The latter was known in England as John Laski, and was responsible for establishing the foreign reformed churches in London, the very institutions whose highly activist members would support Elizabeth Russell's bid to close the Blackfriars Theatre in 1596. Thomas Hoby's association with her father's circle, as well as his ability to use his skills as a linguist to further the cause of reform, appealed to Elizabeth, who would become a formidable translator in her own right. She would indeed go on to marry him, later thanking Philip Hoby, whose 'sister' she had become thanks to his 'judgment', for 'to me your brother Thomas you wanted to wed'. In choosing him over Haddon, Elizabeth was aligning herself with the man whose *Book of the Courtier* would later provide her with a powerful model for her public identity, as well as furnishing William Shakespeare with an important source for his writings.

The Cooke sisters' education at the very heart of the Protectorate would provide them with the skills and confidence to do what so few of their non-royal female contemporaries could: enter an international political arena almost entirely governed by men. In the process they would secure lasting fame. One among many who offered plaudits that were circulated in manuscript, print and paint was the eighteenth-century historian George Ballard, who summed it up best when he called them 'the wonders of the age'. As far back as 1559, when Elizabeth was still a teenager, William Barker singled out 'the daughters of Anthony Cooke' for their proficiency in the ancient languages in his *Nobility of Women*. Seven years later the French translator Jessen, Conte de Malte, went one better and praised them as 'the most learned daughters . . . in both Greek and Latin letters, in all of Christendom'. Queen Elizabeth I's godson,

John Harington, offered in print his wholehearted 'commendation' of Elizabeth Russell, whose talents as a poet placed her 'above all comparison', noting that of the most educated women to be found in Europe, 'three or four in England [come] out of one family, and namely the sisters of that learned Lady [Elizabeth Russell]'.

Looking back to the heyday of Anthony Cooke's household in *The History of the Worthies of England* in 1662, Thomas Fuller observed him 'to be happy in his daughters, learned above their sex in Greek and Latin . . . Indeed they were all most eminent scholars, (the honour of their own, and the shame of our sex) both in prose and poetry.' Further tributes came from Bathusa Makin, who in her *Essay to Revive the Ancient Education of Gentlewomen* of 1673 cited the Cooke sisters as the guiding lights of all women who were passionate about protecting their rights to an education, placing Elizabeth Russell first in the list of the daughters who possessed 'for Poetry, a worthy Character'. This was seconded two years later by Edward Phillips, whose *Complete Collection of Poets* would have remained incomplete without a mention of Elizabeth as one of the 'Women among the Moderns Eminent for Poetry'. In 1803 Mary Hay's multi-volume compendium, *Female Biography*, paid her special attention, stating that she outshone even her learned sisters and was 'celebrated by the first scholars of the age'.

Elizabeth was only thirteen years old when her mother, Anne Fitzwilliam Cooke, died. Her father's influence would thenceforth become ever more pronounced. Watching the progress of his career in public service, she would imbibe both a sense of civic responsibility and an absolute belief in her right to intervene in the policy-making of local and national institutions, even if it meant locking horns with some of the most powerful men of her generation. Anthony Cooke's 'female university' would furnish her with the foundations for that indomitable character which, forged and tested in the flames of her later battles, would give her the edge in her campaign against the most successful theatrical team of all time. In doing so she would marshal against Shakespeare and his business associates the same outspokenness and community spirit that allowed her to become the champion of her oppressed co-radicals, and for which she would be applauded by the poet George Whetsone in 1576:

> Her words of worth doth win her tongue such praise,
> As when she speaks the wisest silent stays . . .
> Her mind is with these noble gifts possessed,
> Her bounty doth beyond her beauty go,
> A care she hath to ease the thrall-distressed.

3.

Monstrous Regiments

On 27 July 1553 Sir Anthony Cooke and John Cheke were taken under armed guard to the Tower of London. Implicated in a plot to put Lady Jane Grey on the throne, they would soon witness the execution of the chief conspirators who had masterminded the scheme. While the autopsy report indicated that Edward VI had died of a 'disease of the lungs' on 6 July, the gossip among the court's foreign envoys was that his untimely death had been caused by poison. Four days later Lady Jane was proclaimed Queen.

The Spanish court heard from one of their spies, who was present at that sombre occasion, that 'among all the faces I saw there, not one showed any expression of joy'. Nor were the public proclamations branding Mary a bastard, shouted through the streets from Cheapside to Fleet Street amid a cacophony of trumpets, met with any warmer reception. As the pendulum of public favour swung towards the Princess Mary, whom Henry VIII had formally proclaimed her half-brother's successor in his 1543 Act of Succession, the Grey faction found themselves outnumbered and outmanoeuvred.

The girl who had been schooled alongside the Cooke sisters would reign for only nine days. While bonfires were lit and street parties held all over London in celebration of Mary I's reclamation of the throne, John Burcher, one of Cooke's reformist circle in Strasbourg, wrote to his fellow radicalist Henry Bullinger, informing him of the fate of their friends, who had been accused of giving 'their consent and sanction' to the crowning of Jane Grey. '[S]hould this prove to be the case,' he lamented, 'it is all over with them.' The new Queen was unaware that Mildred Cecil had previously sent some writings of St Basil to Jane Grey with a letter in Greek which emphasized her 'high birth' and proximity to the royal bloodline. Her husband, however, would be called to account for his part in the treason. Anticipating his own execution, he composed a letter which he placed in the hands of Nicholas Bacon, asking him to deliver it to Mildred after his death. In this heartfelt missive he advised her that should she wish to remarry it must be 'with such a one as hath a true judgement in religion'.

As the axe fell on the prime movers of the Grey faction, Elizabeth, only thirteen at the time, would have been in no doubt of the danger her father and kinsmen were in. It was an early taste of the potentially Faustian nature of court factionalism. In the face of the 'great perils threatened upon us', Cecil protested his innocence to Mary I, citing as his witnesses and defendants those friends who had also been touched by the conspiracy: Anthony Cooke, Nicholas Bacon, John Cheke and Francis Russell, 2nd Earl of Bedford, who would later become Elizabeth's father-in-law. These men, he deftly implied, had all along been secretly working with him to realize the rightful succession, at great danger to themselves. The Cooke sisters were instrumental in helping to reinforce this impression. Anne Bacon and Margaret Cooke entered into Mary's service and were well placed to petition her. The former began acting as a vehement intercessor on Cecil's behalf and proved so successful in securing the much desired royal clemency that she was able to report to him, via his secretary Roger Alford, 'that the Queen thought very well of her brother Cecil', even going so far as to proclaim him 'a very honest man'.

Much to Elizabeth's relief, her father and brothers-in-law were pardoned. However, though they were now free, neither Anthony Cooke nor John Cheke wanted to remain in England to witness the reconversion of the populace to a religion they abhorred. By 14 April of the following year they were both in Strasbourg, where they would take on key roles as members of the Protestant resistance, interrupting their sojourn there briefly in the late summer to undertake a tour of Italy with Thomas and Philip Hoby. On 3

September John Burcher wrote to Henry Bullinger to inform him that the 'noble and learned' Cooke, who had 'lived for some time with me at my house very piously and courteously', would soon be stopping off at Zurich to see him. Cooke was passing through Europe to build up his powerbase, accruing allies in readiness for the long and arduous fight ahead. 'I wish him to find that my recommendation has been of some advantage to him,' Burcher wrote, for Cooke had been 'a fellow-labourer with Cheke in instructing the late King'. After returning to Strasbourg, Cooke established a safe house where those fleeing the Marian persecutions could find shelter. He was being aided in his endeavours by his sons-in-law, William Cecil and Nicholas Bacon, who were supplying him with funds and helping him tap into revenues from his estates in England. Further support came from Francis Russell, who was fast becoming a figurehead for the exiled Protestants.

During the next four years Elizabeth lived with the Cecils at their estate in Wimbledon. There she had to conform, along with the rest of her family and their servants, to the re-established Catholic faith, regularly divulging her sins to a priestly confessor and participating in the sacrament of Holy Communion in the family's chapel. It was to Wimbledon that Thomas Hoby came on 13 May 1558, where, as he noted in his diary, he 'communed with Mistress Elizabeth Cooke in the way of marriage'. He had at this time been occasionally engaged in overseeing his half-brother's ambitious renovations to his home, Bisham Abbey in Berkshire, while Philip was away seeking various medical treatments for a persistent illness. A cure would elude him, for at 3 a.m. on 29 May he died, leaving William Cecil and Thomas Hoby as his executors. His body was conveyed by barge on the waters of the Thames to Bisham on 9 June, where he would be buried in the parish church of All Saints.

'[T]he marriage was made and solemnized between me and Elizabeth Cooke, daughter of Sir Anthony Cooke, Knight. The same day was also her sister, Margaret, the Queen's Maid, married to Sir Ralph Rowlett, Knight.' So recorded a proud Thomas Hoby in his diary entry of 27 June 1558. Never one to pass up the opportunity to steal for himself a little of the limelight due to others, Walter Haddon composed a strange commendatory poem in celebration of the double wedding. Elizabeth may have been amused to note that she did not receive a namecheck. The versifier, having described Margaret as a 'pearl' and a 'precious gem', delivered on the threat made in his anguished missive of spurned love never to name the object of his affections again 'for any reason'.

What began as a summer of such promise for the sisters ended tragically with the death of Margaret Rowlett in unknown circumstances on 3 August. The eighteen-year-old Elizabeth found herself processing in her mourning garments towards the Church of St Mary Staining, London, through streets decorated with banners of black cloth, while inside the chapel four gilt candlesticks burned on either side of Margaret's coffin. Still in exile, Anthony Cooke could not be there to weep over the grave of the young bride or comfort his living children. Elizabeth's grief would have been increased by the fact that the funeral rites were concluded with a Catholic mass.

This bittersweet time of new beginnings and terrible loss was the soil from which Elizabeth's future battles would grow. Thomas Hoby inherited his half-brother's major estates, including Bisham Abbey, vast holdings in Evesham and elsewhere in Worcestershire, and his property in the Blackfriars. The latter was recorded in Philip Hoby's will as 'my mansion house, with the orchards and gardens, in the precinct of the late Black Friars at London'. Part of the network of dissolved priory buildings plundered by Henry VIII in 1538, this Blackfriars residence stood on the corner of Water Lane and Carter Lane. The King had gifted it to Philip in June 1541 as a reward to his Gentleman of the Privy Chamber, and from at least 1550 he had use of two gardens on the site. Elizabeth would in time inherit these estates, a turn of events that would have a huge impact on the life of the as yet unborn William Shakespeare.

The playwright's fate was also bound up with the Cooke family's fortunes in another significant way. The maelstrom that had uprooted Elizabeth's father and his close associates from their homes during Mary I's reign had two important consequences. It brought Elizabeth closer to William Cecil, who took on a fatherly role in Anthony Cooke's absence, a relationship they would maintain until Cecil's dying day and which would provide Elizabeth with one of her primary contacts in the Privy Council in 1596. It also determined the theatrical associations of the Blackfriars in a manner which would eventually give shape to Shakespeare's career.

In 1548 Edward VI had granted the former Buttery and Frater (refectory) of the dissolved monastery of the Dominican Black Friars to Sir Thomas Cawarden. These desirable tenements, in which the friars once stored victuals and dined, abutted on to the western side of what had been the monastery's Great Cloister to the north and Inner Cloister to the south. Determined to exploit these assets, Cawarden had by 1533 leased to John Cheke four rooms which comprised the eastern section of the Upper Frater and part of the hall which extended over the Buttery. Cawarden was Master of the Revels, a post which gave him command of royal entertainments. When Cheke vacated his tenements in the wake of the Grey scandal, Cawarden thought he could do worse than convert these lodgings into the Office of the Queen's Revels, in which costumes and props could be stored and the children of the Chapel Royal could rehearse for court performances. Since the rooms in which the office had previously been located had been leased to another tenant, Cawarden's decision to use Cheke's apartments in this way secured the immediate future of the Revels, ensuring that the Blackfriars would remain the hub of London's theatrical enterprises. In April of the following year the tenement next door to the Revels Office, situated in the northern section of the hall above the Buttery, was conveyed to George Brooke, then 9th Baron Cobham. Already in possession of a house attached to the north end of the Buttery itself, Cobham's investment further augmented the Brooke family's interests in the area. Locating them closer to the building that would become Shakespeare's Blackfriars Theatre, these transactions would lay the foundations for the tensions which would later see Shakespeare and his associates hounded out of the Blackfriars.

Thus began the theatrical legacy of the Blackfriars district. Throughout Elizabeth's life these buildings would maintain these thespian associations. The tenement which housed the Revels Office would eventually become part of what is now known as the First Blackfriars Theatre, established by Richard Farrant. Later, when Shakespeare's business partner, James Burbage, purchased the buildings which would become the Second Blackfriars Theatre in 1596, the sale included those sections of the Upper Frater which had been Cheke's lodgings. The house Elizabeth and her husband had inherited from Philip Hoby, and which she would eventually commandeer, lay less than 139 feet to the north of the Revels Office. When George Brooke died on 29 September of that year, his property holdings in the area were taken over by his successor, William Brooke, 10th Baron Cobham, who would forge an alliance with Elizabeth and her Cecil kinsmen, a collaboration which would have particularly disastrous consequences for Shakespeare. The political turmoils that surrounded the reforming community and turned the Cooke family's world upside down would therefore play a part in placing Elizabeth at the very heart of one of London's most important theatrical districts.

Another of Thomas Hoby's diary entries for the year 1558 records the moment when everything in Elizabeth's life changed for ever: 'The 17 of November died Queen Mary between 6 and 7 of the clock in the morning, and between 9 and 10 was proclaimed at Westminster the Lady Elizabeth, Queen of England, France, and Ireland.'

The birth of the Elizabethan era would make the new Queen's namesake one of the most well-connected women in the country. On the very first day of her reign, Elizabeth I appointed William Cecil her Secretary of State. By the middle of December Nicholas Bacon was knighted and a week later made a Privy Councillor. His elevation to the office of Lord Keeper of the Great Seal of England allowed him to preside over the House of Lords and the Court of Chancery. The Catholic Queen was gone, but just when Elizabeth could begin to look forward to her father's return from self-imposed exile, to an England in which a new day was dawning for the Protestant alliance, a disastrous coincidence nearly annihilated the community of radicals at whose core he stood.

During Mary I's reign the fiery Scottish preacher John Knox authored one of the most infamous books in European history, *The First Blast of the Trumpet against the Monstrous Regiment of Women.* Providing a theological and political justification for the ousting of the Popish Queen, it was published just as Elizabeth I was stepping into her half-sister's place. Women, Knox declared, should not 'presume to use the offices due to men', for 'a woman promoted to sit in the seat of God, that is, to teach, to judge or to reign above man, is a monster in nature, contumely to God, and a thing most repugnant to his will and ordinance'. It is hardly surprising that the Queen was not happy to see such sentiments in print. Anthony Cooke's speedy repatriation became expedient. Assuring her of the continuing commitment of his co-religionists was paramount. Just before leaving Strasbourg Cooke wrote to Bullinger with his hopes for his sovereign's promotion of their cause, urging his comrades to steer the Queen towards a vigorous re-adoption of Protestantism. What could give more 'strength to her army', what be more damaging to her mighty enemies, than the monarch's willingness to embody 'the spirit of a Judith or a Deborah', the Old Testament's warrior-women, wielders of sword and scimitar?

Neither Cooke nor his fellow exiles, who had, in his own words, 'long and sorrowfully lacked our country', were showered with royal favours upon their return. Jean Calvin, the French reformer whose theological writings would exert the most potent influence on the radicals, put this down to Knox's inflammatory tract, which had 'offended' the Queen. The case was so severe that all Protestant refugees had 'just reason to fear, lest . . . by reason of the thoughtless arrogance of one individual, the wretched crowd of exiles would have been driven away not only from this city, but even from almost the whole world'. Calvin was quick to defend himself, assuring William Cecil early in 1559 that while the book had its genesis in a conversation he had shared with Knox 'about the government of women', it did not in any way express his own views. Had not the bible, he insisted, echoing Anthony Cooke's own sentiments, extolled the virtues of the warlike ruler Deborah? Might not a woman therefore be 'raised up by divine authority'? Calvin named Cooke as a witness to his innocence, since it was he who had first been made aware of Knox's tract and he who immediately alerted his co-radical Theodore de Beza to the dangers it posed to their cause. But Cecil had put the matter plainly: 'Of all others, Knox's name . . . is most odious here'; and anyone tainted with the *Blast* could not expect to be bathed in the Queen's good graces. It was a bad start for the forward Protestant movement.

It is with a sense of real vigour and urgency that, during the first years of the new monarchical establishment, Cooke sought to harness the efforts of a pan-European intellectual community in 'expelling the tyranny of the pope . . . and re-establishing true religion', a mission which he felt was 'moving far too slowly'. Appointed to the 1559 session of Parliament, he began working towards passing an unequivocally Protestant bill on religion, but found 'the work is hitherto too much at a stand'. He hoped to influence Elizabeth I directly by providing her with letters from his influential friends, including Martyr and Bullinger, which he had himself 'placed in the Queen's hands'. He watched her shed copious tears while reading them, only to find his hopes frustrated once again. By April her lack of enthusiasm for extreme reform had begun to take its toll on him, and John Jewel was becoming concerned about his lack of tact, writing to Martyr that he 'defends some scheme of his own, I know not what, most obstinately, and is mightily angry with us all'. Knox did little to help matters when he wrote to the Queen on 20 July, insisting that his book was not 'prejudicial to your Grace's just regiment', adding the condescending caveat, 'provided that ye be not found ungrate unto God' and fail 'Christ Jesus in the day of his Battle'. It was an unconvincing apology.

When it came to religion, the Queen would tread more cautiously than either of her siblings. Between 1559 and 1562 Anthony

Cooke had been appointed to various religious commissions to ensure royal supremacy over the Church of England and enforce the uniformity of its clergy, but was disappointed by the limitations placed on the further purification of religion. Disillusioned, he began a slow retreat from the grander spheres of central politics, though he also attended to his local civic duties in Essex less than enthusiastically. It would be up to his daughters to fill the space he left behind. Learned, and tapped into the very centres of power, they were well placed to assure the Queen of the non-conformists' promotion of women.

Just one year into the new reign, William Barker, in his *Nobility of Women*, had recognized Elizabeth Cooke and her sisters as part of a cohesive and independent group of highly educated females which included the Seymour sisters, daughters of the former Lord Protector, Duke of Somerset. Around 1550 Mildred had gifted her translation of a sermon by St Basil the Great to the Protector's wife, Anne Seymour, Duchess of Somerset, intending to assure the Protectorate that the women in their circle could cultivate 'a voice of some signification' which could be 'profitable' to the Somerset regime. Anne Bacon went one better in her own contribution to the pan-European effort, popularizing the reforming theology of Jean Calvin in England through her translation of the sermons of the Italian Calvinist Bernardino Ochino. These first appeared in print in 1548 and were reissued by the printer John Day in 1551, around the time when a young Princess Elizabeth was herself engaged in translating the work of the same author. The Cooke girls were therefore the perfect conduits through which their father's circle could convince their sovereign of their loyalty to her fledgling constitution.

It was a stroke of genius on the part of William Cecil and John Jewel to recognize instantly that Anne Bacon was a fitting choice as translator of one of the most important texts in English ecclesiastical history, Jewel's *Apologia Ecclesiae Anglicanae*, which would be published as *An Apology for the Church of England* in 1564. The Elizabethan establishment's official statement on its religious position, it was designed to assure Europe of the 'concord' and unity of the

44

English Protestants amid Catholic accusations that the Church of England was 'divided into contrary parties and opinions'. Disgruntled Catholics would later murmur that the work was a collaborative effort between Anne and her sister Mildred, part of a 'plot' to turn the English Church into an impregnable 'fortification'. While the Cooke sisters would always tread a fine line, desirous of further religious reform but wary of offending their monarch, behind the formal propaganda they were pursuing a more radical agenda.

They would be aided in this endeavour by other women in their coterie. One of these was Katherine Bertie, Dowager Duchess of Suffolk, who had been an associate of Anthony Cooke and Thomas Hoby on the Continent. As well as patronizing the great Protestant martyrologist John Foxe, whose groundbreaking *Acts and Monuments* would be printed by Anne Bacon's publisher John Day, she had helped John Laski in the task of establishing the foreign churches in London in the 1550s. Returning to England on Elizabeth I's accession, the Dowager Duchess maintained a correspondence with Mildred Cecil and her husband and began working to steer the Queen towards a more hard-line stance in the matter of reform. '[W]e English, in our Elizabeth,' she told her, '[must find] that deliverance of our thralled conscience.'

Katherine Bertie also played an important role in her support of another member of the Cooke sisters' female enclave: John Knox's right-hand woman, Anne Locke. In 1557, having left her family to follow Knox into exile, Anne had heard Jean Calvin's sermons in Geneva and became inflamed with a desire to bring his teachings to an English readership, as Anne Bacon had done. Unwelcome at court, Knox moved to Scotland, where he turned his attention to the forward Protestant campaign in the north. From 1559 Anne Locke and Mildred Cecil began working in parallel to further the Scottish reform movement, the former entrusted by Knox with the responsibility of ensuring that the Protestant soldiers there had a ready supply of funds, the latter assisting the Scottish ambassador William Maitland. The following year Locke published her translation of Calvin's sermons, which she dedicated to Katherine Bertie.

Knowing of her patron's close friendship with the Queen, she hoped the project would lead the monarch to embrace the virtues of a purified Church. Surely reading how her subjects had been so 'tossed with worldly adversity' under Catholicism would encourage her to bring domestic policy into alignment with that of England's more radical neighbours. Surely she could see that her people, 'their minds armed' for the fight ahead, were in desperate need of both a heroic leader and a spiritual healer. And what better physician for the nation's malaise than Jean Calvin, Europe's 'most excellent Apothecary', whose medicines Anne herself had now 'put into an English box'? If only the Queen would open it.

By the time her translation was published Anne Locke was living in Cheapside, close to another female radical who was applying her quill for the benefit of the reformers, Dorcas Martin. She and her husband, Richard Martin, a goldsmith who would later become Master of the Royal Mint and Lord Mayor of London, would determine the structure of the non-conformist community closest to Elizabeth. More significantly, Richard Martin would contribute directly to the tribulations of Shakespeare and his business partners during their battle with Elizabeth in the Blackfriars. In 1560, while these relations were being established under a new and as yet uncertain royal settlement, Elizabeth and her husband were making their own contributions to the cause of reform.

After their marriage, the Hobys moved into Bisham Abbey. There they continued the renovations which had begun under Philip Hoby's stewardship. A freshly appointed suite of rooms had been added to the building's original thirteenth-century boundaries. This included a grand banqueting chamber which neighboured the house's central hall, on the southern side of which stood a room boasting a pristine fireplace. When completed, the hearth would be flanked with spandrels bearing decorative armorial shields, above them a plaster panel on which would be incised the arms of Thomas Hoby, impaled with those of his wife. On 5 November 1560, probably just after a commanding octagonal turret had been erected at the northern end of the abbey, the Hobys departed for London.

They would remain there for thirteen weeks. Their mission, coord-inated no doubt from their Blackfriars home, was to oversee the publication of one of the most influential texts of the English Renaissance: Thomas Hoby's *Book of the Courtier*.

Encapsulating the hopes and aspirations of a new generation of upwardly mobile gentry, Hoby's book was both politically and pedagogically motivated. It was printed in 1561 with a dedication to Henry Hastings, composed before Hastings had acceded to the Earldom of Huntingdon in 1560. The choice of patron is a telling one, for Hastings was mooted as a potential successor to the Crown. Following the debacle surrounding the unfortunate Lady Jane Grey – who was executed on 12 February 1554 after being implicated in another uprising, led by Sir Thomas Wyatt, grandson of Thomas Brooke, 8th Baron Cobham – the Hobys may have begun to look elsewhere for a Protestant insurance policy in the event that the as yet unmarried Queen died without an heir. Their support of Hast-ings may have been intended to thwart the designs of the Queen's favourite courtier, Robert Dudley, soon to be ennobled with the title Earl of Leicester. Dudley's wife, Amy Robsart, had been found dead at the base of a flight of stairs in Cumnor Place, Berkshire, on 8 September 1560. As the rumour mill began to turn, some sus-pected her husband of plotting her murder so he could marry the Queen, while others believed that he had been the victim of a plot designed to shatter his reputation. Strangely, on the very day of Amy's death, Dudley's chief enemies in the Grey, Seymour, Brooke and Arundel families – including Lady Jane Grey's sister Catherine and William Brooke, 10th Baron Cobham – had an all too conveni-ent alibi. They were dining in the very same county, just twenty-three miles away in Bisham Abbey, with Elizabeth and Thomas Hoby.

Dudley had other adversaries. The Spanish ambassador Bishop de Quadra had observed that Hastings 'loves Robert as he loves the devil', and 'is a great heretic', meaning a fervent reformer. 'Cecil says he is the real heir of England,' he added, 'and all the heretics want him.' The Hobys' publication of *The Book of Courtier*, there-fore, made it very clear where they stood on the relative merits of the men who had set their sights on the Crown of England. As well as a letter by John Cheke, Cecil's brother-in-law, to 'his loving friend Master Thomas Hoby', the work was printed with Hoby's own dedicatory epistle to Hastings, in praise of 'the courtly fashions, comely exercises, and noble virtues' that had 'taken custom' in his 'so honourable patron'. There could not have been a more potent public ratification of the Earl of Huntingdon as a fitting national leader.

Elizabeth was a skilled translator and linguist in her own right and may have contributed to this text, which would create a revolution in manners, and even leave its impression on Shakespeare's own drama. She would certainly have taken an interest in its publication and her backing of Hastings indicates that the 21-year-old Lady Hoby was keen to involve herself in projects of national importance. In the wake of their father's retreat from public life, Elizabeth and her sisters would develop an ever-stronger commitment to achieving their father's vision for a purified Church of England, becoming Judiths and Deborahs of the English Reformation. And none was more willing to wield the sword of faith than the future Dowager Lady Russell.

4.

The Ambassador's Wife

It was Sir Nicholas Throckmorton who first suggested that Thomas Hoby should succeed him as Ambassador to France. 'I could remember your brother Mr Thomas Hoby,' he wrote to William Cecil, before realizing the snag in his plan: 'But then your sister will be angry'; and who could stand up to Lady Elizabeth's temper? At his wife's insistence, Thomas Hoby declined the honour again and again. The post was dangerous and costly. It was not until the Queen applied direct pressure that the couple finally relented. As a further incentive, she knighted her new ambassador on 9 March 1566, just ahead of his departure for the French court in Paris.

Nearly two years after the birth of William Shakespeare, Elizabeth and Sir Thomas Hoby set out on their sensitive diplomatic mission. Despite being four months pregnant at the time, Elizabeth insisted on accompanying her husband to France on a demanding journey which had a far from auspicious beginning. It had rained for almost the entire journey from London to Dover via Canterbury, making the roads treacherous. While passing through the outskirts of Sittingbourne, Elizabeth, having failed to navigate her horse in the flowing sludge, had slipped from her saddle and found herself sprawled on the ground, drenched to the petticoats. Sir Thomas reported to Cecil shortly afterwards that the fall was 'without danger, though not without bruise, for a time painful', causing the entire party 'some grief'. In the face of inhospitable travelling conditions and the hazards normally attending pregnancy, Elizabeth decided to press on, for she had no intention of remaining in the background while she and her husband were in Paris. She had a mission of her own to accomplish and no 'rain and foul ways' were going to stop her. Her experiences in France would fundamentally underpin her campaign against Shakespeare's Blackfriars Theatre three decades later.

The clouds still hung menacingly over Dover Castle when the twenty weary travellers in the Hoby party arrived there on Sunday 7 April. Now the promise of dry chambers and warming hearths lay before them. For none of the company was this a more welcome prospect than Elizabeth, whose fall had probably exacerbated a spinal condition from which she was already suffering. She would be plagued by back problems her entire life. Her eldest sister, Mildred, may have had scoliosis, an S-shaped curvature of the spine; and the children of at least three of the Cooke sisters, including the son Elizabeth was now carrying, would inherit varying degrees of spinal malformation. In time to come, Robert Cecil, Elizabeth's nephew, would be mockingly referred to as a 'crookback spider' by his enemies, forever associated in their minds with Shakespeare's Richard III, whom the playwright described as a 'bottled spider' and 'poisonous bunch-backed toad'.

To add to Elizabeth's difficulties, she was travelling with her young children, six-year-old Edward, and two girls: Elizabeth, aged four, and Anne, aged two. The costs involved in bringing the whole family to France were crippling, subsistence charges for the travellers and their horses, as Thomas complained, coming to 'half as much more as the Queen's allowance'. Thomas had failed to convince Elizabeth to remain at home with their infants, despite the obvious financial pressures their accompanying him would bring, which, he confessed, 'at the very first I foresaw, but could not without inconvenience remedy'. It had cost one pence per mile per horse – a total of £9 10s – to convey the train of twenty horses, burdened with supplies and victuals, to Dover. The full receipts of trafficking the Hobys' own goods 'by long seas' to Rouen, carefully recorded by Elizabeth herself, would amount to £6 13s 4d, with a further cost of £14 6s 7d to convey them thence to Paris. But Paris must have seemed a long way away as the party snaked up the strenuous path to the fort, which had kept its hulking vigil over the chalky cliffs and predictably protean seascape since its construction by Henry II in the late twelfth century.

Though Elizabeth was certainly glad to get out of the damp chill, which must have snapped keenly against her aching spine, she and her husband looked around them in dismay as they staggered through the castle's once grand chambers. There was no escape from the rain to be had here. While the edifice had so settled into the surrounding earthwork as to appear to the distant observer to defy the taunts of time (an impression reinforced no doubt by the castle's imposing Great Tower, which extended eighty-three feet in height), at close quarters that illusion was quickly shattered. The castle was crumbling. The roofs of some of the rooms were on the brink of collapse and, as Thomas Hoby lamented, could 'not [be] kept from rain, which hath pierced the very main timber'. Other chambers were entirely open to the elements, their 'roofs, with lead and all, fallen down'. Discomforts of a different sort awaited the couple later that night. Close to midnight they were met in Dover by the Cooke family's kinsman Sir Nicholas Wotton and Anthony Browne, 1st Viscount Montagu, who brought with them to Dover Elizabeth's former suitor, Walter Haddon. It must have been a tense meeting. But since it was already late, everyone tried to make the best of things and settled down for the evening.

The winds licked against the outer walls of the hoary keep. Elizabeth prayed that they would abate by 3 a.m., when they planned to set sail. As she tried to make herself comfortable in her austere surroundings, thoughts of an emotional parting from her brother-in-law, William Cecil, at his home in Westminster, crowded in on her. By the feeble light of a winking candle, she wrote a note to him, thanking him for his 'fatherly care'. It is her earliest surviving letter. While she was keen to cultivate the diplomacy her new role as ambassador's wife now demanded, something of the forcefulness of her character emerged in her defence of the vehemence with which she had executed a task on her husband's behalf before their departure:

> I earnestly desire you, that if any word not fit passed unawares out of my mouth, in my speech used to you (touching my husband) at Westminster, that it will please you to consider upon what point I stood: either to leave my husband's mind and errand undone, for which cause he sent me, or else to hazard myself in offending you, which I have (since my years of discretion) been as loath to do as any possible could do.

This was hardly an apology: her husband's errand would be performed whether Cecil chose to be offended or not. The woman who spent the years of her father's exile as a ward in his household and who, on their final parting, was blessed enough to hear him assure her that he looked upon her as a daughter, was clearly an influential – and forceful, if it came to it – mediatrix in the interests of her husband and children. The practical mind at work beneath the surface formalities of epistolary etiquette is indicated with particular lucidity in Elizabeth's postscript: 'Sir, I pray, at your next occasion of writing to my husband, send me word whether any child born beyond the sea shall inherit any land in England.' Squashed beneath the closing salutation, this apparent afterthought reveals the nascent litigious streak in Elizabeth, which would grow ever more robust in years to come. Her letter was drawn to a hasty conclusion, informing Cecil that Lord Montagu and Sir Nicholas had just arrived. She refrained from mentioning that Walter Haddon was with them.

A brooding and melancholy prescience underscores this relic of Elizabeth's early years, which seems to cut deeper than Haddon's sudden appearance or the fact that her fall had left her 'scarce at this present in health'. As she prepared to set sail, she confided to her brother-in-law that she felt 'uncertain whether my hap will be so good as ever to meet again with you'. Whether it was the growing volatility of the political situation in France or simply the dangers of such a voyage for an expectant mother and her young children, her sense of foreboding and fearful anticipation of impending loss would soon be realized in a manner she could not have foreseen.

The next day, Elizabeth and her scarce-rested fellow travellers gathered their belongings and, leaving behind the pebble-strewn banks of Dover, paid the £6 10s required for the two ships needed to convey them to Boulogne. Montagu and Wotton there parted company with them, bound on a mission to Dunkirk. Elizabeth and Haddon boarded separate ships.

Having set sail, Elizabeth quickly realized that her prayers for fair winds would not be answered. Battling fierce currents, the ship altered course to cross via calmer waters to Calais. Thomas Hoby may have been somewhat amused to discover later that Haddon was not a natural-born seaman and was sick all the way. He made a special point of later mentioning the fact to Robert Dudley, now Earl of Leicester. The Hoby party reached their destination safely at 3 p.m., but their relief would be short-lived.

Taking them by surprise, a volley of gunfire came from somewhere near the gate to the fortifications enclosing the town. It tore over their heads, narrowly missing them but slicing twice through the red and white flag of St George one of their company had been carrying as they processed towards the garrison. The shot had been fired from an arquebus, a long-barrelled gun designed to tear through battle armour.

Calais had been under English rule for two centuries, having been captured by Edward III in 1347. In 1558, eight years earlier than the Hobys' arrival, it had been reclaimed by the French. It was still being fortified against retaliatory assaults, and partially remained a construction site, the unfinished garrison harbouring some seven or eight hundred soldiers, and a further six to seven hundred labourers and builders. This was an intimidating sight for such a small party. The moment Hoby's group arrived, they were under surveillance. Like many of the surrounding towns, which had now practically become military strongholds and were, as Hoby was to discover, 'in a marvelous jealousy of strangers', Calais could not be entered 'without special license' or without two or three armed soldiers to ensure visitors did not get up to any mischief. Elizabeth, drawing her gaze across the length of the fort, would have sensed the hundreds of pairs of suspicious eyes 'privily' watching their every move. She was a long way from the comforts of Bisham or the Blackfriars here.

Outraged at their reception, Thomas Hoby immediately requested a conference with Monsieur d'Argos, lieutenant at the garrison. An argument ensued, with Hoby informing him of the 'discourtesy' and 'breach of amity' shown to their party, and demanding the punishment of the men who had dared to shoot through the Queen's flag. While d'Argos, with some reluctance, began an investigation, the ambassador dispatched some of his men on a reconnaissance mission to scout out the town and survey the churches in the area in order to ascertain the impact of France's recent conflicts on those of the Protestant faith.

The country had been torn in two by two warring factions. The Guise family under Francis, Duke of Guise, and his brother, the Cardinal Charles de Lorrain (both uncles to Elizabeth I's chief rival for the English throne, Mary, Queen of Scots), stood on the Catholic side. Opposing them was a group of militant Huguenots – French Protestants with largely Calvinist leanings – among them Louis de Bourbon, Prince de Condé, and the Châtillon brothers: Gaspard de Coligny, the Admiral of France; François d'Andelot, the Colonel-General of the French Infantry; and Cardinal Ôdet. Matters reached a head on 18 February 1563 when the Duke of Guise, who was considered by many Frenchmen to be a national hero for his instrumental role in the conquering of Calais, was assassinated. His supporters blamed Gaspard de Coligny. A blood-curdling oath was drawn up and subscribed to by key members of the Guise faction. 'I promise,' it ran, 'to use all my strength up to my last breath to expel from this kingdom or to kill those who have made peace without punishing the murder, and to inflict a shameful death on those who shared in the homicide, and I swear also to use all my strength in exterminating those of the new religion.'

Faced with the task of preventing a civil war was Catherine de Medici, who had become regent during the minority of her ten-year-old son, Charles IX, following the death of Francis II in 1560. She fashioned an uneasy truce, known as the Peace of Amboise. Ratified on 19 March 1563, this placed severe restrictions on Protestants' right to worship publicly. While noblemen were allowed 'freedom of conscience' in their own homes, where they were able to 'practise the reformed religion', those of less elevated station were permitted to congregate in only one or two designated meeting places in each region, normally in out-of-the-way locations. The Peace of Amboise was a hollow treaty and did little to stop the Huguenots agitating for freedom from what they came to call 'la tyrannie guisienne'. Elizabeth would see for herself the conditions within which the Protestants were forced to worship. It was an experience that would stay with her.

On Thursday 11 April the Hobys and their entourage left Calais on the next leg of their journey to Paris. They had not gone further than Boulogne when a servant of d'Argos intercepted them with a letter, informing them that the lieutenant had 'set by the heels [in the stocks] seven or eight suspect persons . . . for shooting through our flag'. Hoby was cynical. 'I doubt whether he writ truly' was his assessment of the matter. The next day, after passing through Montreuil on their way to Abbeville, they had a nasty encounter which left Elizabeth shaken. They were overtaken by seven or so riders who thundered past them on 'great horses'. Among them they recognized the infamous Marquis of Baden, brother-in-law to the King of Sweden, who had lately escaped from England after a spell in prison for refusing to pay off £5,000 of debts and for keeping his creditors at bay with loaded pistols and 'other weapons defensive'. Having lopped off his beard and disguised himself 'like a mean man' of low status, he was now riding among these rogues incognito. The boisterous crew stationed themselves on the summit of a hill overlooking the Hobys' party and, retrieving two pistols apiece from their saddles, began brandishing them wildly, shooting into the air and making an unearthly din, before doubling back on the road to Calais. Hoby immediately shifted his attentions to his pregnant wife, who was 'somewhat dismayed'. Nevertheless, she insisted on carrying on, for this was an important opportunity for them to assess the extent of the oppression experienced by their fellow reformers on the Continent as they travelled through this 'Popish country'. On the way it became apparent that many Huguenots had been ejected from their churches and were forced to meet secretly in 'certain houses' which were 'appointed for the assembly of Protestants'.

On Easter Day they joined five or six thousand souls 'devoutly assembled at a sermon and communion' a mile from the town walls of Amiens. News quickly spread of their arrival and the Vidame d'Amiens, Louis d'Allye, whom the Hobys noted favourably was 'a very courteous gentleman and one of the reformed Church', came especially to invite them to his Castle of Pinkenye, where, on the Tuesday, they were entertained with a 'solemn and great feast, served all in silver'. They dined in somewhat faded grandeur, for d'Allye's fortunes were not what they had been. He apologized for this, explaining that a more sumptuously furnished house he once owned in town 'was by the Papists clean pulled down, defaced and spoiled, in the late turmoils of civil wars'. The conversation would no doubt have turned to the heavy price paid by the French reformers for their faith, the factional clashes having resulted in several terrifying massacres in recent years.

Despite these atrocities, Elizabeth I had become increasingly reluctant to intervene in the troubles of her continental neighbours, following the humiliating collapse of the controversial Treaty of Hampton Court in 1564. The treaty promised six thousand troops to the Huguenots in exchange for the port of Le Havre, and was signed in the presence of three of the prime movers of the Huguenot faction: the Prince de Condé; Admiral de Coligny; and Jean II de Ferrières, Vidame de Chartres and Seigneur de Maligny. The agreement ended disastrously when the French Protestants betrayed the Queen by joining with the Catholics in a military campaign to wrestle back the port. In this uncertain atmosphere, d'Allye recognized that the intercession of the Hobys was a valuable means of securing English support for his beleaguered co-religionists, not least of all because Lady Elizabeth was a good friend of the Seigneur de Maligny.

The Hobys parted from d'Allye with a resolve, for a while at least, not to dwell solely on the horrors visited upon their French allies. A little sightseeing on their way to Paris would help lighten their mood. Thomas had long been interested in antiquarian pursuits, having travelled through the Continent recording the epitaphic inscriptions on the tombs of notable historical figures. Now he had an opportunity to introduce his wife to these delights. Together they visited some of the lavish funerary monuments of France's former kings; saw a display of royal paraphernalia which included the 'crown, scepter, robes and other necessaries for the French King's coronation'; and examined the famous collection of sacred curios held at the Church of St Denis, while no doubt fighting the impulse to marvel at the 'great treasure of gold and stone in crosses, chalices, and relics'. The experience would have a profound impact on the young Elizabeth, who would soon acquire lasting fame as the age's most prolific female designer of funerary monuments. Particularly influential was her trip to the Celestine convent in Paris, in which she saw the arresting monument of Charles de Maigny. The work of the sculptor Pierre Bontemps, the unusual seated effigy was clad in full armour, his hand propping up his slightly tilted head. Elizabeth was enchanted and would later use this spectral tomb as a model for her own groundbreaking memorials on English soil.

They reached Paris on 20 April, just after a summons by Catherine de Medici requesting that all foreign ambassadors repair to the royal court. Representatives from England, Venice, Spain and Scotland answered her call. Sir Thomas Smith, Hoby's ambassadorial predecessor in France, was one of them, arriving two days later. Eying the couple, he noticed that they looked exhausted, particularly Elizabeth, who was 'weary of that long travail in a country strange'. Their fatigue would not have been helped by the appearance, on

Friday 26 April, of George Carey, Shakespeare's future patron and the man who would later help Elizabeth close down the Blackfriars Theatre. A graduate of Trinity College, Cambridge, Carey was in the flush of youth, only nineteen, and enjoyed spending money as much as he relished complaining about his limited resources. On 6 March Thomas Smith had informed Cecil in exasperation that Carey had come to him, 'without money', asking for a cash injection, as usual, and being generally tetchy about the fact that neither the Queen nor his father, Henry Carey, 1st Baron Hunsdon (who would precede his son as Shakespeare's patron), had been forthcoming with any funds. As he had done 'divers times' before, to the tune of a hundred crowns in total, he reluctantly handed over a loan, probably aware that he was unlikely to see the money again.

George Carey's visit was not just a social call. He had come for cash. During dinner, Thomas handed over the £50 which George's father had sent him. Far from being grateful, the young profligate merely grumbled that it was hardly enough to cover the cost of transportation for five horses, let alone the bed, board and wages of his men. In addition to this, he had incurred a number of debts in France, which were more 'by a great deal' than the paltry sum he had greedily snatched from Hoby's hands. The complaints did not stop there. He was disappointed at his reception by the King, from whom he had expected a generous allowance but 'hath hitherto had none, nor . . . [was] likely to have'. Concerned about his extravagant ways, Sir Thomas wrote to Cecil on his behalf, asking if it would be possible for Lord Hunsdon to augment his son's allowance, or else find 'some means to diminish all superfluities by sending over some discreet person to be about him for his direction'. Young Carey was out of control and needed to be reined in.

Elizabeth had more on her mind than Carey's financial troubles. While in France she was determined to associate herself with some of the noblewomen on the front line of the reform movement. One of these was Anne de Pisseleu d'Heilly, Duchess d'Étampes. Celebrated in her youth for her sprightliness, quick wit and arresting beauty, she had been the mistress of King Francis I. Having shed her former, racier, image, she became a supporter of many non-conformist preachers and the Hobys viewed her as 'a grave, godly, wise, sober and courteous lady, one of the stays of the reformed religion in France'. Elizabeth went to see her alone and was 'well entertained'. The two discussed the predicament faced by the Protestants, both in France and abroad, and Elizabeth inserted into the conversation such effusive praise of her husband that the Duchess conceived a 'great desire' to meet him. Elizabeth facilitated the encounter, and before too long Hoby was writing enthusiastically to Cecil, offering his opinion that the Duchess was 'one that I cannot commend too much' and assuring him that this pillar of the Protestant cause 'thinketh well of the Queen my Sovereign and all her reformed doing'.

Engineering the 'service' of this influential ally for the English Crown was not the only job Elizabeth had to do in France. On 3 May the Queen of Navarre, Jeanne d'Albret, one of the architects of the French Huguenot movement, came to Paris, sending the nobility pouring in from across the land. The Hobys went to see her, gaining her pledge that she would continue towards 'the perfection of matters of religion'. Another visitor was Elizabeth's acquaintance the Seigneur de Maligny. This probably provided her with the opportunity to fulfil her main objective in Paris: the promotion of the Cooke name as the hallmark of the reform movement.

Maligny was the dedicatee of the 1566 French edition of a treatise on the Eucharist which had been published originally by Anthony Cooke in Strasbourg in 1557. The work's Latin title, *Diallacticon viri boni et literati*, would become *A Way of Reconciliation of a Good and Learned Man* when Elizabeth came to produce her own English translation. Its true author had in fact been John Ponet, Bishop of Winchester, one of the men cultivated by the Lord Protector, Duke of Somerset, during Edward VI's reign. Ponet had followed Cooke into exile after the accession of Mary I, travelling through Strasbourg and Geneva, where he absorbed Calvinistic teaching. After Ponet's death in 1556 Cooke purchased his library from his widow and set about popularizing his anti-Catholic mantra. Echoing its title, the preface to the Latin version of the book identified the author only as a *'viri . . . boni, erudite, moderati'* (a good, learned and modest . . . man); an ambiguity that was no accident.

Concealing Ponet's identity was vital, given his somewhat tarnished reputation. In 1556 he did something that would envelop him in infamy: he published *A Short Treatise of Politic Power*, which dared to argue that the 'deposing of kings' is, when it became necessary, 'most true, just and consonant to God's Judgement', even going so far as to suggest that murdering a monarch could in the right circumstances be both lawful and laudable. Flying in the face of the Divine Right of Kings, which placed royalty beyond all earthly judgement, this work put the Cookes in a perilous position, for they were closely affiliated to the community that was generating Renaissance Europe's most explosive political philosophies.

When the French edition of Ponet's book appeared it was no longer from an anonymous hand. A dedicatory epistle to Maligny by the translator, who identified himself cryptically as Étienne de Malescot, a near-anagram of his real name and honorific title, Jessen, Conte de Malte, claimed that the 'intelligent and wise man' who had authored the work was Anthony Cooke. It can be no coincidence that Jessen had reserved special praise for the Cooke sisters, with whom he had previously corresponded, informing Maligny in print that they were 'held among the English (and not without cause) in great repute' as those 'virtuous and excellent ladies, who have not at all diminished the wisdoms, virtue, and learning of their father'. The epistle is dated May 1566, precisely the time at which Maligny and Elizabeth were in Paris together, and explains why she was so insistent on undertaking such a dangerous mission to France while pregnant. The boldness of this strategy to promote the Cooke legacy, and her sense of confidence as an independent woman, were articulated in her decision to distribute her poetry among leading intellectuals of the French court, inscribed, highly unusually, with the Latin version of her maiden name: 'Elisa Cokia'.

Under Elizabeth's stewardship, Ponet's eucharistic work would become inextricably associated with the Cooke name, both shielding her family from the taint of its original author's reputation and endorsing its call for the purification of the Church and the restructuring of the political order which upheld it. Her success in this regard was in step with the growth of a substantial sympathetic readership by 1566. Between 1559 and 1565 many of France's southern provinces had seen a sharp rise in the number of gentry turning to Calvinism, as well as Normandy, Brie and Champagne. By 1560 an estimated 15 to 20 per cent of Rouen had embraced the Huguenot faith, and by 1565 it boasted a Calvinist congregation of 16,500. La Rochelle, Montauban and Montpellier saw conversions to Protestantism rise to roughly 50 per cent. Because Calvinism emphasized unmediated consumption of religious doctrine, encouraging open religious debate and doing away with the Catholic priest's monopoly on the Latin scriptures, the word could also be spread in inns and taverns, on the streets and in the markets, among ordinary working people. A large proportion of new converts were tradesmen – weavers, dyers, textile-makers, cobblers and tanners. Between 1549 and 1560 most refugees leaving France for Calvin's Geneva were involved in these and similar professions. Elizabeth would later seek the support of many such Huguenot tradesmen in her petition against Shakespeare's Blackfriars Theatre.

In the 1560s the semi-literate merchant and trade classes, alongside those of more elevated station, provided a ready audience for pro-Calvinistic teachings. This did not mean that Elizabeth and her comrades were winning the battle for France's hearts and minds. With only 12 per cent of the total population Protestant at this time, there was a long way to go. The incidence of the conversion of highly influential families, however, such as those of Bourbon, Châtillon, Condé and Rohan, gave the Huguenots a disproportionate amount of political power and a new confidence when circulating their beliefs in print. Elizabeth and her family were taking advantage of, and helping to perpetuate, this cultural revolution.

There was an ulterior motive behind Elizabeth's promotion of the French edition of Ponet's treatise, one in line with her husband's ambassadorial mission. Jessen's dedicatory epistle drew attention to Anthony Cooke's role as 'an exile in Germany because of the great persecutions which occurred in England in the time of Queen Mary'. Reminding its readers of the horrors visited upon the Protestants under Mary I served as a potent warning of the terrors which could be unleashed if France decided to enter into a Faustian pact with Scotland in order to further the aims of the Catholic Mary Stuart. This was very much on Thomas Hoby's mind as he geared himself up for a meeting with Charles IX, now ruling in his own right after his mother had proclaimed the end of his minority prematurely, on 17 August 1563.

A pregnant Mary, Queen of Scots, had been making strenuous overtures to the French royals with the aid of the Catholic faction. The question of the English Queen's marriage was therefore more urgent than ever. News had spread as far as the Spanish court late in January that Charles IX and his mother had bent their efforts on sabotaging the English marriage negotiations with Archduke Charles II of Austria and were assisting the Earl of Leicester in his own bid for Elizabeth I's hand. That same month, the Spanish ambassador, Guzman de Silva, had alarmed Cecil by informing him that 'the French were pressing Leicester's suit'. '[L]ook out,' he added impishly, 'and endeavour to get news of this.' Cecil attempted to intervene directly by blackening Leicester's name, urging his sovereign to abandon all thoughts of attaching herself to a man whose sole purpose was to 'study nothing but to enhance his own particular friends: to wealth, to offices, to lands and to offend others'.

One of these friends was the diplomat Henry Killigrew, who had made his support of the Earl's ambitious suit to the Queen a patriotic matter. 'Englishmen would be glad to find an English husband for her,' he had said, on another occasion warning Sir Nicholas Throckmorton in a coded letter, 'whatsoever you do that tendeth to mislike or disallow of that great liking that some have of my L. R. [Lord Robert] is taken but practise of your own hand, rather of ill will than well meaning to the state'. Killigrew had married Elizabeth's sister, Katherine, in November 1565, a match which Cecil had initially tried to thwart, earning from the groom a passionate 'invective' in retaliation. At length Killigrew and Cecil would develop a regard for each other that would flower into a steadfast friendship. In 1566, however, it was to the Hobys that Cecil looked as fitting instruments for the derailing of the Earl's plans. Thomas would lose many nights' sleep labouring over his commission in France, which included doing everything in his power to prevent Leicester's marriage to the Queen.

On 8 May Thomas Hoby got his chance with the King. With Thomas Smith and Elizabeth's brother Edward, he travelled to the court at St Maur, just outside Paris. Once there they were ushered up a flight of stairs to the Privy Chamber of Catherine de Medici, whom they found reposing regally beneath a cloth of estate, discreetly arrayed between her bed and the wall. Presenting letters of credence from the English Queen, Hoby was keen to sound out Catherine on 'Scottish matters'. He was quickly assured that she and the King were 'well given to entertain the peace' between France and England. The ambassador knew what she was holding back: that Mary, Queen of Scots, was now seeking 'safety in France' after the murder of her beloved Italian Secretary, David Rizzio, by Protestant nobles working in confederacy with her husband, Henry Stuart, Lord Darnley, to whom she had refused to grant co-sovereignty of Scotland. Furthermore, her uncle, the Cardinal of Lorraine, had been secretly sending her funds, having dispatched his own Secretary to Scotland to proffer aid, disguised as a merchant who had been 'spoiled by pirates'. The Queen Mother could not bring herself to speak ill of the Scottish Queen, merely indicating her 'much misliking . . . [of] the unstaidness of the Lord Darnley'.

When Hoby was conducted to the King's bedchamber he was not pleased to find the Cardinal of Lorraine there with the Duke of Nemours and Henry, Duke of Guise, who had vowed revenge against Admiral de Coligny for the death of his father, Francis, the former Duke. Hoby presented the young regent with the English Queen's letters. Such was his haste to read them that, in a frantic attempt to unfold the first, he tore off a large piece, 'whereat the Cardinal of

Lorraine smiled and seemed to make a scoff'. Hoby was less amused and became positively incandescent when the cardinal decided to station himself 'not far off, the better to decipher' the King's response and 'cast continually a glaring' upon the letters. Perceiving this, he interposed himself between them, his back to the cardinal, in order 'to stop his sight'. At this affront the cardinal and the Duke of Nemours began whispering in conspiratorial tones, Hoby's brother-in-law Edward noting this as proof that the cardinal had 'not as yet digested any part of his old malice towards England'.

The meeting had been less than successful. By 11 May Hoby would have better luck in his attempt to undermine the Earl of Leicester's relations with the French; the Venetian ambassador, Barbaro, would become his instrument. The most powerful 'Peers of the Realm', Hoby had informed him, had delivered to the Earl a 'certain sort of prayer mingled with threats, that he must desist from his enterprise, and no longer perform the very assiduous service hitherto rendered by him to the Queen'. Before too long the Spanish court was also awash with the news 'that Leicester was not so deep in the Queen's confidence as formerly, and that he was not a person of whom they [the French] need to make so much as they did'. That Hoby was the source of this gossip may have become apparent to the Spanish ambassador because his sister-in-law Mildred had been working to similar effect during his diplomatic mission to England. '[T]he Queen will never marry Lord Robert,' she had declared, 'or, indeed, anyone else, unless it be the Archduke, which is the match Cecil desires.' The Spanish ambassador was taken aback, but concluded that 'if anybody has information on the matter it is Cecil's wife, and she is clever and greatly influences him'.

By the end of the month the cracks in the fragile peace between the Huguenots and Catholics were beginning to show. Elizabeth must have been greatly worried for her children when rumours of an assassination plot against the Admiral de Coligny and d'Andelot triggered clashes between the rival factions. Suddenly they found themselves surrounded by armed men preparing for war. Hoby sent a dispatch to Cecil, informing him that 'great multitudes of captains, men at arms, soldiers, and others' had begun pouring into the city. He estimated that there were twenty thousand horsemen, besides the scores of footmen 'to the assisting of both factions'. So great was the panic that the noblemen of Paris donned battle armour and mounted watches outside their doors all night, 'thinking verily they should have been assaulted at home'.

Fearing that the new fracas would 'cost some of the best Protestants of France their lives', Hoby leaked news of the escalating hostilities to the Queen Mother. This was a tactical error. Her response was a rapid and rigorous clampdown on the armed supporters of the Huguenots, forcibly removing their 'trains of factions . . . out of the city'. The ambassador began to worry that the royals' actions were only the prelude to what he surmised was their real intention: sending a French army to Scotland to stand behind Mary Stuart. They were better placed to do this than ever, following terrible clashes in the village of Pamiers in Languedoc during which three hundred Catholics lost their lives. The massacre, Hoby knew, would prove powerful ammunition for the anti-Huguenot propagandists.

In this atmosphere of paranoia and peril Elizabeth decided to work her own diplomatic powers on the wives of some of France's most influential men. On Tuesday 18 June she organized a meeting in the Hobys' apartments in the Parisian royal court. On the guest list were Madame de la Foresta; the latter's sister-in-law, Marie Bourdin, wife to Jacques Bourdin, French Secretary of State; and Madame Bochetel, who was married to Jacques Bochetel, French Ambassador to England. Also invited that day were the Bishop of Rieulx and the humanist scholar and schoolmaster Jacques Amyot. The event did not quite go according to plan. The pressing discussions about the dangers posed by rising tensions in Scotland were sidelined when the schoolmaster suddenly asked 'if there was any mass in England'. The question was a trap.

'No,' replied Hoby, with a confidence that would quickly be dashed, 'all popish abuses be as well or better reformed there, than in Scotland.'

'I much marvel,' said the bishop, 'that ye say there is no mass in England. And yet I hear there be altars, organs, crosses . . . surplices; yea, and priests compelled to wear caps and tippets contrary to the manner of all reformed churches. Which, as you now see by us,' he added, gesturing to his own attire, which was mostly that of a layman, apart from a hat and a long taffeta gown of the type worn by lawyers, 'is in this country left to our discretion.'

'Why,' snapped Hoby, choler rising, 'if the Queen's Majesty should maintain both factions, Her Highness should do none otherwise than your King doth.' At this the schoolmaster jumped in to offer his learned opinion.

'Nay . . . your Queen . . . doth maintain in despite of all your reformed ministers, such things which men term abuses of the Church of Rome . . . for when all those matters be about a priest, there wanteth nothing but a Mass book.'

'As for crosses and altars,' Hoby responded defensively, 'ye are misinformed, for by order they are taken away in all places throughout the realm. For organs . . . surplices, corner caps, and tippets, as indifferent things, they were at each man's choice to use or to leave, when I was in England.'

'Nay,' corrected the schoolmaster, 'as many as come from thence say that the cross, altar and organs be always in the accustomed place in your Queen's Chapel, and that diverse of your best ministers be put from their livings, and others of the old religion placed in their stead.'

Elizabeth and her husband could not believe what they were hearing. Could this be true? Were ministers of the reformed Church being ejected from their ministries because they refused to wear the three-cornered hats and surplices that for many committed Protestants smacked of Catholic ritual? Investigating the matter, the Hobys soon discovered the humiliating truth. The English were a laughing stock, the butt of every joke among 'both factions'. They had become a strange hybrid, neither fish nor fowl, worshipping in neither a Catholic nor a purified Church. The Hobys felt betrayed. 'And to be plain with you,' wrote Sir Thomas to Cecil, 'it is against my conscience . . . [and] not a little to my grief to hear.' What the Hobys had been informed about while in France were the first stirrings of the Vestments Controversy in England. It was all Sir Thomas would know of the conflict that would soon envelop his wife.

So it came to pass that during Thomas Hoby's last sleepless days, his mind was filled with blood. The Pamiers massacre, the oppression of the Huguenots in France, the murder of David Rizzio and the pressures and challenges facing the Puritans back home were all mixed up together in his thoughts. In his last surviving dispatch he wrote darkly of a 'secret' conspiracy, a bloody cabal between the Pope, King Philip of Spain and Charles IX, to send an army to France with the intention of enforcing Catholicism: every Protestant soul's worst nightmare.

Shortly afterwards Thomas Hoby fell ill. Elizabeth remained by his side in his final days. A physician, a Monsieur Ballie, was called, but he could do little to improve his patient's condition. On 12 July he hastily drew up his will in the presence of his wife; his brother-in-law Edward Cooke; another of his wife's kinsmen, Hugh Fitzwilliam; and his servants, among them Robert Seton. He made his wife 'my full executrice', giving her licence to oversee his burial and commandeer his primary estates until his eldest son, Edward, came of age. He also left 1,000 marks apiece to his two daughters, Elizabeth and Anne. He bequeathed a further 1,000 marks to his unborn child 'if it be a daughter that my wife goeth withal'. There was one caveat: 'And all that to be paid at the day of their marriages if they marry with my wife's consent, or else not to have anything at all.' Hoby was leaving behind a widow who, he well knew, would have the ability to discipline and guide her children. He could not have known that the money he was hoping would secure his daughters' future would never be paid.

Between five and six o'clock on the morning of 13 July Sir Thomas Hoby died in Paris at the age of thirty-six. Elizabeth's former suitor, Walter Haddon, would later say that he had given up his final breath while lying in his wife's lap.

5.

A Widow's Bed

The oppressive sense of foreboding Elizabeth had felt before leaving England, that some terrible fate would befall her in France, proved all too accurate. Now seven months pregnant, left in a foreign country with three children to take care of, she needed every ounce of courage she could muster to fulfil her husband's dying wishes: the transportation of his body back to England for burial, through a country riven by rival factions and civil broils.

In the immediate aftermath of this personal catastrophe, neither her trusted servant Robert Seton, nor her brother Edward Cooke, was able to remain by her side. Seton had been dispatched to England to inform Elizabeth I of the terrible calamity, while Cooke had hastened to the French King and Queen Mother, who were now residing around six miles from Paris. Cooke's mission would prove the more peculiar of the two.

There was something odd about the French royals' reaction to the news of Hoby's sudden death. Shock, amazement, distress followed fast upon each other. This was the expected response. On the way to inform the royals, however, Cooke discovered that he had been pre-empted in his task and that they had already been told the news by another messenger. 'I know very well, they had intelligence before,' he wrote to William Cecil, perturbed, 'yet they both seemed unto me to have understood nothing thereof but by me.' If they were aware of the ambassador's demise, why were they feigning ignorance? This strange episode has since given rise to rumours that Hoby was poisoned. In the tense political climate, this would not have been a far-fetched hypothesis. Edward Cooke would himself die shortly afterwards, on 16 November, from a mysterious sickness, greatly adding to his sister's sorrow.

In the wake of Hoby's death Edward Cooke's missive painted an atmosphere of danger and half-concealed intentions. As he explained to Cecil, the Admiral de Coligny may also have had his own suspicions, for, despite his wish that he could be there to console Elizabeth personally, he was keeping a low profile and 'durst not come himself'. An apparent plot to assassinate him having been uncovered by the Protestant faction at court, he was taking no chances. He therefore sent on his behalf 'the Queen of Scots' bastard brother', James Stewart, 1st Earl of Moray. Cooke had spoken with him confidentially and was told that when news of Hoby's death had reached the admiral's ears he exclaimed that 'all his purpose was dashed'. 'What he meant by it,' Cooke added cryptically, 'he [Stewart] could not tell.'

Elizabeth and her sister Mildred had been supporting the reformers' efforts in Scotland by working to further the interests of Mary Stuart's half-brother. Stewart, an influential Protestant and iconoclast, was developing ties with the Huguenot faction in France and was therefore a valuable ally. Henry Killigrew, Elizabeth's brother-in-law, had praised him for his 'virtue, manhood, valiantness and stoutness' and that very summer the Scotsman would thank Mildred for her aid in their 'common Cause'. Here he was now, urging Elizabeth 'to be of good comfort, and to take God's visitation thankfully'. There was also a warning. Greater battles lay in wait for the Protestants, but through all these the Admiral de Coligny would stand faithfully by her side.

The King meanwhile was quick to assure Edward Cooke that he was 'very sorry' for Elizabeth's loss and 'that if there were anything in his realm, that might stand her in stead, she might as well command it as if she were in England', sentiments echoed by Catherine de Medici. They stuck by their word, and before long the distraught widow was besieged by well-wishers sent from the Queen Mother, including her royal physician, Dr Castellano, 'an excellent learned man, and a very earnest Protestant'. The Queen of Navarre responded with equal alacrity, sending her chief minister, 'who gave her very wise and godly counsel'. The next day Elizabeth was visited by a succession of foreign ambassadors, with representatives from Venice, Scotland and Florence 'offering her all kind of surety that might be showed'. Others sent word 'every day' to offer encouragement and ask if they could 'show her any pleasure'. 'And to say the truth,' wrote Cooke with some relief, 'she hath received since her husband's death, as much courtesy, at divers men's hands as might be possibly showed to any stranger, wherefore I trust by God's grace (although I feared it very much at the first) she shall overcome her great sorrow well enough by little and little.'

Edward Cooke's initial worries about his sister's emotional state were well founded. Her friend the poet Daniel Rogers had commented how, after Hoby's death, his widow had wildly torn at her hair and cried so much that her 'poor swollen little eyes were red'. Before leaving France Elizabeth composed a heart-wrenching poem, intended for private circulation, which reveals that in those dark times she had contemplated taking her own life:

> O beloved consort, O husband most sweet,
> If it had been permitted, since my thought was fixed,
> Wretched me, to follow after you in your entombment,
> On that journey which everyone fears,
> Dismal, loathed by others, welcome to me,
> I would have already followed you down that path,
> Either as a fellow traveller in death, or as surety in
> exchange for your return.
> But now, because the decrees of most high Jove prohibit it,
> Whether I should live, or vanish into the light
> (No, that is not death, death is but whatever misery,
> Unhappy me, without you – alas, alas! – I deservedly
> drag with me),
> Eternally, in my grief, I will memorialize you, because
> this is permitted,
> Adorning my sorrows with wailing and weeping,
> O beloved consort, O husband most sweet.

In the dense thicket of horrors surrounding her Elizabeth found solace in poetry. This tendency would result in her being dubbed the 'English Sappho', after the greatest poetess in classical history. Her many monuments and epitaphic inscriptions would become tourist attractions, both in her own day and for later generations. The antiquarian William Camden would publish Elizabeth's elegiac verses in his guide to Westminster Abbey in 1603, enshrining them as, within themselves, among the greatest monuments preserved there, and she would feature in at least five other tourist guides over the next two centuries, including Elias Ashmole's *Antiquities of Berkshire* in 1719.

Elizabeth's instinct to turn to verse in her grief was inseparable from her need to memorialize her husband, and together these endeavours formed a lawful alternative to suicide, which was strictly forbidden by Christian doctrine. These sentiments were set in stone in Thomas Hoby's epitaph, which still remains in the parish church of All Saints, Bisham, in Berkshire: 'I could not prevent your death, but to your lifeless limbs / As far as I can, I will always do reverence with honour.' For Elizabeth, honouring her husband's memory would become a means of establishing a legacy for her children. More radically, it would allow her to promote the Anglo-French Protestant alliance the couple had been working together to achieve.

The time had come for Elizabeth to convey her husband's embalmed body back to England. The troupe of twenty travellers was now a funeral cortège, conducting a chariot in which was placed a coffin draped in black cloth. It was an arduous journey, not without dangers. Among the £13 6s 8d for 'intelligences', carefully itemized by Elizabeth, are costs for 'espial at several times'. This would have included payment for spies, sent on ahead of the party to make sure the routes were clear of any possible skirmish or lurking Catholic terrorist.

Now she was the most senior noble in the ambassadorial party, Elizabeth's responsibilities were many. She had to secure lodgings along the way; ensure that she, her children, kinsmen and servants had sufficient food and drink (for which she was paying an average of £3 6s 8d per day); and were provided with efficient means of transportation for themselves and their belongings; not to mention managing the difficulties involved in conveying a heavy lead-lined coffin along dusty roads and across choppy seas. Horses were hired at a cost of £30 to take the train from Paris to Boulogne, and a further £5 secured a ship to Dover. Thence, more horses were acquired to carry them to Bisham Abbey, where part of the lavish heraldic ceremony for Sir Thomas Hoby's burial would be performed.

On English soil the party passed through the Blackfriars, where the Hobys' London neighbours could pay their respects before his coffin. Once Sir Thomas's body was arrayed in state at Bisham Abbey, mourners who wanted to offer condolences filed through an outer gate and into an entryway fringed on either side with braided baize-cloth decorated with 'escutcheons', armorial shields depicting Hoby's coat of arms. The coffin had been placed in Elizabeth's private chapel, and was now covered with more expensive black velvet, also adorned with the Hoby arms. The walls round about it were swathed in mourning cloth; the gold and silver paint on the armorial shields, fastened at regular intervals to the drapery, catching the meagre light as his loved ones and neighbours said their final farewells.

Elizabeth had nearly reached the full term of her pregnancy, and was charged with the task of overseeing a spectacular, though unwieldy, funeral ritual. She would have been relieved when her father, Sir Anthony Cooke, arrived at Bisham. She needed him now more than ever, and he had agreed to take the place of honour as his son-in-law's chief mourner. The English heraldic funeral was managed by the College of Arms, the institution responsible for managing the rites of passage – christenings, marriages and deaths – of the nobility. The elaborate and highly structured observance had nothing whatsoever to do with love and everything to do with power and status. Men and women were strictly segregated throughout the service, and chief mourners were selected according to gender and rank: only a man could serve as a chief mourner for a deceased male and had to be of comparable rank to do so. Such obsequies offered little room for a grieving wife and mother to express her sense of personal loss or to assert her deep emotional ties to a once beloved husband. Throughout her life, however, Elizabeth would prove time and again that she could stretch the College of Arms' regulations to suit her will, and this would be her first experience of negotiating rites which were both socially and politically significant. This was to be another life lesson for Elizabeth and would determine the development of her public identity, as well as her fierce investment in her family's reputation and honour.

As the sun began to rise on Monday 2 September, the temperature rose with it. It was to be an unseasonably warm day and the officers of the College of Arms must have felt more than a little discomfort in their hooded ceremonial gowns of heat-absorbing black cloth. A rotund Elizabeth would have swayed uncertainly beneath the long mourning train she was permitted to wear by the college, as befitting her status. This would not have prevented her from noting how magnificently Sir Thomas Hoby's personal crest, the crowned hobby volant – a hobby hawk with outstretched wings embellished with shimmering argent – shone on the standard being carried in the funeral procession. The image of the proud brown-breasted bird, emblazoned on a waving flag that stretched four yards in length, was commissioned by Elizabeth from the painter Robert Grenewood at a cost of forty shillings, and bore the legend *Disce Mori*, 'Learn to Die'. Carrying this was both an honour and, in these sultry conditions, a burden, one fittingly borne by a 'Mr Burden' (possibly the very same whose family would later become embroiled with Shakespeare's kinsmen in an unusual legal scandal), who walked before a grave troupe of heralds carrying other potent symbols of martial service: a ceremonial sword, a shield and a steel battle-helmet.

Next in the procession was the young Anne Hoby's godfather, Gabriel Goodman, the Dean of Westminster, who had served as a tutor in the home of William and Mildred Cecil during the years in which Elizabeth had lived with them. Behind the coffin, which was carried by six yeomen, walked Anthony Cooke, along with Thomas Hoby's male kinsmen and Sir Henry Neville. A neighbour of Elizabeth's in the Blackfriars, Neville would soon marry her niece, Elizabeth Bacon, and go on to play a significant role in the development of the Blackfriars theatres just a stone's throw away from her own home.

In the stifling parish church of All Saints a pulpit had been erected in the north door 'to avoid the heat of the sun'. It was here that Goodman read a funeral sermon in which he praised Thomas Hoby for his 'zealousness and fervency' towards the reformation of religion. Elizabeth then heard herself extolled in the roundest terms for her own service to the state and heroic conduct in the face of adversity. She had, he declared, fearlessly traversed 'foreign shores to bring him and, according to his desire, to bury him in his natural country', a duty she had performed 'not with any superstitiousness', but with all the rites most befitting a committed Protestant. In her choice of her close friend Goodman to preside over the service, Elizabeth had been able to refashion the death ritual – which ordinarily celebrated patrilineage and masculine heraldic attainments – into a public confirmation of her role as her husband's active co-labourer in the reforming cause.

Sir Thomas Hoby's body was buried beside that of his brother, Philip, beneath the choir of the chancel, on the eastern side of the church. But even as Elizabeth was turning her husband's funeral rites into an outlet for her own political activism, her family's network of co-religionists was putting its weight behind the Vestments Controversy, the eruption of which she had been made aware of in France. That year John Bartlett issued the *Fortress of Fathers, Earnestly Defending the Purity of Religion*, a work which gathered together the writings of Anthony Cooke's circle of exiled scholars and ministers. This 'Fortress' was manned by soldiers of Christ, ready to defend their faith to the death, and included Martin Bucer, Peter Martyr, Henry Bullinger and John Laski, the last explicitly identified in this text as the 'superintendent of the Strangers Church in England'. Uniting the churches of England, France and Geneva, this collaborative project constituted a show of international solidarity among the non-conformists.

John Bartlett, a radical preacher of St Giles' parish, Cripplegate, had been one of more than a hundred ministers who were summoned to appear at Lambeth Palace before the Bishop of London, Edmund Grindal, on 26 March 1566. There they were forced to subscribe to the official dress of the national Church 'or else to do no service'. Bartlett refused and was removed from office. Another thirty-five ministers shared his fate. The issue divided the Church and signalled the flowering of Puritanism as a more cohesive movement. Lending his own voice in support was Henry Hastings, now Earl of Huntingdon, the dedicatee of Sir Thomas Hoby's *Book of the Courtier*. From a secret printing-house abroad he rushed a manifesto into press, *About the Popish Apparel*, inaugurating in the process an altogether more militant tone to the radicals' rhetorical arsenal. Recruiting 'valiant' readers 'to the battle . . . against the Romish relics and rages of Antichrist', it called for nothing less than a holy war with Christ himself as their 'head-Captain'.

The England to which Elizabeth returned after her French embassy was one in which the radicals and their opponents were beginning to turn 'from rough words . . . to blows'. Many of these blows were dealt by women, who responded with special fervour to the plea of those 'who called themselves Puritans or Unspotted Lambs of the Lord'. Sixty women ambushed Grindal on 4 May 1566, demanding Bartlett's reinstatement. A few months later they would stalk him through the streets en masse shouting 'many opprobrious words' after him. On 3 June others organized a public riot in London, and when one minister dared to perform a service at St Margaret Pattens in Roode Lane wearing a surplice, they threw stones at him and, pulling him from the pulpit, began tearing off his priestly vestments and 'scratching his face'. Nurtured in a culture of public protest, Puritanism would unite many women in a shared agenda that would give shape to such female-dominated non-conformist centres as the Church of St Anne's in the Blackfriars. Elizabeth would later become a central figure in the ministry of Stephen

Egerton in that parish. The church's chief administrators would be the very same who would sign her petition against Shakespeare's Blackfriars Theatre, including, astonishingly, his publisher, Richard Field.

The militant non-conformist agenda that emerged as a consequence of the Vestments Controversy began to make itself felt during the period in which Elizabeth had secured her public image as her husband's heroic co-equal in the international fight for a purified Church. Under the guidance of her own and her father's associates, the radicals would begin to develop a cohesive identity and a dynamic sense of purpose. Puritanism had arrived, and it was armed.

Elizabeth's conduct after Thomas Hoby's death would not go unnoticed by the Queen, who would collaborate with William Cecil in an intimate letter, endorsed with the royal signet. Lauding Elizabeth for her admirable 'demeanor' in France, the English monarch would pay the most extraordinary tribute to her namesake:

> And for yourself, we cannot but let you know that we hear out of France, such singular good reports, of your duty well accomplished towards your husband, both living and dead, with other your sober, wise, and discreet behaviours in that court and country, that we think it a part of great contentation [contentment] to us and a commendation of our country that such a gentlewoman hath given so manifest a testimony of virtue in such hard times of adversity . . . And therefore though we thought very well of you before yet shall we hereafter make a more assured accompt [account] of your virtues and gifts, and wherein soever we may conveniently do you pleasure, you may be thereof assured. And so we would have you to rest yourself in quietness, with a firm opinion of our especial favour towards you.

The epistle closed with touching simplicity: 'Your loving friend, Elizabeth R[egina]'. In her hour of grief, Elizabeth must have derived comfort from the Queen's noteworthy description of her as the 'commendation of our country', and she would not neglect to take advantage of her sovereign's offer of further support. She had incurred huge debts as a result of the embassy in France, not to mention the additional costs involved in bringing her husband's body back to England. She proved herself a shrewd accountant, and before too long a bill itemizing her full expenditure reached the Queen. Accorded an honour rarely given to women, Elizabeth had been placed in the ranks of those diplomats, politicians and principal servants of the state who had demanded generous subsidies from the Royal Treasury for the execution of their political missions.

The Queen was not alone in offering vociferous praise to this uncommon lady. There was one lurking in the wings who now saw his opportunity to draw nigh to the widow. Walter Haddon could not help but notice that his former heart's desire was now a free agent (and probably also that she had been placed in command of a substantial fortune). He lost no time in penning an artful elegy for Thomas Hoby. It would probably have come as no surprise to Elizabeth that the bulk of the verse was devoted to her, rather than to the recently deceased:

> Rich, and learned, happy with a distinguished wife,
>> Whom Phoebus would make his, if he could . . .
> With open arms, he undertook an embassy in France,
> And his wife accompanied her man.
> Thus Mithridates' wife wandered in battle-gear,
> Thus a wife joined with Pompey.
> But with unequal fate. An enemy force opposed those men;
>> Thomas is dead, lacking an enemy and threats . . .
>> Placed in the lap of his wife, ill, he dies.
> And a tranquil death has followed a peaceful life.

These compliments were double-edged. Elizabeth is painted as a warrior-woman, clad in 'battle-gear', in emulation of Hypsicratea, the sixth wife of King Mithridates VI of Pontus, who disguised herself as a man, acquired the skills of a soldier and accompanied her husband into exile. Hoby, on the other hand, is hardly the male lead in an epic. His peaceful death follows an equally uneventful and unheroic life, so unlike that of the great Roman general Pompey. Elizabeth is also compared perhaps to Pompey's wife, Cornelia Metella, renowned for her education, though there may also be a buried allusion to Stratonice, a former wife of Mithridates who betrayed him by surrendering her husband's castle on the Bosphorus to his enemy, Pompey. If this was not offensive enough, there was more cheeky double-talk beneath the assertion that 'Phoebus would make [Elizabeth] his, if he could.' Phoebus was the god of poetry, and could easily be read as standing in for Haddon himself.

Elizabeth hardly melted with ardour at this apparent declaration of Haddon's continuing infatuation. Instead she asserted her devotion to Thomas Hoby by undertaking an ambitious commemorative project which took five years to complete. The quaint parish church of All Saints, Bisham, was augmented with a new Hoby Chapel, the purpose of which was to house a magnificent alabaster tomb. Elizabeth commissioned this monument from the celebrated workshop of William Cure, who had already designed a stone fountain for Bisham Abbey in 1563 and who had undertaken building projects for her sister and brother-in-law, Mildred and William Cecil. Stretching around six feet in length and ten in height, the monument consists of an imposing sarcophagus upon which repose two life-size stone effigies, one of Elizabeth's husband, the other of her brother-in-law Philip. Both are dressed in battle-armour, fringed with gold guilloche designs, and at their feet stand two majestic hobby hawks embellished with gold. Sir Thomas lies in front, half turned towards the viewer, his left cheek propped up by a cupped hand. The design's origin is unmistakable: the tomb of Charles de Maigny which Elizabeth saw in Paris at the Celestine convent.

Not for the last time, Elizabeth had masterminded a cutting-edge introduction of the French style into England. Creating a visible synergy between the two nations, the tomb allowed her to write herself into the drama of her husband's ambassadorial mission.

While the epitaphic tradition demanded a certain degree of formulaic hyperbole, the genuine depth of her grief and the unique challenges she faced in the aftermath of Thomas Hoby's death can be gleaned from her Latin tribute (here translated) to him:

> O sweet husband, my soul's best part,
>> Whose life was the centre of my existence,
> Why those so conjoined do the jealous Fates rend apart?
>> Why am I left alone, abandoned to a widow's bed? . . .
> When you were serving your country, when you were working
>> for the common good,
>> You died, a pitiful corpse on foreign ground.
> Our poor children are ablaze with burning fevers.
>> O what shall I do, sinking in so many woes? . . .
> Leaving those lands of death, I plunder from there my wedded corpse,
>> Hauling my children away by their listless limbs.
> So, with my womb swelling, I return over earth and waterways
>> To my country, lost in my despair, death-enamoured.

The tomb that Elizabeth designed is a theatre of loss and reclamation. Bringing to life her own and her children's traumatic experiences in France, the monument is more than just an act of remembrance. It stakes a claim for the Anglo-French Protestant alliance she and Hoby had been cultivating in Paris, and for which the English ambassador had sacrificed his life. In her hands the art of commemoration had become explosive political statement.

Sir Thomas Hoby's death had one other unforeseen consequence. Sir William Cecil had written to him a highly confidential letter which arrived shortly after his demise. The unopened missive was taken by someone in Hoby's party and sent to the Earl of Leicester. Tearing Cecil's seal, he was shocked to read instructions to Hoby asking him to defame the Earl's name in France, and to do everything in his power to drive a wedge between him and the English Queen. Giving vent to his rage, Leicester sought Cecil out and confronted him directly. He now had the incontrovertible proof he so desired that Cecil had been using the Hobys in a diplomatic smear campaign against him. Things had reached the point of no return. The growing rift between them would be inherited by their children, and when Elizabeth came to close the Blackfriars Theatre, three decades later, she would find herself at the very centre of it.

That year, 1566, also gave rise to a further event which would have repercussions for Shakespeare. On Friday 6 September Elizabeth gave birth to the child she was carrying. She called him Thomas Posthumous, because he was born after his father's death. Queen Elizabeth agreed to serve as godmother. The boy would grow to be every bit as zealous as his parents, and his association with Shakespeare would be talked about for centuries to come.

PART TWO

Parliament Woman

6.

The War of Admonition

On 25 February 1570 the Queen attended a lecture which would be one of the most memorable of her reign. The speaker was Elizabeth's friend, the Cambridge theologian and hell-raising evangelical preacher, Edward Dering. A vicious denunciation of the 'abominations' and 'thousand more iniquities' of a corrupt clergy ensued, with Dering accusing the Queen's chief ministers of being 'ruffians', a mere rabble of 'dumb dogs'. Demanding the complete demolition of the Church hierarchy, beginning with the bishops, was not enough for Dering. Having dispensed with the clergy, he turned to address his sovereign in the most profoundly shocking terms:

> And yet you in the meanwhile that all these whoredoms are committed, you at whose hands God will require it, you sit still and are careless, let men do as they list [like]. It toucheth not belike your commonwealth, and therefore you are so well contented to let all alone . . . The hands of the Princes and Rulers are chief in this trespass . . . [A]mend these horrible abuses, and the Lord is on your right hand, you shall not be removed forever. Let these things alone, and God is a righteous God, he will one day call you to your reckoning.

Dering quickly felt the sharp edge of royal displeasure and was forthwith banned from preaching publicly. The damage, however, was done. The lecture sparked a wave of activism in Cambridge, and a chance event would provide the zealots with a new champion for their cause. When John Whitgift stepped down from the office of Regius Professor in Divinity in Cambridge to be replaced by William Chaderton, the latter's post of Lady Margaret Professor became vacant. It was duly filled by the 35-year-old Thomas Cartwright, a man who would soon become closely affiliated with Elizabeth. In a series of lectures on the Acts of the Apostles, Cartwright made the radical proposal that the authority to appoint holders of clerical and university offices should be wrested from the bishops and placed in the hands of the common people. The Queen understood immediately the darker implications of this Presbyterian model of religious constitution, for it would turn the ruler into a servant of the Church, bound to the collective wills of the congregations and their democratically elected ministers. It was a revolutionary idea, and one that found a receptive audience.

It was William Cecil, as Chancellor of Cambridge University, who heard the complaints of Edmund Grindal on 25 June. Now Archbishop of York, Grindal condemned Cartwright's new-found celebrity status, for the 'youth of the University . . . doth frequent his lectures in great number; and therefore in danger to be poisoned by him with love of contention'. If Cartwright could not be brought 'with all his adherents to silence, both in Schools and Pulpits', then there was no other remedy than their 'expulsion out of their colleges'. To William Chaderton, looking down from the lofty heights of his Regius Chair, Cartwright's actions were little short of treason, and threatened not only to rend the Church in two but to dismantle the whole political order. Allowed to flourish unchecked, he would, before too long, Chaderton warned, work 'to overturn and overthrow all ecclesiastical and civil governance that now is, and to ordain and institute a new found policy'.

Panic gripped the conservative members of the establishment, and when a proposal to award Cartwright a doctorate was put forward, the university's vice-chancellor and several college heads banded together to thwart his promotion. By 3 July Cartwright's supporters began to sense the danger he was in and coordinated a petition in his defence. Among the signatories was Edmund Rockray, fellow of Queen's College from 1561. Elizabeth knew him well, for she was one of his patrons and employed him as a tutor to her children. Rockray had drawn the attention of the university authorities at this time because of his fulsome response to one of Whitgift's most controversial enterprises, the revision of the statutes of Cambridge University. Deliberately meant as a challenge to Cartwright's own agenda, these new statutes were designed to increase the powers of the college heads. Some deft legal manoeuvring allowed Whitgift to rig the fine print of the statutes in a manner which, conveniently, made it easier to expel members of the faculty from their posts, especially those deemed, in Whitgift's own words, to be 'dangerous and very inconvenient for the state'.

It did not take long for Cartwright's followers to realize how Whitgift intended to use these new powers, which were endorsed with the royal seal on 25 September. Following a second petition in support of Cartwright, signed by twenty-two of his colleagues, Edmund Rockray among them, Dering jumped into the fray with characteristic zeal. 'I will speak my mind,' he informed William Cecil on 18 November, stating that in his opinion Whitgift's 'affections ruled him, not his learning, when he framed his cogitations to get new Statutes'. If Cecil was not willing to 'stand honourable to Mr Cartwright', then, he declared in a shocking breach of epistolary etiquette, 'it were better for you that a millstone were tied about your neck, and you thrown in the bottom of the sea'.

Dering and Rockray put up a united front, with the latter delivering a stern lecture just over a week later in which he denounced the new statutes as the handmaidens of tyranny, created to give yet more power to 'hypocrites and flatterers'. Whitgift retaliated swiftly. Already successful in having Cartwright 'inhibited from reading', he stepped up his efforts to have him ejected from his office entirely. On 11 December he got his wish. With Cartwright out of the way, he turned his attentions to the Puritans' new spokesman against the statutes. Rockray would need his most influential friends around him, and decided to turn to his loyal patron, Elizabeth.

★

Elizabeth's response to the seismic events in Cambridge was coord-inated within a cluster of quirky buildings which exhibited the collision of ancient and modern that had come to characterize the Blackfriars district. In the years succeeding the Dissolution, walls had been knocked down, new partitions created and additional tenements erected within and around the shell of the monastery that once belonged to the Dominican order of the Black Friars.

Thomas Cawarden died in 1559. The following year the property magnate Sir William More, of Loseley Park, Surrey, acquired his lucrative Blackfriars tenements (and their lessees) from his widow for £2,000. It was a canny purchase, for during the 1550s, as one con-temporary reported, there were around eight hundred inhabitants in the area, many of whom were Cawarden's tenants. Among the tenements More now controlled was the old priory's church porch, known to Elizabeth and her neighbours as the Square Tower. This still formed an eye-catching feature close to the north-western cor-ner of the extinct monastic site and was affixed to the eastern section of a distinctive building 'commonly called the Round House or Corner Shop'. Leased to the French immigrant and goldsmith Lewis de Mare, this stood on the corner of Carter Lane and Water Lane. Lady Elizabeth's home was a complex with an upper-storey gallery which extended over both part of the Round House and a tenement which lay on its north-western side, now under the tenure of one Peter Buram.

By the winter of 1570 Elizabeth had taken up residence in the Blackfriars. Here she intensified her efforts to promote non-conformist ministers, supported their activities with her own financial backing, entertained them in her own home, and facili-tated public lectures and sermons designed to appeal as much to native Englishmen as to the many members of the French and Dutch churches who had settled in the area. She was well placed to do this, for she numbered among her neighbours some of London's most influential immigrants, including the printer and bookbinder Thomas Vautrollier, who was leasing the Square Tower right next door. He and Elizabeth had something in common, for they both knew at first hand the horrors of the recent French wars. Vautrollier had come to England early in Elizabeth I's reign 'for religion', one of many escaping the troubles in France. He was granted his formal letter of denization on 9 March 1562 and was admitted as a 'Brother' of the Stationers' Company two years later. Ratified by official 'letters patents', denization gave the applicant permanent residency in England, the right to own land and property, and permission to operate a business. Vautrollier exploited these benefits not merely for his own profit, but in order to realize his own religious vocation. He and his wife, Jacqueline, were committed Protestants and members of the French Church.

The lectures that Elizabeth had funded in the Blackfriars coincided with Vautrollier's self-promotion from bookseller and bookbinder to printer. One of his earliest outputs, produced that very year, was a translation of the work of the French schoolmaster Jean de Beauchesne, establishing a lifelong pattern of specializing in the publication of French works as a way of promoting Huguenot interests. He would eventually publish an account of the life of Elizabeth's friend, the Huguenot figurehead Admiral Gaspard de Coligny, and issue editions of the writings which emerged from the heart of her father's radical community of former exiles. It is very likely that, by this time, Elizabeth had translated the treatise on the Eucharist written by her father's associate, John Ponet. When this came to be published in 1605 as *A Way of Reconciliation of a Good and Learned Man* she made it clear in its preface that her rendering had followed the book's reincarnation as 'a French creature', indicating the 1566 edition which she must have helped oversee during her ambassadorial sojourn in Paris. Her translation's searing conclusion matched, and thoroughly endorsed, the sentiments that Dering had laid before the Queen in 1570:

> I beseech the God and Father of our Lord Jesus Christ to remove from the minds of pastors, doctors, and ministers of the church, the greatest confusion of the church . . . that is, desire to strive and rule . . . wresting it to the nourishing of contentions and factions. And

vouchsafe to inspire with his Spirit the hearts of princes and magistrates, that they may above all things regard what doth most become the rule committed to their charge, and advance God's glory, and not respect what may grow to their coffers . . . with the cruel vexation of their subjects, and common calamity of their commonwealths.

One of the only published statements by a woman of the Presbyterian agenda conceived in the first flowering of the Puritan movement, this work allowed Elizabeth to promote her father's beliefs, providing her with a means of 'honouring his Cooke's blood', as she would later put it in a letter to her nephew Robert Cecil. The original production and circulation of the text in manuscript form was also intended to send a clear message to the Queen during a period when the Church of England was at a crossroads.

Living next door to a printer, one beginning to augment the reputations of French Huguenots, would have impressed upon Elizabeth the power of the rapidly expanding medium of print to engage new recruits for the Protestant hardliners. Vautrollier would soon take on a young Warwickshire apprentice who would later follow in his footsteps, publishing the works of Protestants with more radical leanings: Shakespeare's publisher and former Stratford neighbour, Richard Field. Both Vautrollier and Field would go on to issue the writings of Geoffrey Fenton, who, in 1570, was benefitting directly from Elizabeth's largesse. A keen follower of the political upheavals in France and the Low Countries, Fenton may have been a member of the Hobys' entourage in Paris. In May he had published *A Discourse of the Civil Wars and Late Troubles in France*, with the intention of providing 'a most true looking glass for the Sovereign' in the hope that this would draw from her a 'vehemency to the cause' of reform. In supporting him, Elizabeth was publicly aligning herself with the men who were agitating in print for the end of the Huguenots' sufferings in France and the Low Countries. Her promotion of the London preachers was intended to bring these concerns to her doorstep and help alleviate the persecution of the non-conformists on home soil.

Having established her public reputation as a champion of these men, it is hardly surprising that Rockray, who had found himself on Whitgift's hit list, sought Elizabeth's aid directly. Before too long her brother-in-law William Cecil was tearing open the seal to a letter containing her fervent complaints on the preacher's behalf. Rockray's 'defence of certain liberties' was, she insisted, 'construed to far other meaning than he thought', and was certainly no slight against the Queen:

[B]e good unto him, for that, having had no small trial of him, both for religion, good nature, and disposition to learning, and other virtues, during the time of his being schoolmaster in my house, me thinketh I durst in my conscience answer in his behalf: that what fond words soever passed him, perhaps in some heat, they proceeded not from a mind desirous of sedition, or otherwise less willing to show himself a most true subject to his prince than any one of his college. And therefore assuring myself that if you knew him so well as I do . . . you would altogether alter your opinion of him to the contrary . . . [and] pardon this his first folly.

She would have to wait some time before she knew if her request would be heeded. In the meantime, other matters required her attention. So all-consuming had been her immersion in the Puritan cause that substantial properties she had inherited from her husband had lain neglected. Among the acres of pastureland and dense forest she now managed in the rural county of Worcestershire and its environs was Evesham, a parish lying close to Stratford-upon-Avon, under the governance of the Hundred of Blackenhurst, and surrounded by the gently lapping waters of the river Avon. Elizabeth now owned most of the town and this privilege came with responsibilities, but also rights, rights it was virtually unprecedented for a woman to have: influence over local courts, control of public thoroughfares – including bridges and the traffic that passed through them – and the power to appoint bailiffs. Now, the bridges were collapsing, the mills falling into disrepair, the waterworks and waterways in need of maintenance. The residents petitioned her with their grievances, for 'the great bridge', which linked Evesham with the neighbouring village of Bengeworth, could not 'without danger be passed over', nor 'the mills serve to any use'.

Elizabeth's tenants would not plead in vain. By January 1571 she was back in Bisham, commissioning surveyors, ordering the quarrying of stone and the cutting down of timber from nearby Shrawnell Park, land inherited by Edward Hoby but placed under her charge during his minority. To move the renovations in Evesham along, she enlisted William Cecil's help, confidently ordering him to get going, since the works 'must of necessity be in hand the beginning of this spring'.

Five years into her widowhood, Elizabeth was proving herself adept at overseeing her unwieldy landholdings as well as keeping in touch with the needs of their inhabitants. This is all the more remarkable given the fact that she was a single mother, charged with the responsibility of raising four children, and often bed-bound because of her spinal condition; in her own words, 'neither [able] to bow my back, nor yet to stir my foot to go once out of my chamber by means of most extreme pain in my back and hip bones'.

Elizabeth's efforts on behalf of the radical reformers, as well as her willingness to embrace her responsibilities as a major figure in the communities over which she held sway, revealed a woman setting her lands in order. Her fantasies of idyllic springtime rejuvenation would, however, be shattered by a terrible tragedy, one that eclipsed anything she had yet experienced.

On 17 February 1571 a small coffin was lowered into the floor of the Hoby Chapel of All Saints Church in Bisham. Inside was the body of Elizabeth's nine-year-old daughter, Elizabeth Hoby. She would not rest there alone. One week later, on the twenty-fourth, her seven-year-old sister, Anne, was buried beside her.

Why the girls died within days of each other is not recorded. Perhaps they were the victims of the plague, or the tuberculosis that had deprived so many parents of their children in the sixteenth century. A faded floor slab, rubbed and scuffed by over four hundred years of worshippers' footfalls, remains as a barely legible monument to their mother's intense grief. Placed together in death at her request, the Hoby daughters' perpetual roof would be engraved with a stylized burial urn, topped with a classical capital. The hand that rendered this simple memorial also carved thereon their mother's arresting Latin funeral dirge:

> My Elizabeth, you lie dead (alas! my own flesh) fated,
>> Scarcely ripened, to be cast down a tender virgin.
> Dear to me when you lived, your mother's daughter,
>> Dear to God hereafter, live on, your father's daughter.
> Death was cruel to you, but still more pitiless in his desire,
>> Smothering at once your younger sister Anne with you.
> Anne, your father's and your mother's ornament, your
>> sister's destiny-chaser,
>> Even after these maternal lamentations, child of light,
>> you lie here still!
> One living mother, one dead father, share with you death's
>> double-vault,
>> Even here where a sole stone now covers two bodies.
> It is for this that your mother determined you should be
>> twinned in one tomb,
>> For I bore you both, trembling with joy, in one womb.

These traumatic events could so easily have crushed the 'spirit' that was such fertile ground for those who were later to praise Elizabeth. Added to this, in 1571 little in her life was stable. Her dream of creating a purified sacred constitution was hanging in the balance. Dering and Cartwright had been disgraced, the former banned from public preaching, the latter banished from Cambridge and now living a self-imposed exile in Calvin's Geneva. Nor would Rockray escape Whitgift's fury. The latter demanded on 15 March 1571 that the preacher publicly apologize for his injudicious lecture. When Rockray refused he was sent the way of Cartwright, forcibly ejected from his post on 18 April. It must have looked to Elizabeth as if even her brother-in-law, to whom she had appealed on Rockray's behalf, had abandoned her, at a time when everything she held dear – her family, her comrades in the reforming mission and the new kingdom of the godly which she was trying to forge – was being taken away from her piece by piece.

The radical wing of the Protestant Church was now weakened by a lack of strong, charismatic male leaders. Instead of withdrawing from the world, Elizabeth took all her grief and anger and, stepping into the breach, channelled them into the reforming cause with remarkable vigour. Once again, she used her role as an influential patron to intensify her promotion of the Hoby legacy. By the summer she had funded Geoffrey Fenton's *Acts of Conference in Religion*, a translation of a work outlining the series of disputations in the Sorbonne in Paris between Catholics and Protestants who met to debate the troubles in France. These had taken place from July 1566, during Elizabeth and Thomas Hoby's ambassadorial mission. The dedicatory epistle to Elizabeth, penned on 4 July 1571, drew attention to her now famed heroism during this time, praising her for 'your wise behaviour amongst the French to discharge the high trust of your husband . . . [and] your unfeigned duty of a wife in his honourable funerals'.

This was more than idle flattery. Fenton's intention was to make an explicit association between his patron and the democratic style of disputation pursued during the 1566 conference, a model for the kind of open religious dialogue embraced by the French Huguenots. The English Puritans had already begun following this continental practice, organizing their activities into what were known as 'prophesyings', during which they met in public squares and markets in order to deliver sermons and engage in theological debate. Whitgift and his followers worked assiduously to shut down such proceedings, but Elizabeth persisted. She was one of the early pioneers who sought to systematize this method in order to propagandize the non-conformist cause. She had, as Fenton noted in the dedicatory epistle to his book, funded lectures and hosted meetings around her own table in the Blackfriars which had become synods of 'deep divines and preachers'. In doing this she had, he continued, 'raised into dignity' the Cooke name by 'your great charges to entertain men of arts and learned faculties, by which your house seems an university of learning'. Elizabeth, a graduate of her father's 'female university', had now established a university of her own. The pupil had surpassed her teacher. Her tireless endeavours were, Fenton concluded triumphantly, 'public monuments which cannot be defaced'.

Geoffrey Fenton composed these sentiments from the Black-friars, possibly while living in Elizabeth's own house, just paces from the building that would become Shakespeare's Blackfriars Theatre. The *Acts of Conference in Religion* placed the Blackfriars as the new border territory of the Puritan mission and was published at an auspicious moment. As Fenton was adding the final flourish to his dedication, Edmund Rockray received news that he was being re-instated, at William Cecil's instigation. Elizabeth's brother-in-law had not abandoned her after all. Emboldened by these developments, Dering took the opportunity to keep the ball rolling and in March 1572 wrote to Cecil requesting that Cartwright be allowed to return to England without fear of punishment. His gamble paid off. In April 1572 Cartwright was back on home soil, just as Geoffrey Fenton was giving further public recognition to his patroness. In his translation of an Italian work on the nature of love, *Monophylo*, Fenton included a dedicatory epistle in which he associated Elizabeth with the great natural philosophers who strive. to 'decipher the secret nature of things' and attain 'perfection in science'. Written in his lodging in the Blackfriars on the sixth, the plaudit was carefully designed to bring to the fore her interest in cosmography and natural history – and not without reason.

Elizabeth became involved at this time with the learned Dr Bartholo Sylva of Turin, a new convert to Protestantism who was seeking protection and favour in the English court. With Dering still facing the royal cold shoulder because of his insulting oration before the Queen, Elizabeth decided to team up with her sisters and

Anne Locke in order to help the beleaguered preacher. The previous year, Locke's husband, Henry, had died, leaving her his sole executor. When Dering heard of this he decided he would claim this 'good possession' for himself. A mutual friend of theirs, the Puritan matron Dorcas Martin, wife to the goldsmith and future Lord Mayor of London Richard Martin, set about arranging the union, and they married in 1572. Sylva had entered the scene at the perfect time, and Elizabeth and her fellow female radicals decided to co-opt him in a rather unusual project.

Sylva had composed a scientific treatise in Italian called the *Giardino Cosmografico Coltivato* (*Cultivated Cosmographical Garden*). A curious mixture of ancient and cutting-edge wisdom, this work laid before the reader, in pages teeming with vibrantly coloured diagrams and cosmographical charts, recently discovered and exotic new worlds: Peruvian Cuzco, Aztec Temistitan, the Straits of Magellan, the Caribbean, South America and Japan. The Cooke sisters and the Derings provided poems in Latin, Greek and other European languages in a lavish presentation copy to the Earl of Leicester. The gift was intented to reach the Queen through her favoured Earl, drawing her attention to the fact that Dering had been responsible for Sylva's conversion. On 24 May 1572 Elizabeth added her own garnish to the work, a poem in Greek in which she described Sylva 'as a friend' and lauded Leicester, his patron, as a 'hero, to whom this gift is given'. If Leicester was prepared to extend his hand to Dering, then couldn't his beloved sovereign also be moved to show the rejected preacher a little grace?

Cartwright was now back in England, Rockray had been restored to his office in Cambridge, and Dering was being supported by Lady Elizabeth and her sisters, and by his new bride, Anne Locke, and her Cheapside neighbours the Martins. The new-won confidence of the non-conformists was being replicated among a growing faction of sympathizers in Cambridge and London, with the occasional support of Elizabeth's brother-in-law William Cecil. These were all the ingredients needed to cause an explosion.

*

Anyone labouring under the misapprehension that Puritans were a dour bunch, a coterie of strait-laced academic types, would have found it difficult to sustain their prejudices when confronted with those Cambridge progressivists who backed the likes of Dering, Cartwright and Rockray in their war against Whitgift's new university statutes.

Young, confident and brash, these men were too nonchalant to remove their hats respectfully in the company of their superiors and could be found stalking the corridors of the colleges attired in 'very unseemly ruffs at their hands, and great galligaskins and barrelled hose stuffed with horse-tails, with scabilonians and knit netherstocks [stockings] too fine for scholars'. Galligaskins were wide, ostentatious breeches; 'scabilonian' is a derogatory term for inappropriate or outlandish dress. This is very far from the popular, and somewhat skewed, image of Puritanism that has entered circulation today.

As the heads of the Cambridge colleges observed, these ruffians were more than willing to 'go abroad, wearing such apparel even at this time in London' and with 'such unseemly going' and 'lewd example' tarnish the reputation of the university. Worse still, they were by 'their own nature given to contention' and enjoyed whipping up their fellow radicals into a frenzy with their public orations. This contributed to the growing number of agitators against the statutes and, when a further petition of complaint was presented to William Cecil on 6 May 1572, it was signed by 164 fellows of the colleges, half the total number in Cambridge. Learning little from his recent spell of unemployment, Lady Elizabeth's trusty schoolmaster, Edmund Rockray, was one of the signatories. To Whitgift and the college heads it was clear that these reckless men had begun 'a petty rebellion'.

It was in this highly tense atmosphere that two of the preachers who would emerge as leaders of the Puritan faction, Thomas Wilcox and John Field, composed one of the most incendiary texts of Elizabeth I's reign: *An Admonition to the Parliament*. This was published shortly after Cartwright's reappearance on English soil and was a response to the failure of a bill put forward in the House of Commons to license some non-conformist forms of worship that deviated from the Church of England's Book of Common Prayer. When it appeared, *An Admonition* caused a storm, due in no small part to its coarse and uncompromising diction. The archbishops and bishops, it argued, were uninterested in their spiritual vocations and preferred to 'toss the Psalms in most places like tennis balls' and endorse a flawed prayer book which was 'culled and picked out of that popish dunghill'. Calling for an Anglo-French alliance, an appended letter by Anthony Cooke's associate Theodore de Beza urged ministers of the French Church in London to join the rebellion by offering 'refuge and succour' to those 'banished' from their native countries by the 'enemies of the Gospel'. Building to a rousing crescendo, this spiky little pamphlet informed fellow Puritans that they were now in open battle with the very forces of darkness. This was no local conflict, it was a world war:

> Is a reformation good for France? and can it be evil for England? Is discipline meet [appropriate] for Scotland? and is it unprofitable for this Realm? Surely God hath set these examples before your eyes to encourage you to go forward to a thorough and a speedy reformation. You may not do as heretofore you have done, patch and piece . . . and never labour or contend to perfection. But altogether remove whole Antichrist, both head, body and branch, and perfectly plant that purity of the word . . .

This small pamphlet lit the touchpaper of what came to be known as the Admonition Controversy. 'Surely the book was fond,' wrote Thomas Norton on 20 October 1572, 'and with unreasonableness and unseasonableness hath hindered much good and done much hurt.' An exasperated Whitgift gave a more damning critique. 'That book,' he declared five days later, 'defaceth the whole state of religion, the whole order of service, the whole ministry, the whole kind of government, used and allowed in this church,' and, worse still, it was now 'in every man's hand'. Instantly divisive, *An Admonition* threatened 'to make schisms and to stir up contentions'. Its authors were quickly rooted out and cast in Newgate Prison, though this did little to bring them to contrition. 'We have used gentle words too long, and we perceive they have done no good,' announced Field during his interrogation that September. 'It is not time to blanch, nor to sew cushions under men's elbows, or to flatter them in their sins.'

Far from putting a stop to the tremors of the controversy, the incarceration of Field and Wilcox fed the earthquake that ensued. The two simply turned their prison into their new centre of operations and were visited there by the most influential radicals of the land. Catching wind of this, Whitgift and his associates recruited the gaoler of Newgate as their spy and pressed him to divulge their names. Elizabeth's closest intimates, Thomas Cartwright and Edmund Dering, were among them. Others included Robert Johnson, personal chaplain to Elizabeth's sister and brother-in-law Anne and Sir Nicholas Bacon; John Browne, chaplain to the Protestant activist Lady Katherine Bertie, the Duchess of Suffolk; and James Younge, 'a common carrier of all the news to them'. These networks allowed the authors of *An Admonition* and their followers to coordinate further publications, spawning tract and counter-tract, with Whitgift and Cartwright trading metaphorical blows in the press.

Cartwright's most controversial contribution to the quarrel was his *Reply to an Answer Made of Master Doctor Whitgift*. Circulated by a secret press by April 1573, this work declared his unambiguous commitment to a holy crusade: 'It is a profane saying of a profane man that an unjust peace is better than a just war.' That month Edwin Sandys, the new Bishop of London, was reporting to William Cecil that the authors of these texts, Cartwright among them, were inciting their influential supporters to arrange themselves in battle formation on their behalf. 'Surely they will make a division not only among the people but also amongst the nobility,' he mused, 'yea, and I fear among men of highest calling and greatest authority, except speedy order be taken therein.'

Many of these supporters who hailed from noble stock were

women. The surviving copies of the texts generated by the controversy were mostly inscribed to female associates of John Field, by
whose own hand they were signed. Lady Mary Grey, sister of Lady
Jane, owned the *Admonition* and other principal works sparked by it.
When Cartwright was forced into hiding by the publication of his
Reply, he was sheltered by Anne Locke's close friend Dorcas Martin
in her house in Cheapside. By 9 December a shocked Edmund Grindal was reporting that not only was Dorcas harbouring this fugitive
but that she had taken on the traditionally male role of becoming,
illegally, the 'stationer for all the first impressions of the book'. Like
Elizabeth and her sisters, Dorcas was a Puritan translator, and would
be lauded by Thomas Bentley in his *Monument of Matrons* as one of
a group of female 'heroical authors' who, 'for the common benefit
of their country', had dedicated themselves to 'the studies of noble
and approved sciences'; achievements which, Bentley adroitly
implied, were wholeheartedly endorsed by Elizabeth's brother-in-
law William Cecil. Dorcas and her husband were financial backers
of the French Church in London (the synodical structure of which
had so influenced the substance of the Admonitionists' aims), whose
congregation had also on occasion been joined by Cecil's sisters-
in-law Katherine Killigrew and Anne Bacon. Anne would become
the unfailing patron of both Field and Wilcox, and the latter would
describe her as a woman 'made truly famous abroad in foreign
Churches and countries'.

On Friday 29 May 1573 Field and Wilcox were ordered to appear
before the Star Chamber. After Dering's name had been flagged up
to the authorities as one of the Puritans who had visited them in
prison, he too was summoned on the same day. Their interrogators,
however, had a difficult time of it, and found it nearly impossible to
make any accusations stick. Elizabeth's brothers-in-law, Nicholas
Bacon and William Cecil, who were presiding over the proceedings,
seemed unwilling to press the witnesses or to accuse them of any
specific crimes. The Archbishop of Canterbury, Matthew Parker,
was furious that 'nothing else would have been done' to bring them
to justice. He no doubt remembered that Dering had, the previous

December, darkly prophesied 'that Matthew Parker shall be the last Archbishop of Canterbury', and now vented his frustrations before Cecil and Bacon, declaring that 'if the matter were but thus wound up, neither should the Queen's Majesty's expectation be satisfied, nor yet the expectation of the city'. Proceedings ended shambolically, and even the pair's suspension from public preaching proved difficult to enforce. When Dr Thomas Wilson forbade Dering to give a lecture just before Christmas, 'in Her Majesty's name', Katherine Killigrew stepped in to berate him for usurping the Queen's own prerogative, leaving him stammering denials 'that ever he spake it, or had any such message'. Dering carried on with his lectures.

The Queen herself had underestimated the effect the support of such influential women and their husbands would have. On 11 June 1573 she issued a royal proclamation against *An Admonition* and any works defending it, requesting that they be submitted to the bishop of the relevant diocese within twenty days, 'upon pain of imprisonment and Her Highness's further displeasure'. On 2 July a dumbfounded Edwin Sandys wrote to Cecil bewailing the fact that the populace had entirely ignored the Queen's edict, for 'the whole City of London, where no doubt is great plenty, hath not brought one to my hands'. No wonder, when the ministers who backed the Admonitionists were preaching radical sermons from St Paul's Cross, just north-east of Elizabeth's home, condemning those who capitulated to the bishops' demands as self-interested 'men pleasers'.

Sandys maintained that the populace's stubborn refusal to betray the Puritans was evidence of a 'conspiracy breeding in London', galvanized by radicals who were shielding Cartwright and his followers with 'promise to stand in the defence thereof unto the death'. He also knew that these Puritan figureheads had become 'Idols who are honoured for Saints, and greatly enriched with gifts'. He had a pretty good idea who was funding them too, having discovered that a 'great resort' of visitors was repairing to Dorcas Martin's home and that there plots were being laid with the support of the foreign Church. It was with a detective's revelatory air that

Sandys reported his findings: 'French ministers are meddlers in these matters.'

In 1572 the French Church had seen a sudden rise in its powerbase as a consequence of one of the worst atrocities in France's history. The St Bartholomew's Day Massacre took place on 24 August following the assassination of Admiral Gaspard de Coligny by Henry, Duke of Guise. The horrors that followed were the culmination of years of seething hostilities against the Protestants, coupled with frustration at spiralling food prices, abysmal harvests, crippling taxes and increasing unemployment. In Paris these tensions coalesced into a lethal ecstasy of pillaging, looting, rioting, burning and killing which lasted nearly a week. The death toll in the capital has been estimated at between two and three thousand.

As news of the massacre spread across France, so did the carnage. In Orléans, Angers, Lyons, Rouen, Bordeaux, Toulouse and many other villages and towns, Catholics took up arms against their Huguenot neighbours. The slaughter continued for well over a month, with estimations of the total death count ranging between five and ten thousand. Francis Walsingham, William Cecil's intelligence operative in France, was a witness to these events, for he and his family, along with as many Huguenots as he could rescue, cowered in his home, close to the Pont aux Meuniers, as hundreds of Protestants were butchered and thrown into the Seine. It was probably he who sent to Cecil the initial lists of the women and children murdered in the massacre, a harrowing document which runs to nearly four pages of densely packed handwritten script.

With Cecil's agents now accusing Charles IX of becoming, largely through the 'motherly persuasions' of Catherine de Medici, a despot who was 'so bloody that it is impossible to stay his thirst to quench the same in innocents' blood', attention quickly turned to the wider consequences of the massacre. 'These evil times trouble all good men's heads and make their hearts ache,' lamented Edwin Sandys, 'fearing that this barbarous treachery will not cease in France, but will reach over unto us.' Huguenot refugees poured into England, bringing with them their heart-stopping tales of the violence and apocalyptic bloodshed. Many exiles quickly entrenched themselves in the foreign churches of London, the numbers of French pastors taking up residence more than quadrupling almost overnight after above sixty ministers arrived seeking shelter. The English Puritans suddenly found themselves with a new army of potential allies and were being roused to greater extremes of activism. They were aided by Thomas Vautrollier, who began circulating disturbing accounts of the massacre in print. Sandys became concerned that the younger radicals in particular, 'unskilful in matters political, yet so carried with zeal', would incite the rest of the populace to acts of sedition. The growing rage of the displaced communities which had come to London was, however, becoming a catalyst for the Huguenot faction in the Low Countries. Coligny's death had been hastened by his strenuous efforts to mobilize French military aid in an invasion of the Netherlands, to liberate the Huguenots there from Spanish rule. Now the Protestant coalition wanted to finish what he had started. Only days after Sandys voiced his concerns, Cecil received requests from the heads of the forces stationed in Flushing (now Vlissingen, in the south-western Netherlands) to give authority to the French churches of London to recruit fit and able men, to equip them with the necessary arms and send them out to the Low Countries to aid the war effort.

The horrible tragedy in France changed the composition of the London population, particularly in areas such as the Blackfriars, and gave further impetus to the war of Admonition. Uprooted from their homes, their families and their livings, some of these refugees would become acquaintances and supporters of Elizabeth Russell. One of them was William de Lawne, who was born just outside Dieppe. In three years he would become a minister of the French Church, settling in the Blackfriars, where he would not only sign Elizabeth's petition against James Burbage's new theatre but also play a significant role in Richard Field's betrayal of Shakespeare.

7.

Lady Russell

Elizabeth almost never became Lady Russell. Not long before she would unite herself with the celebrated house of the Earls of Bedford, the Russell family came close to being utterly disgraced after becoming implicated in one of the most baffling cases of Puritan espionage to have occurred in Queen Elizabeth's reign.

While Elizabeth had been only twenty-six years old when she was widowed, she came to enjoy her independence and had been in no hurry to find a second husband. As the years wore on, however, she may have begun to realize that marriage to another influential reformer could benefit the Puritan cause. She chose the 21-year-old John Russell, son to Francis Russell, 2nd Earl of Bedford, and Margaret St John. Unusually, she was some thirteen years older than her groom. The Russell family's reformist qualifications were impeccable. Francis was a close friend of the Cecils, particularly Mildred, who visited him regularly at Bedford House on the Strand. One of Anthony Cooke's fellow exiles, he had established close ties with Calvin as well as with pastor Nicolas des Gallars, the Queen of Navarre's chaplain, who had become the leader of the French Church in London from 1560.

The most influential members of the Russells' radical coterie were identified in the conspiracy, which shook the Privy Council at its very core. During the winter of 1573 the non-conformists were the focus of the kind of bad press that was music to John Whitgift's ears. After coming fresh from a Puritan lecture, a dagger-wielding zealot, Peter Birchet, had attempted to assassinate the Queen's Navigator, Captain John Hawkins, having mistaken him for Sir Christopher Hatton, a parliamentarian and Gentleman of the Queen's Privy

Chamber whom his attacker believed to be a crypto-Catholic. Before Birchet's execution, his interrogators had come to the conclusion that he had been 'set on by others . . . engaged with him in some dangerous practices' and pointed their accusatory fingers at 'two of the head Puritan preachers'. Weeks later Thomas Asplyn, one of the printers suspected of involvement in issuing Cartwright's *Admonition* text, the *Reply*, had attempted to kill the printer John Day and his wife because 'the Spirit moved him'. By early December a warrant was issued for Cartwright's arrest. The preacher escaped to Calvinist Heidelberg to commune with members of the French and Dutch churches there, leaving his fellow non-conformists at home facing a spate of persecutions and imprisonments. An informant named Humphrey Needham duly materialized from the shadows and began to cash in on these strange events, offering his services as a spy for the bishops who had been seeking to use these calamities to undermine the Puritans. At their head was Archbishop Matthew Parker.

What Parker did not know was that Needham was a double agent. During the following year he delivered into the Archbishop's hands a cache of letters, replete with encrypted messages, aliases and murderous plots, which seemed to incriminate the prime movers of the Puritan faction. These included Francis Russell; Thomas Cartwright; Anne Locke's patroness, the Duchess of Suffolk; and John Browne, the Duchess's personal chaplain. Among the documents were letters to Richard Martin, husband to Dorcas Martin, the woman who acted as the stationer for Cartwright's *Reply*. This is significant because it places the Martins among the Russell enclave and provides yet another link between Elizabeth Russell and Richard Martin, who would later be responsible for the harassment of Shakespeare's company in the run-up to the closure of the Blackfriars Theatre.

Needham's shocking letters revealed that Cartwright had secretly stolen back into England and was preparing to publish a more explosive manifesto from a clandestine press in Southwark. One missive, dated 8 April 1574, purporting to have been written by John Browne to Cartwright, indicated that the entire enterprise was being funded by the Earl of Bedford. Further letters appeared, each more sensational than the last, identifying a mysterious John Undertree as the secret mastermind behind the scheme and hinting at a plot to assassinate William Cecil with the help of Richard Martin, who was called upon 'to dispatch our matters and that as soon as may be'.

Parker sprang into action, arresting some of the Puritan ministers mentioned in the letters. Cecil meanwhile ordered a raid on a building in Southwark, thinking it to be the location of the secret press. They even planned to ambush the mercurial Undertree, believing they had managed to trick him into meeting at Parker's own home, or nearby 'on the water-side'. All they needed to do, they assured themselves, was 'to lay in wait' and take 'possession of him'. It would not be so easy. 'This deep, devilish, traitorous dissimulation, this horrible conspiracy, hath so astonished me,' wrote Parker to Cecil on 19 June, 'I would I were dead before I see with corporeal eyes that which is now brought to a full ripeness.' The next day Cecil drew up a list of suspects for interrogation, including 'Martin, the goldsmith, at the Mint in Milk Street'.

By 30 June, after further failed attempts to capture Undertree, 'either by hook or crook', as Parker had put it, the whole sordid affair had been exposed as a fraud. The letters were forgeries. 'I marvel that Browne's letters, so many, should be counterfeited ever with one hand,' declared an amazed Parker, and not without some relief that 'the realm is not yet corrupted with such sprites as were feared'. No better punishment could be meted out to the man responsible for the charade, he averred, than 'this varlet [to] be hanged'. The Puritan prisoners were immediately released and the Earl of Bedford was back in everyone's good graces: 'innocent men be purged by this examination, and friends be still the same'.

Had the forgery not come to light, the figureheads of the Puritan faction would have lost their heads. The details in the letters were blatantly wrong in so many obvious ways, however, that the affair seemed staged specifically to be uncovered as fraudulent. Could the Puritans have orchestrated the conspiracy to humiliate Parker and Whitgift? Were they acting collectively as agent provocateur, using Needham as their instrument? This is certainly a possibility, for the incident temporarily stayed the systematic oppression of non-conformists. When Elizabeth became Lady Russell in Bisham parish church on 23 December 1574, therefore, she had aligned herself with an activist circle which had recently scored – purposefully or not – some immunity from the machinations of Whitgift and his allies.

Marriage to John Russell had one other advantage. Following the untimely death of his elder brother, Edward, in 1572, he was now heir apparent to the great Bedford Earldom. Elizabeth was in line to become a Countess, outranking even her influential sisters. She did not know it then, but the marriage would be the start of a war over her future honorific title, that of 'Dowager', which would stand as a perpetual monument to her action against the Blackfriars Theatre in her petition of 1596.

London was in the grip of the plague as Elizabeth readied herself to give birth to John Russell's first child in October 1575. Her friend Gabriel Goodman, Dean of Westminster, who had previously led the solemnities at Sir Thomas Hoby's funeral, had come to the rescue, offering the Russells his lodgings in the close abutting Westminster Abbey. The Black Death had wiped out thousands in Venice that year and swept its terrible scythe across parts of northern Europe and England. Of the parishes in the environs of London, Westminster was the most severely affected, with 58 per cent of all deaths in the Bill of Mortality for the week ending 9 September recorded as due to the plague. Elizabeth's Blackfriars home, however, was exposed, and Goodman's relatively isolated rooms offered some security.

Inside this quiet nook of the cathedral complex, as if the expectant mother had determined to oppose her own title against Death's dominion, no expense had been spared to give her every possible luxury 'appertaining to such estates'. In constant attendance were women, stationed in a 'great chamber' next door, coming and going with towels, linen and elaborate silver pitchers of water or caudle, the sweet, fortifying spiced wine (sometimes flavoured with saffron, honey or ground almonds) which was never absent from the bedside of a labouring woman during this period. While the rituals that governed lying-in and childbirth were a female affair, the grander ceremonial elements of the nativities and christenings of the nobility, like their burials, were appointed by the College of Arms. As Elizabeth had done during her first husband's funeral, she decided to manipulate these conventions to suit her own purposes.

She was now a Baroness, her husband a Baron, yet she insisted on lying in a 'rich bed of estate for a Countess'. While men would not normally have entered the birthing-chamber, John Russell was not far away. A nearby room had been theatrically adorned with 'a cloth of estate for an Earl', framing an ostentatious throne, topped with a 'pommel' or decorative finial. The fact that this was prohibited by heraldic custom did not deter Elizabeth, who ensured that such embellishments provided a somewhat premature statement of her status as imminent inheretrix of the privileges due to the Bedford Earldom. This was a bold self-elevation, intended to place the Russells above even her brother-in-law William Cecil, whom the Queen had ennobled with the title Baron Burghley on 25 February 1571.

The privileges of rank and status are, however, no bulwark against the dangers of childbirth, and when Lord Burghley visited his sister-in-law during her lying-in he became worried about her health. On 2 September John Russell reassured him that while Elizabeth may have appeared 'in a bad estate' when he last saw her, she had since 'made amendment' and, apart from a brief scare four or five days previously, she 'had no more pain than hath been common with her ever since her being with child'. Though confident of a 'safe and speedy delivery', his main concern was the recklessness of the servants, whose constant 'straying abroad' was putting their 'small company' in danger of infection from the plague. His desire that Elizabeth 'go out her full time' without any further 'torment' would not be realized. In the early hours of 22 October Lady Russell went into a difficult and near-fatal labour. Her husband would have heard the screams and the panicked hubbub of the midwife and nurse as they struggled to deliver the baby.

To John Russell's great relief, between the hours of six and nine in the morning, the 'noble lady was happily delivered of a daughter'. Elated, the new father penned a hasty missive to Burghley that very moment:

> God having delivered a poor lady of great fear and torment, I do both as joyfully and as speedily as I can, let your lordship know thereof. And though I could have wished, with all my heart, to have had a boy, yet the danger that I stood in of losing both, doth make me rejoice in having a girl.

John Russell could not have foreseen the consequences of not having a son. It would eventually cost his wife the Bedford wealth and titles, their promise so apparent in the sumptuous accoutrements of the Earl and Countess with which the couple had surrounded themselves, in outright defiance of the College of Arms. For now at least he was in high spirits and got up the courage to ask for Burghley's solicitation in the matter of the child's christening. 'I cannot tell what surety I may make of the Queen's acceptation, if I should beseech Her Majesty to be Godmother, which I think best not to leave untried,' he wrote. As to the godfather, Lord Russell seemed convinced that his father, Francis Russell, would be 'neither glad of the matter nor willing to accept it', other weightier affairs having 'drawn his mind' of late. The honour fell instead to the Queen's darling, Robert Dudley, the Earl of Leicester. The choice was a significant one. As Leicester's brother, Ambrose Dudley, 3rd Earl of Warwick, had married John Russell's sister, Anne, Lady Russell was now sister-in-law to the land's most favoured courtier. With such prestigious familial ties, and with the Queen agreeing to act as godmother to one of Elizabeth's children for the second time, no more illustrious, or more auspicious, beginning could have attended a girl's birth.

On Thursday 27 October, at 10 a.m., the christening party

processed from Dr Goodman's lodgings, cutting through the close of Westminster Abbey, into the echoing cloisters, then through to the central nave of the church. In accordance with the birthing ritual, Elizabeth was not with them, the mother not being permitted to stir from her bed until the rite of thanksgiving known as 'churching' had formally reintegrated her back into the community. Much to Elizabeth's disappointment, the Queen was sojourning at Windsor and could not attend on the day. Her sister-in-law Anne Russell, Countess of Warwick, was appointed in her stead 'as Her Majesty's deputy', with Frances Sidney, Countess of Sussex, serving as godmother. Leading the train was a stunning troupe of Earls and Barons, followed by the Earl of Leicester. After him came the midwife, a Mrs Bradshaw, cradling the infant in 'a mantle of crimson velvet' lined with ermine and fastened with golden laces. The morning light, filtering through the leaded abbey windows, shimmered against the child's intricate 'lawn', a fine gauze of linen which covered her face, interwoven with gold lace and studded with gold and white embroidered flowers. Next followed the Countess of Sussex, then the Countess of Warwick, with a long train borne by Elizabeth's sisters Mildred Cecil and Anne Bacon.

After a brief oration by Gabriel Goodman, the baby was baptized in 'a great basin' filled with water and decorated 'with flowers about the brim', set near the altar on a purpose-built frame 'a yard high'. There the Earl of Leicester and the Countess of Sussex 'christened the child by the name of Elizabeth', a double memorial, recalling the name of her deceased half-sister as well as of the Queen. No doubt Elizabeth Russell carefully choreographed the dinner which followed immediately afterwards. As with all the major events managed by her, political considerations would underpin the celebrations. Since the eruption of the Admonition Controversy, Leicester had shown a growing commitment to the Puritan cause and agreed to patronize Elizabeth's friend, the disgraced preacher Edward Dering. When the guests took their places, all eyes would have been turned to the main table. They would have noted that Leicester had been strategically placed next to Mildred

Cecil, who sat to his left. With Lady Bacon placed beside Ambrose Dudley, Earl of Warwick, the event provided Elizabeth with a means of pointedly aligning herself and her sisters with her Dudley kinfolk, with whom she hoped to further her goal of extreme reform in the Church of England.

After a 'costly delicate banquet' of sweets, the guests washed their hands in silver basins before paying a final visit to Elizabeth's chamber to congratulate her on the day's spectacular proceedings. Gifts were also sent up to the jubilant mother, among them a 'great standing cup' from the Queen, who also sent a handsome reward of £3 to the midwife and forty shillings to the nurse, and 'a great bowl' offered by the Earl of Leicester. Marking Elizabeth's status as a Countess in the making, the christening was one of the high points of her career. But she would already have learned that joy was rarely experienced without some sorrow following in its wake.

On 26 June 1576 Edward Dering, one of the leading lights of the radical reformers, died. By his side as he lay on his deathbed at Thobie Priory in Essex was his wife, Anne Locke, who nursed him in his final days. Some of his last known letters had been sent to Elizabeth Russell's sister Katherine Killigrew, detailing the horrifying symptoms of the tuberculosis which had taken hold. Through them she was confronted with vivid portraits of a man who would regularly choke on the blood he was spitting up, whose skeletal frame was rattled by fits of uncontrollable coughing and whose every laboured breath seemed to require a Herculean effort. Katherine did all she could, sending him her physician and as many medicines as she could procure. Those who watched him die noted with awe how the rays of the sun streamed in through the window to bathe his face in a mysterious glow, he taking occasion thereby to confirm the solidarity of the Puritan brotherhood. 'There is but one Sun that giveth light to the world . . . one communion of Saints,' he rasped in an otherworldly voice, urging his followers to continue the fight he had begun, to ease the 'many troubles' of the Puritans. This was a petition he had made not long before to Katherine, whom he asked to stand firm in the 'tower of defence' which was their common cause. This message would acquire additional urgency for Elizabeth and her sisters that very month, following another, yet more personally affecting, tragedy.

On 11 June 1576 the man responsible for the Cooke girls' extraordinary education died. Sir Anthony Cooke made his last will and testament around three weeks before, in the presence of his son-in-law Lord Burghley; Gabriel Goodman; and Katherine Killigrew. Cooke ensured that all his daughters received a suitably fitting intellectual legacy, leaving them a choice of books from his library. 'My daughter Russell shall have two . . . volumes in Latin and one in Greek such as she will choose,' he specified, adding also bequests to her of gilt salt-cellars as tokens of his affection.

Elizabeth got together with her siblings to plan the memorial to her father and, belatedly, to their mother, Anne, who had died in 1553. It is likely that Elizabeth took the lead in these proceedings, for it was Cornelius Cure, son of the William Cure who had fashioned the effigies of Sir Thomas and Sir Philip Hoby in Bisham, who had been called on to create the arresting monument in the Church of St Edward the Confessor in Romford, Essex, which would include relief carvings of Elizabeth and her sisters. The tomb's textual programme makes no mention of the sons' achievements. The daughters are the star attractions, celebrated in a Latin elegy which was certainly composed by the Cooke sisters, if not by Elizabeth herself:

Wherefore, Rome, does your learned Cornelia make you proud?
      How many such, and more, has Cooke?
Five daughters who understand how to combine Greek and Latin,
      To embellish their celebrated and pious deeds.
These to noblemen (a thing well known) you married:
      Who Christ in true faith worship,
And from whose perfect prudence the British profit;
      Who wield legitimate power, and give sober guidance.

The Cooke sisters are presented as outdoing even Pompey's wife, the accomplished Cornelia Metella, to whom Walter Haddon had directly compared Elizabeth in his elegy on Sir Thomas Hoby. A further English epitaph deftly aligns them with the curriculum which Sir Anthony Cooke fashioned for the Protestant Edward VI: 'With sacred skill unto a King he read,/Whose toward youth his famous praises spread.' This learning was, the poem reveals, politically charged, instrumental in keeping the reforming cause alive during periods 'when persecuting rage was rife'. Married to the navigators of England's ship of state, Cooke's daughters are elevated through solid stone into the living embodiments of this activist legacy.

The death of Elizabeth Russell's father nearly frustrated the plans of one theatrical entrepreneur who had firmly set his sights on the Blackfriars. The Queen had been thinking of visiting her namesake at Bisham Abbey during her Progress that summer, and her itinerary was of particular interest to Sir Henry Neville.

A close friend of Elizabeth, Neville had formed part of the elaborate cortège at the funeral of Thomas Hoby and would have been known to her as one of Anthony Cooke's fellow Marian exiles. Adding the post of High Sheriff to his other local offices in Berkshire, Neville was a familiar face. He was also Lieutenant of Windsor Castle and Forest, where one of Elizabeth's tenements was located. They would cement kin ties just two years later when Neville married Elizabeth Bacon, daughter to her brother-in-law Sir Nicholas Bacon and his first wife, Jane Fernley. Neville saw the royal Progress as an opportunity to liaise with William More of Loseley Park in Surrey. The purpose of this was to petition him directly on behalf of Richard Farrant, the enterprising Master of the Children of St George's Chapel, Windsor, who had become Deputy Master of the Children of the Chapel Royal that year (the latter company of young entertainers operating in a more mobile capacity at whichever location the court happened to be residing when their services were required). Farrant had been responsible for adding secular plays to the repertoire of the Queen's choristers, a novelty which would have profound consequences for playing in the Blackfriars.

On 13 April the theatrical speculator James Burbage secured the lease for the land in Shoreditch on which he would build one of the greatest innovations of the age: the Theatre. Burbage was later described by his son Cuthbert as 'the first builder of playhouses'. While it was preceded by two known temporary theatres, probably adapted from existing structures – the Red Lion, constructed by James Burbage's brother-in-law, John Brayne, in Whitechapel in 1567, and a playhouse in Newington Butts – the Theatre was the country's first purpose-built permanent playhouse. It was also the building that would play host to Shakespeare's early career. Hoping to cash in on the popularity of the dramatic arts, Farrant decided to establish a rival theatrical venture.

Practically abutting the south side of Elizabeth's Blackfriars home was the former Porter's Lodge of the Black Friars' monastery, which had been converted into the mansion of Sir William Brooke, Lord Cobham. Attached to this, running some hundred feet along the western end of what was once the Great Cloister, was the former Buttery, now two tenements also occupied by Cobham, the southern section having passed to him from 1571. Three years before that it had belonged to Henry Neville, who had been granted the property in 1560. In the summer of 1576 Farrant heard that Cobham had decided to vacate this tenement and immediately appealed to its former owner, Neville, to help him acquire it. His plan was to commandeer it as a rehearsal and performance space for the Queen's choristers. The two men coordinated their efforts, sending letters to William More on the same day.

'It may do him at this present great pleasure, and no man shall be readier to requite your friendship than he,' wrote Neville to More on 27 August. In the second letter he read of Farrant's intention to 'pull down one partition' in Cobham's former tenement and 'so make of two rooms one', in order to fashion the rehearsal space in which the child players would prepare for performances before the Queen. The dutiful Neville promised to petition More in person at his manor in

Surrey, if their sovereign would be repairing thither after visiting with Elizabeth at Bisham on her summer Progress. The merest hint of royal intercession, he knew, would help Farrant's cause. Sir Anthony Cooke's death may have contributed towards what was already 'a very uncertain Progress', and there is no evidence that the Queen made it to Elizabeth's home. Perhaps the grief-stricken Lady Russell was in no state to entertain a large royal train of courtiers, hangers-on and servants that summer. In any case, the mention of the Queen's possible interest in the transfer of the property to Farrant was enough to convince More. Farrant signed the lease on 20 December, undertaking to pay rent of £14 per annum, coincidentally the very same amount that Burbage had agreed to pay for the land in Shoreditch on which his theatre would be raised.

Both Farrant and Neville, in their letters to More, neglected to mention their real plans for the property. More was not pleased to discover that the windows in his tenement had been blocked out, to create the intimate ambience of the theatre during candlelit performances. Still less was he pleased by the fact that the building could be accessed only via the path leading directly to his own mansion. 'Farrant pretended unto me to use the house only for the teaching of the Children of the Chapel,' he later complained, 'but made it a continual house for plays, to the offense of the precinct.' The damage had been done, however, and since the choristers were under the Queen's protection, the sound of choral harmonies would not be prevented from breathing life into the extinct priory buildings. Farrant's new headquarters, which stood well under 139 feet away from Elizabeth Russell's house, established what has since come to be known as the First Blackfriars Theatre.

In the years after her father's death, Elizabeth would have witnessed these developments at first hand. She may have occasionally seen Farrant or his servants returning from the nearby Royal Wardrobe, located just off Carter Lane to the east of her house; her eye may have caught glimpses of the lush coloured fabrics, embroidery and fine regalia – everything needed to mount a show-stopping play – they were carrying back to the First Blackfriars Theatre.

Established by Edward III in 1361, the Royal Wardrobe stood in what is now Wardrobe Place, opposite the road currently leading up from St Andrew's Hill. During Elizabeth's time it provided storerooms for the costumes, arms and other paraphernalia which were increasingly being plundered for use in court performances. Farrant's theatre was, it seems, a success, for the Queen was so pleased with the first performance, which combined the talents of both the Children of the Chapel Royal and the Children of Windsor, that in January 1577 she paid a handsome £10 'reward' above the standard payment of £6 13s 4d.

The following Christmas season, when rehearsals for the child performers' upcoming royal performance were reaching their most frenetic, Elizabeth judiciously decided to stay well clear of the Blackfriars. Instead she took up residence in Westminster, in the familiar surroundings of Gabriel Goodman's lodging, where she had stayed during the birth and christening of her daughter Elizabeth. Her return was probably prompted by a similar happy event. It was in this year that she gave birth to her second daughter of the Russell marriage. The child was named Anne, after her second-deceased Hoby daughter. Her financial dealings with the Dean of Westminster had also intensified from 1576, thanks to the intercessions of George Burden, possibly the same Mr Burden who was involved in her first husband's funeral, or a close relative. Burden would act as Elizabeth's facilitator in her efforts to patronize the college there, a project which would no doubt help her acquire a place as a prominent memorializer in the nation's grand mausoleum of Westminster Abbey in years to come.

After all the devastating losses Elizabeth had suffered in her life, it must have seemed to her as if the Russells were finally on their way to establishing a living conduit for the Bedford land and titles. In readiness for this, Elizabeth turned her attention to one of the greatest assets in her possession: her home in the Blackfriars. Her decision to establish this property as the new base for herself and her husband would change someone else's destiny too: that of a teenage boy from Stratford called William Shakespeare.

8.

Meet the Neighbours

The Blackfriars was an emporium where the wares of the world came to flaunt themselves. South of St Paul's Cathedral, the meandering streets extending down from the parish of St Anne's to the cluster of buildings which once made up the thirteenth-century priory of the Dominican Black Friars were home to a lively community of tradesmen and instrument makers from all parts of England, France, the Low Countries and Italy. Private residences stood cheek by jowl with shopfronts advertising the merchandise of gold- and silversmiths, feltmakers, apothecaries, clockmakers, blacksmiths, comfit-makers, milliners, shoemakers, crossbow manufacturers, printers and booksellers.

Walking through the Blackfriars was like passing a succession of theatrical sets, where one could survey the latest styles of dress and marvel at mechanical astrolabes and armillary spheres, nautical devices, gilt standing-cups shaped like stags' heads, and fantastical automata. The latter were becoming de rigueur in the cabinets of the most discerning collectors across Europe, who rushed to purchase twittering robotic birds, arrow-shooting centaurs, music boxes, cittern-playing maidens and diminutive silver cows from which mechanical maids drew real milk. For the engineers who made clockwork curiosities and mathematical devices for royalty, the Blackfriars was the district of choice. But others came too, not merely charmed by the age's most cutting-edge technologies, or by the fact that the district had its own water conduit which serviced the community's needs, but keen to be part of the fashionable set. Lingering on the busy streets here, it would not be unusual for one to spot a Lord or a Baron, a Countess or a lady of means. These were Elizabeth Russell's neighbours, and she would soon be seeing a lot more of them.

On 16 January 1581 John Russell was summoned to the Painted Chamber in the Palace of Westminster, the hall in which the Queen presided over the state opening of Parliament. There, in a ceremony made all the more poignant by its lack of pomp, he was appointed to 'his father's place being Lord Russell'. The parliamentary officials were not wearing their usual robes of state that day when, much to Lady Russell's satisfaction, his induction to the House of Lords became a public endorsement of his status as 'son and heir to Francis, Earl of Bedford'. But Lord Russell's elevation was tinged with a sad irony. In 1579 Elizabeth had given birth to a son, Francis; the longed-for living channel of the Bedford lineage. The infant did not survive to fulfil his parents' dreams, dying the following year. Later Elizabeth would memorialize him in England's grandest mausoleum, Westminster Abbey, with the impassioned Latin epitaph of 'a sorrowful mother':

Behold, a grandfather's comfort, a father's most gratifying joy,
    My very soul, overtaken by a miserable fate:
O, if only your mother was lying there, in the darkness
    And you had performed my last rites first.
Yet in vain I do complain, because a higher power has determined this,
    That orphaned from me on earth, I seek you alone in heaven.

At the age of forty-one Elizabeth's chances of having another son were limited. Despite this she continued to put her energies into augmenting her family's public reputation, and her husband's new commitments provided her with the perfect opportunity. Her Blackfriars home was within easy access of the House of Lords but was in a dilapidated state, hardly fit for an Earl and Countess in the making. Realizing that its central location could provide the couple with a headquarters for their forays into the political arena, she took the matter in hand. Soon the Queen's surveyor, master carpenter, mason and plasterer were bustling around the property, taking measurements and drawing up plans for a dining chamber which would extend above the Round House and the tenement leased out by William More to Peter Buram.

It was to More that Elizabeth appealed, lamenting the state of 'mine old house, ready to fall', and putting in an 'earnest request' that he 'pleasure my lord and me so much as to give me leave as to make sufficient foundation for the bearing of that I build, which is my gallery over the way'. Since her brother-in-law, the Lord Treasurer Burghley, had himself arranged for the most skilled members of the Office of the Queen's Works to undertake the project, as Elizabeth did not fail to mention, she was certain More would not refuse. A dining room, ideal for entertaining the courtiers and politicians in their ever-expanding social circle, was therefore fitted out. It would stand virtually parallel to Farrant's theatre, separated by the home of William Brooke, Lord Cobham, which stood between them. The enterprise did not come cheap. Edward Hoby was now twenty-one and, having come of age, had inherited the Blackfriars house which had been in his mother's hands during his minority. Unwilling to let it go, Elizabeth decided to buy the property from him, complaining that the 'purchase and building cost me above £1000' – coincidentally, precisely the same amount that James Burbage would spend on the acquisition and renovation of his theatre in 1596. This was a considerable investment, but one which enabled Elizabeth to entrench herself in the Blackfriars, where she would become such an obstacle to the ambitions of Shakespeare and the Burbages.

By 1581 the Puritan anti-theatricalist Stephen Gosson would write that 'a great many Comedies' had been performed at the Blackfriars, and for a fee members of the public could attend plays featuring spectacular special effects, such as the memorable scene from *The Arraignment of Paris*, probably performed in 1584, during which 'a Tree of gold laden with Diadems and Crowns of gold' magically materialized on stage through a trap door, succeeded by the god Pluto seated on a dazzling throne. We would expect Lady Russell and her distinguished neighbours, William Brooke, Lord

Cobham, and Henry Carey, Lord Hunsdon, to have left some record of a protest against this turn of events. What of More's claim that the residents in the area were dismayed to find a theatre in the vicinity? Lord Cobham's property lay just north of Farrant's theatre and Hunsdon was leasing William More's own mansion and garden, which extended into what was once the monastery's Great Cloister, abutting immediately east upon the playhouse. Yet, as close as they were, there is no evidence that these men made any formal complaint.

Far from objecting to the Queen's choristers' theatre, Lord Cobham seems to have helped keep it going after Farrant's death on 30 November 1580. Anne Farrant, who found herself, in her own words in a letter to More penned on Christmas Day, in 'a poor widow's distressed estate', with 'ten small children' to feed and no experience of running a theatre, decided to sell the lease to William Hunnis, the new Master of the Children of the Chapel Royal, and his business partner John Newman. She was backed in this endeavour by the Earl of Leicester. William More, however, was less than supportive. Frustrated by the repeated failure of Anne's new tenants to meet their payments, he began measures to have them evicted. The ensuing conflict prompted the intervention of the man to whom some believe Shakespeare would later pay homage in the same play in which he would turn his satirist's pen against Elizabeth Russell and her kinsmen: *The Merry Wives of Windsor*.

Henry Evans was a Welsh scrivener who would manage Shakespeare's Blackfriars Theatre after Elizabeth blocked the adult players from taking up residence there in 1596. He would also play a part in the evolution of Farrant's playhouse. Realizing that Evans' legal knowledge and contacts could prove useful, Hunnis and Newman cunningly evaded More by leasing the theatre to Evans. Now in the firing line, Evans adroitly delayed the legal proceedings long enough to arrange the transfer of the lease to the powerful Edward de Vere, Earl of Oxford. The latter in turn gifted it to his protégé, the writer and dramatist John Lyly, around June 1583. The measure was not intended to oust Evans. Quite the contrary, for Farrant's boy actors now became the 'Children of the Earl of Oxford' and continued to mount plays for the Queen under the management of the young Welshman.

More blamed Anne Farrant for Evans' occupation of the theatre, sparking a new round of legal suits from the winter of 1583. Anne attempted to prove that she had 'never made any lease to Evans' and that her unruly tenants were deliberately withholding rent in order to bring about the forfeiture of her lease. It was during these difficult times, after she had been forced to sell her 'plate and jewels' to feed her 'littleons', that she turned to Cobham. He did not ignore her 'humble and pitiful suit', and before too long he had directed his servant to 'tender and pay the rent', which temporarily saved the theatre. Hunsdon may also have come to Lyly's rescue, for when it became clear to the latter that More was on the brink of seizing back the theatre, he decided to make a quick profit by selling the remainder of the lease to Carey, who kept hold of it until around 1590 or 1591.

The Puritan objection to play-going has become something of a commonplace. Anthony Munday had described the theatre as the 'house of Satan'; Stephen Gosson called playhouses 'markets of bawdry . . . full of secret adultery'; while Elizabeth Russell's close friend Geoffrey Fenton insisted that 'Players . . . corrupt good moralities by wanton shows and plays.' Both More and Cobham leaned towards the non-conformist tendencies which animated Elizabeth's sense of public responsibility, yet there is no evidence that they mounted a spirited objection to Farrant's theatre on religious grounds. Cobham had in fact served as patron to a theatrical company variously called the Lord Warden's Players or the Lord Cobham's Players. The child choristers had, of course, the protection of the Queen, who, according to Anne Farrant, was as 'gracious and bountiful' to her in her hour of need as Lord Cobham had been. When More pressed the suit that would allow him to seize back Farrant's property around May 1584, thereby putting an end to Evans' first incursion into the theatre business in the Blackfriars, he was taking a risk. And if he was not objecting to the theatre for any spiritual or moral reason, what drove him to oppose even the Queen? It was the challenge to his authority as the Blackfriars' principal freeholder to which he was responding. Neither should Elizabeth Russell's later campaign against Shakespeare's Blackfriars Theatre be attributed purely to theological considerations. Many of the Blackfriars residents' actions during the tenure of the Farrant–Evans lease ultimately served to protect the theatre because it was a significant counter in a political game of high stakes.

Elizabeth's actions in 1596 were part of a long-standing conflict between the influential inhabitants of the Blackfriars and the Lord Mayor and his aldermen for control of the district which stretched back to the earliest years of her residency in the area. This was a battle which would directly involve the Russells.

The Blackfriars was located in the liberties of London, beyond the control of the City authorities at whose head was the Lord Mayor. The rapid growth of the area from the 1530s made it a serious threat to the City's commercial and financial interests and, time and time again, those who called the Blackfriars home had to defend the rights they claimed as dwellers of the liberties. In April 1580 the residents of the district were agitating for such special privileges as exemption from taxes charged to City-dwellers, freedom from arrest by constables operating outside the liberty, and immunity from any searches made within the precinct without 'the assistance of the inhabitants' working in accordance with the permission of local Justices of the Peace. These requests came a year after Farrant's theatre had come under attack by the City authorities, who dispatched constables to infiltrate the building and forcibly eject the players. This met with little success in the face of the locals' continued insistence on their independent status.

The Blackfriars' tutelary lord William More had been seeking a patent to establish his own legal court and appoint Justices of the Peace to enforce law in the district. Elizabeth's brother-in-law Sir Nicholas Bacon was drawn into the scheme and was sent a list of gentlemen who could be appointed as 'commissioners for the peace within the precinct'. A further list included the name 'L[ord]: Russell' among the potential commissioners. He was joined by William More; Lord Cobham; a 'L[ord]: Lawane'; and one Thomas Browne. Lawane is William de Lawne, the minister who came to England following the St Bartholomew's Day Massacre in 1572, taking up residence in the Blackfriars not long afterwards, and who would go on to sign Elizabeth's petition against the Blackfriars Theatre. The Thomas Browne named alongside John Russell refers to Sir Thomas Browne, who was not merely Elizabeth's neighbour in the Blackfriars but her kinsman, related to both the Cooke and Fitzwilliam families. He must have been the very same who would feature as a signatory on her petition. This is made all the more likely by the fact that he was a resident of St Anne's, where Elizabeth worshipped in the church just south of her own house. This was the same parish that many of her other co-signatories called home. A few years later Sir Thomas would be involved with Elizabeth's close friend and kinsman Sir Henry Neville in the equipping of the 'trained shot' in Berkshire, the troops pressed into the service of the Crown during the attack of the Spanish Armada in 1588. His efforts in Elizabeth's home county at this time would be coordinated with those of Sir Thomas Lucy, of Shakespeare's native Warwickshire, who would soon play an instrumental role in the near-destruction of the playwright's Arden kinfolk. As well as his property in the Blackfriars, Browne also owned an estate in Surrey, Betchworth Castle, making him a neighbour of William More twice over.

Thomas Browne gave further ratification to the 1580 list of commissioners by appending his name for a second time to the base of the document, where it appears alongside those of William More and Lord Cobham. The latter, while not an official signatory of Elizabeth's petition, would be evoked by name in her address to the Privy Council in 1596, indicating his tacit support of her antitheatrical campaign. It is likely therefore that the community's bid to acquire legal control of the Blackfriars, to create a largely self-governing community, was a battle which directly involved at least three men who were later specifically identified as Elizabeth's backers, two of whom signed her petition: Thomas Browne, William de Lawne, and William Brooke, Lord Cobham. When Elizabeth was renovating her home this battle was still raging, amid charges of disorderly activity and 'lewd and evil behaviour' made on both sides.

While plans for a Blackfriars Court, presided over by William More, were never fully realized, the residents had managed to draw the sympathies of the Privy Council, at whose head was William Cecil. This is hardly surprising, given that Cecil's intimates and kinfolk, Elizabeth Russell, William Brooke and Henry Carey, were some of its most powerful inhabitants. The residents approached the Council, claiming that the City authorities' encroachment on their rights was damaging to the Queen's interests, for the Blackfriars had ceded to the Crown in 1538. On 15 May 1580 they received the response they were hoping for. The Lord Mayor was ordered to steer clear of the Blackfriars and 'not to intermeddle in any cause within the said liberties', scoring for the inhabitants a significant victory and, in the process, shielding Farrant's theatre from the City authorities' attempts to shut it down.

By the 1580s the residents of the Blackfriars had become used to the unusual powers the district's lack of formal hierarchical structure gave them. Elizabeth and her husband became part of a community which took responsibility for managing the daily running of the precinct. Along with their neighbours, they paid for a cleaner, or 'scavenger' as he was then called, to maintain the public thoroughfares, and a porter to shut the liberty's gate every evening and open it every morning. They ensured that the lamps were lit at night and that Blackfriars Stairs, leading to the Thames, were kept in good order. They paid for the local bridges to be repaired when needed and for the communal water conduit to be well looked after. They arranged for monthly collections for the poor and, during outbreaks of the plague, they appointed men to seal contaminated houses and carry away the dead. When vagrant individuals disturbed the peace, they made sure that they were whipped at the cart's tail and dispatched to nearby Bridewell Prison. Most significantly, in relation to Elizabeth's later attempt at acquiring the support of key members of the community to help her close down the Blackfriars Theatre, they served as patrons of the local church and its chief minister, ensuring that 'a preacher there maintained by the benevolence of the inhabitants' was also provided with a suitable home. One of these preachers was Elizabeth's later co-signatory, Stephen Egerton.

This was a close-knit community, and the Russells were joined in their endeavours by other neighbours, who can be traced through the Lay Subsidy Rolls. These voluminous documents record the amount of tax due from each household, alongside the estimated value of the land or goods the subsidies were being levied against. The Blackfriars residents were largely classed under two 'wards', those of Farringdon Within and Castle Baynard. Elizabeth's closest neighbours, and most of those whose names match those on her petition, were included in the rolls for Farringdon Within. So how many of those who helped Elizabeth Russell put Shakespeare out of business in 1596 were her neighbours in 1582, and what kind of people were they?

The only Thomas Browne listed in that year's Subsidy Rolls was Elizabeth's kinsman and More's Surrey neighbour Sir Thomas Browne, whose lands were valued at £70, placing him as one of the wealthier of the parish of St Anne's in the Blackfriars, with taxes levied at just over £4. John Robinson was valued at a healthy £20, alongside Andrew Lyon (Lyons) and John Dolling (or Dollin), both valued at a respectable £3 and taxed three shillings. While the last two were born in England, their names indicate that they probably hailed from French families. There were two men called John Edwardes on the 1582 Subsidy Rolls. One was English-born and belonged to the parish of St Olave's in Mugwell Street, recorded with goods worth £5. His foreign namesake was wealthier, being valued at double the amount, and is identified as a tailor in the 1576 Rolls. He is the more likely candidate for Elizabeth's petitioner, being a resident of St Anne's.

The remainder of Elizabeth Russell's future recruits who appear in the 1582 rolls were 'strangers', that is, they were immigrants from foreign shores. The 'bookseller' Askanius Reynolde, the Ascanius de Renialme listed on the 1596 petition, was valued at £10, a sum not to be sniffed at. Ascanius was a friend of Elizabeth's next-door neighbour Thomas Vautrollier, and would later witness his will. He would also become close to Elizabeth, who later described him as an 'honest man and my good neighbour'. A John le Mere, whose goods were valued in the Subsidy Rolls at £20, having doubled since 1576, was probably the John le Mere of Elizabeth's petition. Also appearing on the Subsidy Rolls were the petitioners Robert Baheire, valued at £3, incurring a tax of six shillings, and Harman Buckholt, a 'goldsmith', taxed at four old pence. While not appearing on the 1582 Subsidy Rolls, Henry Boice, recorded variously as Boyes or Boyse, was also in the area, for he is listed in the St Anne's Marriage Registers as having wed 'Annes Barrier', whose name indicates that she may have been a 'stranger', on 20 April 1573.

In 1583 John Russell and his long-standing neighbour, William Brooke, Lord Cobham, would undertake an extraordinary enterprise which would provide the Russells with more detailed information about some of the neighbours who would later join Elizabeth in her mission to put the Blackfriars Theatre out of commission. Armed with patents from the Privy Council, Lords Russell and Cobham appointed Robert Donckin and Thomas Hall, constables of the liberty of the Blackfriars, to conduct a survey 'of the number, names, and trade of living of all Strangers' in the area. The immigrant population settling in the Blackfriars had nearly tripled, from 102 in 1567 to 275 when the audit was conducted. However, there was more to the commission of John Russell and Lord Cobham than a mere census of the area's expanding 'alien' community. Many of those who had settled in the Blackfriars from abroad were Protestants fleeing religious persecution in their native countries and were now attached to one of London's 'Stranger Churches', particularly those belonging to the French and Dutch communities, with which the Russells and Cookes had been closely affiliated.

Donckin and Hall were instructed to find out, when interviewing each 'stranger', 'what Church they are of'. Since the closest thing the Blackfriars had to an administrative hub was the parish of St Anne's, which comprised the church which became a headquarters for Elizabeth Russell and her fellow radicals, the religious affiliations of these immigrants would have been of some significance not only to the Privy Council, who were keen to monitor potentially subversive activities in the liberties, but also to the influential residents of the area who were agitating for religious reform. It is difficult to imagine Elizabeth not taking an interest in her husband's activities at this time. Because some of these immigrants were wealthy, highly committed to the Protestant cause and managed lucrative businesses which appointed many young and impressionable apprentices, they were a potential stock of allies who could be galvanized in support of the ideological aims of the Puritan faction – and they were used in exactly this way by Elizabeth in 1596.

The survey provides a snapshot of the lives of the immigrants who were Elizabeth's neighbours and who would go on to support her political agenda over a decade later. In April 1583 the constables set about their task, and after interviewing a blacksmith, a shoemaker, two feather dressers, a milliner, a tailor, a brush-maker, a painter, and a 'letter caster for printers', among others, they knocked on the door of Harman Buckholt, the goldsmith, who was working in 'Jonson's Shop'. Donckin and Hall asked him where he came from. He answered that he was 'born under the King of Spain's dominion', probably in the Spanish-controlled Netherlands, and that he had come to England as a child. The constables then demanded to know if he had been granted denization. Buckholt insisted that he had, receiving his 'letters patents' on 24 February 1576. Immigrants had to pay a fee and take an oath of allegiance in order to become 'free denizens' and enjoy the rights of other business holders in the area, rights of which this upwardly mobile bachelor had taken full advantage. Buckholt then assured his interrogators that he was of the *right* faith, a committed member of the Dutch Church. Satisfied, the constables moved on.

Four strangers' doors on, they came to Ascanius de Renialme, the bookseller, from Venice, who had been accepted into the honourable ranks of the Stationers' Company of London on 27 June 1580. Though his wife, Elizabeth, and his German servant, Nicolas de Brone, were members of the Dutch Church, he belonged to the French Church, and was made 'free denizen' from 12 December 1579. When asked what had brought him to English shores, he informed his interviewers that he 'came into England 10 years past to see the country'. He may in fact have had another, altogether more secret, reason for settling in London. Ascanius had gained notoriety as an importer of foreign books. According to the English bookseller George Bishop, he was 'an honest young man who knows his business well'. Very well, it seems, for he was eventually 'Licensed to import popish books' from 1586, a commission 'tolerated' by John Whitgift, who was elevated to Archbishop of Canterbury in 1583. Since Whitgift was no friend to the non-conformists, there is a strong likelihood that the bookseller was working as an agent for, and therefore had the protection of, William Cecil, his role being to keep the Privy Council abreast of the latest pro-Catholic publications circulating in Europe. Lady Russell would later recommend Ascanius to her nephew Robert Cecil as a 'book seller, whom my lord your father loveth exceeding well'. Ascanius was one of those 'aliens' who had done well for themselves since settling in the Blackfriars, much like the tailor John Edwardes, who, as this survey revealed, was a member of the Dutch Church, probably born in the Spanish Netherlands, and Robert Baheire, who turns out to be a 'feltmaker' who belonged to the French Church.

During their laborious travels, Donckin and Hall encountered many 'strangers' who had fled the French wars of religion in the late 1560s and early 1570s because of their non-conformist beliefs. Common entries include repeated phrases specifying that an immigrant had left his home nation 'for religion' or 'for his conscience'. Sometimes the event which prompted the move was identified, and none more poignant for the footsore constables than recording that an interviewee had come 'into England when the massacre was in

France'. Among such men was John le Mere, now securely identified as a goldsmith born in Paris. Affiliated to the French Church, he had established himself successfully in his profession, for there would have been work aplenty in the area, with no shortage of shops specializing in luxury items hewn from metalwork and clockwork. Elizabeth's own neighbour Thomas Vautrollier, who had also been interviewed by the constables appointed by her husband, would establish a family of renowned clockmakers in the Blackfriars. This included his son, James Vautrollier, who would become a legatee and stepson of Shakespeare's publisher, Richard Field, after the latter married Vautrollier's widow, Jacqueline.

Later on, the constables imposed upon another refugee from the Paris massacre, the 53-year-old William de Lawne. His interrogators established that he was 'one of the ministers' of the French Church, who had come to England 'for his conscience's sake'. In fact, he had originally established himself in Rye, Sussex, as a minister, coming to London in 1575, where he quickly became assistant minister in the French Church in Threadneedle Street. He had also cultivated ties with the Cambridge non-conformists in the circle of Thomas Cartwright and Edward Dering. But he had another string to his bow. Within the last five months he had been granted a licence from the College of Physicians and would soon gain a reputation as a distinguished doctor. This was a man going places; his elder son, Gideon de Lawne, born in Nîmes, France, would become a distinguished apothecary and, later, minister of the French Church between 1593 and 1596. William de Lawne would play a special role in the creation of Shakespeare's Blackfriars Theatre, for part of the property which James Burbage would purchase, and in which he would create his indoor playhouse, had been leased by the French immigrant. He may also have gone on to exert a particularly potent influence on Richard Field.

William de Lawne had something else in common with Elizabeth Russell. He was a close associate of Richard and Dorcas Martin, the couple who had worked tirelessly to promote and shield the likes of Thomas Cartwright, Edward Dering and Anne Locke. In the very year in which John Russell oversaw the survey of Blackfriars' 'strangers', de Lawne produced an abridged version of the radical work that underpinned the mission of many non-conformists in Elizabeth's circle, Jean Calvin's *Institutes of the Christian Religion*. This was reissued in an English version in 1585 by none other than Thomas Vautrollier. On 18 February 1583 de Lawne wrote his introductory epistle to the work, dedicated to Richard Martin, which he hoped would encourage the reader to emulate his patron's role as a 'Christian champion', one 'better armed to discomfite all the enemies of the truth . . . and to beat down the Monsters of heresies'. Nor did he hold back on his praise of Dorcas Martin, who, with her husband, had supplied her 'gorgeous house' for the 'relieving of the oppressed', its doors ready 'to stand open to all the godly as a common Inn'. The book was printed at Vautrollier's press in Edinburgh, during which time his wife, the industrious Jacqueline, managed his Blackfriars printing press. Like Dorcas before her, who acted as illegal stationer for Cartwright during the Admonition Controversy, she was clearly not afraid to take on the male role in the publishing industry.

The exact location of Vautrollier's London print shop, and that of his successor, Richard Field, has not, until now, been firmly identified. Uncovering Elizabeth Russell's story has provided the best map yet available of the physical arrangement of the buildings which neighboured her own. The deeds and indentures recording the tenements of William de Lawne, Gideon de Lawne, Richard Field and one Paul Buck indicate that the printing press that produced Shakespeare's poems was located right next door to Elizabeth's house. The Square Tower, which William de Lawne would purchase at the end of 1593, was annexed to a 'little shop' called the 'Timber House', for which Field would claim the lease after Vautrollier's death. This was the same tenement which belonged to Vautrollier from at least 1570. Since Richard Field would later take over Vautrollier's business as well as his tenements in the Blackfriars, one of which it is now possible, for the first time, to locate practically next door to Elizabeth's 'gallery', it is likely that this was also the original location of Vautrollier's London press. The publication of the Huguenot immigrant's first known work coincides with his earliest appearance as a lessee of William More.

Vautrollier's business had clearly been growing. By 1574 he had been granted a patent to hire six French or Dutch workmen, and his holdings were assessed at an impressive £15 two years later. Elizabeth would probably have seen Richard Field going to and from the premises just east of her own, for Shakespeare's former fellow pupil of Stratford grammar school became apprenticed to Vautrollier in 1579. This was the same year in which Vautrollier published another book translated by Geoffrey Fenton, Guicciardini's monumental Italian *History*. Fenton originally promised Elizabeth that he would 'bring forth my great work' as a testament to 'the reverent duty I owe you . . . which I hope will more worthily resemble your high virtues'. This book, which would be reissued by Field in later years, would not be dedicated to Lady Elizabeth but to her royal namesake. It is another of the intriguing ironies of Elizabeth's life that the work of Geoffrey Fenton, whom she had so diligently patronized at her own expense, would become hugely influential to Shakespeare, providing material for such plays as *Romeo and Juliet*, *Much Ado about Nothing* and *Twelfth Night*.

By 1583 many of those who made up the cast in the drama of the near-destruction of Shakespeare's career were living and working on Elizabeth Russell's doorstep. The picture beginning to build is more complex than may have been expected. Some of this group were clearly zealously Puritan, and engaged in the combative and militaristic language of which Elizabeth and her sisters were so fond. Some were also drawn to the Blackfriars by the tempestuous wars of religion in France and the Low Countries. There were, however, other factors which brought this largely wealthy community together: their long-standing battle with the City authorities for governance of the Blackfriars area and a shared commitment to the upkeep of the district and its public services and thoroughfares. The skilled professionals represented by Elizabeth's petition – booksellers, printers, tailors, goldsmiths, feltmakers – would also have been particularly desirous to protect their business interests. The influential Blackfriars residents had welcomed these craftsmen as their neighbours and friends. As part of their scheme to maintain the autonomy of the Blackfriars residents, Elizabeth's own husband and her powerful neighbours Lord Cobham, Sir Thomas Browne and William de Lawne had supported the move to protect the rights of 'artificers and craftsmen' in the area by allowing them to 'lawfully exercise their trades, mysteries, and occupations without controlment of the Mayor or other officers of the city'. This must surely have fostered a sense of community spirit between Elizabeth and her local tradesmen, greatly facilitating her dealings with them in the 1590s.

Not long after Elizabeth undertook the renovation of her Blackfriars home, her husband, John Russell, and their neighbour and kinsman, Lord Cobham, were in possession of the personal statistics of many of the men who would go on to support her petition for the closure of the Blackfriars Theatre. Their religious affiliations and ecclesiastical memberships, professional status and level of affluence, political proclivities and business interests were mapped in a way that allowed the Russells to identify who their allies in the area were likely to be.

The screw was beginning to turn.

Adjoining the eastern part of the shops leased to Robert Baheire was the tenement of Robert la Fontaine, also called le Maçon, who, like William de Lawne, had fled the St Bartholomew's Day Massacre in France in 1572. The Church of St John the Apostle no longer exists. It was destroyed in the Great Fire of London in 1666. The southern side of the chancel had, according to John Stow, once been embellished with 'a very fine, neat and well-contrived Monument'. On this tomb were verses by Elizabeth Russell and Fontaine in memory of Katherine Killigrew, who died on 27 December 1583 after giving birth to a still-born baby.

Fontaine's epitaph describes its author as *'Pastor Ecclesiae Londino-Gallicae'*, 'a minister of the French Church of London', the very church that Katherine and her husband had funded. Fontaine was also the dedicatee of *The French Schoolmaster*, written by the Huguenot refugee Claudius Hollyband and published by Thomas Vautrollier. As Hollyband was listed as paying tax on goods valued at £5 10s in the St Faith's parish of Farringdon Within (and therefore in the same ward as the Blackfriars), he was a neighbour of Vautrollier, Fontaine, de Lawne and Elizabeth, placing Katherine as part of this community of activists. Fontaine had also been close to Mildred Cecil, to whom he gifted a copy of the 1583 edition of a work by Sir Anthony Cooke's associate Peter Martyr called the *Loci Communes*. This he garnished with a dedication to Cooke, in which he praised his daughters' achievements. The loss of Katherine deprived the radicals of one of their most active supporters. It also put more pressure on Elizabeth as a surviving pillar of the Puritan community, a struggle which seems almost to make itself felt in her Latin epitaph to a beloved sister:

Dear sister, Adieu, in heaven a death-conqueror;
　　To you death is life, yet to your own it is fatal . . .
As our blood joined us, may Christ unite us in the ethereal plains:
　　Until that time I will be silent, as one made dead by your death.

9.

The Widow and the Necromancer

The wagon carrying the corpse of John, Lord Russell had been buffeted by the storm since 7 p.m. It would be four o'clock the next morning before the angry winds abated and the precarious sodden tracks were rendered visible by other, gentler, means than the flashes of electrified air which tore through the tumultuous darkness during that terrible journey.

William Andrew, who on 27 July 1584 had accompanied his master's body to Westminster for its burial, would always remember the apocalyptic tempest which produced 'a most horrible light[n]ing and thunder as never was the like heard of'. Having braved the treacherous travelling conditions, Andrew was met at Westminster by the dean, Gabriel Goodman. A decade before, Goodman had presided over the christening of Lord Russell's daughter Elizabeth. Now he would officiate over his funeral in the same church. Then the abbey had been decked with crimson curtains of estate; now it would be draped in black.

An impenetrable veil of mystery cloaks John Russell's final days. By 6 p.m. on Thursday 23 July the 'great consumption' which had suddenly taken hold of his body had done its worst. Andrew had seen through 'the beginning and end of his sickness' and would have been present when Dr Alexander Nowell, the Dean of St Paul's, delivered words of religious comfort on his deathbed. But Lord Russell would not be comforted and Andrew later reported that his demise 'should seem to come through a thought or grief'. Unwilling to elaborate further, he has left little clue as to the cause of his depression in his final hours. After all, he had much to live for. He was heir to the Bedford Earldom and estates and father to two beautiful girls.

He was married to Lady Russell, the sister-in-law of the most powerful man in England. His star was in the ascendant.

Lord Burghley's papers record that John Russell drew his final breath in 'Hyghat'. This refers to the Highgate home of John Cholmeley, a man whose name would become entangled with that of the Queen's necromancer and occultist, Dr John Dee. A chemical distiller by trade, Cholmeley was practising medicine occasionally by 1584. He would find himself in trouble with the College of Physicians towards the end of September 1594 for his dubious medical procedures. Dee would come to his aid, securing him a pardon but with the caveat that he desist from administering medicine henceforth. He may have been the same John Cholmeley who was in the service of the committed Puritan Henry Hastings, 3rd Earl of Huntingdon, the man to whom Thomas Hoby had dedicated his *Book of the Courtier*. Elizabeth's prior association with him may therefore have served to cement these fateful ties. Perhaps John Russell had been seeking Cholmeley's medical assistance in his last days, the two drawn together through a shared religious vocation.

Dee's diaries are silent on the matter of John Russell's connection to Cholmeley in 1584, but it seems an eerie coincidence that Elizabeth's husband should die in the home of one of Dee's associates within a year of the Russells' employment in a brief spell of espionage which drew them into the heart of the necromancer's shadowy world.

John Dee was more than a magician. He was a player in the Crown's intelligence service. Always on the lookout for wealthy and well-connected individuals with whose collaboration he could prove his value to the Queen and her chief council, fate would bring him the Polish Count Palatine of Siradia, Albert Laski. Grotesquely charismatic, with a towering vanity to match, the first thing anyone noticed about Laski was his imposing beard, which was reputed to be of 'such length and breadth, as that lying in his bed, and parting it with his hands, the same overspread his breasts and shoulders, himself greatly delighting therein, and reputing it an ornament'.

In the latter part of the 1570s the succession crisis in Poland had thrown the country into turmoil and now Laski was looking to England for aid, having seen an opportunity to make a bid for the disputed Crown. Just in case more persuasive means were required, he had also begun to amass his own army. With the Earl of Leicester as his enabler, Dee began to work on Laski's behalf in the spring of 1583, fully believing him 'to be of God elected to govern him a people'. To confirm this he began a series of séances, some of which involved Edward Kelly, a man of dubious character who had allegedly had his ears lopped off just three years before, following a charge of forgery. Laski was delighted when Kelly claimed to have seen a spectacular vision of a resplendent throne which radiated a beam of dazzling light on to the awesome figure of the angel Raphael. When asked whether Laski would acquire the Polish Crown Raphael answered emphatically: 'Many witches and enchanters, yea many devils have risen up against this stranger. But I will grant him his desire . . . Fear not, therefore. Love together.' Little more encouragement was needed.

Like Elizabeth Russell and her husband, Dee had nurtured a determination to establish a pan-European Protestantism and was drawn in by Laski's grandiose promises of the fervour with which he would institute wide-scale religious reform on obtaining the Polish throne. Elizabeth's father had had a long-standing relation with the Laski family, having worked closely with his kinsman John Laski, who had helped establish the London Stranger Churches. It was not long before Albert Laski won the backing of Lord Burghley, ensuring that the Russells were rapidly conscripted into the scheme to entice him to the English Crown's intelligence network. It was to Elizabeth's Bisham home that the Polish dignitary came on Friday 14 June as part of a diplomatic tour designed to muster support among the dons of Oxford University. Giordano Bruno, the Europe-renowned cosmologist, philosopher and mathematician, had been invited to Oxford, and the Earl of Leicester, as chancellor of the university, had arranged for Laski to be publicly presented, and lauded, at one of Bruno's lectures. Feasts and intellectual disputations were the order of the day and Laski, as Dee logged in his diary, was 'very honourably used and entertained'. The intention was to place Laski at the heart of a progressive community of scholars, but the event was far from a success.

Bruno managed to antagonize his hosts by presenting the vice-chancellor with a letter in which he described himself as 'a stranger with none but the uncivilised and ignoble, a wakener of sleeping minds, a tamer of presumptuous and obstinate ignorance'. His lecture instantly confirmed his unwieldy ego. One auditor who witnessed his performance described him as a mere 'juggler' who 'undertook . . . to set on foot the opinion of Copernicus, that the earth did go round, and the heavens did stand still; whereas in truth it was his own head which rather did run round, and his brains did not stand still'. Nicolas Copernicus's revolutionary new cosmology, which asserted that the earth revolved around the sun, had been published in his *De Revolutionibus Orbium Coelestium* (*On the Revolutions of the Heavenly Spheres*) in 1543. Bruno had pounced on this radical heliocentric theory, fusing it with his own unique brand of occultism.

The Russells' involvement with Dee and Laski at the time of this propagandist campaign in Oxford was no coincidence. It was, however, not Lord Russell but his wife, Elizabeth, who had already demonstrated to the Earl of Leicester her interest in using the cosmological sciences as a means of advancing the Protestant movement. Around a decade before, she had contributed towards a presentation copy of Dr Bartholo Sylva's pseudo-scientific treatise, the *Giardino Cosmografico Coltivato*, dedicated to the Earl as a means of promoting the Puritan cleric Edward Dering. When Laski stayed the night at the Russells' home in Bisham after his trip to Oxford, he knew that his account of the intricate disputations which had followed Bruno's lecture would find a willing ear in the bookish Elizabeth. But Laski's sojourn was all too brief, for the next day he said his farewells to the Lady of Bisham and, with John Russell as his conductor, set out on his journey to Dee's home. At about 5 p.m. they arrived at Mortlake and Dee was impressed when he saw that

Laski and his entourage were being ferried in high state on the Queen's silk-covered barge, serenaded by the royal trumpeters.

The Polish Count may have won Dee and the Russells over with his charm, good looks and veneer of courtliness, but he found it difficult to live up to his inflated promises. It would not be long before Kelly denounced him as a fraud and a charlatan, lamenting that he and Dee had become 'coupled with so ungodly a man'. Burghley's own loss of patience would ensure that Dee's relations with Laski ultimately came to little. The alchemist's association with Elizabeth would, however, continue. She would become one of the many well-heeled noblewomen in his client book, consulting him on her personal problems; and, it seems, she was not averse to a little supernatural solicitation when called for. On 5 April 1592 Dee would record in his diary: 'The Lady Russell robbed a little after midnight of pearls, diamonds, &c. One John Smyth is suspected, a young man of 30 years old, very ingenious in many handiworks, melancholic, auburn-haired &c.' Dee failed to note the outcome of their investigations, but perhaps Elizabeth was pleased with his work, for over the next couple of years his diary records the mysterious comings and goings of her servant Thomas Richardson to Mortlake. As well as undertaking undisclosed errands for Dee, Richardson had also been acting as a go-between, ferrying messages from the magus to Elizabeth's chief steward, Thomas Sharp. These relations stand as a strangely poignant testament to the peculiar demise of her husband, the cause of whose 'grief' before his death remains a mystery.

Yet not long afterwards Elizabeth had complained that relations between them had not always been harmonious. 'What of mere love without the persuasion of any I have done and endured for him,' Elizabeth wrote to Lord Burghley of her wayward son Thomas Posthumous Hoby, 'in not yielding his brother's wardship to my Lord Russell, God and myself best know.' Under laws established during Henry VIII's reign, when a child's father died before he or she reached the age of majority – normally twenty-one for a boy – the monarch had the right to claim revenues from the family estate. A Court of Wards was established to oversee the procedure, and could arrange the sale of wardships to wealthy noblemen or proffer them as gifts to senior courtiers. Wardships could be lucrative, as their guardians were placed in charge of the profits deriving from any properties owned by their young charges while they were under their care. It was therefore a system open to abuse. Following her first husband's death, Elizabeth's son Edward had become a ward of the Crown. After her second marriage, Elizabeth had, unusually, entered into a battle with her own husband over the wardship of her son. Her success in obtaining control of, and revenues from, Sir Thomas Hoby's estates may have been due to the fact that her brother-in-law William Cecil served as Master of the Court of Wards from 1561. With her son's wardship, Elizabeth gained a significant source of income, £220 annually, with the addition of an annuity of £50 until Edward reached fifteen and thereafter £60 yearly until he came of age.

There is no hint in the little surviving correspondence from the years of Elizabeth's marriage to John Russell of a woman who felt herself subject to the law of 'covert baron', the term which designated a wife's legal rights and status. 'A woman as soon as she is married is called covert, in Latin *nupta*, that is, veiled, as it were, clouded and over-shadowed,' as one early legal manual described it, 'her new self [husband] is her superior, her companion, her master'. A feme covert, as she was known, did not own properties in her own right, could not enter into a bargain of sale under her own name, could not sign legally binding contracts or accrue revenues from manors and estates without her husband's express permission. In common-law practice, marriage for a woman of this period meant nothing less than the obliteration of her own identity.

Elizabeth Russell, on the other hand, was unflinchingly possessive about the properties she had inherited. She described the Blackfriars house to Sir William More as 'mine old house' and her surviving itemizations of the value of leases attached to the Hoby manors indicate a woman keen to keep these estates in her own hands and out of her second husband's. Even when Edward reached

the age of majority in 1581, so unwilling was his mother to relinquish control of the Hoby estates that she attempted to trick him
into selling her the lease for his manor of Poden for £1,200 under
the ruse that she had been 'meaning, or at least seeming, to be willing to dwell in Worcestershire', where the property was located.
Keeping hold of these estates was, she protested, 'a matter of no
small importance to my heart'. During her marriage to John Russell
she even expected to benefit from some insider dealing through her
brother-in-law Lord Burghley, asking him to help her undercut a
rival purchaser for the manor of Chew in Somerse by delaying the
sale, 'if any seek it, for that I mean to purchase it if I can'. It is clear
that one thing Elizabeth was not prepared to do was allow herself
to be 'clouded and over-shadowed' by her husband.

While Elizabeth's insistence on her financial independence may
have caused tensions between the couple, could this really have
been so dire as to have been the catalyst for John Russell's premature death? Did his demise have something to do with his association
with Dee and the pseudo-medic and mixer-of-potions John Cholmeley? The elaborate funeral service and commemorative programme
Elizabeth devised for her husband would cast no further light into
these dark corners. Instead, her manipulation of the arts of death
and memory would become her opening salvo in a battle for the
great Bedford fortune and for her right to be recognized as a Dowager Countess.

On 31 July 1584 John Russell's mourning procession set out, a brightly
emblazoned standard waving in front of the sombre train. This
time 'Mr Burden' walked behind the banner, along with Elizabeth's
Fitzwilliam kinsmen and Alexander Nowell, who had comforted
John Russell by his deathbed and who would now deliver the burial
sermon. Other officers from the College of Arms followed, carrying the symbolic accoutrements of John Russell's status: his helmet,
crest, shield and sword. The latter was hired at a cost of ten shillings, and was carried by the York Herald, Sir William Dethick, the
man who would go on to grant Shakespeare a coat of arms for his

father in 1596. Behind him walked his father, Sir Gilbert Dethick, the highest-ranking officer of the college, bearing a large tablet engraved with the Russell arms and clad in the most expensive of the heralds' mourning gowns, procured at a cost of £6. Lord Burghley followed the coffin, probably dressed in his Treasurer's robes, for he 'came without black'. Thirty yeomen all draped in mourning cloaks also conducted the corpse, one for each full year of Lord Russell's life.

For Elizabeth Russell a public ritual was more than a rite of passage. It was a piece of propaganda. In her hands the funeral ceremony would become a defiant statement of her entitlement to the privileges belonging to the wife of the Earl of Bedford's heir. This was necessary, for she instantly realized the danger she and her daughters were in, John Russell having died without a son before he had formally inherited his father's title. If Elizabeth could not prove herself to be a fully fledged Dowager Countess (an honour belonging to the widow of an Earl), then it would be easier for other members of her husband's family to insist that they were the true inheritors of the Bedford estates. In order to stake a claim for her rights publicly she decided to channel the conventions of the College of Arms in a way few women would have dared. The result would stand out among the countless ceremonies staged by the heralds for the burials of the elite. A fantastical hearse was constructed 'at the cost of the Lady Elizabeth' in a manner normally assigned to a high-ranking member of the nobility. A velvet pall thirty-five yards in length was draped over the coffin and garnished with taffeta and 'valences of silk fringe'. Escutcheons and flags bearing the Russell arms punctuated the black drapery with vivid colours and flecks of shimmering gilding. But these markers of status were not enough for Elizabeth.

During the preparations for the funeral she had come into conflict with the Officers of Arms over the nature of the rites due to her husband. She demanded a 'banneroll' for the hearse. This was a three-foot-square panel of decorated silk on which the family's lineage was inscribed, normally provided for the obsequies of Earls. Her request was flatly refused, with a note attached to the College of Arms' outline of the funerary proceedings stating that there would be 'no banneroll as requested', regardless of the plaints of Lord Russell's grieving widow, 'because he died before his father, whereby he had not possession of that degree entirely'. Elizabeth appears at first to have backed down, only to make an even more shocking request – and this time she would not be talked out of it.

Heraldic funerals were strictly organized along gendered lines. The laws of the College of Arms demanded that only a man could act as a chief mourner for a deceased male. In this instance, the honour initially went to John Russell's cousin John St John, Second Baron of St John of Bletsoe. Ordinarily, he would have walked directly behind the hearse in the funeral procession. Instead Elizabeth insisted that her daughters take this privileged place, usurping the role of the male chief mourner. This was a scarce-conceivable breach of protocol, in outright defiance of the college's grave traditions of gendered etiquette. So worried were the heralds by this that they added an apologetic note to the record of the funeral, stating defensively that 'Mistress Elizabeth [and] Mistress Anne went in this place [behind their father's coffin] at the request of their mother.' The radical new arrangement was intended to press the Russell girls' status as rightful heirs to the Bedford wealth, and this had clear implications for their mother's public identity as a Dowager Countess.

Elizabeth Russell had turned the greatest mausoleum in the country – the resting place of kings and queens – into a stage set for her political ambitions. By visibly supplanting the male chief mourner she injected a new drama into the proceedings. While the funeral ceremony was a transitory affair, Elizabeth ensured that her aims would be enshrined for all time on the magnificent Russell tomb, which she designed. The product of Elizabeth's favoured Cure workshop, the imposing monument still stands today in the St Edmund's Chapel of Westminster Abbey. Above a semi-recumbent effigy, relief engravings of young Elizabeth and Anne Russell (by this time most often affectionately referred to by their mother as Bess and Nan) clutch a cartouche into which has been engrafted the

Russell crest, bearing the motto '*In Alto Requies*' ('Rest on High'). Beneath Lord Russell's feet reposes the lost hope of this branch of the Bedford clan, the diminutive effigy of his only son, Francis. Against this crushing disappointment Elizabeth added a legal caveat to the monument's textual programme. Among epitaphs in English and the classical languages, she included a Latin verse ratifying her surviving daughters as the legitimate inheritors of the Bedford estates, exclaiming unflinchingly: 'you have been raised to be like the heir of an Earl'. Her English verse in honour of her husband reinforced his status as Francis Russell's principal beneficiary:

> Right noble twice, by virtue and by birth,
> Of heaven loved, and honoured on the earth:
> His country's hope, his kindred's chief delight,
> My husband dear more than this world's light
> Death hath me reft [bereft]: but I from death will take
> His memory, to whom this tomb I make.
> John was his name (ah, was!), wretch must I say,
> Lord Russell once, now my tear-thirsty clay.

Claiming ownership of the entire memorial production, Elizabeth inscribed thereon a Latin interjection which stands out as a bold testament to her sense of the inequalities experienced by women in the public domain: '*Quod licuit feci, vellem mihi plura licere*' ('All that is lawful I have performed. I wish more were allowed me'). No statement better captures the struggle faced by women of Elizabeth's generation, who found themselves battling against restrictions placed on their freedom of expression by the powerful institutions whose business it was to reinforce the masculine status quo. This would not be the last time the widow would throw down the gauntlet before the College of Arms.

While Elizabeth Russell was coping with the death of her husband, there were new beginnings for Shakespeare. In May 1583 Susanna Shakespeare was born. William, his wife, Anne Hathaway, and the baby were probably living with John Shakespeare and Mary Arden in Henley Street, Stratford, at this time. It would not be long, however, before the family was seriously shaken by events which would darken the Shakespeares' reputation.

The two men who would work to ensure the world would know about the disgrace that had befallen the playwright's kinfolk would be Elizabeth Russell's brother-in-law William Cecil and her next-door neighbour Thomas Vautrollier. The scandal would involve that family name which would become a perennial curse in the mouth of Queen Elizabeth I: the Percy Earls of Northumberland.

PART THREE
Turf Wars

The Arden Trail

The first thing they saw was the body sprawled on the bed. The second was the pistol lying a few feet away on the floor. When the guards broke into the bedchamber, one of a suite of apartments annexed to the Queen's own lodgings in the Tower of London, the smell of charred flesh assailed them. Before his death, its ill-fated occupant, befitting his elevated status, had free rein of five large rooms, comfortably furnished and with pleasant views over the Thames, but he was still a prisoner.

The mutilated remains were examined by Henry Carey, Lord Hunsdon. They were a grisly and baffling sight. In his presence the surgeon conducting the autopsy retrieved three bullets from beneath the left shoulder blade. These had shattered the victim's heart, broken three ribs and nearly severed the spinal column. Bizarrely, the torso was covered in mysterious gunpowder burns and, on the left-hand side of the chest, there was a large wound the width of a spread hand. Whatever caused this had burned the shirt clean away from the scorched flesh beneath. Stranger still, while the injuries sustained suggested the involvement of another unknown party, the Lieutenant of the Tower insisted that the door to the bedchamber had been bolted from the inside. There was no other way into or out of the room.

The victim was Henry Percy, 8th Earl of Northumberland. He had been incarcerated following his alleged involvement in a plot against the Queen's life. This had been masterminded by Francis Throckmorton, it was believed, with the backing of Mary, Queen of Scots, and the Duke of Guise. Hunsdon knew that the death of so eminent a figure was a waiting powder keg beneath the Queen's government. Faced with this impending crisis, he did the only thing he could do. On 23 June 1585, at the inquest in the Star Chamber, he stood before the Lord Treasurer Burghley, the man who had broken the Throckmorton Plot wide open, and returned his verdict on the unusual death. The miserable Earl, he revealed, had taken off his waistcoat, then, charging his pistol with three bullets and more than the usual amount of gunpowder, had lain facing upwards on his bed with the weapon pressed to his chest. Racked with remorse for his crimes against his sovereign and his country, he shot himself, alone in the middle of the night.

That, at least, was the official story.

It was not long before news of Percy's death reached the public domain. Despite the verdict of suicide, many of William Cecil's enemies, drawn from the recusant Catholic community, suspected a cover-up and began to surmise that the Earl had been assassinated on his direct orders. In response, Burghley set about stemming the tide of these 'manifest untruths' by publishing an official statement on the case, *A True and Summary Report . . . of the Earl of Northumberland's Treasons*, which described in unflinching detail how Percy 'most wickedly destroyed and murdered himself'. This did little to intimidate the conspiracy theorists, whose printed rebuttals were circulated in Spain, Italy, France and on native soil. In these explosive pamphlets Burghley was subjected to the full force of his enemies' vituperative might and the public imagination was fed with images of the hapless Earl of Northumberland being brutally murdered in his bed by the Crown's hired guns. Percy's surviving sons never forgot the indignity of their father's blighted name and in the years following his mysterious death the Cecils, and anyone closely associated with them, became synonymous with the secret centres of power from which all conspiracies flowed.

Elizabeth Russell knew enough about the latest Catholic plot to raise her concerns with Cecil over the 'troublesome time' that had descended upon the beleaguered monarch, who, in Elizabeth's own words, had had to endure 'this unnatural conspiracy against herself and [her] country'. Her awareness of the intrigue may have proceeded as much from Lord Hunsdon as it did from her brother-in-law, for she was now related to Shakespeare's future patron through the marriage of her son Edward Hoby to his daughter Margaret Carey. The Queen herself was in attendance at the ceremony, which took place on 21 May 1582. Such was her delight in the match that she knighted Hoby at Somerset House the next day. This union furthered Elizabeth's progress towards the inner sanctum of the royal court, for she noted that her son was now enjoying greater favours from 'the Prince [Elizabeth I], in respect of his wife'. Elizabeth's recent relations with John Dee also placed her in close proximity to the Earls of Northumberland, with whom the necromancing astrologer had been associated. The son of the 8th Earl, also named Henry Percy, would come to be known as the 'wizard Earl' because of his passion for the occult. He would eventually marry Dorothy Perrot, the sister of Robert Devereux, 2nd Earl of Essex. The latter would become one of the most notorious courtiers in history, his association with Shakespeare drawing the censure of Elizabeth's closest kinsmen and, in the process, embroiling her in the clampdown on the playwright's activities in the years 1596 to 1597.

The scandals surrounding the 8th Earl of Northumberland and the Throckmorton Plot had already touched Shakespeare's family, and when Elizabeth dispatched a messenger directly to the Queen with consoling words, she did so little knowing that the spectre of Percy's death, and his sons' long-nursed grudge, would raise its head in the most public fashion eleven years later, when the playwright and his theatrical troupe turned up in her neighbourhood.

The name Francis Arden is not mentioned in any of the major biographies of Shakespeare. Yet in April 1586 the playwright's kinsman was languishing in the Tower of London and 'by reason of his imprisonment dangerously diseased'. The Privy Council met to decide his fate and, in the presence of William Cecil, Francis Walsingham and William Brooke, Lord Cobham, passed a motion that he be released with 'sureties in the sum of £500' because 'there is no sufficient evidence to try him upon the treasons pretended against him'. If the suspect was unable to stretch to the huge bail of £500, then goods and leases 'to that value' would be confiscated and the near-dead prisoner set 'at liberty' on promise 'to be of good behaviour'. Freedom had a bitter taste for Francis Arden, for his two and a half years of incarceration had ruined him.

Following Arden's trail backwards, we find him, on 27 May 1585, listed among the suspects 'indicted for treason' in a conspiracy involving Sir Francis Throckmorton. He was interrogated alongside Henry Percy, 8th Earl of Northumberland, the priest Hugh Hall, the Catholic Sir Henry Howard and a widow named Margaret Somerville. Further back, a letter preserved in the State Papers dated 7 December 1583 reveals the seriousness of Francis Arden's offence, for he was accused 'of high treason for conspiring Her Majesty's death'.

The plot to murder the Queen was orchestrated by the kinsmen and relations of William Shakespeare in October 1583. The astrologers who were charting the movement of the heavenly spheres that year were nervous about the conjunction of Saturn and Jupiter. They believed that the ominous celestial alignment presaged 'the destruction of certain climates and parts of the earth', the advent of 'new found heresies, and a new founded kingdom' which would bring 'much sorrow and heaviness to men'. Before the year was out, it would appear to the Arden family that their world really had ended, for they would be implicated in a plot to destroy the Elizabethan constitution and bring about that 'new founded kingdom' for Mary, Queen of Scots, under the Pope of Rome.

Francis Arden's role in these tragic events is unclear. He is interesting because his imprisonment continued through the Throckmorton Plot and into the succeeding Babington Plot, another attempt by Catholic conspirators to assassinate the Queen, indicating that Shakespeare's kinsmen were under the Privy Council's continual surveillance in the mid-1580s. The instigator of the plot was John Somerville of Edstone, near Stratford, who was probably Francis Arden's nephew. Somerville had married Margaret Arden, daughter of Edward and Mary Arden. The union was in fact facilitated by

Francis Arden, who had entered into a bond with Edward Arden to help the latter pay for the couple's dowry.

Mary Arden's namesake, Shakespeare's mother, was a blood relation of Edward Arden, the head of the chief and most venerable branch of the Arden family, whose seat was Park Hall, in Cudworth, Warwickshire. Edward's wife hailed from one of the most notorious families of the age, for she was daughter to Sir Robert Throckmorton, in whose home Edward had been a ward before their marriage. Shakespeare would have known Edward, Francis and the Arden women as his 'cousins' and such was the Shakespeares' pride in their Park Hall roots that the playwright's father, John Shakespeare, would attempt to have his newly acquired coat of arms combined with theirs in 1599. The grant would be rejected, for this side of the family had been stained with treason.

The Reformation was slow to take root in Shakespeare's Stratford, and little wonder, for the unrepentantly Catholic Throckmortons held court in Warwickshire, supported by the Arden and Somerville families. They were opposed by the powerful Dudley clan, at whose head was the Earl of Leicester. Of his faction were the Lucy family, whose principal seat was Charlecote, just outside Stratford, where Sir Thomas Lucy presided. Elizabeth Russell's own family would eventually become tied to that of Sir Thomas Lucy through marriage, a fact which may have been of some interest to Shakespeare. It was with Lucy that the dramatist, according to a long-standing tradition, was said to have locked swords in his youth, having been caught indulging in a spot of illegal deer poaching on Sir Thomas's estate, after which he was forced to leave Stratford. This story is often dismissed. However, the Ardens' relations with the formidable Lucy suggest that the tale may have emerged as a consequence of very real tensions between the two families. Shakespeare himself would find out in 1583 just how far Lucy was prepared to go to 'see the house of Arden ruinated'.

In *Henry VI, Part 3* Shakespeare left us with an intriguing mystery. In the climactic final act of the play the Earl of Warwick is standing on the walls of Coventry, expecting the arrival of his enemy. He turns to a man beside him and asks, 'by thy guess, how nigh is Clarence now?' Warwick is informed that he is passing through Southam with his forces. 'Then Clarence is at hand – I hear his drum,' exclaims Warwick, before being corrected by his companion with a show of his local knowledge of Warwickshire:

It is not so, my lord. Here Southam lies.
The drum your honour hears marcheth from Warwick.

This cameo is by a man named John Somerville. He has no other part in the play and cannot be confidently associated with any historical figure from the period on which the dramatic events are based. He is the only one of the principal messengers in the scene given a name, his identification serving no discernible function in the plot. For Shakespeare this John Somerville may have been a spectral record of the man who decided, on 25 October 1583, that he was going to murder the Queen.

'His purpose,' as a witness later confessed when questioned about the treasons of John Somerville, 'was to go to London where he was in hope to see the Queen's Majesty and he meant to shoot her through with his dag [pistol] and hoped to see her head to be set upon a pole for that she was a serpent and a viper.' Somerville never made it to London a free man. After recklessly boasting of his intentions he was intercepted en route at an inn near the village of Aynho. By 30 October he was interrogated, before being incarcerated in the Tower. Edward Arden was also arrested, as were Mary Arden and Somerville's wife, Margaret. Following in their wake was Francis Throckmorton, who, being immediately suspected of complicity in the assassination attempt, was apprehended and confined to the claustrophobic torture chamber called Little Ease. They were all joined in the Tower by Francis's brother George Throckmorton. The Privy Council geared itself up for a rigorous inquiry.

On 2 November Thomas Wilkes, the Privy Council's clerk, had been dispatched to Charlecote, the base from which the investigation would be led, under the watchful gaze of Thomas Lucy. The latter, in his capacity as local Justice of the Peace, ordered immediate raids on the houses of the family and close friends of the Ardens and Somervilles, looking for incriminating books and papers. It would not be far-fetched to imagine that the home of the nineteen-year-old Shakespeare was touched by these proceedings. If it was, nothing significant was found there. Seven or eight boxes of 'evidence', however, were confiscated from Edward Arden's home, though even this was not enough to make the Throckmorton mud stick. On 7 November Wilkes wrote to the Queen's spymaster Walsingham from Charlecote, insisting that a more direct approach was required, warning him:

> . . . that unless you can make Somerville, Arden, Hall the priest, Somerville's wife, and his sister, to speak directly to those things which you desire to have discovered, that it will not be possible for us here to find out more than is said already; for that the Papists in this country generally do work upon the advantage of clearing their houses of all shows of suspicion: and therefore unless you can charge them with matter from the mouths of your prisoners look not to wring anything from them . . .

Wrung they would be, for the principal male suspects in the case would be stretched on the rack. Throckmorton was tortured at least three times but, as an amazed contemporary noted, 'they say confesseth nothing'. Edward Arden's torturers made a special effort to ascertain what secret 'speeches' passed between him and Somerville and were keen to compile a list of Arden kinsmen who regularly visited Park Hall. The investigation gathered further impetus when it was discovered that Somerville's sister, Elizabeth, whom the authorities described as 'a very perverse and a malicious papist', had 'of late been beyond the seas', having travelled to St Omer, a notorious hub of recusant activity. The mere suspicion that she may have been a conduit for foreign intelligence put the spotlight on the Arden women, who were now beginning to look like the backbone of a sophisticated operation – or so the authorities wanted them to appear.

One man had managed to slip through Thomas Lucy's fingers. Hugh Hall, derided by the investigators as a 'most dangerous practiser, a conveyor of intelligence to all the capital papists in these parts', was nowhere to be found. The green-fingered priest had a flair for evasion, for he had been conducting his business in disguise 'under the cloak of a gardener' while living at Park Hall and at the home of the Catholic recusant John Talbot of Grafton, in Worcestershire. The Privy Council would eventually hear from one of their spies, William Davison, that Hall had been travelling through Rome and that he had smuggled back to England 'seditious books packed together very cunningly' and concealed 'amongst trees and plants'. The same document claimed that the Queen had accumulated enough damning evidence to 'convict' Lord Henry Howard and that Sir Charles Arundel had been visiting a 'new perfumers' who had been providing him with scented 'gloves and sweet savours' laced with poison as gifts for his unwitting sovereign. Davison was writing on 23 November 1584, but claimed to have received this information some 'two years since and more', indicating that Hall was already on the Privy Council's hit list before Somerville undertook his dangerous mission.

For a while Hall had been hiding out in Idlicote, at the home of a William Underhill. Then, on 7 November 1583, Wilkes wrote to Lord Burghley after receiving a tip-off that the priest had fled to London and taken up residence at the Bell Inn in Carter Lane, just a few paces east of Elizabeth Russell's Blackfriars home. Under interrogation Somerville confessed that it was Hall's influence which had led him down this bloody path. The priest had delivered a searing lecture at Park Hall, in the presence of Edward and Mary Arden and Margaret Somerville, denouncing the Queen's policy against Catholics. When an enthusiastic Margaret relayed the contents of the sermon to her husband it 'wrought in him a hatred towards Her Majesty'. Somerville next approached an acquaintance of Elizabeth Russell's, Sir John Conway, whom he made 'privy unto the trouble of his mind about an intent he had to do somewhat for the benefit of [the] commonwealth'. Conway had felt Elizabeth's wrath two years previously, following his attempt to divest Edward Hoby of his estates of Offenham, Poden and Morton, in Worcestershire, at rock-bottom prices. 'I am come to the understanding of such cozenage,' she had complained 'vehemently' to Burghley, 'as if it please not you forthwith of your own authority to stay, Edward is utterly undone, so wilfully, as never I think was any the like.' Conway's dubious dealings were therefore already known to Cecil through his sister-in-law and it would certainly not have worked in his favour that he had clearly been intimate enough with Somerville to have been 'privy' to his darkest thoughts. Conway escaped a charge of treason, but if he had intended to dissuade Somerville from his cruel mission he did not do a very good job.

By 24 November Hugh Hall had been tracked down and tortured. The investigation would now proceed in a manner which would entangle Elizabeth Russell in its labyrinthine shifts. On 6 December Lady Margery Throckmorton, mother to Francis and George, was interrogated for her suspected complicity in the plot, after Burghley's spies discovered that she had been attempting to make contact with Lady Arundel. The latter was, it seems, involved in a rather interesting export business; for the goods she was trafficking were Catholics. The suspected involvement of Mary, Queen of Scots, in recent plots to kill Elizabeth I prompted the authorities to institute a 'stay and search' policy in England's major coastal ports, in the hope of flushing out her co-conspirators. As the surveillance of recusants intensified, Lady Throckmorton sought a means of smuggling her son Thomas out of the country to a safer life 'beyond the seas'. George Throckmorton had already attempted to flee, but was apprehended and searched; his goods confiscated. Determined to fare better with Thomas, his mother approached the servant of John Talbot, the man who had harboured Hugh Hall, who informed her that the 'Lady of Arundel might pass him over safely' if he could get to Arundel Castle in Sussex. For her fixer in the matter Lady Throckmorton chose Dr Thomas Fryer, who, she later confessed, 'did often resort to that Lady [Arundel] for Physic'. Her purpose, she protested, was to prevail upon the doctor's 'credit with the Lady' to procure safe conveyance for her son, with the intention simply of enabling him to avoid having his 'apparel and other things taken from him' by the harbour officers. She speedily arranged to meet Fryer at her home in Lewisham in order to set her plan in motion. Her attempts to spirit her sons across the oceans, with the aid of the Catholic Arundels, in the immediate aftermath of the Somerville–Arden plot, appeared far from innocent.

Fryer was incarcerated in the Clink, but his naming in the Throck-morton interrogations was just the latest in a long line of suspicious activities that had seen the one-time physician to the Spanish Ambassador to England suffer short spells of imprisonment. He immediately appealed to Elizabeth, later reminiscing in a letter to Robert Cecil that 'after that when I was committed by warrant . . . close prisoner to the Clink . . . through the means of your thrice honourable aunt, the Lady Russell, how speedily the fifteenth day, I was released'. Elizabeth prevailed for a very good reason. Fryer was a spy and informant working for Burghley, as she well knew. It was the Lord Treasurer who had previously sprung him from Newgate when he was 'indicted . . . for recusancy' and who had secured a licence for him to study physic abroad, where he could prove useful as a conveyor of intelligence about the Cyprus wars and, later, on Spanish matters. Perhaps Fryer had betrayed Lady Throckmorton to Burghley, for early in November her home was raided and searched. This would explain the ease with which Elizabeth was able to secure his release from prison. It would not be the last time he would work as an informant for the Crown's intelligence service, for he appears on the 1596 recusant list with a note stating that 'ser-vice [was] expected at his hands for the discovery of Garnett'. This refers to Father Henry Garnett, who would become one of the notorious ringleaders of the Gunpowder Plot, along with Hugh Hall's patron, John Talbot.

Hall's close links with Talbot were not enough to establish a firm connection between him and Francis Throckmorton, despite his involvement in the scheme to help Francis's brother escape the country, apparently with help from the Talbot household. Hall denied having had any 'familiarity' with Francis Throckmorton for next to seven years. A more incriminating association between the chief conspirators of the Throckmorton Plot and the Somerville–Arden debacle was needed. It would be provided by another of those flushers-out of recusants, Sir Edward Stafford, who was acting as an agent and ambassador for Walsingham in Paris in December 1583. During this time Stafford continued to receive intelligence from his predecessor there, Sir Henry Brooke, brother to William Brooke, 10th Baron Cobham. Henry had occasionally been acting as a go-between for Walsingham and providing Stafford with information about the die-hard Throckmortonists who refused to give up on their 'enterprise against their Prince and state'. On 2 December Stafford related a peculiar incident in which Charles Arundel and the brothers Charles and Thomas Paget broke into his apartment in Paris. Stafford had been in his dining chamber at the time and was 'amazed' when he turned to find them standing behind him 'afore anybody was aware of them'. They claimed to have fled England in haste following news 'given out by the traitorous Somerville', who had informed them that they were about to become the targets of 'enemies' who would shortly 'have a hard hand over all papists'. They claimed to be innocent of any wrongdoing, but Stafford was dubious. 'For the Lord Paget and Arundel,' he assured Walsingham, 'I have as good an eye over them as I can.'

With all the suspects in the Somerville–Arden plot rounded up, it was time for Lord Burghley to make a public display of them. On 16 December John Somerville and Edward Arden were tried at Guildhall and convicted of treason. Presiding that day was Elizabeth's kinsman Henry Carey, Lord Hunsdon. On 19 December the captives were transferred to Newgate Prison, whence they would be conveyed to their execution. Within two hours Somerville was 'found (desperately) to have strangled himself', having fashioned a hangman's noose from his garters.

Intercepted intelligence declared that Somerville was 'hanged to avoid a mischief', to protect the identities of the real masterminds behind the plot for which he was made the unwitting scapegoat. Mary, Queen of Scots, was quick to deny all knowledge, insisting that she knew neither 'Sommerfeld ny Arden'. Somerville's wife was also sentenced to death, but was spared, 'she being with child'. For Edward Arden there would be no escape. It was down to Lord Burghley to put the adequate justificatory spin on the proceedings. He immediately composed a propagandist tract, *The Execution of Justice*, in which he described Somerville as a 'furious young man of Warwickshire', lured on by the 'enticements of certain seditious and traitorous persons his kinsmen and allies'. In January 1584 it flew off the presses in English, Latin, French and Italian. The Latin and French editions were commandeered by none other than Thomas Vautrollier.

The energies that had coalesced in the very public disgracing of Shakespeare's family had proceeded from the core of Elizabeth's own coterie: her brother-in-law and her next-door neighbour in the Blackfriars. The printer responsible for the Italian edition of Burghley's *Execution* was John Wolfe, who would later play a significant role in linking the Earl of Essex to Shakespeare's *Richard II* and *Henry IV* plays, lending fuel to the flames of the conspiracy that would form the backdrop of Elizabeth's closure of the Blackfriars Theatre. In some of the other anti-Somerville–Arden propagandist texts issued, Burghley's hand can be discerned. In the most important of these, Raphael Holinshed's *Chronicles*, sections of the Treasurer's tract are quoted verbatim, with the addition of a gruesome vignette of Arden's fate which spared few of the gritty details:

Edward Arden was drawn from Newgate into Smithfield, and there hanged, bowelled, and quartered: whose head with Somerville's was set on London bridge, and his quarters on the gates of the city . . . A dreadful example of God's heavy judgement upon those two offenders; but specially against the last, whom God delivered to a reprobate mind, in so much that his own hands became his hangman . . . Thus much by the way of terror, that the remembrance hereof . . . may make men evil minded, amazed at the rigorous revengement which God taketh (when he seeth his due time) upon the wicked . . .

What must Shakespeare have thought reading this (which we know he must, for Raphael Holinshed was one of the principal sources for so many of his plays)? How must he have felt seeing the name Mary Arden – with the instant pull of its maternal associations – emblazoned alongside those 'traitorous persons', the 'kinsmen and allies' of Edward Arden and John Somerville, who sought 'with full intent to kill the Queen's Majesty'? Still less would Shakespeare have been pleased to see the development of his kinsmen's after-lives, for they would forever be ranked among a list of notorious Catholic conspirators. This included Francis Throckmorton, who was led via Blackfriars Stairs to his execution at Tyburn on 10 July 1584, as well as the likes of William Carter and William Parry, who were hanged, drawn and quartered between 1584 and 1585.

Shortly afterwards the name William Carter would haunt Elizabeth Russell in a most peculiar manner. Shakespeare would have to deal with some ghosts of his own. John Somerville's appearance in *Henry VI, Part 3* may suggest that he had far from forgotten the damage done to the reputation of the Ardens, and their allies the Throckmortons and the Percys, by the houses of Cecil, Cobham and Russell. The latter would have a special involvement in the dis-astrous career of Henry Percy, 8th Earl of Northumberland.

Shock, embarrassment and horror must have been Elizabeth Rus-sell's reaction to the news that her father-in-law, Francis Russell, had been mentioned in an interrogation sparked by the paranoia sur-rounding the 8th Earl of Northumberland on 3 June 1585. The fact that the name of John Talbot of Grafton was also evoked would not have helped matters. There was little substance to the incident, merely a servant's gossip about rivalries between some of the Queen's most powerful courtiers, but it may have arisen due to some known ill feeling between the Percys and the Russells.

On 16 December 1583 Northumberland was put under house

arrest following the sensational discovery of the Somerville–Arden plot. He could therefore no longer be trusted with the Captainship of Tynemouth Castle, in Tyne and Wear, for such a stronghold could easily be used for the concealing of recusants, or worse still as a safe passage for invading troops entering the harbour there from the river Tyne. When Francis Throckmorton was arrested, just over a month before, his home, located close to St Paul's Cathedral, was searched and papers listing the ports suitable for such purposes were discovered. Elizabeth Russell's brother-in-law Sir Francis Russell the younger was ordered to take charge of Tynemouth Castle. Henry Percy, however, was unwilling to relinquish it and ordered his servants to withhold the castle's revenues from the newly appointed captain. The Earl defended himself to the Queen, insisting that losing this vital income would ruin him and be the cause of a shameful 'disgrace and discredit . . . unto him in his own country'. Francis pleaded with Walsingham to provide him with the necessary payments directly and 'not at the hands of any of the Earl of Northumberland's men, because they do nothing but shift me from day to day'. As the tensions escalated he pressed forward with his mission to search every ship that drew near to the castle. 'I fear great evil is wrought here in this harbour,' he wrote to Walsingham on 16 May 1585. He need not have worried: in just over a month Percy would be found dead in the Tower under mysterious circumstances.

Sir Francis Walsingham may have been able to refer to Northumberland's death as the 'unfortunate accident' of a man who 'unnaturally and desperately destroyed himself', but Francis, Lord Russell took a little more convincing. Walsingham sent him a full account, no doubt based on Burghley's version of events, with the intention of using him as a means of quashing the potential retaliatory impulses of the recusants in the area. 'It will hardly be believed in this country to be as you have written,' replied Francis from Tynemouth on 26 June 1585, 'yet I am fully persuaded and have persuaded diverse, that it was no[t] otherwise.' His initial reticence is understandable. Given rumours that the Duke of Guise had been preparing to rescue the Earl with the aid of a French army, his death seemed more than convenient.

On 21 June Henry Percy's son and namesake, who was born at the now confiscated Tynemouth, became the 9th Earl of Northumberland. This associate of John Dee may have been in Elizabeth Russell's orbit at this time, for, just over one month later, she received a shocking message from his steward, one that heralded a dramatic change to her life. '[M]y old man is said to be suddenly dead,' she wrote to Lord Burghley in a state of agitation. 'I hope it be not so. He was well on Friday after dinner. I received a letter written with his own hand on Saturday, and yet reported on Tuesday to my Lord of Northumberland, as his steward told me, to be dead, and that suddenly.' The 'old man' must refer to her father-in-law, Francis Russell, the Earl of Bedford. Elizabeth had every right to be alarmed. The Earl's life was all that was keeping the Bedford wealth from reverting to the next male heir in the family. But there is another mystery here. Francis Russell's death occurred on Wednesday 28 July 1585. How could news of his demise have been reported on Tuesday? The confusion was due to an extraordinary and tragic coincidence.

A Francis Russell did die on Tuesday 27 July. This was not the Earl of Bedford, but his son. Given the 9th Earl of Northumberland's connection to Tynemouth, in the younger Lord Russell's hands at the time of his death, it makes sense that the former would be one of the first to receive news of the tragedy. The Earl of Bedford died only a few hours later and this must have been the reason for Elizabeth's confusion, as news began to spread of the passing of the elder Francis Russell the following day. It is possible that it was knowledge of his son's brutal death that hastened the Earl's end, for young Francis had been shot on the borders of Scotland, not far from Berwick. Shamefully, his demise had occurred during a truce in the military campaign there. A premeditated assassination was instantly suspected and the male members of the Russell family began agitating for a formal investigation. Before its completion, intelligence gathered from France suggested that the sons of the 8th

Earl of Northumberland were preparing to back the Earl of Westmorland in an invasion of the north, and would be provided with
ten thousand men and a hundred thousand crowns for the purpose.
It was rumoured that Thomas Throckmorton would join the campaign, coordinating an attack on the south with 'Spanish forces'
while Charles Arundel orchestrated a pincer movement by raiding
the west.

The infamy surrounding the Throckmortons and the Percys was
not going to die any time soon. It was in the wake of the anxieties
generated by the Somerville–Arden, Throckmorton and Babington
plots against the Queen that Elizabeth Russell's name became
embroiled in a puzzling incident.

On the evening of Thursday 13 October 1586, at around eight
o'clock, James Parrys braved the cold to pay a visit to his neighbour
William Carter in the parish of Aylesbury, in Buckinghamshire. His
arrival interrupted Carter's discussions with a mysterious guest
whom Parrys, when questioned later, insisted vehemently was 'to
him a stranger'. Greeting the newly arrived visitor, the unknown
man introduced himself as John Yates, but gave no fixed address.
They could scarcely believe what he told them next.

Yates claimed that he had just come from the home of Elizabeth
Russell, in nearby Berkshire. Elizabeth may have been known to
Parrys, for upon hearing that he had lately been in the company of
so distinguished a lady he immediately asked him 'what news he
heard out of Flanders'. The remark is an intriguing one. It is unclear
whether Parrys surmised that the enigmatic stranger was one of
Elizabeth's spies, who had recently come from an intelligence-
gathering mission to Flanders, or whether he simply assumed that
Lady Russell was herself the conduit for privy information, perhaps
gleaned from her brother-in-law Lord Burghley or from the Earl of
Leicester, who, as Governor General in the Netherlands, was
charged with the responsibility of dealing with the current crisis in
the Low Countries. High on Leicester's agenda had been the support of the Protestant resistance in Flanders against Catholic Spain.

Just days before John Yates turned up at William Carter's home, the Earl had drawn up a pressing memorandum calculated to wrest £50,000–60,000 from the Queen to help him fight 'the common cause'. The liberation of Flanders in particular was a goal to which Elizabeth was committed, and she would later attempt to convince her sovereign to step up her support for the beleaguered region. Parrys' request for information was, however, met with Yates's impatient reply that he had nothing new to share with him 'from thence'. He had instead something far more alarming to report, which betokened 'evil news for England', for, while at Elizabeth's house, her grooms of the stable had informed him 'that we had now no Queen, for that Her Majesty was dead'.

In the shadow of the Throckmorton and Babington plots, this was no time to be spreading such rumours. The previous year the Act of Surety of the Queen's Person had extended the treason laws to include the 'aiders, comforters, and abettors' of those who merely 'compassed or imagined' the Queen's death. After their guest had departed, it must have occurred to his hosts that if the peculiar incident had been some kind of sting operation, orchestrated by Elizabeth's powerful kinsmen to flush out clandestine recusants in the area, then their heads would roll. By around five o'clock the next day, they had reported the incident to the Buckinghamshire Justice of the Peace, Alexander Hampden. John Yates was 'sought with all diligence' but was nowhere to be found. He vanished into the night and out of the records, leaving an enigma that would be only partially resolved after Elizabeth's death.

On 20 July 1615 an old and frail man presented a petition before the Archbishop of Canterbury and other honourable members of the Privy Council at Whitehall. Though seriously ill, he was a prisoner of the Clink. Some time before 1585 he had become a Catholic priest, having been 'ordained beyond the seas by authority derived from the Bishop of Rome'. Now he was requesting that he be permitted to return home, 'to continue the remainder of his days' in the place of his birth: Buckland, near Aylesbury. His petition was granted, 'with two sureties in £500 a piece' offered by him as collateral, on condition that he 'behave himself in all things as becometh a dutiful subject' and retire to Buckland, there to remain in quiet until his death. The petitioner's name was John Yates.

This must be the same John Yates who had appeared twenty-nine years before in the home of William Carter. His absence from the area prior to 1585 may explain why Carter and Parrys did not recognize him. The pattern is a familiar one. In the 1570s many bright but disillusioned young men were fleeing the country, to be trained and ordained in centres of Jesuit activity abroad, before returning to England on a mission to convert the populace to Catholicism. Coming from a parish close to Bisham, Yates is likely to have known of Elizabeth and her political activities, and his role as a Catholic missionary may even have prompted him to target one of the female leaders of the Puritan faction by implicating her household in treasonous accusations regarding the Queen's supposed demise.

It is one of the peculiar coincidences, if coincidence it be, of this intriguing case that between 1579 and 1584 the Privy Council was investigating the activities of one William Carter, a printer residing in Hart Street in the parish of St Olave's. Carter's home had been raided and among the treasonous books and papers discovered was one which challenged Elizabeth I's claim to the throne, declaring boldly 'that if by parliament the Crown be limited to a Bastard, such act and limitation is void'. Lord Burghley had already been informed by the Bishop of London on 30 December 1579 that Carter had printed 'lewd pamphlets' and 'a very dangerous book' written in French which had named Mary, Queen of Scots, the 'heir apparent of this Crown'. He had also defended the Percy family's treasonous machinations and, as a horrified Cecil learned, directly 'discourseth against you, and the late Lord Keeper', Nicholas Bacon, who had died earlier that year. William Carter was arrested and questioned by the commission for monitoring recusant activity, headed by Elizabeth's father-in-law, the Earl of Bedford; her neighbour in Windsor, the Lord Admiral, Charles Howard; and her brother-in-law Burghley. The charges were damning, but Carter remained tight-lipped about the provenance of the seditious texts. He was eventually 'set at liberty' with bail of a hundred marks, only to be arrested in 1583 after a spy, known only as P. H. W., reported to Walsingham that 'of this I am most assured, that there is neither Jesuit, priest, nor papist of any accompt within England but he knoweth them'. Carter was executed the following year for printing a text that encouraged Catholic women to assassinate the Queen.

There is no known connection between the William Carter who had been circulating seditious material about Elizabeth Russell's kinsmen between 1579 and 1581 and his namesake who confessed to the Buckinghamshire Justice of the Peace in 1586 that news of the Queen's death had been spreading from her house. Could the two Carters have been kinsmen? If there was some connection, then were these men somehow involved in a plot to undermine Elizabeth Russell? The removal of such a powerful Protestant from the region over which she held court would certainly have been a significant victory for the Catholic faction. While it may never be possible to determine if this was the case, what can be gathered from this curious episode is Elizabeth's proximity to the Catholic intrigues which were the source of such paranoia in the 1580s, as well as her neighbours' perception that she was in some way connected with the unfolding military campaign in Flanders. These sympathies would be borne out by her associations with the Blackfriars immigrants who had attached themselves to the Dutch Church in London, some of whom would support her audacious scheme to push the Burbages and their principal playwright, Shakespeare, out of the area.

So what of Shakespeare's 'cousin', Francis Arden? What became of him after his release from prison? It seems there were some who were waiting impatiently on the outside for his enlargement, not to welcome him home but to settle old scores.

In the years immediately following his reappearance in Warwickshire, Arden found himself the target of a series of legal suits. The earliest of these has barely been touched on by historians and biographers in over four centuries. Recounted in three rolls, the longest unfolding to two and a half feet in width and nearly five in length of densely packed legal script, the voluminous case saw Arden pitted against Francis Throckmorton. This was not, however, the same Throckmorton who was executed for plotting against the Queen. He was, rather, the head of a related branch of the family, whose seat was Ullenhall, located west of Henley-in-Arden. The dispute was over a lease for property in Warwickshire which Throckmorton had granted to Arden in 1576. The transaction immediately sparked a fierce legal battle for control of the manor which would engulf other members of the Throckmorton family and many Warwickshire residents. Throckmorton attempted to reclaim his lease, complaining that he was only twenty-one years old when the 'evil dealing' Arden had taken advantage of his youth to obtain his property at exploitative rates with 'crafty . . . indirect practises and subtle confederacy'. As the case dragged on, Arden's accomplices 'empanelled a very partial and affectionate Jury on their behalf', most of whom were 'either of kindred or of alliance . . . or tenants to them', some leasing property in the disputed manor itself. They also gained the backing of the High Sheriff of Warwickshire, to whom they were 'allied either by affinity or consanguinity'. Together, Throckmorton's adversaries set about proving that he had lied about his age.

The case reached its scandalous apex around 1587–8, just after Francis Arden was released from prison. It was then that the validity of the argument put forward in court by Arden and his accomplices was dismantled by the Burden family, almost certainly the same who were intimates of Elizabeth Russell as well as her Fitzwilliam kinsmen. We have previously encountered a 'Mr Burden', who had taken a ceremonial role of honour in the funerals Elizabeth devised for both her husbands. This may have been George Burden, for less than two years before the Burdens appeared in court to challenge the Arden 'confederacy', a man by that name had acted as Elizabeth's intermediary for the payment of renovations she had made to Westminster College, generously funding the repair of chimneys, candlesticks, hangings, 'coverlets and carpets of Arras', among other improvements. He worked alongside Gabriel Goodman in Westminster and his clerical connections indicate that, if he was not the very same described in 1552 as William Cecil's 'servant George Burden, now a canon of Rochester', then he was a close relation.

It was the brothers George and John Burden, identified in the trial documents as 'gentlemen', who came to the rescue when they provided documents signed by their father, a 'Mr Burden' who had been an 'officer at Dover', which confirmed Throckmorton's story and placed his real age beyond doubt. With this advantage, Throckmorton did something extraordinary. Determined to expose what he believed was corruption on a wide scale, he decided to sue Francis Arden, his accomplices and all twelve Warwickshire jurors – seventeen persons in all – in the Court of Star Chamber, where the case could be heard by Elizabeth Russell's brother-in-law William Cecil. It is possible that the Burdens' closeness to the Cecil, Hoby and Russell families – the common link between them of course being Elizabeth herself – may have given Throckmorton the confidence to take this unusual course. With so many Warwickshire residents involved, including Shakespeare's Arden and Throckmorton kinsmen, it is hard to imagine the playwright not being aware of this scandalous case. Ullenhall Manor was close to his Stratford home, and he may even have known members of the jury, which was made up of men 'allied' to Francis Arden's coterie. The case must have at least been the talk of the town, given the involvement of so many men, in Francis Throckmorton's words, 'of light credit and fame in the country'. The nature of this 'fame' is unclear. It is possible that Throckmorton had made the most of the continuing notoriety of the Somerville–Arden conspiracy shortly after Francis Arden's release in order to gain the Privy Council's sympathy. That his opponent's name still packed a political punch is suggested by the fact that this would not be the last time he became the focus of legal controversy.

On 18 November 1591 Francis Arden became entangled in an investigation that touched on his involvement in the circumstances which brought the conspirators Margaret Arden and John Somerville together. The case revolved around the bond he had entered into with Edward Arden, who had borrowed money to pay for the 'parcel of the marriage goods' of his daughter and son-in-law. The simple matter of Margaret's dowry had, curiously, demanded an inordinate number of intermediaries, including the ex-convict. One of the men interrogated confessed that he had 'rode with Mr Francis Arden to Somerville's house', where he witnessed the disputed funds being counted 'upon the table in the parlour', yet did not explain, when asked, 'what was the cause the said [Edward] Arden would not be seen to borrow that money himself'. The fact that the suit was instigated by the Crown, long after the death of the chief suspects in the Somerville–Arden plot, indicates that the authorities were still watching Shakespeare's kinsmen eight years later.

The Queen's Soldier

'Keeper of a Castle in England is Knight's service.' This is how one seventeenth-century manual described the post of Custodian, or Keeper, of a Castle. This office was still classed under the feudal law of tenure known as 'escuage or shield service', designating the right to hold land or property in exchange for military service. The College of Arms' regulations assigned to the Keepers of castles an important martial role. Responsible for a stronghold's armoury, they were required to make battlements and weaponry available for the defence of Crown and country during times of war. As everyone knew, women could not be knights. The poet Edmund Spenser may have been fantasizing about the conquests of the warrior-woman Britomart when writing his epic *The Faerie Queene* in the 1590s, but these were grandiloquent flights of fancy . . . for everyone, that is, except Lady Elizabeth Russell.

Having buried her second husband, Elizabeth was independent once again and able to give free rein to her own ambitions. She turned her attentions to one of her most audacious projects: becoming a captain of her own fortress. Not satisfied with her current arrangement of merely renting Donnington Castle from the Queen, Elizabeth felt that the manors and estates which stood just outside Newbury in Berkshire had more to offer her. Flouting the laws of the College of Arms, she made a bid for the Keepership of the stronghold from around 1588, offering her royal landlord huge bribes in hopes of securing the lucrative post. The list of gifts made an admirable catalogue: 'a canopy of tissue, with curtains of crimson taffeta' embroidered with gold; two hats, each set with a dazzling jewel, one of which, a 'white beaver', cost £100; a 'pendant pearl' worth £30; and, as Elizabeth itemized somewhat testily (but not without a tinge of perverse, but disarming, humour), 'a gown and petticoat of such tissue as should have been for the Queen of Scots' wedding garment, but I got them for my Queen'. In just eighteen weeks Elizabeth had spent a total of £500 on such sumptuous enticements, the equivalent of close to £65,000 in today's money. It was not until Frances Brooke, the wife of William Brooke, 10th Baron Cobham, agreed to petition on Elizabeth's behalf, passing on to the Queen a New Year's gift of 'fair gold' worth £30, that the Dowager finally got her wish.

On 17 March 1590 the Queen granted Donnington to 'our well beloved Elizabeth, Lady Russell'. With the Keepership of the castle, which carried remuneration of two and a half pence per day, Elizabeth acquired powers usually reserved for men alone, including the posts of 'Keeper and Paler of the Park of Donnington', which provided wages of four pence per day, and Bailiff of the Manor of Donnington 'and all other manors . . . in the county of Berkshire', the latter bringing to her coffers a further two pence per day. She also became 'Master of the drift of wild animals of Donnington Park' and Warden and Paymaster of the local almshouses, offices previously held by Thomas Cawarden, the former Master of the Revels. These rights came with some additional perks: rent collection from all the tenants leasing properties on castle grounds, full administrative authority in the area in her role as bailiff, and involvement in any military campaigns which required use of the castle and its artillery. She had become the first woman in England to serve as her Queen's soldier.

It was not merely the allure of becoming mistress of her own castle that prompted Elizabeth to seek the Keepership of Donnington. She desperately needed the money. Her husband's premature death, before formally acceding to his father's Earldom, left the Bedford estates open to competing claims from the late Earl's kinsmen. Elizabeth's daughters were made wards of the Crown, leaving her suddenly shut out of the Russell properties. To further complicate matters, the tragic demise of the old Earl of Bedford and his son, his namesake Francis, Lord Russell, within a few hours of each other, meant that the latter's son Edward Russell had become Earl of Bedford while still a minor. His wardship also reverted to the Queen, and became an instant bone of contention.

In 1585 Elizabeth had appealed to the Earl of Leicester to help her stop her daughters' inheritance being consumed by Edward Russell's wardship. Leicester was looking out for his own interests and pressed the Queen for shared custody of the boy with his brother, the Earl of Warwick. No sooner was the request granted than Warwick began to make overtures to Walsingham, pleading with him to pressure the Queen to give his 'poor afflicted wife' full control of the Bedford properties. His wife was more than capable of speaking for herself, for Anne Dudley, Countess of Warwick, was one of the Queen's oldest and most trusted companions, best placed to petition her royal mistress. She became Elizabeth's chief opponent in the battle for the Bedford fortune, beginning a legal suit to wrest hold of the late Earl's estates on Edward's behalf.

The terms of the dispute were intricate. Elizabeth Russell claimed that, according to the Earl of Bedford's original will, the desirable estates were left to his son and that these would descend to his daughters in 'remainder' in the event of John Russell's death. A 'remainder' meant that Elizabeth's daughters would become 'feoffees', inheriting the Earl's lands until they married, after which they would pass to their husbands. This was challenged vigorously by the Countess of Warwick, who insisted that the Bedford properties should be claimed in 'reversion', that is, they should revert back to the Earl in the event of his son pre-deceasing him, and then pass directly on to his surviving male heir, Edward Russell. Elizabeth's claims were extraordinary in themselves, for many of the properties under dispute were granted by Henry VIII as long-term leaseholds and 'entailed', a legal term which indicated that they could be passed on only to male heirs.

Such legal niceties were unlikely to deter the girls' litigious mother. Aware that she was up against the mighty machinery of a biased legal system which favoured male descendants, she sought to exploit a loophole in the law. Her daughters, she insisted, were 'heirs general' to the deceased Earl of Bedford, a term which designated legitimate heirs of either sex. Her argument rested on the fact that Edward Russell was descended from the former Earl's younger son, while the Russell girls were scions of his elder male offspring, the undisputed 'heir apparent' to the Bedford wealth. Refusing to be intimidated, in her own words, 'by those that favour the heirs male more than the heirs general', she commissioned a survey of the late Earl of Bedford's properties, revenues and debts, with principal estates itemized down 'to the very rents which the tenants at this day pay upon their leases', in the hope of encouraging the Queen to protect her daughters' entitlements. Her efforts were wasted. By March 1587 the Countess of Warwick had taken control of the estates of a boy who was 'sickly and weak and not able to travel without danger of his life'. The Bedford legacies were as good as hers.

Elizabeth Russell refused to give up. Little over a month after acquiring the Keepership of Donnington Castle, she devised a new scheme. Her solution was to recruit the College of Arms in a clever piece of heraldic graffiti. The idea came to her shortly after William Cecil's appointment as one of three deputy earl marshals, an office which involved him in the heralds' enforcement of the law of arms. Cecil, she demanded, should convince his two co-deputy marshals, Henry Carey, Lord Hunsdon and the Lord Admiral, Charles Howard, to enforce the downgrading of Edward Russell's coat of arms:

> Whereupon by my request to the heralds, that the Earl that now is [Edward Russell, 3rd Earl of Bedford], coming of a younger brother to my daughters' father, may have the Bedford arms with some such difference as that my daughters, in time, may not be forgotten to come of the elder brother, and thereby heirs general to the Earl . . . Good my lord, be so favourable to me and mine that justice may be published. I crave no more otherwise for safeguard of my daughters'

inheritance. While my daughters be in my power, they shall live elsewhere rather than in court to the disgrace of my dead husband by suffering the Earl to do them wrong . . .

In heraldry a 'difference' was an addition made to a coat of arms which distinguished between branches of a family. Usurping the heralds' jurisdiction, Elizabeth was seeking to intervene directly in the design of Edward's arms, adding a 'difference' which acknowledged his descent from a younger son of the 2nd Earl of Bedford. It would be an astonishing act of iconoclasm. Elegant as this solution seemed, Elizabeth would soon find that it would not be so simple. The legal suit would drag on, with Elizabeth gaining only the smallest victory when the Queen finally capitulated to her demands, no doubt through her brother-in-law's intercession, for her own daughters' wardship in 1591. She was allowed 'presently to enter into Bedford House and to enjoy it as the Queen's tenant during the minority of her daughters'.

With a stalemate over most of the Bedford inheritance, Elizabeth needed a new, bolder, strategy if she was going to win over the Queen.

Elizabeth I arrived at Bisham on 11 August 1592. She would spend three days there before resuming her summer Progress to the homes of Baron Chandos at Sudley and Henry Norris at Ricote. Despite having her resources stretched by an intimidating entourage, which included the Privy Council, Lady Russell rose to the occasion by composing a lavish entertainment in honour of her royal guest.

An expectant Queen stationed herself at the top of a hill overlooking Bisham as mysterious music emanated from the forest at the base of the valley, played by an orchestra of coronets concealed somewhere beneath its canopy. While she looked on, a ragged figure emerged from the woods. He was a 'wild man', a native of the sylvan world. As he approached her, a strange decorum suddenly came upon him. 'My untamed thoughts wax gentle,' he intoned deferentially, 'and I feel in myself civility: a thing hated because not known, and unknown because I knew not you.' Having pledged his undying allegiance, he led her halfway down the hill to the next stage of her quest, where she encountered two shepherdesses, Sybilla and Isabel, with samplers in their hands, plying their needlework. The Queen instantly recognized the girls. They were Bess and Nan, taking lead roles in their mother's play. Peering closer, she noticed that the designs they were embroidering included eglantine roses, her emblematic flower. With them was Pan, the pastoral god of shepherds, who began a roguish and amorous suit to the maidens. 'Pretty souls and bodies too, fair shepherdess, or sweet mistress, you know my suit, love,' he coaxed. 'I cannot tickle the sheep's gut of a lute . . . but for a pipe that squeaketh like a pig, I am he . . . [B]e not aghast, sweet mice . . . Can you love? Will you?'

Elizabeth's script is precisely as we might expect: the girls responded to Pan's advances with chaste yet worldly wit. 'Alas, poor Pan,' declared Sybilla. 'Look how he looketh, sister, fitter to draw in a harvest wain than talk of love to chaste virgins. Would you have us both?' With that the battle of wits commenced.

'Ay, for oft I have heard that two pigeons may be caught with one bean.'

'And two woodcocks with one spring . . . And all fools with one fair word,' quipped Isabel.

Getting to the anatomical nitty-gritty, Pan then asked the girls to educate him as to the difference 'between men's tongues, and women's'.

Elizabeth could not resist giving Sybilla an avowedly feminist agenda. '[W]omen's tongues,' she retorted sharply, 'are made of the same flesh that their hearts are, and speak as they think. Men's hearts of the flesh that their tongues [are], and both dissemble.'

The sexual banter came to an abrupt end when Pan's eye alighted on the Queen. 'What, does Jupiter come this way?' he remarked in amazement.

'No,' said Sybilla triumphantly, 'but one that will make Jupiter blush,' before making the entertainment's most explicitly political statement:

> What our mother hath often told us, and same the whole world, cannot be concealed from thee . . . This way cometh the Queen of this island, the wonder of the world, and nature's glory . . . By her it is, Pan, that all our carts that thou seest are laden with corn . . . that our rivers flow with fish . . . One hand she stretcheth to France, to weaken rebels, the other to Flanders to strengthen religion; her heart to both countries, her virtues to all. This is she at whom Envy hath shot all her arrows, and now for anger broke her bow . . . heedless treason goeth headless; and close treachery restless . . .

Scripting herself into the entertainment, Elizabeth drew attention to the turmoils in France and the Low Countries. Following the assassination of Henri III in 1589, the Protestant Henri of Navarre – son of the Hobys' one-time ally in France, Jeanne d'Albret, Queen of Navarre – had become Henri IV of France. On his accession the Catholic faction refused to acknowledge him, causing a rift in Henri's armed forces, with many choosing to defect. This reignited the wars of religion, but this time under the threat of a new behemoth: the Catholic League, funded by England's nemesis, Philip II of Spain. In an attempt to crush Henri, Philip organized a new invasion of France from the Spanish-controlled Netherlands in 1590. By January 1592 the governor of the Netherlands, the Duke of Parma, acting under the Spanish King's instructions, made an unambiguous statement of the League's control of Paris by establishing a garrison there. Henri, once the champion of the Huguenots, was backed into a corner and began to see his own conversion to Catholicism as the only way out.

A mere few months after the latest crisis faced by the French King, Elizabeth Russell's entertainment pressed the Queen to take a hard-line stance to liberate those Huguenots suffering under Catholic regimes in France and the Low Countries. In this endeavour she was not acting alone. In 1590 Anne Locke had dedicated to

Elizabeth's sister-in-law Anne Russell her translation of Jean Taffin's Calvinistic text *Of the Marks of the Children of God*. Its purpose was to draw a parallel between the sufferings of the Protestants in these oppressed states and those faced by Puritans on English soil. Her dedicatory epistle may have been deliberately designed to stir up memories of the Admonition Controversy in order indirectly to influence the Queen to pursue a more aggressive internationalist reforming agenda. Locke called upon the faithful to 'admonish' their brothers and sisters, to rouse themselves in readiness for 'the day of trial'. It was well known to Elizabeth's contemporaries – men like James Sandford, who made a point of stating it in print – that she and Anne Locke, along with Mildred Cecil and Anne Bacon, had been working together to inspire their sovereign to 'do greater things' for the purification of religion.

These were precisely the kind of activities that had brought the Cooke sisters to the attention of the Catholic faction in 1592, as they stepped up their efforts to identify and eliminate the architects of the Elizabethan Protestant regime. No work played a more central role in establishing the Church of England than Anne Bacon's translation of Bishop John Jewel's *Apologia Ecclesiae Anglicanae* in 1564. The very year in which Elizabeth was entertaining the Queen at Bisham, Richard Verstegan, one of the Catholic propagandists who had blazed the supposed assassination of Henry Percy, 8th Earl of Northumberland, opened up the case of the authorship of the English edition of Jewel's work. 'The Apology of this Church was written in Latin, and translated into English by A. B. with the commendation of M. C.' was his coded statement on the matter, 'which twain were sisters, and wives unto Cecil, and Bacon, and gave their assistance and helping hands, in the plot and fortification of this new erected synagogue.' By this time Elizabeth was bearing a greater share of the burden of steering foreign policy in the direction of radical reform. Katherine Killigrew had died in 1583 and in April 1589 Elizabeth served as the chief mourner at Mildred Cecil's funeral. Anne Bacon retreated to her manor of Gorhambury, in Hertfordshire, where she occupied herself with sending a constant stream of advice to her sons, Anthony and Francis, who were often far from willing to heed it.

Elizabeth had seen too much to take a back seat while the Privy Council debated the extent of England's involvement in the crusade for religious reform across Europe. She had first-hand experience of the troubles in France during her ambassadorial sojourn there in 1566. Her Blackfriars friends and fellow worshippers were among those affected by the wars of religion. Her own husband, John Russell, had overseen an audit of the 'strangers' in the area, many of whom belonged to the French and Dutch churches in London, and had read their accounts of the horrors which had led many of them to flee their native countries. Elizabeth was living next door to members of the de Lawne family, refugees from the St Bartholomew's Day Massacre, and Richard Field, who had married his Huguenot wife, Jacqueline Vautrollier, in Elizabeth's own church of St Anne's on 12 January 1589. With the Queen as captive audience, therefore, Elizabeth did not pass up the opportunity to remind her of the expectations of England's long-afflicted Protestant neighbours.

In a skilfully choreographed climactic flourish, the Queen was led from this moment of political revelation directly to her hostess. Descending the hill, the monarch, associated in the entertainment with the mythic goddess of chastity and the moon, Cynthia, was about to encounter another legendary Queen: Ceres, maternal goddess of agriculture and fertility. Appearing in a harvest cart, with a train of nymphs, Ceres wore a crown made of wheat ears, set with a dazzling jewel. Beneath the elaborate disguise was the 52-year-old Elizabeth Russell. Queen met Queen inside Bisham, where Elizabeth gracefully removed her diadem and offered it to her royal namesake with a moving final speech:

Greater than Ceres, receive Ceres' crown, the ornament of my plenty, the honour of your peace. Here at Your Highness' feet I lay down my feigned deity, which poets have honoured . . . And this much dare we promise for the lady of the farm, that your presence

hath added many days to her life ... who presents Your Highness
with this toy and this short prayer, poured from her heart, that your
days may increase in happiness, your happiness have no end till there
be no more days.

Elizabeth's reference to herself as 'the lady of the farm' was more
than a rustic flight of fancy. It was a daring allusion to the Roman
author Horace, who was known to Renaissance readers as the poet
of the 'Sabine Farm' because many of his poems were written from,
and roundly eulogized, the rural estate gifted to him by his patron,
the statesman Gaius Cilnius Maecenas, in 33 BC. Since Horace, over
whose satires and epistles Elizabeth had often laboured, was known
for being an astute commentator on the power structures of his
age, the allusion allowed her to showcase herself as a learned political advisor to her sovereign. If, in the process, she could convince
her to rule in her daughters' favour in their legal battle over the
Bedford estates, then so much the better.

Elizabeth's entertainment was not out of step with the civic
machinery which had accompanied the royal Progress to Bisham,
for she knew a thing or two about the 'close treachery' then troubling the state. During the Queen's sojourn her home had become
the powerhouse from which the entire country was being run, and
a politically savvy woman like Elizabeth would have made it her
business to know what was on the Privy Council's agenda. The
members of the Council at Bisham at the time included her
brother-in-law Sir William Cecil; Lord Cobham, Sir William
Brooke; the Lord Admiral, Charles Howard; Sir Francis Walsingham; and the Queen's Latin Secretary, Sir John Wolley, who was
the son-in-law of the Blackfriars' most powerful freeholder, Sir
William More.

Top of the list of the Council's concerns during those days was the
alarming rise in clandestine intelligencing Catholics in More's home
county of Surrey. It was from Bisham, on 13 August, that instructions
were sent to More, John Whitgift and Sir Thomas Browne (Elizabeth's kinsman and later petitioner against Shakespeare's Blackfriars

Theatre), informing them that the Queen was all too aware of 'the notable backwardness and defection in religion' in the area. Royal decree commanded that the 'principal persons of the recusants' be committed, at their own expense, to the houses of trusted individuals who might set about 'to reform them' or else cast in some 'common Gaol'. A missive went to the Earl of Huntingdon on the same day, charging him to deal with the 'dangerous practises' of the recusants in like manner. One signature stands out on these documents: 'Ro: Cecyll'. Before the watchful eyes of the Lady of the Farm, Robert Cecil was beginning to assume his place as a major player in the Privy Council, following in his father's footsteps as one of the Queen's most trusted advisors. In such a context, in the presence of her closest kinsmen and allies on the Privy Council, Elizabeth's politically coded royal entertainments had a special charge and urgency.

Elizabeth had already proved herself one of the Council's enablers in the war against Catholic intrigue. She had facilitated Dr Fryer's continuing employment as an agent for Walsingham and Burghley, following the Somerville–Arden conspiracy. She had also helped ease the path of another spy into the Crown's intelligence services; an operative whom Burghley had recruited as part of the drive to stamp out seditious recusants and who was particularly active between 1589 and 1591. Robert Allatt had formerly been arrested and imprisoned for suspected complicity in the very Catholic plots which he would later help expose, thanks in some measure to Elizabeth's intervention. In December 1578, during Elizabeth's stay in Westminster, Allatt had appealed to her from his cell, remembering 'how bountiful and liberal' she had been to him 'since my abode here', and knowing her 'virtuous inclination and courteous noble mind to be such, as will not disdain the acceptance of any poor man's petition'. He begged her to appeal to her friend Gabriel Goodman, the Dean of Westminster, on his behalf, asking that he grease the palm of an unnamed member of 'Her Majesty's Privy Chamber' who had offered to help accelerate his release and regain his lost fortunes thereafter 'on condition to serve him three or four years'. 'I have right well deserved [this], for service past,' he protested, 'in respect whereof hitherto, I never received one groat of wages, or other benefit or recompense.'

The mysterious individual who had offered to take Allatt into his service was probably connected in some way to Walter Mildmay, a close friend of the Cecil and Hoby families, who had owned lands in Elizabeth's Berkshire. With Elizabeth's help Allatt was released from prison and, on Burghley's instructions, placed under Mildmay's charge, so that he could work towards the 'discovery of the practises of fugitives and other enemies of the state in foreign parts'. He then travelled through Catholic hotspots in Scotland, France, Venice and Rome, sending back privy intelligence to Burghley. In 1591 he infiltrated a Catholic stronghold, the home of Lady Bothwell in Edinburgh, where he learned that James VI had sent assurances that he would 'join in league' with her Spanish confederates, for 'the King and his nobility carried a deadly hatred against certain in England for his mother's death'. As one of the major orchestrators of the demise of Mary, Queen of Scots, who had been executed on 8 February 1587 following the sensational exposure of the Babington Plot, Burghley would not have been pleased to hear this. But there was worse to come, for the chatter among Lady Bothwell's intimates was that the King of Spain had been heard 'often times [to] protest in open audience that he would be revenged of his enemies in England, if the expense of all he had to the cloak of his back would compass it'.

Allatt's most recent missions coincided with the Cecils' increased surveillance of James VI. On 7 October 1589 Thomas Fowler, one of Lord Burghley's spies in Scotland, despite facing 'great trouble and danger of life', had infiltrated a covert operation orchestrated by a mysterious female agent going by the pseudonym 'Ryalta'. She and the Scottish King were conducting their 'secret conference' through a 'cipher' of her own devising, which contained the code names of 'every one that is partaker in the matter'. Burghley soon discovered that Ryalta was Lady Penelope Rich, sister to Robert Devereux, 2nd Earl of Essex. Both were stepchildren to his old nemesis, the Earl of Leicester.

Lady Rich gave her brother the alias 'Ernestus', while James VI was flatteringly called 'Victor'. Among their accomplices was one Mr Ottoman, code name 'Orlando'. This was Dr Jean Hotman, who had formerly been in the service of the Earl of Leicester. His involvement indicated that the young Devereux had begun to take over their stepfather's secretariat following his death in 1588. Ryalta wrote to James VI 'almost every week', assuring him of 'the Earl's service and fidelity', but she was playing a dangerous game. In her encryptions she had initiated a fantasy which was little short of treasonous. The Queen was assigned the mythic appellation 'Venus' and, in mock-chivalric fashion, the Earl was cast as the disillusioned warrior-lover, 'the weary knight'. As Fowler informed Burghley in his sensitive dispatch, 'always that he is exceeding weary, accounting it a thrall he lives now in and wishes the change'. But the siblings 'went too far', he reported, 'in persuading the poor King to hope for hap shortly and that Her Majesty could not live above a year or two by reason of some imperfection'. What was being temptingly dangled before Victor was the throne of England itself, and with it the support of the powerful Devereux.

The young Cecil and Essex had inherited their parents' bad blood. The Devereux' overtures to James VI would have become even more worrying when set against Allatt's discoveries by 1591. As the Privy Councillors listened to Elizabeth Russell's artful speeches at Bisham the following summer, therefore, they were doing so in an atmosphere tinged with paranoia, amid fears that the menacing tentacles of the Catholic League were reaching out towards the Scottish King, while key members of the English nobility were showing every sign of impatience with Queen Elizabeth's regime. Burghley and his son Robert would have been under no illusion that this was a potentially explosive combination. Elizabeth's entertainment, with its imagery of national fertility and fecundity under a bountiful Queen – of harvest carts 'laden with corn', 'rivers flow[ing] with fish' and cattle feeding on abundant pastures – was intended to remind its elite audience that these pleasures were precarious and provisional. Domestic peace depended on the right foreign policy.

Failure to heed this warning, she had implied before her sovereign, would mean that, like the Huguenots in the St Bartholomew Day's Massacre, they too would see 'our rivers flow . . . with blood'.

That very year the theatres would be responsible for imbuing these fears with an alarming reality in Elizabeth's own neighbourhood of the Blackfriars.

Closing Ranks

The surviving records of St Anne's in the Blackfriars reveal something startling that has remained unknown for over four centuries. The episcopal visitation book which itemizes the offices of the men involved in the administration of the parish's church in 1592 and 1593, entirely unexpectedly, includes the name of Shakespeare's publisher, Richard Field.

Field is listed as one of two 'oeconomi' or 'sidemen' – officials working under the church wardens and charged with the task of assisting them in their daily duties, helping with the collection of poor relief and managing some of the church's financial business. Sharing this post with him is Robert Baheire, the immigrant feltmaker who, like Field, would go on to sign Elizabeth Russell's petition. Both men answered to two wardens. The first is their co-signatory Thomas Holmes; the second Robert Donckin, the very same who was ordered, in his capacity as a constable of the Blackfriars, to undertake a survey of the district's 'stranger' community in 1583, under the immediate command of the late John Russell and William Brooke, Lord Cobham. These unearthed records provide us with a direct link between the officials who were policing the immigrant population of the Blackfriars in the 1580s, managed by Elizabeth's intimates, and the men who answered her call to arms in 1596.

With the church's preacher for 1592–3 recorded as Stephen Egerton, who would also back Elizabeth's campaign against Shakespeare's Blackfriars Theatre, the document unites four of the men who would become her supporters three years later, placing them as cogs in the administrative machine of St Anne's. They were not the only ones among Elizabeth's allies who had operated in a similar capacity. Egerton appeared as the parish's 'lecturer' in the church's records three years previously, when he was put under the spotlight for his Puritan leanings and requested to 'show his conformity' to the established Church of England. His name is logged alongside the church warden 'John Dallinges', the John Dollin who signed Elizabeth's petition. The latter was listed in relation to the episcopal investigations into the wearing of the prescribed surplice by the ministry of St Anne's, suggesting that its members were suspected of non-conformism. Later, when Elizabeth began drawing men to her side in her mission to close down the new theatre in her neighbourhood, she turned to those who operated at her principal place of public worship in London, a church which had drawn the attention of the bishops for its subversive activities.

It adds something new to our understanding of the man who printed Shakespeare's narrative poems when he is viewed as part of this group who sailed close to the wind when it came to the Church of England's official prescriptions. Field had sworn an oath that he would conduct his duties in St Anne's honourably. He was clearly serious about these commitments, for he would soon work his way up the administrative ranks there. In 1597 the ancient building which housed the community's local place of worship collapsed. The residents immediately got behind its renovation – and this would have included Elizabeth Russell and Richard Field – and by December an 'enlarged' church was reconsecrated under two new church wardens, 'Willm Watts et Henrici Boyce'. These were the William Watts and Henry Boice whose names had appeared on Elizabeth's missive to the Privy Council the year before. By 1598 they would be replaced by Richard Field, for beside his name in the records for that year is the abbreviation 'gard.', short for 'gardianus': church warden. This was an honour Field would share with one 'Edwardus Lea', the Edward Ley who also participated in Elizabeth's uprising against Burbage and Shakespeare's theatrical troupe. These extraordinary manuscripts demonstrate something we did not previously know about Field. His involvement in Elizabeth's petition was not accidental. It was part of a coordinated effort by a close-knit community, many of whom held positions of responsibility within the church they and Elizabeth were funding. Of those who signed the 1596 petition, at least six are listed in the surviving Blackfriars records as having been church wardens, and two more as serving in other capacities between 1589 and 1598.

Field's entry into the formal echelons of the St Anne's administrators coincided with a period of heightened paranoia and sensitivity in the area, which may have caused him and his fellow petitioners to close ranks against the theatres. Shakespeare emerged from the period of his life now known as the 'lost years' in 1592, taking his place on the London theatrical circuit. Robert Greene's vituperative pamphlet of that year, his *Groatsworth of Wit*, offers a barely concealed allusion to the playwright, calling him an 'upstart crow . . . that with his tiger's heart wrapt in a player's hide, supposes he is . . . the only Shake-scene in a country'. The quip was an allusion to a line in *Henry VI, Part 3*, the play in which the ominous John Somerville has a brief walk-on part.

Greene's reaction indicates that Shakespeare was already making a splash among the play-going public. But these were tempestuous times in which to attempt to earn a living as an actor and dramatist. If Elizabeth Russell had kept away from the Blackfriars in the spring of 1592, she may have been doing so for reasons other than her preparations for the Queen's visit. Shakespeare would come to realize that year that even the pastime of playing was as much about politics as it was about getting paying customers through the doors, for at 8 p.m. on 11 June a riot broke out in Southwark so large that it snowballed uncontrollably, gathering rioters as it went and spilling over into other districts, including the Blackfriars. This event would provide Elizabeth's associates with ammunition against the public theatres and profoundly influence the nature of her petition to the Privy Council in 1596.

The early 1590s were years of recession, abysmal harvests, inflation and increasing competition between London tradesmen. There were simmering tensions among the apprentices, who competed for dwindling business and job opportunities, tensions which finally exploded in the terrifying riot which so shocked the Queen's Councillors in 1592. The chief culprits in the disturbance were apprentice feltmakers, most of whom had come from the Blackfriars 'with a great number of loose and masterless men apt for such purposes'.

The incident started when Henry Carey, in his capacity as Lord Chamberlain and deputy knight marshal, instructed the knight marshal's men to deliver a warrant for the arrest of a 'feltmaker's servant'. In the execution of their task, however, the officers behaved in a 'rough and violent manner', entering the house with daggers drawn and 'affrighting the goodwife who sat by the fire with a young infant in her arms'. The prisoner was confined to the Marshalsea Prison while his friends and fellow apprentices devised a plan to rescue him. A 'rude tumult' ensued, with the knight marshal's officers brandishing daggers and bastinados and 'beating the people'. Passers-by and those who simply stopped to gaze at the spectacle were drawn into the fray, with swords unleashed on both sides.

The Lord Mayor of London, William Webbe, alerted Lord Burghley and an investigation was launched, during which it transpired that 'the said companies assembled themselves by occasion and pretence of their meeting at a play, which . . . giveth opportunity of committing these and such like disorders'. The fracas gave the City authorities the excuse they needed to seek incursions into the liberties, normally beyond the legal control of the Lord Mayor of London. Because the latter had no jurisdiction over playhouses in these peripheral areas, he had to appeal directly to the Privy Council, whose powers extended over all the Queen's dominions. Webbe disclosed to Burghley his fears that from such riots 'great sequels have grown many times', drawing his attention to 'the present discontentment against strangers inhabiting within this city of such as may enjoy their conscience and trades at home, and yet hinder divers trades and occupations of this city'. The racial tensions caused by these foreigners, he averred, 'may give some occasion to such seditious persons to kindle the coals of a further disorder'.

The economic downturn had fuelled a series of alarming race riots beginning that year. As the hostilities escalated, racist slogans were plastered around the city and chanted by menacing mobs, threatening those who worshipped in centres of Huguenot activity such as the French Church in Threadneedle Street and St Anne's in the Blackfriars. 'We'll cut your throats in your temples praying/Not Paris massacre so much blood did spill,' one chilling slogan ran. The French Church had been vigorously supported by Elizabeth's sisters Katherine and Anne, the latter only the previous year having encouraged her son Anthony Bacon to go there to 'hear the public preaching of the word of God' by those who were 'armed so with prayer'. Elizabeth would have felt the tremors in her own parish. The nature of the anxieties which these troubles raised is vividly brought to life in a document which, coincidentally, has left to posterity the only substantial sample of Shakespeare's handwriting: his revisions to the play *Sir Thomas More*. Probably originally composed just after these local tumults, it contains a vivid and timely portrayal of the violent anti-immigrant riots of May Day 1517. The scene in question begins with a gathering of apprentices in the streets, responding to protests that 'if strangers be suffered' the citizens will soon see 'red herring at a Harry groat [four pence], butter at eleven pence a pound, meal at nine shillings a bushel, and beef at four nobles a stone'; prices that would have shocked a Renaissance audience. As the tensions mount the rioters claim they will 'show no mercy upon the strangers', whom they blame for the rise in inflation, the 'undoing of poor prentices', and the spread of disease. Thomas More steps in to appease the mob, holding up a ghastly mirror before their own monstrosity: 'You'll put down strangers,/ Kill them, cut their throats, possess their houses . . . /You shall perceive how horrible a shape/Your innovation bears.' The word 'innovation' can denote a rebellion and is the word Shakespeare would later use in *Hamlet*, perhaps to describe the closure of the Blackfriars Theatre by Elizabeth Russell.

Sir Thomas More did not make it to performance until the reign of James I. It failed to get a licence after the Master of the Revels, Sir

Edmund Tilney, insisted that the play be rewritten and the scene dramatizing the attack on the 'strangers' culled. The sensitivity towards suggestions of rioting in the 1590s would scarcely have been helped by Christopher Marlowe's play *The Massacre at Paris*, which was being performed by 1593. Cashing in on the recent tensions, Marlowe revived memories of the St Bartholomew's Day Massacre of 1572 among a population which included large numbers of Huguenot refugees who had fled the French wars of religion, some of whose number would have been among the audiences watching as a group of 'five or six Protestants' were butchered by the Duke of Guise's men while kneeling at prayer. This incredibly popular play, which was staged by the theatrical company patronized by the Lord Admiral, Charles Howard, notched up ten performances between 21 June and 27 September 1594. To the 'strangers' who witnessed these scenes against the backdrop of the real physical violence unleashed by the race riots, it must have seemed as if London was on the brink of its own St Bartholomew's Day Massacre.

In the wake of the riots begun by the Blackfriars feltmakers, these troubling developments would have been of interest to one particular enterprising individual of the same community, Robert Baheire, who had signed a lease on 18 March 1590 for an extensive range of 'shops, cellars . . . halls, chambers, rooms, yards, [and] entries' at an agreed annual rent of £6 13s 4d. This indicates a substantial investment, and Baheire was therefore probably successful enough to have required the services of feltmaker apprentices. Some of these may have been 'strangers', for Baheire's ties to the immigrant community were close. Before becoming an assistant to the St Anne's church wardens in 1592–3, he was attached to the French Church. He was in fact living and working practically next door to one of its ministers, Robert la Fontaine, alias le Maçon, close friend of Elizabeth Russell and her sisters.

The properties of Baheire and Fontaine were located on a lane leading from the Blackfriars towards Bridewell, a little further south of Elizabeth's home, but abutting on to the side of Water Lane. Baheire clearly had a good relationship with William More, who was listed in the Blackfriars records as a chief patron of St Anne's Church. A touching indication of this arises from More's surviving papers, which reveal that the feltmaker was allowed to discharge his obligations in an unusual way, the More family being pleased to accept samples of exquisite cloth, such as 'one good new bare beaver felt', every year as part payment for the lease. Whether or not Baheire's own apprentices were involved in the riots, as a member of the 'stranger' community and a feltmaker he would have had a vested interest in following the fortunes of the theatres as places of civil unrest, particularly during lean times when apprentices may have been agitating for more rights and higher wages and when immigrants were living under the constant threat of violent racial abuse. This is exactly the kind of stress he would not have wanted to add to his official duties in the Church of St Anne's, even if he did that year have Richard Field to help him. Other immigrant tradesmen in the neighbourhood, including those who signed the 1596 petition, would have shared Baheire's concerns, and Lady Russell herself, as a renowned champion of oppressed Huguenots, would also have had strong views on the matter.

Webbe's dire warning that further race riots were imminent was enough to prompt the Privy Council to take urgent action. When the City's attempts to gain control of the liberties threatened the autonomy of the residents in areas such as the Blackfriars, that was another matter, but when it came to the safety of the populace and, worse still, to a direct threat to the largely Puritan 'stranger' population, there was less resistance. On 23 June the Privy Council sent directives to Lord Cobham in the Blackfriars and to the Surrey Justices of the Peace, among whom were William More and his son, George More, as well as William Gardiner. The same decree went to Richard Martin, member of the Russell enclave. These men were asked to 'take order that there be no plays used in any place near thereabouts . . . or other usual places where the same are commonly used, nor no other sort of unlawful or forbidden pastimes that draw together the baser sort of people'. One of the playhouses specifically targeted was the Theatre in Shoreditch which Shakespeare relied on for his living. These missives put a spin on the riots, transforming them from spontaneous acts into premeditated and highly organized rebellions. A Privy Council order devised on 9 July, and sent to William More and Gardiner, among other justices, urged them 'to use all diligence, care and discretion that the bottom of this outrageous fact and conspiracy may be thoroughly discovered'. They followed this up six days later with a demand that George More, Gardiner and Martin, along with some of the rioters' other interrogators, 'meet together without delay' to proceed in a matter of 'great weight and consequence' towards the swift punishment of the offenders to 'Her Majesty's contentment'.

The very same year in which the Privy Council had convened in her home, the fate of the theatres was being navigated by Elizabeth Russell's own discrete circle, managed from above by the Cecils in the Privy Council. It is also worth noting that Cobham, the Mores, Martin and Gardiner all had something in common with Elizabeth. They were all Puritans. Gardiner would play a particularly intriguing role in the events surrounding Elizabeth's machinations, clashing spectacularly with Shakespeare in the very month the formidable Dowager successfully shut the doors of the Blackfriars Theatre in the faces of the playwright and his business partners. Before all this, however, the Queen's soldier had another war to fight.

13.

Sheriff and Bailiff of the Manor

On 25 March 1593, in anticipation of the start of the legal term, Elizabeth Russell stormed back to London, intent on putting the judges in her daughters' legal battle on trial. Her strategy was to prove they were guilty of corruption.

Her targets were the Lord Chief Justice of the Court of Common Pleas, Edmund Anderson; the Chief Baron of the Exchequer, William Peryam; and Associate Justice of the King's Bench, Francis Gawdy. In the last Elizabeth would make an enemy with whom she would soon clash over her rights to her properties in Bisham and Windsor. These men, Elizabeth divulged to William Cecil, were working covertly 'to pervert the Lord Chief Justice Wray in opinion'. They could not be trusted, she insisted, because they had previously served as counsel for the opposition. In total, twelve common-law judges were required to hear the case, and Elizabeth claimed that the influential men she had singled out would attempt to intimidate those who, 'being inferior, [would] be loath to oppose their opinions against their superiors'.

Elizabeth, who, highly unusually for a woman of that time, had a razor-sharp knowledge of the law, came up with a solution. The judges, whether they liked it or not, would deliver their opinions to the Queen directly *'singulatim'*, a Latin legal term which means 'individually': that is, they should not be allowed to confer before passing judgement. This did not say much for her confidence in the judgement of her sovereign, in whose hands the outcome of the case rested, and was the last thing Cecil wanted to hear. He was ailing with the gout and unable to attend the legal proceedings. His health was a small matter for Elizabeth, however, when set against the great loss of revenue from the lands belonging to the Earldom of Bedford in the eight years since this legal dispute had begun. If he was not up to the task, then he should appoint his son Robert in his place to tie the case up speedily, 'that in being by end of law dispatched, I might be gone and hide my head that owe more than I am worth'.

By May, proceedings having failed to move with the desired alacrity, Elizabeth decided to circumvent the Cecils entirely, appointing the day when the judges should be called to Westminster, where her lawyer, Edward Coke, would be ready to defend her daughters' cause. She had found a powerful advocate in Coke, who had been made Queen's Solicitor General the year before, and promoted to Attorney General this year. The exasperated Treasurer, taxed to the limit, was unable to satisfy the requirements of Elizabeth's tight schedule and passed the matter on to his son. Robert Cecil was equally stumped. He wrote back desperately, 'I pray your Ladyship, send me word what will you have done, for neither the Lord Chief Justice nor Fenner are in town.' The latter was Edward Fenner, Associate Justice of the King's Bench, another of the judges appointed to hear the case. Others were summoned but had not yet arrived. Lady Russell would not be kept waiting. She demanded that Coke appear at once and that Robert Cecil 'command all the judges from the Queen to repair to the court with their opinions in writing'. Proceedings would go ahead as she had planned. Those who were out of town could deliver their responses to the Queen on their return. 'This is all,' she wrote, 'without fail, let Mr Solicitor be sent for.'

Then Elizabeth did something important, something that stands as an indelible sign of a new resolve in the building of her public identity. She signed her letter 'Elizabeth Russell, your loving aunt, Dowager'. It was a gesture of defiance. 'Dowager' is the title given to the widow of an Earl, belonging to a Countess. From now on she would end most of her letters with this confident flourish, flying in the face of all who would oppose the honorific rights she claimed as her due.

Elizabeth's growing confidence in the legible markers of her noble status collided with the outcome of her legal suit. By 23 May it was all over. The Queen ruled against her, in the process authorizing an opposing legal identity for her namesake. Lord Burghley found himself the immediate recipient of his sister-in-law's plaints. She wrote to him accusing her opponent of foul play. It is as plain as day, she lamented, that 'by my Lady Warwick's working, my daughters be disinherited of their father's land, and that by her greatness the judges have wrested the law to her liking'. Later she would curse her, calling to God 'in his justice to reward my Lady of Warwick according to her wrongs, and cruelty done to her brother John, my lord'. Her crimes went deeper than simply rigging the outcome of the legal suit against her nieces. Elizabeth was acting on intelligence that the Countess of Warwick had contrived to have the late Earl of Bedford's original will, made around 1562–3 and unambiguously conveying his property to John, Lord Russell, and his daughters, destroyed. Her story was corroborated by Francis Russell's second wife, Bridget Hussey, who claimed that Lady Warwick had asked her to goad him on to disinherit John's heirs after his death, urging him 'to remember to burn the writing'.

Elizabeth presented Burghley with a thorough list of accounts, itemizing the paltry revenues from the properties promised to the girls and demonstrating that little was to be got from the manors of Denbury, Chalden Hering and Chadwell. The previous year she had fought a case in the Court of Wards for her daughters' rights to the latter two manors. The suit remained notorious as late as 1656, when it was published among the collection of 'remarkable cases' recorded by Sir John Popham. So intricate was the suit that it 'was put ten times to all the Justices to be resolved'. In 1587 Elizabeth had also engaged in another court battle for her rights to Carlisle House, part of the rentable tenements attached to Bedford House, also known as Russell House. Her opponent was her mother-in-law, Bridget Russell, and at stake was an annual yield valued at £16 9s 4d. She was successful but, as she complained to William Cecil, it came at the 'charge of mine own purse more than the rotten houses be worth'. While the Queen had granted Elizabeth the use of Bedford House, which would eventually pass to the girls at the end of their minority, from all their inherited properties they could exploit a total value of only £9 12s per year, with promise of a further £52 10s 6d after the death of Bridget Russell's daughter, Jane Sibylla Grey. This was a pitiful sum, given the entire estate could yield between £3,000 and £4,000 a year, in today's money roughly between £375,000 and £500,000.

Elizabeth's eldest son, Edward, had come into his inheritance in 1581, after which he threw himself with gusto into a number of local offices, becoming a Justice of the Peace for Berkshire, Kent, Worcestershire and Middlesex, and MP for Queensborough and Berkshire. While he was rooting out corrupt officials and generally making an impact in the House of Commons, his 27-year-old brother, Thomas Posthumous, was still very much a burden on his mother. Having wilfully disobeyed her command not to go abroad, he joined the military campaign in the Netherlands with the Earl of Leicester in 1586, before enrolling in Gray's Inn two years later. His first tentative steps into public service saw him twice elected to the constituency of Appleby, in Westmorland, Cumbria, in 1589 and 1593. With the bulk of the Hoby inheritance now out of Elizabeth's hands, she and her daughters were left with a minimal income, and with severely depleted funds following a long and draining legal battle. 'Not so much as the trifles of two diamonds appointed in rings by their grandfather in all these eight years could never be delivered,' she lamented. She was now faced with the challenge of maintaining the girls' upkeep in a world that valued the visible markers of status and conspicuous wealth:

To conclude, my lord, I have brought them up hitherto with mine own charge; I have righted their wrongs with mine own purse; I have defended their cases in law, with uncredible and most untolerable malice to be offered to any Christian being honest. They be now women by law, fit to be married . . . I would know where I shall leave my eldest daughter now at my going out of town and how

provided for, for diet of herself, her maid, and groom, and foot-
man . . . For on my faith, my lord, I am no longer able to endure the
charge without comfort.

This letter stands out among those penned before and after it,
ending simply 'Your lordship's afflicted sister-in-law by malice, Eliza.
Russell'. Finishing the letter, she could not bring herself to follow
her name in the closing salutation with the word 'Dowager'.

One of the most magnificent estates in Elizabethan England had
slipped through Elizabeth's fingers. She was still, however, the
Keeper of Donnington Castle and its environs, a post which made
her a major figure in local politics. Her rights as bailiff over vast tracts
of land in Berkshire was a privilege she began wielding over her
properties at Bisham and Windsor. Such powers were bound to draw
the disapproval of the ruling lords who had, until then, dominated
the territories of Berkshire and neighbouring Buckinghamshire. The
men with whom she would clash were as martial as they came: the
Queen's Lord Admiral, Charles Howard, 2nd Baron Effingham, soon
to be created 1st Earl of Nottingham, and Richard Lovelace, one-time
Sheriff of Berkshire. Howard was now the Keeper of Windsor Castle and Forest and was closely allied to Elizabeth through the
Hunsdon family. He had become son-in-law to Henry Carey, Lord
Hunsdon, after marrying his daughter Katherine in 1563. Since Elizabeth's son Sir Edward Hoby was married to Katherine's younger
sister, he was Howard's brother-in-law.

Lovelace was Howard's second-in-command, the Lieutenant of
Windsor Castle and Forest, and the two men's interests were therefore closely bound together. Elizabeth's elevation caused tensions in
the neighbouring parishes in which she managed estates. The result
was the creation of two competing factions. Representatives of
both sides stalked the forests, fields and tenements of these territories fully armed and ready to shed blood in the protection of their
respective masters' interests. As the conflicts escalated, Elizabeth
would be subjected to repeated attempts to force her out of Windsor and Donnington, and to reduce her rights in their environs.

Howard and Lovelace would find this endeavour harder than they could ever have suspected, for they were up against an opponent who claimed that she was England's only female sheriff and bailiff.

The trouble began with an act of apparent generosity and ended in armed combat and a ferocious legal battle, amid charges of riot, fraud, forgery, kidnapping and violent affray. The legal documents are voluminous and have never been explored in detail until now. They tell an extraordinary story of conduct scarce conceivable for a woman of this period. By the time it was over the conflict would come to the attention of Shakespeare, who would use it as a weapon against the Cecil–Cobham–Russell alliance.

Elizabeth Russell and Richard Lovelace were long-standing neighbours in Berkshire. They had been close friends for over two decades and Elizabeth had supported Richard's children, Anne and John Lovelace the elder, whom she had taken into her employ as 'her servants daily attending upon her . . . for divers years'. On 28 March 1592 she decided to reward them for their dedicated service by granting them, along with another of Richard's sons, John Lovelace the younger, the copyhold to 'certain lands' in Bisham, which included a tenement which could be leased out for the 'term of their natural lives'. It was a magnanimous gesture.

Anne Lovelace immediately took possession of the property, with Elizabeth's permission, and began to reap the profits for herself and her brothers. This felicitous situation continued for two years. Then, as Anne later claimed in court, Elizabeth suddenly had a change of heart and began to conceive 'a desire . . . to get into her hands the said copyhold . . . contrary to sundry her former honourable professions of love and goodwill'. A campaign of entrapment ensued, so Anne deposed, with Elizabeth attempting to 'drive' her servants into 'some undutiful behaviour' by 'hard usage' and general mistreatment, her intention being to find thereby an excuse to seize back her lands. When this failed she channelled her ire against the elder John Lovelace and 'without any just cause' discharged him from her service, demanding the return of the copyhold.

Anne Lovelace protested, but was assured by her mistress that she bore her no ill will. Her intention was simply to strike out John's name and replace it with that of another of Anne's younger brothers, Hobby Lovelace. That done, she would return the copyhold to the Lovelace siblings. Reluctantly, Anne surrendered the property and on 30 March 1594 Elizabeth dispatched her steward to the local court at Bisham to draw up the new terms. Satisfied, Anne, who was clearly not one to allow a potential money-spinner to go unexploited for long, immediately requested a licence to lease the property to one John Rolles. No sooner was this granted than Elizabeth began to display a 'determinate and resolute purpose' to divest the three Lovelaces of their estate. Anne gave no reason for this turn of events, stating only that the indomitable Dowager had subjected her to a tirade of abuse and 'hard terms', during which she informed her that she no longer wished to keep her in her service. Elizabeth now wanted her lands back and the Lovelaces and their tenants out. John Rolles, who had moved into the tenement with his wife and children, refused to go. He could not have predicted the consequences of his obduracy.

The records do not say what John Rolles was doing when they came for him. He was dragged out of his house and taken to an imposing mansion set in the rolling hills of Berkshire. An ominous octagonal tower protruded from the northern end of the building, its crennellated edges casting jagged shadows on the surrounding lawns. Bisham Abbey. He did not reach the main edifice, however, for Elizabeth instructed her men to place him in her Porter's Lodge, a small building in the grounds. Once inside, Rolles discovered that this was not like the ordinary constructions that stood as functional sentinels to most Elizabethan great houses. This Porter's Lodge had been converted into a prison.

It must have been with a sense of mounting horror that the unfortunate villager was conducted to a contraption to which were attached heavy iron locks, the purpose of which he immediately recognized. At Elizabeth's command, her men forced his limbs into its constricting circular apertures and there left him 'imprisoned in the stocks'. Rolles was wretchedly detained in the Dowager's personal gaol for around nine days. During this time Elizabeth sent a searing message to his wife and children: if they wanted to see him again they had to vacate her property immediately. She got her way. By 29 September 'his wife and children through fear . . . departed'.

With the tenement now lying vacant, Anne acted swiftly to protect her interests. She sent two of her father's servants, Hugh Dabornon and William Mitchell, as bodyguards to keep possession of the property 'to her use'. When Elizabeth heard about this affront she was outraged. On Monday 30 September she did something extraordinary. Gathering together some of her servants, around twelve in all, she had them 'all armed and arrayed with unlawful and unusual weapons', and then marched them up to the tenement. On arrival they found the doors barred and bolted against them, Anne Lovelace and the two servants having barricaded themselves inside. Locks and bolts were minor obstacles for the governess of Bisham, who led her private army 'in warlike manner' in a full frontal assault on the edifice. As Anne Lovelace later described the incident, 'by the commandment, incitation, and procurement of the said Elizabeth, Lady Russell', the intimidating crew began 'in most riotous and forcible manner' to 'break down the door of the said copyhold (being fast locked and barred)', and 'with violence . . . did dispossess' the rebellious tenants.

The action did not stop there. As an indignant Anne Lovelace went on to recount, 'Elizabeth, Lady Russell, in most furious, forcible, and riotous manner, did then cause the said riotous persons to pull out of the house . . . Hugh Dabornon and William Mitchell from whence she sent them prisoners to her own house in Bisham.' There they met the same fate as the prison's former inmate, John Rolles, being manhandled and 'fast locked' into the stocks. Their ordeal in this dungeon lasted five hours, though Elizabeth, according to Anne, had other plans for them, 'intending most unlawfully and cruelly so to have detained and kept them some long time to their utter spoil and undoing had there not been means used for their enlargement'. These means were engineered by Richard Lovelace.

In the aftermath of the incident a servant left Hurley in Berkshire, where Lovelace's home was located, and undertook the three-mile journey to Bisham Abbey. Richard Barton had been dispatched on a peace-keeping mission, in the hope that Elizabeth Russell could be 'moved' to compassion and release Hugh Dabornon and William Mitchell without further affray. This was optimistic. Upon arrival he was told curtly by Elizabeth's servants that their mistress was in no mood for a parley. He begged at least to be allowed to speak to Lovelace's incarcerated servants, but this request was also flatly refused. All gentler means having failed, later that same day Lovelace offered a firmer riposte to Lady Russell's turf war. He subsequently told the court that he had heard it credibly reported that his formidable opponent had a habit of allowing men to languish for 'some long time' in her stocks 'to their great spoil and hurt', for, he insisted, 'she had done [so] to some others before'. This 'being known' to him, he decided to concoct an audacious rescue operation. From this point on, the testimony of the complainant (Elizabeth Russell) differs somewhat from that of the defendants (Richard Lovelace and his accomplices).

According to Richard Lovelace, he and another five of his 'ordinary household servants', plus one of his younger sons 'then late from school', set out on the short journey from Hurley to Bisham Abbey. They were armed. On the way they were joined by a mysterious 'gentleman', whose identity was not disclosed in the defendants' depositions, who spoke confidentially with Lovelace before riding out with them to Elizabeth's home. Arriving around 2 p.m., they found the gates to the courtyard of Bisham Abbey open. They stalked their way in, spying only one of Elizabeth's servants in attendance at the Porter's Lodge. This was going to be easier than they had anticipated.

The operation became a quiet stake-out, Lovelace and his men hiding close by and waiting for their opportunity to strike. When Elizabeth's attendant left the Lodge, they seized their chance. With a swift 'thrust with his foot', one of Lovelace's men broke open the door. Inside they were met with the spectacle of Dabornon and

Mitchell 'miserably locked in the stocks'. In court, Lovelace's men later claimed that they had simply happened to come across 'an axe there lying by' which 'in compassion of the said two persons so imprisoned' they put to meritorious service, smashing open the locks and liberating their comrades. Rescue mission accomplished, they rode back to Hurley in 'peace and quiet', not having seen or spoken with Elizabeth or any of her servants. Richard Lovelace's testimony paints a flattering picture of a man not given to violence but shrewd enough to outwit his wily adversary. His nemesis would tell a rather different tale.

In her own witness statement Elizabeth Russell told the Court of Star Chamber how, on the afternoon of 30 September 1594, Lovelace appeared with upwards of seventeen men, perhaps as many as twenty, all 'armed and weaponed, with swords, daggers, long staves, guns, and halberds, and with other weapons as well defensive as offensive'. These were more than just the precautionary weapons which Lovelace's men protested, in their testimony, they 'usually' carried when 'they attended their said master'. These were designed to intimidate. Having 'most forcibly and most unlawfully, and most riotously entered' her property, Elizabeth said, they proceeded to 'break up' the Porter's Lodge while she and her servants looked on in 'very great dismay and fear'. Immediately after the event Elizabeth had sought the aid of the Privy Council, sending them a petition in which she requested that Lovelace be 'called before your lordships: and himself may be committed to prison and fined'. In this document she insisted that she had arrested Lovelace's men because the lieutenant had authorized another of his servants, a Laurence Manfield, to cut down a tree illegally on the grounds of the disputed copyhold. Elizabeth claimed this was 'contrary to law and privilege of her liberties held by charter'. Lovelace had therefore infringed her rights as governess, as she presented in the imperiously expansive rhetoric of her own witness testimony in the Star Chamber, of 'all houses, barns, stables, orchards, gardens, messuages, granges, mills, lands, tenements, meadows, pastures, commons, wastes, fishings, warrens, woods, underwoods, moors, [and] marshes . . . within the parishes of Bisham and Cookham'.

In her petition to the Privy Council Elizabeth went on to say that, upon arrival to inspect the damage to her woodland, she demanded the key to the tenement but was told haughtily that Lovelace had it. It was then that she 'commanded the door to be broken open' and Lovelace's men kidnapped. These she forcibly 'brought home to her house and put them by the heels in her Porter's Lodge, saying that she would teach them to come within her liberties and keep possession against her, where he [Lovelace] knoweth no sheriff to have authority'. The men, it seems, put up some resistance, but the canny Dowager justified her action by maintaining that she had arrested them in accordance with the Queen's vagrancy laws, accusing them of being 'vagrant and wandering persons' who had ensconced themselves in her own tenement and committed 'sundry most foul and most outrageous behaviours and misdemeanours' against her.

Doubtless Elizabeth hoped to get the men to incriminate their master, but they remained tight-lipped. She was not even able to get them to disclose their names. Not having yet fully 'examined' her prisoners to her satisfaction, therefore, it is not surprising that she did not wish to let Lovelace and his men walk out of her Lodge with them. The Lovelace faction responded to Elizabeth's recalcitrance with brute force, 'then and there threatening and menacing' the Dowager and her servants 'in most desperate sort', and offering to 'beat down' anyone who attempted to 'hinder or resist' them. Elizabeth stood down, leaving the intruders to liberate the weary prisoners. In the aftermath, a stung Elizabeth declared to her brother-in-law Lord Burghley and the rest of the Privy Council, that 'so great an indignity . . . hath not been heard of to be committed against any Lady of her calling unpunished, from so mean a Gentleman as Mr Lovelace'.

While Anne Lovelace and the other defendants were cagey about Elizabeth's apparently sudden decision to oust the Lovelaces and their tenants from the copyhold, their rival's own testimony indicates that her actions were a response to pressure tactics designed to challenge her control over significant territories in Bisham and its surrounding environs. The events which took place next reinforce this and hint that a more powerful figure was lurking in the shadows, a man with an interest in limiting the powers of this most indomitable of women.

Four days later, a Thursday, the action moved to Windsor. Here Elizabeth had been residing for most of the year in a 'tower' serving as a rentable tenement attached to Windsor Castle. These lodgings, which also supplied her with a storehouse for her personal possessions, allowed her to follow her Queen when the court was in residence here and gave her a convenient base from which she could provide support for some of her allies in the vicinity.

Richard Lovelace was far from willing to countenance the Dowager's unhampered enjoyment of these advantages. In his capacity as Lieutenant of the Castle, he decided it was time she was pushed out of Windsor. He sent one of his men to bully her into submission, informing her that she had to vacate the premises immediately and leave him the key. Elizabeth refused to go with 'so sudden warning, all her stuff being there', and referred the matter to Charles Howard, Lovelace's superior, offering him 'as much Rent in money as it was worth, and more, as she had sent him before'. Lovelace's servant replied 'that he cared nothing for money'. She was stunned, but dug her heels in, protesting that 'she had paid for it with her friendship and purse already to him and his, and therefore would not remove'.

Two more nights came and went with no help forthcoming from the Lord Admiral, Howard. Was he for or against her? The answer came on Saturday, when Lovelace and his personal army of retainers 'came bravely' to the tower. With tools in tow, they broke open Elizabeth's door and 'clapped on another lock', word being sent round 'command[ing] that none should undo the lock'. Denied access to her lodging and her own possessions, the Dowager was left out in the cold autumnal air.

Shaken, but not defeated, Elizabeth picked herself up and set new legal wheels in motion. Another petition, detailing the recent indignities she had suffered, landed on the Privy Council's table. Charging Lovelace with 'riot', she demanded that he be 'put out of the Commission' of Justice of the Peace. She stopped short of explicitly charging Howard with any offence, but hinted that Lovelace was acting on his authority. It was to be the beginning of what would become an outright war with the Queen's Lord Admiral. She decided to deal with Lovelace first, protesting to the Council that if this 'spiteful injury' were to be left unpunished, then 'it is better to be a mean Justice of Peace than a Noble woman'.

The wronged Dowager resolved to take the matter to the highest court in the land, the Star Chamber, and wrote to her nephew Robert Cecil for advice. He referred the matter to her attorney, Sir Edward Coke. 'I have considered of the state of the cause between my Lady Russell and Mr Lovelace,' replied Coke on 16 October 1594, 'and I take it the Star Chamber is no fit Court for my Lady to complain in.' There was every chance a trial would not go Elizabeth's way because, as he informed Cecil, 'her stocking and imprisonment of his men is not justifiable in law'. It would be better for Lovelace to be summoned before the Privy Council and 'the quality of his offence' explained to him, in the hope that he might wish to reconcile himself to his opponent. This, he believed, was 'the best and safest course for my Lady'.

Elizabeth Russell cared nothing for safe courses. She may have been temporarily forced out of Windsor, but she would not give Howard and Lovelace the satisfaction of allowing herself to be evicted from one of her own Bisham copyholds. Lovelace might lock her out of her possessions and fell her trees, but he was not going to profit from her tenement any longer. She therefore followed Anne Lovelace's example and had one of her own men, a Francis Woodes, placed in the property, to keep any unwanted intruders out. When this came to Richard Lovelace's attention he dispatched Laurence Manfield to Bisham on a mission of 'good will'. He got lucky, for Elizabeth was in one of her more malleable moods and admitted him to her presence, no doubt curious to find out what Lovelace's next move in this feudal game of chess would be. His choice of words was unfortunate.

Manfield entreated her not to continue taking the law into her own hands but instead to 'refer the matter to any learned man in the laws of the realm'. Noticing perhaps from her expression that he had struck a bad chord, he rushed to qualify his meaning, assuring her ladyship that 'if the said learned man would say . . . that the copy of the said copyhold tenement and lands were insufficient and not good in law' then Lovelace would 'yield it up . . . without any further trouble'. This only fanned the flames. Elizabeth, who considered herself to be well versed in the law, spat back at him 'that she herself knew it to be naught', referring to the validity of the copyhold agreement, 'and therefore she would not refer the matter to any man'. Manfield merely interpreted the outburst as evidence of a lack of 'conscience', but, having failed miserably in his suit, decided that Elizabeth would respond better to a woman's touch. Before long his wife was sent to Bisham Abbey, in the hope that she would be more successful. She had the door shut in her face and 'returned home without any answer'.

The best part of a year passed in this stalemate. Richard Lovelace and his daughter put their heads together to find a solution. The strategy they resolved on triggered a new round of conflicts. In order to get Francis Woodes out of the tenement, Lovelace, on Anne's behalf, sued him for trespass. The first step in the suit was to issue him with a 'writ of *Latitat*'. *Latitat* is Latin for 'he who lies hidden'. The recipient of such a writ is deemed to be unlawfully evading the law and is required to present themselves before the Court of King's Bench in Westminster to answer the charges against them. On 2 October 1595, this particular writ was issued, with a demand that Woodes appear before the bench by 10 October. The next step in the process was for the Sheriff of Berkshire, then Richard Hide, to produce a warrant for Woodes' arrest. Elizabeth claimed that it was at this point that Lovelace and his confederate, Laurence Heyden, decided to usurp Hide's privilege by opening the seal on the writ and producing an arrest warrant 'in the name of the said Richard Hide', without the permission of either the sheriff or his undersheriff, Thomas Goodlacke. Heyden duly appeared with this document, which was sealed on 4 October, and presented it to the local bailiff, who was charged with the task of bringing in the accused.

It was not long before Woodes was tracked down. Perceiving the trouble he was in, he pleaded with the bailiff to allow him some respite, until he was 'done sowing of certain seed' on his farm. His request was granted. This was a clever delay tactic, designed to buy him enough time to 'send notice of his arrest' to Elizabeth Russell. She acted quickly, dispatching 'three or four of her servants to fetch him home', seducing the bailiff 'with good words to go with them also'. The bailiff fell for the bait. On 6 October he arrived at Bisham and, keeping a firm hold of his prisoner, was shown into the abbey. A few moments later Elizabeth made a dramatic entrance, 'accompanied with divers of her servants and others'. It was then that the bailiff realized he had walked into a trap.

Dispensing with any pleasantries, the Dowager subjected the bailiff to an avalanche of abuse, during which 'she had in most furious manner reviled, reproached, and rebuked' him. She then made an extraordinary claim. She had sole rights in Bisham, and he was a mere usurper, 'alleging her liberties to be such as that no bailiff or other officer could meddle within the same for the arresting of any'. If anyone was going to do any arresting in her dominions it would be her. A practical demonstration of her power ensued. Without warning, she made a lunge for the prisoner and 'with strong hand, most unlawfully, did rescue and take the said Francis Woodes out of the possession of the said bailiff'. If that was not enough, she proceeded to give the helpless official a taste of his own medicine and had him 'commit[ted] as prisoner unto her said prison or porter's lodge, where she detained and kept him in most cruel manner', demanding a staggering bail of 'two hundred pounds at the least'.

Until she received some kind of satisfaction, the bailiff would not be allowed to go beyond the confines of his prison or speak with anyone except in the hearing of her servants. As Richard Lovelace later revealed, the unlucky bailiff was kept in 'so close a little room' that he was left gasping for the 'open air'. Elizabeth, perhaps taking some pity on him, allowed him to take supervised walks in the garden, while she turned her attentions to the warrant for Woodes' arrest. As she perused it she became convinced it was a forgery. All garden-walking privileges were revoked forthwith, as she began a legal process against the bailiff and his accomplices. 'In truth there was never any such warrant at all made,' deposed Elizabeth in court, and she would 'be able to prove it directly'.

Although made in Richard Hide's name, the document was not embellished 'with the usual seal wherewith the said undersheriff was wont to seal warrants'. Elizabeth summoned and interviewed the undersheriff, Thomas Goodlacke, who denied any knowledge of the warrant, or of giving 'any authority to any other' to produce it. Later in court, in order 'to cover and hide the forgery', he changed his story. He was, Elizabeth insisted, offered 'rewards or promises of rewards' by Richard Lovelace and Laurence Heyden, who had colluded together in the creation of the 'false warrant'. She was not dismayed at this because she had already interrogated Hide and, before witnesses, forced him to remove his seal from his pocket. When she compared it to that which had ratified the warrant it became clear that it 'was not the seal of his office'. Heyden was therefore forced to admit in court that he had unlawfully used his own seal. If these men thought they could fool Elizabeth Russell, they were mistaken. She had proved that her knowledge of legal procedure could rival that of any man.

While the nature of the warrant was under dispute, Elizabeth was determined to keep the bailiff prisoner until she could prove that forgery had been committed. It took the intervention of the Queen to get him released. Through Edward Coke, the Lord Chief Justice of England, she sent a writ of habeas corpus, which required the named individual to appear 'bodily' before her at the Court of King's Bench in Westminster Hall. His hard warden had no choice but to relinquish him. But this was Elizabeth Russell, and not even the manner of his conduct to London would be a straightforward affair.

Eight or nine days after the bailiff had been imprisoned, the Lady of Bisham appointed three of her servants and one of her tenants to accompany him to Westminster. The party set out at the crack of dawn. After a while travelling, the bailiff realized something was wrong. This was not the usual road to London. These were 'unknown ways', hidden from the public thoroughfares. He asked the servants where they were taking him. They replied, tauntingly, 'to the Gallows'. As the byways got knottier and the taunts harsher, he began to 'verily believe . . . that she [Elizabeth Russell] had given them in commandment to have [him] hanged', and was in 'utter despair of his life'. Anne Lovelace theorized, in her deposition, that she had 'cause to suspect' that at the 'commandment of the said Lady Russell', the men had 'most cruelly and despitefully' threatened the bailiff in the hope that he could be led to incriminate himself. The whole affair was 'sinisterly practised' in order to have him committed to the prison of the King's Bench as soon as they got to Westminster.

Despite his harrowing ordeal, the bailiff arrived safely in London and was quickly bailed. His walk to freedom would be a short one. No sooner had he got to Maidenhead, within a mere stone's throw of Lovelace's home in Hurley, than Elizabeth 'caused the said bailiff to be arrested again'. Now that he was back in her dominions she 'refused to accept of any bail', defying the 'men of great sufficiency' who were offering to stand surety for him.

Meanwhile, Francis Woodes, having been liberated by Elizabeth, was apprehended and taken before another of the Dowager's enemies, Judge Gawdy, who decided to enforce the terms of the disputed warrant. Not content with consigning Woodes to prison, he chose to fine Elizabeth for his unlawful release. She remained uncowed, sending him a biting letter informing him that 'the warrant had no authority in my liberty', for neither 'sheriff nor any bailiff hath to deal in the manor of Bisham'. In order to intimidate him she threatened to involve her nephew Francis Bacon, who was beginning to have an impact as a lawyer. 'I care as little for your fine and rigour as yourself, who wallow in wealth,' she declared proudly. 'Let my man lie in prison as long as you list. I will be at no charge nor pay no fine till by law it be proved whether I have offended or not.'

Elizabeth accused Gawdy of venting his 'crabbed . . . spite and rancour' in a personal grudge against her and her children. As evidence she cited his 'malice to my daughters in Chancery for Langley parsonage'. The case to which she was referring was her suit against John Kettle of Hertfordshire for the Rectory and Parsonage of King's Langley, part of the late Earl of Bedford's estate, which she was claiming for her daughters. Beginning with 'suits and controversies' between Elizabeth and the Countess of Lincoln, the case ended with the former accusing Kettle of acquiring the manor 'by indirect and sinister practises and means underhand'. By 17 March 1595 he appeared in court, charging her with intimidation via the influence of William Cecil, 'to his great hindrance, discredit and charges'. After the failure of intermediaries to appease Elizabeth 'both by writing and by word of mouth', the Queen intervened, forcing her to surrender the property back to the Crown. Before the end of the year Elizabeth grudgingly signed the deed, adding with an indulgent flourish the familiar title 'Dowager'.

Elizabeth blamed Judge Gawdy for the loss of the case and had previously accused him of corruption in his handling of her suit for her daughters' rights to other parts of the Bedford estates. Now he was working to divest her of her privileges in Berkshire. She had little choice therefore but to ignore Edward Coke's advice. She decided to make a Star Chamber matter out of the proceedings, requesting a subpoena to be issued against Lovelace and his accomplices 'to appear and be before your Highness in your Highness' court of Star Chamber' to face trial before the Queen's 'honourable Council'. At stake were the extraordinary rights she was defending, the performance of which had profoundly shocked her adversaries, who, in open court, had expressed their disbelief at 'the supposed Privileges, Franchises, and Liberties by her presented to be belonging unto her Lordship of Bisham'.

In possession of her own prison, Elizabeth Russell thought little of usurping the authority of the sheriff and bailiff of the Seven Hundreds of Cookham and Bray, the 'liberty' under which Bisham operated at this time. She had, in effect, created her own autonomous state over which she was ultimate governess. In outright protest against the men who opposed these rights, she commissioned an imposing life-size portrait in which she stands boldly outfacing the world. She is dressed in mourning attire; her widow's hood, made according to the French fashion, flares dramatically outwards around her face. In her left hand is a small embroidered bible, behind her a large folio bible with a cloth cover decorated with eglantine roses, perhaps included to commemorate the Bisham entertainments she had devised for the Queen in 1592. If so, then she may have used the needlework her daughters had embellished with the royal flower to dress these sacred books. Elizabeth chose a Greek inscription for the portrait. It is from Psalm 55 and reads: 'O cast thy burden upon God, and he will uphold thee.' The key to this riddle is in the chilling prophecy to which these words form the prelude: 'he will not suffer at any time the righteous to move./And as for them: thou O Lord, wilt hurl headlong into the pit of destruction. The bloodthirsty and deceitful men shall not live out half their days.'

The 'righteous' Elizabeth Russell's Star Chamber suit against the 'bloodthirsty and deceitful men' who had challenged her authority in Bisham and Windsor would be resolved in 1596, just months before she threw herself into another turf war: her crusade against Shakespeare's Blackfriars Theatre.

PART FOUR

The Battle for Blackfriars

14.

Building Ambitions

Elizabeth Russell and James Burbage were building their dreams in the Blackfriars in 1595. By the close of the year Shakespeare's business partner would seal the deal for the acquisition of the buildings in which he would create the Second Blackfriars Theatre. His aspirations would clash spectacularly with those of Elizabeth, who, that summer, had been waiting to hear from Sir Richard Martin, after having submitted to him a 'request for a way or passage to certain new building in the Blackfriars'. Martin had been elected alderman of Farringdon Within, the ward which included the parish of St Anne's. This was a post he would hold until 1598. On 1 August 1595 he and his fellow aldermen met to decide whether or not to grant a licence for an entryway to a newly erected addition to Elizabeth's property.

The Dowager may have decided to expand her Blackfriars home at this time after finally realizing her long-cherished ambition of placing her daughters in royal service. Bess had become Gentlewoman of the Privy Chamber in 1594 and Nan a maid of honour the following year. This sudden elevation of her status as mother to two girls, in her own words, 'being so near the Queen', may have prompted Elizabeth to undertake these renovations, which would provide her with more room to accommodate them for longer stays during those periods when the court was settled in London. A world of prestige and privilege awaited the sisters and, as the winter months approached, Elizabeth may have been looking forward to bringing them to a freshly appointed suite of rooms during the Christmas season. She was also keen on making the trip to the court to celebrate their first New Year together in their coveted posts.

Now twenty years old, Bess had grown into a vivacious, and somewhat reckless, young woman. She relished the extravagance and sexual intrigue of the court. She had seen the splendour of Elizabeth I's Accession Day Tilt at Whitehall on 17 November 1595 and, since Elizabeth had insisted that her daughters keep her informed of their progress when they were away from Bisham, she may have written enthusiastically to her describing the valour of the jousting knights and the excitement of the twelve thousand or so spectators, who had paid a shilling each to witness the spectacle. Gossip would also have reached Elizabeth's ears about the heart-stopping moment during the post-tilt supper when the Earl of Essex had publicly insulted the Cecils. Knowing how much Robert hankered after his father's former post, he arranged for a servant to dress up as a Secretary of State while posing as one of the minions of Philautia, or Self-Love, in a mocking allegorical pageant. Essex donned the guise of Erophilus, or the Queen's True Love.

Yet the proud matriarch passed no formal comment on the fact that Essex's 'darling piece of love and self-love', as Henry Wotton called it, had been composed by her own nephew Francis Bacon, who, along with his brother, Anthony, had become part of the Earl's intelligence service. Nor did she expect to be tainted by the Queen's anger at having one of her oldest and dearest intimates derided so indiscreetly, despite the fact that the royal auditor of Essex's little play was heard to remark, before storming off to bed, 'that if she [the Queen] had thought there had been so much said of her, she would not have been there that night'. Elizabeth was too preoccupied with visions of her daughters' day in the imperial sun as she rushed to their side in December. Her fortunes, however, would take a sudden downward turn.

Arriving at court in expectation of a private royal audience, she was devastated to find herself snubbed by the Queen, who was in no mood to receive her. Her petitions were blandly returned with the command that any lady wishing to see Her Majesty could do so from afar when it pleased her to make her way in public procession to prayer. Crushed and confused, Elizabeth asked to see her nephew

Robert Cecil, hoping he could make some petition on her behalf. Discovering that he was occupied in a meeting of the Privy Council, she penned him a desperate plea, complaining, 'I came to show my duty, how glad I am to see Her Majesty's face as oft as I can, which by malice I am never afforded but when it pleaseth Her Majesty to be seen of all.' Further humiliations were to follow.

Elizabeth's lukewarm reception began to send ripples through-out the court, and when she attempted to join the procession to prayer, with the intention of catching the Queen on her way to church, she was greeted with haughtiness and disdain by the other female courtiers. Sensing the awkwardness of the situation, she tried to engage them in conversation, asking where she and the other ladies would dine that day. One of the royal hangers-on snapped back at her, accusing her of stalking the court in order to save on household expenses. This was a particularly unkind way of indicating that Lady Russell was not on the restricted guest list. Most galling, however, was the fact that all but one of her detractors – Cicely Sackville, Lady Buckhurst – were of lower, or to use Elizabeth's own sneering term, 'ordinary', social rank. Unable to bear the indignity, she left in a huff, remarking only that she had plenty of food at home and that if the Queen did not wish to make an appearance at prayers she 'would not tarry' where she was not wanted, adding with characteristic caustic wit, 'God bless me from seeking my suit that am such an eyesore.'

Smarting from what she referred to as her 'disgrace' at court, Elizabeth's despair quickly gave way to anger as she began looking for someone to blame. Suspecting that Lord Burghley had been poi-soned against her, she explained to her nephew that she believed herself to be 'maliced thus in respect of your father merely, without desert of my dishonour to my conscience known', adding with almost Shakespearean pathos, 'which sticketh so fast by me, as I shall never wipe it out of the tables of my heart while I live'. Pro-testing her loyalty to her brother-in-law, she reminded his son of her tireless work in support of the Cecils, for which, in recompense, she had acquired a 'multitude of mighty enemies'. In a final irascible flourish she observed that the aging Lord Treasurer 'either thinketh it not, or considereth not, or knoweth not what devilish dealing I have endured for him, to my shame in the world undeserved'.

Tensions between the Lord Treasurer and his sister-in-law at this time may have been due to her role as a catalyst for increasing agitation and activism among the non-conformist faction. Elizabeth was becoming ever more vocal in her antipathy towards John Whitgift, who had found a new way to target her intimates by devising a remodelled *ex officio* oath designed to ensure the uniformity of the clergy. Refusal to subscribe was viewed as an act tantamount to treason. One of those who resisted was Elizabeth's long-standing ally Thomas Cartwright, earning him a spell in the Fleet Prison. So sick and emaciated that he was 'scarce able to bear mine own clothes', the scholar wrote to Elizabeth from his cell on 13 August 1591, seeking her 'honourable mediation' to Lord Burghley. Moved, Elizabeth folded the missive and scrawled on the outside, 'Good my lord, read this through and do what good you can to the poor man,' before sending it to her brother-in-law. While he may not have appreciated being pressured by her in this way, Burghley did not ignore her suit. A grateful Cartwright was released by 21 May 1592.

Elizabeth's activities were seconded by those of her close friend Stephen Egerton, who was active from around 1585 as the preacher of St Anne's in the Blackfriars. Just before his imprisonment Cartwright had accompanied Egerton to a conference of Puritan ministers which convened to debate how best to petition the Queen for the release of those who had already been incarcerated as a result of Whitgift's machinations. Further meetings had taken place in Stephen Egerton's home in the Blackfriars. As a licensed preacher, Egerton was entitled to accommodation funded by the parish of St Anne's. The records of the Blackfriars' leaseholders of 1609 and 1611 reveal that John Wharton, who would become a co-signatory of Elizabeth's petition, was a near-neighbour of 'Stephen Egerton, Preacher'. The latter's home is described in these documents as located south of Farrant's former theatre, but overlooking the part of the premises which was converted into a Pipe Office. William More had become Chamberlain of the Exchequer in 1591 and the Pipe Office was where the financial records of the nation's exchequer were held. If Egerton had been here as early as 1596, he may therefore have been living just south of Elizabeth Russell's home, in a tenement attached to the Church of St Anne's and close to the northern boundary of the building that would soon become Shakespeare's Blackfriars Theatre. Like Egerton, Wharton was a religious activist. He had been a Marian exile along with Elizabeth's father, Anthony Cooke, becoming a schoolmaster on his return to England. In 1578 he published the egotistically entitled *Wharton's Dream*, which was dedicated to the Dowager's friend Alexander Nowell, Dean of St Paul's, praising his 'fervent zeal' and exhorting his readers to wage a fierce battle against the 'riotousness of London', armed with 'the Sword and Breastplate' of faith. In another work he appealed to the righteous to 'cast away the works of darkness, and put on the Armour of light'.

Egerton would emerge as no less a militant leader of the Puritan cause. His 'great congregation' became notorious because, as the diarist John Manningham recorded, it was made up 'specially of women'. In his sermons he urged his female flock to use their education and their voices to forward the true Church, enjoining them to think of themselves as soldiers of Christ. Moses, he informed them, was 'a good orator and a good warrior, mighty in words and in deeds'. He encouraged them to forge themselves in the same mould and use their learning to 'reprove them that do ill', even if it meant reprimanding those who sit in positions of power since the 'policy of man [is] foolishness with God'. When John Donne came to compose his satirical mock-manual, *The Courtier's Library*, he ridiculed Egerton for the attention he paid to the women of his parish. In his list of invented books he placed 'The Spiritual Art of Enticing Women, or Egerton's Sermons beneath Undergarments' beside the sardonically entitled 'Afternoon Belchings of Edward Hoby' on the courtier's imagined bookshelf. The dig was no doubt also meant at the expense of Elizabeth's coterie of activists, one of whose figureheads was the late Sir Thomas Hoby, who had given *The Book of the Courtier* to the English-speaking world.

In 1596 the Church of St Anne's was still a provisional structure. The original building had been pulled down not long after the Dissolution. Elizabeth and the rest of the largely female congregation therefore met in more clandestine fashion, in a rickety and unstable 'lodging chamber above a stair', where, in these intimate surroundings, they plotted the best means to win the hearts and minds of the populace over to the Puritan cause. It is in this space that Elizabeth saw many of her co-signatories. The church was listed as 'newly rebuilt' by 11 December 1597, under the auspices of William Watts and Henry Boice as church wardens, who would pass the honour on to Richard Field and Edward Ley the following year. In a pew that stood in a coveted spot 'right over against the pulpit' of this church worshipped William de Lawne, Elizabeth's neighbour and another of the men who would sign her petition against the nearby Blackfriars Theatre. Her own rank would have meant that she would also have customarily stood in an enviable position not far from the church's other influential worshippers.

Elizabeth was more than willing to follow the kind of radical advice Egerton was doling out in St Anne's Church, and which Egerton, Wharton and de Lawne were circulating in print. She would do so within the context of a Church that had drawn the repeated censure of the ecclesiastical hierarchy for its non-conformist practices. In her response to the latest crisis faced by the Puritans under Whitgift's regime, Elizabeth would prove that she thought little of taking on the Queen of England herself. Even Robert Cecil, who by now would have become habituated to sifting through the Dowager's strongly worded petitions, would have been shocked at the lengths to which she was willing to go to re-balance the power structure. Elizabeth had realized that placing her allies in influential ecclesiastical and civic posts would be the Puritans' only means of defence against their persecutors.

'I trust your divinity stretcheth not so far as to think every man bound in conscience,' she wrote to her nephew on 24 February 1595, 'to impair his own estate to the good of others and to his own disgrace.' She was referring to an old friend of hers, the Puritan prelate and former Provost of Eton, William Day, who 'by commandment of Her Majesty' had been ordered to move from his post as Dean of the Royal Chapel at Windsor to that of Bishop of Worcester. Elizabeth took it upon herself to countermand the order, reminding her nephew that she had tirelessly petitioned for Day's elevation to the Privy Council and promotion to a bishopric in the influential sees of either London or Durham. In suggesting the latter, she had been thinking as a military strategist, for Durham was a northern see, a gateway for Jesuits entering from the Scottish borders, and required rigorous defence.

The Queen had done everything in her power to stay Day's promotion over the years, no doubt because he was of a somewhat non-conformist bent, and became enraged when, just a month earlier, Elizabeth supported his decision to withdraw from the Worcester office where the wily monarch had wanted him safely conveyed, out of harm's way. Day deserved better, Elizabeth averred, in 'recompense of his so many years' service', adding with a smattering of sardonic mischievousness, 'I dare affirm him to have been as learned and good a preacher as any hath been of his time and more fit for a Councillor than either Bourne, Boxall or Whitgift.' Cecil may have permitted himself a sly snigger at this, for Elizabeth was deliberately comparing Whitgift, the bastion of the established Church, to two notorious Catholics who had served under Queen Mary: Gilbert Bourne, formerly Bishop of Bath and Wells, and John Boxall, one-time Dean of Windsor, both of whom had been scandalously removed from office for their treasonous resistance to the fledgling Elizabethan constitution. 'But since my lord your father and you set so slightly by so grave and worthy an old servant, of more worth than as you write,' she concluded sourly, 'I have done.'

The Queen was not impressed with the Dowager's petitions and refused to be pressured. Finding herself barred from the New Year's celebrations, Elizabeth resorted to the measure she knew had prevailed with her royal namesake in the past: bribery. Placing in young Bess's hand a purse containing £20, she asked her to deliver it personally to her royal mistress during the presentation of the New Year's gifts. Exiled from court and feeling ill, she then retired to her bed in her Blackfriars home, where she remained in a state of nervous agitation, worrying about how her daughters would fare now that she was out of favour. In January 1596 the news she had been hoping for finally arrived. Nan sent her word that both she and her sister had been showered with affection and gifts by the Queen and her courtiers, among them the Cecils and the premier ladies-in-waiting, Elizabeth's sisters-in-law, the Countesses of Warwick and Cumberland, who presented Nan with 'two carcanets', elaborate gold necklaces encrusted with jewels. Perhaps most exciting of all for these impressionable girls, the handsome and rakish Earl of Essex gave them each 'honourable New Year's gifts'. Bess, the prettier of the two – with a slender, slightly upturned nose and fuller lips – may have piqued Essex's interest, for the two would later be rumoured to have engaged in an illicit affair.

Keen to draw Cecil's attention to her expertise in courtiership, as widow to Castiglione's most famous translator, Elizabeth thanked Cecil for 'show[ing] yourself a complete courtier at this time . . . by such actions . . . fit at such occasions both for place, person, and times'. He could be assured that she would always live up to the ideals of loyalty espoused in this most influential of manuals, and could not resist dropping a hint that she would like the opportunity to have access to the Queen's 'Privy Chamber, to make me able to give a New Year's gift to Her Majesty'. She was staying put in London until she had thawed the Virgin Queen. Before long, she would get the opportunity she had been hoping for.

Lord Burghley's uncertainty about his sister-in-law's loyalties at this time may also have been due to another, more pressing, reason. This was the very year in which the Earl of Essex emerged as a force to be reckoned with, thanks in part to his association with Elizabeth's nephews, the Bacon brothers. The tensions this caused would soon erupt in a civil war at the heart of the royal court, and the Dowager would be caught in the middle.

On 3 May 1595 Essex and his sister Lady Penelope Rich were dining at Essex House. Around their table sat two of the most notorious intelligence operatives in Europe: the King of Spain's former Secretary of State, Antonio Pérez, and the Catholic agent Anthony Standen, who had once been in the service of Mary, Queen of Scots. The former was on the run from the King of Spain, and wanted for a long list of crimes, from treason to murder. Suspected of arranging the assassination of Juan de Escobedo, secretary of John of Austria, Pérez had managed to ingratiate himself into the French Court from 1593. It was from the November of the same year that he began appearing on Essex's extant record of expenses, with a monthly stipend of £20, extravagant gifts of 'Plate', and generous payments towards his travel and subsistence costs. Presents and alluring letters also came from Lady Rich, who had already acquired by this time the reputation of being one of the most beautiful women in England, due to her fair hair and dazzling black eyes. Muse to many poets and artists, Lady Rich was not only James VI's 'Ryalta' but also the famed 'Stella' of Sir Philip Sidney's sonnet sequence *Astrophil and Stella*. How could Pérez possibly resist?

The purpose of Essex's soirée was to find a way of convincing the Queen to grant the Spanish agent an extension to his commission in England. The Cecils would not have looked favourably on these attempts to augment the Earl's growing private secretariat. By the end of 1595 the Earl had taken on at least four secretaries and was looking to hire more. Pérez's usefulness to the Devereux is summarized by Camden, who reported that 'the Earl of Essex gave him entertainment and supplied him with great cost, making use of him (as an Oracle) that was so well skilled in the secrets of the Spanish Court'. He may already have proved himself an asset in 1594 over the scandalous affair of the Portuguese Jew Dr Rodrigo López, Elizabeth I's physician, who was accused of attempting to assassinate his royal patron and arrange for the murder of Pérez himself. The latter may have helped Essex pin the 'dangerous . . . treason' on López, for he was writing to Lady Rich about it this year. 'When they try to kill me in England, your ladyship arrives with your favour, like those of your letter, one of them sufficient as a strong antidote against the poisons and human violence,' he declared in typically flamboyant terms. 'Is there a fiercer lioness nor crueller beast than a beautiful lady?' Essex's apparent success in unravelling what he claimed was a plot which immediately threatened the throne, and which would eventually lead to the execution of López, allowed him to stake a claim for the utility of his own intelligence networks when pressed into the Queen's service. This made Pérez uniquely dangerous and Robert Cecil could hardly have been pleased by Essex's courting of the turncoat agent who had devised for him (much to the Earl's delight) the nickname 'Roberto il Diavolo'. If anything captures the volatility and eccentricity of the exiled Spaniard's character, it is his own motto: 'The Monster of Fortune'.

Essex was not above dining with monsters if it meant increasing the effectiveness of his burgeoning secret service. Crucial to the scheme to prise Pérez away from the French King was Anthony Bacon. Formerly in the service of Sir Francis Walsingham, he had spent thirteen years on the Continent. He was now Essex's chief spymaster, and the vast store of contacts he had accumulated while abroad made him an indispensable conduit for foreign intelligence to the Essex secretariat. By the end of August 1595 Anthony had taken up permanent residence in Essex House, a course of action his mother, Anne Bacon, had warned him against, insisting that it would bring 'some increase of suspicion and disagreement, which may hurt you privately if not publicly'. Francis's intimate association with a Spanish fugitive who had a reputation for homosexuality was equal cause for concern. On 27 April 1594 Anne demanded that Anthony encourage his brother to abandon 'that Bloody Pérez, as I so told him then, yea as a coach companion and bed companion; a proud, profane, costly fellow, whose being about him I verily fear the Lord God doth mislike'. The faults of the 'old doted pollingest [most thieving or cheating] papist' aside, the Bacons' close association with Essex could only serve, as their mother insisted, to antagonize the Cecils: 'some do think that your Brother and you make too great a note of the Earl's favour'. Anyone found consorting with this unofficial rival secretariat could be seen as a potential threat to the Cecil regime. William Shakespeare would come close to finding himself in such a position after some of his company's members were interrogated for their part in the rebellious activities of Essex and his followers, who attempted to overthrow Elizabeth I's court in early February 1601.

Shakespeare's involvement in Essex's disastrous career may have begun as a consequence of a chance event: the closure of the theatres due to the plague in 1593–4. This brought the playwright into the orbit of Henry Wriothesley, Earl of Southampton. Essex's right-hand man, Southampton would become infamous after joining with him in his ill-advised uprising against the Cecil faction and other architects of the Elizabethan constitution. With the theatres shut down, Shakespeare was unable to make a living from playing and turned his hand to writing poetry as a means of staying financially afloat. The narrative poems *Venus and Adonis* and *The Rape of Lucrece* rolled off Richard Field's press in 1593 and 1594 respectively. (Field was two years older than Shakespeare and a Stratford boy. Their parents knew each other well. The dramatist seems to have renewed an old contact just when he needed it.) Both poems were dedicated to the Earl of Southampton, who some believe to be the mysterious W. H. identified by Shakespeare as the recipient of his sonnets. 'The love I dedicate to your Lordship is without end,' he wrote to Southampton in the prefatory epistle to his *Rape of Lucrece*. 'The warrant I have of your honourable disposition, not the worth of my untutored Lines, makes it assured of acceptance. What I have done is yours, what I have to do is yours, being part in all I have, devoted yours.'

Shakespeare's association with Southampton may have been facilitated by a family connection. The Earl hailed from an activist Catholic background. During the Somerville–Arden scandal he had provided safe harbour for some of the Ardens while the investigation into the plot to murder the Queen, conducted by Sir William

Cecil and Sir Thomas Lucy, was under way. The movements of the young, glamorous and sexually ambiguous Southampton were still being watched by the Cecils in the 1590s, for the flamboyant patron had become one of the Earl of Essex's closest allies. He had also been co-recipient of Pérez's sensational autobiography, in 1593 or 1594, the *Relaciones*, which was dedicated to Essex and published under the pseudonym 'Raphael Peregrino', Raphael the Wanderer. Shakespeare would take a keen interest in the activities of this group, for *Love's Labours Lost* would contain what is undoubtedly a caricature of Pérez. It is no coincidence that the initial vignette of the character of Don Armado is offered by the King of Navarre, whose living counterpart, the Catholic Henri IV, had become Pérez's most recent employer:

> Our court, you know, is haunted
> With a refined traveller of Spain –
> A man in all the world's new fashion planted
> That hath a mint of phrases in his brain;
> One whom the music of his own vain tongue
> Doth ravish like enchanting harmony;
> A man of complements . . .

Shakespeare glances at Pérez's alias Peregrino when the character Holofernes says of him, 'He is too picked, too spruce, too affected, too odd, as it were, too peregrinate, as I may call it.' Shakespeare probably revised *Love's Labours Lost* after the Spanish agent had fallen out of favour with Essex and the Bacons, which explains the satirical edge to the pompous Armado's character. Despite this, Lady Rich remained interested in Pérez's activities, for she had written to Anthony Bacon in 1596 requesting news of 'French affairs' and of her brother's involvement in the campaign for the relief of Calais, taking the opportunity to add a postscript asking: 'I would fain hear what becomes of your wandering neighbour,' a reference to Pérez's alter ego as 'the Wanderer'. Catching the hint, Anthony Bacon wrote back two days later with a stern warning: 'your

Ladyship may well call my neighbour wandering if you knew, as I do against my will, what strange bypaths his thoughts walk in which fester every day more and more in his mind'. Shakespeare's sketch of the Spanish spy was in step with the views of the majority of the Essex circle once he had become more of a liability than a benefit to them.

The Cecils' worries about Southampton in 1594–5 did not initially dampen the Queen's affection for him, despite his explosive temper and tendency to sulk, attributes he shared with Essex. The latter, it seems, did not begrudge his young friend's successes, for Rowland White, Sir Robert Sidney's agent and a notorious gossip, reported that Southampton 'doth receive favours at Her Majesty's hands; all this without breach of amity between them'. It was Southampton's relations with the beautiful and fashionable Elizabeth Vernon, maid of honour to the Queen and Essex's cousin, that would strain his sovereign's patience. White was writing by the end of September that 'My Lord of Southampton doth with too much familiarity court the fair Mistress Vernon.' The two lovers would eventually marry in secret in 1598, with the help of Lady Penelope Rich and her brother, bringing Shakespeare's patron and the Devereux even closer together. It would prove to be an injurious relationship.

A cash-strapped Shakespeare was looking forward to returning to the theatre in the winter of 1594, when his new patron, Henry Carey, Lord Hunsdon, began working to restore the fortunes of 'my now company of Players', as he called them, assembled under the name of the Lord Chamberlain's Men since May of that year. The playwright's hopes, however, would quickly be dashed by Elizabeth Russell's associate Richard Martin.

On 8 October Hunsdon took up his pen in his Privy Council office at Nonsuch Palace, Surrey, in order to compose a letter to Martin at the Guildhall. The latter had been serving as the Lord Mayor of London since the late spring of 1593, reprising the role he had fulfilled in 1589. With the cold months closing in and the company unable to make use of their open-air Theatre in Shoreditch,

Carey's request was that the recently formed Chamberlain's Men be allowed 'to play this winter time within the City at the Cross Keys in Gracious Street'. The Cross Keys was an inn within the City walls and hence under the Lord Mayor's jurisdiction. Sensing that Martin might not look favourably on his appeal, Carey promised that the players 'will not use any Drums and trumpets at all for the calling of the people together', and even assured him that they would provide charitable aid to 'the poor of the parish where they play'. The plague outbreak had resulted in a ban on such recreational gatherings, but now that there was 'no danger of the sickness', as Carey had protested to Martin, he saw no reason why the Chamberlain's Men should not be allowed to play in an indoor venue in the City.

Despite Carey's hope that Martin would 'yield' to the players' 'reasonable conditions', his request was denied. This is hardly surprising, given that, after the terrifying Southwark riots of 1592, which had been started by feltmaker apprentices in the Blackfriars, Martin and his fellow justices William More, George More and William Gardiner had proved themselves to be no friends to the theatres. As well as being close to the Russell and de Lawne families, Martin had participated in Puritan public events with the Vautrolliers and with the Cooke sisters' friend Robert la Fontaine. He was also married to Dorcas Martin, who had engineered the powerhouse alliance between Anne Locke and Edward Dering, and promoted Thomas Cartwright during the Admonition Controversy.

Richard Martin's stubbornness meant that not only Shakespeare but James Burbage and his sons, Richard and Cuthbert, were in danger of losing their livelihood. The lease on their current premises, the Theatre in Shoreditch, was due to expire in April 1597. All attempts to negotiate an extension with the Puritan landlord, Giles Allen, had failed. James Burbage was therefore forced into a new scheme. Late in 1595 he entered into discussions with William More with the intention of purchasing the building which lay south of the Pipe Office, formerly Farrant's theatre, and almost abutting on to the western side of St Anne's Church.

Lord Hunsdon was well aware of Burbage's plans, for the latter had long been under Henry Carey's service and wore his livery. On 9 January 1596 Hunsdon wrote to William More with a business proposition. Having informed him of his 'understanding that you have already parted with part of your house to some that means to make a playhouse in it, and also hearing that you mean to let or sell your other house, which once I had also', he offered to purchase the lease to the latter again, 'giving for it either as much rent, or otherwise as any other shall, and rather more'. The tenement in question was probably next door to the projected theatre. Knowing that More had 'already parted' with the building which would become England's first purpose-built permanent indoor playhouse (if we assume that Farrant had created the short-lived First Blackfriars Theatre under the ruse that it was intended to function primarily as a rehearsal space and not a public playhouse), Hunsdon was not only undaunted by the prospect of owning further properties in the immediate vicinity but had clearly given his tacit agreement to James Burbage's innovative plan.

On 4 February 1596 Burbage signed the deed of sale. A stroke of brilliance, the deal allowed him elegantly to sidestep the prohibitions on playing in the City imposed by the Lord Mayor while acquiring a venue he could exploit all year round. His purchase included de Lawne's 'seven great upper rooms', apartments that had once formed the grand Parliament chamber, with external dimensions totalling 107 feet in length, north to south, and 52 feet in width. Located in what was also known as the Upper Frater of the extinct priory, this space would become the main body of Shakespeare's Blackfriars Theatre and was not much more than 50 feet south of William Brooke's lodgings. The floor below de Lawne's rooms included 'a great room paved', in which the famous fencing master Rocco Bonetti had previously established a school from around 1584.

An evocative description, surviving in George Silver's *Paradoxes of Defence* of 1599, records the air of glamour and sophistication which clung to this desirable property and supplies us with evidence that Burbage's acquisition of the building which had housed Bonetti's former school was on Shakespeare's mind in 1596. Brilliantly decorated round about with the coats of arms of the gentlemen who were 'his scholars', the fencing room had a theatrical flavour, with its bench-lined walls, from where Bonetti's students could view their fellow pupils' dramatic sparring sessions. Bonetti, as Silver informs us, was loved at court. The male glitterati flocked to him, despite the fact that he 'taught none commonly under twenty, forty, fifty, or an hundred pounds'. The fence-master paid for his hubris in 1587; at least, so Silver claimed. Bonetti met his match in the form of one Austen Baggar, who had challenged him to a duel with the taunt that he would out-fence him, though he 'takest upon thee to hit any Englishman with a thrust upon any button'. During or shortly after the construction of Burbage's theatre, the playwright alluded to Bonetti in *Romeo and Juliet* through Mercutio's jest that Tybalt was 'the very butcher of a silk button, a duellist'. Shakespeare at this time may not have lived far away. He is assessed for tax purposes in October of that year, based on goods valued at £5, a respectable sum. Listed as a resident of St Helen's, Bishopsgate, a parish on the same side of the Thames, he was not much more than a twenty-minute walk away from the Blackfriars. He would in any case have been very interested in the business arrangements of James Burbage as the expiry of the theatre's lease drew worryingly near.

By the time Burbage acquired it, Bonetti's school had been converted into a series of 'rooms and lodgings with a kitchen thereunto adjoining'. The chambers above this, once belonging to de Lawne, were knocked through, giving Burbage a total interior space of 101 by 46 feet in which to construct the stage and auditorium. Around this he built at least two tiers of galleries for the seating and provided Lords' rooms, or private boxes, which could be accessed only with keys. A large platform stage was constructed, with a balcony, musicians' room and 'tiring-house', where actors could change costumes and where props and sets could be kept in readiness for each performance.

An altogether more genteel structure than the Theatre in Shoreditch, here, a sense of exclusivity and intimacy predominated. A row of chandeliers set with blazing candles would bathe the galleries and stage in a mysterious glow, an awe-inspiring effect amplified by the high windows, which were, as another source tells us, 'wrought as [in] a church'. The artificial lighting also meant that the atmosphere in each production could be more precisely controlled, lending a further dimension to the play-going experience. This was augmented by the incorporation of machinery into the stage which allowed the application of the latest in special-effects technology. Trapdoors, operated from the rooms below, would allow actors and props to make sudden dramatic entrances, while winches located in specially constructed chambers above would enable gods and spirits to descend from the celestial regions. This was all being built alarmingly close to George Carey's home, which was annexed to the south of the paved hall, in what was once the friars' Infirmary. Despite the fact that Carey's mansion was three storeys in height, due to its being perched on a steep incline, it was located directly beneath the Second Blackfriars Theatre. With his new buildings, the theatrical entrepreneur gained a considerable privilege: 'free liberty' to share 'the ways now used to the said house of the said Sir George Carey', the entrances to both men's properties standing side by side.

Shakespeare was already one of eight principal sharers in the Chamberlain's Men, with a portion probably valued at around £50. As sharers were jointly responsible for a theatre's running costs and its material assets, including stage properties, playbooks, costumes and musical instruments, as well as any rental charges owing, a new venture was always a risk. In addition to the £600 Burbage paid for these buildings, he immediately laid out another £400 for the renovations. The investment promised enviable returns by anyone's standards. Made for a deeper-pocketed clientele, tickets would cost as much as six times more than those at the Globe Theatre. The most expensive seats at the Globe would be around 6d; those at the Blackfriars 2s 6d. The very cheapest ticket at the Blackfriars would buy the grandest Lord's room at the Globe. Years later, after Elizabeth Russell's death, the company would be making £1,000 more for performances during a single winter than they did from the Globe, as much as it initially cost James Burbage to acquire and remodel the whole complex. Sadly, the entrepreneur would not live to enjoy these returns, and it would later be claimed by many that the Chamberlain's Men's nemesis, Elizabeth, was to blame for his untimely demise.

Henry Carey must have wanted Shakespeare's company to succeed, for he did not attempt to put a stop to Burbage's plans. He would also have been keen to capitalize on his theatrical troupe's recent success at court. On 15 March 1595 Shakespeare was listed, alongside Burbage's son Richard, as a joint payee for 'plays performed before Her Majesty' on 26 and 28 December the previous year. It is the first record of Shakespeare as one of the 'servants to the Lord Chamberlain', a post which granted Hunsdon responsibility for the licensing of plays and royal entertainments. Theatrical patronage provided Carey with a valuable means of drawing favour from the Crown through his company's involvement in court festivities. It seems Elizabeth Russell was not so keen to see the Chamberlain enjoy such advancement.

On 27 January 1596 Robert Cecil received an intriguing letter from his aunt. On the face of it, she was up to her old tricks, requesting a place in high government for Henry Grey, Earl of Kent. Cecil's heart must have momentarily sunk. Then it would have occurred to him: his aunt barely knew Grey. The purpose of her petition was not, therefore, simply the promotion of one of her political allies. Reading on, he would have realized that her true motives were buried in an encrypted message, which he immediately understood. 'I beseech you,' she wrote, '*quod facis fae cito* [what you do, do speedily], or else I fear one of the tribe will be before him *Hercules Furens*.' When Elizabeth was conveying sensitive or dangerous information she would often resort to the use of cryptic Latin or Greek. The 'tribe', one of whom she warns would rush to occupy these vacant offices like a 'mad Hercules', if he were not prevented, was a code word for the family who, to those in the know, was nicknamed the 'Tribe of Dan'. The family in question was that of Lord Hunsdon.

The Queen had always been close to Henry Carey, who was her 'cousin'. At least, that is how she wanted him referred to. It was, however, an open secret that he was probably her half-brother, the result of Henry VIII's affair with Mary Boleyn, and thus too close to the royal blood for comfort. She and the Cecils therefore nurtured the prospects of Hunsdon and his sons cautiously, much to their eternal chagrin. By demonstrating her sympathies with the Crown's policy on the Careys, despite her kinship with Henry through her son's marriage to his daughter, Elizabeth was indicating that she was willing to have her loyalties tested. It was a bold gesture and one which came with her unswerving support for Robert Cecil's own advancement, 'wishing yourself Chancellor of the Duchy or Secretary or both with this beginning of the New Year'. While the chancellor's post was prestigious and paid well, it was that of Secretary of State, the most powerful office in the land, which Cecil had always coveted. This was the position his father, Lord Burghley, had occupied so successfully for the first fourteen years of the Queen's reign, and which the Earl of Essex also now had his eye on.

Elizabeth's curtailment of the courtly ambitions of the 'tribe' would extend to Shakespeare's next patron. If Henry Carey was so reluctant to interfere with Burbage's theatrical project, why should his son George, who went on to back Elizabeth in her action against the Blackfriars playhouse, have felt any different? Why did he put his name to the document which nearly brought an end to Shakespeare's career and his own theatrical company in the process? Was he motivated merely by the closeness of his mansion to the proposed theatre, or did he have other reasons? The answers to these questions must lie in the unique political and economic pressures under which he was labouring in 1596.

Shakespeare and Essex

With some help from Richard Field, Shakespeare had been transplanted into the circles of the literary intelligentsia after scoring the patronage of the Earl of Southampton, the man to whom the playwright referred as the 'noble god-father' of his verse. It must also have brought him to the attention of the Earl of Essex, for it was just following Field's publication of the narrative poems that Shakespeare began to compose works which channelled their satirical firepower against the chiefest rivals to the Essex faction.

By the end of 1595 Shakespeare had completed *Richard II*, which would be at the centre of the storm surrounding Essex's attempted rebellion in 1601. This controversial deposition play charted Henry IV's usurpation of the throne from an ineffectual king who had lavished too many favours on his corrupt courtiers. It is possible that Elizabeth Russell had heard about this from her son Edward Hoby before it even reached a public audience. By this time an active member of the Elizabethan secret services, Hoby may have thought of leveraging some favour at court by alerting Robert Cecil to it, for on 7 December 1595 he invited his cousin to a private performance at his home on the Strand where he could expect to see 'King Richard present himself to your view'. Hoby would have been best placed to know about such a production, as the son-in-law of Shakespeare's patron.

It was not until the following year, after the completion of *Henry IV, Part 1*, a sequel to *Richard II*, that the authorities began to take serious notice of the dramatist's output. Probably completed by the spring of 1596, this play has regaled centuries of audiences with the antics of Sir John Falstaff, one of Shakespeare's best-loved creations.

In its original conception, however, this character first stalked the boards by another name: Sir John Oldcastle. It was probably with Oldcastle as the comic lead character that the play hit the stage in London before touring in the provinces from August. The real Oldcastle, born in the late fourteenth century, was a Lollard martyr honoured with the title Lord Cobham. For Puritans such as Elizabeth Russell the Lollard sect's opposition to some of the doctrines of the Catholic Church made Oldcastle an inspiring figurehead, a forerunner of the hard-line Protestants, who was willing to die for his anti-clerical beliefs. On the title page of his *Brief Chronicle concerning the Examination and Death of the Blessed Martyr . . . John Oldcastle*, which shows a heroic Oldcastle sporting Roman armour, John Bale referred to him as 'the worthy Lord Cobham and most valiant warrior of Jesus Christ'. In 1570 a twenty-page defence of Oldcastle had been added to John Foxe's masterwork of martyrology, the *Acts and Monuments*, insisting that charges of treason against him were mere 'rumours and uncertain', perpetrated by 'prelates . . . inflamed against these Lollards' for their unconventional faith.

In 1596 Oldcastle's descendants were prominent courtiers. In fact, one of them lived just south of Elizabeth Russell: Sir William Brooke, 10th Baron Cobham. The parallel between the two Cobhams is something Shakespeare could not have avoided, for one of his principal sources, Raphael Holinshed's *Chronicles*, contained a long treatise on the noble descent of the Cobham line by Francis Thynne which included Oldcastle among the 'famous, good, just, and virtuous ancestors' who laid the foundations for the glories of the house of Cobham in the present day. Elizabeth had been friends with the Cobhams since her marriage to Thomas Hoby and cemented familial ties when Elizabeth Brooke, William's daughter, married Robert Cecil in 1589. Cecil therefore became the brother-in-law of William Brooke's son and heir, Henry Brooke, which served to enflame Essex further against this younger generation, leading him to mutter that he considered these two men to be 'my great enemies'. Essex reserved special venom for Henry, saying that he 'had just cause to hate [him] . . . for his villainous dealings and abusing of me; that he hath been my chief persecutor'. Henry Brooke had no problem returning these sentiments. 'Hearing how disdainfully my Lord of Essex speaks of him in public,' said a contemporary gossip, '[he] doth likewise protest to hate the Earl as much.' Neither Cobham, father or son, would have been amused to see their ancestor ridiculed on stage as a thief, a coward and a drunkard.

Shakespeare's play had forged an indissoluble connection between the living Cobhams, particularly Henry Brooke, and Shakespeare's Oldcastle/Falstaff. Early in 1598, after Brooke had embarked on a doomed affair with Margaret Ratcliffe of Ordsall, Essex wrote to Cecil advising him to inform Sir Alex Ratcliffe that 'his sister is married to Sir John Falstaff'. There is no record of a marriage between the two. Margaret, who had already been of a sickly disposition, pined away and died shortly after Brooke turned his attentions to a rival mistress. Nan Russell was chief mourner at her funeral. Henry's sexual conquests were probably the subject of Elizabeth Vernon's gossipy letter to Southampton in July of 1599, informing him in their shared riddling patter that 'Sir John Falstaff is by his Mrs Dame Pintpot made father of a goodly miller's thumb.'

Vernon perhaps knew that Southampton had good reason to be interested in Shakespeare's *Henry IV*, for the play had originally included a character called Harvey, who was Oldcastle's co-conspirator and joint-roisterer. This happened to be the family name of Sir William Harvey, the man who had been assiduously courting the Earl of Southampton's mother, going on to marry her in 1599. Considerably younger than the object of his affections, by some eleven years, and of limited financial resources, he was seen by Southampton as a parasite and interloper who was putting his inheritance at risk. Rumours that the affair would lead to marriage were already rife by 1597, prompting Essex to come to Southampton's aid by enlisting the help of Lord Henry Howard, who was charged with the task of convincing the Countess not to go through with a marriage that would be to the disgrace of her reputation and her son's honour.

To the right Hon:ble the Lords and others of her
Ma:tie most hon:ble privy Councell

Humbly shewing and besechyng yo:r honno:rs the Inhabitants of the Precinct of the
Blackfryers London. That whereas one Burbage hath lately bought certaine
Roomes in the same Precinct neere adioyning unto the dwelling houses of the said
right honnorable the Lo: Chamberlaine and the Lo: of Hunsdon which Romes the said
Burbage is now altering and meaneth very shortly to convert and turne the
same into a common playhouse which will grow to be a very great annoyaunce and
trouble not only to all the noblemen and gentlemen thereabout inhabiting
but allso a generall inconvenience to all the inhabitants of the same precinct, both by
reason of the great resort and gathering togeather of all manner of vagrant
and lewde persons that under cullor of resorting to the playes will come thither and worke
all manner of mischiefe and allso to the great pestring and filling up of the
same precinct, yf it should please god to send any visitacion of sickenes as heretofore
hath been, for that the same precinct is allready growne very populous;
And besides that the same playhouse is so neere the Church that the noyse of the
drummes and trumpetts will greatly disturbe and hinder both the
ministers and Parishioners in tyme of devine service and sermons, In
tender consideracion whereof, aswell for that there are not at any tyme
heretofore been used any common playhouse within the same precinct But
that now all players being banished by the Lo: Mayor from playing within
the Cittie by reason of the great inconveniences and ill rule that followeth
them, they now thincke to plant them selves in liberties. That therfore it
would please yo:r honno:rs to take order that the same Roomes may be converted
to some other use and that no playhouse may be used or kept there And
yo:r Supplyants as most bounden, shall and will dayly pray for yo:r Lo:rps
in all honnor and happines long to live

Elizabeth Russell
  Dowager
Hunsdon et 9 Sept 1602
Henry Bowes
Thomas Browne
John Crooke
Will: Meredith
Stephen Egerton
Richard Lee
    Smith
william Paddy
William de Lawne
Francis Hinson
John Edwards
Andrew Lyons
Thomas Nayle
Owen Lochard

John Robinson
Thomas Homes
Ric: Field
Will: Watts
Henry Boice
Edward Ley
John Clarke
Will Bispham
Robrt Baheire
Ezechiell Major
Harman Buckholt
John Le mere
John Dollin
Ascanio de Renialmire
John Wharton

227

1. Elizabeth Russell's petition to the Privy Council, signed by her neighbours in the Blackfriars, which prevented the opening of Shakespeare's Blackfriars Theatre in November 1596. Astonishingly, it includes the names of Shakespeare's patron, George Carey, 2nd Baron Hunsdon, and his publisher, Richard Field.

2. Portrait of Elizabeth (Cooke Hoby) Russell, possibly by an artist in the circle of Robert Peake the Elder, *c.* 1596–1600.

3. Portrait of William Cecil, 1st Baron Burghley and Lord Treasurer of England, painted by an unknown artist after 1587. The father of Robert Cecil and husband to Elizabeth Russell's sister Mildred, he was the most powerful man in England.

4. Portrait of Mildred (Cooke) Cecil, Lady Burghley, attributed to Hans Eworth. The wife of William Cecil and mother to Robert Cecil, Mildred was known for her great intellect and influence over her husband.

SERO, SED SERIO

5. Portrait of Robert Cecil, painted by John de Critz the Elder around 1606–8. One of Elizabeth Russell's chief contacts in the Privy Council, Robert became Secretary of State from 1596 and under James I was created Viscount Cranborne, 1st Earl of Salisbury and Lord Treasurer. He married Elizabeth Brooke, daughter of William Brooke, 10th Baron Cobham.

6. Monument of Charles de Maigny, who died in 1557, sculpted by Pierre Bontemps. Elizabeth Russell saw this effigy at the Celestine convent during her ambassadorial mission to Paris in 1566. It had a profound influence on the monuments she would go on to design.

7. Monument of Sir Thomas Hoby and his half-brother Sir Philip Hoby, in the Church of All Saints, Bisham, Berkshire, designed in the French style by Elizabeth Russell and probably completed by the workshop of William Cure around 1570–71.

8. Detail from the tomb of Sir Thomas Hoby and Sir Philip Hoby, Church of All Saints, Bisham, Berkshire.

9. Bisham Abbey, Bisham, Berkshire. Elizabeth Russell's former residence is said to be one of the most haunted houses in England.

10. Silver medal with the portraits of Richard Martin and Dorcas (Eglestone) Martin engraved on either side, made by Steven Cornelisz van Herwijck in 1562. The Martins were part of Elizabeth Russell's circle of radicals. Richard Martin persecuted Shakespeare's company and was involved in measures to shut down the theatre industry.

11. Monument of Sir Anthony Cooke and Anne Fitzwilliam Cooke in the Church of St Edward the Confessor, Romford, Essex. Probably designed by the Cooke sisters, this monument was created under the direction of Cornelius Cure after Anthony Cooke's death on 11 June 1576.

12. Detail from the monument of Sir Anthony Cooke and Anne Fitzwilliam Cooke, showing the four surviving Cooke sisters, from left to right, Mildred Cecil, Anne Bacon, Elizabeth Russell and Katherine Killigrew.

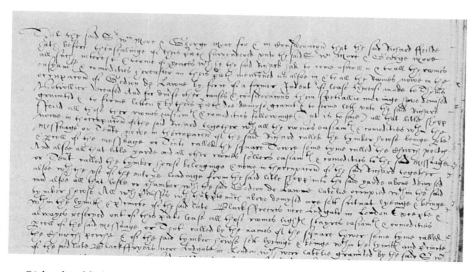

13. Elizabeth Russell's letter to William Moore, composed 9 August *c.* 1580–81. The letter indicates that Elizabeth's home comprised a 'gallery' which extended above the tenements 'let to one Peter Buram, and Lewes' [Lewis's] widow, that was a goldsmith'. The goldsmith was Lewis de Mare, who was lodged in the Round House, just to the west of the Square Tower and Timber House which would be successively occupied by Thomas Vautrollier and Richard Field.

14. Richard Field's lease agreement of 22 September 1592 for his 'little shop' in the Timber House, part of the tenement known as the Square Tower. It indicates that Elizabeth Russell lived practically next door to the printing house first occupied by Thomas Vautrollier and later by Field.

15. Monument of John, Lord Russell, in the Chapel of St Edmund, Westminster Abbey, London, designed by Elizabeth Russell and executed by the Cure workshop after his death on 23 July 1584. Relief engravings of Elizabeth's daughters, Bess and Nan, hold aloft a cartouche bearing the family's coat of arms, while a diminutive effigy of her son, Francis, who died in 1580, reposes at Lord Russell's feet.

16. Portrait of Robert Devereux, 2nd Earl of Essex, painted by Marcus Gheeraerts the Younger around 1596. The Earl sports the square-shaped beard he helped to make fashionable after his return as the hero of Cádiz. Elizabeth Russell was caught in the middle of Essex's bitter rivalry with the Cecils and the Brookes, which threatened the Elizabethan constitution at its very heart.

17. The remains of Donnington Castle, near Newbury, Berkshire. Elizabeth Russell offered huge bribes to Queen Elizabeth I in order to acquire the Keepership of the castle, a post with martial responsibilities, which was, up until then, strictly reserved for men alone. She later waged a fierce war with the Lord Admiral, Charles Howard, over her rights to the stronghold.

18. Portrait of the Lord Admiral, Charles Howard, 1st Earl of Nottingham, painted in 1602. One of Elizabeth Russell's chief enemies and, perhaps not coincidentally, master of his own theatrical troupe, known as the Admiral's Men, he clashed spectacularly with the Dowager over their competing claims to the ownership of Donnington Castle.

19. Portrait of William Shakespeare, attributed to John Taylor and painted in the 1600s. Elizabeth Russell nearly destroyed the dramatist's career after convincing the influential residents of the Blackfriars district to join her in a campaign against the Blackfriars Theatre.

20. Detail from a 1616 engraving by Cornelius de Visscher, with a theatre labelled 'The Globe'. The Globe Theatre may never have been built had it not been for Elizabeth Russell's campaign against Shakespeare's Blackfriars Theatre.

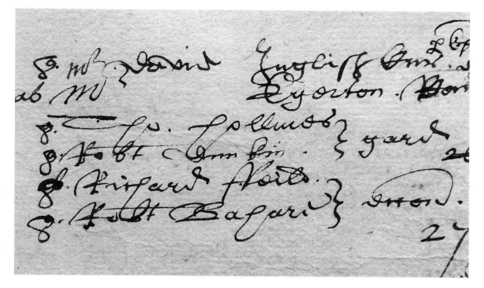

21. Church visitation records of 1592–3 revealing that Richard Field was an 'oeconomus' or 'sideman' in the Church of St Anne's in the Blackfriars. He is listed alongside fellow sideman Robert Baheire, the preacher Stephen Egerton and the church warden Thomas Holmes, all of whom also signed Elizabeth Russell's petition against Shakespeare's Blackfriars Theatre in 1596.

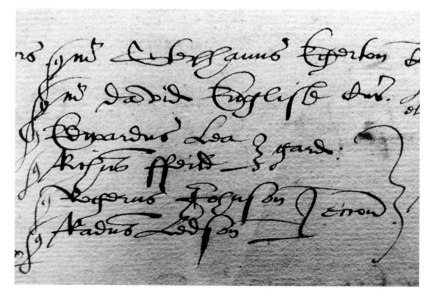

22. Church visitation records of 1598 revealing that Richard Field was a 'gardianus', a church warden, in the Church of St Anne's in the Blackfriars. He appears alongside Stephen Egerton and the church warden Edward Ley, both of whom signed Elizabeth Russell's petition.

23. Section from the *Long View of London*, by Wenceslaus Hollar, issued in 1647, showing the Globe Theatre on the Bankside and the Blackfriars district across the river. The building marked 'Beere bayting' was mislabelled and is actually the Globe Theatre.

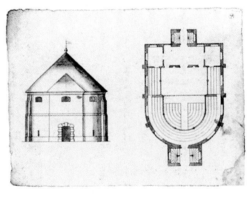

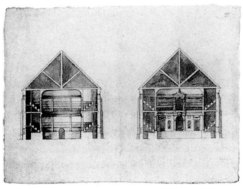

24. Inigo Jones's designs for the Cockpit Theatre, Drury Lane, produced around 1616 and possibly modelled on the Blackfriars Theatre. These schematics are probably the closest we will come to a contemporary rendering of how the interior of Shakespeare's Blackfriars Theatre would have looked.

25. Interior of the Sam Wanamaker Playhouse, London, opened in 2014. The design for this indoor theatre was partly based on what is known about Shakespeare's Blackfriars Theatre.

26. Reconstruction of Shakespeare's New Place, which the playwright purchased in 1597. With its grand courtyard fronted by an elaborate façade, it reveals something of the aspirations of the man who had succeeded in acquiring a coat of arms for his father in 1596.

27. The wedding of Nan Russell and Henry Somerset, Baron Herbert and future Earl of Worcester, attended by Queen Elizabeth I on 16 June 1600, possibly painted by Robert Peake around 1601. Shakespeare's patron, George Carey, stands third from left, holding the white staff of the Lord Chamberlain's office.

28. Monument of Bess Russell, who died on 2 July 1600, shortly after the wedding of her sister Nan. Produced by the Cure workshop for the Chapel of St Edmund in Westminster Abbey, it is the first seated monument of its type in England and sparked a new vogue for such memorials. Though it was commissioned by Nan, it was almost certainly designed by Elizabeth Russell.

29. The Somerset House conference, which took place in 1604. The Spanish delegates are seated on the left. On the right are, from the window, Thomas Sackville, Earl of Dorset; the Lord Admiral, Charles Howard; Charles Blount, Earl of Devonshire; Henry Howard, Earl of Northampton; and Robert Cecil, Viscount Cranborne. As one of the King's Men and a Groom of the Chamber, Shakespeare would have been present.

30. Exquisite miniature of an unknown woman by Nicholas Hilliard, possibly painted in the first decade of the seventeenth century. Could this be a portrait of Elizabeth Russell?

31. Monument of Elizabeth Russell in the Church of All Saints, Bisham, Berkshire. Elizabeth designed this monument to herself and her family. It may have been created under the auspices of William Cure II.

32. Detail from Elizabeth Russell's effigy. The Dowager chose to present herself wearing a Countess's crown, in defiance of the men who opposed her honorific title.

33. (*Left*) Detail from the effigy of Nan (Russell) Somerset, Lady Herbert, draped in sumptuous ermine in anticipation of her husband's inheritance of the Earldom of Worcester.

34. (*Right*) Detail from the effigies of Elizabeth Russell's sons from her Hoby marriage: Edward and Thomas Posthumous Hoby.

Oldcastle and Harvey had yet another companion, a buffoonish and drink-loving comrade-in-arms called John Russell. In the version of *Henry IV, Part 1* now known as the First Quarto, published in 1598, both Harvey and Russell are mentioned as thieves who are about to have the tables turned on them and their ill-gotten gains stolen. The character Poins tells Henry IV's son, Prince Hal, 'I have a jest to execute, that I cannot manage alone. Falstaff, Harvey, Russell, and Gadshil, shall rob those men that we have already waylaid . . . and when they have the booty, if you and I do not rob them, cut this head off from my shoulders.' Southampton was an avid theatregoer and, as one contemporary recorded, was content to pass his 'time in London merely in going to plays every day'. If he had been present at a performance of *Henry IV* he may have been thrilled to see his mother's lover lampooned in this way. One woman would have been less pleased by these unflattering theatrical portraits. John Russell's appearance in Shakespeare's play rounded off a satirical swipe at the combined Cecil–Cobham–Russell family union and could not but have incensed one individual: Elizabeth Russell, widow of the late John Russell.

These were not the only nasty surprises Shakespeare's plays held in store for the Dowager's kinsmen.

In the climactic scene of *Henry IV, Part 1*, Henry Percy, Earl of Northumberland, while conspiring against the King's life, has been killed in battle by Prince Hal. Coming across the body, Sir John Oldcastle deviously takes credit for conquering 'this gunpowder Percy'. Demanding a reward from the King on whose behalf he claims to have assassinated the rebel, Oldcastle informs the Prince, 'If your father will do me any honour, so; if not, let him kill the next Percy himself.' Viewing this scene with growing relish was a nobleman who made no attempt to disguise his identity before the common play-goers. On the contrary, he wanted to make sure he was seen in public attending Shakespeare's plays about the rise of Henry IV's glorious dynasty. This theatregoer was Robert Devereux, the Earl of Essex.

When a controversial book, John Hayward's *Life and Reign of King Henry IV*, was published in February 1599 with an incriminating dedication to the Earl which implicitly compared him to the usurping monarch, the authorities' investigations turned up witnesses willing to testify that Essex was a conspicuous presence at performances of these plays, 'himself being so often present at the playing thereof, and with great applause giving countenance and liking to the same'. Tracing his ancestry back to Henry IV, Robert Devereux was using the theatres to cultivate a public persona as the living embodiment of the royal bloodline which would produce the warrior-prince Hal; the man who would become Henry V and the heroic victor of Agincourt. While cheering on his ancestor as he watched Shakespeare's play, it would have been as clear to him as it was to those viewers who had heard about the scandalous demise of Henry Percy, 8th Earl of Northumberland, that the topical allusion to 'this gunpowder Percy' was intended to conjure the ghastly image of his future namesake's gunpowder-scorched body lying in his apartment in the Tower of London. Shakespeare was playing with fire, dredging up the events that followed in the wake of his family's disgrace in the Somerville–Arden and Throckmorton plots.

Two other noblemen wanted to be publicly associated with Shakespeare's *Richard II* and *Henry IV* plays. These were Sir Charles Percy and Sir Joscelyn Percy, younger brothers to Henry Percy, 9th Earl of Northumberland; the latter kinsman to Essex through the marriage of his sister, Dorothy. It was Charles Percy who would commission Shakespeare's *Richard II* on 7 February 1601, on the eve of Essex's failed coup, paying forty shillings for a performance at the Globe which he and his brother attended. The Percys' connection to a series of plays about their early ancestor would have doubled the impact of dramatic allusions to their father's death, reigniting old rumours of Burghley's suspected hand in it.

After the failure of Essex's rebellion it was suggested that he had commissioned Hayward's book in order to cultivate a popular image in the mould of Henry IV. His intention, his interrogators insisted, was to pepper its pages with the sentiments of 'certain seditious traitors and evil-affected subjects, against the Queen's government' by 'cunningly insinuating that, the same abuses being now in this realm that were in Richard 2 days, the same course might be taken that then was for the redressing of them'. Essex had therefore been 'plotting . . . how he might become another Henry the 4th'. Robert Cecil's own notes indicate that he was pushing for this comparison, affirming that Essex had attempted 'to make his time seem like the time of K. Richard 2 and that they were to be reformed by him like as by Hen. 4th'.

In the aftermath of Essex's botched coup in 1601 this association with the notorious usurper would have been particularly incriminating, evidence of Essex's presence at Shakespeare's *Richard II* and *Henry IV* plays serving to underscore the devilish mimicry. This was, however, a connection that had been made long before, during the interrogations into Hayward's book in July 1600, when it was concluded that the Earl 'selecteth a story 200 year old, and publisheth it this last year, intending the application of it to this time'. More alarming still were the parallels between Richard II and the Queen, as they appeared in Hayward's text:

> [A] king is taxed for misgovernment, his Council for [being] corrupt and covetous . . . The king censured for conferring benefits of hateful parasites and favourites; the nobles discontented, the commons groaning under continual taxation. Thereupon the King is deposed, and by an Earl and in the end murdered.

The damning link goes back further still, even before Hayward's book was published, to the earliest responses by Shakespeare's contemporaries to his plays. In *Richard II* the King of the play's title (probably played by Richard Burbage) recounts how the rise of Bolingbroke, the man who would become Henry IV, had been accelerated by his assiduous 'courtship to the common people':

> How he did seem to dive into their hearts
> With humble and familiar courtesy,

What reverence he did throw away on slaves,
Wooing poor craftsmen with the craft of smiles . . .
Off goes his bonnet to an oyster-wench.
A brace of draymen bid God speed him well,
And had the tribute of his supple knee . . .

In 1598, before Hayward's history hit the bookstalls, Edward Guilpin published his cutting satire against Essex in his *Skialetheia*, its title alluding to a Greek phrase meaning 'shadow of the truth'. What lay beneath the shadows of his account was Shakespeare's own depiction of the people-loving Bolingbroke, who:

. . . passing through the street,
Vayleth his cap to each one he doth meet,
And when no broom-man that will pray for him,
Shall have less truage than his bonnet's brim,
Who would not think him perfect courtesy?
Or the honeysuckle of humility?
The devil he is as soon: he is the devil,
Brightly accoutred to bemist his evil.

Like Shakespeare's Bolingbroke, Guilpin's scarcely veiled Essex-figure is presented as working 'T'entrench himself in popularity', manipulating the 'people's love' in order to feed his 'yeasty ambition'. These accusations were precisely those which were levelled at Essex by the Cecil faction, as well as by another of Elizabeth Russell's nephews, Francis Bacon, who was beginning to entertain concerns about the Earl's designs. On 4 October 1596, not long after Essex's return as the hero of an expedition to Cádiz, Bacon sent him a long treatise of sage advice. He reminded him that his 'popular reputation' should be 'handled tenderly' and that he should 'take all occasions to the Queen to speak against popularity and popular courses vehemently', lest she begin to harbour 'a conceit that you have higher imaginations'. When Hayward came to compose his book, he probably made use of the already established connections between Essex and Bolingbroke/Henry IV, affirming that the latter 'was not negligent to uncover the head, to bow the body, to stretch forth the hand to every mean person, and to use all other complements of popular behaviour, wherewith the minds of the common multitude are much delighted and drawn'.

Guilpin's satire would have made little sense had at least some of his readers not already been aware of a link between Essex and Shakespeare's *Henry IV* cycle of plays, a connection which Hayward was quick to exploit. This is given further credence by the possibility that the play 'Harey the V' (*Henry V*), staged by the Admiral's Men under Lord Admiral Charles Howard's patronage from November 1595, was intended to forge a patriotic association between Henry V's victory at Agincourt and Essex's upcoming military campaign in Cádiz, which had been planned from the autumn of that year. Essex and Howard would take joint command of the mission in the spring of 1596 and it would have made sense for Howard to have backed such a play, which was performed at the Rose Theatre eight times by the end of February 1596.

This play's first performance coincided with the publication of a mysterious text about *The Next Succession to the Crown of England*. This was issued from a foreign press under the pseudonym 'R. Doleman' and was dedicated to Essex. Drawing attention to his apparent patron's descent from the 'noble ancestors' of the Hereford and Essex lineage – the houses associated with Bolingbroke's heritage – Doleman made the dangerous insinuation that 'the people' looked to him for a solution to the uncertain succession for 'no man is in more high or eminent place or dignity at this day in our realm, than yourself'. The publication caused a temporary rift between Essex and the Queen, yet the Earl and his coterie seemed quite happy to think of themselves in relation to the group of plays which spawned the various manifestations of Shakespeare's Oldcastle/Falstaff. In one of his letters Sir Charles Percy reflects on the 'country business' which kept him away from court, saying jocularly, 'If I stay here long . . . you will find me so dull that I shall be taken for Justice Silence or Justice Shallow.' Silence and Shallow are characters from *Henry IV, Part 2* and the popular spin-off to the *Henry IV* plays, *The Merry Wives of Windsor*.

Could Essex have knowingly commissioned Hayward's *Life and Reign of King Henry IV*? It was one thing to cheer on the heroic exploits of your ancestors in the festive surroundings of the theatre, but quite another to be named as a dedicatee of a work which foregrounded the activities of a usurper from whom that familial descent had been claimed. During his interrogation on 11 July 1600, Hayward confessed 'that presently after the book was printed, Wolfe the printer thereof carried the same to the Earl of E[ssex] and about a month after the epistle was taken out'. If the dedicatory epistle was issued with a printed text which Essex had not yet seen, as Hayward implies, then another possibility presents itself.

Two days later John Wolfe was questioned and confessed that when the book first came to him it had no epistle. Seeing this, he 'requested then to dedicate the book to some man of honour and reputation'. He and Hayward then had 'some conference' between them about it, during which Wolfe persuaded him 'it might be dedicated to the Earl of Essex for that he was a martial man'. Dedicating the book to Essex was thus neither the Earl's nor Hayward's idea, it was Wolfe's. Could Essex have been the victim of a sting operation, one which ingeniously turned his own propagandist devices against him?

The printer in question, John Wolfe, was a bit of a maverick. He had left unbroken few of the legal regulations governing printers, and was the kind of man who followed the scent of lucre. He was interrogated and imprisoned for his part in Hayward's book, but was incarcerated for only fourteen days, after which he went about his business. Having been inducted into the Stationers' Company in 1583, Wolfe had printed books for Richard Field and, along with Thomas Vautrollier, had worked on the anti-Catholic projects masterminded by Elizabeth Russell's brother-in-law Lord Burghley. He came to the attention of the latter for engaging in the illegal practice of obfuscating his own identity and misrepresenting the origin of his output in the title pages to his books. Far from punishing him for this, William Cecil swiftly inducted him into his service, employing him to release propaganda with misleading imprints in order to outwit the nation's Catholic enemies. Among the works with which he was entrusted was the Italian edition of the pamphlet that trumpeted the Somerville–Arden conspiracy to the world, Burghley's *Execution of Justice*, which had implicated Shakespeare's kinsmen in the Throckmorton plot. The French and Latin versions of this work were printed by Vautrollier.

William Cecil's strategy had frequently involved employing printers and booksellers who had contacts abroad, including the likes of Vautrollier and Ascanius, and this was true of Hayward's printer. 'Wolfe, leave your Machiavellian devices, and conceit of your foreign wit, which you have gained by gadding from country to country,' said one of his many detractors. Closer to home, he may have known Elizabeth Russell, for he issued a reprint of *The Courtier* in 1588. When in London he operated a stone's throw away from the Blackfriars, just north-east of the homes of the Dowager and Lord Cobham, near the great south door of St Paul's Cathedral – a good location for one of the Privy Council's spin-doctors. He was therefore fully entrenched in the community which was responding to Essex's publicly lauded connection to Bolingbroke's lineage between 1595 and 1601.

It can probably never be proved that Elizabeth's nephew Robert Cecil used Wolfe to frame Essex in 1599. What is clear is that the anxieties which made the printer's text so damaging to the Earl's reputation had their beginning in the years leading up to Elizabeth's closure of the Blackfriars Theatre, the venue which would no doubt have been used to stage Shakespeare's popular *Henry IV* cycle on her very doorstep. That this is the case is indicated by the likelihood that Shakespeare began capitalizing on his recent success with *Henry IV, Part 1* almost straight away, writing the sequel, *Henry IV, Part 2*, replete with further unflattering portrayals of Oldcastle and John Russell, probably even as James Burbage's new theatre was under construction. He had no reason to doubt his new creation would prove as much a triumph as its predecessors, for the man who had licensed these dangerously topical histories was the same who had examined the gunpowder-smeared body of Henry Percy, 8th Earl of Northumberland, in 1585. In short, the chief promoter of the Oldcastle play – the Lord Chamberlain, Henry Carey – was one of the few men in England who knew the intimate details of the Throckmorton conspiracy and Percy's strange death. With Carey's tacit backing of Burbage's latest theatrical enterprise, Shakespeare was looking forward to an explosive opening season at his new playhouse. His fortunes, however, were about to change.

On 21 July 1596 Shakespeare's patron, Henry Carey, finishing his supper, suddenly felt ill. Calling his son George to him, he expressed his dying wish that he be the sole possessor of his worldly fortune. 'Her Majesty hath sent me sundry gracious promises,' he announced, 'that in the word of a Prince, she would fully relieve my estate, which if I shall not live to enjoy, that she will confer it upon mine. And therefore doubt not but she will bestow mine Offices upon you.' By the end of the next day he would be dead and George left with the burden of saving the family from the financial ruin which had been slowly spreading its shadow across the 'tribe'.

With the revenue from George Carey's inheritance amounting to a paltry £366, around £40,000 of purchasing power today, the future of the Hunsdon line depended on the Queen's willingness to keep her promise. While he was given the post of Captain of the Pensioners the day after his father's death, other lucrative offices, including that of Lord Chamberlain, which carried remuneration of £166 13s 4d per year, and a place as a Privy Councillor, were held back. In total the revenues from his father's public posts amounted to a potential £2,147 3s 4d; income Carey could not afford to lose. No doubt it was the intercession of the Cecils which saw the vacant chamberlainship pass immediately to their kinsman William Brooke, Lord Cobham. Shakespeare had lost the man whose protection had nurtured both the Chamberlain's Men and the *Henry IV* plays. With the downturn in the dramatist's professional life came a more personal tragedy. On 11 August 1596 he buried his eleven-year-old son, Hamnet.

George Carey took over from his father as patron of his theatrical troupe, which was now assembled under the name of 'Lord Hunsdon's Men'. This did little to soothe Shakespeare's own anxieties in what must have been one of the most perilous periods of his career. Without Henry Carey's former offices, his son was powerless. But the Cecils were not finished with him yet. When no further grants for the former Lord Chamberlain's other vacated posts were made to George Carey he became desperate. A stream of petitions, growing in urgency, began to land on Robert Cecil's desk. One begged him to intercede to the Queen and 'play that part of a friend to me and of a faithful councillor to her' by reminding her of 'the nearness of my blood' in hopes that she would relieve his 'poor estate' and 'burden of a naked honour'. These pleas fell on deaf ears and by 20 September he was writing to Cecil again, this time with a veiled warning that 'the eyes of the world' were now watching to see 'what respect Her Majesty will carry to our house, so near in blood to hers and so little advanced in her reign of so many years'. The Queen would not have taken this kindly, and it is clear that in another missive, dated 23 November, he was forced to defend himself strenuously against some damning accusations:

> [I]t is neither new nor unusual for Princes to yield more plentiful sap to the small twigs of their own branches, than ever my hopes shall aspire unto, my ambition reaching but not to be thought unworthy to succeed my father . . . which I hold shall be honour for Her Majesty to give and disgrace for me not to receive.

Carey was responding to very troubling charges of treasonous conduct, for Cecil had already informed him, back in April, that the Queen was 'somewhat out of quiet' with him because she suspected his being engaged in 'some vain project' at the instigation of an unnamed 'cozening companion' who had urged him to 'go to sea' without royal leave. Carey was involved in the preparations for the

Cádiz voyage. Could he have been planning on joining Essex without the Queen's permission? She, for her part, was content to deliver a veiled threat, informing him that 'some others that were more maliciously affected, imputed your purpose to be grounded upon some particular cause of discontentment'. A heart-stopping insinuation.

In the weeks leading up to Elizabeth Russell's closure of the Blackfriars Theatre, Hunsdon was walking a tightrope. He could not afford to anger the Queen or his mediators in the Cecil faction. His livelihood depended on it.

16.

Detective Dowager

In 1596 the nation was in a state of crisis and the Earl of Essex was turning this to his advantage. With Henri IV of France having recently converted to Catholicism and under immense pressure to sign a truce with Spain, England was open to an attack from its perennial nemesis, the dreaded Spanish Armada. On 10 April 1596 this looked like a terrifying possibility as news spread that Calais had been raided and taken over by the Spanish. It was rumoured that the Queen had heard the sound of cannons blasting the walls of Calais from her palace at Greenwich. With the nation within earshot of disaster, the people were afraid and needed a champion.

Four days later, with Essex having been appointed leader of a 6,000-strong army 'for the relief of Calais', the Queen stepped aboard the *Due Repulse* to rouse the navy as they prepared to meet the Earl, who had gone ahead to Dover, where he was surveying the French coastline for Spanish ships. While on board she penned a missive of encouragement, urging him to lay aside his squabbles with Robert Cecil and work with him against a common enemy. 'God cover you under his safest wings, and let all peril go without your compass,' she wrote. 'Believe Cecil in the rest.' Cecil, however, had other ideas and persuaded the Queen to limit aid to the Catholic French King. Essex tried to reason with him, sending an impassioned plea in which he explained that without the necessary funds and force of arms the mission was doomed, and the consequences would fall hardest on the Crown. 'I protest I apprehend her dishonour and danger,' he complained, 'as the pangs of death that were gripping my heart.' Cecil remained unmoved and the Calais enterprise met with limited success.

By the end of July an undaunted Essex would find a way to live up to the public persona he had so carefully crafted through his association with Shakespeare, leading an expedition to Cádiz and returning as its hero on 10 August. While he was away news reached the Cecils that between them Essex and the Lord Admiral, Charles Howard, had knighted sixty-three of their comrades-in-arms, thirty-six under Essex's personal jurisdiction. It was one of the largest mass-knightings in Tudor history, and to Burghley and his son it looked as if the eternal thorn in their side was assembling a private army.

The public's response to Essex's success could not have been more different. With the backing of John Whitgift, who had become increasingly sympathetic to Essex's cause, sermons were given in London proclaiming, to the 'great applause' of the congregations who heard them, the Earl's 'justice, wisdom, valour, and noble carriage in this action'. On the streets the hawkers of doggerel rhymes lauded him as greater than Hercules, the conqueror of the bountiful Cádiz. Shakespeare, it seems, was keen to chime with the public mood. In *Romeo and Juliet*, which may have been composed around this time, it is possible that he alluded to the Cádiz raid through the compelling image of Queen Mab, who 'driveth o'er a soldier's neck, / And then dreams he of cutting foreign throats, / Of breaches, ambuscadoes, Spanish blades.' The most explicit allusion comes in another play composed in 1596, *The Merchant of Venice*, in which the Spanish galleon captured in the invasion, the *San Andreas*, makes an appearance as the 'wealthy Andrew'. It is significant that Shakespeare drew attention to one of the prize treasures captured in Essex's raid in a comedy about a devilish Jew. This could only have reminded audiences of Essex's apparent foiling of the plot to poison the Queen, masterminded, so the sleuthing Earl claimed, by the Portuguese Jew Dr Rodrigo López.

Essex's initial jubilation at hearing reports of his growing fame in England quickly turned to dismay when he discovered that the Cecils had taken advantage of his absence to appoint Robert Cecil Secretary of State on 5 July. Worse news awaited him when he landed at Plymouth, where he was greeted with a message from his secretary, Edward Reynolds, informing him that Lord Cobham's son, Henry Brooke, had the Queen's ear and was busy casting a shadow over his exploits in Cádiz. There was no better time for his slanders to take effect. When the English mariners laid siege to the town, they had found the castle and the surrounding houses of eleven of the wealthiest citizens stocked with ducats and fine wares. In addition, merchants' shops, full to the brim with gold and silver plate, tapestries and highly prized silks, velvets and taffetas, chests of sugar, expensive wines and exotic pelts, stood waiting to be pillaged for the Queen's own coffers. When the value of the plunder was calculated, however, the figures did not add up. Suspicions that the lion's share of the booty had been 'embezzled' were aroused when the £2,450 retrieved from the castle did not tally with earlier reports that the keep alone harboured £11,000. The total value of the goods pillaged from the Cádiz raid amounted to £12,838, which paled into insignificance beside the Spaniards' own estimation of a loss of 5 to 6 million ducats.

An investigation was launched and on 7 September Essex was summoned to court. The next day he wrote to his chief intelligence operative, Anthony Bacon, protesting that 'my Lord Treasurer and Sir Robert Cecil did before the Queen contest with me'. Blamed for failing to secure the Cádiz loot 'for Her Majesty's profit', he received a severe dressing-down from Robert Cecil during a tense interrogation. '[T]his day,' he wrote grumpily, 'I was more braved by your little cousin than ever I was by any man in my life, but I am not, nor was angry, which is all the advantage I have of him.' But there was something else troubling Essex: Anthony Bacon's aunt. News had reached his ears that, while he was detained at court, she had been meddling in his political affairs. He was beginning to suspect that she had had a hand in the Cecils' sudden clampdown on the activities of his secretariat. Surely it could be no coincidence that while he was safely under the Cecils' watchful gaze, she had been working to dismantle his spy network from the inside, beginning with Anthony Bacon.

Suddenly Elizabeth's activities over the past three years seemed to take on a new, and altogether more alarming, significance. Essex had been assiduous in his promotion of the Bacon brothers. When Sir Gilbert Gerard died, a rare opportunity presented itself to the Essex faction. Gerard had been Master of the Rolls, an influential judicial office in the Court of Chancery. If the Queen did as she was expected and awarded the newly vacated post to Sir Thomas Egerton, the latter's own office of Attorney General would be there for the taking. In the spring of 1594 this is exactly what happened. Essex made a bid to secure Egerton's former post for Francis Bacon, approaching Robert Cecil directly. Unsurprisingly, they almost came to blows over the issue. 'I wonder your Lordship would go about to spend your strength in so unlikely or impossible a matter,' said Cecil dismissively when Essex brought up the subject. 'Can you name one precedent for the promotion of so raw a youth to so great a place?' Essex's blood began to boil, for Cecil was younger than his 34-year-old cousin. 'Digest me no digestions,' the Earl barked back, 'for the Attorneyship for Francis is that I must have, and . . . whosoever getteth the office out of my hands for any other before he have it, it shall cost him the coming by.'

Perhaps he should have said 'it shall cost her', for a matter of weeks after Essex began petitioning Burghley, Elizabeth Russell attempted to block Egerton's promotion. She had decided the office of Master of the Rolls should be awarded to her 'cousin' James Morrice, who had openly fought against Whitgift's *ex officio* oath in a fiery speech of denunciation delivered in Parliament. He was a powerful Puritan ally and Elizabeth plotted to work on Burghley's latent non-conformist sympathies through his son. 'Oh, good nephew, the gravity, wisdom, care of maintaining law of the land, learning, and piety of the man I find such, as in my very heart,' she wrote grandiloquently to Cecil. 'I could be content to live with bread and water' as long as Morrice was elevated to the Rolls 'for private good of your good father, that lacketh such a one to back him'. But why stop at the Rolls? Elizabeth insisted that Morrice also be made Privy Councillor – and here proceeded an artful jibe at

Whitgift for the inquisitorial nature of his regime – for the good of 'God's church and maintenance of the state by the laws of the realm and not by rigour'. Elizabeth's petition was a low blow to her nephew's prospects of promotion and, if it had struck home with Burghley, would have severely dented Essex's powerbase in the upper reaches of the judicial establishment.

Unfortunately for both Essex and the Dowager, the Cecils remained indifferent to their pleas. Neither, however, would lay down their petitioning pen. The death of Sir John Puckering, Lord Keeper of the Privy Seal, on 30 April 1596, saw Egerton immediately promoted to the vacated office. The post of Master of the Rolls once again came under dispute, and once again Essex championed Francis Bacon's cause. Elizabeth was, as ever, sensitive to the impact that the redeployment of such legal offices could have on the broader political structure, and less than a month later began pulling strings for another of her associates, Matthew Dale, who, like Bacon, had been trained in the Inns of Court and who had been a colleague of James Morrice at the Middle Temple.

Hours after the death of the Master of Requests, Ralph Rokeby, on 14 June, she wrote to Cecil, explaining that Dale was the aptest candidate for the vacated office, which afforded jurisdiction over the legal affairs of the Crown's servants, 'since his white hairs show him to be so ancient a lawyer, so wise men think him most fit'. In a note intended to exploit Cecil's sense of moral obligation to her sister Mildred, she added that the able candidate she had selected 'himself cometh to you in your mother's name'. Success in this venture would have meant having an intimate of hers in a senior office which annually dealt with a larger number of cases than Chancery. With the failure of her previous attempts at acquiring the Mastership of the Rolls for Morrice, this was a shrewd strategy. There was, however, a more calculating purpose behind her pleas. 'And let not Doctor Caesar, a civilian,' she added contemptuously, 'deprive him of the fee due by patent to a temporal lawyer and not to a civilian, who beside hath enough already, if these days could acknowledge what is enough.' The wealthy and influential Julius Caesar was a close friend of both John Whitgift and the Earl of Essex. Lady Rich had conducted a correspondence with him, offering him the unfailing support of the Devereux.

While Elizabeth could not prevent Caesar from becoming Master of the Court of Requests, she was clearly matching Essex's tactical bids for political sway move for move. To Essex, the fact that she was now working her wiles on the fulcrum of his intelligence service while he lay, in his own words, 'tied to this place', an unofficial detainee at court, was troubling. He was unable to reach Anthony Bacon, and there was no telling what damage she could do. To be on the safe side, from now on the Earl would keep a very close watch on the clever Dowager.

On the morning of 8 September 1596, just two months before she targeted Shakespeare's Blackfriars Theatre, Elizabeth Russell took a coach to Paris Garden, where, with only one gentlewoman for company, she boarded a wherry to Essex House near the Strand to visit Anthony Bacon. This was to be no mere social call. Elizabeth had come direct from Nonsuch Palace and what had passed between her and the Lord Treasurer while she was there was a matter of national security. Essex had created his intelligence network in order to put himself forward as a candidate for the Secretaryship. Now that this was no longer a possibility, to what use would he put his secret service? Elizabeth was about to turn detective to find out.

Upon arrival she was shown directly to Anthony Bacon, who had taken up residence with the Earl at Essex House from August of the previous year. Managing the vast quantities of intelligence which passed through Essex's headquarters, relayed by his agents on the Continent, in Ireland, Scotland and on home ground, was a huge undertaking and Bacon had to be on call every hour of the day. Essex House became a satellite court, a meeting place for the discontented young glitterati of the Elizabethan regime, bustling with foreign envoys, spies and, worst of all, Catholics. And Bacon's friends were dangerous. While living in France he had become close to the now Catholic Henri IV and found himself embroiled with the most notorious double agents in Europe. In addition to this, he had been charged with the sexual abuse of male minors in his service. A swift cover-up prevented news of the latter scandal from reaching a wider audience in England. The rest, as the Lord Treasurer and his sister-in-law well knew, presaged a wider crisis which had to be dealt with head on. Now, standing before her nephew, Elizabeth was keenly aware how much depended on her ability to prise Bacon away from Essex's grasp.

'I do exceedingly long to hear,' wrote Essex to his spymaster just after his remarkable interview with Elizabeth, 'the charge of my Lord Treasurer, and your particular answers.' Unable to leave court because of the 'extraordinary business' which followed his return from Cádiz, he asked him 'to set them down in writing'. Not one word that left Elizabeth Russell's lips would escape the Earl's attention. The unfolding events at Essex House mirror closely the charges Elizabeth herself set out in her own letters immediately after her meeting with Bacon. We can be fairly certain, therefore, that his account is accurate.

Elizabeth's opening address came replete with the niceties which Bacon sardonically referred to as his aunt's 'kind enchantments'. He could guess what was coming and braced himself for a tough interview.

'Marry, nephew,' she began, slipping with well-oiled alacrity into the role of the wounded kinswoman, 'my heart . . . is chocked with griefs to hear that which [you] do.' Then she paused, setting her features with the most wistful expression she could muster, scanning his face carefully to see if he was 'dismayed'.

'Nay good madam, go on, I beseech you, and spare not to charge an innocent heart with advertisement of misreports or wrongful imputations,' he coaxed, showing he was equally adept at playing the victim, and no doubt exploiting for effect his weak and perennially sickly frame. All he wanted to do, he assured her, was 'to ease your heart by satisfying you thoroughly'.

'Well, nephew, seeing you so armed,' she replied, 'I will not flatter you a whit, but will tell you that all your bodily pains grieve me not so much as your indisposition or alteration of your mind.' From this point on the meeting became an inquisition – as meetings with Lady Russell were apt to – and she accused him of being 'corrupted in religion, factious and busy, undutiful and unnatural'. When this failed to elicit the desired response more specific charges were made. '[A]nswer my proofs,' she demanded, 'for the first point, your familiarity with Standen, a fugitive, and Wright, a seminary priest . . .'

These were names to conjure with. Standen had lived with Bacon in France and had been arrested on suspicion of spying for the King of Spain. Thomas Wright's career was no less troubling. A Jesuit priest, he was currently in custody in England on suspicion of treasonous dealings with the Spanish intelligence services. Like Bacon, he had previously been in Walsingham's employ, and Burghley had hoped to attract him to his own intelligence service with the intention of tapping him for information on the Spanish court. Snatched from Burghley's grasp, he became another of Essex's growing band of renegade intelligencers. These men were not the only Catholics Bacon and Essex had attracted to their faction.

Losing none of his self-possession, Bacon pre-empted what he knew his aunt was keeping back as her trump card. 'Give me leave to help you, madam,' he offered wryly, 'and my Lord Harry, whom you should have done the honour to have named first.'

'Aye . . . and he too,' she replied tetchily, with some justification on her part, given Lord Henry Howard's reputation as a Catholic who had been secretly nurturing ties with King James VI of Scotland. Elizabeth's sister, Anne Bacon, had already informed her son in an encrypted letter, all incriminating names concealed in Greek cypher, 'Beware in any wise of the Lord H. Howard, he is a dangerous intelligencing man; no doubt a subtle Papist inwardly and lieth in wait. Peradventure he hath some close working with Standen and the Spaniard [Pérez]. Be not too open, he will betray you to divers, and to your aunt Russell.' Though she had always been very close to her sister, Anne was aware that Elizabeth had too much to lose if the Queen's official secret services decided her loyalties to her Bacon nephews conflicted with their interests. Anne warned her son 'to be more circumspect and advised' in his dealings with the Cecils for 'the father and son are affectionate, joined in power and policy', and they had spies everywhere.

Elizabeth made it perfectly plain to Anthony that neither she nor Lord Burghley would countenance his association with these perfidious double agents, who were now clearly 'so inward with you and such companions as none can be greater', least of all Harry Howard. He was a kinsman of the Lord Admiral, Charles Howard, who was making life difficult for her on her estates in Bisham and Windsor. By an extraordinary coincidence, it was at this point in the interrogation that Bacon was interrupted by his servant, who entered the room to inform them that the Lord Harry Howard had come to Essex House requesting a personal conference with Bacon. It must have been with a knowing look of half-concealed amusement that he then went on to tell his master that Howard, upon hearing that the Lady Russell was present, had bolted for the door and taken to his heels, making 'no less haste to go away'. He was fully aware that Elizabeth detested him and he wisely resisted a confrontation. As it turns out, he would not evade her for ever, but for now he had unwittingly played into her hands. Bacon could see, as he later informed Essex, that his aunt 'was glad of such an advantage', and it was all the prompting she needed to drive her point home.

'The daily resort of these unto you makes you odious. The second point,' she added, recovering her former train of thought, 'you are too well known and beloved in Scotland to be a true Englishman, and busy yourself with matters above your reach, as foreign intelligence, and entertainment of spies.' There were more serious allegations to follow. At this time Elizabeth would come closer than anyone else had ever dared – even the Cecils – to openly accusing Essex and Bacon of treason: '[Y]ou do ill offices, not only with the Earl here, but in France, and Scotland by means of your acquaintance. In one word, you oppose yourself more directly than any nobleman in England durst do, how great soever.'

For a moment it looked as if Elizabeth had the upper hand. With these courageous insinuations she had overstepped her original commission in order to give her nephew a stern warning in terms which would be staggeringly prescient. She had, however, under-estimated him.

'I confess to you freely, good madam,' he protested, 'being to plead for the life of my reputation at the bar of so near and dear a friend . . . I am resolute . . . to prove as clearly as daylight myself no way guilty neither in part or in whole.' As for his religion, had he not been honoured by the most pure of faith? Had he not been entertained in Geneva by the great Theodore de Beza, who dedi-cated his *Meditations* to his mother, Anne Bacon, 'for my sake'? With regards to Standen, he had gone to a great deal of effort to entice him to Burghley's service, only to find that the Treasurer showed nothing but 'carelessness and contempt of him', much to the Bacons' own disgrace. Touching Wright, it 'had pleased Her Maj-esty . . . to extend her mercy' to him after receiving 'particular infallible arguments of his loyal and dutiful heart to his Sovereign and country, whatsoever his religion'. He had, in any case, been encouraged to enter the intelligence services by William Cecil, from whom he had received 'nothing but fair words, which make fools fain, and . . . who had inned my ten years' harvest into his own barn without any halfpenny charge'. Far from being a traitor, he had all along, he insisted, been acting in the Queen's interests.

By way of proof Bacon placed before his aunt's eyes a letter of commission from Walsingham, thanking him 'in Her Majesty's name' for his services with 'assurances of her princely favour and good opinion'. As Elizabeth read the epistle her expression changed.

'God's Body, nephew,' she cursed, 'thou art mightily wronged, for here is not only warrant but encouragement.'

With this advantage he began pulling on her heartstrings, claim-ing that Lord Burghley had harboured a secret grudge against him, a fact which had even come to the attention of a perplexed Queen: 'Her Majesty hath censured with admiration, what should make him so loath, yea so backward, to advance his nephews, which God knoweth my brother and I have found most true.' With his interrogator softening, he added a further gloss to his tale, informing her that his mother, her beloved sister, had been spoken to harshly by Robert Cecil, who had promised her that nothing would dampen the flames of his 'deadly feud' with his cousin Anthony, 'swearing that he held me for his mortal enemy, and would make me feel it when he could'.

Hearing this, Elizabeth exploded. 'Ah, vile wretched urchin . . . Is it possible?' Cecil, whom the Queen referred to affectionately as her 'little pigmy', had inherited a condition which left him small in stature, with marked curvature of the spine. Elizabeth, despite her own problems with her back, was always quick to exploit the insecurities of others when she was angry, and Bacon knew it. Chiming in with the sniping edge of her wit, he begged his aunt to pay no heed to Cecil's threats, quoting the Gascon proverb: 'Heaven does not hear the braying of an ass.'

'By God,' she answered, now in a more playful tone, 'but he is no ass.'

'Let him go for a mule then, Madam,' he responded smoothly, 'the most mischievous beast that is.'

With that, she exploded again, but this time with laughter, ending the meeting by singing her nephew's praises and lamenting the 'monstrous insolency' which had brought about the besmirching of his reputation. Bacon, knowing that his aunt always liked a good joke, had deftly managed to change the mood of the interrogation. What Elizabeth did not then understand was that the joke was on her.

For the time being Bacon had turned the tables on the Cecils. But how long would this last? Elizabeth had, as Essex read in Bacon's account, delivered a 'parting blow' to her nephew before leaving. She wanted him to set everything he had told her in writing, for Burghley's approval, and what effect could witty repartee have before the aged councillor's analytical eye? Bacon found an excuse to stall, but he would not dodge his aunt for long. That evening Essex had a restless time of it. As he lay in bed, unable to sleep,

Elizabeth's words, he confessed to Bacon the next day, 'ran in my head all the night after'.

Elizabeth Russell went back to Burghley with a full report of her meeting with Bacon. Offended at the charges that had been laid at his door, he strenuously denied ever having acted against his nephew's interests. With time to reflect on the way she had left things with Bacon, it did not take long for Elizabeth to reassess the situation.

Later that same afternoon she wrote to her nephew again, with an unflinching reiteration of the accusations she had made that morning, challenging him 'to set down wherein justly in any one thing you can charge himself with the least unkindness'. Burghley had been strenuous in his efforts, Bacon's aunt informed him, 'to prefer you in all kindness to Her Majesty', despite which Bacon still continued to consort with 'a bishop and other bad fellows'. He had also fallen out with leading Huguenots in France, whose friendship Burghley was keen to nurture for the benefit of the Crown. 'If you have more than a warrant for these and other dealings,' she added, 'he is glad with all his heart, but he hath great cause to doubt the contrary.' Elizabeth now saw that Bacon's exhibit A, the letter that seemed such compelling proof of his innocence at the time, had been little more than a clever sleight of hand.

What of Cecil's so-called 'deadly feud' with his cousin Anthony Bacon? According to Burghley, he had not heard anything of this until his son had 'told him that you railed on him everywhere, having never deserved ill of you'. He had been entirely unaware that any harsh words had been said 'to your mother or otherwise'. Elizabeth now renewed her demand that Bacon answer these charges more fully in writing, promising that if he so desired he could address his response to her and that she would 'keep it to myself'. This was on condition that in 'respect of secrecy' he could return the favour and send her letter back 'without imparting it to any; lest I reap displeasure for my good will'. The reason for this quickly became clear to Bacon as he read on, for she had introduced an unexpected caveat. While she remained convinced that Burghley was indeed 'well affected' towards him, she claimed to be uncertain about the true motives of another, mentioning no names, but adding what amounted to a textual nudge and wink, 'You know who.'

Who was Elizabeth referring to so conspiratorially? Could she really have been hinting that she distrusted Robert Cecil? She was in a difficult position, caught between her loyalty to two warring nephews and their parents. This she openly admitted to Bacon, stating that she had some sympathy for his predicament for 'you be both my sisters' sons'. But the strong suggestion that this 'other' individual, whom she would judge only 'as his desert shall require', was Robert Cecil made this show of empathy a risky strategy. Could this have been a ploy to extract a full confession from him? Bacon clearly thought so, as he pointedly disobeyed her appeal for utter secrecy. The next day he had the letter copied and dispatched post-haste to Essex along with his own epistolary rebuttal to his aunt, in which he stressed that he had done nothing to be ashamed of and would 'continue my former honest course'.

Essex and Elizabeth received Bacon's letter at the same time. Both responded very differently. The incensed Elizabeth dashed off a surly admonition: 'This letter of yours doth nothing answer my expectation.' As far as she could tell, he had provided no justification at all for his stubborn refusal to cease 'conversing with bad people'. She reminded him that the purpose of her last letter was to inform him, yet again, that he was 'required' to satisfy Burghley in all the charges made against him. 'Therefore you mistake me and my letter to yourself,' she concluded testily, 'if you interpret otherwise.' Essex, on the other hand, was quietly confident that Bacon had skilfully managed, with his evasive response, to undermine Burghley's plans to incriminate him, writing, 'I do find your letter to my Lady Russell to be a very good and a wise letter.' Elizabeth's interrogations could have proved far worse for the Earl and his companions. Her continual frustrated demands for a confession in writing proved that the Cecils had little to go on and were clearly shaken by the solidarity of the Essex House cabal. This would be

confirmed just two weeks later when events took a surprising turn
and the Dowager found herself unwittingly responsible for helping
the Essex faction score a further victory against the Cecils.

On 22 September there was a storm at court. Lord Thomas Buckhurst, Lord High Butler of England, and Sir John Fortescue,
Chancellor of the Exchequer, were cowering – the only permissible
course of action when the Queen was in a rage. The councillors'
ears were assaulted with such 'words of indignity' and 'reproach'
the like of which they could never have believed possible: for the
subject of the great Gloriana's scorn was her ever-faithful Treasurer,
Lord Burghley.

It was with some trepidation that the shaken courtiers broke the
news to Burghley when he came to court. The Queen had railed
uncontrollably, they informed him, calling him 'a miscreant and a
coward'. In a blind panic Cecil stormed back to his manor at
Theobalds, where he found a letter from Elizabeth Russell that
caused him to snap. In it he read her account of her private conference with the Earl at Essex House, during which she was treated to
a damning critique of her brother-in-law. It was, in his own words,
with a 'mind troubled' that he decided to compose a letter to Essex
in a style its recipient could never have imagined would be intended
for his gaze. The Queen's outburst, the Treasurer claimed, was triggered by his defence of the Earl in the controversy surrounding the
distribution of the Cádiz loot. He had endured her 'implacable
displeasure, only for this your cause', and he was now doubly
wronged, being 'farther laden with report of your displeasure also,
whereof my Lady Russell hath advertised me largely'. Burghley was
fawning, ingratiating himself in a manner that would have shamed
even the most servile flatterer at court. He went on to bemoan his
'miserable' fate, trapped as he was between Scylla and Charybdis,
for 'Her Majesty chargeth and condemneth me for favouring of you
against her; your Lordship contrariwise misliketh me for pleasing
of Her Majesty to offend you.' The only remedy he could see was
henceforth to 'live an anchorite', seeking his 'way to heaven' far

from 'the world's eye'. The impossible had finally happened: a wedge had been driven between Burghley and his sovereign – and Essex was the cause.

Elizabeth Russell was fanning the flames. Burghley trusted no one else with the safe delivery of his apology to Essex. At stake was the relationship which had been the scaffolding of the throne for nearly four decades, and if Essex could be convinced to use his influence to appease the Queen, then Elizabeth agreed that bending the baronial knee to the wayward Earl was a price worth paying. It could not have occurred to her that the reply Essex would ask her to return was a time bomb, and that she would be caught in its blast. In this condescending epistle, the Earl thanked the Treasurer for his letter, 'and yet,' he continued in riddling fashion, 'the occasion of writing in so strange a style, [is] less than I think my Lady [Russell] herself, that heard me, did apprehend'. Burghley would have understood exactly what he meant. Put simply, 'my Lady' had got it wrong. She had misled her own brother-in-law for 'both the matter and the manner of my speech was full of reverence to your Lordship . . . I have no ambition but Her Majesty's gracious favour, and the reputation of well serving her.' Ending with another swipe at Elizabeth's expense, he begged him to 'make me know it' if he should 'hear or apprehend anything' to the contrary, for 'I have ever desired, and so do, that your Lordship were well edified of me.' Elizabeth had been cast as the purveyor of misinformation. She was the troublemaker who had 'edified' Burghley incorrectly.

Essex had put Elizabeth back on the Cecils' radar of suspicion and she had been the catalyst for her own disgrace. When the Earl boasted of his exploits to Bacon, Elizabeth's nephew could barely contain his euphoria. Writing to Essex's Venetian spy, Dr Hawkins, he proclaimed jubilantly: 'Our Earl, God be thanked! Hath with the bright beams of his valour and virtue scattered the clouds and cleared the mists that malicious Envy had stirred up against his matchless merit.' He closed with the mocking caricature of Burghley, reporting how the Earl's machinations 'hath made the Old Fox to crouch and whine, and to insinuate himself by a very submissive letter to my Lord of Essex, subscribed in these terms, *Your Lordship's, if you will, at commandment'*. In his aping of Burghley's simpering tone, Bacon had captured what he believed to be the old adage in action: the fall of the mighty. Little did he know that Elizabeth Russell had not yet played all her cards.

17.

'my war between mine own flesh and blood'

Elizabeth Russell did not like losing. It was fortunate for her, therefore, that in 1596 she would be the victor in more than one battle. While she was preparing to take on the entrepreneurial titans that were James Burbage and Shakespeare's theatrical team, her competitive streak was piqued by a controversy of a different kind.

Elizabeth had fought for her children's wardships, for their inheritance and for their honour, and she would continue to fight for their future. Of particular concern to her were her offsprings' marriages. 'God bless them with the best husbands of this land!' was the prayer she must have uttered in exasperation for her daughters, on more than one occasion. But no nuptial was more hard-won than that of Thomas Posthumous Hoby. This would be a triumph, against all odds; the culmination of a long and bitter conflict with her son which had taken all her cunning, patience and persistence to win.

Thomas Posthumous had always been a difficult child. Crippled by an inherited spinal condition, he remained diminutive of size and would always be mocked by his contemporaries, who variously referred to him as a 'spindle-shanked ape' and a 'little knight that useth to draw up his breeches with a shoeing horn'. He had therefore found it difficult to apply himself, still harder to meet his mother's high expectations. Whenever Elizabeth's strictures became too harsh he would make a bid for freedom, running away to the Isle of Sheppey, where his brother Edward had held an estate since 1584. It was always too brief a taste of liberty, for the indomitable matriarch would ride out and fetch him back against his will. 'Again I found my child in Sheppey, and he is now here,' she wrote in complaint to William Cecil in 1585, explaining that the 'cause of his departure to be because he should this next term, by my appointment, have been placed in Inns of Court for his better instruction'. Elizabeth wanted him to train for a life in the legal profession, a respectable and laudable occupation for the son of the Queen's late ambassador. Thomas Posthumous dreamed of adventures on the high seas and heroic military campaigns, preferring to consort with the likes of the valiant Earl of Leicester, whom he idolized. Elizabeth's plans fell through when Thomas Farmer, a Master Bencher of the Middle Temple, urged her to 'forbear till he were bigger, for that he should be reputed as a child'. This was of little consequence to her son, who protested that he could not, in any case, 'frame himself to like or to take that course', no matter what his physical stature.

Elizabeth was damned if she was going to see her son follow in the footsteps of her shady nephew, for the 'example of Anthony Bacon doth make me resolute in no wise to consent to his going over the sea'. He could learn about foreign countries without gadding about in such 'frivolous' fashion, gleaning as much 'here at home by books with less danger'. Not to mention the cost of travel overseas! 'And though I will never be found unnatural,' the frugal noblewoman proclaimed, 'yet will I not, while I live, beggar myself for my cradle, if I may prevent it.' Her solution was to suggest – nay demand – that Burghley take Thomas Posthumous into his service so that he may be prompted, under his guidance, to 'apply himself thoroughly and diligently' to some better occupation. A bribe of £100 per year was offered as a sweetener. Her brother-in-law had little option but to accept. How could he not? The persuasive missive is one of the most passionate accounts of a mother's tortured relations with her children to have survived from the period:

> My lord, though I be not so bad a bird as to defile mine own nest, yet I know my children as well as the wisest shall in time . . . And though my natural inclination have been, by love and reason, to procure my children to love and fear me, yet I have not deserved thereby

contempt, nor showed myself simple in being ignorant of my due, and value of my desert. My lord, I beseech you, think me not passionate. I abhor that humour. But believe me, the unnatural, hard nature and insolency of this boy hath exceeded his brother's . . . [He] hath eaten no bread since his birth, but what my purse hath paid for; neither hath he groat but what my money hath paid for . . . Though both most ungodly and monstrous, I mean to send him to your lordship to hamper, though to avoid the opinion of passion, myself in choler, but coldly, have not uttered a word whereby my servants might discern my war between mine own flesh and blood.

Elizabeth was determined that her son would at least wed well. The opportunity arose in 1591 when the twenty-year-old Margaret Dakins, who had been married to the Earl of Essex's brother, Walter Devereux, became a widow. Barely two years had passed since the solemnizing of their union in 1589, when Walter was sent to France on a campaign to aid King Henri IV against the Catholic League. On 8 September of that year Essex and Elizabeth Russell's brother-in-law Sir Henry Killigrew looked on helplessly as Walter's life drained away. He had received a gunshot wound to the face, as Essex described it, 'in an unfortunate skirmish before Rouen', which had 'robbed me of him who was dearer to me than ever I was to myself'.

Margaret Dakins had much to recommend her as a bride for Thomas Posthumous. An only child, she had inherited vast tracts of land in Hackness, near Scarborough. Much to Elizabeth Russell's liking, Margaret's parents, Arthur and Thomasin Dakins, had determined that she should be raised and educated in the steadfastly Puritan household of Henry Hastings, 3rd Earl of Huntingdon, and his zealous wife, Catherine, in Ashby-de-la-Zouche, Leicestershire.

Hastings was well known to Elizabeth as the dedicatee of her first husband's version of *The Book of the Courtier*. Margaret's training in this disciplined home would ensure that she was well equipped to resist the popish proclivities of most of her neighbours in the primarily recusant-controlled northern territories. Elizabeth Russell would no doubt have calculated that placing her son in command of Margaret's lands, with all the legal privileges and sway over local politics this entailed, would facilitate the creation of a Puritan stronghold in the Catholic north. She lost no time, therefore, in pulling strings to secure the match.

Lady Russell's first act was to write to the Earl of Essex on her son's behalf. This was ill-advised. Essex was furious that a marriage was even being mooted so soon after his beloved brother's death. But sentiments of this nature were of small moment in comparison to the grand Puritan alliance Elizabeth was envisaging. With no help forthcoming from Essex, she turned to her brother-in-law William Cecil to intercede with the Earl of Huntingdon. Cecil did as he was told, writing to Margaret's former guardian on 21 September and putting up a united front, insisting that 'my good Lady and sister-in-law the Lady Russell, maketh me bold to join with her', commending Thomas Posthumous as 'a good and courteous husband, and a keeper and no spender'. All seemed to be going her way, but Elizabeth had miscalculated.

The Countess of Huntingdon was the aunt of another eligible bachelor, Thomas Sidney, brother to the heroic Philip Sidney, the very flower of chivalry, who, since his death in 1586, had become the stuff of legend. The Huntingdons immediately set about steering Margaret in Thomas Sidney's direction. Catching wind of this, Cecil attempted to undercut them by appealing directly to Arthur Dakins. Writing to him with some urgency on 29 October, he made it known that he was 'informed that some have or will shortly attempt to make some request both to you and the young gentlewoman your daughter'. Unwilling to be 'prevented by any delay', he hoped to entice him with assurances that 'my Lady Russell, his mother, hath provided a good portion of livelihood to be left to him' – and here came the crucial, yet inevitable, caveat – 'if he shall content her in his marriage'. A 'speedy answer' was requested. Cecil, who was not a man used to being kept waiting, would be disappointed.

Days passed with no response from the young widow's father. Elizabeth Russell's plan was at a standstill. She insisted that Thomas

Posthumous would have to take matters into his own hands and win the heiress's hand himself. What he needed was a private conference with her. Margaret, however, seemed to have vanished from the face of the earth. Suspecting that the girl had been taken by the Huntingdons, she contacted one of her spies, whom she taxed with the mission of seeking out Margaret's whereabouts. Her recruit was Lady Dorothy Perrot, née Devereux, sister to the Earl of Essex, who dispatched one of her own servants to the Huntingdons' London residence to make enquiries. He was told a flat-out lie. The Huntingdons were not about to let such a prize slip through their fingers and feigned ignorance. Even the well-connected Lady Perrot, sister-in-law to Margaret, 'could learn nothing of her coming up', as she confessed to Thomas Posthumous from London on 1 November. Unbeknownst to Elizabeth, the Huntingdons had already sent Thomas Sidney to Margaret's father with the intention of securing his permission for the marriage. The polar opposite of Thomas Posthumous, Sidney was tall, commanding and rakishly handsome. He had little trouble prevailing with Arthur Dakins, who agreed to a somewhat sinister plan.

On 2 November Margaret was spirited away to London, clutching letters from her father to the Huntingdons giving them permission to marry her to the suitor of their choice. Once inside the house she was locked away in her room. Looking back on these events four years later, in a letter to the Earl of Essex, a bitter Thomas Posthumous insisted that this had been done against her will and that she had been kept a 'close prisoner in her chamber'. Posthumous hinted at deeds even more terrible than this: 'Now what I could say further is fitter for my Lord to imagine, than for me to relate.' What had been so terrible that he could not bring himself to commit it to paper? What had he left to Essex's own darkest imaginings? Had Margaret Dakins, 'closely kept' in a room in the Huntingdons's home by the Countess, been raped by Thomas Sidney? If so, then it would have been almost impossible for her to refuse the match.

Lady Perrot had been working all this while to determine the location of the girl. Her enquiries bore fruit too late, for it was not until 13 November that she wrote to Thomas Posthumous, informing him that 'the gentlewoman you know of is come to my Lord of Huntingdon's'. Elizabeth Russell was not about to give up. She decided to set a trap for the unsuspecting Margaret. 'Now, child, it standeth you appear for your own credit's sake to try your friends,' she wrote to her son, hoping to pique his competitive spirit. 'My Lady Perrot,' she assured him, is 'the wisest, surest, and fittest to your good.' The plan was for Dorothy to gain Margaret's trust, entice her to a pre-appointed meeting place, and then relay the time and location to Thomas Posthumous, who would no doubt lie in wait for her coming. It was to be less of a courtship and more of an ambush.

To convince her son to take the bait, Elizabeth Russell did what came naturally, offering a bribe of £500 a year by way of dowry, and a jointure of £300 for life after her own death. In addition she would supply 'a house presently furnished to bring her to'. Elizabeth was fully aware that the dashing Thomas Sidney, brother to a national hero, could attract any woman. But what if Margaret was really being held against her will? Could she not then afford to be optimistic, given the great influence of Hoby's own kinsmen? 'If in affection she be gone to Sidney, it is one thing,' she mused. 'If by reason she be willing to be led to her own good, you will be found the better match of both.' Then Thomas Posthumous's ambitious mother divulged the wily twist to her plot.

Thomas Posthumous was to enlist the aid of his cousin Sir Anthony Cooke the younger, and together they would kidnap the girl. Elizabeth allowed herself to be carried away by the audacity of the device to, in her own words, 'steal her away' from the Huntingdons and the Sidneys. Outsmarting two powerful families would be fitting revenge for the humiliation of being pre-empted by them in her designs for the heiress. Ignoring Arthur Dakins' own pronouncements to the contrary, she insisted that Margaret 'hath her father's consent to match where she list'. So confident was she of the success of her bold scheme that she had already appointed the musicians for the wedding, though not without first subjecting them to the unique experience of auditioning for her. After they had met with her approval, she paid them five shillings up front, ahead of the upcoming nuptials. Schedules were drawn up, without Elizabeth feeling the need to consult with the happy couple. 'I would you could so use the matter that the widow be here this Christmas,' she commanded, for a Christmas wedding would be so delightful.

The musicians would not play that year at Thomas Posthumous's wedding. Whether by force or, more likely, a genuine 'affection' (as Lady Russell had feared), Margaret married Thomas Sidney by the end of May the following year. This time, Elizabeth was outwitted; but not for long.

Elizabeth Russell blamed her son for his failure to seize the eligible bride and relations between them thereafter were far from smooth. Writing to his cousin Robert Cecil on 3 February 1595, Thomas Posthumous complained that his mother had barred him from her presence after another falling-out between them. With no respite from her 'unkind strangeness', he decided it was wise to stay away from court, giving the 'great feasts' of the New Year's celebrations a miss because he was afraid that if he dared appear before her she would cause an embarrassing scene 'in so public an assembly'.

When Margaret was widowed yet again on 26 July 1595, Thomas Posthumous saw his chance to regain his mother's affection. With Thomas Sidney's manor of Kingston now added to her Dakins fortune, the heiress became an even greater jewel worth fighting for. Thomas Posthumous now found the way to appease the sulking Dowager. A week had not passed since Sidney's death when he wrote to Robert Cecil explaining his intentions. 'I find my mother forwards in the cause,' he declared jubilantly, 'so as I have no reason to doubt of my good success.' If, however, he should find himself 'crossed by some prerogative suitor', he begged his cousin 'to use some means to cross them, if any shall attempt such proceedings'. This time he was taking no chances.

Elizabeth set to work, demanding that the Earl of Huntingdon make up for his previous shifts and do right by her son. In the absence of another obvious suitor, even Huntingdon could now see that the match could serve his own interests as President of the Council of the North. In a landscape riddled with hideaways for plotting Catholic priests and intelligencers, Hackness Hall stood like a proud coastal sentinel for the spying out of conspirators and it needed an able captain with religious fervour in his veins to take the reins. At Huntingdon's insistence, Sir Edward Stanhope, a member of the Council, accompanied Thomas Posthumous to see Margaret in Yorkshire. After a 'long journey into the North for a good cause', the weary travellers arrived on Saturday 20 September 1595.

In York they were disappointed, for the ever-ethereal Margaret had slipped through their fingers once again, having beaten a hasty retreat to Hull. They followed in her wake, arriving three days later. Thomas Posthumous had been knighted in 1594 and was now a peer of the realm. In addition, 'the natural affection borne him of his honourable mother' would bring her closer to Elizabeth's brother-in-law, the most powerful man in England. Surely she would not refuse him this time. But refuse him she did, locking herself away in her room and keeping aloof from the visitors. After much importuning, she agreed to see Stanhope alone. He found her with tear-stained, swollen eyes, complaining of a headache and bursting into tears whenever her late husband's name was evoked. Stanhope nevertheless pressed Thomas Posthumous's suit, showing her the Earl of Huntingdon's letter recommending the match. Margaret's reaction was to let loose a new avalanche of tears, protesting that 'the tender love she bare to him that was dead, made it grievous to her to hear of any new'.

Stanhope had a way with words and marshalled the full arsenal of the romantic poet. Thomas Posthumous, he said, had undertaken this journey 'in desire his eyes to witness that which public report had delivered him, that the gifts of nature had in some sort equalled her virtues'. Margaret did not wilt at these professions of love from a man who had never even seen her in person, but 'in

dutiful regard' to the Earl of Huntingdon's commands she agreed
to meet with him. Stanhope went back down to Thomas Posthumous to deliver the good news . . . and they waited. And then they
waited a little more. Half an hour passed. Still no friendly word
from Margaret. They were beginning to grow impatient when, after
an hour or so, they were finally conducted into her presence. It was
hardly the reception they were hoping for. Margaret was wary and
primly formal, 'courteously and modestly entertaining him with
few speeches'. It became clear to Thomas Posthumous that 'the
favourable access' which he had obtained, thanks to Huntingdon's
intercession, was 'unwillingly performed'. Her duty done, Margaret
made an abrupt exit.

Thomas Posthumous was all for a continued assault on the
widow, but Stanhope persuaded him to 'retire himself into the
south' and await the Earl of Huntingdon's arrival so that he could
resume his role as mediator. Elizabeth had other ideas. Unhappy
with the delay, she decided a little reverse psychology would not go
amiss. Her son panicked and informed his cousin Robert on
29 October, that 'I find my Lady mother so backwards for my preferment; I have no other hope to draw her to do anything, but by
my Lord Treasurer's honourable means.' Elizabeth's strategy
worked, prompting Hoby to secure further letters of recommendation from Burghley and Huntingdon. Just in case these were not
enough, he loaded his satchel with gifts of 'fair jewels and pearls'
and made his way to York. 'I come not so far to be discouraged with
some few repulses,' he declared, his optimism growing, 'so will I
not depart until I have performed the uttermost of my strength in
seeking her.'

Margaret was, however, as stubborn as Thomas Posthumous,
and by December she had had enough. Casting all courtesy to one
side, she wrote to Huntingdon informing him that she wished to be
relieved of the knight's attentions. He could show Thomas Posthumous her letter if he did not believe her. 'I did acquaint him with the
contents of your letter, and at the last I did give him the letter to
peruse,' the Earl assured her on the ninth of that month, 'but it

moved him not to that purpose you desired.' Huntingdon began to worry about the repercussions, knowing how unforgiving Elizabeth Russell could be. 'For God's cause,' he warned her, 'have care of all our credits, and so handle the matter as his coming again may be neither offensive to you nor displeasing to himself.' This was one of the last letters Huntingdon would write. He died just five days later. One of Elizabeth's most powerful mediators was out of the picture, but in dying he had, ironically, provided her with the ammunition she needed to catch the slippery Margaret once and for all.

The late Earl's brother now stepped into the frame. Beginning proceedings for the seizure of Margaret's Hackness estate, he claimed that money originally paid towards its purchase had not been reimbursed. Elizabeth and her son, having petitioned unsuccessfully from February to April of 1596 to get the support of Anthony Bacon and the Earl of Essex, now had the perfect tool at their disposal: blackmail. If Margaret was to fend off this encroachment on her property, and the expensive Chancery suit it required, she would need powerful intermediaries. On 28 May Edward Stanhope wrote to Margaret with his advice. '[H]aving these great folks to stand against you,' he informed her, 'if you would so far use your faithful servant Sir Thomas as direct him by your appointment to try his credit with my Lord Treasurer for you, I know his Lordship may sway the matter wholly.' Now, if she were willing to assure Thomas Posthumous that 'the motion proceedeth from yourself', he was in no doubt that 'he will strike it sure for you'; that is, *if* she were willing to ensure that 'Sir Thomas shall have kind thanks of you for it'. She should also bear in mind that her suitor was 'well supplied by his honourable mother', Burghley's sister-in-law and closest confidante. Who else could prevail with his Lordship to grant the protection that had the full force of the royal seal behind it? What else could the beleaguered widow do?

On 26 June 1596 Thomas Posthumous Hoby wrote a grateful missive to the Countess of Huntingdon which indicated that he had all but won his prize. 'And when I shall prove so happy as to possess the happiness I do now seek for,' he declared jubilantly, 'I will be found as dutifully serviceable, as if I were a natural branch of the stock itself, whereto I shall then be but grafted.' On 1 August his mother wrapped things up, writing to Robert Cecil to invite him to the wedding which would take place on the ninth of the month. 'My meaning is not to make any solemnity, but only a private meeting of good and honourable friends,' she wrote, asking him to attend with his wife, Elizabeth Brooke, 'to be the chief as friends to my son and fairest flower of his garland for friendship when I am gone'. Elizabeth had taken full control of the ceremony. There would be no music, no dancing, no cavorting. Her son would content himself with a godly sermon and a sufficient dinner.

Elizabeth would ensure that one other flower would grace the garland of friendship she was now carefully cultivating. She arranged for a coach to collect her daughters on the wedding day. They would ride on towards the ceremony, stopping on the way to pick up Sir William Brooke, 10th Baron Cobham, who would take pride of place in the nuptials. Elizabeth made sure that even these modest festivities would become a political statement, a showpiece for her growing intimacy with the powerful Cobham clan, who were about to become particularly bothersome to both Shakespeare and the Earl of Essex.

18.

Shakespeare's Nemesis

November 1596. Elizabeth Russell sat at her desk in her home in the Blackfriars, pen in hand and poised to make the first fateful stroke on the single sheet of paper laid out before her. Every inch of this London bolt-hole must have rekindled memories of her late husband, John Russell, for whom she had constructed the upper-storey dining chamber in which they shared so many intimate conversations.

Now everything was different. Her neighbourhood had been invaded by the worst kind of entrepreneurial freeloaders: a theatrical troupe whose political loyalties were up for hire. The conversion of the Blackfriars Theatre had dragged on into the autumn and was now nearing completion. Since James Burbage purchased it from William More, Elizabeth had been forced to endure the constant clattering of the workmen and the rattle of carts bringing building supplies to the tenements which had just been vacated by William de Lawne. Directly opposite her home, the newly erected Swan Theatre in Paris Garden, having only recently reopened its doors after a plague outbreak, served as a reminder of what was awaiting her on her very doorstep: the increased traffic from the rowdy theatregoers pouring into the vicinity from every quarter of London; the thumping of the tabor and ear-piercing pipes keeping time to the boisterous jigs of Will Kemp, the Hunsdon's Men's famous actor and dancer; and, worst of all, the hordes jeering as players in mockery of her husband and her kinsmen, the descendants of the venerable Cobham line, plodded around like buffoons on the stage. But the damage had already been done. With every staging of *Henry IV, Part 1* in one of London's seedy playhouses, or out in the provinces where Shakespeare's company toured, the Russell name in which she took such pride lost a little more of its lustre. As the theatre took shape under her watchful gaze, less than 187 feet south of her own home and gardens, so did her scheme to put a stop to the Hunsdon's Men's best-laid plans.

Elizabeth's hopes were resting on a document half filled with elegant and flowing secretarial script, beneath which was a blank space awaiting the signatures of those who opposed the opening of an indoor playhouse in the district which they believed to be under their independent control. Once completed, this simple piece of paper would make history by forcing a radical change to the course of Shakespeare's career and determining the subsequent fortunes of the theatre industry in England. It would soon be carried 'To the right honourable the Lords and others of Her Majesty's most honourable Privy Council'. After reading it, the Council's members, who included the Cecils and Lord Cobham, would be in no doubt that Lady Russell had taken drastic action, that she had headed a campaign against the theatre's backers, gaining the full support of 'the inhabitants of the Precinct of the Blackfriars'. Firm of purpose, she dipped her pen in ink and signed the petition, not forgetting to add the honorific title 'Dowager' after her name. This act would trigger a chain of events which would nearly drive Shakespeare out of his profession.

If Elizabeth stepped outside her door and stood on Carter Lane, looking down towards the Thames with Ludgate just behind her, she would have seen a stocky building called the Square Tower immediately in front of her. To the right of this, but forming part of the same messuage, was the Timber House, comprising a 'little shop' which must be the long-lost printing-house of Shakespeare's publisher, Richard Field, identified in the title pages to many of his books as being located 'in the Blackfriars by Ludgate'.

A 'great shop' graced the Square Tower on its ground floor; above it, a second storey comprising two chambers built with stone bricks. These were topped with a further loft chamber covered with a lead roof. Two flights of stairs connected the larger shop to the rooms above, and a further flight provided direct access to the 'garret' lying over Field's Timber House. Elizabeth's own mansion, straddling Carter Lane and Water Lane, stood adjacent to, and protruded just beyond, Field's property. Had she rounded the corner and followed Water Lane down, in under two minutes she would have come to the theatre James Burbage was constructing for Shakespeare and his fellow players. Beneath its very shadow lived many of the men who would help her sabotage Burbage's new business venture.

In the years leading up to Elizabeth's mission against the Blackfriars Theatre, the movements of some of her co-petitioners made them her natural accomplices. On 22 September 1590, one year after marrying Thomas Vautrollier's widow, Field renewed his lease for 'that little shop now in the occupation of the said Richard . . . called the Timber House', which was 'part and parcel' of the tenement known as the 'Square Tower, some time called the Church Porch'. Field also gained a yard and access from this to the entry leading to his 'little shop', as well as use of the chamber above the Timber House, which had been occupied previously by William de Lawne's son, Gideon. Just two days before, Gideon had been granted the 'great shop' in the Square Tower and the rooms above it, as well as the right to enjoy 'all those three pair of stairs, one above another, leading out of the entry adjoining into the great shop, up into the stone chambers and garret over the said Timber House'.

The indentures and leases recording these transactions reveal some tantalizing details about the more mundane routines of these men's daily lives. Field had one essential convenience in the Timber House: a privy, or toilet. Gideon was not so fortunate and had therefore agreed with William More that he and his family would have the right to share these facilities with Field. The latter would therefore have seen the de Lawnes regularly passing through the way leading to the Timber House in order to use his toilet. The neighbours were further bound together by their promise to each 'well and truly bear and pay the one half of the charge for the cleansing of the . . . privy'. Perhaps their arrangements were not always harmonious, for there may have been some dispute between them over rights to collect rainwater from the properties. Gideon de Lawne's deed gives him permission to exploit water from Field's yard as well as the roofs of the Square Tower, Timber House and their adjoining garrets, while the indenture produced two days later for the publisher blocked his neighbour's access to the yard for this purpose. As well as bumping into each other when collecting rainwater, they would also have frequently crossed paths in the entryways to their properties. These were clearly attached, for each tenant undertook not to renovate their own path in a manner which might narrow their neighbour's or be 'prejudicial or hurtful' to the other.

The surviving leases indicate that Field was living at very intimate quarters with Gideon, the son of another of Elizabeth's co-petitioners. They were not, however, merely allied by their material living conditions. More spiritual considerations connected them. In accordance with the terms of their agreement with William and George More, both were paying towards the maintenance of the church and its minister, who at this time was Stephen Egerton. The connections between Field and Egerton go further. In 1596 Field may have been preparing to publish the preacher's *A Brief Method of Catechising*, which was printed the following year. Before this, in 1594, he issued the English translation of a work by the French author Matthew Virell, *The Principal Grounds of Christian Religion*, for which Egerton had contributed a preface which he entitled 'an admonition', deliberately reigniting the radical vocabulary of the Admonition Controversy. 'Therefore herein gird up the loins of thy mind, put upon thee the whole armour of God,' he declared therein, urging his readers to fight against the 'rage of our invisible enemy'. He left no doubt as to where his own battle was being fought, signing off from the 'Black Friars'. The book was popular, for it was reissued in 1595 and, like Egerton's treatise on *Catechising*, was sold at the 'sign of the Brazen Serpent' in St Paul's Churchyard, just north-east of

Field's press. Field's work for Egerton must have recommended the printer as a worthy candidate for the post of St Anne's church warden, which he went on to occupy in 1598.

The case for the identification of Field's tenement with the print shop which actually produced Egerton's works is strengthened by his lease agreement, in which he undertook to 'sufficiently keep, uphold, sustain, repair, and maintain all the said little shop' and the additional 'chambers and rooms' which came with it, but with the fairly hefty lease of £7 per year. This was £2 more than the sum agreed by one Paul Buck for the 21-year lease to the 'shop commonly called the Round House or Corner Shop', which he commandeered from Lewis de Mare's widow on 30 June 1591. This indicates that Field's Timber House was substantial enough to house a printing press, though annexed to the modestly sized former church porch. Field was not one of the printers licensed by the Stationers' Company to hold more than one press at this time. A relatively small room could therefore have accommodated his needs. If we have finally found the precise location of Richard Field's print shop, then we can say that Elizabeth Russell was living directly next door to the very building from which not only some of Egerton's tracts were printed, but the words of Shakespeare had their first birth as consumer products.

On 31 October 1593 something happened that would have significant consequences for Richard Field's livelihood, his business and his relation to Elizabeth's petition. Dr William de Lawne's practice had clearly been doing very well; so well in fact that he felt able to extend his investments in the Blackfriars. He therefore approached William and George More and asked to buy the Square Tower in its entirety, including the Timber House, 'now in the several tenures or occupations of Gideon de Lawne, Richard Field, or their assigns, and sometime in the tenure or occupation of Thomas Vautrollier or his assigns'. The sale would also include the adjoining Round House, as well as a tenement above it, which would have been exactly parallel to the second storey of Elizabeth's house. William de Lawne's shelling out of £360 for these tenements had one important repercussion:

Richard Field had a new landlord. His rent, as Field was soon informed, 'henceforth shall be yearly payable to the said William de Lawne, his heirs or assigns, during the continuance of the same lease'. Field's living was now bound to this Huguenot refugee, who shared with his wife, Jacqueline, a common origin, a common religion and a common place of worship in the French Church, the church so diligently funded by the Cooke sisters and their friends.

Richard Field would have had other reasons for agreeing to the action which betrayed his Stratford friend William Shakespeare. He was one of Lord Burghley's agents. Having been admitted to the Stationers' Company on 6 February 1587, he was well placed to follow in Thomas Vautrollier's footsteps after his death. The latter's widow, Jacqueline, was keen to continue publishing books, but her unmarried status put a cap on her activities. She was ordered to 'meddle not with the printing of anything else until she procure herself to be chosen and allowed to print according to the decrees of the Star Chamber'. Before long Field had taken over the company, as well as some of the propagandist work Thomas Vautrollier had been assigned in collaboration with John Wolfe, the man who had also helped to disgrace Shakespeare's family in the aftermath of the Somerville–Arden plot, and who would go on to print the infamous *Life and Reign of King Henry IV*, the text that would contribute to the spectacular downfall of the Earl of Essex.

Burghley seems to have lost no time in securing Field's services, for his very first book, which was described on its title page as having been 'Imprinted at London by J[acqueline] Vautrollier for Richard Field', was the virulently anti-Spanish tract *The Copy of a Letter sent out of England to Don Bernadin Mendoza*. Issued in 1588, the year in which the Spanish fleet sailed out on its mission to conquer England, it purported to be a leaked letter from one Richard Leigh, a seminary priest. The confidential epistle apparently revealed that some of the Pope's followers, disgusted with his bloody and dictatorial regime, were beginning 'to stagger in their minds' in their loyalty to him. The manuscript for this incendiary pamphlet survives in the hand of Lord Burghley. Field's first books as an independent printer would therefore see him taking over Vautrollier's role as the disseminator of the French and anti-Catholic propaganda which was such a pivotal weapon in the Cecils' political arsenal. If we add Field's obligations to Burghley as government spin-doctor to his responsibilities towards William de Lawne as tenant, the pressures placed on him to sign the petition against the Blackfriars Theatre become overwhelming. When taken together with Field's formal duties as a post-holder in the Church of St Anne's from at least 1592, it becomes clear that we have finally solved the mystery of why it was that the printer's commitments to Elizabeth Russell outweighed those to his Stratford comrade, Shakespeare.

With the Dowager living just next door, there was further incentive, for she could wield some influence over the destinies of local printers. This would prove so for another of her supporters who was involved with the publishing industry. Ascanius de Renialme also helped put Shakespeare's company out of business, and his signature once again casts the Cecils' ominous shadow over the Dowager's anti-theatrical campaign. The extent of Ascanius's obligation to Burghley's sister-in-law becomes clear in a letter of 10 July 1598 from Elizabeth to Robert Cecil, seeking support for the man whose contacts across Europe had once provided Burghley with a valuable source of foreign intelligence:

> My neighbour, Ascanius the bookseller, whom my lord your father loveth exceeding well, hath earnestly sued me to speak a good word for him, and to become a most humble suitor to yourself in his behalf, that whereas the whole Hall of Printers made a petition to the Council table that he might be a printer, whereupon the full board writ their letter to the Lord Mayor and his brethren, which they have so smally accompted of as they never so much as called Ascanius before them to satisfy him why they did not grant his desire . . . I refer the sequel to your own wisdom, desiring as much to be done for the honest man, and my good neighbour, as may be performed by you without your own hurt . . . From my house at the Blackfriars . . .

Ascanius was licensed to sell books, not print them. The Stationers' Company, which governed the publishing industry, had to be appealed to in order to admit new printers to their ranks. The company dutifully pressed Ascanius's suit on Sir Richard Saltonstall, the then Lord Mayor of London, and his aldermen to grant his request. Several months passed with no response. Ascanius turned to Elizabeth, hoping she could pressure the Privy Council directly to 'write to the Mayor a letter to show that it is Her Majesty's pleasure that they should admit him' as a licensed printer. He had no reason to doubt she could prevail, given his own involvement in her successful petition to the Privy Council to shut down operations at Burbage's playhouse.

Ascanius and Field were not the only anti-theatrical signatories to have been in the service of the Cecils. It is through Thomas Browne that we gain a striking new insight into the relationships that connected Elizabeth Russell to the world of play-going. Browne had been working as a commissioner for Cecil and the Privy Council, appointed to help uncover Catholic recusants in Surrey in the early 1590s; a project partly coordinated from Elizabeth's Bisham home in 1592. When he put his name to her petition he had less than a year to live. When he died, in 1597, his Blackfriars property passed to his second wife, Helen Harding. The 1599 London Subsidy Rolls confirm that the man who was present in the Blackfriars in 1596 and signed Elizabeth's petition must be this same Thomas Browne, for his name is replaced on the list of tax assessments by that of 'Lady Browne'. The intriguing document suggests some telling neighbourly associations, for next to her own name, and placing them as the Brownes' immediate neighbours in the parish of St Anne's, are those of 'Doctor Paddy' and 'Cuthbert Burbage'.

In the very year in which the physician Dr William Paddy signed Elizabeth's petition, he had been made 'dissector of anatomies to the Barber-Surgeons' Company'. The Barber-Surgeons' Hall was located on Muggle or Monkwell Street, just round the corner from the house on Silver Street which Shakespeare would occupy in 1604. Paddy was certainly working for William Cecil and members of his family by 1595, when he was writing to assure his son Robert that, for his pregnant and sick niece, Elizabeth, Countess of Derby, '[t]here shall be nothing omitted in care (I beseech you be assured) for her further and perfect recovery'. Paddy was also close to Elizabeth and her daughter Nan, for he would be invited to the latter's elaborate wedding in the Blackfriars in 1600.

It is the Browne family's proximity to James Burbage's son Cuthbert which is especially interesting, for it may conceal a relationship that is more than merely neighbourly. Sir Thomas Browne's son, Sir Matthew Browne, inherited his father's estate of Betchworth Castle in Surrey and would cement business ties with the Burbages and Shakespeare. He was one of the trustees of Nicholas Brend, described in the latter's will as among his 'loving friends'. Brend leased the land on which Shakespeare's Globe Theatre would be built; land which in 1601 would be passed on to Sir Matthew, who effectively became Shakespeare's landlord until 1603. Thomas Browne's political career was strongly supported by Sir Thomas Cawarden and Sir William More, the Blackfriars' principal freeholders. Elizabeth would become twice related to the Brownes: through Frances Grey, the wife of her brother William Cooke and niece to Anthony Browne, 1st Viscount Montagu, one of the Brownes of Betchworth; and through Thomas Browne's first wife, Mabel Fitzwilliam, whose family were entrenched in Berkshire and affiliated to the Dowager's Windsor neighbour Sir Henry Neville. The subsequent fate of the Globe Theatre points to very intimate connections between the men who built and funded the playhouse and the Dowager's kinfolk.

That Elizabeth was tapping into networks of mutual support sometimes founded on economic, sometimes on religious, principles when she approached her co-petitioners in the Blackfriars in 1596 is strongly suggested by the available evidence. An indenture of 18 February 1602 was signed by a John Dermer, who may be the John le Mere (also known as John de Mere or de Mer), who was a Paris-born goldsmith and member of the French Church. Dermer gave George More £130 in hand to purchase several tenements, one of which had been in the tenure of the Dutchman Harman Buck-holt, who was also a goldsmith. The document reveals that Buckholt had later passed this property on to John Robinson, a 'cordwainer'. Those working with cordwain or cordovan leather were normally shoemakers. This may be the same John Robinson who knew Shakespeare personally.

In 1609 John Robinson was mentioned in a legal suit involving Alexander Hawkins, son-in-law of Henry Evans, the former impresario of Farrant's theatre. Evans would be granted the lease of Shakespeare's Blackfriars Theatre for his boy players by Richard Burbage in 1600, debates over his subsequent financial responsibilities there sparking the conflict which would reveal that the playhouse was situated immediately north of rooms 'in the tenure and occupation of one John Robinson'. It is possible that he was the same who was mentioned in Shakespeare's will as his tenant in the Blackfriars Gatehouse. This building, which lies only a few paces to the east of the site of the Blackfriars Theatre and close to the King's Wardrobe, was purchased by the playwright in 1613 and left to his daughter Susanna Hall. In the will it is described as 'that messuage or tenement, with the appurtenances, wherein one John Robinson dwelleth, situate, lying and being in the Blackfriars in London, near the Wardrobe'.

Could Shakespeare have had such a forgiving heart as to provide one of Elizabeth Russell's army of petitioners with a lodging? Perhaps his hard nose for business overruled his personal feelings. If the two John Robinsons are indeed one, then he may have been living next door to the building which became the Blackfriars Theatre in 1596 or in another tenement close by. Surviving indentures record William More's granting of the lease for a property in the Blackfriars to Robinson from 1 May 1572, which was still effective on 18 February 1602, when John Dermer entered into his contract with George More. Agnes Lyons, the widow of Robinson's co-petitioner Andrew, left a bequest in her will to 'my cousin John Robinson of Portsmouth' in 1610, though it is unclear whether there is a relation between the two Robinsons. Other petitioners, however, were clearly kinsmen. Ascanius de Renialme's will of 1600 reveals that he was godfather to one of Owen Lockhard's children as well as to a 'Marie Henson', daughter 'to my neighbour Francis Henson'. This is likely to be Francis Hinson, another signatory of the 1596 petition. Ascanius was particularly close to Lockhard, John Dollin and Edward Ley, to whom he left 'rings of gold' in the will, which was witnessed by Ley and Gideon de Lawne.

Some of Elizabeth's backers were brought together through the churches they frequented. Harman Buckholt, for example, was acquainted with other petitioners through the Dutch Church, the registers recording its members in 1594 revealing that he and his wife attended services there with the tailor John Edwardes and the wife of Ascanius de Renialme. Ascanius himself, along with Robert Baheire's widow, Katherine, left bequests to the same church in their wills. In the years following the closure of the Blackfriars Theatre many of Elizabeth's associates were united in a manner which indicates longer-term associations established through St Anne's Church. An indenture of 1607 places William Bispham, John Wharton and Ezekiel Major together as purchasers of rooms in St Anne's, with an arrangement that if the church wardens agreed to pay them £120 within seven years the property would be reserved for the use of local parishioners. The document gives us a snapshot of some of Elizabeth's petitioners as guardians of the public interest under the auspices of the church where she worshipped, where Stephen Egerton held his radical ministry, and where a number of her co-signatories had served as wardens or their supporting 'sidemen'. Little wonder they complained when they discovered, in the words of the petition, that the 'playhouse is so near the church'.

Many of the men who opposed Burbage and Shakespeare's theatrical team needed only to step outside their doors to see each other. Henry Boice would take out a lease in February 1602 for a property close to that of John Robinson. Both men were bound to their new landlord, possibly John le Mere. One 'John Clarke, gent.' was identified in 1610 as residing just north of 'the high way that leadeth towards the . . . mansion house of the right honourable

George, Lord Hunsdon', placing him practically next door to the Blackfriars Theatre. Clarke's ownership of the tenement 'in the parish of Saint Anne's' goes at least as far back as 1601 and, since his residency in the area can be confirmed in February 1592, it is very likely he is the same who signed Elizabeth's petition. A few paces further south of Clarke's residence and one comes to the lane leading to Bridewell. In 1596, just weeks before the Dowager approached the Privy Council with her grievances against the Hunsdon's Men, Thomas Holmes, 'citizen and Merchant Tailor of London', put his name to a 22-year lease for some property there. These may have been the same tenements mentioned in an indenture of 9 August the following year as situated close to the home of Robert Baheire, 'next unto Bridewell Stairs', just south of the lane leading thence from the Blackfriars.

The proximity of Elizabeth's co-petitioners made them the mutual benefactors of the property exchanges and business dealings which took place in the labyrinthine clusters of buildings that formed the Blackfriars. With two goldsmiths, two tailors, a cordwainer, a feltmaker, a bookseller, a printer and two physicians, among others, taking up the gauntlet against the Blackfriars Theatre with her, we would expect an economic impetus to lie behind their action. Many of the Dowager's backers would have signed leases for their own properties which had built into their wording traces of the long-standing battle of the Blackfriars residents for independence from the City authorities. Thomas Holmes' earlier lease of 1596, for example, also enjoined him to 'uphold and to the uttermost of his . . . power maintain and defend [the] privileges, liberties, and jurisdictions of the said precinct of the said Blackfriars'. But the responsibilities were also financial, for tenants in the area were legally bound to ensure the maintenance and upkeep of their properties. Robert Baheire's lease is typical, indicating that a tenant must 'so often as need . . . well and sufficiently repair, sustain, support, glaze, tile, keep, and maintain the said messuage, or tenement, and other premises'. Landlords could strictly enforce this, reserving the right to enter into and explore the said properties and request necessary renovations within a specified time frame. Failure to comply could result in eviction.

The increased traffic in the area, due to the presence of a theatre on their doorstep, and the consequent damage this could cause to houses, shops and public thoroughfares (the charge for the cleaning of which residents were jointly responsible), would have been very worrying to Elizabeth and her neighbours, particularly those whose outlays on their businesses were already cutting deeply into their pockets. In 1619, after the Blackfriars Theatre recovered from Lady Russell's machinations, the residents were still trying to close it down. One of these was Sir Thomas Posthumous Hoby, who signed one of two petitions which cited as precedent the petition of his mother and other 'honourable persons' in November 1596. These documents give a clear indication of the anxieties that would have underpinned Elizabeth's earlier campaign:

> [T]here is daily such resort of people, and such multitudes of coaches . . . that sometimes all our streets cannot contain them, but they clog up Ludgate also, in such sort that both they endanger the one the other, break down stalls, throw down men's goods from their shops, and the inhabitants cannot come to their houses . . . nor the tradesmen or shopkeepers utter their wares, nor the passenger go to the common water stairs, without danger of their lives and limbs, whereby also many times quarrels and effusion of blood hath followed; and that further danger may be occasioned by the broils, plots or practices of such an unruly multitude of people . . .

The later actions against the Blackfriars Theatre deliberately build on the clever strategy established by Elizabeth in her petition to the Privy Council. While one of her complaints was that 'the said playhouse is so near the church that the noise of the drums and trumpets will greatly disturb and hinder both the ministers and parishioners in time of divine service and sermons', this was much more than a protest against the noise pollution a new theatre would bring to the neighbourhood. After all, Farrant had occupied the First

Blackfriars Theatre even closer to Elizabeth's home, with no record of a formal complaint from her or from Lord Cobham, the latter himself not averse to a little theatrical speculation, having served as patron of his own acting troupe in the 1560s. The Dowager certainly would entertain no scruples when it came to marrying her daughter, Nan Russell, into the family behind the theatrical team known as Worcester's Men.

For Elizabeth there were additional, more pressing, reasons to object to the new theatre. She had become convinced that other, much darker, deeds were afoot. The text of her petition makes a daring insinuation that the Blackfriars Theatre, once opened, would become a cover for illicit activities. Her stroke of genius was deftly to insinuate that her assessment was ratified by George Carey, Lord Hunsdon, and by William Brooke, who had by this time taken over Henry Carey's role as Lord Chamberlain:

> That whereas one Burbage hath lately bought certain rooms in the same precinct, near adjoining unto the dwelling houses of the Right Honourable, the Lord Chamberlain and the Lord of Hunsdon, which rooms the said Burbage is now altering and meaneth, very shortly, to convert and turn the same into a common playhouse which will grow to be a very great annoyance and trouble, not only to all the noblemen and gentlemen thereabout inhabiting, but also a general inconvenience to all the inhabitants of the same precinct, both by reason of the great resort and gathering together of all manner of vagrant and lewd persons that under colour of resorting to the plays, will come thither and work all manner of mischief . . .

The words of the petition were carefully chosen to ignite the touchpaper of paranoia gripping the city since the 1592 riots, which, having been triggered by feltmakers in the Blackfriars, were perpetrated by 'masterless men' who had 'assembled themselves by occasion and pretence of their meeting at a play'. Since 1531 at least three separate constitutional acts had been passed against vagrants and 'masterless men'. These 'rogues, vagabonds, and sturdy beggars' were more than just the idle and indigent. They were, according to the terms of the acts which defined them, the root causes of political agitation, disaffection, rioting and rebellious subversion. Between 1594 and 1596 the crises caused by inflation, disastrous harvests, squabbles between cash-strapped apprentices and increasing racial tensions were contributing to the demonization of the capital's 'masterless' citizens.

On 3 November 1594 the anti-theatrical party's campaign took on a more serious tenor when one Francis Langley, an entrepreneur with a dubious past, sought permission to build yet another theatre on the Bankside: the Swan. Writing to Lord Burghley, the Lord Mayor, John Spencer, accused Langley of providing a venue for the 'vagrant persons and masterless men' who were 'practisers of treason', identifying 'our apprentices' as keepers of 'evil and riotous company'. He begged Cecil to find fit means of dispelling 'the stink and contagion not only of this city but of this whole realm' by 'suppress[ing] all such places built for that kind of exercise, than to erect any more of the same sort'. This was the strongest insinuation yet that the playhouses were suspected as the catalysts for sedition, and it demanded the attentions of the Privy Council.

Just one year before Elizabeth's petition reached the Privy Council, in June 1595, the Lord Mayor's fears that London had not seen the last of the civil broils were realized when an estimated 1,800 people laid siege to the districts of Cheapside and Leadenhall 'with a great number of loose and masterless men', some of whom had helped to build a makeshift gallows outside the Lord Mayor's door. As the mayor lay cowering in his home, the rioters called out provocatively to him that 'they would hang him up if he durst come out'. His door would stay firmly bolted the entire day, but he would later hear how another three thousand men lay waiting in the fields, armed with battle-poles and clubs, ready to ambush the authorities.

The panic unleashed by this latest round of rioting intensified the move to suppress the playhouses and, on 13 September, the Lord Mayor and aldermen explicitly identified Shakespeare's Theatre, alongside other playhouses on the Bankside, as the 'great cause' of disorder'. The 'masterless' were again singled out and the theatres blamed for 'the late stir and mutinous attempt of those few apprentices and other servants' who had triggered the recent apprentice and race riots, and who 'drew their infection from these and like places'. Immediate directives were dispatched, ordering 'the present stay and final suppressing of the said plays, as well at the Theatre and Bankside'. By 22 July 1596 the spread of the plague gave the Middlesex and Surrey Justices of the Peace, which included William Gardiner, the excuse they needed to bring the curtain down on the theatres. Some of those who looked on as these events unfolded smelled a campaign of intimidation. The satirist Thomas Nashe, who witnessed at first hand the misfortunes of Shakespeare's theatrical troupe in the September of 1596, commented that 'the players . . . are piteously persecuted', lamenting their over-confidence in believing 'their state settled' because of their association with their former patron, Henry Carey. This did them little good, for their future was 'now so uncertain they cannot build upon it'.

The spectre of the 'masterless' still clung to the Blackfriars when Elizabeth took up arms against the Blackfriars Theatre, demanding that the Privy Council 'take order that the same rooms may be converted to some other use and that no playhouse may be used or kept there'. The petition reveals her insider knowledge of the recent prohibitions against performing, complaining 'that now all players being banished by the Lord Mayor from playing within the city by reason of the great inconveniences and ill rule that follow them, they now think to plant themselves in liberties'. Elizabeth may very well be referring here to the ban on city-playing which had been in force since Henry Carey's application to Sir Richard Martin for permission to mount productions at the Cross Keys Inn. She may have learned of this directly from Martin or from her kinsmen on the Privy Council. In the early 1590s Martin had also coordinated his efforts to close the theatres in the liberties with the Dowager's other Surrey friends William and George More, as well as with William Gardiner, who would turn out to have a particularly interesting connection to both Shakespeare and Lady Russell.

Before Elizabeth continued on her journey through the Black-friars, to draw the support of her influential friends and neighbours, she made her way down Water Lane to visit Edward Hoby's brother-in-law, who lived just beneath Burbage's nearly completed theatre. Her decision to accost Shakespeare's new patron first was characteristically brazen, but she would have been aware of the pressures he was under in the immediate aftermath of his father's death. George Carey signed her petition with a perfunctory 'G. Hunsdon', performing thereby one of the most astounding acts of betrayal in theatrical history. Satisfied, the Dowager continued on her way, armed with the arguments she knew would best prevail among the business holders, lessees, immigrants and activists in her neighbourhood. In doing so she was walking in the footsteps of the constables appointed by her late husband, John Russell, and William Brooke, who had conducted their survey of the area's 'stranger' population thirteen years previously. In the process she would galvanize one of the most ambitious communal protests ever commandeered by a woman.

Elizabeth's petition is extraordinary for its inclusion of so many signatories. Another thirty residents of the Blackfriars community chose to lend their voices to her campaign against a new indoor theatre in the vicinity. It is indicative of her mettle that she did not submit her complaint under a male head signatory (apparently unconcerned by the prospect of being accused of meddling in matters above the reach of women), nor did she stop at the names of one or two prominent local men, as would have been more in keeping with the style of most petitions during this period. The Dowager was taking no chances. It was probably with an unfaltering anticipation of her success that she dispatched the completed document either to Richmond or to Whitehall, where the Privy Council was most frequently in attendance from late October and throughout November. At the heart of the royal court the councilmen would have debated Elizabeth's request. If the Earl of Essex, who had been in regular attendance at the Council table during at least the first three weeks of November, had raised any objections to her plea for the expulsion of Shakespeare's company from the area, he would have been outnumbered and outvoted by her own supporters, with both William and Robert Cecil, as well as her close neighbour Lord Cobham, its most influential members at this time.

Elizabeth was triumphant. Before too long the Privy Council had issued an order prohibiting the use of James Burbage's theatre by George Carey's players. Shakespeare and his business partners were cast out and left to face a cold and unforgiving winter.

19.

In the Name of Love

In 1596–7 the Cecils and William Brooke, as representatives of the Privy Council, had come to believe that in seditious hands the theatres could become the focal points of civil unrest, a view shared passionately by Elizabeth Russell. The Earl of Essex was riding high after his success in Cádiz and, with the opening of the Blackfriars Theatre, would have acquired a new vehicle for the propaganda that was upsetting the balance of power in an ever more volatile court.

It would not have escaped Essex's attention that one of the men responsible for targeting the theatres, Elizabeth's associate Richard Martin, had also been attempting to ruin his family financially from the winter of 1593. Martin was suing his mother, Lettice Knollys, demanding an eyewatering £2,123 from the Earl of Leicester's estate, close to £270,000 today, 'for plate sold to the Earl'. Although Martin's machinations while Lord Mayor had dented the fortunes of Shakespeare's company, it was Elizabeth's petition that abruptly put a stop to any plans the playwright may have had of moving his Oldcastle plays – with their aggrandizing of Essex's ancestral line and mockery of the Cobhams and Russells – to the Burbages' indoor playhouse. Shakespeare would have been aware, because it was included in one of his principal sources, Holinshed's *Chronicles*, that it was 'in the hall of the Black Friars at London' in which the Brookes' ancestor, Oldcastle, had been 'examined . . . [and] denounced an heretic'; the very same room that became Shakespeare's Blackfriars Theatre. In this venue the Oldcastle plays would have acquired a dangerous immediacy. Since Robert Cecil was married to Lord Cobham's daughter, Elizabeth Brooke, he would have also had a vested interest in protecting his children's legacy and was only too eager to believe his aunt's claim that the new theatre would be used as the cover for 'all manner of mischief'.

Already crippled by the closure of the theatres due to the plague, and on the verge of losing their Shoreditch Theatre, Shakespeare's troupe was left without an indoor venue and facing bankruptcy. Elizabeth's kinsmen on the Privy Council chose this time to strike a further blow by intervening to censor the dramatist's plays directly. This could have been skilfully stage-managed only through the intercession of William Brooke, Lord Cobham, who became Lord Chamberlain from 8 August 1596, after the death of Henry Carey. George Carey was frustrated in his attempts at gaining his father's former post, which gave its holder the power to license and censor plays. He had also been denied a place on the Privy Council, which meant he could not follow the elder Carey's example and serve as a buffer between the Queen's Councillors and the players. Henry Carey may have originally licensed *Henry IV, Part 1* with Oldcastle and John Russell in the character list, but this would not stop his successor from subjecting Shakespeare to the humiliating reprimands of censorship. Under investigation by the authorities, the playwright was forced to expunge John Russell and Harvey from his play and change the name Sir John Oldcastle. John Russell became Bardolph, while Oldcastle was replaced with Sir John Falstaff, the names by which they are popularly known to this very day.

In 1625 Dr Richard James looked back on these events and reflected that 'in Shakespeare's first show of Harry the Fifth, the person with which he undertook to play a buffoon was not Falstaff, but Sir John Oldcastle'. 'Harry' here probably denoted the *Henry IV* plays, those dealing with young Prince Hal, future King Henry V. James went on to explain that the censorship was ordered because 'offense' had been 'worthily taken by personages descended from his title, as peradventure by many others also who ought to have him in honourable memory'. He does not say who these 'others' were, but suggests they were acquainted with the scandal surrounding Shakespeare's play and revered Oldcastle's memory. This indicates that they were likely to be Puritans. In 1655 Thomas Fuller condemned Shakespeare for profaning the 'Memory of Sir John Oldcastle', whom he had 'fancied a boon companion, a jovial roister, and yet a coward to boot'. Intriguingly, he hinted that the 'bold' rewriting of Oldcastle's character was 'unjustly' executed as part of a more insidious conspiracy to undermine the Protestant faith, adding that 'it matters as little what petulant Poets, as what malicious Papists have written against him'. One of Fuller's detractors, Peter Heylyn, responded to these charges by saying that he was only making these claims because he himself was a Puritan.

We do not know precisely when one of history's most famous acts of censorship actually took place. It must have been some time before the death of the new Lord Chamberlain, William Brooke, on 6 March 1597. It was probably also before this date that Elizabeth Russell began engineering a marriage between his son, Henry Brooke, and her daughter Bess. 'It was told to me very secretly today,' wrote Rowland White on the seventh of that month, 'that the now Lord Cobham shall marry Mrs. Russell of the Privy Chamber'. This did not come to pass, perhaps because the mooted marriage was part of a compact between the late Lord Cobham and Elizabeth which Henry was not interested in honouring. It is very likely therefore that while Shakespeare was being investigated by the living descendant of Oldcastle, the Russells and the Brookes were planning a new alliance. It is a strong indication that the former Lord Cobham and the Dowager had been coordinating their activities in the policing of both Shakespeare and Essex in 1596–7.

Henry IV, Part 2 was either completed or still being written when Shakespeare was commanded to make changes to the text. The play may well have been left in limbo until the dramatist proved he had carried out Cobham's wishes and, just to add insult to injury, complied with his demand that he end the play with an embarrassing apology, which was probably spoken by the actor playing Falstaff:

> If my tongue cannot entreat you to acquit me, will you command me to use my legs? . . . All the gentlewomen here have forgiven me . . .

One word more, I beseech you. If you be not too much cloyed with fat meat, our humble author will continue the story with Sir John in it . . . where, for anything I know, Falstaff shall die of a sweat, unless already a [he] be killed with your hard opinions. For Oldcastle died martyr, and this is not the man.

The 'hard opinions' to which Shakespeare refers are evidence that his Oldcastle plays had caused offence. If the critic Violet A. Wilson was right, then one offended gentlewoman would not be so forgiving. It was Wilson who first suggested that *The Merry Wives of Windsor* contained allusions to the Dowager's legal dispute with her neighbour Richard Lovelace. In the very opening scene an actor dressed as a pompous country Justice of the Peace bounds on to the stage, bellowing angrily: 'I will make a Star Chamber matter of it. If he were twenty Sir John Falstaffs, he shall not abuse Robert Shallow, Esquire.' Justice Shallow's complaint against Falstaff is that he had been the catalyst for a 'riot', a crime for which he seeks the intercession of the Privy Council in order to initiate a suit in the Star Chamber. A Welsh parson, Sir Hugh Evans, attempts in his native patter to persuade him otherwise:

SHALLOW The Council shall hear it; it is a riot.
EVANS It is not meet the Council hear a riot. There is no fear of Got in a riot. The Council, look you, shall desire to hear the fear of Got, and not to hear a riot [. . .]
SHALLOW [*To Falstaff*] Knight, you have beaten my men, killed my deer, and broke open my lodge.
FALSTAFF But not kissed your keeper's daughter? . . .
SHALLOW The Council shall know of it.
FALSTAFF 'Twere better for you if it were known in counsel [*in secret*]. You'll be laughed at.

Wilson argued that the Windsor setting, the reference to the breaking open of a lodge and the appeal to the Privy Council to pursue a charge of 'riot' in the Star Chamber must have alluded to

Elizabeth Russell's war with Lovelace, which shook Bisham and Windsor. This has never gained wide-scale acceptance among Shakespeare scholars. But is there further evidence, untapped by Wilson, that might suggest the playwright really did intend for Elizabeth Russell to 'be laughed at' in his play?

It is most commonly believed that Shakespeare's *Merry Wives* was written for the investiture of George Carey to the venerable Order of the Garter on 23 April 1597 at Whitehall, probably performed during the evening of the Garter Feast, coincidentally on or near Shakespeare's thirty-third birthday. Among the twenty-four Knights of the Order in attendance was the Lord Admiral, Charles Howard, whom Elizabeth believed was behind her ejection from her Windsor property. But why should Shakespeare have felt the need to resurrect an incident that had occurred some years previously? Wilson, not having consulted the original Star Chamber transcripts of the trial, had misdated the Lovelace dispute to 1593. In fact, these conflicts had occurred between 1594 and 1595, with Elizabeth's Star Chamber suit, charging Lovelace with 'riot', dragging on until June 1596, when it was concluded in her favour. Lovelace was fined £40 and served a humiliating spell in prison. In the summing-up of the case Lord Keeper Egerton said 'he was not a fit or meet man to be a Justice of the Peace', while Lord Burghley called him 'an ungrateful man, for he and his father are greatly indebted to the said Lady [Russell] and Sir Edward Hoby, the chief founders of him and his ancestors'. Such indignities must have touched Lovelace's friend and commander, Charles Howard. The latter may therefore have been particularly amused by a witty allusion which mocked the formidable Dowager for her role in the events that had caused such trouble for his second-in-command. As Lieutenant of Windsor Castle and Forest, it is certain that Lovelace was himself involved in the celebrations that took place in Windsor at the ceremony for the installing of the knights on 24 May. He may have been among the 600-strong cavalcade of men who followed behind George Carey and Lord Thomas Howard in the procession to Windsor, wearing blue coats lined with orange-coloured taffeta or 'sad sea-colour green taffeta', with plumes of orange, green or purple ostrich feathers in their hats, draped with sparkling chains of gold. Shakespeare was among the handsome troupe so dressed, an orange plume in his hat, following proudly behind his patron.

That Shakespeare may have been intending to draw some of these men into camaraderie against the controversy-loving Dowager is perhaps indicated in a clever quip that almost always goes unnoticed. It is another of Shakespeare's characteristic plays on names, which indicates that he probably had at least begun writing the comedy before it was censored by William Brooke and that his intention was to make the character John Russell part of the action. The clue comes just a few lines after Justice Shallow's charge of 'riot':

FALSTAFF Pistol, did you pick Master Slender's purse? . . .
PISTOL . . . Word of denial! Froth and scum, thou liest! . . .
SLENDER By this hat, then he in the red face had it. For though I cannot remember what I did when you made me drunk, yet I am not altogether an ass.
FALSTAFF What say you, Scarlet and John?
BARDOLPH Why, sir, for my part, I say the gentleman had drunk himself out of his five sentences –

Bardolph is a name which appears thanks to the machinations of Lord Cobham. The joke here does not make sense unless the audience knows that the name Russell forms a pun on 'russet', the colour 'red'. Will Scarlet and Little John were two of Robin Hood's band of merry men. By calling Bardolph 'Scarlet and John', Falstaff alludes to his ruddy complexion – brought about by his fondness for drink – and the russet connotations of the name Russell. The jibe is perfectly fitted to a character who was originally called John Russell. If Shakespeare had intended such a character to be on stage during the comedic shenanigans involving the charge of 'riot' against Falstaff/Oldcastle, then this would have added to the relevance of the opening scene's mischievous topicality.

John Russell would have therefore shared the stage with the Welshman Hugh Evans. This is intriguing, for Evans is also the name of the Welsh scrivener and manager of Farrant's former theatre who had been responsible for the combined companies of boy players which included the Children of the Chapel at Windsor. *Merry Wives* culminates in an all-singing, all-dancing number by boys dressed as 'fairies', who bless Windsor Castle and the Chapel of St George and are instructed by the Fairy-Queen (a common mythic representation of Elizabeth I) to tend to the 'several chairs of Order', indicating those prepared for the investiture of the Knights of the Order of the Garter. Using the Queen's choristers, once managed by Evans, for the climactic scene of retribution, in which Oldcastle/Falstaff is hilariously pinched and taunted by the 'fairies', would have especially tickled the Brooke family's enemies.

That a seam of half-concealed allusion runs through this play is also indicated by the fact that Falstaff's gulling is matched by that of a fellow dupe, a character called Ford who disguises himself as 'Brooke' in order to test his wife's fidelity. Both end up being tricked by Mistresses Ford and Page, the 'merry wives' who prove their chastity and their superior intelligence. Once again, Shakespeare appears to have been subjected to the rigours of the censors and was forced to change the controversial name Brooke to Broome. This is hardly surprising, given that Brooke recalled the Cobham family into which Robert Cecil had married, the same family with whom Elizabeth Russell had been negotiating the marriage of her daughter to Henry Brooke just weeks before the garter feast. Shakespeare could not have chosen a better way to get at Elizabeth and her kinsmen if he'd tried, for his play brought on stage together the doppelgängers of the men who had lived in the immediate vicinity of the Blackfriars, practically next door to each other: John Russell, the Brookes and Hugh Evans. But there is one figure missing: Richard Lovelace. Can his presence be felt in this play?

Historians have been perplexed by the play's apparent autobiographical reference to an incident which allegedly occurred in Shakespeare's youth. The first act of *The Merry Wives of Windsor* seems to contain comic allusions to the Lucy family, whose patri-arch, Sir Thomas Lucy of Charlecote, was said to have once prosecuted the playwright for poaching on his land. As the mayhem in the first scene of the play continues, the Queen and knights are treated to a mocking exposition of Shallow's venerable pedigree. Shallow's nephew, Abraham Slender, praises his coat of arms:

SLENDER . . . a gentleman born, Master Parson, and writes himself Armigero – in any bill, warrant, quittance, or obligation, Armigero.

SHALLOW Ay, that I do, and have done any time these three hundred years.

SLENDER All his successors gone before him hath done't, and all his ancestors that come after him may. They may give the dozen white luces in their coat.

SHALLOW It is an old coat.

EVANS The dozen white louses do become an old coat well. It agrees well passant. It is a familiar beast to man, and signifies love.

Many critics believe the 'luces' – a luce was a fresh-water pike – refers to the coat of arms of the Lucy family. 'Armigero' meant to bear the arms of a gentleman. The three silver luces on the Lucy crest served as a fitting pun on their ancestral name. The confusion between luces and 'louses' would therefore be particularly cutting. But why should such an early episode in Shakespeare's life – if it had occurred at all – have appeared in a play of 1596/7? This question has led critics to doubt the veracity of the tale that describes Shake-speare's brief career as a poacher.

Few biographers of Shakespeare know, however, that in 1597 Sir Thomas Lucy's granddaughter Joyce married Elizabeth Russell's nephew William Cooke of Higham Court in Gloucestershire, son to her brother, also called William Cooke. The younger William Cooke was a blood relative of the Brownes of Betchworth, one of whom signed Elizabeth's petition against the Blackfriars Theatre. The mar-riage probably took place in Shakespeare's native Warwickshire, in

Charlecote itself. Shortly after Elizabeth targeted Burbage's play-house, therefore, the Lucy family had married into the Cooke family. It was the elder Sir Thomas Lucy who so mercilessly perse-cuted Shakespeare's kinsmen during the breaking of the so-called Somerville–Arden plot. Commandeering the investigation, he ensured that the family would be disgraced and touched with the infamy of treason. Elizabeth may have known the Lucy family, because both she and Sir Thomas senior commanded extensive estates in Worcestershire and her friends in the Burden family had intervened directly in the legal suits that pursued Francis Arden and many of his Warwickshire acquaintances after the conspiracy. It is hardly surprising that both the Lucys and the Russells should be satirized together in the play which grew out of the *Henry IV* cycle. Shakespeare may have viewed the match as a compact between an old nemesis and his new persecutors.

Shakespeare may also have intended his first audience to decode another ingenious puzzle in the 'luce' joke, one which alluded spe-cifically to Elizabeth's dispute with Lovelace. Just three months after she won her Star Chamber case, Richard Field published one of the most scurrilous books to appear in Elizabeth I's reign: *The Metamorphosis of Ajax*, written by the Queen's godson, John Haring-ton. This text was truly groundbreaking, as it was a book about a cutting-edge piece of technology which would change the world; for Harington was an inventor and he had designed the first modern flushable privy or toilet. 'Ajax' is a pun on 'a Jakes', the slang word for a privy. But Harington had a mischievous streak. He had acquired a reputation as a satirist and libeller and used the occasion of his indecorous theme to turn his *Ajax* into a comic satire. Alongside his account of the construction of England's first modern flushable toi-let he created a cryptic gallery of caricatures mocking the great and the good of Renaissance society. Harington had attended Eton with Edward Hoby, but was also incredibly close to his mother, whom he addressed affectionately as 'my best Lady that have even from my childhood ever so specially favoured me'.

On 14 August 1596 Harington looked to the Dowager for support with the progress of this book, saying that his work was a mere 'toy' which he thought 'would give some occasion to have me thought of and talked of'. It certainly did that. He was writing in some consternation for his 'fantastical treatise', as he termed it, had been put 'to the print under a covert name', but not before part of it was sent to William Cecil, who was far from pleased with the fruits of Harington's labours. The book sparked the fury of the Queen, who exiled its author from the court, accusing him of attempting to libel the memory of Essex's stepfather, the Earl of Leicester (though this did not stop her from having a flushable toilet of her own installed in Richmond Palace in Surrey).

Harington begged Elizabeth to speak to Cecil and 'to deliver your favourable censure of it, at least so far, that it is pleasant and harmless'. He asked her, by way of bribe, to inform Burghley that he could call upon him to install a privy for him at Theobalds at his earliest convenience. Always a pioneer, Elizabeth would have appreciated Harington's engineering prowess. She and her first husband, Sir Thomas Hoby, had fitted one of the country's first plumbing systems in their Bisham home. She would also have relished being one of the few people in the country who knew the true identities behind the witty parodies in Harington's book, as he had read 'the most part of it' to her. She may even have had something to do with a riddling reference to her which has remained undecoded until now. This quip is squashed in the margin of the main text and reads:

> There is a noble and learned Lady, dowager to the Lord John Russell, that will not name love without save reverence.

To say 'save reverence' in the Renaissance meant to ask forgiveness, or beg one's pardon, normally after uttering something blasphemous or crude. Here Harington is implying that for Elizabeth even the *name* of 'Love' is a profanity. The joke is at the expense of Richard *Love*lace, the Lieutenant of Windsor Castle. During the very year in which he helped to close down the Blackfriars Theatre, therefore, Field was printing texts which lauded Elizabeth Russell as both Dowager and successful litigant.

So what of Shakespeare's *Merry Wives*? Hugh Evans hits the mark when he identifies the meaning of the luce/louse. The intricate connotations of this creature meander through the scene's comic shifts and turns until we finally alight on the punchline: this beast 'signifies 'love', it is a *love*-luce. Shakespeare's picking up on Harington's joke, published just before the first performance of his play, makes sense of Evan's climactic final word on the matter, giving us the identity of Elizabeth's antagonist 'Love*lace*'. As the real Henry Evans had been the Dowager's near-neighbour in the Blackfriars, knowledge of the scandalous conflict would probably not have escaped him and, coming from his namesake, the snappy quip would have been especially effective. The likelihood that Shakespeare was aware of Harington's text and engaged with its satire is increased by his possible allusions to it in *As You Like It*. It has long been thought that the play's melancholy Jaques, whose name puns on 'jakes', is a caricature of Harington himself (in allusion to his 'Ajax'). Shakespeare's creation appears to be in self-imposed exile from the court and describes himself as a satirist-figure by whose invective the 'wise man's folly is anatomized'. When the play's feisty heroine, Rosalind, encounters Jaques in the forest of Arden, a contest of wits follows, one which conceals a cryptic statement that has gone entirely unnoticed:

ROSALIND They say you are a melancholy fellow . . .

JAQUES I have neither the scholar's melancholy, which is emulation,
nor the musician's, which is fantastical, nor the courtier's, which
is proud . . . but it is a melancholy of mine own . . . extracted
from many objects, and indeed the sundry contemplation of my
travels . . .

ROSALIND A traveller! By my faith, you have great reason to be
sad . . . Farewell, Monsieur Traveller.

The allusion is to a sequel to Harington's pamphlet, *An Anatomy of the Metamorphosed Ajax*, also published by Richard Field in 1596. The author is anonymous, simply identifying himself as 'T. C. traveller'. Shakespeare's joke, like that in the *Merry Wives*, ranges over several lines, as Rosalind artfully turns Jaques' penchant for travelling into a name: 'Monsieur Traveller'. Shakespeare's name-play would have been a fitting homage to Harington, who closes the *Anatomy* with a cryptic emblem and a challenge to his reader. 'Now riddle me what name is this,' writes the author, drawing the reader's attention to an image of a hare with a ring in its mouth standing on a barrel or 'tun'. Beneath this a poem:

> Fly sin with fear, as harmless (hare) doth hound,
> Like precious (ring) embrace more precious truth,
> As (tun) full of good juice, not empty sound . . .

When setting the text to type, Field placed brackets around certain words: hare, ring, tun. Har-ing-ton. The fact that Shakespeare responded to such encrypted wordplay and enjoyed using it himself makes it all the more likely that he had included a riddling reference to Elizabeth Russell's Lovelace disputes in his play. It was probably composed only shortly after Harington's *Ajax* referred to the termination of her case, and it is unlikely that members of the elite audience who witnessed the *Merry Wives* would not have interpreted the charge of 'riot', the breaking open of a lodge and the threat of a Star Chamber suit, with an eye towards the Dowager's recent scandals. If the play had originally been composed with the intention of having John Russell on stage while these events unfolded, then the allusions would have been all the more striking. Harington would have known that the case was notorious enough to have garnered a chuckle from those in the know after reading about Elizabeth's new-found hatred of the name of 'love'. Shakespeare follows suit, scoring a small victory against his female nemesis.

Around one week before his investiture to the Order of the Garter, an honour which Henry Carey had also held, George Carey was made Lord Chamberlain and granted a place on the Privy Council. Less than six months after he had helped close down the Blackfriars

Theatre, he was finally being awarded his father's most influential offices. Shakespeare's satirical targets and his celebration of his patron in the *Merry Wives* indicate that there were probably no hard feelings between them. Carey was now in a place of greater security, and perhaps they both felt that they could laugh themselves out of the awkwardness caused by his role in the closure of the Blackfriars Theatre.

In the 1930s the critic Leslie Hotson suggested that another figure lurked behind the character of Shallow: that of William Gardiner, the Puritan Justice of the Peace who had been involved in repeated attempts to close the theatres along with Elizabeth's associates, Lord Cobham, William More, George More and Richard Martin. His first wife was Frances Wayte, whose family name was Luce or Lucy. This meant that he was entitled to display on his coat of arms the three luces, or fresh-water pike, which also appeared on the crest of Sir Thomas Lucy. Gardiner's role as one of the Surrey Justices of the Peace who had responded so vigorously to the 1592 riots – the very tumults which provided Elizabeth with the potent precedent that underpinned her own petition – would have given Shakespeare additional reason to detest the name of Lucy. It was in the very year in which James Burbage's playhouse slipped through his grasp that the playwright became entangled with Gardiner in a mysterious incident which has continued to defy explanation.

Towards the end of November 1596 Shakespeare was accused of little short of attempted murder and was summoned to give sureties of the peace in court with four other accomplices, one of whom was Francis Langley, the owner of the newly built Swan Theatre. The popular image of England's 'gentle Shakespeare' is incompatible with that of the man accused of threatening his victim with 'fear of death and mutilation of limbs'; yet this is the very wording of the writ of attachment returnable on 29 November.

It was some time in the middle of the month when William Wayte appeared before the Court of King's Bench to swear that his life was placed in danger by Shakespeare, Langley and their confederates. A sheriff of Surrey was then dispatched to apprehend these persons. Once located, they were issued with a command to appear before the court, where they were forced to swear to uphold the peace on pain of fine or imprisonment. Wayte was Gardiner's stepson and was described by a contemporary as 'a certain loose person of no reckoning or value, being wholly under the rule and commandment of the said Gardiner'. Gardiner was scarcely regarded in better light by those who knew him. His own son-in-law, as he expired on his deathbed, accused him of causing his demise through witchcraft. It is possible that Wayte had served the writ on his stepfather's behalf, for on two consecutive days, 21 and 22 May, Gardiner had clashed spectacularly with Langley. Angry words were exchanged between them, and Langley, who reviled his antagonist as 'a false perjured knave', was quick to get his writ in first. In October 1596 both Gardiner and Wayte received notification that their opponent was seeking 'sureties of the peace' against them. About two weeks later Wayte countered with his own writ, targeting, along with Shakespeare and Langley, three unidentified individuals: Anne Lee, Dorothy Soer and John Soer, the last two husband and wife.

The Soers may in some way be related to the owners of the tenements in Paris Garden Lane, on the Bankside, called 'Soer's rents'. These were probably once owned by Francis Langley and were let out to a number of actors. It is possible that Shakespeare was leasing lodgings from the Soers for, after Elizabeth Russell had forced him out of the Blackfriars, he decided to move across the Thames to the Bankside, close to the site of Langley's Swan Theatre. Wayte's writ places Shakespeare in this area, over which the Surrey justices held sway, by mid-November, when the writ was probably issued. It therefore gives us a likely date for Elizabeth's petition of early November.

Langley was accused of a range of criminal activities, from dealing in stolen goods to keeping a brothel. His connection to Shakespeare adds a sordid note to the playwright's machinations at this time; all the more so since Langley was being tailed by Elizabeth's brother-in-law and nephew, the ubiquitous Cecils. These peculiar events unfolded in the same month that the Dowager mounted her operation against Shakespeare's Blackfriars Theatre. Can this be a coincidence? Could it have had anything to do with the fact that the storm which engulfed Langley at this time was blown in by the Earl of Essex?

The events which had embroiled Francis Langley culminated in the interrogation of Essex for the missing Cádiz loot in September 1596. It was Sir Anthony Ashley, one of the many whom Essex had knighted during the Cádiz mission, who would be instrumental in implicating the Cecils' adversary in the scandal. Ashley had illegally confiscated valuable treasures from the Cádiz raid, including a ship's cargo of oil. He was aided in the theft by Essex's steward, Sir Gelly Meyrick, also one of the Earl's new knights. Before Ashley had even returned to England, Robert Cecil was suspicious and dispatched his spy, Richard Drake, to stake out his home in Holborn. Hiding out in the shop of a nearby shoemaker, he waited for Ashley to incriminate himself. On 4 August he reported strange goings-on at 2 a.m. Men were seen carrying eight heavy trunks into his lodgings under cover of darkness. Cecil ordered a raid and Ashley eventually made a full report to the Privy Council, revealing that in Cádiz 'great spoils hath been made and robberies of riches'. Ashley's confessions helped the Cecils keep Essex under their thumb while Elizabeth worked on his spymaster, Anthony Bacon. But there was more to Cecil's interest in Essex's renegade knight. He had been trailing Ashley for quite some time, on the hunt for a fabulous diamond. Cecil had pursued this prize for four years and, in 1596, he finally found it in the hands of Ashley's brother-in-law, Francis Langley.

The treasure had been seized in the Azores voyage of 1592. When Sir Walter Ralegh's fleet captured the Portuguese carrack the *Madre de Dios*, they found it laden with silks, carpets, spices, precious stones, musk and ambergris. Among the jewels of incalculable value was a 'great diamond'. The stone slipped through Cecil's grasp, vanishing shortly after its confiscation from the ship. It was not until 15 May 1596 that he learned of Francis Langley's involvement in the diamond's theft, from his own brother-in-law. Ashley confessed that he and Langley had planned to sell it for a staggering £2,600, close to £300,000 today. In order to pressure Ashley into giving up the whereabouts of his brother-in-law, Cecil employed William Brooke, Lord Cobham, to apply some none too gentle pressure. Cobham obeyed, writing a fierce letter to Ashley, terrifying him out of his wits and keeping him awake the whole night after. At 3 a.m. on 16 May Ashley found and confronted Langley, thrusting Cobham's letter in his face, 'whereat (I assure you) he was so far gone out of himself', he reported, 'that for a time I knew not what to make of him, fish or flesh, wise or foolish, protesting solemnly he would rather choose to rot in prison than betray or deliver the thing'. Ashley importuned him but Langley refused to 'repair to the Lord Cobham . . . doubting thereby some danger intended to us both'.

Francis Langley double-crossed Ashley, reaping not only his own but his brother-in-law's share of the profits. Humiliated and cheated of the diamond, Cecil and Cobham now waited for any excuse to make Langley pay. In the very same month that Elizabeth Russell shut down the Blackfriars Theatre, he and Shakespeare found themselves targeted by William Gardiner, a co-justice with Elizabeth's friend William More. There is perhaps a more intimate connection between Elizabeth and Gardiner. The latter's son and namesake would marry the daughter of the Puritan Christopher Yelverton, the Queen's Sergeant. Yelverton's son Henry would inherit the family's non-conformist leanings and establish close ties with Elizabeth; so close, in fact, that she intended to make him a benefactor in her will. She would also place him in a position of great trust as co-executor of property in Eyfforde Pastures, in Gloucestershire, for he is named in the indenture that conveys her portion of the estate to her children 'for their better preferment' in 1608. A longer-term association between them is suggested by the fact that both Yelvertons, father and son, were Gray's Inn men, like Thomas Posthumous Hoby, and worked to support Puritan preachers.

While the extent of Elizabeth's association with Gardiner in 1596–7 must remain speculation, what is clear is that Shakespeare felt the need to move across the river to the Bankside during or just after the Dowager's intervention in his plans for the Blackfriars Theatre, where he became involved, wittingly or not, in the scandal surrounding Langley. If the playwright's company had moved to the Swan Theatre by the middle of November 1596, having been evicted from their new indoor theatre, then Wayte's persecution of Shakespeare and Langley, almost certainly with Gardiner's support, may have been an attempt to dismantle Langley's business dealings with George Carey's troupe, which would be renamed the Chamberlain's Men after William Brooke's death. Tellingly, Gardiner would be involved, along with other Surrey Justices of the Peace, in an aggressive move to close down the Swan on 28 July 1597. That the beleaguered playwright found it difficult to settle near the Swan is indicated by the fact that he appears again in the tax assessments for the parish of St Helen's in Bishopsgate the following year, having moved back to the other side of the river. This must have been a terrifying time for him. Prevented by Elizabeth Russell from making use of the Blackfriars Theatre, he was facing legal prosecution by the Surrey authorities. With the lease for the Shoreditch Theatre about to expire, an uncertain future without a playing venue loomed. History's most famous dramatist was facing his own terrible tragedy.

PART FIVE

The Birth of the Globe

20.

Aftermath

Lady Elizabeth Russell was precisely the type of person about whom it was wise to speak in code. She had powerful intimates and knew much they would rather have kept hidden from the world. Because she was not one to understand her kinsmen's political peccadilloes without attempting to do something about them, Sir Robert Sidney's agent, Rowland White, had the good sense to use an encrypted method of communication when discussing her exploits with his employer. His dispatch of 4 March 1597 becomes a secret cypher after the general gossip gives way to matters of greater sensitivity:

> And now I will acquaint you with something which I hear of the secrets in court.
>
> 24 hath been very often very private with 1000 and is the mediator of a peace between him and 200, who likewise hath been private with him; 24 alleges how much good may grow by it. 1500 continual unquietness will turn to contentments. Dispatches of all matters of war and peace for the safety of the land, will go forward, to the hurt of the common enemies; 1000 was yesterday in the afternoon two hours at my lady Russell's house in Blackfriars. How —— will like of this, when it is known, you may in your own wisdom judge of; but 1000 wearied with not knowing how to please, is not unwilling to harken to those motions, made unto him for the public good.

Following her success in preventing the Blackfriars Theatre from opening, Elizabeth did not slacken her involvement in the intrigues that were continuing to shake the royal court. The mysterious individual, assigned the code number 1000, who visited her in the Blackfriars for a clandestine conference lasting two hours was the Earl of Essex. Factional squabbles between the latter and Sir Robert Cecil, code number 200, had become so intense that even Essex's other enemy Sir Walter Ralegh, referred to here as 24, had been attempting to bring about a reconciliation. This was needed now more than ever. The Queen, 1500 in White's cypher, was drawing her best military commanders together with the intention of arranging a pre-emptive strike on the Spanish fleet in the port of Ferrol, following fears that King Philip was out for English blood after suffering the humiliation of the Cádiz raid. Elizabeth would shortly have something to say about this, but her pressing business with Essex in the Blackfriars (and the reason for White's cautious use of secret code) was due to a matter altogether closer to home. Less than sixty-six feet south of her own property to be more precise, for it was in his mansion here that William Brooke, Lord Cobham, the man who censored Shakespeare, lay dying.

The missing name in White's cypher is no doubt that of Lord Cobham's son, Henry (Harry) Brooke, Essex's rival and the real Falstaff. On 2 March White had written to Sir Robert Sidney of the ailing Baron that 'it is now held certain he cannot live', informing him that Essex was doing everything in his power to ensure that Cobham's post of Warden of the Cinque Ports would pass to Sidney. 'For the Cinque Ports,' wrote White, 'as I hear, Mr Harry Brooke stands for that place . . . If my Lord of Essex is able to do anything, it will now appear,' Essex did not wait for fate to decide the outcome. He set about poisoning the Queen against Henry, 'laying before Her Majesty his unworthiness, and unableness to do her service'. Around midnight on 5/6 March Lord Cobham died. 'The court is now full of, who shall have this and that office,' White rushed to tell an expectant Sidney, 'but most voices say, that Mr Harry Brooke shall have . . . the Cinque Ports.' If Essex had hoped in his private meeting with Elizabeth to charm her into supporting his friend's bid for the disputed office, he was mistaken. Henry Brooke would win this little battle.

The solidarity of the Cecil–Cobham–Russell alliance can be felt in the closure of the Blackfriars Theatre, and in the censorship of Shakespeare's *Henry IV* plays and *The Merry Wives of Windsor*. It was, however, a bond which would be weakened by more than the tragedy of Lord Cobham's death. Perhaps Shakespeare's use of the name of Brooke in *The Merry Wives* would have felt like even more of a rebuke to Robert Cecil after he had lost a living link to the family of the real Oldcastle. On 24 January 1597 his wife, Elizabeth Brooke, died in childbirth. It says something about Cecil's relationship with his aunt that, at his lowest ebb, he decided to write to her. His letter is not extant but Elizabeth's fulsome reply, written the very next day, is. It is a learned treatise – peppered with a good smattering of Latin and Greek – on the dangers of grief, a subject in which she herself was well schooled. 'I speak by experience,' she wrote, 'and know too well that to be true which I say.' Her words show something of the robustness of her personality, her stoicism in the face of devastating loss:

> [Y]ou [will] find this *daemonius meridianus* [noonday demon] to creep so far into your heart, with his variety of virtues, seeming good to be yielded to (melancholy I mean) as in end will shorten life, by cumbrous conceits and sickness, and when it is rooted so, as with peevish persuasions . . . it will bring forth the fruit of stupidity, forgetfulness of your natural disposition of sweet and apt speeches, fit for your place, and instead thereof breed and make you a sullen, sharp, sour plum, and no better than in truth a very melancholy mole and a misanthropos; hateful to God and man . . .

Warning him against the 'dissembling devil' of despair, Elizabeth quoted one of her favourite authors, the poet Horace, '*Tu, Romane, caveto*' ('You, Roman, beware'). Not content with that, she sent him a separate poem, one of Horace's *Epistles*, which had been poignantly altered in a manner which referred to its recipient as her 'sweet foster-child'. As she had done many times before, she used her letter to foreground her identity as wife to the translator of *The Book of the Courtier*, urging her nephew to hold fast to his role as 'a wise councillor and cunning courtier'. Hold fast he did, for, even during his greatest hour of grief, he did not abandon his duties nor his significant work, the weight of which made his desk bow.

On 1 June it had come to Cecil's ears through an Italian agent that the astronomer Rizza Casa had predicted that the Queen was about to be poisoned. England's Catholic enemies had needed less encouragement in the past. 'The Earl of Essex ought to be strong,' said the dispatch, advising him to make immediate haste to intercept the Spanish fleet before it attacked England. By 22 June Cecil was rousing the commanders of the mission, sending them a handwritten prayer by the Queen in 'delicate style', and confirming that Essex's 'purpose is to burn the fleet at Ferrol'. Cecil was drawn into temporary camaraderie with his nemesis, allowing himself to believe that their joint efforts would 'free us of an evil neighbour, and make Mercury [his code name for the mercurial King of Spain] stoop'.

Busy making predictions of her own, Lady Russell was less pleased about the news. Although she had been in favour of a hard-line stance when it came to England's intervention in France and the Low Countries, she felt this strategy was too risky. 'I in no wise like of the enterprise toward,' she said. 'It may have good beginning, but I fear ill success in end by lives and loss of more than the King of Spain and all his is worth.' She waited for Cecil's response. None came. She would not be ignored, think though he may that such matters were above the reach of a woman. She wrote back on 24 June demanding a reply, protesting that it was the least he could do, given that 'I took a great deal of pain to mitigate your melancholy.' Needless to say, her advice was not heeded. Cecil should have listened, for the mission became a national embarrassment after Essex's fleet was shipwrecked off the Bay of Biscay during ferocious storms.

Elizabeth had an ulterior motive for demanding her nephew's attention. Looking towards storms closer to home, she had resolved to end the dispute over her family's right to claim honorific title by acquiring for one of her daughters the undisputed coronet of a

Countess. It had come to her attention that William Somerset, Baron Herbert, the eldest son of Edward, 4th Earl of Worcester, was on the marriage market. Her attempts at securing a match for her daughter with Henry Brooke having failed, she now issued a new command: 'it will please you in your best opportunity to persuade the Earl so as my daughter Bess may be wife to my Lord Herbert, his eldest son'. She promised in return a jointure of £200 per annum after her death, in addition to the £100 yearly inheritance 'presently enjoyed'. This should be, by her calculation, 'a sufficient portion for an Earl of so small revenue and so many children as the Earl of Worcester hath'.

The Earl may have paused in considering this, for Bess was as headstrong and stubborn as her mother. She was unlike her mother, however, in her attraction to the extravagance of court life, and her desire to keep up with the other female courtiers meant she was constantly short of funds. Their relationship would be tested in 1599 when Elizabeth conveyed to her daughters' use Russell House on the Strand, the title to which had belonged to the Queen. Dissatisfied with its rental returns, Bess was particularly keen to sell the property as soon as it came into her hands. Robert Cecil lived practically next door, in Burghley House, and quickly began proceedings to purchase it from the girls. The sale, as Elizabeth explained forcefully to her nephew, 'bitterly forbidden was by me . . . whereby I shall have your inward malice to me for not agreeing to it'. She blamed the mastermind behind the scheme. 'But this is all the comfort that ever I yet received of Bess since her breath,' she wrote angrily, 'to be detriment to me by all means [that] lie in her.' This did not satisfy Cecil, who asked Sir Edward Hoby to try to change his mother's mind. Hoby dutifully 'reasoned the case with her'. In return his mother 'gave way to many humours', berating him for his 'unthriftiness'. She was determined, he exclaimed with some sourness to his cousin, forever to keep possession of the 'rotten house of Russell'. Cecil refused to accept this as her final answer. He commanded her to think more carefully about his offer and return to him with her decision within three days.

Before the deadline expired Elizabeth sat mournfully at her desk in the Blackfriars. It was nine o'clock on a Sunday morning. As she began to write, her resolve hardened. 'I, that had ever told Bess and her sister, long since and often, that whensoever they weeded out their father's name out of Russell House, they should root out my heart from them,' she declared defiantly, 'must either consent or bring the burden of a mighty Councillor, my nephew, upon me.' Let it be so, *'perfecto odio oderis me'* ('hate me with a perfect hatred'), Russell House would never be pulled up from her 'dead husband's name . . . by the roots' while she could do anything about it. She would rather 'sell all I am worth' than 'not to give all due to my dead darling while I breathe'. Since Nan had protested 'with tears' that she would not sell 'to any creature' without her mother's consent, then 'God reward Mistress Elizabeth, much good shall she get by her presumptuous disobedience.'

Elizabeth made it clear that her battle with Bess over Russell House was only the latest in a long history of misdemeanours which had brought them into conflict. She would not even be satisfied in her daughter's proposed marriage, for she did not get the opportunity to wear down the Earl of Worcester. William Somerset, Baron Herbert, died in 1598, leaving his brother Henry in Elizabeth's line of sight. This would not be the last the Somersets heard from the ambitious Dowager. The next time she entered into negotiations about her daughters' marriages, however, she would do so with more political savvy.

In the months immediately following her closure of the Blackfriars Theatre, Elizabeth's interest in her daughters' marriages was prompted by another cause. Her recent machinations had left her exhausted, physically weak and drained. In June 1597, at the age of fifty-seven, she turned her sickbed into her office and thence set about securing her girls' future by arranging a £600 yearly inheritance to be paid to them after her death. 'I am mortal and sickly,' she wrote to Thomas Egerton, wasting no time in requesting that he 'be an overseer of my will'. But this was Elizabeth Russell and things were rarely straightforward. 'I make a gentlewoman sole executrice,' she said, 'which, by your lordship's assistance, may be supported every way with justice and law.'

Elizabeth was aware that conferring such a responsibility on one of her daughters – by this time Bess and Nan were aged twenty-two and nineteen respectively – would be straining the law, but she was a defender of women's legal rights. Just after her brush with Anthony Bacon the previous September, she had proved this by attempting to shield a niece of Robert Bacon from the latter's greed. Robert was a cousin of Anthony and had sought Elizabeth's aid in a Chancery case involving the wardship of his niece's children. Worded in collaboration with Anthony, the request was that she contact Lord Treasurer Burghley and Lord Keeper Thomas Egerton on Robert's behalf. The petitioner, it seems, wanted to enjoy the revenues from the wardship but evade the responsibility of providing for their mother, who had been left with £1,400 debts, close to £160,000 today, and only a meagre revenue from a leased property to help her bear the charge. Elizabeth's response remains a rare and most affecting instance of female solidarity to have survived from the period:

> You shall pardon me, I will neither speak to the Lord Treasurer nor send to the Lord Keeper in your behalf, for that I think this so unreasonable an allotment as that the widow that was your niece hath just cause to think you no way to have loved her. What shall she pay debts with? . . . How shall she live when this lease is expired? . . . And shall her cradle be beholding to you for that which is her own and yours but in trust . . . ? Did not you tell me that it should be to her good and her children's? What good hath the mother out of the third or halfpenny benefit by your friendship, but undone and made contemptible . . . and abused by putting her whole trust in you? . . . God bless my daughter from such a kinsman . . .

Elizabeth's refusal to help an influential member of the Essex–Bacon cabal left Anthony fuming, and he wrote two days later to the Earl of Essex with his detractions against his aunt's 'most violent, passionate partiality, and dishonourable inconstancy'. Essex threw his weight behind the Bacons' cause and even visited Elizabeth in the Blackfriars shortly afterwards, but to no avail. Her desire to defend Robert Bacon's niece against such mighty opposition, as well as her insistence on appointing a female executrix for her will, say something about her belief that women had as much right to manage, and benefit from, landed estates as men.

Despite the weariness that had followed in the wake of her clash with the backers of the Blackfriars Theatre, in 1597 Elizabeth found the strength to engage in a legal battle with the widow of a draper called May and an upholsterer named Barrodell over services which they claimed had remained unpaid. Pursued through a process normally reserved for those of lower rank, she was served a writ which made her an 'outlaw' if she failed to appear to answer charges when apprehended by a sheriff. This piqued her customary defence of her status as Dowager Countess, and it was the ever-patient Robert Cecil who received her protest that the motion was 'not lawful . . . my husband being known to be more than a Baron'. The case had not dented her sense of humour, for she ended in lively style, declaring, 'as lately as I have been at death's door, I would rather marry someone that lacketh one of his five senses rather than carry so great an indignity . . . Thus, nephew, may you see, how weak soever my body is made by sickness, my mind is the same it was.' Cecil did as he was told and put pressure on Mistress May's counsel to drop the suit. A jubilant Elizabeth thanked her nephew for taking the time to 'rattle up the attorney'.

With May and 'that varlet Barrodell' put in their places, Elizabeth decided she was going to serve all the undesirables in an entire London district in like fashion. In a mission to secure greater independence for the residents of the Blackfriars than had ever been achieved by William More, she began negotiations with Lord Burghley to tighten security there, to be effected by officers appointed by her. She ordered the Cecils' man, William Necton, to undertake a survey of the area and, armed with the results (no doubt slanted in her favour), she asked Robert Cecil to inform his father that 'there hath been, and is needful to be, a steward and a Bailiff in the Black-friars to maintain the liberties of Her Majesty, and to keep all things in order which now for want of a governor are too bad out of course'. A woman undertaking the policing of a densely populated London district in this way was entirely unprecedented. The outcome is unrecorded, but it is clear that in reminding the Cecils of her concerns about local disorder, she was continuing her bid for political sway in the area in a manner which drew on the tenor of her Privy Council petition little more than eight months previously. Shakespeare and Burbage had stood in the way of those plans and they had paid the price.

The year 1596 marked the termination of Richard Field's business dealings with William Shakespeare. After issuing the fourth edition of *Venus and Adonis* that year, he never published a stand-alone work by Shakespeare again. The only known potentially personal connection between them after this time emerges from a cryptic reference in Shakespeare's late play *Cymbeline*. Donning a masculine disguise, the play's heroine, Imogen, assumes the French name Fidele and claims that her master is one 'Richard du Champ', Richard of the Field. Fidele is a near-anagram of 'Field'. This, compounded with the fact that, in his Spanish publications, the Stratford printer called himself 'Ricardo del Campo', indicates that Shakespeare must have been alluding to Richard Field.

This touching moment in the play has always been seen as a compliment to Field: a testament to an enduring bond of friendship, for *fidèle* is French for 'loyal, faithful, constant, trustworthy'. Field would have appreciated the French connotations, having been married to the Huguenot Jacqueline Vautrollier. After his introduction to Imogen in her guise as Fidele, the character Lucius responds, 'Thou dost approve thyself the very same:/Thy name well fits thy faith; thy faith thy name:/ . . . The boy hath taught us manly duties.' If Shakespeare was aware of Field's betrayal, had he forgiven him by 1610, the potential date of the play's composition? By this time he had regained the Blackfriars Theatre, and perhaps he felt he had the luxury of forgiveness. If so, then why did he not turn to Field for the publication of his sonnets in 1609? There is another, as yet unexplored, possibility. Could the allusion have been intended to hurt Field, to remind him of just how far he had fallen from his faith, from his fidelity, by showing him a taunting exemplar of faithfulness in the character of the loyal Fidele? The pun on Fidele's name, though obvious enough not to require much overstating, is harped on extravagantly by Lucius. Does Shakespeare, in other words, protest Fidele's/Field's fidelity too much?

By helping Elizabeth Russell block Shakespeare's occupation of the Blackfriars Theatre, Field was partly responsible for the crisis into which this plunged the playwright in 1596. Shakespeare must have known that his patron, George Carey, had signed Elizabeth's petition too. Since Carey's father, Shakespeare's previous patron, had given his tacit agreement to James Burbage's theatrical scheme, it would have been almost impossible for his son to hide his objection to the plans after commandeering the company. Shakespeare had suffered a double betrayal, and the abrupt ending of Field's role as his publisher may indicate that he was keenly aware of this. Whatever the truth behind the enigmatic Fidele, Shakespeare would have had no doubt about the danger he was in by January 1597, when a bitter and bankrupt James Burbage died. His death, some would later claim, was due to his grief at the loss of the Blackfriars Theatre.

Little more than three months remained of the lease of the Theatre in Shoreditch when the Hunsdon's Men lost one of history's greatest theatrical innovators. Thanks to Elizabeth Russell, the Blackfriars was out of bounds and Shakespeare had found any association he may have had with Francis Langley at the Swan Theatre far from untroubled. Burbage's sons, Richard and Cuthbert, moved fast to attempt to secure an extension to the lease of the Theatre from the landlord, Giles Allen. The latter's recalcitrance sparked a lawsuit at the Court of Requests. During these trials it was revealed that around 13 April 1576 James Burbage had signed the lease for the grounds in Hollywell, in the parish of St Leonard's, Shoreditch, upon which his Theatre would be built. He had agreed to pay £14 per annum with the proviso that Allen consent, in writing, after ten years, to renew the lease for a further twenty-one years. After the initial term Burbage continued an uncertain occupation of the theatre, making several requests for the formal extension of the lease, only to be refused on the grounds, according to Allen, that 'the premises were not bettered by James Burbage according to his covenant, and that there were arrearages of rent behind and unpaid'.

The impact of these events on Burbages' sons is preserved in later legal suits over shares in the King's Men's playing company undertaken in 1635. Their testimony foregrounds the years of trauma and financial uncertainty following James Burbage's construction of the Theatre, 'with many hundred pounds taken up at interest . . . upon leased ground, by which means the landlord and he had a great suit in law and by his death, the like troubles fell on us, his sons'. Their woes were compounded by Elizabeth Russell's campaign in 1596. 'Now for the Blackfriars that is our inheritance,' they recalled, 'our father purchased it at extreme rates and made it into a playhouse with great charge and trouble.' It would be the beginning of '35 years' pains, cost, and labour' and, by 1635, it had all become too much. The Burbages begged the court for succour so that 'they may not further be trampled upon than their estates can bear, seeing how dearly it hath been purchased by the infinite cost and pains of the family of the Burbages'. From these legal documents it is viscerally apparent just how close the Burbage boys came to losing everything after the Blackfriars Theatre was prevented from opening its doors to the Hunsdon's Men in 1596.

Things could scarcely have been much better for Shakespeare. These pressures would have been transferred to him as a sharer in the ailing theatrical troupe. He would have been liable for a portion of the costs or loans involved in keeping the company going during these difficult times, as well as bearing some of the burden for the lawsuits which rose out of the disputes with Allen, who would soon be pursuing the Burbages for £800 in damages. How the playwright responded to this crisis, and who he may have turned to for help, tell us a great deal not only about his character but about his potentially dangerous affiliations.

Shakespeare was a risk-taker. He did not, as he may have been expected to, tighten his belt at this time. Instead, in the spring of 1597, he decided to invest in his family's future by purchasing New Place in his native Stratford. After acquiring a coat of arms for his father in October 1596, he was beginning to think like a gentleman and wanted a house to match. Recent archaeological excavations of New Place reveal the grandeur of his aspirations, for the property had an impressive courtyard bounded with an imposing façade which fronted on to the street, in imitation of the stately country piles of Elizabeth I's chief courtiers. Shakespeare's plan to take possession of the building which he would eventually convert into one of English history's most celebrated homes brought him back into contact with one of the Stratfordians entangled in the notorious Somerville–Arden plot. His interest in procuring such investments also cemented his association with the martial coterie of the Earl of Essex.

The trail begins only a few paces from Elizabeth Russell's door at the Bell Inn in Carter Lane, the same Bell Inn to which the priest Hugh Hall had fled after Shakespeare's kinsmen John Somerville and Edward Arden had been arrested on suspicion of plotting the Queen's assassination in 1583. On 25 October 1598 Richard Quiney, a Burgess of Stratford, wrote a letter from his lodging in the Blackfriars. It is an important document, for it is the single extant letter addressed to the playwright and provides the only evidence that Shakespeare may have been a visitor to Elizabeth's neighbourhood before this date. Quiney was a trusted friend, and his son Thomas would eventually go on to marry Shakespeare's daughter Judith. A sense of urgency underpins the message, scrawled in Quiney's tight, brisk hand:

> Loving countryman, I am bold of you as of a friend, craving your help with £30 upon Master Bushell's and my security or Master Mytton's with me. Master Roswell is not come to London as yet and I

have especial cause. You shall friend me much in helping me out of all the debts I owe in London, I thank God, and much quiet my mind which would not be indebted. I am now towards the court in hope of answer for the dispatch of my business. You shall neither lose credit nor money by me . . . My time bids me hasten to an end and so I commit this [to] your care and hope of your help. I fear I shall not be back this night from the court. Haste. The Lord be with you and with us all. Amen.

Having folded the letter, Quiney dashed off an instruction on the outside: 'H[aste], To my loving good friend and countryman Master William Shakespeare deliver these.' The assurances that Shakespeare's credit would be safe in the hands of Quiney and the man chosen as co-surety belie one fact: Quiney was lying. He was not seeking this loan for himself alone, but for some venture which involved one Abraham Sturley, who wrote to Quiney at the Bell Inn on 4 November to inform him that 'Your letter of the 25 October came to my hands the last of the same at night . . . which imported . . . that our countryman Master William Shakespeare would procure us money, which I will like of as I shall hear when, and where, and how.' This leaves us with something of an enigma. Quiney's letter to Shakespeare was, it seems, never sent, for it was later discovered among Quiney's own papers. How then did Shakespeare hear of this loan and give some indication that he might honour it in time for Quiney to report this to Sturley on the same day? Quiney felt the need to inform Shakespeare that he may not be returning to Carter Lane that evening, strongly implying that the playwright knew exactly where to find him and that he would ordinarily have expected him to visit immediately upon news of his presence in London. The most obvious explanation is that Shakespeare turned up at Quiney's door before the letter was sent. The scenario is made more likely by the near-certainty that the two men had seen each other on previous occasions when Quiney was in London representing the interests of the Stratford Corporation, which was seeking exemption from hefty taxation after much of

Stratford was devastated by fires in 1594–5. In a letter of 24 January 1598 Sturley indicated that he had heard from Richard Quiney's father, Adrian:

> ... that our countryman, Mr Shakespeare, is willing to disburse some money upon some odd yardland or other at Shottery or near about us; he thinketh it a very fit pattern to move him to deal in the matter of our tithes. By the instructions you can give him thereof, and by the friends he can make therefore, we think it a fair mark for him to shoot at, and not unpossible to hit. It obtained would advance him indeed, and would do us much good.

The letter hints at meetings between Quiney and Shakespeare before this date, when Shakespeare would have made known to the former that he was looking for more investments. Quiney was charged with the task of convincing the dramatist to divert his credit into the Stratford Corporation. Since he had visited London during the winters of 1596/7 and 1597/8 he may have told Shakespeare about the financial troubles of a man known to them both: William Underhill, the owner of New Place. Languishing under crushing debts, Underhill had been vigorously pursued by the corporation for unpaid tithes since 1595. Multiple subpoenas served against him had failed to flush him out.

While it cannot be proved that Quiney was the conduit for valuable insider information that helped Shakespeare acquire New Place for a good price, it is clear that the latter's decision to enter into this business transaction brought him back into contact with a man who had been implicated in the Somerville–Arden plot. Underhill was a diehard Catholic and had helped Hugh Hall, one of the chief suspects in the case, evade the authorities. While Sir Thomas Lucy and Lord Burghley's agent, Thomas Wilkes, scoured the neighbourhood looking for incriminating evidence, Hall had been hiding out in Underhill's home in Idlicote. At some point in the investigations he fled to the Blackfriars' Bell Inn, clearly a favoured spot for the Stratford crowd. If Shakespeare had not been helped in his purchase of New Place by Quiney, he may have exploited his own family's links with Underhill. Either way, he would acquire the second largest house in Stratford from a suspected conspirator in the scandal associated with the Throckmorton Plot, that which led to the death of Henry Percy, 8th Earl of Northumberland. Things did not improve for William Underhill. Around two months after the sale of New Place he was dead, apparently poisoned by his own son, Fulk Underhill.

One question remains. Why did Quiney conceal the identity of the man who would benefit from Shakespeare's loan on 25 October 1598? Sturley had close connections with Sir Thomas Lucy, having spent time in his service before becoming a bailiff of Stratford in 1596. This may not have been a connection he wanted to foreground. Instead he decided to draw Shakespeare's attention to Richard Mytton and Peter Roswell, who were servants of Sir Edward Greville. It was to Greville that Quiney had sued for support with his petition to Parliament to ease Stratford's tax burdens, and his letter indicates that Shakespeare would have trusted these men and may even have been expecting to meet with Roswell when he finally arrived in London. Greville was a powerful figure in Stratford, having served as a magistrate in Warwickshire from 1592, then as sheriff in 1594–5. He was also one of the Earl of Essex's creatures.

When the Earl was looking to procure men and supplies for the Cádiz mission in 1596, he turned to Greville, and trusted him to stand co-surety on £1,620 worth of victuals. Essex called him personally to 'Her Majesty's service' on 27 March 1596, assuring him of his 'affection' and promising him 'that you cannot be anything more acceptable unto me than by using your credit and best endeavours therein'. His fidelity would, he insisted, draw from the nobleman 'my best thankfulness'. Thankful he proved, for, after joining him on his Azores mission in 1597, Greville became one of Essex's knights. The Earl's interest in Greville reveals that the former was keen to follow in the footsteps of his stepfather, the Earl of Leicester, as one of the titular lords of Warwickshire.

Quiney expected his association with Greville's men to be looked upon favourably by his addressee, who was also happy to receive advice about further investment opportunities from him. These complex transactions give some indication of the kind of men with whom Shakespeare was willing to do business – and to whom he chose to turn in the face of an uncertain future – in the immediate aftermath of Elizabeth Russell's petition against the Blackfriars Theatre. The agents of a member of the Essex cabal; a conspirator in the Somerville–Arden plot: these were relations that could only be regarded with suspicion by Elizabeth's friends in the Cecil faction.

21.

'this distracted Globe'

The men who entered Shoreditch as darkness fell on a snowy 28 December in 1598 were taking no chances. Armed with swords, daggers, battle staves and axes, they made their way to London's first permanent playhouse, the Theatre, built by the entrepreneur James Burbage. They were an intimidating crew, around sixteen in total, and they had no intention of pursuing their cause quietly. The Queen would later be informed that they had broken into the site 'in a very riotous, outrageous, and forcible manner, and contrary to the laws of Your Highness's realm'. The brave souls who attempted to resist them were dealt with severely and 'with great violence'. These were the actions of desperate men, and they had been brought to these extreme measures by one woman: Lady Elizabeth Russell.

The gathering crowd watched helplessly as the trespassers began 'pulling, breaking, and throwing down' the Theatre beam by beam. These were, however, no common criminals. They were the Chamberlain's Men, the country's premier theatrical company, and they were acting in accordance with the wishes of William Shakespeare. Their intention, to use the confiscated timber from the Theatre in order to construct a new playhouse on the Bankside: the Globe. It was a risky venture, but Lady Russell had left James Burbage's sons, Richard and Cuthbert, with little choice but to take up arms with 'divers and many unlawful and offensive weapons' as they dismantled the amphitheatre in Shoreditch, overlooked by old Burbage's widow, who had braved the chilly air in support of the men who were now stumbling through the slippery compacted snow with the skeletal remains of the playhouse that had nurtured Shakespeare's early career.

The company's star playwright may very well have been there, along with the other men whose future was riding on the bold enterprise, the actor-sharers John Heminges, Augustine Phillips, Thomas Pope and Will Kemp. The Burbages believed that while the land on which the Theatre had been built belonged to Giles Allen, the man who had refused to extend the Chamberlain's Men's lease, the materials used to construct the playhouse were their property. They appointed Peter Street, a carpenter, to oversee the project, and he directed the twelve labourers who worked under guard to retrieve the £800 worth of oak beams and other fixtures. The show of brute force was unfortunate but necessary since the Burbages had, correctly as it turns out, expected resistance from the freeholder's supporters. The Chamberlain's Men's cause could not have been helped by the fact that, like Elizabeth Russell, Allen was a staunch Puritan, of the radical non-conformist milieu that was now persecuting Shakespeare's company. The Bankside, an area of bear-baitings, brothels and bawdy entertainments, without the extensive Puritan presence of the Blackfriars and free from both Allen's and Elizabeth's control, offered the chance of a fresh start.

The land on which the Globe would be built was leased from Nicholas Brend, who would later pass it on to Elizabeth's kinsman Sir Matthew Browne, son of the Sir Thomas Browne whose signing of the Dowager's petition had helped bring them to this shift. Nor was this the only irony surrounding this epoch-making moment. The course to which Shakespeare and the Burbages had been brought, thanks to Elizabeth, would ultimately secure the playwright's future in a manner no one could have foreseen. The loss of both the Blackfriars playhouse and the Theatre, which had been lying empty for most of 1597–8, meant that the Burbages were left with heavy debts, nowhere to store costumes, stage properties and other accoutrements of playing, and an expensive legal battle with Allen. The troupe's costs were also increased by their need to rent the Curtain Theatre as a temporary venue after the lease for their nearby Shoreditch premises had expired. Later, in court, Curthbert Burbage would lament the great 'costs and charges' they all went to over the creation of the Globe, claiming that the outlay totalled £1,000, over £120,000 of purchasing power today.

The Burbages needed capital, and quickly. This is when they hit on an entirely unprecedented business model. They offered a larger interest in the playhouse to Shakespeare and his co-sharers than had ever before been negotiated. Five of the sharers (in addition to the investment of the Burbages, which included the old Theatre's valuable oak timbers – all they had left to offer after the loss of the Blackfriars Theatre had so impoverished them) each paid £100 towards the cost of completing the building of the Globe. Most of the members of this company therefore became part-owners of a theatre that was built largely by players for the benefit of players, and were now able to reap 10 per cent of the total profits. The innovative agreement would fashion the identity of history's greatest playwright, who would forever be known as the Shakespeare of the Globe. It was an arrangement that would also bring him into closer association with the Earl of Essex.

In 1598 the ever-watchful satirist Edward Guilpin painted a mournful picture of the abandoned Theatre, a vignette which follows a telling piece of encrypted wordplay:

> There comes one in a muffler of Cadiz-beard,
> Frowning as he would make the world afeard,
> With him a troupe all in gold-daubed suits,
> Looking like *Talbots*, *Percies*, *Montacutes*,
> As if their very countenances would swear,
> The Spaniard should conclude a peace for fear . . .
>   But see yonder,
> One like the unfrequented Theatre
> Walks in dark silence, and vast solitude . . .

Who is the man sporting a 'Cadiz-beard'? It is none other than the Earl of Essex, who returned from his victorious Cádiz raid in 1596 with a striking square-shaped beard which became all the rage among the courtiers who aspired to emulate the naval hero. Guilpin hits on the historical parallelism which surrounded Essex and his entourage, including the Percys, whose living descendants had become his closest allies and kinsmen following his sister's marriage to Henry Percy, 9th Earl of Northumberland, in 1595. That the Percys associated themselves with Shakespeare's own depiction of their ancestors in *Richard II* and the *Henry IV* plays would soon become perilously apparent when they decided to pay for a showing of *Richard II* on the eve of Essex's uprising. The proximity of the Theatre in Guilpin's thinking seems eerily prescient, suggesting perhaps a theatrical dimension to Essex's public identity.

By 1597 the feud between Essex and Cecil had spread its shadow over other leading courtiers. After the Earl's uncle, Sir William Knollys, had been elevated to Comptroller of the Royal Household, and Essex himself promoted to Master of the Ordnance, the power balance seemed to have evened out just enough to allow an uneasy reconciliation between the opposing factions. At a dinner at Essex House on 18 April they managed to patch up their differences, at least on the surface. Sir William Knollys, however, was not convinced and warned Essex to be wary. 'If we lived not in a cunning world,' he told him, 'I should assure myself that Mr Secretary were wholly yours, as seeming to rejoice at everything that may succeed well with you, and to be grieved at the contrary.'

It did not take long for tensions to bubble to the surface once again, and when they did it was Elizabeth Russell who waded into the fray, writing to her nephew, 'I hear of words passed between you and Master Comptroller, and between the other two Earls,' the two Earls being Essex and Charles Howard. On 23 October Howard had been made Earl of Nottingham, adding to his privileges as Lord Admiral and Lord Steward of the Queen's household. These offices meant that Howard outranked his former ally. Essex was furious and challenged the new Earl to armed combat. To appease Essex the Queen granted him the post of Earl Marshal of England on 18 December, restoring his pre-eminence. The Earl of Nottingham responded by resigning his post of Lord Steward and storming out of the court. As usual, Elizabeth was determined to do something about this recent rupture in the courtiers' relations. 'If you will have me to come to court to do you any good offices, who have had ever a natural instinct to be honest and natural in time of trial,' she continued, and here Cecil would have almost heard his aunt's palpable sigh at the thanklessness of the task ahead, 'however it hath been deserved, let me know your mind.' This was a brave undertaking, for the weather was particularly bad that winter, with a cold, rough tide whipping up the Thames and making it unsafe for travel. She would come regardless, though she demanded that George Carey provide her with 'convenient lodging' close to the court for the purpose, 'otherwise, upon the least wet of my feet or legs, by long clothes or cold, my pate is so subject to rheum that my hearing will be so bad as that I am fit for no company or other place than my own cell'.

While Essex and Howard were still thrashing out their differences Elizabeth continued to find outlets for her philanthropic urges. Her efforts 'abroad amongst the distressed saints' in France and the Low Countries came to the attention of Edward Vaughan, a preacher of St Mary Woolnoth whom she had been patronizing in January 1598. Praising her in print, he explained that these endeavours had made her 'a wonder in this world', who was building the 'temple' of true religion alongside her fellow activists 'with weapons in one hand and trowels in the other'. Closer to home, that very month she was also engaged in a new 'business in law' which was a work of no less wonder. It was with watery eyes, continual thumping headaches and weakness in her limbs that she staggered through to the end of a most radical and unusual campaign for a woman.

Elizabeth had made it her personal goal to reform the law in the Hundred of Beynhurst, the liberty that included Bisham. The communities there had long been terrorized by the statute of 'hue and cry', a form of taxation levied against inhabitants whenever a robbery had taken place. In the event of such a theft a 'hue and cry' would be raised, the neighbourhood's call to locate and bring to justice the criminal and restore the stolen goods to their owner. If the perpetrator was not found the local populace was forced to cover a proportion of the costs towards the recompense of the victims. Elizabeth believed this to be an unfair burden on the poor of these parishes and enlisted the support of the Cecils, Sir Walter Ralegh and two further members of the House of Lords: Lord Keeper Thomas Egerton and William Brydges, 4th Baron Chandos. The latter needed little convincing, for his servant had only recently 'hardly escaped robbing there'.

The Dowager was victorious, and a bill was passed which modified the law. The reformed statute now stated that as long as everything reasonable was done to recover the stolen items the community no longer had to foot the bill. It was, she felt, a triumph for common sense and decency. Despite her poor health, she was elated, thanking Robert Cecil profusely for his support 'for which you are like to have no other reward but the prayers of the poor which pierceth heaven'. Burghley would not perform many more charitable acts. On 4 August 1598 the man upon whom Elizabeth had relied almost her entire life, and who had looked upon her as a daughter, died.

With Burghley gone, the animosity between Essex and Cecil intensified, and so did the paranoia in court. Who was really on the Earl's side and who was on the Secretary's? Even Elizabeth came under suspicion, as Cecil began to burrow into men's souls, making windows on to their darkest ambitions. Her attempts to effect a reconciliation between her nephew and his detractors were not looked upon favourably. The French Ambassador, André Hurault, Sieur de Maisse, seeing that Essex's 'quarrel' with 'the Admiral and the Secretary cannot yet be settled', did something which may have put a further strain on her relationship with Cecil. He sent Robert la Fontaine, her neighbour and the Cooke sisters' associate, to the Earl, urging him to attend a meeting of the Privy Council which he had boycotted, being 'unwilling to take part in any Council where they [Cecil and his followers] would be the greater party'.

Fontaine was Essex's agent for the illegal dissemination of a controversial piece of propaganda in France, the *True Relation* of the Earl's voyage to Cádiz written by his secretary Henry Cuffe, with help from Edward Reynoldes, under his own instruction and designed to counter the negative spin Robert Cecil had put on his recent mission. After the double-crossing Anthony Ashley revealed the existence of the work, it was swiftly banned, but Elizabeth's association with Fontaine may have planted a seed of doubt in her nephew's mind. In March 1599 he sent her a fierce letter, accusing her of siding with his 'powerful enemies'. She was stunned. 'I answered not your last letter,' she wrote to him, after leaving some time to let his temper cool, 'because it seemed to be fruits of a troubled mind.' Protesting her innocence, she assured him that 'Since your father's death, I meddle with no matters but my own and my children's, which have beggared me.' What damage could a poor widow, who could not even afford to keep a coach in London on most days, do to the reputation of one so much in the Queen's favour? Was she not made practically deaf by age and illness? When did she ever now venture to court, daring not to stray too far from a warming hearth? Yet she was loyal and she would prove it.

'I have heard a thing not fit, in my conceit,' she confided to Cecil conspiratorially, 'for the eyes or ears of any living but Her Majesty's only.' This news she imparted for his good and was even willing to risk her health by coming to court to divulge her secret. Then he would see 'that nature will not suffer me to like of any that shall go about to wrong you, if I may any way right you'. He would soon realize that he had merely swallowed 'a bait' contrived by practisers 'of these broils' into which the court had been plunged who were bent on driving a wedge between them. Not long afterwards she wrote to offer her services again, adding an ominous postscript: 'Some will kill me, and therefore my kingdom is not of this world. God preserve our Sovereign.'

This claustrophobic atmosphere of intrigue was not helped by mutterings that Spanish troops had overtaken the Isle of Wight and were preparing to invade England. Panic descended upon London. Elizabeth had now more or less taken up permanent residence in the Blackfriars, with six servants, to her mind 'very few' for a lady of her calling, leaving her Bisham home to her son Edward Hoby. With nowhere else to go, she turned to Cecil for aid. 'Friend me so much as to procure me a lodging in court in this time of misery,' she began, stepping into the role of the weak and vulnerable old woman with accustomed alacrity. 'Here I remain where none be left but artisans, myself a desolate widow, without husband or friend to defend me or to take care of me.' If he could not provide her with a 'place to fly unto for safety' – and here the Dowager's real mettle began to surface – then he should take note of the shopping list of weaponry she was sending him and have the items promptly sent, at the Queen's own expense, to her Blackfriars home. Supplying her with 'shot [guns], pikes, and halberds' should not be too much of a chore for Her Majesty's most trusted councillor. What else was a widow to do but defend herself from those 'that would eat us up'?

Elizabeth was always most herself when she was preparing for battle, and as her resolve hardened Cecil again saw that sharp wit which must have assured him that his aged aunt had some life in her veins yet, 'promising you that if God deliver me out of this plunge of danger and misery alive, though I be both blind, deaf and a stark beggar, yet will I . . . take me to a[n] evil mischief and marry to avoid the inconvenience of being killed by villains'. The incident was a false alarm, but Elizabeth's fighting spirit was back and she conveniently forgot her promise to Cecil not to meddle in matters concerning his enemies at court.

'I hear what I am not willing to commit to paper,' wrote Elizabeth to her nephew in a state of agitation in October 1599, 'yet as an aunt, near in blood, I cannot with conscience but to let you know that it is brought to my ears here in my very cell that most vile words have been openly uttered of you at an ordinary.' An 'ordinary' is a public house or restaurant, and in this instance the libellous words were spoken directly in the hearing of one of Elizabeth's own spies. It would leave the Dowager in little doubt that what was said in the hubbub of a place of common resort was at best slanderous, at worst treason. Robert Cecil could not but have been alarmed, for this missive had come at a time of real danger.

The relationship between Essex and the Queen had suffered in the last year. Lady Penelope Rich, the Earl's sister, had come under surveillance, for at least two of her letters ended up on Robert Cecil's desk. Both of these were addressed to Henry Wriothesley, Earl of Southampton, Shakespeare's former patron. The reason for Cecil's piqued interest may have been the clandestine marriage of Southampton and one of the royal maids of honour, Elizabeth Vernon, which Essex and his sister arranged at Essex House in the summer of 1598. Lady Rich was Lady Vernon's cousin and became godmother to the daughter born on 8 November. One of the letters which fell into Cecil's hands closes with a touching postscript, probably alluding to this child and Lady Rich's hopes for Southampton's future offspring: 'Your L[ordship's] daughter is exceeding fair and well and I hope by your son to win my wager.' With evidence like this, Cecil would have been in no doubt that the Devereux had disobeyed royal edict by facilitating this prohibited union.

There was worse to come the following year when Essex, against the express orders of the Queen, promoted Southampton to Master of the Horse during his disastrous campaign in Ireland, whither he had been sent as Governor General to resolve the perennial threat of insurgency from England's Catholic neighbours. While there, secret words passed between him and the leader of the Irish rebels, the Earl of Tyrone, resulting in the two warlords reaching an unauthorized agreement. Worried about his reputation at court, Essex decided to explain his actions directly and, on the morning of Friday 28 September, having abandoned his commission in Ireland without royal leave, he stormed back to Nonsuch Palace, bursting in on the Queen in her private apartments before she was fully dressed. Within a few hours he was under house arrest, and on 2 October he was confined to York House, where his health began to deteriorate rapidly. The Earl's redoubtable sister Lady Rich took charge of Essex House and began to galvanize fellow agitators in a campaign to effect his release. It did not take long for the discontented community of Essex's supporters, who were becoming increasingly visible, to attract the attentions of the Privy Council.

On 11 October 1599 Rowland White informed Sir Robert Sidney that Essex's 'very Servants are afraid to meet in any place to make merry, lest it might be ill taken'. Ill taken it was, by Elizabeth Russell, who informed Cecil that their activities betokened both 'our Sovereign's disquiet and your own peril'. Without realizing that there was a spy in their midst, one whom Elizabeth conspiratorially referred to as being 'tied to me in duty, and other ways', Essex's supporters vented their frustrations about the Earl's treatment and Cecil's role in his disgrace. Loyal to Cecil, the spy 'reproved' their words and immediately returned to Elizabeth with his intelligence, saying 'he was sorry that he was in their company to hear a Councillor so spoken of'. Understanding the gravity of the situation, Elizabeth made a daring claim:

> What the words were, I list not to write, but will tell yourself when I see you. In the mean time, I sorrow in my heart [for] my Sovereign's hurt, your peril I fear, and danger to come to Her Majesty's disquiet and trouble. I can but pray, which I am sure is most devoutly done here daily in the [Black]Friars in most reverent manner for Her Majesty and her Council.

This is by all accounts an extraordinary assessment of the situation, for it is one of the earliest documents to implicate Essex and his followers in a direct threat to the Queen's own life. If Cecil was in any doubt about Elizabeth's credentials, then he should, she reminded him, consider that she had previously acted as Burghley's agent in a similar capacity: 'to no small detriment to myself in the like, I have received in your father's life for friending him in such cases by his own desire'. Perhaps she was also hinting that her informant was not present at this gathering by chance. There is a suggestion that others in the Church of St Anne's in the Blackfriars were aware of these ill-omened proceedings and were working with Elizabeth for the Queen's benefit. Among them would have been the preacher Stephen Egerton and, of course, Richard Field and fellow petitioner Edward Ley, who had become church wardens that very year. Determined to prove that she was not a double agent working for Essex, Elizabeth conveyed her most alarming revelation in her accustomed Latin code:

> This I mean, to cause you, being warned and thereby half armed, to take heed to yourself and life, lest, as the poet saith, *Ille dies primus, Lethi, primusque malorum: causa fuit*, wherein the Earl of Essex was committed, to whom I never sent since return, neither, God is witness, doth any know of this I do, but God and my pen.

Elizabeth quotes from the classical text that most exemplified the themes of war and regime change, Virgil's *Aeneid*. The Latin extract comes from the portentous moment when a ferocious storm forces Dido into a cave with Aeneas, where the tragic lovers consummate their doomed union: 'This day was the beginning of her death, the first cause of all her sufferings.' Significantly, in Virgil's tale, the tempest was first noticed by Ascanius, 'grandson of Venus'. Was Elizabeth hinting at the name of her informant in the Blackfriars, the man who had signed her petition against Shakespeare's Blackfriars Theatre? This is not so far-fetched as it may seem, for her neighbour Ascanius de Renialme had also been one of Burghley's agents and Elizabeth may have wanted to alert Cecil to the identity of so trusted a servant of his father without putting him in danger by explicitly naming him. Either way, Elizabeth's pointed use of Virgil was a powerful rhetorical tool, and the next Latin quote, again from the *Aeneid*, must have made Cecil's blood run cold. In translation it reads:

> As when disorder arises among the people of a great city and the common mob runs riot, wild passion finds weapons for men's hands and torches and rocks start flying.

Cecil, learned in Virgil's Latin, knew that the sentiments which immediately succeeded this moment matched the kind of accusations levelled at Essex in Guilpin's *Skialetheia*, itself borrowing from

333

Shakespeare's *Richard II*. The Virgilian quote continues: 'at such a time if people chance to see a man who has some weight among them . . . they fall silent, standing and listening with all their attention while his words command their passions'. Cecil would have taken Elizabeth's hint that Essex had the power to bend the 'common mob' to his will. 'Thus I manifest that to be true long since written,' she added, for no coded missive would be complete without a smattering of her beloved Horace *Epistles*, '*naturam expellas furca, tamen usque recurret*' ('You may drive out Nature with a pitchfork, yet she will ever hurry back . . .'). As always, with Elizabeth, the key to the code lies in the words immediately following the quote, which, she knew, her learned interlocutor would either know by heart or find in his library: '. . . and, ere you know it, will burst through your foolish contempt in triumph'. The message was crystal clear: Essex was temporarily tamed by the four walls of his prison, but nothing could tame the wildness of his nature. Cecil had been warned. Elizabeth's appraisal of the situation would prove more accurate than she could possibly have imagined.

There was some urgency to Elizabeth's counsel, for earlier in 1599 Shakespeare had offered his audiences a very different view of Essex's exploits. It was probably not long after 27 March, when the Earl left for Ireland to quell Tyrone's rebellion, that the playwright turned his pen to an even more outspoken support of Cecil's great enemy in his *Henry V*. With the Globe still not open for performances, this sequel to the *Henry IV* plays was probably first showcased at the Curtain Theatre. Strengthening Essex's association with the familial line which gave birth to England's heroic victor of Agincourt, the play rides the tidal wave of national pride in the military hero whose anticipated glories in Ireland are celebrated in a rousing vignette:

> Now London doth pour out her citizens.
> The Mayor and all his brethren, in best sort . . .
> With the plebeians swarming at their heels . . .
> As, by a lower but high-loving likelihood,

Were now the General of our gracious Empress –
As in good time he may – from Ireland coming,
Bringing rebellion broachèd on his sword,
How many would the peaceful city quit
To welcome him! Much more, and much more cause,
Did they this Harry [King Henry V].

The 'gracious General' is Essex, every inch the people's champion. Shakespeare's celebratory rhetoric was somewhat premature, but testimony to his willingness to engage his dramatic powers in the pro-Essex propaganda that was augmenting the Earl's public reputation in the mid-1590s. One significant difference was that by 1599 Shakespeare had reneged on his promise, made at the end of *Henry IV, Part 2*, to include Falstaff in a sequel to the historical cycle. Perhaps the infamy of Oldcastle, which still lingered around Falstaff, made him too nervous of offending, or he had been leaned on to abandon all thoughts of resurrecting the rowdy knight, whose pathetic death he described in *Henry V*. It can be no coincidence that during the very same year the Admiral's Men staged a public riposte to Shakespeare's *Henry IV* plays, *The First Part of the True and Honourable History of the Life of Sir John Oldcastle, the Good Lord Cobham*. Its purpose, to restore the reputation of Oldcastle and his descendants:

It is no pampered glutton we present,
Nor aged counsellor to youthful sin,
But one, whose virtue shone above the rest,
A valiant Martyr, and a virtuous Peer:
In whose true faith and loyalty expressed
Unto his Sovereign and his country's weal,
We strive to pay that tribute of our love
            . . . Let fair truth be graced,
Since forged invention former times defaced.

The 'forged invention' can only refer to Shakespeare's Oldcastle/Falstaff and is further indication that a war was being played out on

335

the public stages, one that raged between Essex and his enemies in the Cecil–Cobham–Russell alliance. This play has all the makings of a Cobham commission. Since Shakespeare was ordered to remove Old-castle from his *Henry IV* series by the end of March 1597, why was this play mounted two years later? The reason may lie with the fact that it was performed by the acting troupe under the patronage of the Lord Admiral, Charles Howard, who had recently become Essex's bitter enemy, their animosity flaring again in January of 1599 when 'high words passed' between them. The incident was sparked by Howard's jealousy of the Queen's open flirtation with Essex, with whom she danced at the Twelfth Day feast 'very richly and freshly attired'.

Even as *Henry V* was being performed Essex was up to his old tricks. While in Ireland he had, reported John Chamberlain on 23 August, 'made many new knights', including 'two Lovelaces', one of these being the son and namesake of Elizabeth's arch-enemy Richard Lovelace, and 'Sir Ajax Harington' (Chamberlain's cheeky nod towards his controversial *Metamorphosis of Ajax*). While the admiral may have been far from willing to act in a manner that would benefit Elizabeth Russell, he knew that fighting back against the theatrical team that was supporting his rival at court that year would have been pleasing to the powerful Robert Cecil, who was ever willing to curtail Essex's ambitions. That Shakespeare may also have come under pressure at this time is indicated by the fact that his *Henry V* had an unusually short first run. The play's printing was initially 'stayed' and then commenced in 1600 with potentially offen-sive scenes censored, including those alluding to Essex and his ill-fated campaign in Ireland. This did not stop the playwright com-posing another public rebuttal to Elizabeth around this time.

The timber plundered from the old Theatre had been patiently waiting out the harsh winter months of 1598/9 in Peter Street's Thames-side warehouse, located close to Bridewell Stairs. As soon as the weather improved, the building work commenced. Lath and plas-ter gradually filled the wooden frame until the polygonal playhouse took its now iconic shape. By the late summer of 1599 the Globe Theatre was open for business on the Bankside. By 1601 audiences were listening there enraptured as Richard Burbage – one of the greatest actors of all time, who had played Richard III, and who would go on to define the roles of Othello and King Lear – promised his father's ghost that he would remember him 'while memory holds a seat/In this distracted globe'. This was Burbage, in the guise of Hamlet, proudly drawing attention to the Chamberlain's Men's new theatre. This celebrated moment – which the audience experienced beneath a thatched roof, for the tight budget of the Burbages and their business partners could not stretch to the relative luxury and expense of tiles – would not have existed had it not been for Elizabeth Russell's machinations against Shakespeare's company. In fact, this play, if it had existed at all, would have looked very different, for it would have lacked one of its most memorable scenes.

That there was lingering ill-feeling over the Dowager's successful bid to prevent Shakespeare's troupe from occupying the Blackfriars Theatre is clear from the dramatist's well-known criticism of the adult players' main competitors, the Children of the Chapel, who had risen to prominence after Richard Burbage had granted the vacant playhouse's lease to Henry Evans in September 1600. Having already incurred huge losses in the four years since Elizabeth's campaign, he realized that 'if the said hall were converted from a playhouse to any other ordinary use, it would be of very little value'. Shakespeare was forced to watch as Evans's child-players took London by storm, and from the very venue which should have been the setting for his own plays, had Elizabeth not had other ideas. In *Hamlet*, the eponymous hero's fellow student Rosencrantz informs him that the itinerant 'players', the 'tragedians of the city', are on their way to entertain the court. The exchange is Shakespeare's most self-conscious summation of the state of the English theatre as he laments the diminished fortunes of the adult playing companies:

HAMLET How chances it they [the players] travel? Their residence, both in reputation and profit, was better both ways.
ROSENCRANTZ I think their inhibition comes by the means of the late innovation.

HAMLET Do they hold the same estimation they did when I was in
the city? Are they so followed?

ROSENCRANTZ No, indeed, they are not.

HAMLET How comes it? Do they grow rusty?

ROSENCRANTZ Nay, their endeavour keeps in the wonted pace. But
there is, sir, an aerie of children, little eyases [young hawks], that
cry out on the top of question, and are most tyrannically clapped
for't. These are now the fashion, and so berattle the common
stages – so they call them – that many wearing rapiers are afraid
of goose-quills, and dare scarce come thither.

It has been suggested that this was the Burbages' clever advertising for the theatre, which they were now leasing to Evans for
£40 annual rent. This was, however, a mere fraction of the profit
which could have been theirs had they been allowed to mount their
own plays there. It is also difficult to ignore the tragic image the
scene conjures before the audience: the adult players homeless,
ejected from their permanent playhouses and doomed to a rootless
existence, losing business by the day to the more successful child
actors. Worse still, as the passage implies, the authors of the boys'
company's plays had been using their productions to attack their
rivals, driving their business away. Hamlet wonders who is the victor in this battle of the stages, and asks Rosencrantz, 'Do the boys
carry it away?' He is answered, 'Ay, that they do, my lord – Hercules
and his load too.' The emblem of Hercules carrying the world
was the sign of the Globe Theatre. That Hamlet's role was probably
taken on by Henry Evans' landlord, who was sharing the burden for
the botched Blackfriars project, adds a poignant personal note to this
moment. The playwright Ben Jonson, who had written plays for the
Chapel Children, may have glanced at these misfortunes in his *Poetaster*, performed in 1601 by Evans' players, in which the character
Histrio conspires to mount a performance with adult actors which
'will get us a huge deal of money . . . and we have need on't; for this
winter has made us all poorer, than so many starved snakes: Nobody
comes at us; not a gentleman.'

With the loss to posterity of Elizabeth Russell's story, centuries of audiences have missed the personal frisson with which these lines may have originally been invested by Shakespeare. The 'inhibition' of the players – that is, their suppression – which allowed the Black-friars Children to thrive, could only refer to the Privy Council's ban. The 'late [recent] innovation' – 'innovation' in Shakespeare's day carrying the potential meaning of 'disturbance' or 'insurrection' – may therefore be a pointed reference to the uprising of the Blackfriars' residents led by the feisty Lady Russell. We will never know if the playwright had read the wording of Elizabeth's actual petition. However, it is suggestive that he has Rosencrantz reiterate the derogatory term 'common' for the stages occupied by the adult players, the very players who, as the petition informs the Queen's Councillors, hoped to tread the boards of their new 'common playhouse' in the Black-friars. If Shakespeare had been deliberately echoing that petition, then it is just possible that a ghostly trace of Elizabeth's own words has ended up in the world's most famous literary masterpiece.

While Shakespeare was drawing attention to Essex's exploits and the adult players' ejection from the Blackfriars Theatre around 1599–1601, Elizabeth was proving herself equally adept at using public performance for political ends. She would offer her own response to Essex's growing popularity by creating one of the most memorable spectacles in Elizabethan history. The Queen herself would be in attendance and the unity of the three powerful families who had supported Elizabeth's closure of the Blackfriars Theatre would be on display for all to witness. By the time she was through, an unambiguous message would be sent to the supporters of the ambitious Devereux.

22.

Wedding Belles and Rebels

No apparition could have been stranger or more captivating than that which greeted the Queen as she approached the Blackfriars Stairs in her royal barge: a pale silhouette of a young and elegant woman, the light catching the trembling jewels in her hair and playing over the delicate white brocade of her wedding dress. The great Gloriana was making her way to one of the most lavish nuptials of her reign. The 'great marriage', as it would come to be known, was staged by Elizabeth Russell for her daughter Nan.

The Queen wanted to wield absolute control over her courtiers' marriages. Bitter experience of the dangerous political alliances that could be forged among chief branches of the nobility had taught her to be cautious. Despite this, by 21 April 1600, she had nominally agreed to the wedding of Nan Russell and Henry Somerset, the eldest surviving son of the Earl of Worcester; a match the girl's doting mother had been negotiating hard to arrange since the death of William Somerset. The unmarried Queen, as she did with many of her maids of honour and other female servants on the brink of wedlock, found it difficult to let go of Nan and kept her a virtual prisoner at Greenwich Palace.

Elizabeth had already, somewhat presumptuously, appointed 11 May for the wedding day and she was keen to fetch her daughter so that she could commence the preparations for the event. She asked Cecil to prevail with the Queen and 'not to leave her till she have granted me leave'. Her instincts told her, however, that it would not be this simple. She therefore devised a ruse to deceive her daughter's royal warden. Cecil would conceal the real cause of Nan's business from court. Instead he would say that she was suffering with a troublesome ailment in her eyes. This was true enough, though a few dramatic plaints and swoons would convince the Queen that Nan could 'do Her Majesty no service, her eyes being so bleared'. Her mother would then swoop in heroically to take her to a physician for treatment. If all went according to plan, she would have her daughter back within two days. She should have known that the Queen could not be played so easily.

The eleventh of May came and went, and Nan was still at court. 'The marriage,' reported Rowland White, 'is at a stay till it please Her Majesty to appoint a day.' Elizabeth did not wish to wait upon the royal pleasure and marched down there to confront her directly on 1 June. She returned home without Nan. By this time the nattering courtiers were watching from the wings, somewhat amused by the proceedings, wondering if Elizabeth would get her way. They need not have doubted. She had, as it turned out, been very persuasive. Her sovereign had softened enough to give her permission 'to fetch home my bride', as the relieved Dowager had put it, on Monday 9 June. Once the date had been set she immediately began putting everything in motion. 'I find it will be honourably solemnised,' said White. 'The feast will be in Blackfriars, my Lady Russell making exceeding preparation for it.'

An indication of Elizabeth's purpose can be gleaned from her instructions to Cecil, in anticipation of the return of the bride, that there would be an intimate gathering to mark the occasion: 'I entreat none but such as be of the bride's and bridegroom's blood and alliance to supper that night.' Blood and alliance would be her themes, for she insisted that Cecil take the leading role, acting 'as my husband to command as the master of my house . . . and to bring my Lord Thomas [Cecil] and my Lord Cobham with you'. The presence of Thomas Cecil, Burghley's son by his first wife, Mary Cheke, and Henry Brooke, Lord Cobham, was intended to make the outspoken political statement that Elizabeth had chosen on which side of the political fence she and her family had planted themselves. As further assurance of their solidarity Cobham agreed to take centre stage in Nan's wedding celebrations and, because

Elizabeth's property was 'too little for such company' and probably less luxurious, offered to allow the Queen to lodge at his home, just under sixty-six feet south of the Dowager's, during the three days of planned feasts and entertainments. Elizabeth ended her invitation to Cecil in fine fettle, promising him that 'your welcome shall be in the superlative degree', and adding teasingly, 'You thought that I should never have bidden you to my marriage. But now you see it pleaseth God otherwise.'

So it was, in accordance with Elizabeth Russell's wishes, that Nan prepared to take her leave of the court. Elizabeth came to collect her, bringing with her a huge entourage, many complete 'strangers to the court', as Rowland White reported to a news-hungry Robert Sidney. Before their departure, the Queen made a grand public oration in praise of the bride, addressing 'her [with] as gracious speeches as have been heard of any'. She then commanded all the maids and gentlemen of the court to accompany them to London, for the sovereign herself would be the guest of honour. The spectacular cortège consisted of eighteen coaches; a veritable army of Elizabethan glitterati who '[a]ll went in a troupe away'. An astonished White declared that 'the like hath not been seen among the maids'.

As they rode back to the Blackfriars, Elizabeth must have felt a sense of relief that this day had finally come. The court could be a perilous place for young noblewomen, who often found themselves attracting the attentions of Elizabeth I's red-blooded courtiers. The Queen could be intensely jealous of her young maids and waiting-women, particularly when they succeeded (willingly or not) in garnering the affection of her favourite Earl, who was never reticent in flaunting his numerous sexual conquests. On 23 May 1597 John Harington learned that Lady Mary Howard had incurred her sovereign's displeasure because 'she has much favour and marks of love from the young Earl, which is not so pleasing to the Queen, who doth still much exhort all her women to remain in virgin state as much as may be'. Lady Mary was warned to stay well away from Essex, to 'shun his company' should he seek her out, and to be more comely in her attire, which the Queen thought designed 'to win the Earl'.

In the same year Bess had been caught in the crossfire of the scandal caused by Elizabeth Brydges, the latest bright young thing to have had the temerity to begin an affair with the wayward Earl under the royal roof. When she and Bess were caught spying on the young gallants of the court as they played ball games – the handsome and athletic Earl probably among them – this proved the final straw for the Queen, who rained down blows on Brydges and summarily dismissed both women from her service for three days. Bess's reputation would later be darkened by rumours that she had herself succumbed to Essex's charms and become another of his paramours. A year later Rowland White sent a coded letter to Robert Sidney, revealing that it was 'spied out by Envy, that 1000, is again fallen in love with his fairest B. It cannot choose but come to 1500 ears; then is he undone.' White's accustomed code number for Essex was 1000; 1500 was the Queen. But who is the 'fairest B'? Most commonly she has been identified as Elizabeth Brydges, but she could have been Bess herself. White's letter includes an as yet undecoded comment which adds a further layer of mystery to these sexual intrigues: '7000 daughter that lives in court is said to be the instrument of these proceedings; you know whom I mean.' It is tempting to think that 7000 might be the code number for Elizabeth Russell, though this must remain speculation. What is clear is that Essex's recklessness had not escaped the attention of Elizabeth's sister Anne Bacon, who wrote to him towards the end of 1596 to remind him that God had laid a 'heavy threat' on 'fornicators and adulterers', warning him that his persistent infidelities would prove to him a 'great danger hereby both of soul and body'. Nan, who had publicly received favours from the Earl, had navigated her way through this treacherous sexual minefield, and was on the brink of fulfilling her mother's long-held ambition: becoming heiress to an Earldom and a Countess in the making.

On 16 June 1600 the Virgin Queen boarded her elaborate gilded barge and took to the water in as sumptuous a floating procession as had ever been witnessed by her English subjects. The royal train glided past the trembling trading vessels of livery companies, past upholstered wherries and tilt-boats for hire, past the countless spectators lining the banks, eager for a glimpse of their sovereign, until they reached the Blackfriars. There they were greeted at the landing by the young bride and some of the nation's finest court gallants, dressed in splendid ruffs and embroidered doublets, their swords hanging proudly by their sides. Among them were six knights, carrying a chair of state topped with a canopy of finely worked floral motifs. This 'curious chair', as John Chamberlain had called it, had been provided by Lord Cobham to carry the Queen in splendid style to the wedding ceremony and then to Elizabeth Russell's home.

The excitement of that day is captured for all time in what is perhaps the most iconic painting to have survived from the reign of Elizabeth I, known as *Queen Elizabeth being carried in Procession (Eliza Triumphans)* and attributed to Robert Peake. The bride, shimmering in white, is depicted following directly behind the Queen's litter, a tiara of orient pearls on her head. In the foreground stands the groom's father, Edward Somerset, 4th Earl of Worcester. The bridegroom poses in white, closest to Nan, bearing up the rear of the Queen's triumphal chair. To the viewer's far left stands the white-bearded Lord Admiral, Charles Howard; next to him, holding the white staff of the office of Lord Chamberlain, is Elizabeth's co-petitioner, George Carey, Lord Hunsdon.

Nan Russell and Henry Somerset were married at St Martin's Church in Ludgate. Lord Cobham and Lord Herbert of Cardiff, future Earl of Pembroke and the man who would become the patron of Shakespeare's collected works (known as the First Folio of 1623), accompanied the bride to the church. Thence the joyful procession wreathed its way back to the Blackfriars. Did they pass the Blackfriars Theatre that day? If so, it is tempting to wonder whether Lord Hunsdon may have felt a tinge of guilt seeing again the building from which Shakespeare and his fellow actors were barred, thanks in part to his own allegiance to the bride's mother.

Any such thoughts would have been forgotten once the wedding party arrived at Elizabeth's Blackfriars home. A 'sumptuous and great' banquet awaited them, consisting of six courses at the 'bride's table'. Elizabeth herself dined in more intimate surroundings, laying out dinner for herself and Robert Cecil in her 'drawing chamber', while the larger party enjoyed themselves in what was probably the room directly above the portion of the Round House now belonging to William de Lawne and next door to Richard Field's Timber House. Surely these two men, who also signed Elizabeth's petition, would have been guests at this wedding. This is made all the more likely by the fact that Dr William Paddy, their co-signatory, was present, and entertained the Queen briefly at his home that very evening, presenting her with a fan, before she 'went through' to Lord Cobham's house.

There was something else striking about that day, which would set tongues wagging at court for weeks afterwards. As with the Bisham entertainment before the Queen in 1592, Elizabeth probably authored the 'memorable masque of eight ladies' that followed the banquet. White reported that, as part of the elaborate spectacle, Elizabeth had devised 'a strange dance newly invented'. As a patroness of the arts, she was used to fostering the talents of men such as John Dowland, one of the most accomplished musicians in the country, who had honoured her with a composition called 'The Lady Russell's Pavane' (the pavane is a stately dance with a marching air, fitting for this martial woman), and would have been keen to manage the content of the entertainment. Under her direction, therefore, her home, so close to the Blackfriars playhouse, became a temporary theatre in which the choicest ladies of the court danced before the Queen wearing embroidered bodices 'wrought with silks of gold and silver', hooped over the arm with capes of carnation taffeta. With skirts fashioned from cloth-of-silver swaying to every graceful step, their hair loose down to their shoulders and 'curiously knotted and interlaced' at the ends, they would have made a mesmerizing group. One of these was Nan's sister, the vibrant and mischievous Bess. The eight principal dancers played the muses of

Apollo, who engaged in a dramatic search for their ninth sister – who was of course the Queen. '[D]elicate it was to see eight ladies so prettily and richly attired,' wrote an enchanted White, who also recounted a most astonishing incident which followed.

The dances were led by Mary Fitton, maid of honour since 1595, who would soon be publicly disgraced for her scandalous affair with one of the wedding party, Lord Herbert of Cardiff; the same Mary Fitton who has been identified by some as the mysterious Dark Lady of Shakespeare's sonnets. Leaving the others to 'dance the measurers' with eight more ladies, Fitton approached the Queen, hands outstretched in invitation, and 'wooed her to dance'. Amused, the Queen asked her 'what she was'. 'Affection,' answered the maid. 'Affection,' the Queen snapped back. 'Affection is false.' The scene must have seemed to grind to a halt for the revellers who witnessed the outburst, for everyone would have instantly understood to whom she was referring. Who else but the Earl of Essex? 'Yet Her Majesty rose and danced'; what else could she do? The music and the revelry, however, were unlikely to chase away thoughts of the 'false' courtier, who was conspicuously absent.

Essex was still under arrest when Nan's marriage took place. Just eleven days before, on 5 June 1600, he had entered the great chamber of York House and approached the long Council table around which were seated the eighteen men who had been summoned to hear the charges against him. The group was made up of the Queen's Privy Councillors and four judges of the law. A further two hundred spectators watched as the Earl knelt before the assembly on the cold bare floor, where he remained until the Archbishop of Canterbury, John Whitgift, asked for a cushion to be fetched for the prisoner to rest his knees upon. The charges were read by Francis Bacon, who, unlike his stubborn brother, Anthony, had wisely realigned his allegiances in these perilous times.

Along with an investigation into the Earl's handling of the crisis in Ireland and his brokering of an unauthorized truce with the rebel Tyrone, the interrogations focused on his role in the circulation of an explosive letter written with a 'violent and mineral spirit of bitterness' in his defence. The epistle, as the investigation revealed, claimed that the 'Lo[rd of Essex] suffered under passion, and faction, and not under justice mixed with mercy'. The Queen, who was its recipient, had never before been addressed in so shocking a manner and, to make matters worse, the letter had been illegally published with the intention of galvanizing support for Essex. The author of this offending text was Essex's sister, Lady Penelope Rich.

During Essex's imprisonment Lady Rich and her sister Dorothy had been acting as 'suitors' to the Queen on his behalf. With Lady Essex, they formed a striking community, appearing in the dead of winter 1599 'all in Black', clad in the habiliments of mourning, and requesting that 'the Earle [be] removed to a better air'. When this failed to secure his release, in late January 1600 Lady Rich composed her desperate missive, in which she condemned those 'combined enemies' whose 'malice and counsels' had led them to 'glut themselves in their private revenge' against her brother. Cecil knew that to this she had cunningly attached a secret cypher meant for royal eyes only, containing the names of all those involved in the 'faction' against her brother. The Queen had burned this document without divulging its contents to him, prompting him to exclaim bitterly, 'I doubt not but I was and am in her Ladyship's contemplation the person on whom all the figures of that letter did principally play.'

By the end of May copies of Lady Rich's epistle were printed with one of Essex's former propagandist pamphlets, *An Apology*, addressed to Anthony Bacon and offering a rebuttal to the Cecils' foreign policy (in this instance, 'apology' meaning a defence). '[T]he poor Lady is like to have the worst of it,' wrote John Chamberlain on 28 May, 'being sent for and come to answer and interpret her riddles.' The Queen read the transcript of her interrogation carefully and concluded that while she may not have taken her letter to press, she had demonstrated a 'shrewd' and 'voluntary negligence' by turning a blind eye when Essex's agents did. Now any hope that the Earl's friends 'should see him a cockhorse again', Chamberlain realized, much less reconciled to Cecil, 'was but a kind of dream, and false paradise'.

The 'great marriage' organized by Elizabeth Russell was a skilfully choreographed piece of propaganda that had little to do with love and everything to do with politics. In her hands the wedding celebrations became a potent commentary on the seismic events which formed their immediate backdrop. Like the distinguished family into which her Nan was marrying, Elizabeth had felt an increasing need to shield herself from the taint of the disgraced courtier's gargantuan ambitions. Having previously aligned himself with the hero of Cádiz, the Earl of Worcester had deftly begun to shift his affiliations. There was some urgency to this for, shortly after Essex's ill-advised return from Ireland, Worcester, along with Lord Henry Howard and Lady Rich's husband, Lord Robert Rich, had been seen attending a dinner with the Earl. Worcester's discomfort gave Elizabeth an ideal opportunity to strike, brokering the marriage which would secure the gentrified status of her descendants, while depriving Essex of one of his most powerful allies. This time Worcester did not put up any resistance, seeing the advantage to the union that would make him kinsman to Robert Cecil.

By the time the wedding was over it would generate, according to White's estimate, gifts of plate and jewels valued at a staggering £1,000 'at least', and 'my Lady Russell much commended for . . . the solemnities'. The celebration marked the height of the Dowager's powers, but Elizabeth rarely experienced joy without some calamity occurring in its wake. On 1 July Chamberlain reported the devastating news that 'Mistress Elizabeth Russell lies at the last cast and is either dying or dead.' Young Bess's aunts, the Countesses of Warwick and Cumberland, 'watched with her by turns', tending to the once vivacious 25-year-old girl who had danced before the Queen at her sister's wedding only two weeks before. But they had already 'give[n] her over as past hope'. It was left to Rowland White to report the tragic news on 5 July: 'Mistress Elizabeth Russell died 4 days ago, and great lamentation is made by my lady her mother.'

When Bess Russell's tragic story became the stuff of legend is unclear. In Charles Dickens's novel *The Old Curiosity Shop*, Mrs Jarley, the proprietress of the waxworks, describes a fantastical exhibit to an awestruck Little Nell. This ghostly wax effigy of 'an unfortunate Maid of Honour in the time of Queen Elizabeth, who died from pricking her finger in consequence of working upon a Sunday', represented Elizabeth Russell's daughter.

At least as far back as 1755 a manuscript account by John Boswell records how, like a princess in a fairy tale, Bess had pricked her finger while plying her needlework and slowly bled to death. But what raised this girl, cut off before her prime, to this mythic status? It was, of course, Elizabeth Russell. In a gloomy corner of St Edmund's Chapel in Westminster Abbey stands the memorial to young Bess. An extraordinary testament to her mother's vision, the innovative memorial would earn its eternal resident the title of 'Child of the Abbey' and become the focus of the enchanting story that has developed in the absence of a record revealing the real cause of Bess's death. The first seated effigy of its type in the country, it would influence monumental design for centuries to come. Within the first thirteen or so years alone, it sparked a trend, with its arresting style copied on women's tombs in Fulham, Lincolnshire, Hertfordshire, Kent and Elizabeth's native Essex. The fact that all of these tombs were dedicated to mothers who had died in childbirth indicates that those who commissioned them recognized the aura of maternal anguish that surrounded Bess's tomb.

When conceiving its design, Elizabeth returned to the monument created by Pierre Bontemps for the memorial of Charles de Maigny which she had seen during her embassy in Paris. Bess adopts a melancholy stance, leaning her cheek against the palm of her right hand, an eternally suspended tear just about to trill from her eye. Her left hand points downwards towards a skull, index finger extended. It may have been this enigmatically pointing finger, now missing due to the ravages of time, which inspired her strange legend. The tomb was commissioned and paid for by Nan Russell, but is almost certainly her mother's design, as is the monument of Lord Russell and his son Francis which stands next to it. Unlike its neighbouring tomb, Bess's is inscribed with a brief but nonetheless affecting statement: '*Dormit non mortua est*' ('She is asleep not dead'). Perhaps the myth of Bess's demise, stepping in to fill the unusual gap in Elizabeth's poetic self-expression, developed in homage to the girl's greatest hour: the Bisham entertainments of 1592, when she sat sewing the royal flower, the eglantine rose, on a sampler before her beloved sovereign.

The story of this Renaissance sleeping beauty is probably a romantic fabrication, but the tragedy for Elizabeth, coming so soon after Nan's spectacular wedding, was all too real. On 8 December she decided to pay a visit to Robert Cecil, whose comforting presence she felt she needed at this time. She wrote to say she would be arriving by boat because the expense of the wedding had left her unable to hire a coach and horses. '[M]y heart will not yet serve me to come to court,' she explained, for she could only 'fill every place there . . . with tears by remembrance of her that is gone'. What courage it must have taken for the widow to end the missive with their shared personal joke: 'You must not blaze my beggary, for then you will mar my marriage forever.'

23.

'I'll be revenged . . .'

One of Shakespeare's most celebrated creations is the yellow-stockinged, cross-gartered, cantankerous Puritan Malvolio of *Twelfth Night*. Today this character has become closely associated with Elizabeth Russell's son Sir Thomas Posthumous Hoby. The incident some critics believe was the catalyst for this instance of robust theatrical lampooning took place in the summer of 1600. Hoby's spectacular turf war that year was with his arch-enemies in Yorkshire, the notorious Catholic family the Ewres, at whose head was Ralph, 3rd Lord Ewre, and his brother, Sir William.

After Thomas Posthumous's marriage to Lady Margaret, the Russell–Hoby family drew new battle-lines for the forward Protestant movement across Yorkshire. Hoby was soon sweeping through the 'frozen parts' of the northern territories, as he called them, rooting out Catholic dissenters and generally earning the eternal reproaches of his neighbours. For years afterwards he would acquire a reputation as an unpleasant figure, mocked for his diminutive size, scoffed at for his childlessness, branded with impotency, and even accused of murdering his own wife.

While he may have been a disappointment to his mother in his youth, Thomas Posthumous now had a vocation, and one that had answered her own concern about the policing of the borders of the northern sees, the gateways for Catholic missionaries returning from training camps abroad. And if Thomas was raising hell and making life difficult for the stubborn recusants, then so much the better. Elizabeth was keen on his marriage to the Hackness heiress, not just because she was wealthy, but because she was of strong Puritan convictions, having been raised by the zealous Huntingdons. She had

351

also inherited a ready-made headquarters in the North Riding of Yorkshire, the ideal place from which her husband could set up operations as a spy for Robert Cecil's intelligence network. Sir Erskine Perry would later write about Hoby's relations with Lady Margaret that, according 'to the traditions still existing at Hackness, he accelerated her end by kicking her down stairs' and that he had 'often tried to efface the spots of his wife's blood in the old hall but in vain'. This is a fabrication, a testament to his neighbours' undying venom, for despite their outward incompatibility he and his wife were united in their beliefs and made an excellent team. She had forged a close and lasting bond with his mother, with whom, on her trips to London, she would attend Stephen Egerton's sermons in St Anne's Church in the Blackfriars, where no doubt she would have seen many of her mother-in-law's co-petitioners of 1596, including Richard Field. Her diary records a woman who is obedient, self-disciplined, skilled in medicinal crafts and concerned for her husband's well-being and happiness.

Thomas Posthumous's importance as the Privy Council's chief persecutor of Catholics in the north can be felt in the impact of his absence in April of 1599. John Ferne, who was part of the operation to uncover dissenters in those territories, was utterly bereft without him. He wrote to Cecil on the twenty-seventh of that month, complaining that without him he would require a 'great strength of people' to help him lay siege to a suspected recusant stronghold in nearby Whitby, for 'Sir Thomas Hoby being now at London I do not know of any faithful assistance in the country.' His plan was to stake out the house, and then pounce on the rebels when they least expected it. However, he feared that the servants and tenants of Henry Cholmeley, one of the Ewre family's closest allies and a local Justice of the Peace, would attempt to rescue the concealed recusants. Just five days before, Cholmeley's supporters, numbering forty in total and 'all weaponed', had succeeded in pulling off such a daring rescue attempt, liberating their comrades from the clutches of two officers who had warrants to apprehend them. The rebels informed the officials that the next time they tried to pull a similar stunt 'they should be slain'. They had no doubt who was behind the arrest. Before the fracas subsided the defiant Catholics 'threatened revenge against Sir Thomas Hoby'.

Hoby had locked horns with the whole Cholmeley family in a feud that would last generations. He had clashed with Henry Cholmeley's son, Richard, as well as his grandson, Hugh. The latter later recorded in his memoirs that Hoby, his 'father's old enemy', was 'a troublesome and vexatious neighbour' who was 'of such a nature, unless a man became his very slave, that there was not any keeping friendship, for he loved to carry all things after his own way and humour, how unjust or injurious soever'. With 'a full purse and no children', Hugh Cholmeley went on, the fanatical Puritan 'delighted to spend his money and time in lawsuits'. The apple did not fall far from the tree.

It was a particularly scandalous lawsuit that may have provided Shakespeare with more grist to his mill. In the official trial transcripts, Thomas Posthumous had complained that 'the kinsfolk and allies, servants, retainers, followers and especial friends and favoured persons' of Ralph Ewre had long been in receipt of 'favours' at his hands. Blind eyes were turned to their recusant activities; 'exemptions' given; special kinds of 'protection' offered. Hoby had put a stop to all that. His technique was to target individual families who controlled key areas of Yorkshire. Top of his hit list was Henry Cholmeley, who commandeered most of Whitby. Not one to go in for the softly-softly approach, Hoby had eighty of Cholmeley's relations and 'allies' swiftly 'indicted and convicted for obstinate popish recusancy'. Faced with the prospect of imprisonment, some conformed, including Henry and his wife. As proof of their contrition, they had to attend divine service in their local Protestant church, taking communion there after an estrangement of three years. Hoby then demanded, none too gently, that Henry 'discharge' those servants of his who stubbornly refused to return to the lawful religion. The lapsed Catholic capitulated, 'though very unwillingly'.

Henry Cholmeley did not consider himself a strayed sheep, now returned to the fold. He was still every inch a Catholic and 'conceived in his heart a deep and rooted malice' against the orchestrator of his recent humiliation. Many of his friends felt the same way. Sir Christopher Hylliard was another discontented Catholic for whom merely venting steam with 'violent speeches' against his persecutor was not enough. He began to rouse the recusant community against Hoby, firing up 'a company of youths' who threatened to 'play' their Hackness neighbour a bad turn, one which 'should be so handled as he should not be able to mend himself'. Others followed suit, agitating for an end to their maltreatment. They would all come together to exact their revenge on an unsuspecting Hoby and his wife.

On 26 August 1600 there was a commotion in the Manor of Hackness. Upwards of twenty men appeared on the Hobys' doorstep. This included Will Ewre, son of Ralph Ewre, and the latter's brother Sir William; Richard Cholmeley, son of Henry Cholmeley, and the latter's nephew, John Cholmeley; William Hylliard, nephew of Sir Christopher Hylliard; and 'divers other ruffianly servingmen and boys all weaponed with swords, rapiers, and daggers'.

The intimidating crew dismounted from their horses, all the while talking boisterously about the joys of killing. The discussion continued as they entered Sir Thomas Posthumous's hall and passed into his dining room, without waiting anyone's leave, where they continued in raised tones to boast about 'the sport they had that day' during the hunt in the forest of Pickering, from which they had just returned, or so they claimed. Hoby certainly did not feel he was on friendly enough terms with his unwanted guests to have warranted, or welcomed, such an intrusion. He eyed them suspiciously. Where was their quarry, their kill? For that matter, the paraphernalia one would normally expect to see as 'ordinary preparation for hunting' was notably absent. Following perhaps the line of his stare to their waists, where the hunting-daggers would have hung, they began to make excuses. 'They had lost their daggers that day,' they said, but left their huntsmen behind to find and fetch them. No huntsmen came. '[I]n truth,' Hoby concluded, 'had they not hunted at all that day.' This was little more than a 'pretence', concealing a darker 'plot and confederacy' among his popish neighbours to bring him to 'some intolerable disgrace and outrage in his own house'.

It became quickly apparent that Hoby's guests were not going anywhere for a while. Nervously, he offered them what hospitality lay within the bounds of etiquette as lord of one of the region's principal manors. In return his visitors decided to amuse themselves, their serving men producing cards and dice from their satchels and setting about their usual roistering in high spirits. Hoby was appalled. They knew full well that he detested this kind of 'disorderly play'. He left them to their 'unlawful games' and went to tell his wife what was happening. The news was even less welcome than it would ordinarily have been, because she was under the weather and confined to her bed, having recorded in her diary the night before that she was feeling 'very heavy'. Despite the intrusion, the guests were offered supper, during which there was more talk of hunting, horses and dogs, and chit-chat of a more 'lascivious' nature, 'where every sentence was begun or ended with a great oath'. Then there was 'inordinate drinking unto healths' all round, as one by one the assembled company began to toast each other, raising their mugs in high style. Stephen Hutchinson, one of the company, drank a health to Sir Thomas Posthumous. Sir William Ewre drank a health to the lady of the house. The company then set about attempting to force Hoby 'to carouse and drink healths contrary to his dispositions'.

There was nothing for it but to try to carry on as normal. Hoby insisted that his servants attend evening prayer in the hall, as was their 'usual custom'. He abstained, having decided to stay by his wife's bedside. No sooner had the domestic congregation begun to sing a psalm when a thunderous rumble was heard overhead. This was not the sound of the trumpet signalling the final judgement. It was the almighty reverberation of Ewre & Co. stamping loudly with their feet in the dining chamber above the hall. Hoby's servants tried to continue with their hymns, only to be faced with a new challenge: a cacophony of singing – or some kind of approximation – emanating from the floor above. To make matters worse, those underneath could just make out that what was being chanted was 'a black sanctus', a demonic inversion of the sacred service. Hoby's household listened in horror as devilish 'song making' gave way to further 'wild and strange noises in disturbance and profane derision of prayer'. Then suddenly faces appeared in the window which opened from the stairs on to the hall. It was some of the carousing party, laughing their heads off. They were joined by three of the visitors' servants, who appeared in the hall and began causing a commotion. Hoby could hear the discord and sat there seething, refusing to be goaded by 'riotous and dispightful usage' into a show of inhospitable behaviour which could later be used against him. Surely things would be better tomorrow.

Things were not better on the morrow. Having already taken their places at the dining table for breakfast, the visitors called for more wine. More healths were drunk each to each, with many a cup of beer or wine knocked back. Richard Cholmeley filled his glass 'so full as it ran over into the rushes', prompting mock-Puritan cries from one of his comrades that it was a mortal sin to spill drink. Sir Thomas Posthumous had the cellar locked and informed them testily that 'they would come by no more wine from him'. He was concerned that, his wife's chamber being so close, the 'great noise' of their 'halloing and shouting' would disturb her rest. He sent a message to young Will Ewre, informing him that 'if they were pleased to use his house in gentlemanly and friendly manner and leave off their disorderous courses they should be welcome to him'. This simply 'enraged' them. They stepped up their drinking, 'and pursuing their first intended plot, entered into railing, malicious, and reviling speeches'.

Ewre refused to leave until he and his company had been admitted to Lady Margaret's chamber to see her. Perturbed by the request, she sent word via her servant Robert Nettleton that she would see him on condition that he come alone. Ewre took these 'scurvy messages' as an insult and promised to 'set a pair horns at the gate and be gone'. In Renaissance folk custom horns were nailed to the gates or doors of men whose wives were adulterous. It was part of a local humiliation ritual known as Charivari, or Rough Ridings. The remark could only have been seen as a threat to the honour of Hoby's wife.

At this time the intruders had posted themselves in a small room between the dining chamber and Lady Margaret's bedroom, boasting that 'they were strong enough to keep that chamber if there came twenty or forty against them'. Having given permission for Will Ewre to speak privately with Hoby's wife, Nettleton attempted to bolt the door behind him, to prevent the others from following in his wake. His reward was to be assaulted by Ewre's men, who 'threw him against the ground and thrust him forth by force out of the said chamber'. By no means cowed, Margaret demanded to know what Ewre meant by saying he would 'set up horns at the gate'. He retorted that 'he could wish she would give her husband forty pair, for he was a scurvy ape, and a spindle-shanked ape, and a scurvy urchin, and his best friends of the Privy Council should tell him what he was'. That was the final straw. She ordered him to leave, noting later in her diary that he 'was so drunk that I soon made an end of that I had no reason to stay for'. Depart he would, but not without first causing criminal damage and threatening to rape the lady of the house.

On his way out, Ewre grabbed Hoby's servant and asked him to deliver his master a message: 'the next time I meet him,' he said, making an illustrative lunge for his chin, 'I will pull him by the beard'. Then the party, leaving the premises, threw stones at the house, breaking glass windows 'in sundry places'. Ewre stationed himself on a vantage point at the top of a hill and also began to fling stones, shouting that he 'would play young Devereux' to Margaret; in other words, perform her former husband's office between the sheets. One of the party, George Smith, broke down a freshly appointed hedge before the front gate, pulling up two stiles in the process. He then proceeded to ride 'to and fro' with his horse 'in such sort as he greatly spoilt' the couple's newly laid courtyard, before attacking Hoby's authority in the parish directly by knocking down the 'common stocks' which stood outside the local church, stocks which had no doubt humiliated many a fellow Catholic. When a member of the parish restored them to their former place, Smith returned and 'brake them all in pieces and said that if any shall dare to set them up again, I will set him in them'. In a last parting shot he hurled a piece of wood at a 'poor widow's chimney', threatening to 'pull down the parish church' and burn the entire village to the ground. Then suddenly they were gone, leaving Lady Margaret marvelling, in her own words, at 'the abuse offered by Mr Ewre and his company'. The Hobys immediately sought redress through the Star Chamber, refusing to have their case heard before the Council of the North, where their enemy had too many friends.

The Hobys had come to believe that Ewre and his henchmen had performed this raucous ritual humiliation on them with the intention of attacking the Puritan enclave in the North Riding, protesting that despite the fact their unwanted guests had 'received entertainment for fare and lodging every way answerable to their places and calling yet did they not refrain from any sinful course that could be practiced in that place'. During their invasion of Hackness Hall, they had mounted a search for the Hobys' chaplain Richard Rhodes, promising that they 'would have gelded him'. On 26 September 1600, Hoby wrote to Cecil, complaining that the Ewres were targeting Rhodes in other ways. It was during a meeting of the Council of the North that Will Ewre decided to 'imitate my preacher, by using such gestures as my preacher did use in his evening exercises'. Hoby was offended, for Cecil, he later heard, 'did laugh very heartily at it'.

There may have been a reason for the Yorkshiremen's interest in Rhodes. Just weeks before Lady Margaret's uncomfortable encounter with the Ewres and Cholmeleys, the very day after she had 'heard news of the Death of my Sister, Elizabeth [Bess] Russell', Rhodes had drawn her attention to a controversial work by the Earl of Essex 'in defence of his own Causes'. This may have been the propagandist *Apology* to which Lady Rich's 'violent' letter on behalf of her brother had been appended. They had read and discussed this together and it is clear that Rhodes and the Hobys were keeping a close eye on Essex's machinations and their far-reaching impact in Yorkshire, clearly suspecting that some of his supporters lay concealed in their own neighbourhood. It would not be long before they would be proved right.

On 2 February 1602 a diarist and student at the Middle Temple, John Manningham, wrote about a play he had seen. 'At our feast we had a play called *Twelfth Night, or What You Will*,' he recorded, marvelling at the staging of a 'good practice in it to make the steward believe his lady widow was in love with him'. This was certainly Shakespeare's play, yet Manningham's account is somewhat puzzling. Malvolio, the Puritan 'steward' who is duped into this declaration of love, did not pursue a 'widow' but the Countess Olivia, who was mourning the loss of her brother, not her husband. Was this accidental, or did Manningham see a play that was slightly different to that which has survived today?

If *Twelfth Night* was performed at the Middle Temple, then there is every chance that Shakespeare may have wanted to incorporate a topical scandal which the legal set would have recognized. Ever alert to opportunities for humiliating the woman who had denied him the use of the Blackfriars Theatre, perhaps he chose a notorious case which involved Elizabeth Russell's son and beloved daughter-in-law. The play was probably composed during 1601 and, with the Hobys' suit dragging on until 26 February 1602, when it terminated in Ewre's defeat, Shakespeare had plenty of time to weave into it comedic allusions to these escapades. Both Thomas Posthumous and Will Ewre had been members of Gray's Inn, the former having been admitted in 1588, perhaps with the help of the Earl of Leicester, with whom he had embarked on a mission to the Netherlands two years previously. The rivalry between Hoby and his Catholic nemesis would have been just the kind of gossip the Middle Temple crowd would have enjoyed seeing on stage.

In the first act of the play the carousing Sir Toby Belch turns up at the home of his kinswoman Olivia and insists on 'drinking healths to my niece'. 'I'll drink to her as long as there is a passage in my throat and drink in Illyria,' he adds, determined to engage the household in some fine 'revels'. In the next act he reappears with his companion, Sir Andrew, and the two set about quaffing gargantuan quantities of wine and singing with discordant boisterousness until they are interrupted by Maria, Olivia's waiting-gentlewoman, who protests against the cacophony: 'What a caterwauling do you keep here! If my lady have not called up her steward Malvolio and bid him turn you out of doors, never trust me.' Sir Toby responds by announcing that 'My lady's a Cathayan,' probably his slurred and drunken malapropism for 'Catharan', deriving from 'Cathari', meaning 'pure', which was the term often applied to the Puritan sect. The commotion soon brings in Malvolio, who loses no time in sharing his opinion on such pastimes:

> MALVOLIO . . . Do ye make an alehouse of my lady's house, that ye squeak out your coziers' [cobblers'] catches [tunes] without any mitigation or remorse of voice? Is there no respect of place, persons, nor time in you? . . . My lady bade me tell you that though she harbours you as her kinsman she's nothing allied to your disorders. If you can separate yourself and your misdemeanours you are welcome to the house, if not, an it would please you to take leave of her she is very willing to bid you farewell . . .
>
> SIR TOBY . . . Dost thou think because thou art virtuous there shall be no more cakes and ale?
>
> FESTE Yes, by Saint Anne . . .

The play's clown, Feste, chimes in with an oath which glances at the Church of St Anne's in the Blackfriars; the very Puritan powerhouse that Elizabeth Russell and Margaret Hoby had made their London headquarters. A disgusted Malvolio storms off in a huff after Sir Toby calls for 'a stoup of wine', leaving the revellers to mock his religious proclivities and delusions of grandeur. 'Marry, sir, sometimes he is a kind of puritan,' says Maria jocularly. 'The dev'l a puritan that he is, or anything constantly but a time-pleaser, an affectioned ass that cons state without book and utters it by great swathes.' It is at this point that they decide to 'gull him . . . and make him a common recreation', seeking to subject him to a communal shaming ritual. This culminates in Feste posing as a parson whose 'sportful malice' tortures the poor Puritan into virtual madness; a humiliation which draws from Malvolio the famous promise: 'I'll be revenged on the whole pack of you.'

The comic shenanigans in the play mirror aspects of the shaming ritual orchestrated by Will Ewre and his accomplices on Thomas Posthumous Hoby and his wife. If Malvolio was intended to caricature Elizabeth's son, then perhaps John Manningham had seen a play in which the connections between the real Puritan and Malvolio – incidentally, probably played by Richard Burbage – were strengthened by the latter's courtship of a widow; a union which in the play is as ridiculous and ill-matched as that between Lady Margaret and Thomas Posthumous had seemed to many of their contemporaries. The other possibility is that Manningham recognized the allusion and when setting down an account of the play in his diary confused Olivia with Hoby's bride by calling her a widow. If the former scenario is true, then it is possible that, as with the *Henry IV* plays and *The Merry Wives of Windsor*, Shakespeare's little digs at Elizabeth's closest kinsmen were censored.

An attack on the Hobys would have been particularly galling for the Dowager, who had become incredibly close to Margaret during the period of the play's composition. The first months of 1601 in particular saw the two intensifying their efforts in the Blackfriars, increasing the frequency of their visits to Stephen Egerton's lectures and taking more occasions to dine together, engaging in passionate discussions about the Puritan cause. Margaret's diary also records that her reading practices, no doubt influenced by her mother-in-law, began to include texts which hailed back to the Admonition Controversy, in which Elizabeth had been heavily involved, such as works by Thomas Cartwright, and perhaps also the 'register' of Puritan sufferings, possibly being funded by Elizabeth's sister Anne Bacon. Elizabeth was looking into procuring property for her daughter-in-law and son at this time, and it is clear that she was preparing the former to take over her role as Puritan figurehead after her death. The two were also cultivating their alliance with Cartwright in the run-up to his appointment as a representative of the hardliners at a conference to debate the religious question in Hampton Court in 1604. This culminated in Egerton's own petition to the Lower House of Convocation for a reformed prayer book, which was signed by around one thousand non-conformists. Cartwright died before the conference took place, but Elizabeth and Margaret continued their association with his activist widow, Alice Cartwright. If Shakespeare's sustained mockery of the Puritan temperament in *Twelfth Night* was coupled with a satire against the family who were increasing their political activism in both London and Yorkshire at the time, neither Elizabeth nor her children would have been pleased.

While revenge may have eluded Malvolio, it would not be so for Thomas Posthumous. His opportunity would come when Shakespeare's company became entangled in the greatest scandal to rock Elizabeth I's throne: the rebellion of the Earl of Essex.

24.

'from the Stage to the State'

Sir Charles and Sir Joscelyn Percy paid a visit to the Globe Theatre around the end of the first week of February 1601. Augustine Phillips, actor and co-sharer in Shakespeare's theatrical troupe, testified later that the Percys had spoken to 'some of the players' in his presence, requesting a special command performance of 'the play of the deposing and killing of King Richard the Second'. Asking for a staging the following Saturday, they promised them forty shillings more than their customary payment. Phillips and the players were confused and questioned why they wanted a play 'so old and so long out of use as that they should have small or no company at it'. At last, after further entreaty, they relented, saying they were 'content to play it'. That was a terrible mistake.

The performance would take place during a period of heightened tension following the release of Essex from house arrest. Shakespeare's history plays had already introduced the theatregoing populace to a Machiavellian villain suspiciously like Sir Robert Cecil, the crookback Richard III, who was described as a 'bottled spider' and 'poisonous bunch-backed toad'. The culture being bred by the warring factions at court had become no less theatrical. Since Essex's imprisonment his supporters had begun circulating scandalous libels which rebuked Cecil as a 'Proud and ambitious wretch that feedest on naught but faction', a 'Dissembling smooth-faced dwarf', a 'Crookback spider', whose 'Machiavellian skill' had been bent towards the utter destruction of the innocent and maligned Earl. Some of these were written in encrypted form, but were intended to be broken easily by those close to the drama in court. One, dated 20 December 1599, ran as follows:

Admire all ['Admiral', Charles Howard, Earl of Nottingham],
   weakness wrongs the right,
Honour in general loseth her sight.
Secret are ['Secretary', Robert Cecil] ever their designs
Through whose desert true honour pines.
Award ['A ward', i.e. office of Master of the Court of Wards]
   in worth that is esteemed
By virtue's wrack must be redeemed.
Pride, spite and policy taketh place,
Instead of conscience, honour and grace.
No **cob am** ['Cobham', Henry Brooke] I that worketh ill
Or frame my tongue to enemies' will.
God's ordinance must govern all.
Let no man smile at virtue's fall,
Care you ['Carey', George Carey, Lord Hunsdon] that list
   [who listens]. For I care not
By crooked ways true worth to blot . . .
Action's factions now we find.
They that see nothing must be blind.

Most of Essex's bitterest enemies – Elizabeth Russell's closest associates – make an appearance: Robert Cecil; Henry Brooke, Lord Cobham; George Carey, Lord Hunsdon; and even the Lord Admiral, Charles Howard, who had cleverly shifted his allegiances in the years following the Cádiz raid. It is certainly notable that the first three of these were in some way involved in blocking Shakespeare and his fellow players from commandeering the Blackfriars Theatre just three years before. The poem's anonymous author also vents his anger at Cecil's success in gaining the lucrative Mastership of the Court of Wards on 21 May of that year, a post Essex had long coveted. Not content with circulating such libels in multiple copies, Essex's allies enjoyed scrawling defamatory graffiti where influential courtiers were likely to see it. In his accustomed secret code Rowland White reported, just two days after the composition of the encrypted libel, that 'At court, upon the very white walls, much villainy hath been written against 200 [Robert Cecil]. 1500 [the Queen] doth not send to 1000 [Earl of Essex] but thinks all to be cunning.'

On the morning of the performance of Shakespeare's *Richard II*, Saturday 7 February 1601, the Earl of Essex's household steward, Gelly Merrick, had been stockpiling ammunition, gunpowder, muskets and other weapons at Essex House on the Strand, very close to Elizabeth's beloved Russell House. Having fortified and barricaded the building, he made his way to another nearby dwelling, where he dined with Sir Charles Percy, Sir Joscelyn Percy, Essex's secretary Henry Cuffe and other accomplices. Merrick later confessed under interrogation that from there 'they went all together to the Globe, over the water where the Lord Chamberlain's Men use to play and were there somewhat before the play began'. The entertainment that day had been selected by Sir Charles, son of Henry Percy, 8th Earl of Northumberland, who met his mysterious end after the Somerville–Arden and Throckmorton plots. Percy was a devoted follower of Essex, who had knighted him in 1591, and his ancestral lineage was represented in the drama they were going to see, and he informed the company that 'the play would be of Henry the 4th . . . and of the killing of King Richard the second, played by the Lord Chamberlain's players'.

By the end of the following day Essex and his followers mounted a coup against the Queen's Council, taking to the streets and calling the populace to arms. But the Earl, who according to John Chamberlain had 'ever lived popularly', overestimated the people's love. The residents of London kept their doors firmly shut. With no support forthcoming, the attempt ended shambolically with the rebels barricading themselves into Essex House, where they were soon surrounded by the Queen's officers. Along with the Earl of Southampton and Lady Penelope Rich, the conspirators included Sir Richard Lovelace, son of Elizabeth Russell's nemesis.

Elizabeth and Lady Margaret were probably in London together when these tragic events unfolded. Margaret's diary entry recording the uncovering of 'the treason of the Earls of Essex, Southampton and . . . their associates', follows a particularly busy period of inter-action between her and her mother-in-law. This was succeeded, following the capture of the insurgents, by Margaret suffering a sudden unexplained sickness and extreme weakness. It is hardly sur-prising that the impact of these events would prove virtually crippling. Through her first marriage, she was sister-in-law to the Earl of Essex, and just weeks before had been seen at a meeting with his sister, Lady Rich, the extent of whose involvement in the scandal would soon become horrifyingly apparent.

The list of principal suspects includes a note that 'Lady Rich is with Mr Sackford', having been placed under arrest at the home of the Keeper of the Privy Purse. In the tense period following, Essex made a shocking confession, blaming her for the entire rebellion: 'I must accuse one who is most nearest to me, my sister, who did con-tinually urge me on with telling me how all my friends and followers thought me a coward and that I had lost all my valour,' adding omi-nously, 'she must be looked to, for she had a proud spirit.' On the same day the Lord Admiral, Charles Howard, sent a warning to Lady Rich's lover, Lord Mountjoy, from the Queen: 'I think Her Majesty would be most glad to look upon your black eyes here so she was sure you would not look with too much respect on other black eyes.' The reference is unmistakably to the dark eyes of the renowned beauty.

Elizabeth would also have been concerned. She had extended favours in the past to Dorothy Devereux, wife to the 9th Earl of Northumberland. The Dowager had been accused of working cov-ertly for Essex, with whom she had regularly held private conferences in the Blackfriars and in Essex House. The stubborn loyalty of Eliza-beth's nephew, Anthony Bacon, to the Essex faction did not help matters. Worse still, in the very heat of the Essex uprising, Lady Rich had been responsible for drawing another of Elizabeth's kins-men into the treasonous plot.

After dining with the Earl of Essex, the Earl of Southampton and other conspirators on the eve of the failed coup, Lady Rich sent a messenger to one Henry Bromley, requesting a 'secret conference' at Walsingham House, during which, as Bromley's brother Edward confessed under interrogation on 2 March 1601, she informed him that a summons her brother had received to appear at court that day was a trap. When Elizabeth's nephew, Edward Russell, the Earl of Bedford, was interviewed about his part in the conspiracy on 11 February, he revealed that Lady Rich had been forceful in her insistence that the Earl's life was in danger. Three days later he confessed to the Privy Council that on Sunday 8 February, just after 10 a.m. prayers, 'the Lady Rich came into my house, desiring to speak with me speedily'. While the sermon was being read, she spoke to him in secret 'in the next room' and urged him to accompany her to a meeting with Essex, 'whereupon I went presently with her in her coach, none of my family following me out of the sermon room'. Essex and Lady Rich – the ambitious Devereux siblings – had done all they could to make it appear as if their subsequent enterprise was a panicked and improvised response to a direct threat to the Earl's safety. Margaret Hoby had different ideas, believing that the rebellion was a premeditated 'treason', which should 'appear to the view of all that were not over partially blind'. Robert Cecil agreed, accusing Essex of cunningly concealing his true intentions by 'publishing [that] he should have been slain in his bed by Cobham, Ralegh, and Cecil'.

This was all the prompting Elizabeth's nephew needed to rake up Essex's involvement in Hayward's *Life and Reign of King Henry IV*. The Earl, he maintained, sought to have the court 'reformed by him like as by Henry 4th', and would therefore 'have removed Her Majesty [and] stepped into her chair'. He also claimed that 'this popular traitor' had cultivated both Puritan and Catholic loyalties, 'making them believe that if he came to be Lord of England, he would grant liberation of conscience'. Cecil had already gathered privy intelligence that Essex had been courting the Jesuit priest Thomas Wright, through whom he established contact with the Catholic activist Robert Parsons (an enemy to the Cooke, Cecil and Bacon families). He had even used Wright – or so the Queen's Secretary wanted the Privy Council to believe – to send a message to the Pope: 'if I could be persuaded that your church did not seek my blood, I could like your religion well'.

Even before Essex's execution, Cecil set about ordering preachers across the land to deliver special sermons which appraised the populace of the Earl's desire to become a new 'Henry the 4th', by 'cunningly insinuating that the same abuses being now in this realm . . . were in Richard II's days'. In the immediate aftermath of the coup both Elizabeth and her daughter-in-law must have been worried that they too could be brought in for questioning. This anxiety was no doubt increased by the fact that one preacher may have taken to heart Essex's recent promises of freedom of conscience for Puritans. Stephen Egerton found himself in trouble with the authorities for failing to deliver the anti-Essex sermons. 'Touching the late Earl,' he wrote to Cecil in answer to the charge, 'I protest I never had so much as any purpose or thought to justify either his action or his intention, yea rather, my purpose and endeavour was in express terms to condemn both.' Elizabeth's kinsman William Fitzwilliam also jumped to Egerton's defence, and the Secretary backed down.

It was not until 19 February, when Margaret Hoby recorded in her diary 'the Earl of Southampton and Essex arraigned and condemned', that she began to recover her health. By this point it was clear that Lady Rich had nothing more incriminating to say and that she would escape punishment. This may have been due to the fact that her lover had been sent to Ireland to deal with the crisis Essex had been unable to resolve. The Queen may have thought it unwise to risk enraging Lord Mountjoy, who was now in command of a substantial army. It would also have been unclear how much Lady Rich really knew about her brother's personal grievances against Cecil and his allies. On 18 February 1601 Sir John Peyton sent a letter, which Robert Cecil had read, containing a further enclosure which revealed that, just before he was arrested, Essex had burned a 'book of his troubles all written with his own hand' and a tantalizing 'catalogue of divers names . . . in the presence of my lady his wife [and] the Lady Rich'.

This must also have been a relief to Elizabeth, who, with members of both factions among her close kinsmen, had long been caught in the middle of Essex's machinations. Thomas Posthumous's response to the crisis would have helped reassure his cousin Robert Cecil of his family's loyalty. It also gave him the opportunity to claim the revenge for which he had so longed. One of Essex's co-conspirators was none other than Richard Cholmeley, Will Ewre's confederate. Following Cholmeley's arrest Hoby moved fast to ensure that the scandal would be as damaging to his reputation as possible. He wrote to Cecil, declaring that this traitor (who had clearly proved himself to be of dubious character after acting as one of the 'outrageous defendants' to Hoby's bill in the Star Chamber) was 'one of the rebellious Earl's assistants' and, though 'his friends would have it thought that he was there by chance, and that he was a man of no power', he had evidence to the contrary. He reminded Cecil that Cholmeley had the ability, from the recusant strongholds of the north, to 'raise 500 men, if they should show themselves as traitorous as they do already show themselves disobedient unto Her Majesty's laws'. Cholmeley's properties were all located 'in the most dangerous parts of Yorkshire for hollow hearts, for popery', surely very 'apt to entertain bad intelligenced strangers'. Had he not, after all, harboured Catholic priests? Religion was not his only motive, however, for Cholmeley was a man for hire, who had assisted the 'rebellious Earls Essex and Southampton for money'. Unsurprisingly, Hoby would win his case against Ewre and his friends in the Star Chamber in the opening months of the following year. Perhaps it did not escape Shakespeare that the Hoby–Russell enclave had driven the knife in deeper after Essex's botched coup, or that one of the men who arrested him was Elizabeth's new kinsman, the Earl of Worcester. It may explain why the dramatist was keen to get his own back through *Twelfth Night*.

Essex's demise left a triumphant Cecil the unchallenged superpower at court, revelling as his half-brother, Thomas, the new Lord Burghley, read out the public proclamation with the charges against the Earl and his accomplices. Robert Devereux was thirty-three years old when he met his end on 25 February, Ash Wednesday, 1601. Fearing a public backlash, the Queen had decided on a private execution inside the walls of the Tower of London. The unusual quiet which attended this occasion was broken only by the chaplain's reading of the 51st psalm and the echo of the three full blows of the axe which the executioner needed to complete his heavy task.

The death of the Queen's former favourite did not stop his supporters from continuing to defame the Cecils and their allies in their own libellous proclamations. In particular, Shakespeare's patron, Lord Chamberlain George Carey, came under fire as a traitor and sycophant:

> Chamberlain, Chamberlain,
> One of her Grace's kin,
> Fool he hath ever been . . .
> Raw without and Foul within . . .
>
> Little Cecil trips up and down,
> He rules both Court and Crown,
> With his great Burghley Clown,
> In his long fox-furred gown,
> With his long proclamation,
> He saith he saved the town.

It is possible that the alliances represented here, those which go back to 1596 and Elizabeth Russell's petition against the Blackfriars Theatre, had the unforeseen consequence of helping the Chamberlain's Men escape punishment. Shakespeare must surely have been troubled. Had he not satirized Essex's enemies in his *Henry IV* plays? Had he not praised Essex to the skies in *Henry V*? Had he not declared his love and devotion to Essex's chief co-conspirator, the Earl of Southampton, in his dedicatory epistles to his narrative poems? After his colleague Augustine Phillips was questioned, and his former patron Southampton was incarcerated in the Tower, it must have dawned on the playwright that he stood in danger of losing his livelihood, more so since the role of *Richard II* in these deplorable events was, humiliatingly, made public knowledge.

The formal account of Essex's treasons was written by none other than Elizabeth Russell's nephew Francis Bacon, and quickly flew off the presses as *A Declaration of the Practices and Treasons attempted and committed by Robert, late Earl of Essex, and his Complices*. Bacon revealed that 'on the afternoon before the Rebellion, Merrick, with a great company of others, that afterwards were all in the action, had procured to be played before them, the play of deposing King Richard the second'. This was not, he averred, merely a 'casual' choice, but 'a play bespoken by Merrick', despite the fact that it was 'old, and they should have loss in playing it'. But retribution, he explained, was close at hand: 'so earnest he [Gelly Merrick] was to satisfy his eyes with the sight of that Tragedy, which he thought soon after his Lord [the Earl of Essex] should bring from the Stage to the State, but that GOD turned it upon their own heads.'

The pro-Essex libels reveal something important: Essex's allies had viewed George Carey and Robert Cecil as confederates in the Earl's downfall. This alliance may have shielded Shakespeare from Cecil's wrath in the immediate aftermath of the coup, for the Chamberlain's Men are not explicitly named in Bacon's damning report. This could also explain why it was that on 22 June 1600 the Privy Council agreed to grant a licence for only two playhouses: the Globe, under the auspices of George Carey, and the Fortune, whose patron was Charles Howard, another of the enemies of Essex identified along with Hunsdon in previous libels. When Howard applied for permission to build the Fortune it is significant that below his own name on his petition are those of 'G. Hunsdon' and 'Ro: Cecyll'. Though the birth of the Globe was a troublesome one indeed, Elizabeth Russell's action against the Blackfriars Theatre had ensured Shakespeare's future financial success as a principal shareholder in this lucrative duopoly. She also unwittingly helped provide the justification for the new restrictions, for this neat business arrangement built on former petitions that had highlighted the dangers of 'common Stage plays' as the fountainheads of 'riotous' activity among masterless men, foremost among these being that of 1596.

The Dowager's feelings about this are not recorded, though one thing is certain: she would not have been happy about any increase in the fortunes and influence of the Lord Admiral, for he was about to become her nemesis in a battle that would last the rest of her life.

PART SIX

Shakespeare's Countess

25

The Last Stand for Donnington

Towards the end of 1601 Elizabeth Russell once again found herself at the centre of a 'horrible riot' as she entered into a new round in the bitter turf war with the Lovelace family. Anne Lovelace, who had sparked the original conflict in 1594, appeared to have reconciled herself to Elizabeth, the opponents reaching an arrangement of mutual consolation. Anne continued in her mistress's service and in return was given properties, which she began leasing out. This pleasant situation would not last.

One of Elizabeth's chief delights lay in giving vent to those deep maternal instincts which had all too often been thwarted by the headstrong children of her blood. These normally manifested themselves in her attempts at procuring suitable spouses for young unmarried men and women and, with Anne still to wed, Elizabeth found her perfect project. Her eye alighted on William Latton, a Berkshire gentleman who was going places. Anne may have taken exception to having her destiny managed in this way (though Elizabeth would soon suspect there were other causes), and left her service. Outraged by her desertion, Elizabeth revoked the grant to the copyhold. Anne would not give it up willingly.

The fact that the court had initially decreed in Elizabeth's favour in the legal suit which followed made little difference to Peter Warburton, the associate Judge of the Court of Common Pleas. While her counsel was out of town, he took occasion to revoke the order 'which by law he could not', protested the Dowager to Robert Cecil on 12 October 1601, 'being a record of court'. Before Elizabeth could make her counterplea, Anne decided she was going to profit from the disputed lands no matter what the cost. Under her direction, one hundred rioters invaded the Dowager's land and 'reaped and carried away twenty acres of wheat'. The looters were guarded by 'thirty well weaponed persons' carrying poles, pikes and battleaxes, who formed a protective ring around the interlopers as they hacked away at the harvest. Elizabeth's men attempted to resist them in vain. Blood was shed, with two of her servants injured, 'the rest cast down and not suffered to carry any of my corn out of the field'.

Elizabeth demanded that Cecil summon the 'insolent' Warburton and have him 'unjusticed', or at the very least, 'sharply to take him up for doing me an open wrong, as better learned than himself affirm'. Who would restore the hundred marks' worth of corn she had lost? Who would recompense her for the £40 she had spent on her damaged barn? 'I hold my honour more dear than my life,' she declared defiantly, 'Neither list [will] I, while I breathe, to be thus bearded by a girl's tearing out of my teeth what I meant to her preferment in my own parish, if she had kept my favour.' To be 'bearded' was normally the prelude to a dual or challenge to armed combat between two men, consisting of the provocative pulling of the opponent's beard. Elizabeth, typically, imagined herself and Anne as two male combatants squaring up to each other for a fight.

It is possible that Justice Warburton was leaned upon by Richard Lovelace and his powerful master, Charles Howard. Elizabeth suggested this when she protested to Cecil, 'thus in mine own manor to be cozened for my kindness, I think it too great a dishonour and disgrace for me to bear by my Lord Admiral's maintenance, or Mr Warburton's wrong'. Howard had been working to snatch Donnington from her grasp, petitioning the Queen to grant him the 'fee simple' to the estate, which would confer it upon himself and his heirs. Elizabeth had written to Cecil on 5 March 1600, before Bess's death, urging him to transfer the rights to the hard-won property to her daughter. She also had an ultimatum for Howard.

A year before Essex's coup, Elizabeth planned a rebellion of her own. She had succeeded in whipping up opposition to the admiral's scheme among all the 'tenants that have been under my government these twenty years'. So many were they that Elizabeth referred to them as a 'swarm', and their purpose was to descend upon the Queen with the intention of convincing her to allow her namesake to keep possession of the castle. She had 'stayed' the rebellious tenants for now, but if Howard did not 'desist' in his pursuit of her castle she would have no choice but to unleash them. Her request was not merely due to her desire to maintain her role as Keeper of Donnington and its surrounding parklands. She was concerned that two property magnates of Berkshire, Sir Thomas Parry and Thomas Fortescue, were planning to buy up parts of Donnington from Howard 'to the hurt of the tenants'.

The Lovelaces, meanwhile, were working to challenge Elizabeth's authority in her Berkshire lands, probably as a means of making it easier for Howard to seize control of Donnington. In the early months of 1600 the undersheriff of Berkshire made the journey to the Blackfriars. Turning up at Elizabeth's door, he served her with a writ from the Lord Chief Justice, Sir John Popham, charging her with the illegal and enforced enlargement of a prisoner in a bailiff's custody and the subsequent arrest of the bailiff. This was an attempt to prosecute her for her extraordinary actions in the first round of the Lovelace disputes, during which she detained the bailiff in her own prison. 'I have known many noblemen in my days would have been glad to have had the execution of such a writ upon me,' she declared imperiously, 'having freed myself from so great a danger so many years it would go hard to attach me now.' It was as plain as day, she averred, that 'great ladies' persons' were not in any way subject to 'a base undersheriff or High Sheriff'.

Elizabeth had become convinced that, since the admiral had started his suit for Donnington, she was being subjected to a sustained campaign of intimidation by men who wanted to divest her of her lands. Such assaults were, it seems, coming from all directions, for she had entered into a dispute with one William Childe of Pool Court, Worcestershire, in 1599, over lands she had rented to him. Elizabeth believed that he was maliciously working to cause her 'trouble and hindrance' by 'his personal countenancing' of others' machinations against her. What these were she did not say, but the accusation coincides with the period of Howard's suit for Donnington, which ended in 1601 with his successfully gaining the coveted grant for the castle from the Queen. Childe had, according to Elizabeth, been 'giving any help or information that he conveniently might to this defendant's [Elizabeth's] adversaries, whereby to do harm or prejudice to this defendant and her cause'. The intention behind this was to weaken her financially and thereby force her to sell her lands. She demanded that Childe remove himself and his livestock from her estate. When he refused she forcibly ejected him in her characteristically forthright manner.

In the dead of night Elizabeth made 'entry to . . . the grounds and premises' of Childe's farm and evicted eight hundred ewes and lambs, five hundred sheep, and 'forty other beasts at the least'. The animals were cast out of their enclosure, leaving a breathless Childe scrambling to gather them before they disappeared into the darkness. He later complained in court that he was forced 'to sell a great part of them (wanting other pasture for the same cattle) and as yet her ladyship keepeth the possession of the premises'. Childe found himself without a farm in which to pursue his livelihood and facing the formidable Dowager in the Court of King's Bench.

These would not be the last assaults on her property rights Elizabeth would have to fend off. Her fight with the Lord Admiral was far from over. The next time they locked horns it would be after the death of the Queen who had offered Elizabeth great comforts in her grief, had served as godmother to her children, and had awarded her the controversial post of Keeper of Donnington Castle in defiance of the limitations normally placed upon women's public roles. Acceding to the throne in 1603, the new King, James I, would intervene directly in the continuing war between Lady Elizabeth Russell and the Lord Admiral, Charles Howard.

Elizabeth was surrounded. There were seventeen armed men, each carrying a halberd, their battle helmets glinting in the daylight. When two of the assailants drew their swords against her the irony of the situation became apparent. The weapons had been stolen from Donnington Castle; *her* castle. It beggared belief – 'mine own weapons against myself'.

The incident began on 3 September 1603 as Thomas Dolman, Elizabeth's neighbour in Donnington, was preparing to receive the newly crowned King of England as his honoured guest. Shaw Place was a magnificent brick mansion, built around half a mile from Donnington Castle, near Newbury, but even its stately proportions were not large enough to accommodate the entire royal train. Two years previously, James's predecessor had granted Donnington Castle to Charles Howard, in the Queen's words, 'forasmuch that he did render very great services to us and our kingdom, with our ships and our royal fleet'. Typically of Elizabeth I, she failed to explain precisely what this meant for Elizabeth Russell. Was she to give up the castle immediately, or remain in possession until the end of her life? This uncertainty sparked more clan warfare. Without an express royal command to leave the fortress, Elizabeth would be staying put, and not all the devils in hell would drive her out.

With the King's visit drawing near, Dolman appealed for help to the Earl, who replied that it would be his pleasure to 'have lodgings provided for him within the castle' so that the unwieldy retinue could be more comfortably housed. The admiral sent his servants with supplies and victuals to prepare the fortress. Knowing Elizabeth all too well, he had their cart kitted out with a few additional essentials: a crowbar, iron poles and other accoutrements best suited to making a forceful entry into such an edifice. The group of around thirty men trundled along to the castle. On arrival they found their way barred by two of Elizabeth's servants, whom she had placed inside to guard it while she was away in Wales with her daughter and son-in-law Anne and Henry Somerset. When asked what they were carrying in their cart by the servants, the Lord Admiral's men answered that they were merely bringing 'provision for the Queen's dinner the next day' and demanded to be let in. Immediately suspicious, the servants refused their request. It was then that, according to Elizabeth's own testimony, 'in very riotous and outrageous manner, being all of them weaponed', they charged the castle gates, battering them down with 'their bars of iron and other engines'. After they 'entered and took the castle', they decided to 'break into many rooms', including Elizabeth's 'own closet'. Sifting through her 'writings and other things of great charge and importance', they stole the rolls which pertained to her 'office' of 'collection of rents' for the manor of Donnington. Her servants were thrown out unceremoniously and told 'to go seek their lodging abroad'. They then began compiling an 'inventory' of Elizabeth's possessions. Seizing what they liked the look of, they commandeered some of the comelier chambers for the admiral's use.

When news of the break-in reached Elizabeth's ears she made the journey down from Wales post-haste with the intention of reclaiming her stronghold. Finding her way barred by the admiral's men, she retreated to nearby Newbury, where she began to formulate a plan. On her return she brought back with her Henry Cox, the Mayor of Newbury, his wife and 'divers other her friends'. This would be no peace-keeping mission. Since 1600, Elizabeth's tenants had been standing at the ready to challenge the Lord Admiral's claim to her estate on her command. Now was the time for them to make good on that promise. On the way she rallied further troops, collecting 'divers clothiers', who were no doubt worried about what would become of their livelihood if the castle and its manors changed hands. Equipping them with weapons, she marched them up to the Porter's Lodge, having realized that it was now occupied by her evicted servants.

Sensing that she was amassing an attack force, the admiral's men rushed to intercept them. Now swelled to forty in number 'at the least', they 'set upon' Elizabeth's army, 'being weaponed with swords, halberds, long pick-staves, and pitchforks'. Before her eyes, most of her servants were violently dispossessed of the lodge and surrounding park. She found herself with two swords drawn against her, as seventeen of the attackers closed in, and was told that 'she should not pass any further that way'. In the chaos she heard some of the admiral's followers give the order for the shins of her servants' horses to be hacked and her men to be killed if they dared approach the lodge.

Those few of Elizabeth's servants who had managed to barricade themselves into the lodge 'for fear of their lives' would be starved out. Before too long her opponents had driven out all her cattle and taken possession of the lodge and park. Elizabeth refused to leave, preferring 'to lie without doors, by and under the lodge walls all that night and all the next day'. In an attempt to force her out, the admiral's men patrolled the grounds menacingly, refusing to remove their hats in her presence, and 'in very uncivil sort, taunting and scoffing at her in such unseemly and barbarous manner as was not fitting to be used to any gentlewoman of far meaner state and degree'. Her tormentors did not prevail, and the armed stand-off which ensued lasted 'three days and three nights'.

Charles Howard's servants claimed that only one sword had been drawn, 'and no more hurt done'. Elizabeth begged to differ, for she had found herself facing 'the force of two drawn swords, twenty-four halberds, and as many headpieces out of the castle', and sued the Earl's servants for causing a riot. She also claimed that James Bellingham, the Lord Admiral's man, had abused her with 'saucy taunts' and insolent questions, attempting to goad her into an undignified verbal sparring. Refusing to give him ammunition which he could later use against her, she, 'scorning to [de]file my mouth with a servant', remained silent. This angered Bellingham all the more. 'Oh,' he retorted. 'Belike [perhaps] you think me like some of your kin, that delight to hear themselves speak.' Elizabeth resisted even this barb and decided instead to send for Thomas Dolman, in his capacity as Justice of the Peace for Berkshire. This was a tactical error.

Upon Dolman's arrival, Elizabeth immediately 'willed him to restore her possession, to commit the rioters, and to bind the rest to the peace'. He would do nothing of the sort, for as far as he could tell there had been 'no force nor ill-beseeming words or usage' offered to her. He asked her to retire to her lodging or take up Bellingham's offer, which was that if she could find it in her heart to 'acknowledge' herself subject to the Lord Admiral she would be very welcome, 'with her gentlewoman, and such other necessary attendants as she would have', to reside in the castle or lodge as his guest. She snapped back that 'she would not, for she scorned to be keeper to any subject whatsoever'. At that she took up a one-woman protest and, 'of wilfulness merely', posted herself outside the castle walls, a brooding presence scowling and watching all night in her coach. She was sixty-three years old at the time.

James I and his Queen, Anne of Denmark, had arrived at Shaw Place on 21 September. Elizabeth took the opportunity to petition the King directly. If she thought she would merit as much grace at his hands as she had enjoyed from Elizabeth I, she was mistaken. He simply made answer that 'the castle, park or manor, were none of his, but the Lord Admiral's by the grant of the late Queen Elizabeth' and suggested she 'refer it to some honourable personages' to act as judges in the matter and 'make some good end between them'. Wouldn't she prefer to avoid a messy suit in law? She refused to accept these terms, protesting still that she 'desired justice that the law might end it'. Her royal interlocutor began to lose patience.

'Madam,' he interjected, 'is there none within the kingdom that you dare or will trust?'

'I beseech Your Majesty,' she replied, 'let me have justice, and I will trust the law.'

With that, completely ignoring the King's advice, she began a legal suit through the King's Bench 'for custody of the castle and park'. During the first hearing of the case, it appeared as if all would go in the Dowager's favour when the court 'found against the rioters'. The judges, however, refused to fine them or offer any restitution until a further hearing. Elizabeth decided to pursue the matter in the Star Chamber. Objections were raised all round, but 'she would not be stayed in any kind'. The scandal became the talk of the court. On 11 September Sir Thomas Edmonds had written to the Earl of Shrewsbury, informing him that the Lord Admiral had 'recovered the possession of Donnington Castle from the Lady Russell'. Three days after James I arrived at Shaw Place, her daughter's father-in-law, the Earl of Worcester, gossiped to the Earl of Shrewsbury that Elizabeth's nemesis 'keepeth the castle and her Ladyship out of doors, who complained to the King, but found little redress, and so is turned to the Law'.

As Elizabeth geared herself up for another long legal battle, she began to sense that this might be her last big fight. On 4 October 1603 she wrote to Sir William Dethick, Garter Principal King of Arms, to prepare her own funeral, asking him to 'set down advisedly and exactly in every particular by itself the number of mourners due for my calling, being a Viscountess of birth'. The subtext of her request was obvious: she was demanding to be buried as a Dowager Countess. She had already decided that ten female mourners would accompany the funeral train, and she wanted 'my preacher' there, perhaps Stephen Egerton, as well as her physicians. The latter may have included her other Blackfriars neighbour and co-petitioner Dr William Paddy. 'Good Mr. Garter,' she concluded prophetically, 'do it exactly, for I find fore-warnings that bid me provide a pickaxe.' He may have been a little too exact for her liking, for the 'order of mourners' and 'allowance and quantity of cloth' he sent her was for 'an Earl's eldest son's wife', rather than for that of an outright Dowager Countess.

The woman who had memorialized the great and the good of Elizabethan society was turning her attention to her own legacy; but she wanted that legacy to include the castle she had fought so long to attain. It was with some trepidation that on 13 May 1606, the eve of the hearing for her suit over Donnington, she wrote to Robert Cecil, begging him to attend. As a Privy Councillor, Cecil normally audited Star Chamber trials, but he had refused to deal with his aunt's case for fear of being accused of partiality. She persisted, reassuring him that she only expected that in his 'place as a Councillor and judge you will censure according to justice and equity'. It would do her no good. When she attended court the next day it would be without the man who had been her bulwark during so many of her previous battles. Though she would have felt isolated, exposed and outnumbered by her enemies, sensing that the

King too opposed her, she refused to be intimidated. Before the day's proceedings were over the Star Chamber would become the stage for one of the most extraordinary performances of her life, and a stunned contemporary would exclaim that Lady Elizabeth Russell was scarcely female at all; she was indeed 'more than womanlike'.

It was Henry Howard, the Earl of Northampton, who got more than he bargained for when he decided to challenge Elizabeth Russell in the Star Chamber. Before he knew it, the 66-year-old noblewoman had grabbed him by the cloak and pulled him towards her, before berating him sharply. The Earl's crime was to have had the temerity to defend his kinsman Charles Howard, the Earl of Nottingham, and, even more heinous, to challenge her right to the title she claimed was her due.

'[F]irst, out of the place I hold, as one to whom the office of Earl Marshal is committed,' he had declared, imperiously laying his credentials before the court, 'by the law of arms you are no Lady Dowager, nor [are there] none under the degree of an Earl's wife.' His outburst came in response to Elizabeth's attack on the Lord Admiral, who had begun his address to the court that day in somewhat comedic vein, knowing precisely how to goad his opponent to incriminate herself. When asked by the judge to answer the charges of the complainant, he replied dryly that there was no case to answer, for the complainant in question did not exist. In fact, 'there was not at the time . . . nor at any time after, neither as yet is, any person in being named the Lady Elizabeth Russell Dowager . . . neither ought the said title of Dowager to be given or used to or by any person whatsoever of meaner estate than a Countess'.

Elizabeth played right into his hands, choler mounting, answering that she 'had been Lady Dowager before Nottingham was, and that if the Lord Russell had lived, both for worth, honour and judgment, he had far excelled the Lord of Nottingham; and that he had dealt very dishonourably with her in getting the castle and park from her'. The Lord Admiral had been created Earl of Nottingham in 1597, while her husband had died some thirteen years before that. In comparison to the ancient and noble house of Bedford, Nottingham's title was, to her mind, a vulgar innovation. Henry Howard offered a bold rebuttal in defence of Nottingham's claims. '[T]he Lord Russell, your husband, was a noble gentleman,' he said in polished tones, 'but ill beseeming you with so many unfitting detractions to compare him to the Earl of Nottingham; and he died in his father's lifetime, so you could not be a Lady Dowager, for your husband was never an Earl.' Northampton's unrestrained support of the admiral unleashed in Elizabeth a blind fury and he quickly found himself nose to nose with her when she plucked him by the cloak.

The Dowager's temper was not soothed by the efforts of the Lord Chancellor, Sir Thomas Egerton, to bring the day's proceedings to a speedy conclusion by questioning Elizabeth's ownership of the lodge and casting some doubt on whether a riot really had taken place in her presence. She stopped him mid-flow, telling the court that she 'desired to be heard'. Loud objections to this were raised by the assembled lords, to little effect, for she 'violently and with great audacity began a large discourse, and would not by any means be stayed or interrupted', treating her unprepared auditors to a hair-raising speech that lasted 'for the space of half an hour or more'. Women were very rarely granted licence to speak for themselves in a court of law. Because female outspokenness was shunned, women's words were almost always filtered through a legal representative. Elizabeth's decision to hold the entire court to ransom with her extempore oration was virtually unprecedented, yet she was determined to press her claim for her castle in her own words, evidently feeling that her legal counsel was not up to the task. She had, she insisted, in total paid £1,500 in bribes for the fortress and claimed that 'when she informed the Queen that the Lord Admiral would be a suitor for the same, Her Majesty's answer to her was, "God's death! my castle of Donnington! I think he will have my crown and all."' Then Elizabeth overstepped the mark by protesting that her royal namesake had breached her promise in granting the castle to Charles Howard without returning her money.

The lords were horrified and 'much distasted these fond speeches, but she still went on'. The rest of the court then began to object audibly, 'murmuring and making great noise', yet still she went on. Her own counsel, embarrassed by her outburst, began to remove themselves from the bar, 'yet she went on, without any change, or any way abashed at all, in a very bold and stout manner'. All the while she was being watched by a stunned legal commentator, John Hawarde, who recorded the unfolding events, which have preserved for posterity Elizabeth's extraordinary behaviour in court. Hawarde was appalled and impressed in equal measure, marvelling at this female rhetorician who demonstrated such 'a very great spirit and an undaunted courage, or rather will, more than womanlike, whose revenge by her tongue seemed to be the sum of her desire'. So uncommon a sight was this that he felt compelled to interrupt his factual summary of the case to indulge in an extended analysis of the otherworldly creature before him. 'In a meaner personage,' he mused, 'it is usually termed "malice" and "envy", but in her, being honourable, learned, and endowed with many excellent gifts, we grace it with "a great spirit" which I fear the world conceiveth to be more than blemished, if not utterly extinguished, with extreme pride.' The fact that Elizabeth was facing some of the most power-ful men in the land did not seem in the least irksome to her, despite their continued objections to her unauthorized speech. An amused Hawarde noted in a marginal comment: 'the Lords try to stop her, but in vain'. At length Lord Chancellor Egerton intervened.

'Madam,' he bellowed, 'you must give us leave; we have suffered you to wrong yourself, this court, and our Master his service.'

Then the Earl of Northampton chimed in to express his obser-vation that this kind of behaviour 'was never offered to the court before, such violent interruption of any judge delivering his sen-tence'. Elizabeth was about to open her mouth when the Lord Treasurer, Thomas Sackville, 1st Earl of Dorset, forestalled her, 'for she was beginning again'. She had, he said, 'greatly wronged the dead Queen, his Mistress', and then came the sting in the tail:

'She,' he said, meaning the Queen, 'was so far from breach of any promise . . . which you shall give me leave to believe that there was never any such thing, nor you could never speak more dishonourably of her.'

Then the court exploded, with the Lord Chancellor and the 'rest of the Lords' all shouting at once, each strenuously condemning 'the Lady for those words' and praising the Lord Admiral to the heavens: he was 'as loyal a hearted man as any within the kingdom', he was 'every way very honourably accounted', he was 'of exceeding good merit'. And the complainant, what was she but a headstrong woman and a liar? The Chancellor and the judges 'all wished it had been ended, and never brought to this, all condemning greatly the pride and wilfulness of the plaintiff'. The proceedings were thus chaotically deferred until the precise nature of Elizabeth's ownership of the castle, park and lodge could be determined, leaving an irate Dowager in suspense until the next hearing.

'Vouchsafe me your presence, I beseech you, at the Star Chamber tomorrow,' wrote Elizabeth to Robert Cecil on 6 November 1604. 'Wherein I beseech that Dolman, Justice of the Peace, may be punished,' and Bellingham too, for his 'saucy performance' outside her own lodge. Again her nephew resisted his aunt's pleas. Again she would have to attend court without him. Unsurprisingly, after her previous outburst in the Star Chamber, the judges were less than willing to rule in her favour. Charles Howard was immediately cleared 'from the procuring of any riot'; far from it, for it was concluded that he 'had done honourably and discretely'. More humiliating for Elizabeth, it was formally decreed that Donnington Castle was the Lord Admiral's possession. He was her 'master' and 'the master may break the house' if he chooses so to do, for 'the Lady Russell is the Lord Admiral's servant, and keeper of his house; if he or his servants break the locks or doors, it is no wrong, for she hath but the bare custody, for him and not against him'. Though the court conceded that Elizabeth had 'custody of the park', it could not be legally determined that the same rights extended to the lodge. Any concession meant little, for the court poured further doubt on the Dowager's claim that a riot had taken place. Dolman was much 'commended' for his conduct and, 'if he did not see the force' which Elizabeth insisted had taken place, then he could not be expected to charge anyone nor make restitution.

Then the admiral played the winning card. '[T]he king,' he declared, 'by his prerogative may take up any house in his Progress,' adding a disturbing legal caveat: 'By the Civil law the wives are favoured in cases of treason, *propter imbecillitatem sexus*.' The Latin phrase means 'due to the weakness of the sex'. Elizabeth was no wife, but a widow. As the blame for resisting the King's will could not be shifted on to her husband, Elizabeth was trapped, and she knew it. She could now only remain silent as the Archbishop Richard Bankcroft, John Whitgift's successor, acquitted all of her opponents. Ordered to pay damages, Elizabeth lost her case and her castle. What had begun with one of the most radical appointments made in English history, a woman granted the Keepership of her own castle, ended with Elizabeth dying by the very sword by which she had lived: the Star Chamber.

The new King had inaugurated an altogether more misogynistic culture which would not brook such incursions by women into male spheres of influence. The glory days of Elizabeth I, years which saw a relative increase in the privileges enjoyed by noblewomen, were over and the late Queen's namesake found herself in a world in which she did not belong. From this point on she would be subjected to continued incursions upon her property rights by James I's ambitious male courtiers. Having wrestled Donnington from her grasp, the King turned his attentions to the rest of her estates. Five years into his reign, and looking for innovative ways to fund his profligate lifestyle, he gave his backing to a bill which allowed him to extort money from the nobility by invalidating, and thereupon forcibly seizing, expired grants of lands issued under the Tudors. There would be something in it for the canny courtiers who helped him effect this scheme: revenues from confiscated properties and leases to be pocketed. The King duly set them to work, dredging up the descendants of long-forgotten grantees and rooting out the owners of dissolved monastic estates.

On 19 April 1608 the profiteer and pirate Sir Thomas Shirley the younger convened a commission to investigate the validity of Elizabeth's claim to her Worcestershire manors. Her meticulous record-keeping and intimate knowledge of the law allowed her to sabotage Shirley's plans, for she had 'sought up my evidences' and proved beyond doubt the legitimacy of her ownership. Hearing that other leading courtiers were planning to mount similar challenges to her estates, she wrote to Cecil, who had been elevated to Lord Treasurer from 6 May, begging him 'to stay [their] further proceedings'. James's bullies had no right, she averred indignantly, 'to bring me to trial . . . upon a false information'. Cecil, it seems, agreed, and came to his aunt's rescue.

No sooner had she conquered the engineers of the King's new commission than the local constable materialized on her Worcestershire estate of Poden, 'with four – more, with five – iron prongs', and ordered the impounding of her flock. The Dowager's shepherd attempted to intervene but was 'violently set upon', while thirty-two ewes were taken hostage and held to ransom. Elizabeth was told she would have to pay thirty shillings for the repair of nearby Upton Bridge or lose her livestock. The enterprise was a pretext devised by her 'open enemies in law', Sir Samuel Sandys and Francis Dingley, two powerful Worcestershire landowners. The pair had recently been made Justices of the Peace, an office which conveniently allowed them to get even with the widow, who had taken them to court two years previously for unpaid tithes incurred on her property holdings in the area.

Elizabeth, though sixty-eight years old, would not allow herself to be 'contemptuously trodden on and overbraved by my malicious inferiors and adversaries', finding a legal loophole that enabled her to wriggle out of the Justices' grasp. She was, however, doing more than merely looking to her own financial interests. Her rights were bound up with the freedoms of all other women who wanted to remain independent of men; freedoms that would be jeopardized by such a precedent. 'My lord, my honour [is] dearer to me than my life,' she declared resolutely to Cecil, and if such men are permitted to get away scot-free, then 'by my example, few will be widows so long as I'. Elizabeth's insistence that marriage was a second-best scenario, one to be entered into only when forced by the need to fend off the exploitation of other men, says much about her love of those liberties afforded by her widowed status. It was just like her, though so close to her final days – largely bed-bound, suffering from perennial back problems, crippled by migraines and pains in her eyes that were sometimes so bad she could barely see – to use this as an occasion to take a stand for the rights of women as independent property-owners.

It was perhaps during these final years that Elizabeth may have commissioned from the prodigious miniaturist Nicholas Hilliard an unusual portrait of herself in a bed of estate, wearing her accustomed 'Paris hood' and draped in the ermine cloak of a high-ranking noblewoman. Above her is a Latin quote – *Virtutis Amore* – intended to be every bit as incendiary as that on her earlier Bisham portrait, whose import it resembles. Lifted from one of her favourite texts, Horace's *Epistles*, the phrase, meaning 'for the love of virtue', became something of a rallying call for Puritans, appearing in a number of works either printed or authored by men in Elizabeth's coterie; two of these issued by her next-door neighbour Richard Field. Epistle 16, from which the phrase derives, celebrates Horace's 'Sabine Farm', with its 'hills, quite unbroken', its 'shady valley' and 'rich crop of ruddy cornels and plums'. The relevant section that provides the context for the quote is translated in one version as:

Good men stand in fear to commit offences, through that love which by divine grace they bear to virtue: wicked men are loath to do wickedly because they stand in fear of that punishment which is limited by the laws.

No statement could have been a sharper riposte to the 'wicked men' who had exploited the law to oppose her rights to her Dowager title and her castle of Donnington. The glittering miniature of Elizabeth in her 'widow's bed' is her final act of vengeance, dextrously uniting her two public personae as Horatian 'Lady of the Farm' and Puritan activist as a means of asserting her nobility.

No wonder she felt so strongly. The last years of her life were shot through with the bitterness of having to witness the gradual annihilation of Donnington, which was now no longer 'habitable', as she complained to Cecil in June 1608, 'for stink and ruins made to my wrong by the Lord Admiral's people'. The English Civil Wars would complete what Howard had begun, for all that remains of the once grand fortress now is the gatehouse; a mournful testament to the Dowager's war with the Lord High Admiral of England. From the advent of James I's reign, Elizabeth's rights were constantly threatened by the men whose worldly speculation and profiteering must have seemed to her to go so much against the grain of the values espoused in her husband's translation of *The Book of the Courtier*. Yet during these troubling years support came from an unexpected source. An old nemesis would jump to her defence in the most spectacularly public fashion: the man whose career Lady Russell had nearly destroyed in 1596, William Shakespeare.

26

All's Well That Ends Well

The Dowager Countess has a problem. Her wayward son is a 'rash and unbridled boy' who scorns her strenuous endeavours to find him a suitable wife. Worse still, since his father's death, he keeps bad company and thinks nothing of gadding about with a 'very tainted fellow, and full of wickedness'. Now he has run away to the wars, and plans to indulge in a dissolute life until he is ready to choose his *own* wife. That is the final straw. 'He was my son,' she exclaims in exasperation. 'But I do wash his name out of my blood.' Of course, these words are spoken in anger. She has no intention of abandoning her son. She decides instead to hatch a plot to bring him into blessed matrimony with the woman of *her* choice.

This may sound like a summary of Elizabeth Russell's labours with her son Sir Thomas Posthumous Hoby, but the Dowager Countess in this instance is really a boy actor dressed as a woman, performing in Shakespeare's *All's Well That Ends Well*. Is this similarity coincidental, or did the playwright intend his Dowager Countess of Roussillon to represent Robert Cecil's aunt? Around 1605 Elizabeth began to style herself publicly using her Latin name *Elizabetha Russella*. This coincides precisely with the play's potential earliest dating of around 1604–5 though some critics have recently placed it closer to 1606–7. In the edition of Shakespeare's *Henry IV, Part 1* known as the First Quarto, John Russell's name was originally rendered 'Rossill'. This may be due to the Russells' descent from the family of 'Rosel' or 'Rozel' who, hailing from Lower Normandy in France, proudly traced their pedigree back to the noble Bertrand family. The coat of arms of the Rosel/Rozel branch of the Bertrands boasted the lion rampant, which derived from the heraldic emblem of the Bertrand Barons of Briquebec. Is it possible that Shakespeare had imagined a connection between the 'Rossill' family and the region of south-western France that was the home of his Dowager Countess?

The only authoritative source for *All's Well* derives from the 1623 Folio edition of Shakespeare's collected plays. Here Roussillon appears as 'Rossillion'; probably the dramatist's own spelling, since the base text used for the First Folio printing of this play is likely to have been his own manuscript copy, or 'foul papers', as Shakespeare critics term it. Significantly, the Dowager Countess's son is called Bertram, a name closely related to the French 'Bertrand'. This is a change from Shakespeare's primary source, a story from Boccaccio's *Decameron*, which he probably knew from William Painter's English version of the tale in *The Palace of Pleasure*, in which the protagonist's name is Beltramo. More compelling still is the fact that the figure of the Countess of Roussillon does not appear in any of Shakespeare's sources. She is the playwright's own invention and, moreover, is the only female character in his entire oeuvre whose speech opens a play (other than the gender-ambiguous witches of *Macbeth*).

Would Shakespeare, who had got himself into hot water for his inclusion of 'Rossill' in his *Henry IV* plays, have risked mounting a play containing characters indelibly associated with the near-homonym of 'Rossillion', with a possible allusion to the Bertrand-derived family of the Russells, when Elizabeth Russell and the Earl of Bedford were still living? If this is what he did, then surely it follows that he must have been paying a compliment to the real individual behind the character of the Dowager Countess of Roussillon/Rossillion. Her age, coupled with the play's allusions to the dead Queen Elizabeth's 'withered' and fruitless 'old virginity' (which would no doubt have been pleasing to James I), indicate that the audience may have been expected to recognize the Dowager as having been a *grande dame* of the Elizabethan regime. By 1604–5 there were few noblewomen left who could fit this profile, making Elizabeth Russell a more likely candidate.

The Dowager Countess of Roussillon appears in the opening

scene, clad in the widow's funereal black. She is part of a mourning train which includes her son, Bertram, and her ward, the orphaned Helen. The first words that ring out through the auditorium are delivered by the Countess: 'In delivering my son from me, I bury a second husband.' The Dowager is referring to her son's leaving court to attend the King of France, whose ward he has become following his father's death. Yet the phrasing seems strained, somewhat tortuous. Might Shakespeare have wanted some members of the audience to be reminded of the twice-widowed Elizabeth Russell who was famed for burying two husbands and garnishing their memorials with her accomplished poetry? In his tremendously influential translation of the *Orlando Furioso*, published in 1591, a text which Shakespeare knew, John Harington took the occasion to praise the kind of woman who would write 'some verses in manner of an Epitaph upon her husband after his decease: in which kind, that honourable Lady (widow of the late Lord John Russell) deserveth no less commendation, having done as much for two husbands'. Around the time Shakespeare was writing *All's Well*, the real Dowager was again drawing attention to her prowess as a memorializer, engaging in at least two large public projects which greatly augmented her reputation.

In 1605 Elizabeth Russell did something incredibly unusual for a woman. She commandeered the publication of her own book, a translation of a eucharistic tract by John Ponet published in English as *A Way of Reconciliation*. This was the work her father had originally published in a Latin version in Strasbourg, and which was then issued in a French edition probably overseen by Elizabeth herself during her embassy to Paris in 1566. The purpose of the book, which had been, in her own words, a 'French creature', was to bring together feuding religious factions that had disagreed over the nature of the sacrament of Holy Communion, while insisting on the lawful nature of the Puritan position. Publication was considered an unseemly occupation for respectable women and on the occasion that they did go into print it was either anonymously or with the caveat that the text carried a formal apology insisting that the work had ended up on the booksellers' stalls at the insistence of a scholarly male friend or relative. Elizabeth was flying in the face of convention when she announced in the text's dedicatory epistle that she had taken command of the publication, issuing 'the copy of mine own hand' in print, 'fearing lest after my death it should be printed according to the humours of [an]other'. More shocking still, she made no attempt to hide her identity, proudly emblazoning in capital letters her own name in Latin: 'ELIZABETHA RUSSELLA, Dowager'. Her sisters had been far less radical in their publications.

Making a statement about her right to bear the title of Dowager Countess, Elizabeth dedicated her book as 'a New-year's gift' and 'last legacy' to Nan Russell. By drawing attention to the fact that her daughter was now wife to the 'heir apparent' of the 'most noble Earl of Worcester', and therefore herself a Countess in the making, she was doubling the impact of her family's gentrified status. Intriguingly, Roussillon had a special connection to the New Year theme in Shakespeare's day. While in England the New Year began on 25 March, the Feast of the Annunciation, until 1752, Charles IX's 'Edict of Roussillon' standardized 1 January as the start of the New Year throughout France in 1564, the very same year in which the French King and Elizabeth's father-in-law, Francis Russell, 2nd Earl of Bedford, were jointly inducted into the venerable Order of the Garter.

It may be straining the evidence to suggest that Shakespeare had incorporated these intricate connections into his play. Elizabeth's association with France, French politics and fashions, however, was as well known as her pride in her 'Russella' name. Her monumental programmes had often been based on French models, particularly the tombs of her first husband in Bisham and her daughter Bess. This proclivity is reflected in her commitment to the French edition of John Ponet's tract, which was infused with borrowings from the *Book of Bertram*, composed by the monk known as Bertram, or Ratramnus, who lived near Amiens in France. If the playwright was looking for an occasion to get the attention of the Dowager and her powerful nephew, Robert Cecil, then he could not have selected a better instrument than the publication of her book.

It was probably from around 1604–5 onwards that Elizabeth also engaged in the elaborate memorial programme to herself and her family in the Bisham parish church of All Saints. There Elizabeth's life-size effigy still stands, surrounded by stunning sculptures of her children. In her widow's garments, draped in the striking 'Paris hood' which again displays her abiding interest in the French style, she kneels before a lectern on which is balanced a book. Peering over her shoulder at the pages of this tome, one will see that it is inscribed with simple epitaphs in Latin and Greek, signed 'Elizabetha Russella, Douager'. Like her *Way of Reconciliation*, the monument ratifies her daughter's enviable position as wife to the future Earl of Worcester and her own standing as Dowager. Nan, as in the Hilliard miniature Elizabeth may have commissioned of herself in her final years, wears the sumptuous ermine cloak of a high-status woman. Her mother, meanwhile, in a brazen challenge to the College of Arms' decrees, boasts a fabulous Countess's crown.

What could have been more flattering to Elizabeth than to be publicly presented in her onstage doppelgänger as a fully fledged Dowager Countess? But why would Shakespeare want to pay such elaborate compliments to the woman who had nearly destroyed his career? Could this have had something to do with the theme of her book? Elizabeth maintained that her purpose in publishing the translation was, as she stated in the printed work itself, to 'study to make enemies friends'. In doing so she may have been prompted by an event at which Shakespeare himself was present. In August 1604 a committee of Spanish delegates, led by the constable of Castile, came to England to confer with James I and his Privy Council with a view to ending the perennial wars between the two nations. They were entertained at Somerset House, where the conference took place. By this time Shakespeare's company had become the King's Men, the playwright and his fellow co-sharers in the theatrical troupe having been elevated to Grooms of the Chamber from May 1603. During the Spanish delegates' eighteen-day sojourn the dramatist would have stood watching from the wings, wearing the scarlet cloak and doublet of the King's livery.

At these proceedings was Robert Cecil and at least three men who had been involved in Elizabeth's Donnington disputes: the Lord Admiral, Charles Howard; Thomas Sackville, 1st Earl of Dorset; and Henry Howard, the Earl of Northampton, who had been physically assaulted by the Dowager in the Star Chamber. This event may have given Elizabeth the impetus to publish a work which opposed Catholic eucharistic doctrine and sought to strengthen the Protestant faith by reconciling differing theological positions *within* the reformed Church. The fact that she sent the publication to Cecil as a gift only a few months later may indicate that she wished to deliver a warning about the dangers of opening the nation's door too readily to the old religion. It was probably the very same book she had sent to the Catholic Mary Talbot, Countess of Shrewsbury. 'Be not, good madam, like the deaf adder, that stoppeth her ears and refuseth the voice of the charmer,' she censured her gently, 'charm he never so wisely.' England was sailing close to the rocks and Elizabeth, as always, hoped to navigate the ship of state to her liking through her writings.

The Somerset House Conference brought Shakespeare closer than ever before to Elizabeth's coterie, and to those most intimately connected to her Donnington suit. Surely these men, working together at the precise period when Elizabeth's war with the Lord Admiral was ongoing – a conflict which had been intertwined with her right to bear the title of Dowager Countess – could not have failed to indulge in gossip about this challenging woman's latest exploits. Shakespeare would also have known that by far the most powerful man around the conference table was Cecil, who, since the Earl of Essex's demise, had risen to even greater prominence under James. Around the time of the conference, on 20 August, he was made Viscount Cranborne, prompting congratulatory commendations from Elizabeth. He would also address his first letter as newly created Earl of Salisbury to her, as his emotional aunt observed, 'from your own hand', after being granted the honour on 4 May 1605.

It must have been with some apprehension that Shakespeare came face to face with Cecil at this time. The dramatist had previously satirized Essex's enemies, including the Cobham family into which Cecil had married, and had intended to give the world a drunken buffoon who was his late uncle's namesake, John Russell. His *Richard III* had provided Cecil's detractors with a treasure-house of unflattering imagery they could use against him and his *Richard II* was commissioned by Essex's followers on the eve of their aborted coup. What better way to placate the King's new chief councillor than by turning his pen to a pleasing portrait of his aunt? Alluding to her identity as Dowager Countess *Elizabetha Russella* through the close-sounding Dowager Countess of Roussillon would therefore have allowed him to hold her to the very theme which underpinned her book, that of 'reconciliation', in the hope that all would indeed end well. Is there more evidence for these potential associations in Shakespeare's play?

The Dowager Countess of Roussillon's first few verbal exchanges in the opening scene are in prose, while the bustle and business of establishing the play's context commences. After the first sixty lines her speech suddenly changes into more stately verse, as she offers her son some solemn advice which reveals that this learned woman is proficient in a particular kind of text:

> Be thou blessed, Bertram, and succeed thy father
> In manners as in shape. Thy blood and virtue
> Contend for empire in thee, and thy goodness
> Share with thy birthright. Love all, trust a few,
> Do wrong to none. Be able for thine enemy
> Rather in power than use; and keep thy friend
> Under thy own life's key. Be checked for silence,
> But never taxed for speech . . . [*To Lafeu*] Farewell, my lord.
> 'Tis an unseasoned courtier. Good my lord,
> Advise him.

Unusually for a woman, Shakespeare's Dowager is presented as an oracle on the arts of courtiership, skills she insists her own son can attain by following the example of his father. The learned members of the audience would have instantly recognized the source for this kind of advice: *The Book of the Courtier*, translated by Elizabeth's first husband, Thomas Hoby, father of Thomas Posthumous. This was a work Shakespeare is known to have used in other plays. The words of wisdom offered match closely in tone to the counsel imparted to the would-be courtier in the famous manual. On the subject of friendship, for example, Hoby writes, 'I would have our Courtier therefore to find him out an especial and hearty friend . . . [and] to have an eye to his friend's profit and estimation.'

If the Dowager Countess of Roussillon represents a real woman, then we might expect her to have a reputation for dispensing advice on courtiership, even for having some kind of connection to Hoby's *Book of the Courtier*. Elizabeth Russell described herself, somewhat unconventionally, as 'a courtier and parliament woman' and her letters are full of sage suggestions on how to become a 'cunning courtier', delivered in a manner that suggests her pride in her first husband's achievements. In 1596 Thomas Lodge, whose works had provided sources for Shakespeare, dedicated to Elizabeth his fictional work *A Margarite of America*, in which he drew attention to her expertise in courtiership as Hoby's wife. His acquaintance with her, he suggested, had been a valuable source for his own education in these arts, 'shutting up my English duty under an Italian copy of humanity and courtesy', a reference to Castiglione's *Il Cortegiano*. The courtly associations surrounding 'our English Sappho', claimed Lodge, were so well known that 'whilst the memory thereof shall live in any age, your charity, learning, nobility, and virtues shall be eternized'.

As Shakespeare's *All's Well* progresses, the Dowager Countess's connection to *The Courtier* is strengthened through her witty repartee with her Clown, who enjoys mocking those who misunderstand the courtier's calling. 'Truly, madam, if God have lent a man any manners, he may easily put it off at court,' he jests. 'He that cannot make a leg, put off's cap, kiss his hand, and say nothing, has neither leg, hands, lip, nor cap; and indeed such a fellow, to say precisely, were not for the court . . . Ask me if I am a courtier; it shall do you no harm to learn.' The Clown is quoting, almost verbatim, from Hoby's translation of Castiglione's text, which censured the misguided courtier in just this way by condemning those who 'would fain counterfeit their fashion, and can do naught else but shake the head in speaking, and make a leg with an ill grace'. The nobleman who thinks that bowing, scraping, affected speech and fine clothing make him an ideal courtier has failed to realize that the values to which he should be aspiring are less material: learnedness, honour, moral probity and ability to serve King and country. Prompted by the Dowager Countess's question – 'I pray you, sir, are you a courtier?' – the Clown goes on to give her a practical demonstration of the fashionable and foppish speech used by the foolish hangers-on of the court. The implication is that the Dowager knows full well the difference between the true courtier and the counterfeit, establishing her credentials as an astute reader of Hoby's *Book of the Courtier*, the publication of which Elizabeth Russell may have helped oversee.

So Shakespeare's Dowager Countess of Roussillon is a loquacious widow, appears on stage clad in black mourning garments, is closely associated with France and is well versed in Hoby's famous manual, but is she also a Puritan? The sharp-witted banter between her and the Clown provides subtle hints that she may be. When the Clown sings a misogynistic song that ends with the refrain that of all women there is 'yet one good in ten', the Dowager berates him for corrupting the ditty. He counters by suggesting that she should be pleased with those odds, for it is an improvement on the reality. Imagining himself as a 'parson', he quips that 'One good *woman* in ten, madam . . . is but a purifying o' th' song.' The Countess, annoyed by his mock-Puritan antics, calls him a 'knave' and commands him to leave. The Clown's response is interesting:

That man should be at woman's command, and yet no hurt done!
Though honesty be no puritan, yet it will do no hurt: it will wear the
surplice of humility over the black gown of a big heart.

The intensifying of Puritan imagery, which seems designed to
goad the Dowager Countess, culminates in this reference to a specific historical event: the Vestments Controversy. This was the war
between the non-conformists and the Church of England over the
wearing of the surplice prescribed by official statute. The Clown's
joke is that some of the Puritans hypocritically conformed only out-
wardly, while wearing the non-conformists' black Geneva gown
beneath the required dress. But why should Shakespeare remember
a controversy which raged in the 1560s? This could hardly have had
much comedy value some forty or more years after the scandal had
first emerged. Could Shakespeare have referred to it because it had
sparked the rise of Puritanism as a more cohesive movement among
Elizabeth Russell and her allies? Her *Way of Reconciliation* was probably originally composed just after the first wave of Puritan agitation
over vestments that sparked the Admonition Controversy. These
references come hot on the heels of the Clown's clever treatment of
religious difference:

> If men could be contented to be what they are, there were no fear in
> marriage; for your Chairbonne the puritan and old Poisson the pap-
> ist, howsome'er their hearts are severed in religion, their heads are
> both one: they may jowl horns together like any deer i' th' herd.

The joke is that when it comes to women's infidelities, all men
are equal, and all men, whether Puritan or Catholic, equally capable
of being cuckolded, the male's growing of horns being the traditional emblem of the husband whose wife had engaged in an
adulterous affair. Added to the Clown's other mocking treatments
of non-conformism in particular, this may have been intended as a
gentle quip at the expense of the Dowager Countess of Roussillon,

suggesting that there was no essential difference between Catholics and Puritans. The audience would have recognized that Clowns had special licence to address their noble employers in a manner which cut close to the bone. Their exchanges would have acquired a special charge, therefore, if the actor playing the Dowager Countess had done so in a manner that indicated a Puritan disposition.

The likelihood that Shakespeare's Countess, if she does represent a real woman, is connected to the Cecil coterie is increased by the play's interest in the wardship system. Bertram's very first words, after his mother's opening statement, refer to his new status as ward to the Crown: 'I must attend His Majesty's command, to whom I am now in ward, evermore in subjection.' Lafeu rushes to correct him: 'You shall find of the King a husband, madam; you, sir, a father. He that so generally is at all times good must of necessity hold his virtue to you, whose worthiness would stir it up where it wanted rather than lack it where there is such abundance.' This would have been flattering to both the King and Robert Cecil. The latter had been granted the post of Master of the Wards in 1599, an office under the cloud of endless corruption charges. Shakespeare may also have been well aware that Elizabeth Russell's own kinsmen had been severely criticized in the press for their historical control of the Court of Wards.

In 1592 the Jesuit Robert Parsons published a vicious treatise, *An Advertisement written to a Secretary of my [L]ord Treasurer's of England*, attacking the 'instruments of all misery to England'. The very fountainhead of this corruption, claimed Parsons, was Elizabeth Russell's father, Sir Anthony Cooke, who had engineered the rise of both Nicholas Bacon and William Cecil. It was through his intercession that Bacon had gained the post of Attorney of the Court of Wards and then Lord Keeper of the Privy Seal, posts in which he had 'showed himself so corrupt, and partial for bribery'. In 1561 the Mastership of the Court of Wards was given to William Cecil, who was no less the focus of Parsons' vituperative venom, described as possessing the 'spirit of Beelzebub', as an 'egregious bloodsucker', and a 'monster' who relished the 'tortures, and other violences' meted out to his Catholic enemies. During 1604 Parsons renewed his public attacks on Anthony Cooke and his sons-in-law. Shakespeare's treatment of the wardship system in the play would have served as a robust defence of Cecil and, implicitly, the male kinsmen of Elizabeth Russell who had been involved professionally with the Court of Wards.

It is primarily through the Dowager Countess of Roussillon that this institution is presented as benevolent and free from all corruption. She is concerned for the happiness and welfare of Helen, who had been 'bequeathed to my overlooking' after the death of her father, the great surgeon Gérard de Narbonne, declaring, 'I have those hopes of her good that her education promises.' Countering the kinds of critique that were often levied at those who skimmed off profits from their wards' estates, she protests that 'There is more owing her than is paid, and more shall be paid her than she'll demand.' Through the Dowager the grand civic network which legally binds wards to their guardians becomes a familial one. When Helen responds to the Countess's assurances that 'I am a mother to you' with the more appropriate address, 'Mine honourable mistress', the elder woman replies with passion:

> Nay, a mother.
> Why not a mother? When I said 'a mother',
> Methought you saw a serpent. What's in 'mother'
> That you start at it? I say I am your mother,
> And put you in the catalogue of those
> That were enwombed mine . . .
> I say I am your mother.

This 'mother's care' is demonstrated in the Dowager's scheme to win the unruly Bertram as a husband for the girl in her charge. If Shakespeare was defending Cecil through Elizabeth Russell, then he had selected a woman who had been closely associated with the Court of Wards for most of her adult life. She had fought for the wardships of her children, even against the claims of her own husband, John Russell. She had also been keen to serve as a guardian to orphans whenever she could and saw their welfare as a matter of familial honour. In 1604, for example, she had written to Cecil, offering to take in his daughter Frances, whom Cecil had planned to send to the home of his late wife's twin sister, Frances Brooke Stourton, for her further education. 'I being loath that any of my father's blood should be infected with bad religion, whereof her aunt, my Lady Stourton, hath been suspected,' she wrote, knowing the proposed guardian's Catholicism, 'if it please your lordship to have her with me, I will use her as I would mine own.' In the same letter she showed her concern for Hercules Francis Cooke, son to her nephew Sir Anthony Cooke. The latter had been 'killed by butchery for surgeon's practice' after seeking medical treatment in Cambridge for a persistent ailment. Cecil's willingness to take the boy into his service was, his aunt insisted, to the 'grace and comfort [of] your mother's father's house'.

At some point after 4 May 1605, the heroic Dowager had thrown herself into a dispute in defence of two wards of the Crown and their widowed mother, who was possibly Anne Steward, the daughter of the one-time royal physician and president of the College of Physicians, Robert Huicke. Addressing a letter pointedly to the 'Fairest flower of my garland . . . Master of the King's Majesty's most honourable Court of Wards', she begged Cecil to help her 'overthrow as wicked a cozenage as ever was offered by an executor to a brother'. The executor of the will was another physician, a Dr Steward, brother to the deceased Mark Steward, who was 'devilishly' hoarding the estate and its revenues for himself, turning the widow and her children into 'renegades, not having a place to hide their head in', a turn of events which she protested would 'make the gentlewoman stark mad'. Elizabeth demanded that the dispossessed family have use of their own property in which 'they may dwell all their life' and asked for a suitable jointure of £200 to be provided for the widow, in addition to a 'yearly portion of £40 to discharge her meat and clothes out of Steward's living'.

Elizabeth refused to sit back and allow the poor woman to become 'a slave in subjection' to her wicked brother-in-law. Could Shakespeare's play, which focuses on the Dowager Countess's machinations on behalf of Helen, a physician's daughter, carry echoes of Elizabeth Russell's own interventions with this real medical family from 1605, or at least gesture towards her well-known association with the wardship system?

The same impulse that animated Elizabeth's desire to help unfortunate wards underpinned her other favoured pastime. Like Shakespeare's Dowager Countess, Lady Russell was very fond of arranging marriages. As well as procuring suitable spouses for Thomas Posthumous Hoby and Nan Russell, she tried to secure a match for her legal opponent Anne Lovelace, with disastrous results. She also engaged in numerous negotiations for the marriage of her daughter Bess. While rebuffing the unwanted attentions of the Earl of Hertford (who, Elizabeth complained, 'hovereth so about her, and shall go without her'), she hatched a plan to wed her to either Sir Thomas Egerton or his son; she was not being choosy. In her letter to Egerton she had stepped into her accustomed role as expert on the ways of the courtier, gently chiding him for his pretended melancholy and stand-offishness by calling him 'an arrant hypocrite and a deep dissembler, fit to be a courtier and a Councillor'. She knew full well he could be 'merry, when occasion requireth', but no matter, 'my daughter shall take your lordship with all your faults'.

Elizabeth's most telling matrimonial intervention was in the troubles of Peregrine Bertie, Lord Willoughby, and his wife, Mary de Vere, in 1597. Mary was sister of Edward de Vere, the Earl of Oxford, himself husband to Elizabeth's niece, Anne Cecil. Rumours had reached Bertie's ear that Mary had been having an affair and that she had spoken unkindly of him to the Queen. Elizabeth immediately sprang to the defence of the unfairly slandered woman she referred to as 'my daughter'. There had indeed been 'divers reports told of your lordship's usage hard of her', declared Elizabeth to Bertie, but these did not proceed from Mary's lips, who was 'without stain or touch of dishonour'. She urged him to take her back, 'to the credit and good of you both and to the daunting of your scant friends or enemies to you both'. News of the rocky marriage had preoccupied the Queen, who had talked with Mary 'privately' about it. The scandal had been sufficiently well known, for Elizabeth hinted that she had her own spies in court, perhaps her daughters, who had related to her matters of which 'Her Majesty spoke . . . in secret'. Could the name Bertie have been associated with that of Bertram? Could Shakespeare have been thinking of Elizabeth's involvement in this piece of courtly sexual intrigue when writing *All's Well*? This must remain pure speculation, yet perhaps we have, in the Dowager Countess of Roussillon, a reflection of Elizabeth Russell's intense maternal instincts, which prompted her to attempt to arrange, or to rescue, the marriages of others, and saw her intervening directly in the work of the Court of Wards in her role as champion of orphaned children and widows.

Shakespeare's Countess is every bit the widow, poet, memorializer, mother-figure and authority on courtiership Elizabeth Russell was. Yet, if the playwright was trying to flatter her and her nephew Robert Cecil into releasing the Blackfriars Theatre from the Privy Council's legal stranglehold, she may not have been particularly impressed with her theatrical avatar. Shakespeare would not get the indoor playhouse back until around 1608 and would not mount plays there until the following year; the very year in which Elizabeth, vacating the Blackfriars for good, drew her final breath in Bisham Abbey.

Will the Dowager Countess Elizabetha Russella breathe again through future stagings of Shakespeare's Dowager Countess of Roussillon? This would be poetic justice, some recompense for the popular reputation Elizabeth Russell has since undeservedly acquired as a murderess.

By June 1608 Elizabeth Russell had begun the slow decline which would lead to her death. Though too ill to leave her bed in the Blackfriars, she was desperate to attend service at St Anne's Church and hear a sermon for what she may have believed would be the last time. 'Now, my lord, if in your honour you will help to bring a widow to church to serve God and to pray for you,' she wrote to Robert Cecil, 'your lordship seeth the way; if not, I must patiently expect God's good leisure.'

One of the unforeseen consequences of her war with the Lord Admiral, Charles Howard, was to leave her exposed during a plague outbreak which had resulted, in her own words, in the 'death of seven already, even to my doors, since the last Sabbath', a calamity which was like 'nothing heard of before'. She could not retreat to Donnington, now that it had been left unfit for human habitation by the Lord Admiral, nor could she go to Bisham, for James I was expected there any day now, to be entertained by Sir Edward Hoby during his summer Progress. 'Behold how it pleaseath God continually to exercise me in his school of discipline,' she complained to her nephew, knowing she was no longer favoured at court. 'I have no other house to put my head in.' Despite the danger she was in, she ended with a most remarkable turn of wit, reminding Cecil of their shared joke: 'Only I promise, if your lordship bring me to church, I will not challenge any contract from you for a husband.'

Elizabeth had managed to secure a lodging in Windsor by the end of July, hoping to ride out the plague there. Retiring to her bed again, she kept herself alive by sucking lemons and sipping water, on her doctor's advice. In her last surviving letter she tells her nephew 'in truth, I am weak here in the forepart of my head, unfeignedly, with shooting pain, and swimming brain maketh me, on my faith, to fear a sudden death . . . I sleep little, eat less, nor drank a draught of ale, beer, or wine since my coming to Windsor.'

There were, it seems, some reserves of energy left in the old Dowager. That month James I and Anne of Denmark embarked on their royal Progress. Cecil was part of the train, following until Windsor, where he stopped off to visit his sick aunt with the intention, as she reflected gratefully, 'to comfort my daunted spirits'. Upon his arrival, she jumped out of bed and attended him for the duration of his visit, almost miraculously standing the whole time. Cecil, witnessing her sudden verve, told her that she could not have been as ill as she had claimed. She had, he taunted gently, been complaining 'without cause of pity'. It must have been difficult for Cecil to watch the woman whose battles he had followed his whole life, and for whose causes he had often found himself conscripted into her private army, losing her vitality as she approached her final hour. Perhaps he knew a comment like this would draw a spirited defence, allowing him to see again, just for a wondrous brief moment, that feisty, infuriating, endearing, challenging and argumentative woman he knew and loved. 'I would not willingly deserve to be thought a dissembler or hypocrite,' she declared in answer, having assured him that her exertion had 'made me faint and sweat, truly.' How Cecil must have laughed when he received the gift which came with Elizabeth Russell's last tender missive: 'I am bold to send your pale, thin cheeks a comfortable little breakfast against the contagion of this time.'

On 23 April 1609, at the age of sixty-nine, Elizabeth Russell signed a document in the Blackfriars. It was her last will and testament. Well, not quite her 'last', for not even the approach of death could diminish the unworldly force of the Dowager's character. Combative to the very end, days or possibly even hours before her death she amended her will. On 25 May she took up the pen herself and, with a frail and trembling hand, on her deathbed in Bisham Abbey, struck out the names of a number of individuals against whom she had conceived some kind of offence. These included one of the original witnesses to the will made in the Blackfriars: Sir Henry Yelverton, brother-in-law of William Gardiner junior. The latter was son to the Surrey Justice of the Peace William Gardiner, who had persecuted Shakespeare in 1596 and vigorously worked to drive the theatres into the ground. 'I have put out with my own hand, Henry Yelverton,' wrote Elizabeth in a final addition to the revised will.

One name which was not removed from her initial list of beneficiaries was that of the divine who galvanized the community's female radicals – Elizabeth's fearless sister-soldiers of Christ – in the Church of St Anne's. 'I will and bequeath,' declared the unchanged terms of her original will, 'unto Mr. Stephen Egerton, late preacher at the Blackfriars, London, ten pounds yearly during his life.' Her affection for the man who helped her keep Shakespeare out of the Blackfriars Theatre, and who had worked with Richard Field in a formal capacity in his parish church, held firm until her final breath. It seems fitting that the day Elizabeth confirmed this bond by signing her original will was, as it is commonly believed, Shakespeare's birthday.

Elizabeth died at Bisham, where her body lay in state for a full day before being prepared for the burial, which took place on 2 June 1609. She predeceased the last remaining Cooke sister, Anne Bacon, by a year. The Dowager's monument stands in the parish Church of All Saints, and seems most alive when the light from the stained-glass window, commissioned in her honour, throws its dancing colours over her effigy, which, according to her wishes, wears still the eternal crown of a Countess.

Epilogue

Afterlife of a Murderess

Bisham Abbey has been accorded the dubious honour of being labelled one of the most haunted houses in England. Its troublesome ethereal resident is none other than its former owner, Lady Elizabeth Russell. Her spectral agent has come to be known by various names, the 'Grey Lady', the 'Lady in the Abbey', the 'Wicked Lady Hoby'; for the woman who became famed throughout Europe during her lifetime as an influential memorializer has herself acquired a lasting memory as a murderess.

The rumours surrounding Bisham's ghost have been passed down through the generations. Elizabeth Russell, the story goes, was a hard task-master when it came to educating her children, as befitting the daughter of Sir Anthony Cooke, tutor to Edward VI. She was particularly tough with a son called William, whom it is said she bore during her marriage to Sir Thomas Hoby. William was less adept at learning than his siblings and always blotted his copybooks. Unfortunately for him, his mother could not tolerate sloppiness of any kind. Giving vent to her fury, she took up a heavy wooden ruler and beat him till his lifeless body was bathed in his own blood. There had, apparently, been witnesses, for the Hoby children's lessons were conducted in a 'bower', constructed on the abbey grounds, close to the river. Directly opposite was a towpath from where passing villagers could easily see the calamitous events unfolding. One horrified neighbour later recounted that he had seen the terrible punishment meted out to 'my lady's boy', who had collapsed on to the ground, his blood saturating the grass bank.

Another variation of the gruesome tale makes Queen Elizabeth an unwitting accessory to the murder. The children that inclement day were taking their lessons in the abbey's tower room. As usual, William made a mess of his copybooks and was given his customary beating. Not content with this, his mother tied the boy to his desk, demanding that he continue to work on his grammatical exercises. To calm her nerves she went out riding, where she was accosted by her sovereign, who convinced her to join her in Windsor. There Elizabeth remained for three days. She returned to find her neglected son dead, still tied to his desk, his blotted copybooks before him.

On this matter the parish registers of Bisham are stubbornly silent: there is no evidence of a William Hoby ever having been born. No surviving record confirms that such a child lived out his meagre years in Elizabeth's custody. Suspicious deaths could be brushed under the carpet, of course, officials bribed, records destroyed, witnesses silenced. As a woman of prominence, Elizabeth could not risk such a blemish to her reputation. This 'cover-up' conspiracy acquired some credence after an enigmatic discovery made, supposedly, in 1840. While carrying out essential repairs at Bisham Abbey, workmen found a secret compartment hidden beneath one of the windows of the dining room. The brick dust and rubble gradually settling, a stash of papers which had been carefully concealed inside became visible. These turned out to be copybooks used in children's lessons. The documents were examined by Mrs Vansittart, the then owner of Bisham, who reported that 'In one of William Hoby, I think, every leaf had some blot,' the book containing corrections in Elizabeth Russell's distinctive hand. Frustratingly, despite Mrs Vansittart's credibility as a witness, the story cannot be materially corroborated. The papers are no longer extant, having disappeared shortly after their discovery, thought to have been sold by the workmen, hoping to cash in on the antiquated manuscripts.

Little proof survives to corroborate the unfounded allegation that Elizabeth Russell was guilty of infanticide. Mrs Vansittart was herself not entirely certain she had seen the name William Hoby on the copybooks. The peculiar coincidence of Elizabeth's having insisted on representing the effigy of her infant son, Francis Russell, on both the Westminster Abbey and Bisham family monuments may have given rise to speculation, particularly among the residents of Bisham and its immediate environs, that one of these stone portraits represented a long-lost son who had suffered an untimely death in mysterious circumstances. It is also possible that Elizabeth's tempestuous relationship with Thomas Posthumous Hoby may have fanned the flames of these speculations. During his early years in particular, Thomas Posthumous was the focus of his mother's endless displeasure, and the notoriously diminutive size of his sickly body may have been attributed to the effects of severe physical punishment by those who heard about, or helped to generate, these tales.

The legends surrounding Elizabeth Russell appear primarily to have taken root from around the time when Mrs Vansittart reported the existence of the blotted copybooks, and were perhaps further stimulated by the Dowager's growing reputation among scholars and antiquaries as a woman of formidable intellect and firm self-discipline. Her penchant for tomb design and elegiac poetry may also have inspired the popular imagination, accustomed as it was to the fashion for all things Gothic which had emerged in the late eighteenth and early nineteenth centuries. The Vansittart family were the catalyst for the numerous ghost stories which developed around Bisham Abbey from this time. One of the earliest sightings was recounted by Admiral Edward W. Vansittart, son to Vice-Admiral Henry Vansittart. Edward had been playing chess with his brother one evening in the room in which Lady Russell's portrait hung. 'We had finished playing,' he recalled, 'and my brother had gone up to bed. I stood for some time with my back to the wall, turning over the day in my mind. Minutes passed. I suddenly realised the presence of someone standing behind me. I looked round. It was Dame Hoby [Elizabeth Russell]. The frame on the wall was empty. Terrified, I fled the room.'

In the succeeding decades further disturbing encounters were recorded. During the First World War Captain Alastair Mackintosh, as he later reported in his memoirs, hosted a party at Bisham Abbey at which Adelina Drysdale, fiancée to the Cambridge-educated

Prince Mario Colonna, brother to the Governor of Rome, was in attendance. Not long after Adelina had retired to bed, her toilet set was propelled from her dressing table and exploded in a shower of glass and cosmetics. Her diamond wristwatch, a love token from the Prince, was also flung from the bedside table and smashed against the opposite wall. Before she could scream the heavy curtains of her four-poster bed were ripped away, and in the flurry of fabric and shadow she was confronted with the apparition of a woman dressed entirely in white. Later on she identified her phantom intruder from the imposing portrait of Lady Elizabeth Russell. Adelina survived her ordeal and went on to marry her Prince in 1917. Their union, however, would end tragically. On Sunday 10 July 1938 Mario Colonna died when his plane crashed close to the river Tiber in Rome.

The thousands of tourists who visit the picturesque village of Marlow each year are regaled with tales of the horrifying events which lie behind the strange manifestations at Bisham. They hear of the eerie green lights seen flickering in the vacant tower room of the abbey, and of the peculiar blue mist that wreathes its way across the Thames towards the south-west of the village on midsummer nights, when the apparition of a hooded woman in a small rowing boat appears on Marlow's banks. They are told about the haunted portrait of Lady Russell which still keeps its tireless vigil over the abbey's grand hall, and whose subject still walks the ancient mansion, materializing – one might say in the manner of Lady Macbeth – sometimes before a flowing rivulet, at other times before a silver basin of water, in which she repetitively washes her hands as if trying to scrub away the remnants of some terrible crime. There is a strange footnote to these tales: both Elizabeth Russell and Shakespeare's Lady Macbeth employed a servant named 'Se[y]ton'.

The veracity of these legends is less significant than the fact that Elizabeth Russell's formidable personality and unrelenting wilfulness have burned through the centuries, searing themselves on to the collective consciousness not only of succeeding generations of

Bisham's residents but on the wider world. The myth of the abbey's 'wicked' resident, the character fashioned through the many ghost stories and murder mysteries which have added to Elizabeth's growing notoriety, has eclipsed her true importance as a political activist, religious radical, influential patron, gifted poet and linguist, and pioneer of women's rights. Most of all, it has obscured her pivotal role in shaping the legacy of William Shakespeare.

In the battle between Elizabeth Russell and the backers of the Blackfriars Theatre, the playwright won the greater war. Shakespeare's words would resound again in the reclaimed indoor playhouse from 1609, the year of the Dowager's death. In the August of the previous year he had entered into a syndicate as part-owner-sharer of the theatre, in a consortium that included the Burbage brothers, Richard and Cuthbert, and the two men who would go on to memorialize him by commandeering the publication of the 1623 First Folio of his collected plays: John Heminges and Henry Condell. In possession of both the Globe and the Blackfriars theatres the King's Men could mount plays all year round, significantly increasing Shakespeare's fortunes. The reacquisition of the Blackfriars Theatre also sparked a new phase in the dramatist's career, resulting in the works now known as the Romances: *Pericles, The Winter's Tale, Cymbeline, The Tempest* and *The Two Noble Kinsmen.* Filled with magic, seafaring adventure, intricate staging tricks and mesmerizing illusions, perhaps inspired by the capabilities of the better-appointed indoor playhouse, these plays pushed the boundaries of the dramatic arts. Yet, had Elizabeth Russell not forced Shakespeare out of the Blackfriars Theatre, his style may have evolved in this direction much earlier, and perhaps we would not now have the great tragedies – *Hamlet, Othello, King Lear* and *Macbeth* – which were produced in the first six years after the opening of the Globe. That would have been an incalculable loss indeed.

While Shakespeare's company had never originally intended to create the amphitheatre-style open-air Globe Theatre, it proved to be a huge success; so much so in fact that after it burned down in 1613, when the thatched roof caught fire during a performance of

Shakespeare's *All is True (Henry VIII)*, it was almost immediately rebuilt. The Second Globe Theatre opened for business the following year and was fitted out with an innovation its predecessor lacked: a tiled roof. It seems that the King's Men, whose members could not bear to part with the Globe, were keen to ensure that the playhouse would have a long life. Shakespeare may have sold his own share in the Globe as he approached retirement, yet today he remains associated with the iconic theatre, which would never have come into being had it not been for Elizabeth Russell's audacious campaign in 1596. We might therefore say that we owe a great deal to the Dowager Countess.

One would like to think that, after more than four centuries, Elizabeth Russell can now be recognized for her real achievements, that the apparition of the 'wicked' murderess can at last be dispelled, allowing her to step out from behind the curtain of history which has all too often obscured women's roles as the co-creators of England's rich and wonderful heritage; a heritage now enjoyed across the entire globe.

Notes

Prologue: A Blackfriars Mystery

For the site of Shakespeare's Blackfriars Theatre in London today, see Bowsher, *Shakespeare's London Theatreland* (2012), pp. 203–9. The location of Elizabeth Russell's home has been determined from my own research, presented in the chapters that follow.

Elizabeth Russell's petition is NA, SP 12/260, f. 176r, November 1596. The names on the petition, in the order in which they are presented to the Privy Council, are:

Elizabeth Russell, Dowager

G[eorge] Hunsdon	John Robbinson [Robinson]
Henry Bowes	Thomas Homes [Holmes]
Thomas Browne	Ric[hard] Field
John Crooke	Will[iam] Watts
Will[iam] Meredith	Henry Boice
Stephen Egerton	Edward Ley
Richard Lee	John Clarke
[ ] Smith	Will[iam] Bispham
William Paddy	Robert Baheire
William de Laun[n]e [de Lawne]	Ezechiell [Ezekiel] Major
Francis Hinson	Harman Buckholt
John Edwards [Edwardes]	John Le Mere
Andrew Lyons	John Dollin
Thomas Nayle	Ascanio de Renialmire [Ascanius de Renialme]
Owen Lochard [Lockhard]	John Wharton

(Names in square brackets represent the forms mainly used in this book.)

The counter-petition of William Shakespeare and the players is NA, SP 12/260, f. 178r. It was originally classed under 'Bundle, No. 222, Elizabeth, 1596'. The results of the investigations into the counter-petition's authenticity are recorded in NA, SP 12/260, f. 177r, 30 January 1860 and 2 February 1860.

Collier's claim to have discovered the Shakespeare petition is made in Collier, *History of English Dramatic Poetry* (1831), vol. 1, pp. 297–300. N.E.S.A. Hamilton's attack on Collier

began in *The Times*, in two articles on 2 and 16 July 1859, and was followed by a longer treatise, Hamilton, *An Inquiry* (1860). The journalists' activities against Collier and Hamilton's
scandalized response are quoted from a review of Hamilton's *An Inquiry* in the *Athenaeum*,
no. 1686, 18 February 1860, pp. 229–33. Robert Lemon's assessment of the petition is NA,
SP 12/260, f. 177r, December 1860. Criticism of Lemon's handling of the *Calendar of State
Papers* is in *The Times*, 14 May 1859, p. 12. Collier's letter to the editor of the *Athenaeum* on
14 February 1860 and Ingleby's own critique are from Ingleby, *A Complete View* (1861), pp.
295–7. The investigation into Elizabeth Russell's petition is recorded in Ingleby, *A Complete
View* (1861), pp. 309 and 312–14. For the authenticity of Elizabeth Russell's petition, see
Gurr, *Playgoing in Shakespeare's London* (1996), pp. 23–6 and Dobson and Wells, eds., *Oxford
Companion to Shakespeare* (2001), p. 48. For more on the Collier forgeries, see Shapiro, *Contested Will* (2010), pp. 71–4 and Wells, *Shakespeare* (2002), pp. 312–13.

Shaw on the Dowager Countess of Roussillon is from *Shaw on Shakespeare*, ed. Wilson
(1961), p. 10. Elizabeth Russell's appearance is reconstructed from her portrait in Bisham
Abbey, Berkshire, and her effigy on the Hoby family monument in All Saints Church,
Bisham, Berkshire. The description of Shakespeare as the 'sweet swan of Avon' comes
from Ben Jonson's memorial verse to him in the First Folio of Shakespeare's plays; see
Shakespeare, *Mr William Shakespeare's Comedies, Histories, and Tragedies*, eds. Heminges and
Condell (1623), sig. A4v.

Chapter One: A Radical Beginning

The Hoddesdon riot is described in the official Star Chamber record NA, STAC 2/15, f. 95r,
with the fines against Robert Mitchell and his accomplices tabulated in NA, STAC 2/15,
f. 96r. A second version of the events exists in NA, SP 2/Q/no. 12, f. 42r, 1534. The account
of the riot as presented here is based on the Star Chamber record, with interpolations from
the version in the State Papers. For Sir William Fitzwilliam, John Cooke and the early years
of Anthony Cooke, see McIntosh, 'Sir Anthony Cooke . . .' (1975); McIntosh, 'Some New
Gentry . . .' (1977); and Harvey, *The Cooke Sisters* (1981), pp. 27–8.

For Bourchier's protection of the Hoddesdon rioters, see NA, SP 1/85, f. 119r, 23 August
1534. The quoted letter to Cromwell is NA, SP 1/85, f. 173r, 23 September 1534. For the
impact of Henry VIII's divorce on the inhabitants of Hoddesdon, see Harvey, *The Cooke
Sisters* (1981), pp. 48–9. For more on the divorce, see Fraser, *Six Wives of Henry VIII* (1992),
pp. 133–56 and Weir, *Six Wives of Henry VIII* (2007), pp. 248–9. Two particularly useful
accounts of the Reformation are Haigh, *English Reformations* (1993) and Duffy, *The Stripping
of the Altars* (1992). Elizabeth Russell's birth date is recorded erroneously as 1528 in the
DNB and ODNB. For more on the correct dating of her birth, see Laoutaris, 'Transla-
tion/Historical Writing' (2010), pp. 309 and 324, n. 54; Laoutaris, 'The Radical Pedagogies . . .'
(2011), p. 67; Russell, *Letters*, ed. Farber (1977); Gladstone, *Building an Identity* (1989); and
Russell, *The Writings*, ed. Phillippy (2011), p. 5.

On Margaret Pennington Cooke, see McIntosh, 'Some New Gentry . . .' (1977), pp. 133–6
and Harvey, *The Cooke Sisters* (1981), pp. 29–32. Margaret's post is itemized in NA, LC 2/2,
f. 58r. For Margaret's gifts to Princess Mary, see Madden, *Privy Purse Expenses* (1831), pp. 48,

71, 102, 121, 151 and 167. Princess Mary's letter in support of Margaret Cooke is BL, Cotton MS Vespasian FIII, 'Book of Hands', no. 223, f. 280r. For the backing Margaret received from Cromwell and others in her Risebridge disputes, see letter from Dr John London to Thomas Bedell, NA, SP 1/123, ff. 188r–189r, 3 August 1537.

The reference to Elizabeth marching in 'battlegear' is from Walter Haddon's Latin elegy for Sir Thomas Hoby, in Haddon, *Poemata* (1567), pp. 118–19. The English translation is by Jaime Goodrich.

Chapter Two: The Female University

Lloyd's quoting of Cooke is from *States-men* (1665; 1670 edition), p. 375. For Gidea Hall as a 'female university', see Schleiner, *Tudor and Stuart Women Writers* (1994), p. 34. Cooke's annuity and appointment as Edward VI's tutor is NA, E315/221, f. 131r. Martyr's letter praising Cooke is recorded in Nichols, *Literary Remains* (1857), vol. 1, p. li, with an account of Cooke's role as tutor on pp. xlix–li. Strype's account of Cooke's influence on Edward VI's religion is from *Life of the Learned Sir John Cheke* (1705; 1821 edition), p. 89.

On Edward VI's coronation, the influence of Edward Seymour and Thomas Cranmer and the revised coronation oath, see *Writings of Edward the Sixth* (1836), p. 5; Skidmore, *Edward VI* (2008), pp. 56–61; Hoak, 'The Coronations . . .' (2003), pp. 114–51; and Weir, *Children of England* (2008), p. 31. The ceremony of the Knights of the Bath is described in Nichols, *Literary Remains* (1857), vol. 1, pp. ccxviv–ccxcix and Strype, *Ecclesiastical Memorials* (1822), vol. 2, pp. 34–6. John Cooke's role as Knight of the Bath is recorded in McIntosh, 'Sir Anthony Cooke . . .' (1975). Anthony Cooke's appointment as one of Henry VIII's 'spears' is in NA, SP 1/156, f. 43v. His involvement in welcoming the Admiral of France is BL, MS Cotton Vespasian C/XIV/1, f. 86r. His supplying of footmen in Flanders and France are, respectively, NA, SP 1/180, f. 2r; NA, SP 1/184, f. 96v; and NA, SP 1/184, f. 222r. For Cooke's posts as Sheriff of Essex and Hertfordshire, see Gairdner and Brodie, eds., *Letters and Papers, Foreign and Domestic*, vol. 17, 1542, Henry VIII (1900), p. 642 and vol. 21, part 2, 1546, Henry VIII (1910), p. 222. For his role as Havering Justice of the Peace, see McIntosh, 'Sir Anthony Cooke . . .' (1975), p. 237. Cooke also sat on the Essex commissions for investigations into heresy and was involved in the execution of Joan Bette and others: see NA, SP 1/218, f. 139r, 14 May 1546 and Gairdner and Brodie, eds., *Letters and Papers, Foreign and Domestic*, vol. 21, part 2, 1546, Henry VIII (1910), p. 417, 16 May 1546.

Seymour's appraisal of Cooke is from Lloyd, *States-men* (1665; 1670 edition), pp. 376–7. On the birth dates of Cooke's children, see Harvey, *The Cooke Sisters* (1981), pp. 386–8; the family tree in Gladstone, *Building an Identity* (1989); and Russell, *The Writings*, ed. Phillippy (2011), p. 15. Mildred's birth date is fixed in HH, CP 334, f. 2r. Haddon's visit to Gidea Hall and his account of the Cooke sisters' education is from *Lucubrationes, Orationes, Epistolae* (1567), p. 131 (my translation from the Latin). A description of Gidea Hall is to be found in Barnes, 'The Cookes . . .' (1912) and McIntosh, 'Sir Anthony Cooke . . .' (1975). For the education of William Cecil and Thomas Hoby, see Harvey, *The Cooke Sisters* (1981), pp. 76, 110 and 118. For women's roles in Hoby's translation of Castiglione's text, see Hoby, *The Book of the Courtier* (1561), ed. Whitfield (1975), pp. 185–95.

Cooke's belief in the equality of souls is from Lloyd, *States-men* (1665; 1670 edition), p. 374. My reconstruction of the Cooke sisters' pedagogical training is based on evidence of their reading from their later letters, epitaphic inscriptions, translations and manuscript projects; on the regimen outlined in Ascham, *The Schoolmaster* (1576); on Anne Fitzwilliam Cooke's views as reported by Anne Bacon in the dedicatory epistle to her mother in her *Sermons of Bernadine Ochyne* (1570), sigs. A3r–A5v; and on bequests made in Anthony Cooke's will, NA, PROB 11/59, f. 72r, 22 May 1576, with copy in BL, Lansdowne MS 23, no. 64, ff. 133r–142r, 22 May 1576. Anthony Cooke's translation of St Cyprian is NA, SP 6/13, ff. 14r–15v. Hyde's *Instruction* (1530) is quoted in Trill et al., eds., *Lay By Your Needles* (1997), pp. 24–5. On Elizabeth's reading of Aristotle, see Allen, *The Cooke Sisters* (2013), p. 40. Allen also gives an account of the Cooke sisters' education on pp. 18–55. For the education of the royal children, see Weir, *Children of England* (2008), pp. 1–19.

Ascham's descriptions of Edward VI and Princess Elizabeth are from *Works*, vol. 1, part 1, ed. Giles (1865), p. lxx, 14 December 1550 and pp. lxiv–lxv, 4 April 1550. More's letter to Gonell is from More, *Selected Letters*, ed. Rogers (1961), pp. 103–4, conjecturally dated to 22 May 1518. On the education of More's daughters, see Laoutaris, 'Translation/Historical Writing' (2010), pp. 298–306; see also Guy, *A Daughter's Love* (2008). Coke's comparison of More's daughters with Anne Cooke is from *Debate* (1550), sig. K1. Thomas Birch's 'catalogue' is BL, Additional MS 4344, f. 22. Ascham's descriptions of Lady Grey and Mildred Cecil are from his Letter to Sturm, *Works*, vol. 1, part 1, ed. Giles (1865), pp. lxx–lxxi, 14 December 1550.

Cooke's account of his daughters' dowries is from Lloyd, *States-men* (1665; 1670 edition), p. 377. On the marriages and background of William Cecil and Nicholas Bacon, see ODNB entries for both; Harvey, *The Cooke Sisters* (1981), pp. 103–53 and 393–5; and Loades, *Cecils* (2007), pp. 18–26. On Nicholas Bacon and Philip Hoby benefitting from the Dissolution, see Harvey, *The Cooke Sisters* (1981), pp. 113–14. Cooke's nomination for a royal gift is recorded in NA, SP 10/14, f. 99r and a copy in NA, SP 10/14, f. 101r, 19 June 1552. Richard Goodrich reflects on this honour in his letter to William Cecil, NA, SP 10/14, f. 155r, 28 August 1552. On Philip Hoby's posts and contacts, see ODNB entry and Harvey, *The Cooke Sisters* (1981), pp. 119–20. Philip Hoby's letter to William Cecil is HH, CP 151, f. 43r, 21 August 1552. For another letter from Philip Hoby to William Cecil, arranging a meeting with Mildred, see BL, Lansdowne MS 3, no. 53, f. 113r, 1 July 1556. Haddon's first courtship letter asking for Cecil's aid is BL, Lansdowne MS 3, no. 10, f. 19r, 11 November 1552, translated from the Latin by Jaime Goodrich. Anne Cooke's letter to Elizabeth Cooke in Haddon's hand is BL, Lansdowne MS 104, no. 59, f. 156r, translated by Jaime Goodrich. The latter letter is misdated to 1571 in the Calendar of BL MSS. Haddon's letter to Elizabeth Cooke after his rejection is BL, Lansdowne MS 98, no. 36, f. 252r, probably composed autumn/winter 1552. Scholars are in disagreement about whether Elizabeth Cooke really was the object of Haddon's affections. Harvey and Allen believe that he was courting Anne Cooke. See, respectively, Harvey, *The Cooke Sisters* (1981), pp. 389–91 and Allen, *The Cooke Sisters* (2013), pp. 2 and 205. Elizabeth is identified as the subject of the courtship in Russell, *Letters*, ed. Farber (1977) and Russell, *The Writings*, ed. Phillippy (2011). Jaime Goodrich and I have conducted a detailed analysis of the letters and believe that a Greek inscription in a contemporary hand stating that the letter was composed by 'Anne Cooke to her sweetest sister' is authentic. Goodrich has also noticed a crossed-out inscription at the base of the letter which reads 'Dom[y?]ne T. Ho[by?]' (Master T. Ho[by?]), which may indicate that the letter was shown to Haddon's love-rival. I am also basing my interpretation of the court-ship on the subsequent strangeness of the relationship between Elizabeth and Haddon, as well as on the fact that Elizabeth and her sister Margaret were married in a double wedding in 1558, which indicates that a suitor had not yet been found for the elder sister in 1552.

On Thomas Hoby's travels, see Hoby, *Travels*, ed. Powell (1902) (this is a printed tran-scription of Hoby's manuscript diary preserved in BL, Egerton MS 2148). On Peter Martyr's dedication to Anthony Cooke, see Allen, *The Cooke Sisters* (2013), p. 40. Cooke's ecclesiastical commission is noted in NA, PC 2/4, f. 408r, 6 October 1552. On John Laski, see Collinson, *Godly People* (1983), pp. 247–8. Elizabeth's identification of Philip Hoby as the orchestrator of her marriage to Thomas Hoby is from her Latin epitaph on the tomb of the 'Hoby Knights' in All Saints Church, Bisham, Berkshire (the translation is my own).

The various plaudits to Elizabeth and the Cooke sisters are from Ballard, *Memoirs*, ed. Perry (1752; 1985 edition), p. 189; Barker, *Nobility of Women*, ed. Bond (1559; 1904 edition), p. 155; Jessen, *Diallacticon* (1566), quoted in Russell, *The Writings*, ed. Phillippy (2011), pp. 323–4; Harington, *Orlando Furioso* (1591; 1607 edition), p. 314; Fuller, *History of the Worthies of England*, vol. 1, ed. Nuttall (1662; 1840 edition), p. 509; Makin, *Ancient Education of Gentle-women* (1673), p. 20; Phillips, *Theatrum Poetarum* (1675), p. 256; and Hay, *Female Biography* (1803), quoted in Harvey, *The Cooke Sisters* (1981), p. 11. For additional tributes, see Camden, *Reges, Reginae* (1603), sigs. G1v–G2r and Gerbier, *Elogium Heroinum* (1651), pp. 39–46. On Anne Fitzwilliam Cooke's death, see BL, Lansdowne MS 118, f. 82v. Whetstone's poem in honour of Elizabeth is from the *Rock of Regard* (1576), pp. 123–4. For more on the Cooke sisters' reputation, see the pioneering article by Lamb, 'The Cooke Sisters . . .' (1985), pp. 107–25.

Chapter Three: Monstrous Regiments

The incarceration of Cooke and Cheke in the Tower is related in Machyn, *Diary*, ed. Nich-ols (1848), p. 38. The autopsy report on Edward VI is outlined in a draft letter to the Privy Council, in Lodge, *Illustrations of British History* (1838), vol. 1, p. 225. An early report of Edward VI's disease can be found in Sir Richard Morison's letter in Greek cypher to Wil-liam Cecil, NA, SP 68/12, no. 652, f. 307r, 11 April 1553. The circumstances surrounding the proclamation of Jane Grey as Queen, the suspicion that Edward VI had been poisoned and the reclamation of the throne by Mary I are recounted in Machyn, *Diary*, ed. Nichols (1848), pp. 35–8; in the ambassador Jehan Scheyfve's dispatches to the Emperor Charles V in CSP Spain, vol. 11, 1553, ed. Tyler (1916), pp. 69–109; and in ODNB entries for Jane Grey, John Dudley and Edward VI. The legal 'device' which altered the succession in Jane Grey's favour is ITL, Petyt MS 538/47, f. 317r.

Burcher's letter to Bullinger is from OL, vol. 2, p. 684, 16 August 1553. Mildred Cecil's Greek letter to Jane Grey is SP 10/15, f. 178r (the translation is my own). The Cooke sisters would later claim to be kinsmen of the Grey sisters; see Loades, *Cecils* (2007), p. 65. William Cecil's letter to Mildred in the event of his own execution is BL, Lansdowne MS 104, no. 2, ff. 3r–4v, 13 June 1553. Cecil's 'apology' to Mary I is BL, Lansdowne MS 104, no. 1, ff. 1r–2r, 1553. Alford's report is BL, Cotton MS Titus B.II, ff. 374r–377v.

Burcher's letter to Bullinger is from OL, vol. 2, pp. 686–7, 3 September 1554. Cooke's travels with the Hobys are recorded in Hoby, *Travels*, ed. Powell (1902), pp. 116–20. On Cooke's activities in Strasbourg, see McIntosh, 'Sir Anthony Cooke . . .' (1975) and Cooke's letters to William Cecil: HH, CP 151/141, 10 January 1557; HH, CP 2/11, 17 May 1557; HH, CP 152/12, 12 July 1557; HH, CP 152/6, 24 January 1558; and NA, SP 70/1, f. 78r, 17 May 1557. For Elizabeth's residency with the Cecils, see 'Wimbledon Easter Book', NA, SP 11/8, f. 1r, 5 April 1556 and BL, Lansdowne MS 118, f. 36r. For Thomas Hoby's marriage negotiations, the death of his brother and the double wedding of Elizabeth and Margaret, see Hoby, *Travels*, ed. Powell (1902), pp. 126–7. Haddon's marriage poem is from Haddon, *Poemata* (1567), p. 82 (the English translation is by Jaime Goodrich). Margaret (Cooke) Rowlett's funeral is described in Machyn, *Diary*, ed. Nichols (1848), pp. 169–70. A poem by Richard Edwards supplies what little we know about Margaret: 'Cooke is comely and thereto in books sets all her care / In learning with the Roman dames of right she may compare', BL, Cotton MS Titus A.XXIV, f. 79r. Philip Hoby's will is NA, PROB 11/40, f. 34r, 2 July 1558. The King's grants to Philip Hoby of property in the Blackfriars are itemized in Gairdner and Brodie, eds., *Letters and Papers*, vol. 16, 1540–41, Henry VIII (1898), p. 456, 15–16 June 1541 and vol. 17, 1542, Henry VIII (1900), p. 485, 4–10 September 1542. For his use of these properties, see Rent Roll FSL, Lb.390, 1553–4; FSL, Lb.463; and Smith, *Shakespeare's Blackfriars Playhouse* (1964), pp. 436, 440 and 450. The fortunes of Cheke's property, the Revels Office and George Brooke's purchases are reconstructed from Smith, *Shakespeare's Blackfriars Playhouse* (1964), pp. 102 and 119–23; SHC, LM/347/4, 25 April 1554; FSL, Lb.400, c.1555 and Lb.462, c.1558; and Feuillerat, *Blackfriars Records* (1913), pp. 16–20 and 117.

Thomas Hoby's recording of Elizabeth I's accession is Hoby, *Travels*, ed. Powell (1902), p. 127. The ODNB entries for William Cecil and Nicholas Bacon record their appointments at the start of the new reign. Knox's views on female rulers are in *The First Blast of the Trumpet* (1558), ff. 11r–17r. Cooke's militant letter to Bullinger is ZL, vol. 2, pp. 1–2, 8 December 1558. Cooke's preparations for returning to England and the feelings of the exiled reformers who had 'lacked our country' is NA, SP 70/1, f. 58r, 12 December 1558. Jean Calvin's letter to William Cecil outlining the threat to the reformist cause as a result of Knox's tract is ZL, vol. 2, pp. 34–5, after 29 January 1559. Cecil's own response is ZL, vol. 2, p. 34, n. 2. Cooke's letter to Peter Martyr expressing frustration at the slowness of reform and his petitioning of the Queen is ZL, vol. 2, pp. 13–14, 12 February 1559. Jewel's letter to Martyr about Cooke is ZL, vol. 1, p. 21. Knox's letter to the Queen is NA, SP 52/1, f. 123r. For Cooke's posts, see *Calendar of Patent Rolls, Elizabeth I*, vol. 1, 1558–60 (1939), pp. 33–4 and for his gradual retreat from politics, see McIntosh, 'Sir Anthony Cooke . . .' (1975), p. 246.

On the Cooke sisters' coterie in 1559, see Barker, *Nobility of Women*, ed. Bond, (1559; 1904 edition), p. 155. Mildred's translation of St Basil is BL, Royal MS 17Bxviii, ff. 3r–4r. For Mildred's skills as a linguist, see Giles Lawrence's account in Strype, *The Life and Acts of Matthew Parker* (1711), p. 404. On Princess Elizabeth's translation of Ochino, see Elizabeth I, *Translations*, eds. Mueller and Scodel (2009), pp. 291–4 and Allen, *The Cooke Sisters* (2013), p. 58. Anne Bacon's pronouncements on the unity of the English Church are Bacon, *Apology* (1564), sigs. A4v, C5r–C6v and M8. On Anne Bacon as translator, see Stewart, 'The Voices of Anne Cooke . . .' (2000), pp. 88–102. On the political utility of translation, see Laoutaris, 'Translation/Historical Writing' (2010), pp. 296–327; Goldberg, *Desiring Women* (1997), p. 75; and Ammos, *Early Theories of Translation* (1920; 2007 edition), pp. 81–121. Anthony Cooke also gave a translation of a work by Gregory Nazianzen to the Queen as a New Year's gift on 7 January 1561, BL, Royal MS 5 E.xvii. The reference to the Cooke sisters' 'fortification' of the English Church comes from Verstegan, *Declaration* (1592), p. 12.

On Katherine Bertie, see Hogrefe, *Women of Action* (1977), pp. 82–103. Her letter to the Queen is NA, SP 12/2, ff. 17r–17v. Evidence of Katherine Bertie's correspondence with Mildred comes from her letter to William Cecil, NA, SP 12/3, f. 28r. On Anne Locke, see Felch, 'The Exemplary Anne Vaughan Lock' (2011), pp. 15–27; Felch, ' "Noble Gentlewomen . . ." . . .' (2003), pp. 14–16; and Collinson, 'The Role of Women . . .' (1965), pp. 258–72. Anne Locke's funding of Scottish soldiers is from Knox's letter to her, CSP Foreign, Elizabeth I, 1559–60, vol. 2, p. 294, 18 November 1559. On Mildred Cecil's involvement in the Scottish reform movement, see Allen, *The Cooke Sisters* (2013), pp. 126–31. Anne Locke's dedication to Katherine Bertie is from *Sermons of John Calvin* (1560). On Dorcas Martin, see White, 'A Biographical Sketch . . .' (1999), pp. 775–92. Renovations to Bisham Abbey are reconstructed from VCH, Berkshire, vol. 3, eds. P.H. Ditchfield and William Page (1923), pp. 139–52; Compton, *The Story of Bisham Abbey* (1979), p. 67; and Hoby, *Travels*, ed. Powell (1902), pp. 128–9. The latter pages also provide evidence that the Hobys went to London to oversee the publication of the *Courtier*. Jane Grey's execution is recorded in Hoby, *Travels*, ed. Powell (1902), pp. 102–3 and Weir, *Children of England* (2008), pp. 244–5. See also ODNB entry for Thomas Wyatt. The best account of the death of Amy Robsart and Dudley's relationship with Queen Elizabeth I is Skidmore, *Death and the Virgin* (2011). On the peculiar coincidence of Elizabeth's dinner party on the day of Robsart's mysterious demise, see Hoby, *Travels*, ed. Powell (1902), p. 128. De Quadra's observations are from CSP Spain (Simancas), vol. 1, 1558–67, ed. Hume (1892), pp. 122 and 174. Cheke's letter and Hoby's dedicatory epistle to Hastings are printed as the prefatory matter in Hoby, *Courtier* (1561). For more on the men who coveted the Crown of England, see Ross, *The Men Who Would be King* (2005).

Chapter Four: The Ambassador's Wife

Throckmorton's letter to Cecil is NA, SP 70/14, ff. 62r–63r, 10 May 1560. Thomas Hoby's unwillingness to go to Paris and the Queen's recourse to pressure tactics can be seen in letters from William Cecil to Thomas Smith, BL, Lansdowne MS 102, no. 63, f. 116r, 30 August 1565 and BL, Lansdowne MS 102, no. 66, ff. 121r–122v, 30 August 1565.

Elizabeth's fall and the travelling conditions to Dover are recounted in Thomas Hoby's letter, NA, SP 15/13, f. 15r, 7 April 1566. On the Cooke family's hereditary spinal conditions, see Croft and Hearn, ' "Only matrimony . . ." . . .' (2003), pp. 19–20. I owe my knowledge of Mildred's hereditary scoliosis to Pauline Croft, who also informed me that Robert Cecil may have suffered from 'splayed legs' caused by a 'click hip'. The reference to Robert Cecil as a 'crookback spider' comes from the anti-Cecil libel, Bodleian, MS Don. c. 54, f. 20r. Richard III is referred to as a 'bottled spider' and 'poisonous bunch-backed toad' in *Richard III*, ed. Jowett (2000), 1.3.242–6. Hoby's complaints about the cost of the mission are from his dispatch NA, SP 70/84, f. 172r, 11 June 1566. Throughout, the costs itemized for the journey to and from Paris are from Elizabeth's own record of expenses, BL, Additional MS 18764. The expenses are also printed in Russell, *The Writings*, ed. Phillippy (2011), pp. 64–7. The descriptions of the state of Dover Castle are from NA, SP 15/13, f. 15r, 7 April 1566. Elizabeth's letter to William Cecil is NA, SP 15/13, f. 14r, 7 April 1566.

Hoby's dispatches outline the party's departure from Dover, Haddon's seasickness, landing in Calais, shooting through the group's flag, and French fortifications: NA, SP 70/83, ff. 159r–160r, 9 April 1566 and NA, SP 70/83, f. 166r, 12 April 1566. The best account of the religious factionalism in France is Treasure, *The Huguenots* (2013); see also Rady, *France* (1988), p. 53. The Guise oath is quoted in Knecht, *The French Wars* (1996), p. 106. The limited rights of the French Protestants and the Peace of Amboise are discussed in Rady, *France* (1988), pp. 66 and 73. Charles IX's minority is placed in context in Garrisson, *A History* (1991), p. 263. D'Argos's stocking of the soldiers, the Hobys' encounter with the Marquis of Baden and their exploration of the religious communities of France are reported in NA, SP 70/83, f. 165r, 11 April 1566. Accounts of the Marquis of Baden's debts, his use of weapons, his fleeing the country and his disguise are in NA, SP 12/39, f. 133r; NA, SP 12/39, ff. 151r–151v; and NA, SP 15/13, f. 11r.

The meeting with the Vidame d'Amiens, the Hobys' sightseeing and their arrival in Paris are described in NA, SP 70/83, ff. 212r–212v, 25 April 1566. Hoby's interest in recording the transcriptions of tombs on his travels is attested to in BL, Egerton MS 2148. The recent massacres included that which took place on 1 March 1562, when the Duke of Guise's men raided a barn in the village of Vassy in which hundreds of Huguenots were praying and killed more than thirty. Three months later, a number of Huguenots were butchered at Sens, with some of the victims hanged from the windows of the town hall; see Treasure, *The Huguenots* (2013), pp. 118 and 146; Guy, *My Heart is My Own* (2004), p. 160; and Knecht, *The Rise and Fall* (1996), p. 353. For the Treaty of Hampton Court and the debacle over Le Havre, see Knecht, *The French Wars* (1996), pp. 35–8 and 104 and Knecht, *The Rise and Fall* (1996), pp. 373–4. For more on Maigny's monument, see Russell, *The Writings*, ed. Phillippy (2011), pp. 80–81 and 279.

Thomas Smith's arrival and his description of the Hobys is NA, SP 70/83, ff. 231r–231v, 28 April 1566. Smith's complaint about George Carey is NA, SP 70/83, f. 15, 6 March 1566. The Hobys' meeting with Carey and Thomas Hoby's endeavours on his behalf are outlined in NA, SP 79/83, ff. 240r–241r, 29 April 1566. Evidence of Elizabeth's meeting with the Duchess d'Étampes and Hoby's description of her come from NA, SP 70/84, ff. 211v–212v, 21 June 1566. On the Duchess, see Knecht, *The Rise and Fall* (1996), pp. 149 and 238. Other influential female Protestants included Marguerite d'Angoulême, sister to King Francis I; Louise de Montmorency, mother of Gaspard de Coligny; Marguerite's daughter, Jeanne d'Albret, later Queen of Navarre, who made Protestantism the official religion of Béarn in 1565; Eleanor de Roucy de Roye, wife of the Prince of Condé; and Eleanor's mother, Madeleine de Mailly, Countess of Roye. For more on the role of women in the Huguenot movement, see Treasure, *The Huguenots* (2013), pp. 129–31 and Knecht, *The French Wars* (1996), pp. 14–16 and 35.

The arrival of the Queen of Navarre and the Hobys' meeting with her are referred to in Thomas Hoby's dispatches NA, SP 70/84, f. 8r, 4 May 1566; NA, SP 70/84, f. 9r, 4 May 1566; and NA, SP 70/84, ff. 57r–58v, 16 May 1566, with enclosure of 8 May. More gossip on the Queen of Navarre is reported by Hoby in NA, SP 70/84, f. 94r, 21 May 1566. For Ponet's career, see ODNB. For the sale of Ponet's books to Anthony Cooke, see OL, vol. 1, pp. 118–19. Ponet's controversial views on regicide are from Ponet, *A Short Treatise of Politic Power* (1556), sig. G3r. For the background to Cooke's editions of Ponet's *Diallacticon* and the English translation of the 1566 French edition's dedicatory epistle to Maligny, see Russell, *The Writings*, ed. Phillippy (2011), pp. 318–26. For more on Ponet's connection to the

Cookes, see Laoutaris, 'The Radical Pedagogies . . .' (2011), pp. 74–5. A surviving poem by Elizabeth, signed with her maiden name, is in the Bibliothèque Nationale de France, Collection Dupuy 951, f. 122v. See also Russell, *The Writings*, ed. Phillippy (2011), pp. 49–50. The poem is in the hand of Daniel Rogers, a poet and diplomat, who also circulated poems dedicated to Elizabeth which addressed her as 'Elizabeth Cooke'. These are preserved in Huntington, MS HM 31188, ff. 171r–76v. I would like to thank Jaime Goodrich for translating these Latin and Greek poems for me. For evidence of Rogers' diplomatic mission to France, see NA, SP 70/106, ff. 19r–22r. For more on the complexities of Renaissance manuscript culture, including useful accounts of the involvement of women in manuscript exchange, see Lamb, *Gender and Authorship* (1990) and Woudhuysen, *Sir Philip Sidney and the Circulation of Manuscripts* (1996).

The statistics illustrating the rise of Protestantism in France are from Garrisson, *A History* (1991), pp. 285–8; Rady, *France* (1988), p. 56; and Knecht, *The French Wars* (1996), p. 7. The belief that Dudley had gained the support of the French royal family and de Silva's warning to William Cecil are in CSP Spain (Simancas), vol. 1, 1558–67, ed. Hume (1892), pp. 511 and 540–43, January to April 1566. Cecil's list of arguments against Dudley's marriage to the Queen are in HH, CP 155, f. 38r. Killigrew's defence of Dudley after Amy Robsart's death is recorded in a letter to Nicholas Throckmorton, NA, SP 70/19, ff. 46r–48v, 10 October 1560. Throckmorton's report to Cecil on the French response to Robsart's death is NA, SP 70/19, ff. 130r–131r, 28 October 1560. Killigrew's letter to Northampton promoting Dudley's marriage to the Queen is NA, SP 70/19, f. 57r–58r, 15 October 1560 and his warning to Throckmorton is NA, SP 70/22, ff. 55r–55v, 13 January 1561. On Cecil's 'invective' against Killigrew, see Miller, *Sir Henry Killigrew* (1963), p. 100.

Thomas Hoby's meeting with Catherine de Medici and Charles IX is recounted in NA, SP 70/84, ff. 57r–58v, 16 May 1566, with enclosure of 8 May. Edward Cooke's impressions are given in NA, SP 70/84, ff. 40r–40v, 12 May 1566. On Mary, Queen of Scots, seeking safety in France, Rizzio's death and on her being funded by the Guise faction, see CSP Venice, vol. 7, 1558–80, eds. Brown and Bentinck (1890), pp. 375–80, 2–30 April 1566 and NA, SP 70/84, ff. 202r–203v, 19 June 1566. See also Tweedie, *David Rizzio* (2007). For Hoby's knowledge of Mary, Queen of Scots' relations with her husband, see his dispatch NA, SP 70/83, f. 240r, 29 April 1566. Ambassador Barbaro's account of the gossip surrounding Dudley is from CSP Venice, vol. 7, 1558–80, eds. Brown and Bentinck (1890), pp. 380–81, 11 May 1566. Rumours of Dudley's lack of favour with the French royals in the Spanish court and Mildred Cecil's views are reported by Guzman de Silva in CSP Spain (Simancas), vol. 1, 1558–67, ed. Hume (1892), respectively pp. 571–2, 10 August 1566 and pp. 543–5, 22 April 1566.

Thomas Hoby's accounts of the factional tensions in Paris, the assassination attempts against chief Huguenots and the Queen Mother's response to these are NA, SP 70/84 ff. 57r–58v, 16 May 1566; NA, SP 70/84, f. 162r, 10 June 1566; NA, SP 70/84, ff. 157r–158r, 10 June 1566; and NA, SP 70/84, ff. 172r–174r, 11 June 1566. Hoby's letters reporting the Pamiers massacre are, respectively, to Cecil, NA, SP 70/84, f. 182r, 14 June 1566, and to the Queen, NA, SP 70/84, ff. 200r–201r, 19 June 1566. Hoby's letter to Cecil with the description of Elizabeth's dinner and the discussions having taken place there is NA, SP 70/84, ff. 202r–203v. Some of the individuals at the dinner party are identified in Allen, *The Cooke Sisters* (2013), pp. 139–40. Hoby's last letter is NA, SP 70/84, ff. 211r–212r. Thomas Hoby's will, detailing his bequests and those present at his death, is NA, PROB 11/48, f. 419r, 12 July 1566. The date and time of Hoby's death are recorded in College of Arms, MS 1, 13, ff. 77r–78v. Haddon's description of Hoby's final hours is from his elegy, in Haddon, *Poemata* (1567), pp. 118–19 (translated by Jaime Goodrich).

Chapter Five: A Widow's Bed

Elizabeth's sense of foreboding is from her letter NA, SP 15/13, f. 14r, 7 April 1566. Robert Seton's mission to London is listed in Elizabeth's itemization of the costs of travelling to and from Paris, BL, Additional MS 18764. For Edward Cooke's sickness and death, see the dispatches of his cousin Hugh Fitzwilliam in NA, SP 70/87, ff. 25r–26r, 12 November 1566 and NA, SP 70/87, ff. 60r–62v, 25 November 1566. See also Monsieur de Foix's condolences on the deaths of both Hoby and Cooke in NA, SP 70/87, f. 117r, 10 December 1566. Edward Cooke's letter to William Cecil detailing the French royal family's response to news of Thomas Hoby's death is NA, SP 70/85, ff. 41r–41v, 17 July 1566. For rumours of Hoby's poisoning, see Compton, *The Story of Bisham Abbey* (1979), p. 70. For Mildred's support of Stewart, see Allen, *The Cooke Sisters* (2013), pp. 129–30. Elizabeth's aiding of Stewart is indicated by their conversation as outlined in NA, SP 70/85, ff. 41r–41v. Killigrew's assessment of Stewart is in NA, SP 52/3, f. 67r, 15 April 1560. Rogers' poem recording Elizabeth's reaction to her husband's death is part of the collection of poems to Elizabeth in Huntington, MS HM 31188, ff. 171r–176v, with translation provided by Jaime Goodrich. Elizabeth's poem on her husband's death, signed 'Elisa Cokia', is Bibliothèque Nationale de France, Collection Dupuy 951, f. 122v (the translation into English is my own). For Elizabeth as the 'English Sappho', see Lodge, *A Margarite of America* (1596), dedicatory epistle to Elizabeth, sig. A4r. For Elizabeth's monuments and epitaphic inscriptions as tourist attractions, see Camden, *Reges, Reginae* (1603), sigs. G1v–G2r. For a list of other early tourist guides in which Elizabeth's poems appear, see Russell, *The Writings*, ed. Phillippy (2011), pp. 34–5. The English translation of Thomas Hoby's Latin epitaph on his monument in All Saints Church, Bisham, Berkshire, is my own.

The account of the transportation of Hoby's embalmed body back to England and his subsequent funeral, including Goodman's sermon, are derived from BL, Additional MS 18764 and College of Arms, MS 1, 13, ff. 77r–78v. On details of Renaissance embalming procedure in France, see the account given by the sixteenth-century French physician Ambrose Paré, printed in Giesey, *The Royal Funeral Ceremony* (1969), p. 27. For more on the heraldic funeral and its gendered construction, including an analysis of Elizabeth Russell's influence as a memorializer, see Laoutaris, *Shakespearean Maternities* (2008), pp. 212–67. For the ceremonial procedures of heraldic burials and their encoding of gender differences, see book of funeral proceedings, College of Arms, Vincent MS 151, esp. ff. 58r–59r and 327r–329r; Nicholas Charles, 'Book of Proceeding at Funerals', BL, Additional MS 14417, f. 6r; pictorial records of heraldic funerals, BL, Additional MS 35324, esp. ff. 4v and 20r; 'Antiquarian Collections' of Francis Tate, Secretary to the Society of Antiquaries from 1590 to 1600, BL, Stowe MS 1045, f. 104v; commonplace book of Francis Thynne, Lancaster Herald from 1602 to 1608, BL, Stowe MS 1047, ff. 246v–247r; and proceedings at funerals in WAM MSS 6348 and 6351. For a useful overview of Renaissance burial customs, see Gittings, *Death, Burial and the Individual* (1984). Elizabeth's skills as a memorializer are also explored in Phillippy, *Women, Death and Literature* (2002), pp. 179–210 and Malay, 'Elizabeth

Notes

Russell's Textual Performances of Self' (2006), pp. 146–68. For Goodman's presence in the Cecil household during Elizabeth's own sojourn there, see 'Wimbledon Easter Book', NA, SP 11/8, f. 1r, 5 April 1556. The list of defenders of Bartlett's *Fortress of Fathers* (1566) is in sig. A1r. The removal of Bartlett and the other ministers for refusing to subscribe to the official dress is recounted in Stow, *Memoranda*, ed. Gairdner (1880), pp. 135–6; Collinson, *Elizabethan Puritan Movement* (1967), p. 76; and Collinson, 'Letters of Thomas Wood ...' (1960), pp. 1–2, Wood's letter to William Cecil of 29 March 1566. Huntingdon was the patron of *About the Popish Apparel* (1566), which was probably written by Anthony Gilby, the quotes here taken from sigs. A2r and C1v. The tract expanded upon the militant discourse used in the first cohesive Puritan manifesto, Crowley's *Brief Discourse against the Outward Apparel* (1566); see particularly sigs. B3v, B6r and C4r. For an overview of the Vestments Controversy, see Collinson, *Elizabethan Puritan Movement* (1967), pp. 71–83 and 92–7.

The account of the increasing violence and 'blows' among religious factions is recorded in Stow, *Memoranda*, ed. Gairdner (1880), pp. 137–43. For the ambushing and abuse of Grindal and the riot in St Margaret Pattens, see Grindal, *Remains*, ed. Nicholson (1843), pp. 288–9 and Stow, *Memoranda*, ed. Gairdner (1880), pp. 139–40. For more on the work of English Puritan women, see Collinson, *Elizabethan Puritan Movement* (1967), pp. 93–4. Many of the non-conformists arrested for dissenting were women; see Burrage, *Early English Dissenters* (1912), vol. 2, pp. 9–11, for a list of the women incarcerated in Bridewell Prison in 1568.

The Queen's letter to Elizabeth is collated from an incomplete draft in Cecil's hand, NA, SP 70/85, f. 78r, and a later copy, BL, Harley MS 7035, f. 161r. Haddon's elegy for Thomas Hoby is in Haddon, *Poemata* (1567), pp. 118–19 (translated by Jaime Goodrich). I am very grateful to Dr Goodrich for her insights into this poem, particularly her knowledge of Hypsicratea and Cornelia Metella. On Stratonice, see Rollin, *Ancient History* (1780), vol. 2, p. 455. For a description of the tomb of the Hoby 'knights', see Russell, *The Writings*, ed. Phillippy (2011), pp. 77–81. For the first time it is possible to suggest a precise date for this tomb, thanks to the poems of Daniel Rogers, translated for use in this book. The poem in Huntington, MS HM 31188, f. 172r indicates that the tomb was completed around five years after the death of Thomas Hoby. I am grateful to Jaime Goodrich for translating this poem for me. For an account of William Cure's associations with the Hobys and the Cecils, see Gladstone, *Building an Identity* (1989) and Llewellyn, *Funeral Monuments* (2000), pp. 69–81 and 176–9. I have translated the Latin epitaphs on the tomb of Thomas and Philip Hoby. I am grateful to Patricia Burstall of Marlow for her expertise on the Hoby tombs and for personally showing me around the church of All Saints, Bisham.

Dudley's discovery of Cecil's letter to Hoby after the latter's death is CSP Spain (Simancas), vol. 1, 1558–67, ed. Hume (1892), pp. 571–2, 10 August 1566. For Hoby's birth and baptism, see Powell, ed., *Register of Bisham* (1898), pp. 1–2 and Russell, *The Writings*, ed. Phillippy (2011), pp. 17 and 44, n. 9.

Chapter Six: The War of Admonition

Dering's lecture is printed in Dering, *Works* (1597), pp. 27–8. For more on the background to the scandals surrounding Dering and Cartwright, see Pearson, *Thomas Cartwright* (1925); Haller, *The Rise of Puritanism* (1957), pp. 10–14; Reese, *The Tudors and Stuarts* (1940), pp. 148–9;

and Read, *Lord Burghley* (1960), pp. 11–12. Grindal's letter to Cecil is NA, SP 12/71, ff. 54r–54v, 25 June 1570. Chaderton's letter to Cecil with his complaints is NA, SP 12/71, ff. 24r–24v, 11 June 1570. The move by the vice-chancellor to block Cartwright's promotion is recorded in NA, SP, 12/71, ff. 62r–62v, 29 June 1570. The petition by Cartwright's supporters is NA, SP 12/71, f. 79r, 3 July 1570. Rockray's role as tutor to Elizabeth's children is NA, SP, 12/77, f. 20r, 31 January 1571. For more on Rockray, see Pearson, *Thomas Cartwright* (1925), pp. 39–42. On Whitgift's new statutes, see NA, SP 12/73, f. 76r, 19 August 1570 and NA, SP 12/74, f. 79r, 7 November 1570. Whitgift's own view on the utility of the statutes is in NA, SP 12/73, f. 29r, 11 August 1570 (this manuscript also provides evidence of Cartwright's prohibition from preaching).

The date when the articles were endorsed is recorded in Pearson, *Thomas Cartwright* (1925), p. 39. The second petition is NA, SP 12/73, f. 31r, 11 August 1570. Dering's explosive letter to Cecil is BL, Lansdowne MS 12, no. 86, ff. 190r–191v, 18 November 1570. Rockray's lecture of protest against Whitgift's statutes is recorded in his ODNB entry. Cartwright's being 'inhibited from reading' is recorded in NA, SP 12/74, ff. 79r–79v, 7 November 1570.

On the sale of Cawarden's estates to More and the number of residents in the area, see House, *The City of London* (1993), p. 124. The precise location of Elizabeth Russell's home, presented here for the first time, is calculated from the lease agreement between William More and Lewis de Mare, SHC, LM 348/68, 3 September 1570 (identifying the precise location of Peter Buram's property in relation to Lewis de Mare's tenement, 'the Round House or Corner Shop'); the indenture of Paul Buck, SHC, LM 348/216, 30 June 1591 (which gives the locations of the Round House and the Square Tower); a second indenture of Paul Buck, SHC, LM 348/234, 31 January 1594 (outlining the location of the late Lewis de Mare's properties); and Elizabeth Russell's own letter, SHC, HC 6729/6/98, dated only 9 August but probably written around 1580–81 (which clearly states that the tenements below her 'gallery' are 'let to one Peter Buram, and Lewes' [Lewis's] widow, that was a goldsmith'). Lewis de Mare is identified as a goldsmith in SHC, LM 348/68. Business was clearly going well for de Mare in 1570, for his payment of £10 down and 20 shillings per annum for a property running to the east of Elizabeth's home was in addition to a renewal of his existing leases in the area, which included a further yearly rent of 26 shillings and 7 pence to continue his occupation of the Round House. That Lewis de Mare was indeed 'deceased' by the time Elizabeth wrote her letter is indicated in Buck's indenture of 1591, SHC, LM 348/216.

Elizabeth's residency and activities in the Blackfriars are recorded in the dedicatory epistle to her in Fenton, *Acts of Conference* (1571), sigs. A2v–A3r. The location of Elizabeth's home relative to Thomas Vautrollier's has been determined from Richard Field's lease agreement with William and George More, SHC, LM 333/12, 22 September 1592 (which mentions Vautrollier's previous occupation of the Square Tower); Lewis de Mare's lease, SHC, LM 348/68 (which places Vautrollier's property immediately to the east of de Mare's Round House); and the indenture specifying the agreement between William de Lawne and William and George More, FSL, Lb.349, 31 October 1593 (which outlines the extent of the properties in the occupation of Richard Field). A rental list for 1590 also mentions Vautrollier's previous residency, FSL, Lb.456.

For Vautrollier's background and denization, see Page, ed., *Letters of Denization* (1893), p. 244; Worman, ed., *Alien Members of the Book Trade* (1906), pp. 67–8; and ODNB entry for Vautrollier. For Vautrollier's earliest publications of French works in English, see

Pollard, 'Claudius Hollyband . . .' (1915), pp. 77–93. Vautrollier's publication of a work on Coligny is Golding, *The Life of the Most Godly* (1576). Vautrollier also issued the works of others in Anthony Cooke's activist circle, including Theodore de Beza and Jean Calvin. Elizabeth's outline of the origin of Ponet's tract and the section of her translation quoted are from Russell, *A Way of Reconciliation* (1605), dedicatory epistle to Anne (Russell) Herbert, sigs. A2r–A3r and pp. 102–3. For the dating of Elizabeth's translation, see Laoutaris, 'Translation/Historical Writing' (2010), pp. 309 and 324, n. 54 and Laoutaris, 'The Radical Pedagogies . . .' (2011), pp. 74–5. Her desire to use the translation as a means of 'honouring' her father is expressed in her letter to Robert Cecil, HH, CP 197/53, probably composed sometime after 4 May 1605. For Fenton's possible mission to France and residency in the Blackfriars, see ODNB entry. For Fenton's attempt to influence the Queen, see his dedicatory epistle to Henry Sidney in Fenton, trans., de Serres, *A Discourse of the Civil Wars* (1570), sigs. A3v–A4r.

Elizabeth's letter to William Cecil on behalf of Rockray, which also outlines the reparations in Evesham, is NA, SP, 12/77, f. 20r, 31 January 1571. On Elizabeth's rights in Evesham, see Russell, *Letters*, ed. Farber (1977), p. 81. Elizabeth's letter detailing her spinal condition is NA, SP 12/44, f. 81r, 8 November 1567. I have translated Elizabeth's elegy for Elizabeth and Anne Hoby myself. The floor slab on the church of All Saints, Bisham, Berkshire, upon which the epitaph is engraved, records the death dates of the two girls. The transcription of the now faded engraving is preserved in Ashmole, *The Antiquities of Berkshire* (1719), vol. 2, pp. 470–71.

On Rockray's ejection from his post, see his ODNB entry. For Fenton's dedication to Elizabeth, see *Acts of Conference* (1571), sigs. A2v–A3r. On the 'prophesyings', see Collinson, *Godly People* (1983), pp. 343–4 and Collinson, *Elizabethan Puritan Movement* (1967), pp. 168–76. Dering's letter to Cecil requesting a pardon for Cartwright is NA, SP, 12/85, f. 173r, 24 March 1572. Fenton's dedication to Elizabeth is in Fenton, trans., Pasquier, *Monophylo* (1572), sigs. A2r–A4r. For Anne Locke's marriage to Dering and Dorcas Martin's involvement, see Collinson, 'The Role of Women . . .' (1965), pp. 258–72 and White, 'A Biographical Sketch . . .' (1999), pp. 775–92. For the Cooke sisters' relation to Bartholo Sylva, along with a description of the illuminated manuscript for which they provided dedicatory poems, see Laoutaris, 'Translation/Historical Writing' (2010), pp. 306–8; Laoutaris, 'The Radical Pedagogies . . .' (2011), pp. 77–8 (both of which contain an illustration from the manuscript); and Schleiner, *Tudor and Stuart Women Writers*, (1994), pp. 39–45. For a finely nuanced reading of the Cooke sisters' individual contributions to the manuscript, see Allen, *The Cooke Sisters* (2013), pp. 170–72. The Sylva manuscript is CUL, MS Ii.5.37. I have taken Elizabeth Russell's Greek poem directly from the MS and translated it myself.

For the account of the young and rebellious Cambridge Puritans, see Heywood and Wright, eds., *Cambridge University Transactions* (1854), pp. 112, 63 and 110 respectively. On the petitions of 1572–3 against the statutes, see Porter, *Reformation and Reaction* (1958), pp. 167–8 and 208–9 and Heywood and Wright, eds., *Cambridge University Transactions* (1854), pp. 61–2 (containing a full list of signatories, which includes Rockray). The quotations from Field and Wilcox's *An Admonition to the Parliament* (1572) are from Frere and Douglas, eds., *Puritan Manifestoes* (1907), pp. 29, 21 and 19 respectively, with Beza's letter printed on pp. 43–55.

Thomas Norton's comments about the *Admonition* are in ITL, Petyt MS 538/38, ff. 65r–65v, 20 October 1572. Whitgift's response is ITL, Petyt MS 538/38, ff. 65r–67r, 25 October 1572. Field's statement of defiance was made during his interrogation in prison; see Peel, ed., *The Second Part of a Register* (1915), vol. 1, pp. 87–8. The visitors to Field and Wilcox in prison are listed in ITL, Petyt MS 538/47, f. 481r. For Robert Johnson's role as backer of the French Church, see Collinson, *Godly People* (1983), p. 269. For summaries of the contents of the *Admonition* produced as evidence of its seditious nature, see ITL, Petyt MS 538/47, ff. 463r–465v. For Whitgift's attack on the Admonitionists, see Whitgift, *An Answer to . . . An Admonition* (1572), sig. A3r. Cartwright's response is in *Reply to an Answer Made of Master Doctor Whitgift* (1573), sig. B3v. Sandys' letter to Cecil is BL, Lansdowne MS 17, no. 30, f. 61r. For the female owners of the *Admonition* texts, see Collinson, *Elizabethan Puritan Movement* (1967), pp. 136 and 149. For Grindal's report of Dorcas Martin's activities, see Grindal, *Remains*, ed. Nicholson (1843), pp. 347–8. Dorcas Martin's endeavours as a translator are lauded in Bentley, *Monument of Matrons* (1582), sig. B1. On the Martins' and Killigrews' support of the French Church, see Collinson, *Godly People* (1983), pp. 270 and 263 respectively. Wilcox's praise of Anne Bacon is from his dedicatory epistle to her in Wilcox, *A Short Yet Sound Commentary* (1589), sigs. A3r–A4v.

For an outline of the Star Chamber proceedings against Field and Wilcox and Katherine Killigrew's intervention, see Collinson, *Godly People* (1983), pp. 309–11. Dering's examination and Parker's complaint is ITL, Petyt MS 538/47, f. 479r. Dering's dark prophecy is recorded in ITL, Petyt MS 538/38, f. 68r, dated 'Tuesday night' 11 December 1572. The Queen's proclamation against the *Admonition* texts is recorded in Frere and Douglas, eds., *Puritan Manifestoes* (1907), pp. 153–4. Sandys' letter to Cecil is BL, Lansdowne MS 17, no. 37, f. 81r, 2 July 1573. The sermons of the St Paul's Cross preachers are recorded in ITL, Petyt MS 538/47, f. 476r, 19 July 1573. Sandys' reports of a 'conspiracy' involving French ministers are from his missive to Cecil and the Earl of Leicester, BL Lansdowne MS 17, no. 43, ff. 96r–96v, 5 August 1573.

For the St Bartholomew's Day Massacre, see Treasure, *The Huguenots* (2013), pp. 167–75 and Knecht, *The Rise and Fall* (1996), pp. 413–38. The initial lists of women and children killed are BL, Additional MS 48126, ff. 101r–103r, 24 August 1572. The assessments of the role of the French royal family in the massacre, as presented to William Cecil by his agents, are preserved in BL, Harley MS 260 ff. 335r–335v, 25 September 1572 and NA, SP 70/125, ff. 50r–51r, September 1572. Sandys' letter to Cecil expressing his fears that the massacre would be repeated in England is BL, Lansdowne MS 15, f. 79r, 5 September 1572. The numbers of French pastors coming to England are recorded in Collinson, *Godly People* (1983), p. 247. On Vautrollier's role as a Protestant propagandist, see Parmelee, 'Printers, Patrons, Readers . . .' (1994), p. 856. The request for aid to the Low Countries is itemized in NA, SP 70/125, f. 36r, 27 September 1572. On de Lawne, see ODNB entry for 'Delaune, William'. For an important account of Queen Elizabeth I and her response to English Puritanism, see Ronald, *Heretic Queen* (2012), pp. 91–115 and 192–7.

Chapter Seven: Lady Russell

On Francis Russell's Puritan credentials and his relation to Gallars, see Collinson, *Elizabethan Puritan Movement* (1967), pp. 52–3; Collinson, *Godly People* (1983), pp. 249–51 and 260; and Harvey, *The Cooke Sisters* (1981), p. 271. For John Russell's background, including his early political posts, see Wiffen, ed., *Historical Memoirs of the House of Russell* (1833), vol. 1, pp. 493–506.

For Birchet's assassination attempt, see Nicholas, ed., *Memoirs of . . . Christopher Hatton* (1847), pp. 31–2, Sir Thomas Smith's letter to William Cecil, 15 October 1573. Birchet's interrogations are recorded in BL, Harley MS 6991, ff. 71r–71v, 11 November 1573 and the specific instructions for his examination are BL, Lansdowne MS 17, no. 24, f. 49r, 11 November 1573. See BL, Lansdowne MS 16, ff. 191r–191v for an assessment of Birchet's character. For Birchet's execution, see Pearson, *Thomas Cartwright* (1925), p. 9. For the attempt to murder Day, see BL, Lansdowne MS 17, no. 56, f. 126r, 13 November 1573. See also Read, *Lord Burghley* (1960), pp. 117–18.

The Needham/Undertree scandal is reconstructed from Parker, *Correspondence*, ed. Bruce (1853), pp. 460–46, 19–30 June 1574; BL, Lansdowne MS 19, no. 7, f. 14r, 19 June 1574; BL, Lansdowne MS 19, no. 8, f. 16r, 23 June 1574; BL, Lansdowne MS 19, no. 10, f. 19r, 26 June 1574; BL, Lansdowne MS 19, no. 11, f. 21r, 30 June 1574; and from the following manuscript letters (the forged missives given by Needham to Parker): BL, Lansdowne MS 64, no. 23, f. 69r, Thomas Cartwright to John Browne, 8 April [1574]; BL, Lansdowne MS 64, no. 24, f. 71r, John Westermann to Thomas Cartwright, 17 April [1574]; BL, Lansdowne MS 64, no. 25, f. 73r, William Clarke to Thomas Cartwright, 28 April [1574]; BL, Lansdowne MS 64, no. 26, f. 74r, John Browne to Thomas Cartwright, 18 April [1574]; BL, Lansdowne MS 64, no. 27, f. 76r, Richard Martin to John Browne, 27 May [1574]; BL, Lansdowne MS 64, no. 28, ff. 78r–78v, John Browne to Richard Martin, 13 June [1574]; and BL, Lansdowne MS 64, no. 29, f. 80r, John Browne to Richard Martin, 13 June [1574] (the conjectural year of 1590 for these letters, given in the calendar of Lansdowne MSS at the BL, is clearly incorrect. I have therefore supplied the correct dating). Cecil's list of suspects in the case, which included Martin, is presented in HH, CP 160/7, 20 June 1574. For more on the Needham plot, see Collinson, *Elizabethan Puritan Movement* (1967), pp. 154–5 and Pearson, *Thomas Cartwright* (1925), pp. 125–9. For Elizabeth's marriage to John Russell, see Powell, ed., *Register of Bisham* (1898), p. 19.

The account of the plague is Shrewsbury, *A History of Bubonic Plague* (1970), pp. 205–6. The description of Elizabeth's lying-in, appointing of the Russells' chambers and the christening of Elizabeth (Bess) Russell are derived from NA, SP 12/105, no. 65, ff. 143r–143v and copy in BL, Hargrave MS 497, no. 24, ff. 57r–60r. For Elizabeth's payments to the Dean of Westminster via William Cooke, see WAM, MS 39412, 26 November 1576. William Cecil's elevation to Lord Burghley is included in his ODNB entry. For more on Renaissance birthing, christening and churching rituals, see Cressy, *Birth, Marriage and Death* (1997), pp. 15–148 and Laoutaris, *Shakespearean Maternities* (2008).

John Russell's letter to Lord Burghley on his wife's pregnancy is NA, SP 12/105, no. 35, f. 86r, 2 September 1575. John Russell's letter to Lord Burghley on the child's birth and potential godparents is BL, Lansdowne MS 20, no. 51, f. 132r, 22 October 1575. Elizabeth's kinship with the Dudleys is outlined in Harvey, *The Cooke Sisters* (1981), p. 294, n. 48. Dering's letters to Katherine Killigrew are in Dering's *Certain Godly and Very Comfortable Letters* of 1590, printed in Dering, *Works* (1597); see letters dated 1575. Dering's death is also recounted in Dering, *Works* (1597), sigs. I4v–K1r; see also Collinson, *Godly People* (1983), pp. 318–19. Anthony Cooke's will is NA, PROB 11/59, f. 72r, 22 May 1576, with copy in BL, Lansdowne MS 23, no. 64, ff. 133r–142r. On the composition of the Cooke monument in Romford, see Russell, *The Writings*, ed. Phillippy (2011), pp. 158–70. On Cornelius Cure, see Llewellyn,

Funeral Monuments (2000), pp. 169–78 and 187. The English translation of the Cooke sisters' Latin epitaph is my own.

On Neville, see the entry in ODNB and Wallace, *Evolution of the English Drama* (1912), p. 130. For the repertoire of Farrant's players and accounts of their performances mentioned in this chapter, see Wallace, *Evolution of the English Drama* (1912), pp. 149–51, 206 and 218–20. On James Burbage, London's earliest temporary playhouses and the King's Wardrobe, see Bowsher, *Shakespeare's London Theatreland* (2012), pp. 29, 49 and 206. Farrant's acquisition of the theatre and the location of the properties belonging to Neville and Cobham are outlined in Smith, *Shakespeare's Blackfriars Playhouse* (1964), pp. 120–27, 130–41 and 148–50; Wallace, *Evolution of the English Drama* (1912), pp. 130–146; and Adams, 'The Conventual Buildings of Blackfriars . . .' (1917), pp. 66–82. I have calculated the relative position of Elizabeth Russell's house based on the location of the properties of Lord Cobham/Farrant, Philip Hoby and the Harper, Onslowe and Pitcher families as itemized in Feuillerat, *Blackfriars Records* (1913), pp. 27–35, 106–7 and 115–16 and on a comparison between these properties and those mentioned in the following: SHC, LM 348/68; SHC, LM 348/216; SHC, LM 348/234; and SHC, HC 6729/6/98 (itemized in full in the notes to chapter six). Neville's letter to More is SHC, HC 6729/1/71, 27 August 1571. Farrant's letter to More is FSL, Lb.466, 27 August 1576. An inquisition of 11 June 1571 which relates to the Harper, Onslowe and Pitcher properties and in addition mentions the late Philip Hoby's house was also useful: see Madge, ed., *Abstract of Inquisitiones Post Mortem* (1901), pp. 138–40. The lease for the property which Farrant acquired from More, itemizing the rental charges, is FSL, Lb.350, 20 December 1576; also printed in Feuillerat, *Blackfriars Records* (1913), pp. 28–35. More's displeasure is recounted in Adams, 'The Conventual Buildings of Blackfriars . . .' (1917), p. 81 and printed in Smith, *Shakespeare's Blackfriars Playhouse* (1964), p. 467. Elizabeth's residence in Westminster is revealed in a letter from Robert Allatt to Elizabeth, WAM, MS 5520, December 1578. Elizabeth's association with George Burden is recorded in WAM, MS 39412, 26 November 1576. George Burden's later involvement in Elizabeth's renovations to Westminster College is outlined in WAM, MS 40086, December 1585.

Chapter Eight: Meet the Neighbours

For the Blackfriars, particularly St Anne's, as a location favoured by goldsmiths and tradesmen, see Harkness, *The Jewel House* (2007), pp. 125–7. For examples of Renaissance automata, see Mauriès, *Cabinets of Curiosities* (2002). For the Blackfriars water conduits, see House, *The City of London* (1993), p. 126. The ceremony for Lord Russell's induction into the House of Lords is outlined in NA, SP 12/147, f. 18r. Elizabeth's Latin epitaph for Francis Russell is preserved on the tomb of John Russell, St Edmund's Chapel, Westminster Abbey. I have translated it myself. The renovations to Elizabeth's Blackfriars home are listed in her letter to William More, SHC, HC 6729/6/98, dated 9 August (probably around 1580–81). The location of the properties of Lewis de Mare and Peter Buram are identified in SHC, LM 348/68, 3 September 1570. Buram's property is also included in SHC, LM 346/216, 30 June 1591. Elizabeth's statements on the cost of purchasing and renovating the Blackfriars home are in her letter to William Cecil, BL, Lansdowne MS 10, no. 38, ff. 136r–137r. Gosson's observation is quoted from Wallace, *Children of the Chapel* (1908), p. 24, n. 1. The performance of *The Arraignment of Paris* is described in Smith, *Shakespeare's Blackfriars Playhouse* (1964), pp. 141–2, and Wallace, *Evolution of the English Drama* (1912), pp. 181–2 and 209. On the location of William More's mansion, see Adams, 'The Conventual Buildings of Blackfriars . . .' (1917), pp. 67–8 and Feuillerat, *Blackfriars Records* (1913), pp. 117–18.

Anne Farrant's letter to William More is FSL, Lb.448, 25 December 1580. For Leicester's support of Anne and Hunnis, see his letter to More, SHC LM COR/3/316, 19 September 1581. The transfer of the theatre to Evans and its subsequent history, as well as transcriptions of the documents which pertain to William More's legal battles, are presented in Wallace, *Evolution of the English Drama* (1912), pp. 156–77, with Anne's testimony outlining Cobham's support and the sale of her jewels to pay her debts taken from her 'Answer . . . to the bill of complaint of Will[ia]m Hunnis and John Newman', made on 27 January 1584, pp. 162–6.

For Puritan views of the plays, see Munday, *A Second and Third Blast* (1580), p. 56; Gosson, *Plays Confuted in Five Actions* (1582), sig. G6r; and Fenton, *A Form of Christian Policy* (1574), quoted in Chambers, *The Elizabethan Stage* (1923), vol. 4, p. 195. For Anne's claim that the Queen had been supportive, see Wallace, *Evolution of the English Drama* (1912), p. 159.

The privileges sought by Blackfriars residents are listed in NA, SP 12/137, no. 74, ff. 141r–142r, April 1580. On the battle of the Blackfriars inhabitants and the attempt to close Farrant's theatre in 1579, see House, *The City of London* (1993), pp. 127–38. The initial list of potential commissioners is FSL, Lb.382, which House dates to between 1572 and 1576. The names William More and Thomas Browne are clearly visible on the manuscript. The second list of commissioners, with the names of John Russell, Lord Cobham and William de Lawne, is included in NA, SP 12/137, no. 74, ff. 141r–142r.

Elizabeth was probably twice related to the Brownes of Betchworth: she was sister-in-law to Frances Grey (who married Elizabeth's brother William in 1569), niece of Anthony Browne, 1st Viscount Montagu (who met with Elizabeth and Thomas Hoby during their mission to Paris). Montagu was related to the Brownes of Betchworth Castle in Surrey, who probably also had a kinship with the Fitzwilliams on Elizabeth's mother's side of the family. See the potential relations of the following namesakes as outlined in the ODNB: Sir Anthony Browne (d. 1548); Anthony Browne, Viscount Montagu (d. 1592); William Fitzwilliam, Earl of Southampton (d. 1542); Sir William Fitzwilliam (d. 1559), a Gentleman of the Privy Chamber under Edward VI and father of Thomas Browne's first wife, Mabel Fitzwilliam; and Sir William Fitzwilliam (d. 1599), Lord Deputy of Ireland, born in Milton. These three William Fitzwilliams should not be confused with Elizabeth Russell's grandfather of the same name, but some, perhaps all, were kinsmen. See also the notes to chapter eighteen relating to Thomas Browne.

For Sir Thomas Browne's mustering of the 'shot' in Berkshire, see SHC, LM COR/3/428, 2 May 1588. Evidence that the two Thomas Brownes are the same, based on his association with both the Blackfriars and Betchworth Castle in Surrey, can be found in SHC, LM COR/3/427, 28 April 1588; SHC, LM COR/3/428, 2 May 1588; and SHC, LM COR/3/429, 10 May 1588. The charges of 'lewd and evil behaviour' are quoted in House, *The City of London* (1993), p. 135.

The Privy Council's verdict on City involvement in the Blackfriars is NA, PC 2/13, f. 13r, 15 May 1580. The Russells' responsibilities in the Blackfriars are derived largely from NA, SP 12/137, no. 74, ff. 141r–142r; from the leases I have read in SHC, which commonly reiterate these responsibilities; with additions from House, *The City of London* (1993), p. 139. The lives of Elizabeth Russell's petitioners and evidence of their presence in the Blackfriars are unearthed from: Kirk and Kirk, eds., *Returns of Aliens* (1900–1908), 4 vols., primarily vol. 2, pp. 179–82, 252–3, 291, 462 and vol. 3, pp. 49–51; Lang, ed., 'Two Tudor Subsidy Rolls for the City of London: 1541 and 1582' (1993), pp. 181–7; Scouloudi, *Returns of Strangers* (1985); the survey of 'strangers' in the Blackfriars organized by John Russell and William Brooke, Lord Cobham, HH, CP 208/7, 28 April 1583; Whitebrook, 'Huguenots of Blackfriars . . .' (1941), pp. 254–6; Register of Baptisms, St Anne's, Blackfriars, 1560–1700, vol. 1, LMA, MS 4508; Register of Marriages, St Anne's, Blackfriars, 1562–1726, vol. 1, LMA, MS 4509; and Register of Burials, St Anne's, Blackfriars, 1566–1700, vol. 1, LMA, MS 4510.

Elizabeth Russell's letter in which she describes Ascanius de Renialme is HH, CP 63/7, 10 July 1598. John Edwardes' presence in St Anne's is poignantly attested to by his appearance in the parish Register of Burials, in which he is recorded as having attended the funerals of two daughters and two servants between 25 August and 3 September 1582, probably during a plague outbreak. The previous year he had also buried a newborn baby. The Register of Baptisms for St Anne's reveals that John le Mere had baptized a daughter called Elizabeth on 1 May 1575, little over three months after Thomas Vautrollier had christened his son Thomas. A John Clarke appears on the 1582 Subsidy Rolls valued at £100. He was a 'clothworker' of St Matthew's parish who had clearly been doing a roaring trade, for the value of his holdings had increased by £20 since he was assessed in 1576. It is not clear if he is the same John Clarke who would go on to sign Elizabeth's petition. The 1599 rolls indicate that a John Clarke, residing in St Anne's, was valued at a more modest £5. See the 'Lay Subsidy Returns for London, Middlesex, Surrey (north) 1593–1600', transcribed by Alan H. Nelson at www.socrates.berkeley.edu/~ahnelson/SUBSIDY/subs. A Puritan physician named John Clarke (*c.*1582?–1653) was a resident of the Blackfriars, but he is unlikely to have been Elizabeth's petitioner, due to his age in 1596 and to the fact that he was studying at Cambridge University until around 1615.

On St Anne's as the administrative centre of the Blackfriars and the immigrant population statistics, see House, *The City of London* (1993), pp. 142–7. On de Renialme's background, profession and denization, see also ODNB entry (which includes George Bishop's assessment of him from Plantin-Moretus MS 77, f. 715r); Whitebrook, 'Huguenots of Blackfriars . . .' (1941), p. 255–6; and Elizabeth's own letter, HH, CP 63/7, 10 July 1598. On the Vautrolliers as clockmakers, see Whitebrook, 'Huguenots of Blackfriars . . .' (1941), p. 256. For background to William and Gideon de Lawne, see ODNB entries for 'Delaune, William' and 'Delaune, Gideon'. William de Lawne's dedicatory epistle which praises the Martins is in de Lawne, *An Abridgement of the Institution of Christian Religion* (1585), ff. 5v–6r.

The location of Richard Field's printing press relative to Elizabeth Russell's home has been calculated from the following: Richard Field's rental agreement with William and George More, SHC, LM 333/12, 22 September 1592; William de Lawne's purchase agreement with William and George More, FSL, Lb.349, 31 October 1593; and Paul Buck's two indentures, SHC, LM 348/216, 30 June 1591 and SHC, LM 348/234, 31 January 1594. These have been compared with Lewis de Mare's agreement with William More, SHC, LM 348/68, 3 September 1570 and Elizabeth's letter in SHC, HC 6729/6/98, 9 August, *c.*1580–81.

On Vautrollier's hiring of 'stranger' servants and workmen, see Worman, ed., *Alien Members of the Book Trade* (2006), pp. 67–8 and Kirk and Kirk, eds., *Returns of Aliens*

(1900–1908), vol. 2, p. 182. Fenton's promise to dedicate his *History* to Elizabeth Russell is from Fenton, trans., Pasquier, *Monophylo* (1572), sigs. A2r–A4r. For the influence of Fenton on Shakespeare, see Dobson and Wells, eds., *Oxford Companion to Shakespeare* (2001), p. 137 and Gillespie, *Shakespeare's Books* (2004), pp. 32–41. The commitment of John Russell and William Brooke, Lord Cobham, to protecting the rights of Blackfriars tradesmen is articulated in NA, SP 12/137, no. 74, ff. 121r–122r.

The location of Fontaine's home is derived from the indentures for lease agreements between Robert Baheire and William and George More, SHC, LM 333/1, 18 March 1590 and LM 348/205, 18 March 1590. For more on Fontaine, see Pollard, 'Claudius Hollyband . . .' (1915), pp. 255 and 263; HH, CP 208/7, 28 April 1583; Lang, ed., 'Two Tudor Subsidy Rolls for the City of London: 1541 and 1582' (1993), pp. 181–7; Kirk and Kirk, eds., *Returns of Aliens* (1900–1908), vol. 2, pp. 181 and 252; and Scouloudi, *Returns of Strangers* (1985). For Fontaine's editing of the *Loci Communes* and dedications to the Cookes, see Allen, *The Cooke Sisters* (2013), p. 22. The epitaphs composed by Fontaine and Elizabeth for Katherine Killigrew are preserved in Stow, *Survey of London* (1633), pp. 259–260 (I have translated the Latin epitaph by Elizabeth Russell). That Katherine was every bit as combative as her sister Elizabeth is revealed in her poem to Mildred Cecil, requesting that she persuade her husband, William, to allow Henry Killigrew to remain in their Cornwall home rather than be sent on a diplomatic mission abroad (recorded by Harington in his *Orlando Furioso* (1591; 1607 edition) and preserved in a contemporary translation by W. Kytton in CUL MS Ff.5.14, f. 107; see also Schleiner, *Tudor and Stuart Women Writers* (1994), p. 45:

> If Mildred thou return, my joy to me again,
> Thou shalt be good, and better too, my only sister then;
> But if thou him detain, and to the sea assign,
> Thou shalt be ill, and more than ill, no sister then of mine.
> To Cornwall if he come, great pleasure shall ensue,
> But if to sea, to Cecil then I war proclaim, Adieu.

Chapter Nine: The Widow and the Necromancer

William Andrew's account of John Russell's last days and his body's subsequent transportation for burial, along with Alexander Nowell's sermon, are recounted in BL, Egerton MS 2148, ff. 183r–184v (appended to the end of the manuscript version of Thomas Hoby's *Travels*). John Russell's death in Highgate is recorded in Burghley's papers, HH, CP 140/13, f. 15r. On John Cholmeley, see ODNB entry for Hugh Cholmeley and entry for 'Chomley, John', in Margaret Pelling and Frances White, *Physicians and Irregular Medical Practitioners in London: 1550–1640*, database by the University of London, Institute of Historical Research, 2004.

For Laski, and his relation to Dee and Kelly, see Woolley, *The Queen's Conjuror* (2002), pp. 207–39 and Dee, *The Diaries*, ed. Fenton (1998), pp. 332–4; see pp. 85–92 of the latter text for Dee's séances and the Earl of Leicester's involvement with Laski. On Laski's Oxford tour, Bruno's letter to the vice-chancellor, Bruno's lecture and the response to it, see Pellegrini, 'Giordano Bruno and Oxford' (1942), pp. 303–16; McNulty, 'Bruno at Oxford' (1960), pp. 300–305; Dee, *The Diaries*, ed. Fenton (1998), p. 92; and Woolley, *The Queen's Conjuror*

(2002), pp. 209–10. For Bruno's cosmology and a cautionary note about his 'progressivism', see Feingold, 'Giordano Bruno . . .' (2004), pp. 329–46 and Nicholl, *The Reckoning* (1992), p. 207. Elizabeth's contribution to Sylva's cosmological work is in CUL, MS Ii.5.37. Laski's time in Bisham is from Dee, *The Diaries*, ed. Fenton (1998), p. 92. Kelly's doubts about Laski and Elizabeth Russell's continuing involvement with Dee are described in Dee, *The Diaries*, ed. Fenton (1998), pp. 178, 255, 260, 264 and 266–7.

Elizabeth's letter to Lord Burghley is BL, Lansdowne MS 10, no. 38, ff. 136r–137r, dated 25 August, year uncertain, could be between 1584 and 1586 (my conjectural date-range); on the problems of dating this letter and the possibility that the day and month are also incorrect, see Russell, *The Writings*, ed. Phillippy (2011), p. 103, n. 35. On the wardship system, see Hurstfield, *The Queen's Wards* (1958). Elizabeth's revenues from her son's wardship are itemized in Harvey, *The Cooke Sisters* (1981), p. 255. The law of 'Covert Baron' is outlined in E[dgar], *The Law's Resolutions of Women's Rights* (1632), pp. 124–5. Elizabeth's reference to her Blackfriars home is in her letter to William More, SHC, HC 6729/6/98, 9 August (c.1580–81) and her attempts to purchase Poden and Chew are in her letter to William Cecil, BL, Lansdowne 33/85, ff. 203r–204v, 8 November 1581. Her calculations of the value of the Hoby manors are in both BL, Lansdowne MS 33/85, ff. 203r–204v and BL, Lansdowne MS 10, no. 38, ff. 136r–137r.

The account of John Russell's funeral is in the College of Arms manuscript of the 'Dethick Funerals', 1586–1603, MS 1, ff. 44r–45r and 215r–217r. A second copy is BL, Stowe MS 586, f. 2v. The funeral and epitaphs on John Russell's tomb are also transcribed in Russell, *The Writings*, ed. Phillippy (2011), pp. 135–46 and 171–7. I have provided my own English translations for the Latin epitaphs which Elizabeth commissioned for John Russell's monument in St Edmund's Chapel, Westminster Abbey. I would like to thank Dr Anthony Trowles, archivist at Westminster Abbey Library, for providing me with information about and transcriptions of Elizabeth's epitaphs on the Russell monuments. For Edward Hoby's concerns about his mother's emotional state at this time, see the exchange of letters between him and William Cecil: HH, CP 13/61, 1 October 1584 and HH, CP 163/59, 10 November 1584. For the early years of Shakespeare's marriage in Stratford-upon-Avon, see Weis, *Shakespeare Revealed* (2007), pp. 38–69 and Duncan-Jones, *Ungentle Shakespeare* (2001), pp. 16–22.

Chapter Ten: The Arden Trail

The account of Percy's death, the inquest and Henry Carey's involvement in the autopsy and official verdict are in Anon. (but probably written or orchestrated by William Cecil, Lord Burghley), *A True and Summary Report* (1585). For a gruesome image of Northumberland's death in a pro-Catholic work claiming he was assassinated, see Verstegan, *Theatrum Crudelitatum* (1587), p. 75. For more on *A True and Summary Report* and the circulation of rebuttals to this text, see Scoufos, *Shakespeare's Typological Satire* (1979), pp. 114–20. For the intrigues surrounding the Throckmorton Plot, see Guy, *My Heart is My Own* (2004), pp. 397–479, and Weir, *Elizabeth the Queen* (2008), pp. 331–59. On William Cecil's response to accusations that he and his coterie were at the centre of the conspiracy and had established what their enemies called a '*regnum Cecilianum*', see NA, SP 12/181, ff. 158r–160v, 14 August

1585. Elizabeth's letter to Cecil is BL, Lansdowne MS 10, no. 38, ff. 136r–137r (the dating of this letter is uncertain, but I believe it was composed in July 1585). On the Queen's presence at Edward Hoby's wedding, see Chambers, *The Elizabethan Stage* (1923), vol. 4, p. 99. See also ODNB entry for Edward Hoby. On Dee's relation to the Earls of Northumberland and on the 'Wizard Earl', see Nicholl, *The Reckoning* (1992), pp. 193–201. See also ODNB entry for Henry Percy, 9th Earl of Northumberland.

The Privy Council's decision about Francis Arden is NA, PC 2/14, f. 45r, April 1586. The record of the imprisonment of Francis Arden and other co-conspirators is NA, SP 12/178, ff. 173r–173v, 27 May 1585. The accusation of high treason is in NA, SP 12/167, ff. 91r–93r, 7 December 1583. Francis Arden's involvement in the plot is also mentioned in NA, SP 12/163, f. 63r, 31 October 1583. The astrological prophesy is in Holinshed, *The Third Volume of Chronicles* (1586), p. 1356. For potential Arden family relations, see ODNB entry for Edward Arden. On Francis Arden's role in the marriage of John Somerville and Margaret Arden, see the records of the Exchequer documents in bundle NA, E 133/7/983, 1591. For John Shakespeare's attempt to combine his coat of arms with those of the Park Hall Ardens and the report that the 'house of Arden [is] ruinated' (which is quoted from a letter by the Lord Paget to Mary, Queen of Scots), see Wilson, *Secret Shakespeare* (2004), pp. 104–7.

The quote from *Henry VI, Part 3*, also known as *Richard Duke of York*, is from Shakespeare, *The Norton Shakespeare*, eds. Greenblatt et al. (1997), 5.1.7–13. The Somerville–Arden conspiracy and the interrogations of the main suspects have been reconstructed from the following documents: NA, SP 12/163, f. 57r, 28 October 1583; NA, SP 12/164, ff. 81r–81v, 20 December 1583; NA, SP 12/163, f. 138r, 7 November 1585; NA, SP 12/163, f. 160r, 18 November 1583; NA, SP 12/163, f. 129r, 5 November 1583; NA, SP 12/164, f. 78r, 20 December 1583; NA, SP 12/163, f. 127r, 5 November 1583; NA, SP 12/163, ff. 140r–141r, 7 November 1583; NA, SP 12/163, f. 125r, 5 November 1583; and Wood, *In Search of Shakespeare* (2003), p. 92. See also Wilson, *Secret Shakespeare* (2004), pp. 104–25. The activities of Hall, Talbot, Howard and Arundel have been reconstructed from the following: BL, Cotton MS Caligula C/VIII, ff. 204r–206r, 23 November 1584; NA, SP 12/163, ff. 140r–141r, 7 November 1583; NA, SP 12/163, ff. 67r–67v, 31 October 1583; and NA, SP 12/164, ff. 141r–141v, 31 December 1583 (the last reveals that Hall's interrogators discovered that he had lived in Talbot's house for fourteen years). Elizabeth Russell's complaints against Conway are in her letter to William Cecil, BL, Lansdowne MS 33, no. 85, ff. 203r–204v, 8 November 1581. Lady Margery Throckmorton's testimony is NA, SP 12/164, ff. 16r–16v, 5 December 1583. Fryer's role as physician is reported in NA, SP 70/62, f. 183r, 26 August 1563. On the searching of Lady Throckmorton's home and an overview of her interrogations, see Alford, *The Watchers* (2012), pp. 159–61. Fryer's letter to Robert Cecil is HH, CP 118/159, 1606. Fryer's inclusion in the recusant list is HH, CP 48/46, 1596.

Hall's denial of familiarity with Francis Throckmorton is made in NA, SP 78/10, ff. 113r–115r, 27 December 1583. Evidence of Henry Brooke's former ambassadorial role in Paris can be found in BL, Harley MS 6993, f. 44r, 12 June 1583. Stafford's testimony is from NA, SP 15/28/1, f. 96r, 2 December 1583 and NA, SP 78/10, ff. 113r–115r, 27 December 1583. On the sentencing of Somerville and Arden, Somerville's suicide and the sparing of Somerville's wife, see Holinshed, *The Third Volume of Chronicles* (1586), p. 1356 and NA, SP 94/2, f. 20r, December 1583. The intercepted intelligence about Somerville is in NA, SP 12/185, ff. 131r–131v, 1585. Mary, Queen of Scots' denial is in HH, CP 133/36, 28 January 1584.

Cecil's account is taken from *The Execution of Justice* (1584), sig. D4v. Vautrollier is identified as the printer of the Latin and French editions of the *Execution*; see Cecil, *Justitia Britannica per quam liquet perspicue* (1584) and Cecil, *L'execution de iustice* (1584). Wolfe is identified as the printer of the Italian edition; see Cecil, *Atto della Giustitia d'Inghilterra* (1584). On the execution of Arden and the inclusion of the Somerville–Arden conspiracy among the plots involving Throckmorton, Carter and Parry, see the following: Munday, *A Watchword to England* (1584), pp. 34–5; Holinshed, *The Third Volume of Chronicles* (1586), p. 1356; Crompton, *A Short Declaration* (1587), pp. C1r–C3r; Stow, *The Abridgement* (1618), pp. 348–52; Camden, *Annals* (1625), pp. 47–8; Cecil, *A Collection* (1675), pp. 70–72; and ODNB entries on these figures. On the intrigues surrounding the Throckmorton Plot and the principal conspirators' association with the Duke of Guise, see BL, Additional MS 48029, ff. 64v–68r, 1583–4.

The manuscript outlining the gossip involving Francis Russell and John Talbot of Grafton is NA, SP 12/179, f. 3r, 3 June 1585. The papers dealing with Francis Russell the younger's troubles with the 8th Earl of Northumberland over Tynemouth Castle are: for the argument over castle revenues, see NA, SP 15/29, f. 14r, 27 April 1585; NA, SP 15/29, f. 18r, 16 May 1585; and NA, SP 15/29, f. 20r, 23 May 1585; and for a list of the Earl of Northumberland's reasons for refusing to give up the keys to the castle, see NA, SP 15/28/2, f. 144r. Francis Russell's letter to Walsingham outlining his surveillance of the port is SP 15/29, f. 18r, dated 16 May 1585. Walsingham's account of the 8th Earl of Northumberland's death is NA, SP 52/347, f. 73r, 23 June 1585. Francis Russell the younger's response is NA, SP 15/29, f. 27r, 26 June 1585. On the Duke of Guise's plot to rescue Northumberland, see Edward Wotton's letter to Walsingham, NA, SP 52/37, no. 352, ff. 97r–97v, 22 July 1585.

Elizabeth Russell's letter reporting news of the death is BL, Lansdowne MS 10, no. 38, ff. 136r–137r. This letter is dated 25 August but without indication of year and is often interpreted as reporting the death of her husband, John Russell. Elizabeth precedes the news with the words: 'If your lordship hear that I marry, think it not strange, for I live without comfort of any living, God and yourself excepted. All other I find more cumbrous and dangerous than comfortable.' This strongly suggests that she was already widowed when the letter was written. It is possible, therefore, that the letter reports the death of her father-in-law, Francis Russell, 2nd Earl of Bedford, in July 1585 and that, in her distress, she had written 'xxvth' instead of 'xxviiiith' for the day, also giving the incorrect month. The details of Francis Russell the younger's assassination and fears of a plot by the Percys are derived from NA, SP 52/38, f. 6r, 5 August 1585; NA, SP 59/23, f. 219r, 31 July 1585; and NA, SP 53/16, no. 104, ff. 51r–51v, 8 October 1585.

The report of the peculiar incident involving Elizabeth Russell and the confession of James Parrys is derived from NA, SP 12/294, ff. 66r–67r, 14 October 1586. On the Flanders mission and the Earl of Leicester's role in it, see the following dispatches for September 1586: NA, SP 84/10/1, f. 85r; NA, SP 84/10/1, f. 122r; and NA, SP 84/10/1, f. 85r. For the 'Act of Surety of the Queen's Person', see Tanner, ed., *Tudor Constitutional Documents* (1951), pp. 413–21.

The document detailing the Privy Council's consideration of John Yates's petition is NA, PC 2/28, f. 61r, 20 July 1615. The investigations into William Carter's activities, the searching of his home and his seditious output are derived from BL, Additional MS 48029, ff. 58r–72r, 1583–4; BL, Lansdowne MS 28, f. 177r, 30 December 1579; and NA, PC 2/13, f. 415, 14 June 1581. P.H.W.'s report is NA, SP 12/154, f. 107r, 19 July 1582. On Carter's execution and encouragement of Catholic women, see his ODNB entry.

The voluminous case between Francis Throckmorton and Francis Arden and his accomplices is in the Records of the Court of Star Chamber, NA, STAC 5/T4/23, 1587. For a letter suggesting that a member of the Fitzwilliam family had a connection to a 'Mr Burden', see NA, SP 15/3, f. 61r, 22 October 1566. On the role of a 'Mr Burden' in the funerals of Elizabeth's husbands, see College of Arms MS 1, 13, ff. 77r–78v (Thomas Hoby) and College of Arms, 'Dethick Funerals', 1586–1603, MS 1, ff. 44r–45r and 215r–217r, with copy in BL, Stowe MS 586, f. 2v (John Russell). George Burden's role as intercessor for Elizabeth is in WAM, MS 39412, 26 November 1576. Elizabeth's renovations to Westminster College, with George Burden as intermediary, are itemized in WAM, MS 40086, December 1585. On the George Burden who was Cecil's 'servant', see the Latin letter in SP 10/15, f. 112r, 27 November 1552 (translation from CSP Domestic, 1547–53, Edward VI, ed. Knighton (1992), p. 275). On the Crown's suit against Francis Arden, see records of the Exchequer documents pertaining to the case in NA, E 133/7/983, 1591.

Chapter Eleven: The Queen's Soldier

The role of Keeper of Castle is defined in Kitchin, *Jurisdictions* (1651), p. 408. On escuage, see Wyrley, *The True Use of Armoury* (1592), p. 19 and OED. On representations of Elizabeth I and fantasies of female power in works such as Spenser's *The Faerie Queene*, see Hackett, *Virgin Mother* (1995). Elizabeth Russell's bribes to the Queen are itemized in her letter to Robert Cecil, HH, CP 178/132, 5 March 1600. For Elizabeth's grant, legal rights and posts in Donnington, see Hawarde, *Les Reportes*, ed. Baildon, (1894), pp. 434–5.

Elizabeth's appeal to the Earl of Leicester is quoted in Russell, *The Writings*, ed. Phillippy (2011), p. 7. On the Queen's possession of Edward Russell's wardship, see NA, SP 12/193, f. 84r, 12 September 1586 and NA, SP 12/195, f. 93r, December[?] 1586. For the Earl of Leicester's appeal for joint wardship, see NA, SP 12/181, ff. 145r–145v, 12 August 1585 and NA, SP 15/29, f. 64r, 5 September 1585. The Earl of Warwick's petition to Francis Walsingham is NA, SP 12/181, f. 238r, 31 August 1585. Anne Dudley's own missive to Walsingham is NA, SP 12/182, f. 115r, 29 September 1585. For the terms of Elizabeth Russell's legal dispute over the Bedford inheritance, see College of Arms, Vincent MS 92, ff. 260r–262r; HH, CP 1949, c.May 1593; Russell, *Letters*, ed. Farber (1977), p. 115–18; Russell, *The Writings*, ed. Phillippy (2011), p. 117, nn. 8–9; and Popham, *Reports and Cases* (1656), pp. 3–4. Elizabeth Russell's own letter to William Cecil outlining her case is College of Arms, Vincent MS 92, f. 263r, c.1590. The surveys commissioned by Elizabeth Russell include that itemized by John Hare, sent to Elizabeth, in HH, CP 146/54, 5 March 1586 and the accounts of the late Earl of Bedford's lands as itemized for 'heirs general' in HH, CP 146/82, 1585; HH, CP 146/83, 1585; HH, CP 146/96, 1585; and HH, CP 146/98, 29 December 1585. Money paid in rents to the Court of Wards from these lands is itemized in HH, CP 146/61, 1 March 1586. A summary of the value of the late Earl of Bedford's estates, written in William Cecil's hand, is in HH, CP 146/74, 1585. On Edward Russell's sickly state, see NA, SP 15/29, f. 64r, 5 September 1585. On the Countess of Warwick's control of Edward's inheritance, see NA, SP 12/199, f. 32r, 6 March 1587 and NA, SP 12/202, f. 53r, June 1587. Elizabeth's attempt to change Edward Russell's coat of arms is in her letter to William Cecil, College of Arms, Vincent MS 92, f. 263r, c.1590. For 'difference' as heraldic term, see OED. On Elizabeth's gaining of her daughters' wardship and the right to occupy Bedford House as the Queen's tenant, see NA, SP 12/83, f. 135r, 1591 (this is misdated in CSP to 1571). A further summary of the Queen's provision for Elizabeth's daughters from the Bedford estates is itemized in HH, CP, 146/88, 1585.

The account of Elizabeth's Bisham entertainments for the Queen is derived from Russell, *Speeches Delivered to Her Majesty This Last Progress* (1592; Bisham entertainment), sigs. A2r–A4v. The Queen's Progress schedule, including her sojourn at Elizabeth Russell's Bisham home, is itemized in Chambers, *The Elizabethan Stage* (1923), vol. 4, pp. 106–7. On the background to the crisis in France at this time, see Rady, *France* (1988), pp. 94–5 and Knecht, *The French Wars* (1996), pp. 76–7. For Locke's dedicatory epistle to Anne Russell, see her *Of the Marks of the Children of God* (1590), sigs. A2r–A4r. Sandford's praise of Locke and the Cooke sisters as a cohesive group is in his *Hours of Recreation* (1576), sigs. A4v–A7v. On the impact of Locke, see Laoutaris, 'Translation/Historical Writing' (2010), pp. 306–12 and White, 'Renaissance Englishwomen . . .' (1999), pp. 375–400. Verstegan's suspicions are in *Declaration* (1592), p. 12. For the proceedings at Mildred Cecil's funeral and Elizabeth's role in it, see HH, CP 203/88, 21 April 1589. For Anne's final years, see Stewart, 'The Voices of Anne Cooke . . .' (2000), pp. 88–102. The audit of Blackfriars 'strangers' undertaken by Elizabeth's husband and Lord Cobham is HH, CP 208/7, 28 April 1583. Richard Field's marriage is recorded in the Register of Marriages, St Anne's, Blackfriars, 1562–1726, vol. 1, LMA, MS 4509.

For Horace's farm, see Horace, *Satires, Epistles*, trans. Fairclough (1926), p. xi. For examples of Elizabeth Russell's uses of Horace, see poem to Robert Cecil adapted from Horace's *Epistles*, HH, CP 175/118, 22 October 1597; letter to Robert Cecil, quoting Horace, HH, CP 175/92, c.June 1597; and letter to Robert Cecil, quoting Horace, HH, CP 179/92, October 1599. For other readings of Elizabeth Russell's Bisham entertainment, see Kolkovich, 'Lady Russell . . .' (2009), pp. 290–314; Johnston, 'The "Lady of the Farme" . . .' (2002), pp. 71–85; and Laoutaris, 'The Radical Pedagogies . . .' (2011), pp. 69–70.

For Sir John Wolley, see ODNB. For missives to More, Whitgift and Browne from Bisham Abbey, see SHC, HC 6729/10/86, 13 August 1592. The instructions to the Earl of Huntingdon are in NA, SP 12/242, f. 192r, 13 August 1592. For the activities of the Lord Admiral, Charles Howard at Elizabeth's home during this time, see his letter to William More, SHC, HC 6729/7/89, 14 August 1592 (his manipulation of 'secret intelligence' to protect his interests in Surrey indicates his possessiveness over his lands, a trait which would later fuel his clan warfare with Elizabeth). Elizabeth's role in Fryer's career is outlined in HH, CP 118/159, 1606. Allatt's letter to Elizabeth is WAM, MS 5520, December 1578. For Mildmay's posts and lands, see ODNB. Allatt's association with Mildmay, his travels abroad and his infiltration of Lady Bothwell's home are derived from the following documents: intelligence on Catholic recusants, including contents of papers supplied by Allatt, NA, SP 12/226, ff. 121r–124v, September[?] 1589; Allatt's report to William Cecil from Venice, NA, SP 99/1, f. 84r, November 1589; notes by Thomas Phellipes on Allatt's progress in Scotland, NA, SP 12/240, ff. 230r–231v, c.1591; Allatt's letter to William Cecil, NA, SP 12/238, f. 203r, April[?] 1591; and Robert Bowes' missive to William Cecil about Allatt's activities, NA, SP 52/47 f. 40r, 13 April 1591.

Thomas Fowler's reports to William Cecil are HH, CP 18/15, 7 October 1589 and HH, CP 18/55, 20 October 1589. The list of the Earl of Leicester's servants, compiled 21 July 1587, on which Jean Hotman appears is BL, Cotton MS Galba *C VIII*, f. 102r. For a biography of

Hotman, see Adams, *Household Accounts and Disbursement Books* (1995), pp. 475–6. For more on the 'Ryalta' affair involving Lady Rich and the Earl of Essex, see Laoutaris, '"Toucht with bolt of Treason" . . .' (2013), pp. 201–36.

Chapter Twelve: Closing Ranks

The episcopal visitation record which reveals Richard Field's role as 'sideman' alongside Robert Baheire and the posts of Thomas Holmes and Robert Donckin is LMA, MS 9537, vol. 8, f. 77r, 1592. Donckin's role as constable in 1583 is in HH, CP 208/7, 28 April 1583. That Donckin rented property very close to Richard Field is revealed in his lease agreement, SHC, LM 333/3, 18 March 1590; this lease reveals that Donckin had become a 'cordwainer' by trade (working with cordovan leather, perhaps as a shoemaker). Stephen Egerton's identification as 'lecturer', and his involvement with John Dollin in the episcopal investigation, are preserved in LMA, MS 9537, vol. 7, 1589, f. 106v. The consecration and rededication of St Anne's after its reconstruction, along with the posts of William Watts and Henry Boice, are listed in the Latin record LMA, MS 9531, vol. 13, part 2, f. 297r (the translations are my own). For the church's rebuilding, see also Burch, 'The Parish of St Anne's . . .' (1969), pp. 5 and 11 (which also includes an account of Stephen Egerton's non-conformism on pp. 22–3) and Smith, *Shakespeare's Blackfriars Playhouse* (1964), p. 122. The record revealing Richard Field's role as a church warden of St Anne's, alongside Edward Ley, is LMA, MS 9537, vol. 9, f. 158r, 1598. Richard Field was also sworn in as one of the 'jurati' or 'swornmen', faithfully promising on oath to do his duty. I would like to thank Arnold Hunt (British Library), Richard Rex (Cambridge University) and John Craig (Simon Fraser University, Canada) for their feedback on the Latin abbreviations in these manuscripts. I owe my knowledge of the specific role of the 'oeconomi' and 'jurati' to John Craig.

Greene's account of Shakespeare is *Greene's Groatsworth of Wit* (1592), sig. F1v; John Wolfe was involved in the printing of this work. The account of the Southwark riot is derived from William Webbe's letters to William Cecil, BL, Lansdowne MS 71, no. 15, f. 28r, 12 June 1592 and BL, Lansdowne MS 71, no. 17, f. 32r, 11 July 1592. The anti-immigrant slogan is quoted from Nicholl, *The Lodger* (2007), p. 178. On Katherine Killigrew's support of the French Church, see Collinson, *Godly People* (1983), p. 263. Anne Bacon's praise of the French preachers is LPL, MS 651, f. 310r, 3 August 1595; see also f. 326r of the same manuscript collection for Anne's further support of the French Church. The extracts from *Sir Thomas More* are from the 'Passages Attributed to Shakespeare', reproduced in Shakespeare, *The Norton Shakespeare*, eds. Greenblatt et al. (1997), pp. 2015–19, Add.II.D, ll. 1–161; for the context of the play's original composition and its censorship, see Walter Cohen's introduction to the play in ibid., pp. 2011–14. The scene described in Marlowe's *Massacre at Paris* is from Marlowe, *The Complete Plays*, ed. Steane (1986), 2.3. For the context and staging history of the play, see Nicholl, *The Reckoning* (1992), pp. 41–2 and 170–73 and Henslowe, *Diary*, ed. Foakes (2002), pp. 20–24, 76, 82 and 183–7.

Robert Baheire's business activities and the location of his home relative to that of Robert la Fontaine are calculated from his lease agreements with William and George More, SHC, LM 333/1, 18 March 1590 and SHC, LM 348/205, 18 March 1590. For Baheire's attachment to the French Church in 1582–3, see Kirk and Kirk, eds., *Returns of Aliens* (1900–1908), vol. 2, p. 291. For Fontaine's association with the French Church, see Scouloudi, *Returns of Strangers* (1985), p. 190. For the Mores' willingness to accept from Baheire a 'beaver felt', see the attached note to his lease agreement, SHC, LM 348/205. Baheire's role as assistant in St Anne's Church is itemized in LMA, MS 9537, vol. 8, f. 77r, 1592.

The directive sent to Lord Cobham and the Surrey Justices of the Peace is recorded in Chambers, *The Elizabethan Stage* (1923), vol. 4, p. 310, 23 June 1592. The Privy Council missive sent to William More and William Gardiner is NA, PC 2/19, f. 466r, 9 July 1592; that sent to George More, William Gardiner and Richard Martin is NA, PC 2/19, f. 474r, 15 July 1592.

Chapter Thirteen: Sheriff and Bailiff of the Manor

Elizabeth Russell's letter to William Cecil is HH, CP 170/54, before 25 March 1593. I follow Phillippy in dating this letter based on the beginning of the legal year in England being Lady Day, 25 March; see also Russell, *The Writings*, ed. Phillippy (2011), pp. 109–12. Elizabeth restated her request in a letter to Robert Cecil, HH, CP 170/53, c.May 1593. Robert Cecil's note to Elizabeth is scrawled on one of her own letters to him, which he had returned to her, HH, CP 1949, c.May 1593. The latter epistle is the one in which Elizabeth demands that the judges deliver their 'opinions in writing'. Elizabeth's outrage against Lady Warwick is expressed in her letter to William Cecil, NA, SP 12/245, f. 36, 23 May 1593. Her accusation regarding the burning of the Earl of Bedford's original will is made in HH, CP 90/151, December 1601.

Elizabeth's letter to William Cecil itemizing the value of her daughters' meagre estates is NA, SP/245, f. 36r, 23 May 1593. Elizabeth's legal battle for Chalden Hering and Chadwell is outlined in Popham, *Reports and Cases* (1656), pp. 3–4. For the dispute over Carlisle House, see the account of rents belonging to Elizabeth for the manor in NA, SP 12/206, f. 117r, December 1587; see also SP 12/83, f. 135r, 1591 for the provision of Bedford properties to Elizabeth and her daughters. The total value of the properties left to Bess and Nan Russell is based on the calculations made by William Cecil on the back of Elizabeth's letter NA, SP 12/245, ff. 36v–37r, 23 May 1593; see also corresponding CSP entry. The girls were, in addition, promised an inheritance from their aunt Jane Sibylla Russell Grey, widow of Edward Russell, 3rd Baron Russell, after her death. Elizabeth valued this, in her own letter, at £56. Jane died in 1615. See also Russell, *Letters*, ed. Farber (1977), p. 116. The political activities of Edward and Thomas Posthumous Hoby are from their biographical entries in Hasler, ed., *The History of Parliament* (1981). Elizabeth's complaints about raising the Russell girls with limited funds are from NA, SP 12/245, f. 36r.

On the relation between Charles Howard and Henry Carey, see their entries in the ODNB. The dispute between Elizabeth Russell and the Lovelace family is reconstructed from the following Star Chamber records of the case: NA, STAC 5/L4/26, containing 1. testimony of Anne Lovelace, 2. testimony of Elizabeth Russell, 3. testimony of Richard Lovelace; NA, STAC 5/R15/31, containing the answer of Lawrence Heyden and others to Elizabeth Russell's complaint; STAC 5/R36/31, containing 1. list of questions to be asked of the witnesses in court, 2. notes of the witness testimonies of Richard Lovelace,

Lawrence Heyden and others; Elizabeth Russell's petition to the Privy Council, addressed directly to William Cecil, against Richard Lovelace, which also contains details of Lovelace's attempt to evict her from Windsor, NA, SP 12/245, f. 217r; and Elizabeth's petition to the Privy Council in HH, CP 186/135, October 1594. I believe that the CSP has misdated Elizabeth's petition in the state papers (SP 12/245, f. 217r) to 1593, based on her claim that the incident had taken place 'On Monday the first of October'. It is likely that Elizabeth misremembered the date, since the trial documents reveal that the events took place on 30 September 1594. This was also a Monday. The petition in Hatfield House makes it evident that Elizabeth was not entirely clear about the date, stating that the events in question had taken place 'about the beginning of the instant month of October' (HH, CP 186/135). The State Papers petition and its conjectural dating in the CSP has resulted in the misdating of this important incident in Elizabeth Russell's life.

Edward Coke's assessment of Elizabeth's case is HH, CP 28/94, 16 October 1594. That Elizabeth interrogated Hide in the presence of witnesses is revealed in her angry letter to Francis Gawdy, FSL, X.c.87. I have based my reading of this very damaged manuscript on the transcription with useful interpolations by Patricia Phillippy and Heather Wolfe in Russell, *The Writings*, ed. Phillippy (2011), pp. 119–21. I have dated the letter to late 1595, because it refers to incidents which are revealed in the trial documents to have taken place before that date and because the case for Langley Parsonage terminated in 1595. Elizabeth's battle for King's Langley is derived from the Chancery records, NA, C 2/248/17, comprising 1. Elizabeth Russell's testimony, 2. John Kettle's testimony; and the record of the Office of the Auditors' of Land Revenue, which shows Elizabeth's signature on the document surrendering the manor to the Queen, NA, LR 14/1003. See also NA, C 78/87/4 for more on the conflict between Elizabeth Russell and John Kettle. For more on the Seven Hundreds of Cookham and Bray, see VCH, Berkshire, vol. 3, eds. P.H. Ditchfield and William Page (1923), pp. 137–8. The translation and context of the Greek inscription on Elizabeth's Bisham Abbey portrait are taken from Parker, *The Holy Bible* (1568).

Chapter Fourteen: Building Ambitions

Elizabeth's submission to Martin, suggesting that she had undertaken a renovation and building project to her Blackfriars home (revealed here for the first time), is included in the 'Book of Grants', vol. 1, 1589–1616, LMA, CLA/008/EM/02/01, f. 18r, 1 August 1595. For Richard Martin's official posts, see White, 'A Biographical Sketch . . .' (1999), pp. 775–92. Elizabeth Russell was also busy with other local property disputes at this time, over 'the possession of . . . manors, lands, and tenements', including her engagement in cases between her and George Harvey and Peter Haughton, the last an Alderman of London; see Somerset Heritage Centre: MSS DD/MI/18/54, 11 July 1595 and DD/MI/18/55, 1595.

It has previously been thought that Bess and Nan Russell were both 'maids of honour'. Jane Lawson has discovered that this was not the case; see Lawson, 'The Queen's Maids . . .' (2013). I would like to thank Jane Lawson for supplying me with information about the Russell girls' actual posts. Elizabeth Russell's comment about her daughters' closeness to the Queen is from Elizabeth's letter to Henry Brooke, who succeeded his father as Lord

Cobham, NA, SP 12/255, f. 36r, September 1599. Elizabeth's desire that her daughters keep writing to her is indicated in her letter HH, CP 68/11, January 1596 (she is particularly upset that Bess has neglected to write). For the Accession Day Tilt, Wotton's comment and the Queen's reaction see, Strong, *The Cult of Elizabeth* (1999), pp. 139–46 and Weir, *Elizabeth the Queen* (2008), p. 420. Elizabeth Russell's letter to Robert Cecil outlining tensions with the Queen and other female courtiers is NA, SP 12/255, f. 37r, December 1595.

Cartwright's letter to Elizabeth Russell is BL, Lansdowne MS 68, ff. 131r–132r, 13 August 1591. For more on William Cecil's involvement in Cartwright's release, see Pearson, *Thomas Cartwright* (1925), pp. 346–7 and 357. On the complexities surrounding the Cecils' religious beliefs, see Hurstfield, 'Church and State . . .' (1965), pp. 119–40 and Croft, 'The Religion of Robert Cecil' (1991), pp. 773–96. For Stephen Egerton's presence in the Blackfriars, see Burch, 'The Parish of St Anne's . . .' (1969), pp. 5–11, 22–3 and its appendix table of St Anne's ministers. On the conference of Puritan ministers, see Collinson, *Elizabethan Puritan Movement* (1967), p. 412. The potential location of Egerton's home and its relative position to Elizabeth Russell's home and Shakespeare's Blackfriars Theatre has been calculated from Feuillerat, *Blackfriars Records* (1913), pp. 94 and 126 and the following leases and indentures: SHC, LM 348/68, 3 September 1570 (Lewis de Mare); SHC, LM 348/216, 30 June 1591 (Paul Buck); SHC, LM 348/234, 31 January 1594 (Paul Buck); SHC, LM 333/12, 22 September 1592 (Richard Field); FSL, Lb.349, 31 October 1593 (William de Lawne); and Elizabeth Russell's letter to William More, SHC, HC 6729/6/98, 9 August, c.1580–81[?]. More's post as Chamberlain of the Exchequer is recorded in Smith, *Shakespeare's Blackfriars Playhouse* (1964), p. 156.

On Nowell and Wharton, see ODNB entries for both. Wharton's dedicatory epistle to Nowell is in his *Wharton's Dream* (1578); see also his letter 'To the Christian Reader' (Wharton's period of exile during the Marian persecutions is also described in his prefatory material to this text). Wharton contributed an epistle 'To the Christian Reader' to Smith's *A Mystical Devise* (1575), from which the latter quotation is taken. John Wharton's presence in St Anne's in the Blackfriars is attested to in the 1599 Subsidy Rolls; see the returns for those living in the ward of Farringdon Within in 'Lay Subsidy Returns for London, Middlesex, Surrey (north) 1593–1600', transcribed by Alan H. Nelson at www.socrates.berkeley. edu/~ahnelson/SUBSIDY/subs. Egerton's female congregation and his sermon are recorded in Manningham, *Diary*, ed. Bruce (1868), pp. 101–2 and 74 respectively. Donne's *Courtier's Library* is reproduced in Brown ' "*Hac ex consilio meo via progredieris*" . . .' (2009), pp. 833–66. On the history of St Anne's Church and its congregation, see Stow, *A Survey of London* (1598; 2005 edition), p. 291. For the rebuilding and rededication of the church, see LMA, MS 9531, vol. 13, part 2, f. 297r. The rebuilding and the location of William de Lawne's pew are detailed in Burch, 'The Parish of St Anne's . . .' (1969), pp. 11 and 17.

Elizabeth's letter to Robert Cecil on behalf of William Day is HH, CP 25/51, 24 February 1595. On the Queen's fury, see Day's letter to Robert Cecil, with enclosure itemizing his poverty and debts, HH, CP 30/80 and CP 30/81, 20 February 1596. See also Russell, *Letters*, ed. Farber (1977), pp. 141–2, which gives an account of the careers of Bourne and Boxall on p. 143, n. 3. Elizabeth's attempt to bribe the Queen, her account of the New Year's gifts to her daughters and her praise of Robert Cecil's qualities as a courtier are derived from her letters to the last, NA, SP 12/255, f. 37r, December 1595 and HH, CP 68/11, January 1596. Bess Russell would later become involved in some courtly sexual intrigue involving Essex, as reported by Rowland White in Collins, ed., *Letters and Memorials of State* (1746), vol. 2, pp. 38–9; also Devereux, *Lives and Letters* (1853), vol. 1, pp. 475–6. On the possibility that the 'Mistress Russell' who was the subject of these scandals became Essex's mistress, see Lacey, *Robert, Earl of Essex* (1971), pp. 59–60. On Bess Russell as the 'Mistress Russell' in question, see Borman, *Elizabeth's Women* (2009), p. 365–6.

The account of the Essex House dinner party is from a letter by Anthony Standen to Anthony Bacon, LPL, MS 651, no. 68, f. 111r. For Standen's career, see Lea, 'Sir Anthony Standen . . .' (1932), pp. 461–77. Pérez's controversial life is recorded in his, *A Spaniard in Elizabethan England*, ed. Ungerer (1974–6). The payments to Pérez are outlined in LPL, MS 651, no. 68, f. 111r; for a printed version of the 'Expenses of the Earl of Essex for the Maintenance of Antonio Pérez', see Pérez, *A Spaniard in Elizabethan England*, ed. Ungerer (1974–6), vol. 1, pp. 295–6. For a survey of the many poets who have composed works either dedicated or alluding to Lady Rich, see Hudson, 'Penelope Devereux as Sidney's Stella' (1935), pp. 89–129; see also Craig, *The Amorous Songs*, (1606), sig. C3v. For more on Lady Rich, see Freedman, *Poor Penelope* (1983) and Varlow, *The Lady Penelope* (2007). The gifts from Lady Rich are mentioned in Hammer, *The Polarization of Elizabethan Politics* (1999), p. 310 and Pérez, *A Spaniard in Elizabethan England*, ed. Ungerer (1974–6), vol. 1, p. 82, n. 4.

On Essex's secretaries, see Hammer, 'The Uses of Scholarship . . .' (1994), pp. 26–51. The utility of Pérez and his motto are in Camden, *Annals* (1625), pp. 103–6. Essex's letter discovering the 'treason' and identifying López as the Queen's would-be 'executioner' is LPL, MS 653, no. 171, f. 312r. For more on the López plot and on Cecil's nickname of 'Roberto il Diavolo', see Devereux, *Lives and Letters* (1853), vol. 1, pp. 307–10 and 442 and Read, *Lord Burghley* (1960), pp. 497–9. Pérez's letter to Lady Rich is translated by Alexander Samson (University College London), from the Spanish published in Pérez, *A Spaniard in Elizabethan England*, ed. Ungerer (1974–6), vol. 1, no. 48, pp. 87–9. On Anthony Bacon's involvement in procuring Pérez's services for Essex, see LPL, MS 651, no. 68, f. 111r. On Anthony Bacon's career, see Harrison, *The Life and Death of Robert Devereux* (1937), p. 71, and du Maurier, *Golden Lads* (1975; 2007 edition). Anne Bacon's warnings are taken from her letters LPL, 653, no. 187, f. 330r; LPL, MS 653, no. 175, f. 318r; and LPL, MS 653, no. 177, f. 320r.

On the closure of the theatres due to the plague, see Chambers, *The Elizabethan Stage* (1923), vol. 4, pp. 313–16. On the publishing history and reception of Shakespeare's *Venus and Adonis* and *Rape of Lucrece*, see Straznicky, ed., *Shakespeare's Stationers* (2013), pp. 19–20, 114–16, 251–4 and 274 and Dobson and Wells, eds., *Oxford Companion to Shakespeare* (2001), pp. 510–12 and 367–8 respectively. On the acquaintance of the Field and Shakespeare families in Stratford, see Shapiro, *1599* (2005), p. 150. For a sustained account of Shakespeare's association with Southampton, see Akrigg, *Shakespeare and the Earl of Southampton* (1968). Shakespeare's dedicatory epistle to Southampton is in his *Rape of Lucrece* (1594), sig. A2r. On Southampton's role in the Somerville–Arden plot, see Wood, *In Search of Shakespeare* (2003), p. 147. For Southampton's relation to Elizabethan Catholic intrigues, see also Wilson, *Secret Shakespeare* (2004), pp. 134–41. Southampton's receipt of Pérez's *Relaciones* is mentioned in Akrigg, *Shakespeare and the Earl of Southampton* (1968), p. 37. The quotations from *Love's Labours Lost* are taken from Shakespeare, *The Norton Shakespeare*, eds. Greenblatt et al. (1997), 1.1.163–9 and 5.1.14–15. Lady Rich's request for news about Pérez from Anthony Bacon is from her letter LPL, MS 657, no. 46, f. 61r, 13 May 1596. Bacon's response to Lady Rich's request is LPL, MS 657, no. 88, ff. 133r–133v, 15 May 1596. White's assessment of the relationship between Essex and Southampton is in Collins, ed., *Letters and Memorials of State* (1746), vol. 2, p. 62. His gossip about Southampton's courting of Elizabeth Vernon is in Collins, ed., *Letters and Memorials of State* (1746), vol. 1, p. 348. On the Devereux' involvement in the clandestine marriage of Southampton and Elizabeth Vernon, see Devereux, *Lives and Letters* (1853), vol. 1, p. 474.

For Henry Carey's appeal to Richard Martin and a transcript of his letter (from which the quotes here are taken), see Gurr, 'Henry Carey's Peculiar Letter' (2005), pp. 51–75, with transcription of letter on p. 54. Martin's machinations against the theatre, along with the other Surrey Justices of the Peace, are revealed in Chambers, *The Elizabethan Stage* (1923), vol. 4, p. 310; NA, PC 2/19, f. 466r, 9 July 1592; and NA, PC 2/19, f. 474r, 15 July 1592. For Martin's activities with the Vautrolliers and French ministers, see BL, Additional MS 4736, f. 166v; also White, 'A Biographical Sketch . . .' (1999), pp. 775–92. Burbage's service under Carey is outlined in Gurr, *The Shakespeare Company* (2004), p. 1. Carey's letter to William More is quoted from Wallace, *The Evolution of the English Drama* (1912), pp. 195–6. The lease agreement between William More and James Burbage is FSL, Lb.356, 4 February 1596. The relevant extracts from George Silver's *Paradoxes of Defence*, describing Bonetti's school, are from Adams, 'The Conventual Buildings of Blackfriars . . .' (1917), pp. 64–87. For Shakespeare's allusion to Bonetti, see Shakespeare, *Romeo and Juliet*, ed. Weis (2012), 2.4.23–4. The dimensions of the Second Blackfriars Theatre and its construction have been derived from the following: Burbage's lease (FSL, Lb.356); Smith, *Shakespeare's Blackfriars Playhouse* (1964), esp. pp. 155–73; Bowsher, *Shakespeare's London Theatreland* (2012), pp. 118–22; Gurr, *The Shakespeare Company* (2004), p. 5; Gurr, *Playgoing in Shakespeare's London* (1996), pp. 27–8; and some aspects of Wallace, *The Children of the Chapel at Blackfriars* (1908), pp. 1–72 and Adams, 'The Conventual Buildings of Blackfriars . . .' (1917), pp. 64–87. (Wallace and Adams differ in places from Smith and later historians on their reconstruction of Shakespeare's Blackfriars Theatre.) The church-like nature of the windows in the old Parliament building which Burbage acquired is recorded in *Pierce the Ploughman's Crede* (c.1394), part of which is reproduced in Adams, 'The Conventual Buildings of Blackfriars . . .' (1917), pp. 75–6. The seven rooms formerly belonging to William de Lawne and Burbage's rights of way are quoted directly from the lease, FSL, Lb.356. For Shakespeare's tax assessments, see Kirk and Kirk, eds., *Returns of Aliens* (1900–1908), vol. 2, p. 483 and vol. 3, p. 10; see also Nicholl, *The Lodger* (2007), p. 40.

Shakespeare's share in the Chamberlain's Men, his responsibilities and the comparison of ticket prices and profits are derived from Gurr, *The Shakespeare Company* (2004), pp. 89 and 106–11; Wallace, *The Children of the Chapel at Blackfriars* (1908), pp. 35–6; and Gurr, *The Shakespearean Stage* (2007), pp. 12 and 71. On the first record of Shakespeare as a servant of the Lord Chamberlain, see Schoenbaum, *A Compact Documentary Life* (1977), p. 183. Elizabeth Russell's letter to Robert Cecil is HH, CP 30/26, 27 January 1596. On Elizabeth's relation to Henry Grey, see Russell, *Letters*, ed. Farber (1977), pp. 157–8. An example of the use of the word 'tribe' as a code for the Hunsdon/Carey family comes from a letter of 5 December 1595 by Rowland White, CKS, MS U1475, C12/36, from the de Lisle and Dudley manuscripts (Penshurst Place/Centre for Kentish Studies, Maidstone), in which he makes this comment: 'Truly I heard, that if my Lord of Pembroke should die, who is very pursive and maladive, the tribe of Hunsdon do lay [in] wait for the wardship of the brave young Lord.' I would like to thank Margaret Hannay (Siena College), who generously supplied me with her own unpublished transcriptions of the manuscript letters of Rowland White, among which was this letter. The epistle is also included in Collins, ed., *Letters and Memorials of State* (1746), vol. 1, pp. 371–3. For Henry Carey's genealogy, see ODNB.

Chapter Fifteen: Shakespeare and Essex

Shakespeare's lauding of Southampton is in the dedicatory epistle to his *Venus and Adonis* (1593). Edward Hoby's letter to Robert Cecil is HH, CP 36/60, 7 December 1595. For a consideration of the 'Richard II' Edward Hoby had intended to 'present' to Cecil, see Duncan-Jones, *Shakespeare: Upstart Crow to Sweet Swan* (2011), pp. 211–28. For Bale's view of Oldcastle, see title page to *A Brief Chronicle* (1544). The quotations from Foxe's work are from Foxe, *Acts and Monuments* (1570), pp. 680–81. Thynne's eulogy of the Cobham line is in Holinshed, *Chronicles* (1587), beginning on p. 1499; Holinshed's own defence of the 'valiant captain' Oldcastle can be seen on p. 544. For the full background to the censorship of Oldcastle, see Taylor, 'The Fortunes of Oldcastle' (1986), pp. 85–100. For traces of Falstaff's original identity and name, as Oldcastle, surviving in the censored versions of the plays, see Shakespeare, *Henry IV, Part One*, ed. Bevington (1987), 1.2.40–41, 1.2.136–8, 2.4.419–21 and 2.4.480 and Shakespeare, *Henry IV, Part Two*, ed. Weis (1997), 1.2.173–5.

The animosity between Essex, Robert Cecil and Henry Brooke is reported by Rowland White in Collins, ed., *Letters and Memorials of State* (1746), vol. 2, pp. 26 and 30. Nan Russell's attendance at Margaret Ratcliffe's funeral is mentioned in Collins, ed., *Letters and Memorials of State* (1746), vol. 2, p. 142. For Essex's letter about Ratcliffe, and a discussion of these allusions, including the idea that Shakespeare's Harvey may relate to Sir William Harvey, see Scoufos, *Shakespeare's Typological Satire* (1979), pp. 202–5; Shapiro, *1599* (2005), pp. 20–21; and Jowett, 'The Thieves in 1 *Henry IV*' (1987), pp. 325–33. Elizabeth's letter to Southampton is HH, CP, 101/16, 8 July 1603. For White's gossip on the marriage of William Harvey to Southampton's mother, see Collins, ed., *Letters and Memorials of State* (1746), vol. 2, p. 53. Poins' First Quarto speech is from *The History of Henry the Fourth* (1598), sig. B1r. Southampton's daily enjoyment of plays is remarked upon by Rowland White in Collins, ed., *Letters and Memorials of State* (1746), vol. 2, p. 132.

Falstaff's claim to have defeated 'gunpowder Percy' is from Shakespeare, *Henry IV, Part One*, ed. Bevington (1987), 5.4.120–38. Essex's presence at performances of the *Henry IV* plays is mentioned in NA, SP 12/275, ff. 55r–57r, 22 July 1600. My reading of the allusions to the 8th Earl of Northumberland in *Henry IV, Part 1* and Shakespeare's interest in the Essex circle as evidenced in this play is anticipated in places by that of Scoufos, *Shakespeare's Typological Satire* (1979), pp. 70–133 and 221–45 (though we make very different claims about Shakespeare's direct allusions to Elizabeth Russell herself and do not hold similar views on the dating of some of the plays in the cycle). My interpretation of the chronology of Essex's connection to Bolingbroke and Henry V agrees with that in Hammer, 'Shakespeare's *Richard II* . . .' (2008), pp. 1–35 and Bate, 'Was Shakespeare an Essex Man?' (2009), pp. 1–28. For a further reading of Essex's relation to the theatre, see Ioppolo, 'Robert Devereux . . .' (2013), pp. 63–80. For the Percys' involvement in the staging of *Richard II* before Essex's coup, see the interrogations of the Chamberlain's Men's Augustine Phillips in NA, SP 12/278, f. 139r, 18 February 1601. The attempt to forge a direct link between Essex and the usurper, Bolingbroke, is manifest in NA, SP 12/278, ff. 108r–9v, 14[?] February 1601. Robert Cecil's notes, which do the same, are NA, SP 12/278, ff. 79r–80r, 13 February 1601. The parallels between Essex, *Richard II* and Hayward's book are made in the manuscript account of Hayward's own interrogation and confessions, NA, SP 12/275, ff. 41r–41v, 11 July 1600.

The quote from Shakespeare's play is from *Richard II*, ed. Forker (2002), 1.4.24–36. For

Guilpin's satire against Essex, see *Skialetheia* (1598), sig. C3v. Bacon's advice to Essex is reproduced in Devereux, *Lives and Letters* (1853), vol. 1, p. 400. The quote from Hayward's text can be found in *The First Part of the Life and Reign* (1599), p. 71. For a further analysis of Essex's relation to Hayward's book, see Tipton, '"Lively Patterns . . . " . . .' (2002), pp. 769–94. For the staging of 'Harey the V' and its context, see Ingram, *A London Life* (1978), p. 121. Charles Percy's letter is NA, SP 12/275, f. 240r, 27 December 1600. On the uncertainty of the dating of this letter and for more on Essex's own association with the lineage of Henry IV and Henry V, see Bate 'Was Shakespeare an Essex Man?' (2009), pp. 9 and 14, and Hammer, 'Shakespeare's *Richard II* . . .' (2008), pp. 1–35. The dedicatory epistle to Essex is signed 'R. Doleman'; the text is identified as being by William Allen in EEBO; see Allen, *A Conference* (1595), sigs. A2r–A3r.

Hayward's confession about Wolfe is in NA, SP 12/275, ff. 41r–2v, 11 July 1600. Wolfe's interrogations are preserved in NA, SP 12/275, ff. 45r–46r, 13 July 1600. Wolfe's activities are derived from Hoppe, 'John Wolfe . . .' (1933), pp. 241–89; his entry in ODNB; and Straznicky, ed., *Shakespeare's Stationers* (2013), pp. 20–29 and 301. For William Cecil's use of Wolfe, see Parmelee, 'Printers, Patrons, Readers . . .' (1994), pp. 854–5 and 858–60. Wolfe's edition of the *Execution* is Cecil, *Atto della Giustitia d'Inghilterra* (1584); those printed by Vautrollier are Cecil, *L'execution de iustice* (1584) and Cecil, *Justitia Britannica per quam liquet perspicue* (1584). It is also intriguing that John Wolfe was responsible for printing the work of Elizabeth Russell's late husband just four years later: see Hoby, *The Courtier*, trans. Castiglione (1588); could the publication of her husband's translation by Wolfe have been overseen by her? I agree with Weis's chronology and dating of the *Henry IV* and *Merry Wives* plays; see Shakespeare, *Henry IV, Part Two*, ed. Weis (1997), pp. 9–15.

Henry Carey's last words are recorded in his will, NA, PROB 11/88, ff. 14r–14v, 21 July 1596. The revenues from Henry Carey's estate and offices are derived from the accounts in HH, CP 43/23, July 1596. For Hamnet's death, see Schoenbaum, *A Compact Documentary Life* (1977), p. 224. On William Brooke's role as Lord Chamberlain, see Shakespeare, *Henry IV, Part Two*, ed. Weis (1997), p. 9 and Dobson and Wells, eds., *Oxford Companion to Shakespeare* (2001), p. 259. Carey's petitions to Cecil are HH, CP 43/23, July 1596; CP 173/111, before 26 July 1596; CP 44/113, 20 September 1596; CP 46/66, 23 November 1596; and copy CP 46/64. Cecil's report of the Queen's scandalous accusation was made in NA, SP 12/257, f. 53r, 22[?] April 1596. Carey's involvement in preparations for Cádiz is recorded in NA, SP 12/259, f. 151r, 16 July 1596.

Chapter Sixteen: Detective Dowager

The Queen's letter from the *Due Repulse* is NA, SP 12/257, f. 46r, 14 April 1596. Essex's letter to Robert Cecil is NA, SP 12/257, f. 47r, 14 April 1596. On the loss of Calais, the Cádiz voyage and the creation of knights by Essex and Howard, see Devereux, *Lives and Letters* (1853), vol. 1, pp. 357–72; Harrison, *The Life and Death of Robert Devereux* (1937), pp. 108–14; and Lacey, *Robert, Earl of Essex* (1971), pp. 137–64. On Whitgift's support of Essex, see Hammer, 'Myth-Making . . .' (1997), p. 636. The celebration at Essex's return and Henry Brooke's slanderous accusations are outlined in Devereux, *Lives and Letters* (1853), vol. 1, pp. 378–80. For the possible allusion to the Cádiz voyage by Shakespeare, see *Romeo and*

Juliet, ed. Weis (2012), 1.4.82–5. Shakespeare's reference to the *San Andreas* is in *The Merchant of Venice*, ed. Brown (1955), 1.1.27; see also Weis, *Shakespeare Revealed* (2007), pp. 201–2. The estimation of the value of goods plundered from the Cádiz raid is derived from Devereux, *Lives and Letters* (1853), vol. 1, pp. 375–7.

Essex's letter to Anthony Bacon complaining of his treatment by Robert Cecil is LPL, MS 659, no. 99, f. 142r, 8 September 1596. The argument between Cecil and Essex over the attorneyship is recounted in Devereux, *Lives and Letters* (1853), vol. 1, pp. 283–6. Elizabeth Russell's promotion of Morrice is in her letter to Robert Cecil, HH, CP 170/53, May 1593. See also ODNB entry for 'Morice, James'. For Essex's support of Francis Bacon, including promoting him as a candidate for the Mastership of the Rolls, see Laoutaris, '"Toucht with bolt of Treason" . . .' (2013), p. 212. Elizabeth's letter to Robert Cecil on behalf of Matthew Dale is HH, CP 41/74, 15 June 1596. She had previously petitioned on Dale's behalf in HH, CP 30/26, 27 January 1596. On the affiliation of Dale and Morrice with the Middle Temple, see Russell, *The Writings*, ed. Phillippy (2011), p. 187, n. 9. Caesar's friendship with the Essex circle is attested to in Lady Rich's letter to him, BL, Additional MS 12506, f. 421r.

Elizabeth Russell's journey to Essex House is reconstructed from LPL, MS 659, no. 21, ff. 23r–26v. For the scandals surrounding Anthony Bacon in France, see du Maurier, *Golden Lads* (1975; 2007 edition). Essex's desire to read a full account of Elizabeth's interview with Anthony Bacon is expressed in his letter to the last, LPL, MS 659, no. 99, f. 142r, 8 September 1596. Elizabeth's interrogation of Bacon on 8 September 1596 is reconstructed from his own account of their conversation in LPL, MS 659, no. 21, ff. 23r–26v. For Standen, see Lea, 'Sir Anthony Standen . . .' (1932), pp. 461–77; for Wright, see Russell, *The Writings*, ed. Phillippy (2011), p. 193, n. 9. For evidence of King James's closeness to Henry [Harry] Howard, see Bruce, ed. *The Correspondence of King James VI* (1861), pp. xxxviii, 2, 11, 17 and 19. For more on Howard, see Allen, *The Cooke Sisters* (2013), p. 103. Anne Bacon's coded letter in Greek cypher is LPL, MS 651, f. 108r, 1 April 1595 (the translation from the Greek is my own). Essex's worries and insomnia are recorded in Devereux, *Lives and Letters* (1853), vol. 1, p. 321.

Elizabeth Russell's letter to Anthony Bacon is LPL, MS 659, no. 75, ff. 104r–105r, 8 September 1596. Anthony Bacon's letter in response to his aunt's charges is LPL, MS 659, f. 199r, 8 September 1596; see also ibid., f. 199v, 9 September 1596. Elizabeth Russell's dissatisfaction with Bacon's response is LPL, MS 659, no. 76, f. 106r, 9 September 1596. Essex's response to the same letter is LPL, MS 659, no. 99, f. 142r, 8 September 1596. The Queen's argument with Lord Burghley and Elizabeth Russell's subsequent involvement are reconstructed from Devereux, *Lives and Letters* (1853), vol. 1, pp. 389–92 (which includes a transcription of Bacon's letter to Hawkins); Burghley's letter to Essex, LPL, MS 659, no. 136, f. 201r, 22 September 1596; and Essex's letter to Burghley, LPL, MS 659, no. 133, 196r, 23 September 1596.

Chapter Seventeen: 'my war between mine own flesh and blood'

For the kinds of mocking names used against Thomas Posthumous Hoby, see the Star Chamber records pertaining to his later legal conflicts, NA, STAC 5/N16/2. Elizabeth Russell's letter to William Cecil about Thomas Posthumous is BL, Lansdowne MS 10, no. 38, ff. 136r–137r, July 1585 (the conjectural dating of this letter is my own). Edward Hoby's estate in the Isle of Sheppey is mentioned in Elizabeth's letter to William Cecil in BL, Lansdowne MS 33, no. 85, ff. 203r–204v, 8 November 1581. For Essex's response to Walter's death, see Devereux, *Lives and Letters* (1853), vol. 1, pp. 233–4. For the background to the raising of Margaret Dakins, and her marriages, see the useful introductions in Hoby, *Diary*, ed. Meads (1930), pp. 1–61 and Hoby, *The Private Life of an Elizabethan Lady*, ed. Moody (1998), pp. xv–lii. Most of the correspondence pertaining to Thomas Posthumous's courtship of Margaret Dakins survives in Gardiner, ed., *The Fortescue Papers* (1871), pp. v–xx. The letters preserved in the latter text form the basis for the account presented here, with the exception of the following documents: Thomas Posthumous's letter to Robert Cecil, complaining of his mother's 'unkind strangeness', HH, CP 25/14, 3 February 1595; his epistle to Cecil initiating his second attempt at courting Margaret and asking for 'some means to cross' any rival suitor, HH, CP 33/76, 3 August 1595; Thomas Hoby's complaint to Cecil that his mother is 'backwards for my preferment', HH, CP 35/96, 29 October 1595; Thomas Posthumous's recourse to showering Margaret with 'fair jewels and pearls', Collins, ed., *Letters and Memorials of State* (1746), vol. 1, p. 361; Elizabeth Russell's letter of invitation to Robert Cecil, HH, CP, 43/44, 1 August 1596; and Thomas Posthumous's letter to Cecil, which also outlines the humble nature of the proposed wedding, BL, Additional MS, 4120, f. 77r.

Chapter Eighteen: Shakespeare's Nemesis

The quotations from Elizabeth Russell's petition are taken directly from NA, SP 12/260, f. 176r, November 1596. On the opening of the Swan Theatre, see Chambers, *The Elizabethan Stage* (1923), vol. 4, pp. 316–17. Field's 'little shop' is described in his lease agreement with William and George More, SHC, LM 333/12, 22 September 1592; the details describing the structure of Field's property are derived from this document. The agreements specifying the shared rights of Field and Gideon de Lawne to parts of the Square Tower and Timber House are outlined in Field's lease (SHC, LM 333/12), as well as that of Gideon de Lawne, SHC, LM 333/11, 20 September 1592. The location of these properties relative to Elizabeth Russell's house has been determined from her letter indicating the position of her 'gallery' (SHC, HC 6729/6/98, 9 August c.1580–81[?]); the indenture of Lewis de Mare, SHC, LM 348/68, 3 September 1570; and the indentures of Paul Buck, SHC, LM 348/216, 30 June 1591 and SHC, LM 348/234, 31 January 1594. (See notes to chapter six for a full account of the indentures used to map Elizabeth's home in relation to the Round House and Square Tower, as well as to the property of Thomas Vautrollier, whose 'shop' Richard Field came to occupy.)

Egerton's *A Brief Method of Catechising* (1597) was initially issued with the printer's initials only: R[ichard] F[ield]; the 1615 edition clearly specifies that the work was 'Imprinted by Richard Field'. Egerton's preface is in Virell, *A Learned and Excellent Treatise Containing all the Principal Grounds of Christian Religion* (1594), sigs. A2r–A3v. For Field's posts of assistant warden or 'sideman' and warden of St Anne's Church, see LMA, MS 9537, vol. 8, f. 77r, 1592 and LMA, MS 9537, vol. 9, f. 158r, 1598. The comparison between Field's and Buck's properties is based on SHC, LM 333/12, 22 September 1592 and SHC, LM 348/216, 30 June 1591. I would like to thank Sir Brian Vickers for providing me with information about

Richard Field's printing licence. William de Lawne's agreements with William and George More and his role as Field's landlord are derived from his indenture FSL, Lb.349, 31 October 1593.

On Richard Field's career and the limitations placed on Jacqueline Vautrollier's aspirations as a printer, see Kirwood, 'Richard Field . . .'(1931), pp. 1–32 (Kirwood was unaware that Field was also a church warden). For the quote from Burghley's anti-Spanish tract, see Cecil, *The Copy of a Letter* (1588), p. 3; the manuscript copy in Burghley's hand, with his own revisions and corrections, is BL, Lansdowne MS 103, no. 55, ff. 134r–49r. Elizabeth Russell's letter to Robert Cecil on behalf of Ascanius de Renialme is HH, CP 63/7, 10 July 1598. For Saltonstall's role, see ODNB. For Sir Thomas Browne's work as a commissioner for William Cecil, see SHC, LM COR/3/428, 2 May 1588. For Thomas Browne's career, association with the Browne family of Betchworth, marriages and death, see his entry in Hasler, ed., *The History of Parliament* (1981). For the inclusion of Harding, Paddy and Burbage on the 1599 Subsidy Rolls, see the 'Lay Subsidy Returns for London, Middlesex, Surrey (north) 1593–1600', transcribed by Alan H. Nelson at www.socrates.berkeley. edu/~ahnelson/SUBSIDY/subs. For William Paddy's career, see his entry in the ODNB. For more on Shakespeare's residence in Silver Street, see Nicholl, *The Lodger* (2007). Dr Paddy's letter to Robert Cecil is HH, CP 37/16, 1595. For Matthew Browne, see the biographical entry in Hasler, ed., *The History of Parliament* (1981) and his will, NA, PROB 11/III, f. 267r, 2 August 1603. For Nicholas Brend's will, see NA, PROB 11/98, ff. 325r–326v, 10 October 1601. For Brend's role in the leasing of the site on which the Globe Theatre was built, see the testimony of Cuthbert Burbage in the 1632 legal dispute over the theatre in NA, REQ 2/706, printed in Gurr, *The Shakespeare Company* (2004), pp. 251–2; see also Shapiro, *1599* (2005), pp. 3 and 88. For the relation of Elizabeth Russell to the Brownes through the marriage of her brother William Cooke to Frances Grey, daughter of John Grey of Pirgo and Mary Browne (the latter being sister of Anthony Browne, 1st Viscount Montagu), see the will of William Cooke, PROB 11/74, ff. 362r–367r, 6 March 1588. In the latter document, Cooke makes bequests to members of Elizabeth Russell's extended family, including James Morrice, as well as £10 'to the afflicted French and Dutch Church[es]'. See the notes to chapter eight for the potential relations between the Browne and Fitzwilliam families.

The indenture of John 'Dermer' is SHC, LM 348/294, 18 February 1602. John le Mere's profession and affiliation with the French Church are itemized in Kirk and Kirk, eds., *Returns of Aliens* (1900–1908), vol. 2, pp. 180, 252 and vol. 3, p. 50; Scouloudi, *Returns of Strangers* (1985), p. 190; and survey of 'strangers' in the Blackfriars, HH, CP 208/7, 28 April 1583. John Robinson's inclusion in the Burbages' legal disputes and Henry Evans's role are derived from Smith, *Shakespeare's Blackfriars Playhouse* (1964), pp. 517–19; and the Burbages' 1610 legal disputes, including NA, REQ 4/1/1/1, 8 February 1610 ('Bill of complaint' of Robert Keysar); NA, REQ 4/1/1/2, 12 February 1610 (testimony of Richard Burbage, Cuthbert Burbage, John Heminges and Henry Condell); NA, REQ 4/1/1, 22 May 1610 (reply of Keyser to Richard Burbage, Cuthbert Burbage, John Heminges and Henry Condell); and REQ 4/1/1/4, 19 June 1610 (further rejoinder by Richard Burbage, Cuthbert Burbage, John Heminges and Henry Condell). Shakespeare's will is NA, PROB 1/4. For Shakespeare's Blackfriars Gatehouse, see Dobson and Wells, eds., *Oxford Companion to Shakespeare* (2001), p. 49.

Notes

William More's grant of a lease to John Robinson is recorded in the 'Dermer' indenture, SHC, LM 348/294, 18 February 1602. John Robinson's presence in the Blackfriars is revealed in the numerous instances in which children belonging to a 'John Robinson' are recorded in the registers of baptisms and deaths for St Anne's, though there is a possibility that there could be more than one John Robinson in the area, given the frequency of such occasions (the register of births, for example, records seven children born to a John Robinson from 1591 to 1600); see Register of Baptisms, St Anne's, Blackfriars, 1560–1700, vol. 1, LMA, MS 4508 and Register of Burials, St Anne's, Blackfriars, 1566–1700, vol. 1, LMA, MS 4510. Agnes Lyons's will is NA, PROB 11/117, f. 4r, 18 January 1621. The will of Ascanius de Renialme is NA, PROB 11/95, ff. 127v–128v, 29 February 1600. Evidence that 'Francis Henson' is likely to be Francis Hinson comes from the will of Katherine Hinson, who was probably Francis's widow, who left a bequest to 'my sister Marie Hinson', NA, PROB 11/169, ff. 19r–19v, 21 May 1635.

For the attendance of Buckholt, Edwardes and Ascanius at the Dutch Church, see the 'Dutch Church Registers of Members', printed in Kirk and Kirk, eds., Returns of Aliens (1900–1908), vol. 2, p. 462. Ascanius de Renialme would leave £5 to the Dutch Church and £10 to the French Church in his will (NA, PROB 11/95, ff. 127v–128v), while Katherine Baheire, Robert's widow, would leave a bequest of £20 to the Dutch Church, NA, PROB 11/125, ff. 8v–9r, 7 November 1614. Elizabeth's petitioners may also have encountered each other regularly through the religious rituals that punctuated their lives which would have been performed at St Anne's. Between 1590 and 1591, for example, John Robinson, John Edwardes and William de Lawne all buried children within seven months of each other, such sad coincidences turning up frequently in these records. Such occasions may also have provided opportunities for the less elevated co-signatories of the 1596 petition to come into contact with the noble families of the Russells, Brookes, Careys and Brownes, who had solemnized their servants' burials in the same church. A number of these obsequies took place in St Anne's between 1585 and 1597, Elizabeth herself having buried two servants (John Elton and Rafe Marshal) in that period. Sometimes happier rites joined the community in celebration. William Meredith, John Robinson and Ezekiel Major all christened children between April and August of 1596, just months before signing the Dowager's petition. See Register of Baptisms, St Anne's, Blackfriars, 1560–1700, vol. 1, LMA, MS 4508 and Register of Burials, St Anne's, Blackfriars, 1566–1700, vol. 1, LMA, MS 4510.

The agreement between Bispham, Wharton and Major is in SHC, LM 349/40, 1607. Henry Boice's lease is mentioned in SHC, LM 348/294, 18 February 1602. For John Clarke's property, see Feuillerat, Blackfriars Records (1913), pp. 70 and 77. A John Clarke is recorded as having buried a son in St Anne's in February 1592 and, five years later, was married to Alice Bonfoy (presumably after the death of a previous wife), who may have been the daughter of the French 'featherdresser' Sebastian Bonffoye; see Register of Burials, St Anne's, Blackfriars, 1566–1700, vol. 1, LMA, MS 4510; Register of Marriages, St Anne's, Blackfriars, 1562–1726, vol. 1, LMA, MS 4509; and survey of 'strangers' in the Blackfriars, HH, CP 208/7, 28 April 1583. Thomas Holmes's lease agreement, which mentions his occupation, is SHC, LM 333/17, October 1596; the indenture of 9 August 1597 is SHC, LM 333/18. My calculation of the relative positions of the properties of Holmes and Baheire is derived from Holmes's leases and those of Baheire (SHC, MS LM333/1 and SHC, LM 348/205, 18 March 1590).

The 1619 petition which was signed by Thomas Posthumous Hoby is reproduced in Smith, Shakespeare's Blackfriars Playhouse (1964), p. 491. The quotation from Elizabeth

452

Russell's petition is from NA, SP 12/260, f. 176r, November 1596. The constitutional acts against 'masterless men' are outlined in Tanner, ed., *Tudor Constitutional Documents* (1951), pp. 475–88. John Spencer's letter to William Cecil, with his attempt to prevent the Swan Theatre from opening, is in Chambers, *The Elizabethan Stage* (1923), vol. 4, pp. 316–17. The account of the 1595 riot is derived from NA, SP 12/252, f. 178r; Gurr, 'Henry Carey's Peculiar Letter' (2005), p. 70; and Fogg, *Hidden Shakespeare* (2012), pp. 162–3. The Lord Mayor's petition to the Privy Council of 13 September 1595 and Thomas Nashe's letter are printed in Chambers, *The Elizabethan Stage* (1923), pp. 318–19. The edict of 22 July 1596 to the Middlesex and Surrey Justices of the Peace is NA, PC 2/21, f. 314r. The demand that 'no playhouse' be allowed in the Blackfriars and the insistence that the Lord Mayor had banished players from the city are from Elizabeth Russell's petition, NA, SP 12/260, f. 176r, November 1596. For Martin's involvement in previous attempts to close the theatres, see NA, PC 2/19, f. 474r, 15 July 1592 and notes to the end of chapter twelve. For the possible location of the Privy Council meetings, see NA, PC 2/22, f. 4r, at Richmond, 31 October 1596 and NA, PC 2/22, f. 26r, at Whitehall, 21 November 1596.

Chapter Nineteen: In the Name of Love

Richard Martin's suit is outlined in NA, SP 12/246, f. 16r, 16 November [?] 1593. For Oldcastle in the Blackfriars, see Holinshed, *Chronicles* (1587), p. 1499. Elizabeth Russell's claim that the Blackfriars Theatre would be the cause of 'mischief' is from her petition, NA, SP 12/260, f. 176r, November 1596. Dr James's account is quoted from Schoenbaum, *A Compact Documentary Life* (1977), pp. 195–6. Fuller's views are stated in his *The Church History of Britain* (1655), pp. 167–8. Heylyn's response is in his *Examen Historicum* (1659), pp. 66–7. Fuller made a further reply to Heylyn over the Oldcastle controversy in his *The Appeal of Injured Innocence* (1659), pp. 39–40. I owe my knowledge of Elizabeth Russell's attempt to match Henry Brooke with Bess Russell to John Jowett; see his 'The Thieves in 1 *Henry IV*' (1987), pp. 325–33. White's gossip about the proposed marriage is in Collins, ed., *Letters and Memorials of State* (1746), vol. 2, p. 26; see also McKeen, *A Memory of Honour* (1964), p. 759. For Shakespeare's apology, see the epilogue to *Henry IV, Part Two*, ed. Weis (1997), ll. 17–31. For Wilson's views on the potential allusion to Elizabeth Russell's legal disputes in *The Merry Wives*, see Wilson, *Society Women* (1925), pp. 12–15 and 223–37. The quotations from the *Merry Wives* used in this chapter are Shakespeare, *The Merry Wives of Windsor*, ed. Craik (1990), 1.1.1–3, 1.1.31–110, 1.1.137–158 and 5.5.60. Elizabeth Russell's Lovelace disputes are preserved in NA, STAC 5/L4/26; NA, STAC 5/R15/31; NA, STAC 5/R36/31; NA, SP 12/245, f. 217r; and HH, CP 186/135. (See notes to chapter thirteen for a fuller account of the content of these sources.)

For the dating of Shakespeare's *Merry Wives* and for the account of the Garter celebrations used here, see Hotson, *Shakespeare versus Shallow* (1931), pp. 111–22, esp. pp. 117–19; for dating of the play, see also the introduction to Shakespeare, *The Merry Wives of Windsor*, ed. Craik (1990), pp. 1–13. For Lovelace's punishment, see Hawarde, *Les Reportes*, ed. Baildon, (1894), p. 49. For the wordplay on Russell/russet, see Jowett, 'The Thieves in 1 *Henry IV*' (1987), pp. 325–33. For more on the possibility that Shakespeare alludes to Henry Evans in his *Merry Wives* and for the theory that the boy players used were actually under his own management, see Scoufos, *Shakespeare's Typological Satire* (1979), pp. 188–220, (Scoufos's reading of the significance of this potential allusion is based on a later dating of 1599, and a differing context, for the play.) On the censorship of 'Oldcastle' and 'Brooke', see Taylor, 'The Fortunes of Oldcastle' (1986), pp. 85–100 and the introduction to Shakespeare, *The Merry Wives of Windsor*, ed. Craik (1990), pp. 9–11; see also pp. 6–8 of the latter text for the idea that Shakespeare was alluding to Sir Thomas Lucy's coat of arms in *Merry Wives*. For the marriages of William Cooke the elder to Frances Grey (daughter of Mary Browne, who was kinswoman to the Brownes of Betchworth, Surrey) and William Cooke the younger to Joyce Lucy, see the entries for both William Cooke senior and junior in Hasler, ed., *The History of Parliament* (1981); see also the will of William Cooke the elder, PROB 11/74, ff. 362r–367r, 6 March 1588.

Harington's letter to Elizabeth Russell is BL, Lansdowne MS 82, no. 88, f. 186r, 14 August 1596. On the Queen's belief that Harington had 'aimed a shaft at Leicester' in his satire, see Harington, *Nugae Antiquae*, eds Harington and Park (1804), vol. 1, p. 240. The allusion to Elizabeth Russell's Lovelace disputes is in Harington, *The Metamorphosis of Ajax* (1596), p. 71. Shakespeare's possible allusion to Harington is in *As You Like It*, ed. Brissenden (1993), 4.1.3–30. The riddling poem referring to Harington's name is in [Harington], *An Anatomy of the Metamorphosed Ajax* (1596). For George Carey's new posts, see his entry in ODNB. For Hotson's reading of Shakespeare's Shallow as a representation of Gardiner, see his *Shakespeare versus Shallow* (1931); this text also contains an account of the writ served against Shakespeare in November 1596, from which the details about this used in this chapter are primarily taken. Gardiner's family crest is explained in Schoenbaum, *A Compact Documentary Life* (1977), p. 108, which includes a summary of the mysterious writ on pp. 198–200. For details of 'Soer's rents' and Shakespeare's moves between Bishopsgate and the Bankside, see Hotson, *Shakespeare versus Shallow* (1931), pp. 12–13 and 21–3. Shakespeare's residency in Bishopsgate is also recorded in Kirk and Kirk, eds., *Returns of Aliens* (1900–1908), vol. 2, p. 483 and vol. 3, p. 10. Applying the findings made by Hotson, Kirk and Kirk gives us a more accurate potential date for Elizabeth Russell's petition than has hitherto been possible.

For the scandalous career of Francis Langley, see Ingram, *A London Life* (1978). The knighting of Ashley is recorded in BL, Lansdowne MS 81, no. 73, f. 188r, 1596. The stake-out of Ashley's home and the capture of the *Madre de Dios* are described in Ingram, *A London Life* (1978), pp. 133–4 and 95–103 respectively. For a scintillating account of the culture of piracy and merchant adventuring in Elizabethan England, see Ronald, *The Pirate Queen* (2007). Ashley's confession of Langley's involvement in the theft and attempted resale of the diamond is made in HH, CP 40/88, 15 May 1596. The uncomfortable encounter with William Brooke, Lord Cobham, and Langley's response are recorded in HH, CP 40/89, 16 May 1596. The subsequent fate of Ashley and Cecil's continuing hunt for the diamond are recounted in NA, CP 44/21, 28 August 1596; HH, CP 44/5, 23 August 1596; and NA, CP 45/52, 7 October 1596. For the marriage of Gardiner's son to Christopher Yelverton's daughter Mary in 1597, see Gardiner's will, printed in Hotson, *Shakespeare versus Shallow* (1931), p. 337. Elizabeth Russell's original will, in which she intended to make Henry Yelverton an overseer and benefactor, is PROB 11/113, ff. 435r–436r, 23 April 1609. Elizabeth's granting of Eyfforde Pastures, with Yelverton as co-executor, for her children's 'better preferment' is among the Records of the Exchequer, NA, E44/191, 21 March 1608. For the careers and religious leanings of the Yelvertons, see, for Christopher Yelverton, Hasler, ed., *The History of Parliament* (1981), and for

Henry Yelverton, Thrush and Ferris, eds., *The History of Parliament* (2010). For Gardiner's attempt to close down the Swan Theatre, see Hotson, *Shakespeare versus Shallow* (1931), pp. 22–3 and Chambers, *The Elizabethan Stage* (1923), vol. 4, pp. 321–3. For Ingram's evidence that Shakespeare's troupe was playing at the Swan, see his *A London Life* (1978), pp. 139–50.

Chapter Twenty: Aftermath

The activities of Essex and Elizabeth Russell and the circumstances surrounding William Brooke's death are reported by White in Collins, ed., *Letters and Memorials of State* (1746), vol. 2, pp. 29 and 24–5 respectively. That Robert Cecil had written to his aunt after his wife's death is indicated in Elizabeth's letter to him, HH, CP 52/52, 24 June 1597. Elizabeth's letter to Robert Cecil with advice on managing his grief is HH, CP 175/92, before 24 June 1597. The adaptation of a poem from Horace's *Epistles* is HH, CP 175/118, 22 October 1597. Casa's prophecy is recorded in CMS, vol. 7, 1597, ed. Roberts (1899), p. 229, 1 June 1597.

Robert Cecil's letter confirming Essex's plans is NA, SP 63/199, f. 274r, 22 June 1597. Elizabeth Russell's appraisal of Essex's mission is in HH, CP 175/92, before 24 June 1597. Elizabeth's letter with her marriage plans for Bess is HH, CP 52/52, 24 June 1597. For the fate of the Ferrol mission, see NA, SP 12/263, f. 185r, June[?] 1597; NA, SP 63/200, f. 321r, 17 September 1597; and Devereux, *Lives and Letters* (1853), vol. 1, pp. 451–65. Elizabeth's letters to Robert Cecil with the account of the disputes over Russell House and her appraisal of Bess are HH, CP 73/27, 26 August 1599 and HH, CP73/115, September 1599; for Elizabeth's rights to the property, see NA, SP 12/83, f. 135r, 1591 (which outlines the Queen's grant to Elizabeth and her daughters). For Cecil's residency in Burghley House on the Strand, see Russell, *The Writings*, ed. Phillippy (2011), p. 231, n. 4. Edward Hoby's letter to Robert Cecil about Russell House is HH, CP 73/19, 25 August 1599. Elizabeth's defiant letter to Robert Cecil with her refusal to part with Russell House is HH, CP 74/1, September 1599. Elizabeth's letter to Thomas Egerton with arrangements for her daughters' inheritance is EL, MS 45, 27 June 1597. See also the useful notes in Russell, *The Writings*, ed. Phillippy (2011), pp. 207–9.

Robert Bacon's letter to Elizabeth seeking her aid and Anthony Bacon's own edited draft are LPL, MS 659, no. 43, f. 41r and LPL, MS 659, no. 44, f. 42r. Elizabeth's response to Robert Bacon's request is LPL, MS 659, no. 103, f. 148r, 22 September 1596. Anthony Bacon's complaints about Elizabeth to the Earl of Essex are quoted from Allen, *The Cooke Sisters* (2013), p. 144, which includes an account of the context of Robert Bacon's machinations on pp. 143–4. Elizabeth's disputes with May are recounted in her letters to Robert Cecil, HH, CP 53/89, c.early July 1597; HH, CP 53/26, 11 July 1597; and HH, CP 53/88, after 11 July 1597. The last letter is also the same in which Elizabeth arranges the policing of the Blackfriars.

On the termination of the dealings between Field and Shakespeare, see Plomer, 'The Printers of Shakespeare's Plays and Poems' (1906), pp. 146–66. The quotations from Shakespeare's play are taken from *Cymbeline*, ed. Nosworthy (1997), 4.2.376–97. For James Burbage's death, see his ODNB entry. The Burbages' testimony about their legal and financial troubles is from NA, REQ 2/184/45, 15 May 1600 and 'The Sharers' Papers', NA, LC/5/133, 1635; these are also transcribed in Gurr, *The Shakespeare Company* (2004), pp. 249 and 278–9, which contains a useful summary of the financial burdens on the Burbages and Shakespeare after

the closure of the Blackfriars Theatre, on p. 31. For another account of these financial burdens, see Greer, *Shakespeare's Wife* (2008), p. 214.

I am grateful to Kevin Colls, Archaeological Project Manager, Staffordshire University, for
information about the recent archaeological digs at New Place in Stratford-upon-Avon and
for sharing with me the preparatory report for the excavations: 'New Place, Stratford-upon-
Avon, Warwickshire, Archaeological Desk-based Assessment and Evaluation', *Birmingham
Archaeology* (2009), pp. 1–70. My account of Shakespeare's purchase of New Place and his
dealings with Quiney are derived from Bearman, 'Shakespeare's Purchase of New Place'
(2012), pp. 465–86; Schoenbaum, *A Compact Documentary Life* (1977), pp. 228–40; and Weis,
Shakespeare Revealed (2007), pp. 239–45. For Hall's use of the Bell Inn during the Somerville–
Arden plot, see Wilkes's letter to William Cecil, the Earl of Leicester and Francis Walsingham,
NA, SP 12/163, ff. 140r–141r, 7 November 1583; for more on his role in the conspiracy, see
chapter ten and corresponding notes. For Edward Greville's career, see the entries in Hasler,
ed., *The History of Parliament* (1981) and Thrush and Ferris, eds., *The History of Parliament*
(2010). For Greville's association with Sir Thomas Lucy and his role in Warwickshire, see also
HH, CP 47/102, 1596. Essex's appointment of Greville to stand co-surety is in NA, SP 12/259,
f. 29r, 8 June 1596. The Earl calls Greville to service personally in HH, CP 47/109,
27 March 1597.

Chapter Twenty-one: 'this distracted Globe'

The dismantling of the Theatre in Shoreditch and the construction of the Globe are
derived from NA, STAC 5/A.32, printed in Wallace, 'The First London Theatre . . .' (1913),
pp. 277–9. See also Shapiro, *1599* (2005), pp. 1–7. For an account of the Bankside district, see
Brandon and Brooke, *Bankside* (2013). For Brend's association with the Globe, see notes to
chapter eighteen and his will, NA, PROB 11/98, ff. 325r–326v, 10 October 1601, which
reveals his connection to Matthew Browne. For the Burbages' costs and the new business
model which made Shakespeare part-owner of the Globe, see Dobson and Wells, eds.,
Oxford Companion to Shakespeare (2001), pp. 165–6 and Gurr, *The Shakespeare Company* (2004),
pp. 31–5 and 251–2 (which includes a transcription of Cuthbert Burbage's testimony at the
Court of Requests, NA, REQ 2/706, 28 January 1632). Guilpin's view of the abandoned
Theatre is in *Skialetheia* (1598), sigs. D5v–D6r.

On the temporary truce between Essex and Cecil and Knollys' doubts, see Hammer,
The Polarization of Elizabethan Politics (1999), pp. 374–82 and Collins, ed., *Letters and Memorials of State* (1746), vol. 2, p. 42. Another of Essex's enemies, Sir Walter Ralegh, wrote a
jocund letter to Cecil, hinting that there was camaraderie between the three of them, but
there was an ominous note almost anticipating the tragedy to come in Ralegh's observation that Essex 'was also wonderful merry at your conceit of Richard the 2 [Richard II]',
NA, SP 12/264, f. 12r, 6 July 1597. Elizabeth Russell's letter to Robert Cecil with her attempt
to intervene in the feuding of the courtiers is HH, CP 176/88, January 1598[?]; the dating
is based on the first round of the arguments in 1597, though it is possible the letter was
written in 1599, after a further explosion of tensions in the January of that year; see Chamberlain, *Letters*, ed. Thomson (1965), p. 10. For the argument between Howard and Essex,
see Devereux, *Lives and Letters* (1853), vol. 1, pp. 466–70. Elizabeth draws attention to the

rough weather in her letter to Robert Cecil, HH, CP 58/53, January 1598[?]. It is possible that Elizabeth was convalescing in Windsor at the time, as her decision to sojourn in the country is indicated in her letter HH, CP 53/89, July 1597; see also Russell, *Letters*, ed. Farber (1977), p. 218.

Vaughan's praise of Elizabeth Russell is from his dedication to her in his translation of Palladius's *An Introduction into the Books of the Prophets* (1598), sigs. A2r–A2v. The indication that Elizabeth had new 'business in law' that year is from her letter to Robert Cecil, HH, CP 58/53, January 1598[?]. Elizabeth's efforts on behalf of those suffering under the 'hue and cry' law are recounted in her letter to Robert Cecil, HH, CP 49/13, January 1598. For the context of 'hue and cry', see Russell, *Letters*, ed. Farber (1977), pp. 223–5. For the death of William Cecil, Lord Burghley, see ODNB.

De Maisse's observations are from de Maisse, *Journal*, ed. Harrison (1931), pp. 64–5. For the *True Relation* and la Fontaine's involvement in its dissemination, see Hammer, 'Myth-making . . .' (1997), pp. 630–35. Elizabeth's letter to Robert Cecil in which she defends herself and mentions his angry epistle to her is HH, CP 49/92, March 1599. (The date of this letter is corrected by Phillippy from the erroneous one given in the corresponding CMS; see Russell, *The Writings*, ed. Phillippy (2011), p. 277, n. 1.) Elizabeth's letter hinting that 'Some will kill me' is HH, CP 74/1, September 1599. The rumour of Spanish troops on the Isle of Wight is reported in Collins, ed., *Letters and Memorials of State* (1746), vol. 2, pp. 112–13. Elizabeth's letter to Robert Cecil with her order for weaponry is HH, CP 73/69, August 1599.

Elizabeth's letter to Robert Cecil with her report of words said at an 'ordinary' is HH, CP 179/92, October 1599. The letters of Lady Rich which ended up in Cecil's hands were HH, CP 99/167 and HH, CP 101/205. On the involvement of Lady Rich and the Earl of Essex in Southampton's secret marriage, see Devereux, *Lives and Letters* (1853), vol. 1, p. 474. Lady Rich's letter to Southampton is HH, CP 99/167, dated 10 May but without indication of the year. Essex's unauthorized return to England is recounted in Harrison, *The Life and Death of Robert Devereux* (1937), pp. 248–9. For Essex's house arrest, see Devereux, *Lives and Letters* (1853), vol. 2, pp. 88–9. On the duration of Essex's illness and White's report on the surveillance of Essex's 'Servants', see Collins, ed., *Letters and Memorials of State* (1746), vol. 2, pp. 153 and 132 respectively. The quotations from Elizabeth's highly allusive letter are from HH, CP 179/92, October 1599. The English translations from the relevant sections of Virgil's *Aeneid* (4: 169–70 and 1:147–58) are taken from Virgil, *The Aeneid*, trans. West (1991), pp. 85–6 and 8 respectively. For an excellent reading of these allusions, different to my own though no less valid, see Lamb, 'The Cooke Sisters . . .' (1985), pp. 107–25. The translations of the quotations from Horace's *Epistles* are taken from Horace, *Satires, Epistles*, trans. Fairclough (1926), 1.10.24, p. 317.

The quotation from Shakespeare's play is Shakespeare, *Henry V*, ed. Taylor (1982), 5.0.9–35; see also the introduction of ibid. for the context of Shakespeare's allusion to Essex and the dating of the play, pp. 4–12. The pro-Cobham sentiments from the Admiral's Men's play are from Munday [, Drayton, Hathaway, and Wilson], *Sir John Oldcastle, the Good Lord Cobham* (1600; play first performed by the Admiral's Men in 1599), sig. A2r. On the animosity between Essex and the Lord Admiral, Charles Howard, and Essex's creation of new knights, see Chamberlain, *Letters*, ed. Thomson (1965), p. 10 and 15–16 respectively. On the short run of *Henry V* and on its being 'stayed' and censored, see Shapiro, *1599* (2005), p. 103. The quotations from *Hamlet* are taken from Shakespeare, *Hamlet*, ed. Hibbard (1987),

1.5.96–7 and 2.2.326–40. I am working on the assumption that the passage about the child players in *Hamlet* was cut from the version of the play now known as the Second Quarto (Q2) of 1604 and then restored to the First Folio version of the text in 1623; for more on this and the dating of the play, see Shakespeare, *Hamlet*, eds. Thompson and Taylor (2006), p. 52 and Appendix 1, pp. 468–70. The comment that the Blackfriars Theatre would be of 'very little value' if converted to another use is from the 'Plea of Richard Burbage and John Heminges' in their Chancery case over the playhouse, 8 July 1612, quoted in Smith, *Shakespeare's Blackfriars Playhouse* (1964), p. 536; see also pp. 175–209 of ibid. for a discussion of Shakespeare's *Hamlet* and the Blackfriars Theatre. For the idea of the Burbages' clever advertising, see Knutson, 'Falconer to the Little Eyases . . .' (1995), pp. 1–31. For further discussion about the scene, see Menzer, 'The Tragedians of the City? . . .' (2006), pp. 162–82. Histrio's comments are from Jonson, *Poetaster* (1601; performed by the Children of Blackfriars in 1601). The use of the term 'common playhouse' is from Elizabeth Russell's petition, NA, SP 12/260, f. 176r, November 1596.

Chapter Twenty-two: Wedding Belles and Rebels

Elizabeth Russell's letter to Robert Cecil with her plan for extracting Nan from court is HH, CP 180/77, 21 April 1600. White's reports about the progress of the marriage preparations are in Collins, ed., *Letters and Memorials of State* (1746), vol. 2, pp. 195 (16 May 1600) and 197 (31 May 1600). Elizabeth's letter to Cecil indicating that she had persuaded the Queen personally, with her arrangements for the celebratory supper, is HH, CP 186/134, June 1600 (given the dates of White's reports, the letter was probably composed on or around 2 June). The use of Cobham's house for the Queen's lodging, due to the relatively small size of Elizabeth's home, is mentioned in Collins, ed., *Letters and Memorials of State* (1746), vol. 2, p. 202. Elizabeth and Henry Brooke had a brief falling-out in the autumn of the previous year but had patched up their differences by the time of Nan's wedding: see Elizabeth's letter to him, NA, SP 12/255, f. 36r, September 1599 (for the dating of this letter, see Russell, *The Writings*, ed. Phillippy (2011), p. 237, n. 1). The account of Elizabeth Russell's collecting of her daughter from court, the conveying of the Queen and subsequent wedding festivities is derived from John Chamberlain's letter to Dudley Carleton, NA, SP 12/275, ff. 20r–20v, 24 June 1600; Elizabeth Russell's letter to Robert Cecil, HH, CP 186/134, June 1600; and White's dispatches to Robert Sidney of 11, 14 and 23 June 1600, which are reproduced in Collins, ed., *Letters and Memorials of State* (1746), vol. 2, pp. 200–204. White's letters correspond to the manuscripts in CKS, de Lisle and Dudley collection, MS U1475, C12/252 (11 June); MS U1475, C12/253 (14 June); and MS U1475, C12/254 (23 June).

The letter to John Harington composed 23 May 1597 is printed in Fulkus, ed., *The Private Lives of the Tudor Monarchs* (1974), pp. 118–19. On the brief dismissal of Bess Russell (identified only as 'Mistress Russell' in White's letter) and Elizabeth Brydges from court, see Collins, ed., *Letters and Memorials of State* (1746), vol. 2, pp. 38–9, reported on 13 April 1597. For the persistent rumours of scandals surrounding Essex and the 'Mistress Russell' who was in trouble with the Queen, see also Devereux, *Lives and Letters* (1853), vol. 1, pp. 475–6 and Lacey, *Robert, Earl of Essex* (1971), pp. 59–60. White's coded letter of 12 February 1598 is Collins, ed., *Letters and Memorials of State* (1746), vol. 2, p. 90. Anne Bacon's letter of warning to

Essex is LPL, MS 660, f. 149r. On Peake's painting recording Nan Russell's wedding, see Strong, *The Cult of Elizabeth* (1999), pp. 17–43 and Strong, *Gloriana* (2003), pp. 153–5. For Elizabeth's more intimate dinner with Robert Cecil, see her letter to him, HH, CP 186/134, June 1600. For the relative location of Field's 'Timber House', see Field's lease agreement, SHC, LM 333/12, 22 September 1592; Gideon de Lawne's lease agreement, SHC, LM 333/11, 20 September 1592; the indenture of Lewis de Mare, SHC, LM 348/68, 3 September 1570; Elizabeth Russell's letter to William More, SHC, HC 6729/6/98, 9 August c.1580–81[?]; the indentures of Paul Buck, SHC, LM 348/216, 30 June 159 and SHC, LM 348/234, 31 January 1594; and notes to chapters six and eighteen. The Queen's passing 'through' to Dr Paddy's house is mentioned in Collins, ed., *Letters and Memorials of State* (1746), vol. 2, p. 203 and indicates that Elizabeth's co-signatory of 1596 lived somewhere between her and Henry Brooke. For Mary Fitton's court post, see Lawson, 'The Queen's Maids . . .' (2013).

For the treatment of Essex at the York House meeting, see Lacey, *Robert, Earl of Essex* (1971), pp. 253–6 and Harrison, *The Life and Death of Robert Devereux* (1937), pp. 262–75. The results of the interrogations and the report on Lady Rich's letter are from 'The Proceedings of the Earl of Essex', an account of the York House meeting, BL, Harley MS 6854, f. 179r. The support of Lady Rich and other female relatives is reported by White in Collins, ed., *Letters and Memorials of State* (1746), vol. 2, pp. 132 (11 October 1599), 139 (4 November 1599) and 149 (8 December 1599); in the last, White reported that Lady Essex rose 'almost every day, by day light, to go to my Lord Treasurer's, and Sir John Fortescue' to petition on her husband's behalf. Lady Rich's letters to Robert Cecil on her brother's behalf are HH, CP 68/10, HH, CP 75/83 and HH, CP 178/117. Lady Rich's controversial epistle is BL, Stowe MS 150, f. 140r. (I have based my transcriptions on this text, with interpolations from the printed version of the letter in Anon., *An Apology of the Earl of Essex* (1600)); for further copies of Lady Rich's letter, see BL, Additional MSS 40838, 25707 and 34218. James Daybell in his thorough study of the letter convincingly argues for a date of late January 1600 for its composition; see Daybell, 'Women, Politics and Domesticity . . .' (2010), pp. 111–30, esp. p. 119. Cecil's knowledge of Lady Rich's cypher and the account of the Queen's own response is reported in his letter to Lord Buckhurst, HH, CP 181/62, May or June 1600. (This is a draft letter in Cecil's hand, containing numerous deletions and corrections. For the sake of clarity I have followed the reconstructed text in the corresponding CMS, vol. 10, p. 167, with small emendations from my own transcription of the manuscript.) Chamberlain's report that Lady Rich was summoned to answer her 'riddles' is from Chamberlain, *Letters*, ed. McClure (1939), vol. 1, p. 96; his realization that Essex and Cecil were beyond reconciliation is in his letter NA, SP 12/274, f. 67r, 28 May 1600. For more on Lady Rich's letter and its consequences, see Laoutaris, ' "Toucht with bolt of Treason" . . .' (2013), pp. 201–36. On the Earl of Worcester's presence at a dinner with Essex, see Strong, *The Cult of Elizabeth* (1999), p. 28. On the Earl of Worcester's interest in the fate of Essex's vacated posts (perhaps including that of Master of the Horse), see HH, CP 107/121, 13 November 1599[?]; for the possibility that the letter's anonymous recipient is Essex and that it was composed in 1599, see Strong's account of Worcester's political uses of the Blackfriars wedding and his commissioning of the Peake painting to celebrate his investiture in Essex's former post of Master of the Horse, *The Cult of Elizabeth* (1999), pp. 17–55.

Chamberlain's report of Bess's illness is NA, SP 12/75, f. 35r, 1 July 1600. White's breaking of the news of her death is Collins, ed., *Letters and Memorials of State* (1746), vol. 2, p. 205. The quotations from Dickens's novel are from *The Old Curiosity Shop*, ed. Easson

(1985), p. 283; see also p. 694, n. 3. Boswell's recording of the myth surrounding Bess Russell is from his 'A Description of the Royal Tombs . . . of St Peter, Westminster', BL, Additional MS 33379, f. 20v. For the impact of Bess Russell's monument and the trends it sparked across the country, see Laoutaris, *Shakespearean Maternities* (2008), pp. 212–67. Elizabeth Russell's letter to Robert Cecil is HH, CP 82/50, 8 December 1600.

Chapter Twenty-three: 'I'll be revenged . . .'

For the theory that Shakespeare's Malvolio is a caricature of Thomas Posthumous Hoby and that elements of *Twelfth Night* echo the Hobys' feud with their Catholic neighbours in Yorkshire, see Wilson, *Society Women* (1925), pp. 238–56 and Arlidge, *Shakespeare and the Prince of Love* (2000), pp. 105–7. Elizabeth Russell's disappointment in Thomas Posthumous Hoby is expressed in her letter to William Cecil, BL, Lansdowne MS 10, no. 38, ff. 136r–137r; her concern with policing the northern territories is indicated in her letter to Robert Cecil, HH, CP 25/51, 24 February 1595. For Elizabeth Russell's closeness to Lady Margaret Hoby and their attendance together at the sermons of Stephen Egerton in the Blackfriars, see the numerous entries in Lady Hoby's diary for the period 1599–1605 in Hoby, *The Private Life of an Elizabethan Lady*, ed. Moody (1998). Sir Erskine Perry's assessment of Thomas Posthumous Hoby and John Ferne's account of his importance to the rooting-out of dissenters in Yorkshire are in Gardiner, ed., *The Fortescue Papers* (1871), pp. xx–xxii; Hugh Cholmeley's views on Hoby are recorded in Perry's own account (ibid., p. xxi). The reconstruction of the disputes between the Hobys and the Ewres, Cholmeleys and other neighbours is derived from the following: the Star Chamber records pertaining to the legal case, NA, STAC 5/N16/2 and NA, STAC 5/H22/21; Thomas Posthumous's petition to the Privy Council, HH, CP 88/19, 5 September 1600, with enclosure outlining the events in question, HH, CP 88/17; his letter to Robert Cecil complaining about the mocking of his preacher, HH, CP 251/39, 26 September 1600; evidence given by Thomas Posthumous against Will Ewre, son of Lord Ewre, CP 90/80, 1601; summary of the 'cause' between Thomas Posthumous and Will Ewre, HH, CP 141/357, 29 October 1601[?]; with some interpolations from Hoby, *The Private Life of an Elizabethan Lady*, ed. Moody (1998), pp. 239–45; and Lady Margaret Hoby's response to Ewre's behaviour from her diary in ibid., p. 108. For a useful analysis of Hoby's feud in relation to Renaissance concepts of honour, see Heal, 'Reputation and Honour in Court and Country . . .' (1996), pp. 161–78. The Hobys' refusal to have the case heard by the Council of the North is in HH, CP 88/19, 5 September 1600. Lady Margaret Hoby's reference to the death of 'my sister, Elizabeth Russell' and her reading of a work by the Earl of Essex are recorded in her diary entries for 15 and 16 July 1600; see Hoby, *The Private Life of an Elizabethan Lady*, ed. Moody (1998), pp. 98–9.

For Manningham's account of *Twelfth Night*, see Manningham, *Diary*, ed. Bruce (1868), p. 18. For the significance of the Middle Temple context for the play, see Arlidge, *Shakespeare and the Prince of Love* (2000), pp. 105–7. For Thomas Posthumous's enrolment at Gray's Inn and mission to the Netherlands, see his entry in Hasler, ed., *The History of Parliament* (1981). The quotations from the play are taken from Shakespeare, *Twelfth Night*, eds. Warren and Wells (1994), 1.3.13–39, 1.4.127, 2.3.68–138, 5.1.356 and 5.1.368. For meetings between Elizabeth Russell and Lady Margaret Hoby in the Blackfriars at the start of 1601, see Hoby, *The Private Life of an Elizabethan Lady*, ed. Moody (1998), pp. 134 and 136–7; see pp. 54 and 56 of ibid. for Lady Margaret's reading of Cartwright and p. 137 of the same text for Elizabeth Russell's seeking of a house for her son and daughter-in-law. For the political significance of Lady Margaret's reading, see Crawford, 'Literary Circles and Communities' (2010), pp. 49–53. For Egerton's petition and Elizabeth's and Lady Margaret's association with Alice Cartwright, see Hoby, *The Private Life of an Elizabethan Lady*, ed. Moody (1998), pp. 207–9. For Cartwright's involvement in preparations for the Hampton Court conference, see Pearson, *Thomas Cartwright* (1925), p. 390 and Collinson, *Elizabethan Puritan Movement* (1967), p. 455; see the latter for more on Egerton's involvement, pp. 449–54.

Chapter Twenty-four: 'from the Stage to the State'

The interrogations of Augustine Phillips are NA, SP 12/278, f. 139r, 18 February 1601. The unflattering descriptions of Richard III are from Shakespeare, *Richard III*, ed. Jowett (2000), 1.3.242–6. The anti-Cecil libel which echoes *Richard III* is Bodleian, MS Don. C. 54, f. 20r. The libel dated 20 December 1599 is Bodleian, Rawlinson MS, Poetry, 26, f. 20v; the dating is from the copy in BL, Additional MS 5956, f. 23r. Shortly after Cecil was granted the Mastership of the Court of Wards Elizabeth proudly wrote to him with an address to 'my good nephew . . . Master of Her Majesty's honourable Wards and Liveries', HH, CP 73/69, August 1599. White's coded letter is in Collins, ed., *Letters and Memorials of State* (1746), vol. 2, p. 153.

The background to the events surrounding the coup is based on the very useful accounts in Hammer, 'Shakespeare's *Richard II* . . .' (2008), pp. 1–35 and Bate, 'Was Shakespeare an Essex Man?' (2009), pp. 1–28, with my own transcriptions from the original manuscripts recording the subsequent interrogations as specified in these notes. Merrick's confession is NA, SP 12/278, f. 130r, 17 February 1601. Chamberlain's appraisal of Essex is in Chamberlain, *Letters*, ed. Thomson (1965), p. 18. For Lady Margaret Hoby's response to the calamity, see her diary entries in Hoby, *The Private Life of an Elizabethan Lady*, ed. Moody (1998), p. 138; for her dining with Lady Rich, see ibid., p. 135. The record of the suspects in the Essex uprising and Lady Rich's house arrest is NA, SP 12/270, f. 57v; the second document, recording fewer conspirators' names, is NA, SP, 12/278, f. 55r (both of these are given a conjectural date of 10 February 1601 in the corresponding CSP). Essex's blaming of Lady Rich and the Queen's warning are recorded in Brewer, *The Court of King James the First* (1839), vol. 1, pp. 14–20. Evidence of Elizabeth Russell's support of Dorothy (Devereux Perrot) Percy can be found in Dorothy's letter to Elizabeth in which she seeks her 'honourable favour' in order to prevent the 'ruin and overthrow of us' after her family had been landed with £3,000 debt and 'all manner of disgraces', HH, CP 168/123, June[?] 1592. That Elizabeth had been accused of collaborating with the Cecils' enemies is strongly suggested in her letters to Robert Cecil HH, CP 49/92, March 1599 and HH, CP 179/92, October 1599. For Elizabeth's meetings with Essex, see notes to chapters sixteen and twenty and a letter from the Earl to Anthony Bacon indicating that he intended to visit her, LPL, MS 659, no. 235, f. 342r, 13 October 1596. Edward Bromley's confession is NA SP, 12/279, f. 131r, 2 March 1601. Edward Russell's confession is NA, SP 12/278, f. 71r, 11 February 1601. Edward Russell's address to the Privy Council is HH, CP 76/67, 14 February 1601. For more on Lady Rich's involvement in the events of that day, see the confession of John Davies, NA, SP 12/278, f. 65r, 10 February 1601 and Laoutaris, ' "Toucht with bolt of Treason" . . .' (2013), pp. 201–36. Lady Margaret Hoby's assessment of the rebellion is in her diary entry in Hoby, *The Private Life of an Elizabethan Lady*, ed. Moody (1998), p. 138. Robert Cecil's view of the coup and his reassertion of the Hayward scandal are recorded in his notes, NA, SP 12/278, ff. 79r–80r, 13 February 1601. Cecil's apparent discovery of Essex's cultivation of the Pope, Parsons and Wright is recounted in NA, SP 12/275, ff. 55r–57r, 22 July 1600. Cecil's instructions to the preachers are outlined in NA, SP 12/278, ff. 108r–109v, 14[?] February 1601. Stephen Egerton's letter to Cecil is HH, CP 104/125, 4 April 1601; see also HH, CP 85/145, 8 April 1601, for his further justifications. For the intervention of William Fitzwilliam, Elizabeth Russell's kinsman, in Egerton's troubles, see Croft, 'The Religion of Robert Cecil' (1991), p. 775; further background to this incident can also be found in Collinson, *Elizabethan Puritan Movement* (1967), pp. 446–7.

Lady Margaret Hoby's diary entry recording the fate of the conspirators and her subsequent recovery is recorded in Hoby, *The Private Life of an Elizabethan Lady*, ed. Moody (1998), pp. 138–9. Sir John Peynton's letter is HH, CP 83/86, with enclosure HH, CP 83/85, 18 February 1601. Thomas Posthumous Hoby's letter to Robert Cecil is HH, CP 180/16, 10 February 1601. For Essex's execution, see Lacey, *Robert, Earl of Essex* (1971), pp. 1–5 and 311–20, and Devereux, *Lives and Letters* (1853), vol. 2, pp. 184–91. The libel against George Carey and Thomas Cecil is BL, Harley MS 2127, f. 34r; see also NA, SP 12/278, f. 31r for another copy. The importance of these anti-Cecil/pro-Essex libels within the culture of 'libelling' has only recently become clear, thanks to such immensely valuable projects as the 'Early Stuart Libels' database, eds. Alastair Bellany and Andrew McRae, with assistant eds. Paul E. J. Hammer and Michelle O'Callaghan, and electronic publishing manager, Chris Boswell: see www.earlystuartlibels.net. Francis Bacon's account of Essex's coup is taken from Bacon, *A Declaration of the Practices and Treasons* (1601), sigs. K2v–K3r. On the lucrative duopoly of the Globe and the Fortune, see Chambers, *The Elizabethan Stage* (1923), vol. 4, pp. 326–31 (which reproduces the official documents which ratified it) and Gurr, 'Henry Carey's Peculiar Letter' (2005), pp. 51–75.

Chapter Twenty-five: The Last Stand for Donnington

The account of Elizabeth Russell's dispute with Anne Lovelace is derived from Elizabeth's letters to Robert Cecil, HH, CP 88/120, 12 October 1601; HH, CP 114/115, after 12 October 1601; and HH, CP 90/152, after 12 October 1601. On Latton, see Russell, *The Writings*, ed. Phillippy (2011), p. 287, n. 3. Elizabeth's letter to Robert Cecil asking him to prevent the Lord Admiral's suit for Donnington is HH, CP 178/132, 5 March 1600. Elizabeth's account of Popham's serving of the writ against her is from her letter to Thomas Egerton, EL, MS 46, c. February or March 1600; see also the notes in Russell, *The Writings*, ed. Phillippy (2011), pp. 243–5. (I follow Phillippy's dating of the letter.) The account of the dispute with Childe and Elizabeth's expelling of his animals is taken from the Chancery records NA, C3/263/26, 1599.

Elizabeth's extraordinary battle with the Lord Admiral, Charles Howard is reconstructed from the following documents: Elizabeth's letter to Robert Cecil outlining the plundering and use of her own weapons from her castle and Bellingham's treatment of her, HH, CP 119/73, 6 November 1606 (another letter to Cecil provides evidence that Thomas Dolman was a near-neighbour, HH, CP 106/39, 3 August 1602); Elizabeth's letter to Cecil, requesting his presence at the hearing of 14 May 1606, HH, CP 119/74, 13 May 1606; her witness testimony in the Star Chamber records, NA, STAC 8/245/7, 1606; the Lord Admiral's witness testimony in the Star Chamber records, NA, STAC 8/245/7, 1606; and the account of the trial, Elizabeth's bold conduct and the outcome of the case, in Hawarde, *Les Reportes*, ed. Baildon, (1894), pp. 270–78 and 309–12; see also ibid., p. 434, for Queen Elizabeth I's original grant of Donnington Castle to Charles Howard and the gossip about Elizabeth's dispute spread by Sir Thomas Edmonds and the Earl of Worcester.

Elizabeth's letter to William Dethick with the latter's outlines for the funeral proceedings he felt more appropriate to her rank is College of Arms, Vincent MS 151, pp. 325–9; pp. 373–4 of the same manuscript contain the proceedings for 'The Funeral of a Countess', which was what Elizabeth really coveted. Elizabeth's encounter with Shirley the younger is outlined in her letter to Robert Cecil, HH, CP 126/127, after 6 May 1608. For Shirley's scandalous career, see ODNB. Elizabeth's conflict with Sandys and Dingley is recounted in her letter to Cecil, NA, SP 14/69, f. 26r, *c*.after 6 May 1608. For Sandys and Dingley, see Russell, *Letters*, ed. Farber (1977), pp. 347–50. For a fuller account of my theory that Nicholas Hilliard's miniature of a woman in a bed of estate is Elizabeth Russell, see my article '*Virtutis Amore*: Hilliard's Lady in a Bed of Estate Revealed', forthcoming in the *British Art Journal* in early 2015. The quotations from Horace's Epistle 16 come from Horace, *Satires, Epistles*, trans. Fairclough (1926), pp. 351–7. The Renaissance translation of the section from which the '*Virtutis Amore*' phrase is taken is from Barnes, *Four Books of Offices* (1606), p. 131. Richard Field twice printed works which expounded upon the phrase '*Virtutis Amore*': see Abbot, *An Exposition upon the Prophet Jonah* (1600), p. 634 and Estienne, *A World of Wonders* (1607), p. 61. Elizabeth's letter to Robert Cecil lamenting the destruction of Donnington is HH, CP, 126/126, June 1608. (Phillippy has corrected the erroneous dating in the CMS; see Russell, *The Writings*, ed. Phillippy (2011), p. 314.)

Chapter Twenty-six: *All's Well That Ends Well*

The quotations from Shakespeare's play used in the opening of this chapter are from Shakespeare, *All's Well That Ends Well*, ed. Snyder (1993), 3.2.28; 3.2.66–7; and 3.2.87. On the 1623 First Folio edition of *All's Well* as based primarily on Shakespeare's manuscript copy or 'foul papers' and for the likely earliest possible dating of the play, based on stylistic features, see Dobson and Wells, eds., *Oxford Companion to Shakespeare* (2001), p. 10. The recent controversy over the play's later possible dating of 1606–1607 (with some critics dating it as late as 1609) and an overview of the argument that Shakespeare had written *All's Well That Ends Well* in collaboration with Thomas Middleton are presented in a *TLS* article of 19 April 2012, by Laurie Maguire and Emma Smith, 'Many Hands – A New Shakespeare Collaboration?'. For John Russell's name in the First Quarto version of *Henry IV, Part I*, see Shakespeare, *The History of Henry the Fourth* (1598); see also Jowett, 'The Thieves in 1 *Henry IV*' (1987), pp. 325–33. On the connection between the Russell family and the families of Rosel/Rozel and Bertrand, see Wiffen, ed., *Historical Memoirs of the House of Russell* (1833) vol. 1, pp. 1–7. For examples of 'Rossillion' in the First Folio of Shakespeare's plays see Shakespeare,

Mr William Shakespeare's Comedies, Histories, and Tragedies, eds.Heminges and Condell (1623), pp. 230, 239, 242 and 243. On the connection between the names Bertram and Bertrand, see WNWCD. For one of the sources of *All's Well* as *The Palace of Pleasure* and the Beltramo character, see Appendix E of Shakespeare, *All's Well That Ends Well*, ed. Snyder (1993), pp. 225–32; the quotation from the play referring to 'old virginity' is from ibid., 1.1.162.

The first words of the play are quoted from Shakespeare, *All's Well That Ends Well*, ed. Snyder (1993), 1.1.1–2. For Harington's praise of Elizabeth Russell as a memorializer, see his *Orlando Furioso* (1591; 1607 edition), p. 314. For Elizabeth's overseeing of the French version of the work she translated as *A Way of Reconciliation*, see chapter four. Elizabeth's reference to her translation as having been a 'French creature' and her account of her managing its publication are from Russell, *A Way of Reconciliation* (1605), dedicatory epistle to Anne (Russell) Herbert, sigs. A2r–A3r. On the career of Francis Russell, 2nd Earl of Bedford, see Wiffen, ed., *Historical Memoirs of the House of Russell* (1833), vol. 1, pp. 397–520. For Charles IX's investiture in the Order of the Garter, see BI., Cotton MS Titus B/II, ff. 191r–193r, 1564. For the *Book of Bertram the Priest* by Bertram or Ratramnus, and Elizabeth Russell's use of this source, see Russell, *The Writings*, ed. Phillippy (2011), pp. 376–81. For Elizabeth Russell's creation of the Hoby tombs, see Gladstone, *Building an Identity* (1989). I am indebted to the staff at the Weiss Gallery, particularly Mark and Catherine Weiss, for providing me with information about Elizabeth Russell's widow's attire and the French influences behind her chosen style. For the Somerset House Conference in 1604 and Shakespeare's involvement as a Groom of the Chamber, see Gurr, *The Shakespeare Company* (2004), pp. 51–2. Elizabeth Russell's sending of her book as a gift to Robert Cecil is indicated in her letter addressed to him as 'Lord Salisbury', HH, CP 197/53, composed after 4 May 1605 (when Cecil was created Earl of Salisbury). Elizabeth's letter to Mary Talbot, Countess of Shrewsbury, is LPL, 3203, no. 410, also composed after 4 May 1605. Elizabeth's letter addressed to Cecil as 'the Lord Viscount Cranborne' is HH, CP, 109/27, after 20 August 1604.

The Countess of Roussillon's address to Bertram is from Shakespeare, *All's Well That Ends Well*, ed. Snyder (1993), 1.1.61–72. The quotation from Hoby's translation of Castiglione's work is from Hoby, *The Courtier* (1561), sig. P3r. Elizabeth's description of herself as a 'courtier and parliament woman' is in HH, CP 90/151, December 1601; she also calls herself a 'courtier' in NA, SP 12/255, f. 371, December 1595. Elizabeth refers to Cecil as a 'cunning courtier' in HH, CP 175/92, June 1597 and praises him as a 'complete courtier' in HH, CP 68/11, January 1596. Lodge's lauding of Elizabeth is in his dedicatory epistle to her, *A Margarite of America* (1596), sig. A4r. The Clown's mocking of the courtier and his exchanges with the Dowager Countess of Roussillon which refer to Puritanism are Shakespeare, *All's Well That Ends Well*, ed. Snyder (1993), 2.2.8–40 and 1.3.50–95 respectively. The quotation from Hoby's text which Shakespeare may have borrowed for the Clown's speech is in Hoby, *The Courtier*, trans. Castiglione (1561), sig. Q3v. The quotation from the play in which Bertram refers to his status as the King's ward is Shakespeare, *All's Well That Ends Well*, ed. Snyder (1993), 1.1.4–11. The attack on Elizabeth Russell's family is in [Parsons], *An Advertisement* (1592), pp. 13–19 and 50–57. On the renewal of the attacks on Elizabeth Russell's family by Parsons in 1604, though not specifically connected to the wardship system, see the important findings in Goodrich, *Early Modern Englishwomen as Translators* (2008), pp. 368–85. The Dowager Countess of Roussillon's efforts on behalf of Helen and the quotations bespeaking her maternal role are from Shakespeare, *All's Well That Ends Well*, ed. Snyder (1993), 1.1.38–40, 1.3.103–5 and 1.3.139–53.

Elizabeth's offer to take in Frances is made in HH, CP 109/27, after 20 August 1604; that Sir Anthony Cooke was ill and seeking medical treatment is clear from HH, CP 108/63, 1604. Elizabeth's intervention in the wardships of the Steward family is expressed in her letter to Robert Cecil, HH, CP 197/54, after 4 May 1605; for useful notes on this case, see Russell, *The Writings*, ed. Phillippy (2011), pp. 303–306. Elizabeth's attempt to manage the matrimonial destiny of Anne Lovelace is in HH, CP 90/152, 12 October 1601; her efforts to rebuff the advances of the Earl of Hertford are recounted in EL, MS 47, before 14 May 1600; and her overtures to Thomas Egerton on her daughter's behalf are in her letter to him, EL, MS 46, February or March 1600. Elizabeth's intervention in the marriage problems of Peregrine Bertie is in LA, 10ANC/333, 1597; see also Russell, *The Writings*, ed. Phillippy (2011), pp. 199–201, for useful context to this letter. On Sir Edward Hoby's entertainment of the royals during their Progress, see his letter to Robert Cecil, HH, CP 125/170, 16 June 1608. Elizabeth Russell's letter to Robert Cecil, asking his aid to be brought to church, is HH, CP 126/126, June 1608. Elizabeth's last surviving letter, from her lodgings at Windsor, which gives details of her health and her nephew's visit, is BL, Lansdowne MS 76, no. 82, f. 183r, July 1608. Elizabeth's burial is recorded in Powell, ed., *Register of Bisham* (1898), p. 31. Elizabeth Russell's original will is NA, PROB 11/113, ff. 435r–436r, 23 April 1609. The revised version of her will, dated 25 May 1609, is NA, PROB 10/266, A–W and is printed in Russell, *The Writings*, ed. Phillippy (2011), pp. 431–42, from which the revisions to the will are quoted here. For Elizabeth's dealings with Yelverton, see NA, E44/191, 21 March 1608 and chapter nineteen and accompanying notes, which outline the relationship between the Yelvertons and the Gardiners.

Epilogue: Afterlife of a Murderess

The legends surrounding Elizabeth Russell are recounted in Compton, *The Story of Bisham Abbey* (1979), pp. 103–5, and Chambers, *The Book of Days* (1879), vol. 1, p. 475. Adelina Drysdale's encounter with Elizabeth's ghost is in Mackintosh, *No Alibi* (1961), pp. 53–4. The fate of Prince Mario Colonna is reported in the *Catholic Herald*, p. 14 (obituary), 15 July 1938 and in the *Northern Star*, p. 7, 11 July 1938. For Elizabeth Russell's servant named 'Seton', see BL, Additional MS 18764, 1566 and Sir Thomas Hoby's will, PROB 11/48, f. 419r, 12 July 1566. The Macbeths' servant 'Seyton' appears in Shakespeare, *Macbeth*, ed. Brooke (1990), 5.3.28–61 and 5.5.16; it is Seton who announces Lady Macbeth's death following her ghostly somnambulism. (Brooke in his note to Seyton's first entry draws attention to the character's possible connection to the family of the 'Setons', 'armour-bearers to the kings of Scotland', p. 199, n. 29.) For a more recent paranormal investigation, conducted in February 2007, into the spooky goings-on in Bisham Abbey, see http://www.southernparanormal.com/reports/bisham.html. For Shakespeare's involvement in the syndicate for the Blackfriars Theatre and his purchase of the Blackfriars Gatehouse in 1613, see Dobson and Wells, eds., *Oxford Companion to Shakespeare* (2001), pp. 48–9. For the possibility that Shakespeare sold his shares in the Globe after it was rebuilt, see Gurr, *The Shakespeare Company* (2004), p. 30. The First Globe Theatre's destruction occurred on 29 June 1613; on the end of the First Globe and construction and opening of the Second Globe in 1614, see Schoenbaum, *A Compact Documentary Life* (1977), pp. 276–7; Fogg, *Hidden Shakespeare* (2012), pp. 278–80;

and the anonymous ballad of 1613 which indicates just how much the London populace had taken the Globe to their hearts; the ballad here quoted (my own edited version of that presented in the *Gentleman's Magazine*, no. 86 (1816), p. 114) contains a deliberate pun on the original title of *Henry VIII*, a play which Shakespeare probably composed in collaboration with John Fletcher and was performed as *All is True*. The ballad also refers to some of the theatre's co-sharer-owners:

> Out run the knights, out run the lords,
> And there was great ado.
> Some lost their hats, and some their swords,
> Then out ran Burbage too.
> The reprobates, though drunk on Monday,
> Prayed for the fool and Henry Condye [Condell];
> *O sorrow, pitiful sorrow, and yet all this is true.*

> The periwigs and drumheads fry,
> Like to a burning firkin [keg of butter].
> A woeful burning did betide
> To many a good buff jerkin.
> Then with swollen eyes, like drunken Fleming's,
> Distressèd stood old stuttering Heminges.
> *O sorrow, pitiful sorrow, and yet all this is true.*

The final stanza of this ballad of the 'great renowned house' of the Globe advised the King's Men that if they wished to have the theatre rebuilt then they should:

> Go draw you a petition,
> And do you not abhor it,
> And get with low submission
> A licence to beg for it,
> In churches, sans [without] church wardens' checks,
> In Surrey and in Middlesex.
> *O sorrow, pitiful sorrow, and yet all this is true.*

Could this be a mocking glance at the theatrical troupe's previous trouble with the church wardens who backed Elizabeth Russell in her 1596 petition, a petition signed by the church warden Richard Field, which led to the creation of the Globe?

Bibliography

Abbreviations

BL: British Library, London

Bodleian: Bodleian Library, Oxford

CKS: Centre for Kentish Studies, Maidstone

CMS: *Calendar of the Manuscripts of the Most Honourable the Marquis of Salisbury, Preserved at Hatfield House, Hertfordshire*, 24 vols. (London: Royal Commission on Manuscripts, 1833–1976)

CSP: Calendar of State Papers

CUL: Cambridge University Library, Cambridge

DNB: *Dictionary of National Biography*

EEBO: *Early English Books Online*

EL: Ellesmere Manuscripts, Collection of the Duke of Sutherland, Mertoun, Roxburghshire, Scotland

f./ff.: folio/folios

FSL: Folger Shakespeare Library, Washington

HH, CP: Hatfield House, Hertfordshire, Cecil Papers

Huntington: Huntington Library, San Marino, California

ITL: Inner Temple Library, London

LA: Lincolnshire Archives, Lincoln

LMA: London Metropolitan Archives, London

LPL: Lambeth Palace Library, London

MS/MSS: manuscript/manuscripts

NA, C: National Archives, Kew, Records of the Court of Chancery

NA, E: National Archives, Kew, Records of the Exchequer and Court of Augmentations

NA, LC: National Archives, Kew, Lord Chamberlain's Office Papers

NA, LR: National Archives, Kew, Office of the Auditors of Land Revenue

NA, PC: National Archives, Kew, Privy Council Registers

NA, PROB: National Archives, Kew, Prerogative Court of Canterbury Wills

NA, REQ: National Archives, Kew, Court of Requests Proceedings

NA, SP: National Archives, Kew, State Papers

NA, STAC: National Archives, Kew, Star Chamber Proceedings

ODNB: *Oxford Dictionary of National Biography*, 60 vols., ed. H.C.G. Matthew and Brian Harrison (Oxford: Oxford University Press, 2004)

OED: *Oxford English Dictionary* (Oxford: Oxford University Press, 1989)

OL: *Original Letters relative to the English Reformation . . . chiefly from the archives in Zurich*, 2 vols., ed. Hastings Robinson (Cambridge: The Parker Society, 1846)

SHC, HC: Surrey History Centre, Historical Correspondence

SHC, LM: Surrey History Centre, Loseley Manuscripts
sig./sigs.: signature/signatures
TLS: *Times Literary Supplement*
VCH: *Victoria County History* (Oxford: Oxford University Press, 1911–)
WAM: Westminster Abbey Muniments
WNWCD: *Webster's New World College Dictionary*
ZL: *The Zurich Letters, Comprising the Correspondence of Several English Bishops and Others . . .*,
   2 vols., ed. Hastings Robinson (Cambridge: The Parker Society, 1845)

Primary Manuscript Sources

Bibliothèque Nationale, Paris, France
   Collection Dupuy
Bodleian Library MSS, Oxford
British Library, London
   Additional MSS
   Cottonian MSS
   Egerton MSS
   Hargrave MSS
   Harleian MSS
   Lansdowne MSS
   Royal MSS
   Stowe MSS
Cambridge University Library MSS, Cambridge
Centre for Kentish Studies, Maidstone, Kent
   De Lisle and Dudley Collection
College of Arms MSS, London
Duke of Sutherland MSS, Mertoun, Roxburghshire, Scotland
   Ellesmere MSS
Folger Shakespeare Library, Washington
   Cawarden and Loseley Collections
Hatfield House, Hertfordshire
   Cecil Papers
Huntington MSS, Huntington Library, San Marino, California
Inner Temple Library, London
   Petyt MSS
Lambeth Palace Library MSS, London
   Bacon Correspondence
Lincolnshire Archives, Lincoln
London Metropolitan Archives
National Archives
   C 2, C 3 and C 78: Records of the Court of Chancery
   E 44 and E 133: Records of the Exchequer and Court of Augmentations
   E 315: Court of Augmentations Papers

LC 2: Lord Chamberlain's Office Papers
LR 14: Records of the Office of the Auditors of Land Revenue
PC 2: Privy Council Registers
PROB 11: Prerogative Court of Canterbury Wills
REQ 2 and 4: Court of Requests Proceedings
SP 1: State Papers, Foreign and Domestic, Henry VIII
SP 2: State Papers, Foreign and Domestic, Henry VIII
SP 10: State Papers Domestic, Edward VI
SP 11: State Papers Domestic, Mary I
SP 12: State Papers Domestic, Elizabeth I
SP 15: State Papers Domestic, Edward VI–James I: Addenda
SP 63: State Paper Office: State Papers Ireland, Elizabeth I to George III, 1558–1782
SP 68: Secretaries of State: State Papers Foreign and State Papers Calais, Edward VI, 1547–53
SP 70: State Papers Foreign, Elizabeth I, 1558–77
SP 78: Secretaries of State: State Papers Foreign, France, 1577–1780
SP 94: Secretaries of State: State Papers Foreign, Spain, 1577–1780
STAC 2, 5 and 8: Star Chamber Proceedings
Somerset Heritage Centre Archives, Taunton
Surrey History Centre, Woking, Surrey
    Historical Correspondence
    Loseley MSS
Westminster Abbey Library, London
    Westminster Abbey Muniments

Newspapers and Magazines

Athenaeum
Catholic Herald
Edinburgh Review
Gentleman's Magazine
Northern Star
The Times
Times Literary Supplement

Primary Printed Sources

Abbot, George, *An Exposition upon the Prophet Jonah contained in Certain Sermons, Preached in St Mary's Church in Oxford* (London: Richard Field, 1600)
Adams, Simon, ed., *Household Accounts and Disbursement Books of Robert Dudley, Earl of Leicester, 1558–61, 1584–86*, vol. 6 (Cambridge: Cambridge University Press, 1995)

Allen, William, *A Conference about the Next Succession to the Crown of England* (Antwerp[?]: A. Conincx, 1595)

Anon., *An Apology of the Earl of Essex* (London[?]: for J. Smethwick[?], 1600)

Anon., *A True and Summary Report of the Declaration of Some of the Earl of Northumberland's Treasons Delivered Publicly in the Court at the Star Chamber* (London: C. Barker, 1585)

Ascham, Roger, *The Schoolmaster* (London: John Day, 1576)

—, *The Whole Works of Roger Ascham*, vol. 1, part 1, ed. Rev. Dr Giles (London: John Russell Smith, 1865)

Ashmole, Elias, *The Antiquities of Berkshire* (London: E. Curll,* 1719)

Bacon, Anne, trans., John Jewel, *Apology or Answer in Defence of the Church of England* (London: Reginald Wolfe, 1564)

—, *Sermons of Bernadine Ochyne . . . concerning the Predestination and Election of God* (London: John Day, 1570)

Bacon, Francis, *A Declaration of the Practices and Treasons Attempted and Committed by Robert, Late Earl of Essex and His Complices* (London: Robert Barker, 1601)

Ballard, George, *Memoirs of Several Ladies of Great Britain*, ed. Ruth Perry (Detroit: Wayne State University Press, 1985; original edn 1752)

Barker, William, *The Nobility of Women*, ed. Warwick Bond (London: Chiswick Press, 1904; original edn 1559)

Barnes, Barnaby, *Four Books of Offices Enabling Private Persons for the Special Service of All Good Princes and Policies* (London: A. Islip for G. Bishop, T. Adams and C. Burbie, 1606)

B[artlett], J[ohn], *The Fortress of Fathers* (Emden: Egidius van der Erve, 1566)

Bentley, Thomas, *The Monument of Matrons* (London: H. Denham, 1582)

Brewer, John S., ed., *The Court of King James the First; by Dr Godfrey Goodman*, vol. 2 (London: Richard Bentley, 1839)

Bruce, John, ed., *The Correspondence of King James VI of Scotland with Sir Robert Cecil and Others in England, during the Reign of Queen Elizabeth* (London: The Camden Society, 1861)

[CMS] *Calendar of the Manuscripts of the Most Honourable the Marquis of Salisbury, Preserved at Hatfield House, Hertfordshire*, vol. 7, 1597, ed. R.A. Roberts (London: HMSO, 1899)

[CSP Domestic] *Calendar of State Papers, Domestic Series, of the Reign of Edward VI, 1547–53*, ed. C.S. Knighton (London: HMSO, 1992)

[CSP Spain] *Calendar of Letters and State Papers relating to English Affairs: Preserved Principally in the Archives of Simancas*, vol. 1, Elizabeth I, 1558–67, ed. Martin A.S. Hume (London: HMSO, 1892)

[CSP Spain] *Calendar of Letters, Despatches and State Papers, relating to the Negotiations between England and Spain*, vol. 11, Edward VI and Mary I, 1553, ed. Royall Tyler (London: HMSO, 1916)

[CSP Venice] *Calendar of State Papers and Manuscripts, relating to English Affairs, existing in the Archives and Collections of Venice, and in Other Libraries of Northern Italy*, vol. 7, 1558–80, eds. Rawdon Brown and G. Cavendish, Bentinck (London: HMSO, 1890)

Calendar of Patent Rolls, Elizabeth I, vol. 1, 1558–60 (London: HMSO, 1939)

Camden, William, *Reges, Reginae, Nobiles et alij in Ecclesia Collegiata B. Petri Westmonasterij Sepulti* (London: E. Bollifantus, 1603)

—, *Annals, The True and Royal History of the Famous Empress Elizabeth, Queen of England, France and Ireland* (London: George Purslowe, Humphrey Lownes and Miles Flesher for Benjamin Fisher, 1625)

Cartwright, Thomas, *Reply to an Answer Made of Master Doctor Whitgift* (Hemel Hempstead[?]: John Stroud[?], 1573)

Cecil, William, *The Execution of Justice in England for Maintenance of Public and Christian Peace* (London: Christopher Barker, 1584)

—, *L'execution de iustice faicte en Angleterre pour maintenir la paix publique & chrestienne* (London[?]: Thomas Vautrollier, 1584)

—, *Atto della Giustitia d'Inghilterra, esseguito, per la coseruatione della commune [e] christiana pace contra alcuni seminatori di discordie* (London[?]: John Wolfe, 1584)

—, *Justitia Britannica per quam liquet perspicue* (London[?]: Thomas Vautrollier, 1584)

—, *A Collection of Several Treatises concerning the Reasons and Occasions of the Penal Laws* (London: Richard Royston, 1675)

Chamberlain, John, *The Letters of John Chamberlain*, vol. 1, ed. Norman Egbert McClure (Philadelphia: American Philosophical Society, 1939)

—, *The Chamberlain Letters: A Selection of the Letters of John Chamberlain concerning Life in England from 1597–1626*, ed. Elizabeth McClure Thomson (London: John Murray, 1965)

Coke, John, *The Debate between the Heralds of England and France* (London: Robert Wyer for Richard Wyer, 1550)

Collins, A., ed., *Letters and Memorials of State . . . Written and Collected by Sir Henry Sidney, Sir Philip Sidney, Sir Robert Sidney*, 2 vols. (London: T. Osborne, 1746)

Collinson, Patrick, ed., 'Letters of Thomas Wood, Puritan, 1566–1577', *Bulletin of the Institute of Historical Research*, Special Supplement, no. 5 (London: The Athlone Press, 1960)

Craig, Alexander, *The Amorous Songs, Sonnets and Elegies* (London: William White, 1606)

Crompton, Richard, *A Short Declaration of the End of Traitors, and False Conspirators against the State* (London: J. Charlewood for Thomas Gubbins and Thomas Newman, 1587)

Crowley, Robert, *A Brief Discourse against the Outward Apparel* (Emden: Egidius van der Erve, 1566)

Dee, John, *The Diaries of John Dee*, ed. Edward Fenton (Oxfordshire: Day Books, 1998)

Dering, Edward, *M. Dering's Works* (London: J. R[oberts] for Paul Linley and John Flasket, 1597)

Devereux, Walter Bourchier, *Lives and Letters of the Devereux Earls of Essex*, 2 vols. (London: John Murray, 1853)

Dickens, Charles, *The Old Curiosity Shop*, ed. Angus Easson (Harmondsworth: Penguin, 1985)

E[dgar], T[homas], *The Law's Resolutions of Women's Rights: or the Law's Provision for Women* (London: Miles Flesher for John More, 1632)

Egerton, Stephen, *A Brief Method of Catechising* (London: R[ichard] F[ield] for Robert Dexter, 1597)

—, *A Brief Method of Catechising* (London: Richard Field for Henry Fetherstone, 1615)

Elizabeth I, *Elizabeth I, Translations, 1544–89*, eds. Janel Mueller and Joshua Scodel (Chicago and London: University of Chicago Press, 2009)

Estienne, Henri, *A World of Wonders: or An Introduction to a Treatise Touching the Conformity of Ancient and Modern Wonders: or a Preparative Treatise to the Apology for Herodotus* (London: Richard Field for John Norton, 1607)

Fenton, Geoffrey, trans., Jean de Serres, *A Discourse of the Civil Wars and Late Troubles in France* (London: Henry Bynneman for Lucas Harrison and George Bishop, 1570)

—, *Acts of Conference in Religion, Holden at Paris* (London: H. Bynneman for William Norton and Humphrey Toye, 1571)

—, trans., Estienne Pasquier, *Monophylo* (London: Henry Denham for William Seres, 1572)

Feuillerat, Albert, *Blackfriars Records* (The Malone Society, Oxford: Oxford University Press, 1913)

Frere, Walter Howard, and Charles Edward Douglas, eds., *Puritan Manifestoes: A Study of the Origin of the Puritan Revolt* (London: Society for Promoting Christian Knowledge, 1907)

Fulkus, Christopher, ed., *The Private Lives of the Tudor Monarchs* (London: The Folio Society, 1974)

Fuller, Thomas, *The Church History of Britain* (London: John Williams, 1655)

—, *The Appeal of Injured Innocence: unto the religious, learned and ingenuous reader in a controversy betwixt the animadvertor Dr Peter Heylyn and the author Thomas Fuller* (London: W. Godbid for John Williams, 1659)

—, *The History of the Worthies of England*, vol. 1, ed. P. Austin Nuttall (London: Thomas Tegg, 1840; original edn 1662)

Gairdner, J., and R.H. Brodie, eds., *Letters and Papers, Foreign and Domestic, of the Reign of Henry VIII*, vols. 16–21, 1540–46 (London: HMSO, 1898–1910)

Gardiner, Samuel Rawson, ed., *The Fortescue Papers, consisting Chiefly of Letters relating to State Affairs* (London: The Camden Society, 1871)

Gerbier, Charles, *Elogium Heroinum, or, The Praise of Worthy Women* (London: T.M. and A.C. for William Nott, 1651)

Gilby, Anthony, *About the Popish Apparel* (Emden: Egidius van der Erve, 1566)

Golding, Arthur, *The Life of the Most Godly . . . Jaspar Colignie* [Coligny] (London: Thomas Vautrollier, 1576)

Gosson, Stephen, *Plays Confuted in Five Actions* (Oxford: Thomas Gosson, 1582)

Greene, Robert, *Greene's Groatsworth of Wit, Bought with a Million of Repentance* (London: John Wolfe and J. Danter, 1592)

Grindal, Edmund, *The Remains of Edmund Grindal*, ed. William Nicholson (Cambridge: Cambridge University Press, 1843)

Guilpin, Edward, *Skialetheia, or, A Shadow of Truth, in Certain Epigrams and Satires* (London: J[ames] R[oberts] for Nicholas Ling, 1598)

Haddon, Walter, *D. Gualteri Haddoni . . . Poemata* (London: Gulielmum Seresium, 1567)

—, *Lucubrationes, Orationes, Epistolae, Poemata . . .* (London: Gulielmum Seresium, 1567)

Harington, John, *A New Discourse of a Stale Subject, called the Metamorphosis of Ajax: written by Misacmos, to his friend and cousin Philostilpnos* (London: Richard Field, 1596)

[Harington, John], *An Anatomy of the Metamorphosed Ajax* (London: Richard Field, 1596)

—, trans., Ludovico Ariosto, *Orlando Furioso* (London: Richard Field, 1607; original edn 1591)

—, *Nugae Antiquae: Being a Miscellaneous Collection of Original Papers, in Prose and Verse, Written during the Reigns of Henry VIII, Edward VI, Queen Mary, Elizabeth and King James, by Sir John Harington*, eds., Henry Harington and Thomas Park, vol. 1 (London: J. Wright, 1804)

Hawarde, John, *Les Reportes del Cases in Camera Stellata, 1593 to 1609*, ed. William Paley Baildon (London: Alfred Morrison, 1894)

Hayward, John, *The First Part of the Life and Reign of King Henry the Fourth* (London: John Wolfe, 1599)

Henslowe, Philip, *Henslowe's Diary*, ed. R.A. Foakes (Cambridge: Cambridge University Press, 2002)

Heylyn, Peter, *Examen Historicum: or a Discovery and Examination of the Mistakes, Falsities and Defects in Some Modern Histories* (London: Henry Seile and Richard Royston, 1659)

Heywood, James, and Thomas Wright, eds., *Cambridge University Transactions during the Puritan Controversies of the 16th and 17th Centuries*, vol. 1 (London: Henry G. Bohn, 1854)

Hoby, Margaret, *Diary of Lady Margaret Hoby, 1599–1605*, ed. Dorothy M. Meads (London: George Routledge and Sons, 1930)

—, *The Private Life of an Elizabethan Lady: The Diary of Lady Margaret Hoby, 1599–1605*, ed. Joanna Moody (Gloucestershire: Sutton Publishing, 1998)

Hoby, Thomas, trans., Baldassare Castiglione, *The Courtier* (London: William Seres, 1561)

—, trans., Baldassare Castiglione, *The Courtier* (London: John Wolfe, 1588)

—, trans., Baldassare Castiglione, *The Book of the Courtier*, ed. J.H. Whitfield (London: J.M. Dent & Sons, 1975; original edn 1561).

Holinshed, Raphael, *The Third Volume of Chronicles* (London: Henry Denham, 1586)

—, *The Chronicles of England, Scotland and Ireland* (London: Henry Denham, 1587)

Horace, *Satires, Epistles, Ars Poetica*, trans. H.R. Fairclough, Loeb Classical Library (Cambridge, Massachusetts, and London: Harvard University Press, 1926)

Jonson, Ben, *Poetaster, or The Arraignment as it Hath been Sundry Times Privately Acted in the Blackfriars, by the Children of Her Majesty's Chapel* (London: R. Bradock for M. L[ownes], 1602)

Kirk, Richard Edward G., and Ernest F. Kirk, eds., *Returns of Aliens Dwelling in the City and Suburbs of London from the Reign of Henry VIII to that of James I* (Aberdeen: Publications of the Huguenot Society of London 10, 4 vols., 1900–1908)

Knox, John, *The First Blast of the Trumpet against the Monstrous Regiment of Women* (Geneva: J. Poullain and A. Rebul, 1558)

Lang, R.G., ed., 'Two Tudor Subsidy Rolls for the City of London: 1541 and 1582', London: *The Record Society*, 29 (1993), pp. 181–7

Lawne, William de, *An Abridgement of the Institution of Christian Religion written by M. John Calvin. Wherein brief and sound answers to the objections of the adversaries are set down. By William Lawne, minister of the word of God* (Edinburgh: Thomas Vautrollier, 1585)

Lloyd, David, *State-worthies, or, The States-men and Favourites of England since the Reformation* (Thomas Milbourne for Samuel Speed, London, 1670; original edn 1665)

Locke, Anne, *Sermons of John Calvin* (London: John Day, 1560)

—, *Of the Marks of the Children of God, and Their Comforts in Afflictions* (London: Thomas Orwin for Thomas Man, 1590)

Lodge, Edmund, *Illustrations of British History*, vol. 1 (London: John Childley, 1838)

Lodge, Thomas, *A Margarite of America* (London: A. Jeffes for John Busbie, 1596)

Machyn, Henry, *The Diary of Henry Machyn: Citizen and Merchant-taylor of London, from AD 1550 to AD 1563*, ed. John Gough Nichols (London: The Camden Society, 1848)

Mackintosh, Captain Alastair, *No Alibi* (London: Frederick Muller Limited, 1961)

Madden, Frederick, *Privy Purse Expenses of the Princess Mary* (London: W. Pickering, 1831)

Madge, Sidney J., ed., *Abstract of Inquisitiones Post Mortem for the City of London*, part 2, 1561–77 (London: The British Record Society, 1901)

Maisse, de, *A Journal of All that was Accomplished by Monsieur de Maisse, Ambassador in England from King Henri IV to Queen Elizabeth, Anno Domini 1597*, ed. G.B. Harrison (London: Nonesuch Press, 1931)

Makin, Bathusa, *Essay to Revive the Ancient Education of Gentlewomen* (London: J.D. for Thomas Parkhurst, 1673)

Manningham, John, *The Diary of John Manningham*, ed. John Bruce (London: J.B. Nichols and Sons, 1868)

Marlowe, Christopher, *The Complete Plays*, ed. J.B. Steane (Harmondsworth: Penguin, 1986)

Miscellaneous, *Writings of Edward the Sixth, William Hugh, Queen Catherine Parr, Anne Askew, Lady Jane Grey, Hamilton and Balnaves* (London: The Religious Tract Society, 1836)

More, Thomas, *St Thomas More: Selected Letters*, ed. Elizabeth Frances Rogers (New Haven and London: Yale University Press, 1961)

Munday, Anthony, *A Second and Third Blast of Retrait from Plays and Theatres* (London: Henry Denham for William Seres, 1580)

—, *A Watchword to England to Beware of Traitors and Treacherous Practices* (London: John Charlewood for Thomas Hacket, 1584).

Munday, Anthony [and Michael Drayton, Richard Hathaway, and Robert Wilson], *The First Part of the True and Honourable History of the Life of Sir John Oldcastle, the Good Lord Cobham* (London: V[alentine] S[immes] for Thomas Pavier, 1600)

Nicholas, Harris, ed., *Memoirs of the Life and Times of Sir Christopher Hatton, Vice-chamberlain to Queen Elizabeth* (London: Richard Bentley, 1847)

Nichols, John Gough, *Literary Remains of King Edward VI*, vol. 1 (London: J.B. Nichols and Sons, 1857)

Page, W., ed., *Letters of Denization and Acts of Naturalization for Aliens in England, 1509–1603*, vol. 8 (London: The Huguenot Society, 1893)

Parker, Matthew, *The Holy Bible containing the Old Testament and the New* (London: Richard Jugge, 1568)

—, *Correspondence of Matthew Parker, D.D., Archbishop of Canterbury*, ed. John Bruce (Cambridge: The Parker Society, 1853)

[Parsons, Robert], *An Advertisement Written to a Secretary of My L[ord] Treasurer's of England* (Antwerp[?]: S.N., 1592)

Peel, Albert, *The Second Part of a Register: being a Calendar of Manuscripts under the Title Intended for Publication by the Puritans about 1593*, vol. 1 (Cambridge: Cambridge University Press, 1915)

Pérez, Antonio, *A Spaniard in Elizabethan England: The Correspondence of Antonio Pérez's Exile*, 2 vols., ed. Gustav Ungerer (London: Thamesis Books, 1974–6)

Phillips, Edward, *Theatrum Poetarum, or, A Complete Collection of the Poets, Especially the Most Eminent, of All Ages* (London: Charles Smith, 1675)

Ponet, John, *A Short Treatise of Politic Power* (Strasbourg: the heirs of W. Köpfel, 1556)

Popham, John, *Reports and Cases, collected by the Learned Sir John Popham, Knight, Late Lord Chief-justice of England* (London: Thomas Roycroft for Henry Twyford and John Place, 1656)

Powell, Edgar, ed. *The Register of Bisham, County Berkshire* (London: The Parish Register Society, 1898)

Russell, Elizabeth, *Speeches Delivered to Her Majesty This Last Progress, at the Right Honourable, the Lady Russell's, at Bisham . . .* (Oxford: Joseph Barnes, 1592)

—, *A Way of Reconciliation of a Good and Learned Man Touching the Truth, Nature and Substance of the Body and Blood of Christ in the Sacrament* (London: R.B., 1605)

—, *Letters of Lady Elizabeth Russell (1540–1609)*, ed. Elizabeth Farber (New York: Columbia University, unpublished doctoral thesis, 1977)

—, *The Writings of an English Sappho: Elizabeth Cooke Hoby Russell*, ed. Patricia Phillippy, with translations by Jaime Goodrich, The Other Voice in Early Modern Europe: The Toronto Series, 14 (Toronto: Centre for Reformation and Renaissance Studies, 2011)

Sandford, James, *Hours of Recreation, or Afterdinners, Which May Aptly be Called The Garden of Pleasure* (London: Henry Binneman, 1576)

Shakespeare, William, *Mr William Shakespeare's Comedies, Histories, and Tragedies, Published according to the True and Original Copies*, eds., John Heminges and Henry Condell (London: Isaac Jaggard and Edward Blount, 1623)

—, *The Norton Shakespeare*, eds. Stephen Greenblatt, Walter Cohen, Jean E. Howard and Katharine Eisaman Maus (New York and London: Norton, 1997)

—, *All's Well That Ends Well*, ed. Susan Snyder (Oxford: Oxford University Press, 1993)

—, *As You Like It*, ed. Alan Brissenden (Oxford: Oxford University Press, 1993)

—, *Cymbeline*, ed. J.M. Nosworthy (Surrey: Arden, 1997)

—, *Hamlet*, ed. G.R. Hibbard (Oxford: Oxford University Press, 1987)

—, *Hamlet*, eds. Anne Thompson and Neil Taylor (London: Arden, 2006)

—, *The History of Henry the Fourth, with the Battle at Shrewsbury, between the King and Lord Henry Percy, surnamed Henry Hotspur of the North. With the humorous conceits of Sir John Falstaff* (London: Peter Short for Andrew Wise, 1598)

—, *Henry IV, Part One*, ed. David Bevington (Oxford: Oxford University Press, 1987)

—, *Henry IV, Part Two*, ed. René Weis (Oxford: Oxford University Press, 1997)

—, *Henry V*, ed. Gary Taylor (Oxford: Oxford University Press, 1982)

—, *Macbeth*, ed. Nicholas Brooke (Oxford: Oxford University Press, 1990)

—, *The Merchant of Venice*, ed. John Russell Brown (Surrey: Arden, 1955)

—, *The Merry Wives of Windsor*, ed. T.W. Craik (Oxford: Oxford University Press, 1990)

—, *The Rape of Lucrece* (London: Richard Field, 1594)

—, *Richard II*, ed. R. Forker (London: Arden, 2002)

—, *Richard III*, ed. John Jowett (Oxford: Oxford University Press, 2000)

—, *Romeo and Juliet*, ed. René Weis (London: Arden, 2012)

—, *Twelfth Night*, eds. Roger Warren and Stanley Wells (Oxford: Oxford University Press, 1994)

—, *Venus and Adonis* (London: Richard Field, 1593)

Shaw, George Bernard, *Shaw on Shakespeare: An Anthology of Bernard Shaw's Writings on the Plays and Production of Shakespeare*, ed. Edwin Wilson (New York: Dutton & Co., 1961)

Smith, Jude, *A Mystical Device of the Spiritual and Godly Love between Christ the Spouse and the Church or Congregation* (London: Henry Kirckham, 1575)

Stow, John, *The Abridgement of the English Chronicle, first collected by M. John Stow . . . by E.H.* (London: Edward Allde and Nicholas Okes for the Company of Stationers, 1618)

—, *Survey of London* (London: Nicholas Bourn, 1633)

—, [*Memoranda*] *Three Fifteenth-century Chronicles with Historical Memoranda by John Stow*, ed. James Gairdner (London: The Camden Society, 1880)

—, *A Survey of London* (Gloucestershire: Sutton Publishing, 2005; original edn 1598)

Strype, John, *The Life and Acts of Matthew Parker* (London: John Wyatt, 1711)

—, *The Life of the Learned Sir John Cheke* (Oxford: Clarendon Press, 1821; original edn 1705)

—, *Ecclesiastical Memorials, relating Chiefly to Religion and its Reformation* . . . , vol. 2 (London: Samuel Bagster, 1822)

Tanner, J.R., ed., *Tudor Constitutional Documents, AD 1485–1603* (Cambridge: Cambridge University Press, 1951)

Trill, Suzanne, Kate Chedgzoy and Melanie Osborne, eds., *Lay By Your Needles Ladies, Take the Pen: Writing Women in England, 1500–1700* (London and New York: Arnold, 1997)

Vaughan, Edward, trans., Peder Palladius, *An Introduction into the Books of the Prophets and Apostles* (London: G. S[haw] for William Holme, 1598)

Verstegan, Richard, *Theatrum Crudelitatum Haereticorum Nostri Temporis* (Antwerp: Adrianum Huberti, 1587)

—, *Declaration of the True Causes of the Great Troubles* (Antwerp: J. Trognesius[?], 1592)

Virell, Matthew, *A Learned and Excellent Treatise containing all the Principal Grounds of Christian Religion, set down by way of conference in a most plain and familiar manner* (London: Richard Field, 1594)

Virgil, *The Aeneid*, trans. David West (Harmondsworth: Penguin, 1991)

Wharton, John, *Wharton's Dream, containing an Invective against Certain Abominable Caterpillars as Userers, Extortioners, Leasemongers and Such Others, Confounding Their Devilish Sects* (London: John Charlewood for Paul Conyngton, 1578)

Whetstone, George, *The Rock of Regard* (London: Robert Waley, 1576)

Whitgift, John, *An Answer to . . . An Admonition* (London: Henry Binneman, 1572)

Wiffen, Jeremiah H., ed., *Historical Memoirs of the House of Russell: From the Time of the Norman Conquest*, vol. 1 (London: Longman et al., 1833)

Wilcox, Thomas, *A Short Yet Sound Commentary, Written on that Worthy Work Called the Proverbs of Solomon* (London: Thomas Orwin for Thomas Man, 1589)

Worman, Ernest James, ed., *Alien Members of the Book Trade during the Tudor Period* (London: Bibliographical Society, 2006)

Wyrley, William, *The True Use of Armoury* (London: J. Jackson for Gabriell Cawood, 1592)

Secondary Printed Sources

Adams, Joseph Quincey, 'The Conventual Buildings of Blackfriars, London, and the Playhouses Constructed Therein', *Studies in Philology*, 14, no. 2 (April, 1917), pp. 64–87

Akrigg, G.P.V., *Shakespeare and the Earl of Southampton* (London: Hamish Hamilton, 1968)

Alford, Stephen, *The Watchers: A Secret History of the Reign of Elizabeth I* (London: Allen Lane, 2012)

Allen, Gemma, *The Cooke Sisters: Education, Piety and Politics in Early Modern England* (Manchester and New York: Manchester University Press, 2013)

Ammos, Flora Ross, *Early Theories of Translation* (Charleston: Bibliobazaar, 2007; original edn 1920)

Arlidge, Anthony, *Shakespeare and the Prince of Love: The Feast of Misrule in the Middle Temple* (London: DLM, 2000)

Barnes, Stephen J., 'The Cookes of Gidea Hall', *The Essex Review*, 81, vol. 21 (January, 1912), pp. 1–9

Bate, Jonathan, 'Was Shakespeare an Essex Man?', *Proceedings of the British Academy*, 162 (2009), pp. 1–28

Bibliography

Bearman, Robert, 'Shakespeare's Purchase of New Place', *Shakespeare Quarterly*, 63, no. 4 (winter, 2012), pp. 465–86

Borman, Tracy, *Elizabeth's Women: The Hidden Story of the Virgin Queen* (London: Jonathan Cape, 2009)

Bowsher, Julian, *Shakespeare's London Theatreland: Archaeology, History and Drama* (London: Museum of London Archaeology, 2012)

Brandon, David, and Alan Brooke, *Bankside: London's Original District of Sin* (Gloucestershire: Amberley, 2013)

Brown, Piers, ' "*Hac ex consilio meo via progredieris*": Courtly Reading and Secretarial Meditation in Donne's *The Courtier's Library*', *Renaissance Quarterly*, 61, no. 3 (autumn, 2009), pp. 833–66

Burrage, Champlin, *The Early English Dissenters in the Light of Recent Research (1550–1641)*, vol. 2 (Cambridge: Cambridge University Press, 1912)

Chambers, E.K., *The Elizabethan Stage*, vol. 4 (Oxford: Clarendon Press, 1923)

Collier, John Payne, *History of English Dramatic Poetry to the Time of Shakespeare*, vol. 1 (London: John Murray, 1831)

Collinson, Patrick, 'The Role of Women in the English Reformation Illustrated by the Life and Friendships of Anne Locke', *Studies in Church History*, 2, ed. G.J. Cuming (London: Thomas Nelson and Sons, 1965), pp. 258–72

—, *The Elizabethan Puritan Movement* (London: Jonathan Cape, 1967)

—, *Godly People: Essays on English Protestantism and Puritanism* (London: The Hambledon Press, 1983)

Compton, Piers, *The Story of Bisham Abbey* (Bath: Thames Valley Press, 1979)

Crawford, Julie, 'Literary Circles and Communities', *The History of British Women's Writing: 1500–1610*, eds. Caroline Bicks and Jennifer Summit (Houndmills: Palgrave, 2010), pp. 34–59

Cressy, David, *Birth, Marriage and Death: Ritual, Religion, and the Life-cycle in Tudor and Stuart England* (Oxford: Oxford University Press, 1997)

Croft, Pauline and Karen Hearn, ' "Only matrimony maketh children to be certain . . . ": Two Elizabethan Pregnancy Portraits', *British Art Journal*, 3, no. 3 (autumn, 2003), pp. 19–20

Croft, Pauline, 'The Religion of Robert Cecil', *Historical Journal*, 34, no. 4 (December, 1991), pp. 773–96

Daybell, James, 'Women, Politics and Domesticity: The Scribal Publication of Lady Rich's Letter to Elizabeth I', *Women and Writing c.1340–c.1650: The Domestication of Print Culture*, eds. Anne Lawrence-Mathers and Phillipa Hardman (York: York Medieval Press, 2010)

Dobson, Michael and Stanley Wells, eds., *The Oxford Companion to Shakespeare* (Oxford: Oxford University Press, 2001)

Duffy, Eamon, *The Stripping of the Altars: Traditional Religion in England c.1400–c.1580* (New Haven and London: Yale University Press, 1992)

Du Maurier, Daphne, *Golden Lads: A Study of Anthony Bacon, Francis and Their Friends* (London: Virago, 2007; original edn 1975)

Duncan-Jones, Katherine, *Ungentle Shakespeare: Scenes from His Life* (London: Arden, 2001)

—, *Shakespeare: Upstart Crow to Sweet Swan 1592–1623* (London: Arden, 2011)

Feingold, Mordechai, 'Giordano Bruno in England, Revisited', *Huntington Library Quarterly*, 67, no. 3 (September, 2004), pp. 329–46

Felch, Susan M., ' "Noble Gentlewomen Famous for Their Learning": The London Circle of Anne Vaughan Lock', *ANQ*, 16 (2003), pp. 14–16

—, 'The Exemplary Anne Vaughan Lock', *The Intellectual Culture of Puritan Women, 1558–1680*, eds. Johanna Harris and Elizabeth Scott-Baumann (London: Palgrave, 2011), pp. 15–27

Fogg, Nicholas, *Hidden Shakespeare: A Biography* (Gloucestershire: Amberley, 2012)

Fraser, Antonia, *The Six Wives of Henry VIII* (London: Quality Paperbacks Direct, 1992)

Freedman, Sylvia, *Poor Penelope: Lady Penelope Rich, An Elizabethan Woman* (London: The Kensal Press, 1983)

Garrisson, Janine, *A History of Sixteenth-century France, 1483–1598: Renaissance, Reformation and Rebellion* (London: Macmillan, 1991)

Giesey, Ralph E., *The Royal Funeral Ceremony in Renaissance France* (Geneva: Librairie E. Droz, 1969)

Gillespie, *Shakespeare's Books: A Dictionary of Shakespeare's Sources* (London and New York: Continuum, 2004)

Gittings, Clare, *Death, Burial and the Individual in Early Modern England* (Sydney: Croom Helm, 1984)

Goldberg, Jonathan, *Desiring Women Writing: English Renaissance Examples* (Stanford: Stanford University Press, 1997)

Goodrich, Jaime, *Early Modern Englishwomen as Translators of Religious Literature, 1500–1641* (Illinois: Northwestern University, unpublished doctoral thesis, 1987)

Greer, Germaine, *Shakespeare's Wife* (London: Bloomsbury, 2008)

Gurr, Andrew, *Playgoing in Shakespeare's London* (Cambridge: Cambridge University Press, 1996; 2nd edn)

—, *The Shakespeare Company 1594–1642* (Cambridge: Cambridge University Press, 2004)

—, 'Henry Carey's Peculiar Letter', *Shakespeare Quarterly*, 56, no. 1 (spring, 2005), pp. 51–75

—, *The Shakespearean Stage 1574–1642* (Cambridge: Cambridge University Press, 2007; 3rd edn)

Guy, John, *My Heart is My Own: The Life of Mary, Queen of Scots* (London: Harper Perennial, 2004)

—, *A Daughter's Love: Thomas and Margaret More* (London: Fourth Estate, 2008)

Hackett, Helen, *Virgin Mother, Maiden Queen: Elizabeth I and the Cult of the Virgin Mary* (Houndmills: Macmillan, 1995)

Haigh, Christopher, *English Reformations: Religion, Politics and Society under the Tudors* (Oxford: Clarendon Press, 1993)

Haller, William, *The Rise of Puritanism* (New York: Harper Torchbooks, 1957)

Hamilton, N.E.S.A., *An Inquiry into the Genuineness of the Manuscript Corrections in Mr J. Collier's Annotated Shakspere, Folio 1632; and of certain Shaksperian Documents likewise published by Mr Collier* (London: Richard Bentley, 1860)

Hammer, Paul E.J., 'The Uses of Scholarship: The Secretariat of Robert Devereux, Second Earl of Essex, c.1585–1601', *English Historical Review*, 109, no. 430 (February, 1994), pp. 26–51

—, 'Evidence from Confidential Instructions by the Earl of Essex, 1595–6', *English Historical Review*, 111, no. 441 (April, 1996), pp. 357–81

—, *The Polarization of Elizabethan Politics: The Political Career of Robert Devereux, 2nd Earl of Essex, 1585–1597* (Cambridge: Cambridge University Press, 1999)

—, 'Shakespeare's *Richard II*, the Play of 7 February 1601 and the Essex Rising', *Shakespeare Quarterly*, 59, no. 1 (2008), pp. 1–36

Bibliography

Harrison, G.B., *The Life and Death of Robert Devereux, Earl of Essex* (Bath: Cedric Chivers, 1937)

Harvey, Sheridan, *The Cooke Sisters: A Study of Tudor Gentlewomen* (Indiana: Indiana University, unpublished doctoral thesis, 1981)

Hasler, P.W., ed., *The History of Parliament: The House of Commons 1558–1603* (London: Boydell and Brewer, 1981)

Heal, Felicity, 'Reputation and Honour in Court and Country: Lady Elizabeth Russell and Sir Thomas Posthumous Hoby', *Transactions of the Royal Historical Society*, 6th series, 6 (1996), pp. 161–78

Hoak, Dale, 'The Coronations of Edward VI, Mary I and Elizabeth I and the Transformation of the Tudor Monarchy', *Westminster Abbey Reformed: 1540–1640*, eds. C.S. Knighton and Richard Mortimer (Aldershot: Ashgate, 2003)

Hogrefe, Pearl, *Women of Action in Tudor England* (Iowa: Iowa State University Press, 1977)

Hoppe, Harry R., 'John Wolfe, Printer and Publisher, 1579–1601', *Library*, 14, no. 3, 4th series (December, 1933), pp. 241–89

Hotson, Leslie, *Shakespeare versus Shallow* (London: Nonesuch Press, 1931)

House, A.P., *The City of London and the Problem of the Liberties c.1540–c.1640* (Oxford: Oxford University, unpublished doctoral thesis, 1993), Bodleian Library, shelfmark MS. D.Phil c.22058

Hudson, Hoyt. H., 'Penelope Devereux as Sidney's Stella', *Huntington Library Bulletin*, 7 (April, 1935), pp. 89–129

Hurstfield, Joel, *The Queen's Wards: Wardship and Marriage under Elizabeth I* (Cambridge, Massachusetts: Harvard University Press, 1958)

—, 'Church and State, 1558–1612: The Task of the Cecils', *Studies in Church History*, vol. 2, ed. G.J. Cuming (London, Thomas Nelson, 1965), pp. 119–40

Ingleby, C.M., *A Complete View of the Shakespeare Controversy* (London: Nattali and Bond, 1861)

Ingram, William, *A London Life in the Brazen Age: Francis Langley, 1548–1602* (Cambridge, Massachusetts, and London: Harvard University Press, 1978)

Ioppolo, Grace, 'Robert Devereux, 2nd Earl of Essex, and the Practice of Theatre', *Essex: The Cultural Impact of an Elizabethan Courtier*, eds. Annaliese Connolly and Lisa Hopkins (Manchester: Manchester University Press, 2008), pp. 63–80

Johnston, Alexandra, 'The "Lady of the Farme": The Context of Lady Russell's Entertainment of Elizabeth at Bisham, 1592', *Early Theatre*, 5.2 (2002), pp. 71–85

Jowett, John, 'The Thieves in 1 *Henry IV*', *Review of English Studies*, New Series, 38, no. 151 (1987), pp. 325–33

Kirwood, A.E.M., 'Richard Field, Printer, 1589–1624', *Library*, 4th series, 12, no. 1 (1931), pp. 1–32

Knecht, R.J., *The French Wars of Religion 1559–1598* (London and New York: Longman, 1996)

—, *The Rise and Fall of Renaissance France* (London: Fontana Press, 1996)

Knutson, Roslyn L., 'Falconer to the Little Eyases: A New Date and Commercial Agenda for the "Little Eyases" Passage in *Hamlet*', *Shakespeare Quarterly*, 46, no. 1 (spring, 1995), pp. 1–31

Kolkovich, Elizabeth Zeman, 'Lady Russell, Elizabeth I and Female Political Alliances through Performance', *English Literary Renaissance*, 39 (2009), pp. 290–314

Lacey, Robert, *Robert, Earl of Essex, An Elizabethan Icarus* (London: Phoenix Press, 1971)

Bibliography

Lamb, Mary Ellen, 'The Cooke Sisters: Attitudes toward Learned Women in the Renaissance', *Silent but for the Word: Tudor Women as Patrons, Translators and Writers of Religious Works*, ed. Margaret Hannay (Kent, Ohio: The Kent State University Press, 1985), pp. 108–25

—, *Gender and Authorship in the Sidney Circle* (Madison, Wisconsin: University of Wisconsin Press, 1990)

Laoutaris, Chris, *Shakespearean Maternities: Crises of Conception in Early Modern England* (Edinburgh: Edinburgh University Press, 2008)

—, 'Translation/Historical Writing', *The History of British Women's Writing: 1500–1610*, eds. Caroline Bicks and Jennifer Summit (Houndmills: Palgrave, 2010), pp. 296–327

—, 'The Radical Pedagogies of Lady Elizabeth Russell', *Performing Pedagogy in Early Modern England: Gender, Instruction and Performance*, eds. Kathryn M. Moncrief and Kathryn R. McPherson (Aldershot: Ashgate, 2011), pp. 65–86

—, ' "Toucht with bolt of Treason": The Earl of Essex and Lady Penelope Rich', *Essex: The Cultural Impact of an Elizabethan Courtier*, eds. Annaliese Connolly and Lisa Hopkins (Manchester and New York: Manchester University Press, 2013), pp. 201–36

Lawson, Jane, 'The Queen's Maids: Information Gained from the New Year's Gift Exchanges', unpublished paper delivered at the South Central Renaissance Conference, Queen Elizabeth I Society, 21–3 March 2013, Omaha, Nebraska

Lea, Kathleen M., 'Sir Anthony Standen and Some Anglo-Italian Letters', *English Historical Review*, 47, no. 187 (July, 1932), pp. 461–77

Llewellyn, Nigel, *Funeral Monuments in Post-Reformation England* (Cambridge: Cambridge University Press, 2000)

Loades, David, *The Cecils: Privilege and Power behind the Throne* (London: The National Archives, 2007)

Malay, Jessica, 'Elizabeth Russell's Textual Performances of Self', *Comitatus*, 37 (2006), pp. 146–68

Margetts, Michele, 'Lady Penelope Rich: Hilliard's Lost Miniatures and a Surviving Portrait', *Burlington Magazine*, 130, no. 1027 (October, 1988), pp. 758–61

Mauriès, Patrick, *Cabinets of Curiosities* (London: Thames and Hudson, 2002)

McIntosh, Marjorie Keniston, 'Sir Anthony Cooke: Tudor Humanist, Educator and Religious Reformer', *Proceedings of the American Philosophical Society*, 119, no. 3 (June, 1975), pp. 233–50

—, 'Some New Gentry in Earl Tudor Essex: The Cookes of Gidea Hall, 1480–1550', *Transactions of the Essex Archaeological Society*, 9 (1977), pp. 129–38

McKeen, David, *A Memory of Honour: A Study of the House of Cobham of Kent in Elizabeth I's Reign*, 2 vols. (Birmingham: University of Birmingham, unpublished doctoral thesis, 1964)

McNulty, Robert, 'Bruno at Oxford', *Renaissance News*, 13, no. 4 (winter, 1960), pp. 300–305

Menzer, Paul, 'The Tragedians of the City? Q1 *Hamlet* and the Settlements of the 1590s', *Shakespeare Quarterly*, 57, no. 2 (summer, 2006), pp. 162–82

Miller, Amos C., *Sir Henry Killigrew: Elizabethan Soldier and Diplomat* (Leicester: Leicester University Press, 1963)

Nicholl, Charles, *The Reckoning: The Murder of Christopher Marlowe* (Chicago: Chicago University Press, 1992)

—, *The Lodger: Shakespeare on Silver Street* (London: Allen Lane, 2007)

Parmelee, Lisa Ferraro, 'Printers, Patrons, Readers and Spies: Importation of French Propaganda in Late-Elizabethan England', *Sixteenth-century Journal*, 25, no. 4 (winter, 1994), pp. 853–72

Pearson, A.F. Scott, *Thomas Cartwright and Elizabethan Puritanism 1535–1603* (Cambridge: Cambridge University Press, 1925)

Pellegrini, Angelo M., 'Giordano Bruno and Oxford', *Huntingdon Library Quarterly*, 5, no. 3 (April, 1942), pp. 303–16

Phillippy, Patricia, *Women, Death and Literature in Post-Reformation England* (Cambridge: Cambridge University Press, 2002)

Piper, David, 'The 1590 Lumley Inventory: Hilliard, Segar and the Earl of Essex', *Burlington Magazine*, 99, no. 654 (September, 1957), pp. 298–303

Plomer, H.R., 'The Printers of Shakespeare's Plays and Poems', *Library*, 2nd series, 7, no. 26 (1906), pp. 146–66

Pollard, Alfred W., 'Claudius Hollyband and his *French Schoolmaster* and *French Littelton*', *Library*, 3rd series, 6, no. 21 (1915), pp. 77–93

Porter, H.C., *Reformation and Reaction in Tudor Cambridge* (Cambridge: Cambridge University Press, 1958)

Rady, Martyn, *France 1494–1610: Renaissance Religion and Recovery* (London: Hodder and Stoughton, 1988)

Read, Conyers, *Lord Burghley and Queen Elizabeth* (London: Jonathan Cape, 1960)

Reese, M.M., *The Tudors and Stuarts* (London: Edward Arnold, 1940)

Rollin, Charles, *The Ancient History of the Egyptians, Carthaginians . . .*, vol. 2 (London: J. Rivington, 1780)

Ronald, Susan, *The Pirate Queen: Queen Elizabeth I, Her Pirate Adventurers and the Dawn of Empire* (New York and London: Harper Perennial, 2007)

—, *Heretic Queen: Queen Elizabeth I and the Wars of Religion* (New York: St Martin's Press, 2012)

Ross, Josephine, *The Men Who Would be King: Suitors to Queen Elizabeth I* (London: Phoenix, 2005)

Schleiner, Louise, *Tudor and Stuart Women Writers* (Bloomington and Indianapolis: Indiana University Press, 1994)

Schoenbaum, S., *William Shakespeare: A Compact Documentary Life* (Oxford: Oxford University Press, 1977)

Scoufos, Alice-Lyle, *Shakespeare's Typological Satire: A Study of the Falstaff–Oldcastle Problem* (Athens, Ohio: Ohio University Press, 1979)

Scouloudi, Irene, *Returns of Strangers in the Metropolis, 1593, 1627, 1635, 1639: A Study of an Active Minority*, Quarto Series, vol. 57 (London: The Huguenot Society of London, 1985)

Shapiro, James, *1599: A Year in the Life of William Shakespeare* (London: Faber and Faber, 2005)

—, *Contested Will: Who Wrote Shakespeare?* (London: Faber and Faber, 2010)

Shrewsbury, J.F.D., *A History of Bubonic Plague in the British Isles* (Cambridge: Cambridge University Press, 1970)

Skidmore, Chris, *Edward VI: The Lost King of England* (London: Phoenix Press, 2008)

—, *Death and the Virgin: Elizabeth, Dudley and the Mysterious Fate of Amy Robsart* (London: Phoenix Press, 2011)

Smith, Irwin, *Shakespeare's Blackfriars Playhouse: Its History and Its Design* (London: Peter Owen, 1964)

Stewart, Alan, 'The Voices of Anne Cooke, Lady Anne and Lady Bacon', *'This Double Voice': Gendered Writing in Early Modern England*, eds. Danielle Clarke and Elizabeth Clarke (Houndmills and New York: Macmillan, 2000), pp. 88–102

Straznicky, Marta, ed., *Shakespeare's Stationers: Studies in Cultural Bibliography* (Philadelphia: University of Pennsylvania Press, 2013)

Strong, Roy, 'Queen Elizabeth, the Earl of Essex and Nicholas Hilliard', *Burlington Magazine*, 101, no. 673 (April, 1959), pp. 145–9

—, *The English Renaissance Miniature* (London: Thames and Hudson, 1983)

—, *The Cult of Elizabeth: Elizabethan Portraiture and Pageantry* (London: Pimlico, 1999)

—, *Gloriana: The Portraits of Queen Elizabeth I* (London: Pimlico, 2003)

Taylor, Gary, 'The Fortunes of Oldcastle', *Shakespeare Survey*, 38 (1986), pp. 85–100

Thrush, Andrew, and John P. Ferris, eds., *The History of Parliament: The House of Commons 1604–1629* (Cambridge: Cambridge University Press, 2010)

Tipton, Alzada J., ' "Lively Patterns . . . For Affayres of State": Sir John Hayward's *The Life and Reigne of King Henrie IIII* and the Earl of Essex', *Sixteenth-century Journal*, 33, no. 3 (autumn, 2002), pp. 769–94

Treasure, Geoffrey, *The Huguenots* (New Haven and London: Yale University Press, 2013)

Tweedie, David, *David Rizzio and Mary, Queen of Scots: Murder at Holyrood* (Gloucestershire: Sutton, 2007)

Varlow, Sally, *The Lady Penelope: The Lost Tale of Love and Politics in the Court of Elizabeth I* (London: André Deutsch, 2007)

Wallace, Charles William, *The Children of the Chapel at Blackfriars 1597–1603* (New York, AMS Press, 1908)

—, *The Evolution of the English Drama up to Shakespeare: With a History of the First Blackfriars Theatre* (Berlin: Georg Reimer, 1912)

—, 'The First London Theatre: Materials for a History', *University of Nebraska Studies*, 13 (1913), pp. 1–297

Weir, Alison, *The Six Wives of Henry VIII* (London: Vintage, 2007)

—, *Children of England* (London: Vintage, 2008)

—, *Elizabeth the Queen* (London: Vintage, 2008)

Weis, René, *Shakespeare Revealed: A Biography* (London: John Murray, 2007)

Wells, Stanley, *Shakespeare: For All Time* (London: Macmillan, 2002)

White, Micheline, 'A Biographical Sketch of Dorcas Martin: Elizabethan Translator, Stationer and Godly Matron', *Sixteenth-century Journal*, 30, no. 3 (autumn, 1999), pp. 775–92

—, 'Renaissance Englishwomen and Religious Translations: The Case of Anne Lock's *Of the Markes of the Children of God* (1590)', *English Literary Renaissance*, 29 (September, 1999), pp. 375–400

Whitebrook, J.C., 'Huguenots of Blackfriars, and Its Neighbourhood, in Shakespearian Days', *Notes and Queries*, 8 (November, 1941), pp. 254–6

Wilson, Richard, *Secret Shakespeare: Studies in Theatre, Religion and Resistance* (Manchester: Manchester University Press, 2004)

Wilson, Violet A., *Society Women of Shakespeare's Time* (New York: E.P. Dutton, 1925)

Wood, Michael, *In Search of Shakespeare* (London: BBC, 2003)

Woolley, Benjamin, *The Queen's Conjuror: The Life and Magic of Dr Dee* (London: Flamingo, 2002)

Woudhuysen, Henry, *Sir Philip Sidney and the Circulation of Manuscripts 1558–1640* (Oxford: Clarendon Press, 1996)

Index